CREATING NEW HEALTH CARE VENTURES

The Role of Management

Regina E. Herzlinger, DBA
Nancy R. McPherson Professor of Business Administration
Graduate School of Business Administration
Harvard University
Boston, Massachusetts

AN ASPEN PUBLICATION®
Aspen Publishers, Inc.
Gaithersburg, Maryland
1992

Library of Congress Cataloging-in-Publication Data

Herzlinger, Regina E.
Creating new health care ventures : the role of management/
Regina E. Herzlinger.
p. cm.
Includes bibliographical references and index.
ISBN: 0-8342-0232-8
1. Health services administration—United States. 2. Public health administration—United States. 3. Health Planning—United States. 1. Title. [DNLM: 1. Delivery of Health Care—economics. 2. Delivery of Health Care—organization & administration. 3. Economics, Medical. 4. Health Services—organization & administration. 5. Hospital—Physician Joint Ventures. W 84.1 H582c]
RA971.H48 1992
362.1'068—dc20
DNLM/DLC
for Library of Congress
91-22413
CIP

Case material of the Harvard Graduate School of Business Administration is made possible by the cooperation of business firms and other organizations which may wish to remain anonymous by having names, quantities, and other identifying details disguised while maintaining basic relationships. Cases are prepared as the basis for class discussion rather than to illustrate either effective or ineffective handling of an administrative situation.

Editorial Services: Ruth Bloom
Library of Congress Catalog Card Number: 91-22413
ISBN: 0-8342-0232-8

Printed in the United States of America

1 2 3 4 5

To
George Herzlinger

Table of Contents

Preface

Health care systems in the United States and other developed countries have long faced daunting economic, social, and technological pressures for change: health care costs that inflate more rapidly than the rest of the economy; health care consumers who voice growing discontent with the orientation, efficiency, and convenience of the system; and health care technology that plays a Dr. Jekyll and Mr. Hyde role, simultaneously enabling medical miracles for many sick people and yet requiring massive expenditures for interventions of questionable efficacy. A transformation has seemed inevitable.

But the long-awaited transformation has yet to occur. Consider the U.S. health care system as an example. Although its size grew enormously, from a staggering $70 billion of expenditures in 1970 to an incomprehensible $604 billion in 1989, the structure of the system changed very little: In 1970, hospitals consumed 37 percent of the total, physicians 19 percent, and other professional services 8 percent, and in 1990, they consumed 39 percent, 19 percent, and 6 percent of the total, respectively.[1] No structural revolution is in sight.

As I write this, health care costs continue to inflate wildly, growing 11.1 percent in the United States from 1988 to 1989 alone, consumers remain dissatisfied, and technology still plays its schizophrenic role. The revolution has yet to occur.

What explains the delays in transforming troubled health care systems worldwide? On the basis of my experiences during the 20 years I have had the good fortune to research, teach, and serve as a board member in the field, my answer is simple: a failure of management. The ventures created by many visionary and daring innovators who attempted to effect this revolution faltered for two managerial reasons: misspecification of the need for the innovation or of the managerial skills critical for fulfilling that need.

The following anecdote is all too typical. A few years ago, a world famous venture capitalist told me of his plan to start a new type of health insurance company:

> Health care costs are killing businesses. We can help them by signing up a whole bunch of physicians and hospitals that agree to charge lower prices for providing care to the patients we send them from our new health insurance firm. We will pass some of the resulting savings on to the employers who buy our health insurance, and keep the

rest as profits. Pretty soon, we will be making a ton of money.

One year later, the new venture filed for bankruptcy. What went wrong? In retrospect, the explanation is ludicrously simple. The new insurance company's management was inexperienced in selling its concepts to physicians and hospitals. It found them understandably reluctant to discount their fees, and it signed up only a few takers. Employers did not want to buy a health insurance policy that provided their employees with such a small choice of physicians. And the rest of the story is in the new business graveyard.

If the explanation for the failure is so clear, why did the seasoned venture capitalist not anticipate the hazards? Because he was so dazzled with this opportunity to provide lower cost health care that he neglected the details of management that would realize its potential. But, in health care, as elsewhere, God is in the details.

The purpose of this book is to help the many able, energetic, talented people in the health care sector to create its much needed transformation by identifying the three major opportunities for change and the seven skills of management they require.

In this preface, I briefly describe the three opportunities and seven skills that will transform the health care system. But before I do so, permit me to digress. Some of you no doubt feel that factors other than failures of management contribute to the perceived failures of health care systems. Many cite the shortcomings of the mechanisms used to fund their country's health care. But while U.S. policy analysts complain that our funding mechanism causes inequitable access and an unduly large growth in the proportion of the GNP devoted to health care expenses, British citizens complain that their funding mechanism causes long waits for needed health care services and a critical shortage of technology, and Canadian doctors go on lengthy, disruptive strikes in order to settle payment disputes with the government, their sole source of support.[2] Although each of these three countries employs a different funding mechanism for health care, each system suffers from serious problems.

It is undoubtedly true that national funding mechanisms can be improved and possibly true that the problems of health care systems worldwide can be corrected with different funding mechanisms; but presently no country exemplifies such an ideal model. In the absence of this magic funding formula, health care managers must step into the vacuum and take responsibility for producing better results from the resources that are presently available.

OPPORTUNITIES FOR CHANGE

When I began researching this book in the mid-1980s, three new opportunities had emerged for changing the health care system. One opportunity was based on the possibility of forming ventures to reduce the cost of providing health care services and products; the second was based on the unmet needs of new classes of health care consumers; and the third was based on the existence of dazzling new technologies waiting to be developed.

All three opportunities had immense potential because of the enormous size of the health care industry. In 1989 alone, the United States spent $604 billion on health care. As one investor noted, "In other industries, you struggle to find a billion dollar market; but in health care you keep tripping over such opportunities."

Health care cost control presented the most obvious challenge. The costs of the American system were enormously large with rates of increase two or three times the rate of general inflation. When I surveyed corporate chiefs in 1983, they were optimistic about their ability to limit costs. When I repeated my survey in 1989, most had conceded defeat. The health care cost monster was beyond their control. In that year, corporate health costs equaled after-tax profits.[3]

Yet, many consumer needs were left unmet, despite these huge expenditures. Two consumer groups were particularly noteworthy. One consisted of a large, new class of health care activists fully confident of their ability to master themselves and their environment, including their health status. Although they respected the traditional health care establishment—physicians, hospitals, and pharmaceutical companies—their attitude was hardly deferential. For the health care activist, "Doctor knows best" was replaced by "I know best." This group eagerly purchased health care products and information but found the current system deficient in meeting their needs.

Working families composed the second new health care consumer group. Enlarged by the growth in two-career and one-head-of-household families and characterized by an increasingly aged and feminized labor force, this group values convenience above all else. Domino's Pizza owes its success to them. Its promise of a 30-minute delivery time provides the convenience they prize. Working people changed the face of many other industries but have not yet had a notable effect on health care. The wait in a physician's office was the second highest source of patient dissatisfaction in a recent survey.[4]

The third major opportunity was in new technologies. These range from computer technologies embodied in new medical instruments, devices, and information systems; to biomaterials that hold the promise of creating real bionic people; to biotechnology products that can alter the genetic information in our bodies and prevent or cure many of the diseases that cursed our forebears. Their potential to alter life is dazzling. Some of the new technologies can even help recreate the five senses; one device already provides a sense of sound for people who cannot hear. Other new technologies can correct genetic defects; for example, children with the genetic malady of dwarfism can now reach more normal heights through treatment with the biotechnology product human growth hormone.

At this time, visionary managers have already eagerly responded to the three areas of opportunity. They have created huge vertically and horizontally integrated organizations to reduce the costs of health care. Many of the thousands of American hospitals formed chains to take advantage of economies of shared administration. Many nursing homes and other providers of inpatient services, pharmaceutical companies, and independent physicians followed suit. Through vertical integration—the union of producers and sellers—new organizations were created that simultaneously sold health insurance and offered health care services. (These organizations were variously known as HMOs [health maintenance organizations]; IPAs [independent practitioner associations]; and PPOs [preferred provider organizations].) Health activists were served with powerful new self-administered drugs, diagnostic and therapeutic devices, and health promotion services. Harried working people were offered new convenient sites for health care services, such as neighborhood cancer therapy and minor surgery centers. They could now order drugs by mail, and health care services were sometimes delivered at home. Finally, hundreds of new biotechnology and medical device ventures were formed, funded by investments totaling billions of dollars.

But many of these new ventures have already failed. The costs of many cost-controlling health care ventures continued their unrelenting climb. New consumers found the reality of new health care services to fall far short of the promise. And all too few of the technological marvels delivered on their potential, as managers of new technology companies found themselves enmeshed in unanticipated legal, marketing, and research complications.

THE SEVEN MANAGERIAL SKILLS

Why such dismal results? Sometimes, managers misspecified the nature of the opportunity they were attempting to fulfill. For example, although at-home kits for diagnosing medical conditions frequently result from advances in technology, their primary purpose, in many cases, is to serve the needs of new consumers for convenience and control of their health care. If an at-home kit is presented as a new technology to this group of users, its success is less likely. For example, an at-home pregnancy detection kit sold as a wonderful new technology for physicians to resell to their patients is much less likely to succeed than one sold directly to activist consumers. Indeed, the intended consumers in this case are the very ones who are least likely to seek out a doctor's advice.

More frequently, however, the failure to fulfill the promise of the three opportunities was caused by poor management. Although entrepreneurs accurately envisioned the opportunities for change and developed appropriate strategies for exploring these opportunities, they failed to implement appropriate managerial skills.

Sometimes founders were so dazzled by the opportunity they created that they thought the business would manage itself. For example, some drug or medical device entrepreneurs became so enamored with their technological innovations that they imagined that little effort was required to persuade the market to share their enthusiasm. Genentech, the first company to bring the much-touted blood clot dissolver TPA to the market, was surprised when regulators and physicians questioned its value; Genentech had assumed there would be ready market acceptance for TPA. In other cases, managers were so fixated with one managerial activity that they neglected others. Some other biotechnology managers were so obsessed with finding the huge amounts of capital they needed to finance research that they paid little heed to the many other managerial skills that are critical to the success of health care technology ventures.

From my experience with many new health care ventures, I have distilled the seven managerial skills that are most frequently associated with success. They include *marketing*, to create awareness of the new product or service; *finance*, to obtain the pool of capital needed to organize and operate the new venture; *managerial control systems*, to ensure that the cost and quality of the new venture are as intended; *operations management*, to deliver the product or service in a smooth and timely fashion; *human resource management*, to develop a group of employees who are committed to the principles of the new venture and who will act in accordance with the founders' vision; *regulatory management*, to ensure that the many regulators of capital, personnel, reimbursement, and technology in the health care system understand the merits of the proposed venture; and, last, a *leadership philosophy* consistent with the style of the top management and the needs of the organization.

PURPOSE OF THIS BOOK

The purpose of this book is to help innovators identify the breathtaking opportunities that currently exist for revolutionizing the health care system and to fully appreciate the painstaking details of management appropriate for their implementation.

This book is addressed to two audiences: executives and students presently involved in the health care system and those tantalized by the prospect of becoming involved. For the former, it presents the seven managerial skills that I have found critical to successful innovation in the system and many real-life examples of their implementation. It was written in response to the many physicians, health service personnel, medical scientists, and health care administrators who say, "I know the system needs change. I know what changes are needed. But I do not know how to manage the organizations that would create these changes."

For those outside the system who are intrigued by the possibility of changing it, this book contains detailed descriptions of the three new opportunities for revolutionizing the provision of health care. The descriptions contain sufficient data to enable most would-be innovators to identify and measure the magnitude of the entrepreneurial opportunity they wish to explore. Furthermore, I have tried to write the descriptions in English, not medical shorthand.

This book differs importantly from others that bear similar titles. Despite their names, many books on health care administration deal primarily with issues of public policy, not administration. They focus on issues such as the health care costs of victims of acquired immune deficiency syndrome and the efficacy of government payments for expensive new health care technologies. These are very important issues, but they are not managerial in nature. This book, in contrast, deals with management—the great challenge of breathing life into the clay figure of a new health care product or service.

Then, too, my description of the health care system differs from others. The system is most frequently depicted from the vantage point of the *providers* of health care, but I view it from the opposite side—as a series of opportunities to fulfill the unmet needs of the *consumers* of health care. The book is thus organized around the opportunities inherent in the market rather than around the needs of those who provide health care. Put another way, this book focuses on demand while others examine supply. My market focus embraces a broad gamut of health care services and products—antacid tablets and weight-loss clinics are as much a part of the health care system I describe as is coronary artery bypass surgery at the Mayo Clinic. I also consider all forms of organization, whether administered by businesses, nonprofit organizations, or the government.

I hope this book will motivate readers to explore the new opportunities for changing the health care system and will identify the managerial skills that are needed. It is not my purpose to produce "entrepreneurs" mindlessly salivating at the almighty dollar, but rather to help those who hope to restructure creatively the system that presently exists. Their goal is a noble and important one.

GENESIS

This book emerged from the Harvard Business School MBA course "Creating New Health Care Ventures" that I introduced in 1986. The course, like this book, focused on attractive, newly emerging opportunities for revolutionizing the provision of health care services and products. Its central question was how to manage these opportunities and create effective and efficient health care organizations.

The unusual case-method pedagogy of the Harvard Business School shaped this book. The school's founders believed that descriptions of managerial decisions, which they called "cases," would be more effective for teaching management than lectures or texts. They rejected conventional academic presentations of orderly business "principles" and "techniques" as ill-suited to the messy reality of the conduct of business. The preface to each case underscores this message: "This case was prepared as the basis for class discussion rather than to illustrate either effective or ineffective handing of an administrative situation."

The case-method pedagogy they evolved is difficult for some to accept. All of us crave certainty. We want to be given the ten rules for making a million dollars, winning friends, and being a successful parent. But in our heart of hearts we know that such prescriptions are bilge, that life is ultimately too complex to be reduced to simple rules. The case method of education fulfills our deeper needs for guidance and illumination rather than quick fixes. For example, the case describing the thoughts of Health Stop's management about how to provide ambulatory care services (Case Study 6) contains more valuable lessons about managing costs than most neat textbook presentations of cost-volume relationships.

The course initially focused on some 20 case studies of new health care ventures, many of them presented in this book. These case studies exemplified the three new opportunities. Some of the companies described in the case studies became wildly successful. For example, the New England Critical Care case study, written in 1985, describes a new company that has grown to become the second largest in its industry. Other ventures, however, headed in the opposite direction. For example, Boston Sobriety Development Inc., the subject of a 1989 case study, is now out of business.

Whether describing success or failure, each case study provides useful information. Medical schools teach anatomy as well as pathology so that their students can differentiate the normal anatomical state from the diseased pathological one. The case studies in this book serve the same purpose. They illustrate two important lessons—how to achieve success and how to avoid failure.

My case studies experiences were amplified by those learned as a board member of many health care organizations, including organizations large and small; private and public; start-up and well-established; for-profit, nonprofit, and "no-profit-as-yet"; and providers of health services or technology. (I discuss two of them, Wel Med and Salick Health Care, Inc., in this book.)

From these diverse experiences and the many generous people who graciously shared their wisdom with me, I distilled the lessons of success and failure. Their essence is in the seven skills of management described herein.

My being a professor of business, rather than health care management, also inevitably shaped the content of this book. I do not specialize solely in health care—I also teach management control (the Harvard Business School's euphemism for accounting) to our MBA and executive students. This functional specialty familiarized me with many different industries and enabled me to apply the lessons to be learned from their successes and failure to the health care arena.

A broad business background is helpful to those who hope to be innovators in the health care system. For one, health care is subject to the same social and demographic trends as other sectors. Then, too, the lines between traditional businesses and health care ventures are already blurring, as exemplified by the entrance of companies like Proctor and Gamble, the consumer retailing giant, into the health care industry.[5] My readers should not be surprised, nor insulted, to find analogies in this book between the delivery of health care services and the delivery of fast food, hotel services, and consumer products. Such analogies are intended to illuminate the practices of management in industries facing challenges similar to those of health care.

CONTENTS

The purpose of this book is to enable better management of the health care organizations created to take advantage of the three areas of new opportunity. Part I is an introduction to the three new opportunities and the seven skills. Part II describes the three opportunities in greater detail. Part III fully describes each of the seven managerial skills and illustrates its application to each of the three areas of opportunity. Part IV describes the process of evaluating new ventures. Appendixes A, B, and C provide background information on the structure, financing, and technology of the American health care system. The book ends with 20 relevant case studies.

Despite its bulk, this book is but an introduction. Mastery of business or health administration usually requires at least a year of full-time education. No one book can replicate such scope and depth. For those interested in additional insights into the three areas of opportunity and each of the seven managerial skills, suggestions for further reading are included at the end of most chapters.

Because the book is addressed to a broad audience, individual readers may find some of the parts more relevant than others. I have run the risk of being repetitive and written each part so that it can be read separately.

NOTES

1. 1970 data: *Statistical Abstract 1990* (Washington, D.C.: U.S. Government Printing Office, 1990), p. 93, Table 136. 1989 data: Office of the Actuary, Health Care Financing Administration, *HHS News*, December 20, 1990.

2. Regina E. Herzlinger, "Healthy Competition," *The Atlantic Monthly*, August 1991, 63–83.

3. Katherine R. Levit, Mark S. Freeland, and Daniel R. Waldo, "Health Spending and Ability to Pay," *Health Care Financing Review,* Spring 1989, 39.

4. Lynn K. Harvey, Stephanie Shubat, *AMA Public Opinion on Health Care Issues* (Chicago: American Medical Association, April 1990), 15.

5. Alecia Swasy and Richard Keonig, "P&G Adds Maalox to Pepto-Bismol–Metamucil Stomach Arsenal," *Wall Street Journal*, March 14, 1990, B1.

Acknowledgments

Many people assisted in the preparation of this book. For 2 years, Dr. James Rhea, Associate Professor at the Harvard University Medical School, and Nancy Kane, Associate Professor of the Harvard School of Public Health, helped me to teach the course on which this book is based, and supervised the writing of some of its cases. Joyce Lallman, my research associate from 1985 to 1986, wrote many of the cases, and Rick Siegrist, Richard Benedict, Agnes Connolly, and Ellen Ratner ably assisted as well. Sherrie Epstein, my research associate from 1986 to 1989, wrote the original versions of the book's appendixes, and Jane Noonan and Sarah Collins provided library research assistance. Donna Hohmann and Aimee Hamel ably prepared the manuscript. Diana Gaeta, my assistant, put it all together.

I am very grateful to the organizations that permitted me to prepare case studies about them and to the men and women within them who shared their experiences and wisdom with me. I was first set along this path by the late Dr. Jack Connolly, who generously guided my initial health care case study in 1971, which was set in his visionary neighborhood health center (it appears herein as the Hyatt Hill Health Center). I also appreciate the gracious counsel of Sherif S. Abdelhak and Debra Caplan of the Allegheny General Hospital; Les Bell of Salick Health Care, Inc.; Norwood Davis of Virginia Blue Cross-Blue Shield; Steve Diamond of Management Analysis Center; Dr. Thomas Frist, Jr., of the Hospital Corporation of America; Mark Finkelstein of Health and Rehabilitation Properties Trust; Chuck Hartman of CW Ventures; Roy Goldman, Esq., of Fulbright, Jaworski; Bill Hokanson; Dr. Richard Horman and Dan Marawitz of Adler and Shaykin; David Jones of Humana, Inc.; Jack Kordash of MediQual Systems; Ben Lytle of the Associated Group; Sharon Kleefeld of the Brigham and Women's Hospital; the late Phil Petitt of Shearson Lehman Brothers; Joan Pinck; Bama Rucker of Hambrecht and Quist; Dr. Earle Shouldice of the Shouldice Hospital; and Professors James Heskett, William Sahlman, and James Austin of the Harvard Business School. (Professor Heskett also graciously allowed me to reprint his Shouldice Hospital case study in this book.)

My students were very helpful in providing feedback and information, particularly Richard Benedict, Craig Brooks, Wende Hutton, Elizabeth Lobo, Susan White Oberymeyer, Glenn Reicin, Mark Simon, Chris Spinella, and

Drs. Jeffrey Dann, Brandon Fradd, Lawrence Gelb, Jeffrey Jay, Mary Kraft, and Alvaro Salas.

I am also grateful to the Harvard Business School for permitting me to devote 3 years solely to the teaching, course development, and research in the health care field that resulted in this book and my forthcoming book on health care policy.

Despite all the help I received, the responsibility for this book is, of course, entirely mine.

Part I

The Three New Opportunities and the Seven Skills of Management

1

Introduction

One of my childhood memories was of watching the actor Louis Jourdan serenade Gigi, the young heroine of the movie, in recognition of her recently acquired beauty. "Gigi," he sang,"While you were trembling on the brink, was I out yonder somewhere blinking at a star? Oh, Gigi, have I been standing up too close or back too far?"[1] Meanwhile, a beaming Hermione Gingold, the creator of Gigi's transformation, observed the scene.

The present health care system is like the young Gigi; many of its spectators, like Louis Jourdan, may be standing "too near" or "too far" to see clearly the opportunities for its transformation; and the entrepreneurs are potential Hermione Gingolds. If, like her, they succeed in recognizing the opportunities for change and responding appropriately to them, they too will effect a miraculous transformation.

THE THREE NEW OPPORTUNITIES

The most noticeable opportunity for change came with the growth of health care costs—in the United States alone, they grew from 3.5 percent of GNP in 1929 to 11 percent in 1988. These few percentage points may obscure the magnitude of the change. They amount to an absolute growth of over $500 billion in health care expenditures a year.[2]

This growth exacted a devastating price from the economy. U.S. health care costs, as a percentage of GNP, are the highest in the world—nearly twice those of the Japanese and 50 percent higher than those of developed European countries. But health care cost increases are not unique to the United States. The health care costs of most developed countries grow at rates exceeding those of their economy or general rate of inflation.[3]

The American public has expressed greater satisfaction with its health care system than the citizens of Germany, Great Britain, Sweden, and Japan,[4] but even here three complaints persist. Activist health care consumers, who tend to participate aggressively in maintaining their excellent state of health, find the system overly focused on treatment of disease rather than promotion of health. Over 40 percent complained of insufficient emphasis on prevention of illness in a recent survey.[5] Their perceptions are supported by the meagerness of health promotion spending, which is not large enough to register even as a blip in the huge $600 billion of expenditures in the health care system.

Working people are also displeased. Many of the 120 million Americans in the 1987 labor force rated the system as inconvenient. For one thing, health care providers are hard to find at convenient locations during nonworking hours (such as evenings and weekends). The inadequate availability of health care after hours and on weekends was most frequently noted as a shortcoming by respondents to a recent survey.[6] Then, too, the system is not organized around patients' needs. For example, the millions of people suffering from bad backs cannot easily locate the right source of care. Instead, patients travel from orthopedic surgeons, to neurologists, to radiologists, to physical therapists, to laboratories, to sports medicine specialists, to the designers of various back support devices. Few "back stores" exist to provide the multispecialty teams these patients need at one convenient site.

For these working people, the current health care system is akin to the retail grocer before the advent of the 24-hour supermarket. In the old days, Americans could buy food only in small, inconvenient, expensive stores that offered limited choices and hours. Supermarket creators recognized the need for convenience, and they bundled an enormous range of food and consumer products under one roof and kept their doors open 24 hours a day. No analogue to the supermarket currently exists in the American health care system.

The last major consumer complaint about the system is in its efficiency. Although the health industry claims that cost increases are an inevitable artifact of our aging population and expensive new technological innovations, many do not agree. In a 1990 survey, Americans rated hospitals as the worst value for the money; hospitals were ranked well below other expensive purchases, like a college education or an automobile, and even below items whose costs have traditionally been suspect, like automobile repair costs and legal fees.[7]

As health care costs grew, the cost of American hospitals zoomed ahead. In 1989,

U.S. hospital costs increased 11.8 percent; in contrast, health care costs rose 8.0 percent and the general rate of inflation was only 4.3 percent.[8] Meanwhile, use of hospitals plummeted. In 1985–1987, American hospitals attained a paltry 65 percent occupancy rate—one out of three beds was always empty.[9] Consumers obviously questioned why hospital room cost indices grew fifteenfold from 1960 to 1988 while occupancy declined by 14 percent.[10]

Not all aspects of the system are so gloomy. For example, Americans greatly admire their physicians, whose proficiency attracts patients from around the world, and the advances in medical knowledge that have greatly enhanced the diagnosis and treatment of disease. Heart disease victims can now survive longer and lead richer lives than was possible 20 years ago. Last year alone, 1,500 Americans received new hearts, and hundreds of thousands more functioned with less pain and restriction as a result of new surgical techniques, devices, and drugs. Computer-based devices have restored the sense of hearing to some and may soon be used to restore other senses, like sight. Those once destined to go through life crippled can now lead more normal lives because of advances in implant and biomaterials technology. And genetically engineered drugs hold the promise of reversing cruel genetic defects, like cystic fibrosis.

But despite this admiration, many American physicians are currently unhappy with their career choice. Nearly 40 percent would not make the choice if given another chance.[11] Even in the case of medical technology, there is a sense of lost opportunities, of promising science left unexplored or conceded to competitors. For example, Genentech, the brilliant California start-up company that many thought was destined to become the first large independent biotechnology firm, chose instead to sell a majority interest to an established pharmaceutical company. And many innovative ideas are left undeveloped, hobbled by shortages of capital and unanticipated regulatory and marketing difficulties.

Is the glass half empty or half full? Every problem presents a corresponding opportunity.

What opportunities correspond to these problems?

There are three. First is the opportunity to create organizations that constrain health care costs. Because of the prominence of hospitals in the cost equation, the most readily apparent cost-reducing techniques are those that increase hospital efficiency and offer alternate health service sites. The second opportunity is to create organizations that serve the currently unfilled needs of health care activists and working people. These organizations would allow activists greater control over their health and would provide working people with greater convenience. The third opportunity is to create organizations that effectively develop the brilliant promises of medical technology.

In the past 20 years, many ventures emerged to take advantage of these opportunities. Some succeeded. Some failed. In the subsequent parts of this chapter, I describe some of these organizations, the characteristics of their founders, and how the seven skills of management contributed to their success or failure. Almost universally, the successful new ventures implemented these seven managerial skills, and the failures did not.

THE SEVEN SKILLS OF MANAGEMENT

To illustrate the seven skills that make the difference between success and failure, I discuss them in the context of a hypothetical venture, Newco, created to serve a relatively new type of American consumer: two-career or one-head-of-household families residing in towns that are neither sufficiently affluent nor large enough to attract many physicians. Such families may either lack a regular physician or are unable to find one available before or after standard working hours or on weekends. Instead, they reluctantly use hospital emergency rooms for relatively minor medical needs, like small cuts and sprains. Many characterize emergency rooms as hard to reach, expensive, and rarely able to provide timely service. They would prefer to use health care centers that are located nearby and open at convenient hours.[12]

The founders of Newco believe they can fill these needs with a chain of centers that provide fast, high-quality, relatively inexpensive health care services at convenient times and in convenient locations, such as shopping malls. The centers would be open from 8 A.M. until 8 P.M., located in underserved communities, and fully staffed with a doctor, a nurse, and x-ray and laboratory technicians to treat routine medical problems.

The centers' costs would be lower than hospital emergency rooms because of the economies achieved by administering a chain, because the centers would be located in shopping malls rather than in expensive downtown hospitals, and because the staff would be trained to fill multiple responsibilities thus reducing the number needed. Quality would be ensured through the use of clinical audits, consumer satisfaction surveys, and training for providers.

So far, so good. But what managerial skills would translate these promises to reality? *Marketing* would clearly be critical. Newco is intended to provide a new kind of health care service: new hours, new settings, new types of organizational arrangements. Identifying its potential consumers and the channels best suited for reaching them would not be simple. Marketing health services directly to consumers and employers has rarely been attempted.

Newco would run focus groups to identify its clients and experiment with many alternative marketing channels: radio and television advertising, direct mail, billboards, newspaper ads, coupons, special days for free blood pressure and cholesterol measurement, physician panels, community events, and industry conferences to inform potential patients of Newco's services. It also would advise insurance companies and businesses of the desirability of its new alternatives to higher priced emergency room care.

The new organization requires extensive amounts of *financing*. Large capital needs are partially created by the novelty of the venture. A long time would elapse before it could attract the number of consumers necessary to make it profitable, and capital is needed to keep it afloat while it was building up to this critical number. Capital is also needed to finance the creation of a chain of such centers. The substantial economies of scale to be captured with a chain—economies in marketing, purchasing, design, hiring, billing, and so on—require a substantial initial investment.

Other managerial skills are also important. *Managerial control systems* would ensure that costs were in line with those of competitors and that quality was at a satisfactory level. *Operations management* would provide patients arriving for unscheduled visits with timely and satisfactory services. *Human resource management* would ensure consistency between the vision of the service providers—the physicians, nurses, and technologists—and the founders' vision of efficient, high-quality services.

Newco also needs to *manage* its *regulatory* environment so that health insurance companies would pay for its services, it complies with health care construction regulations, and its personnel were performing the functions for which they are licensed. Finally, as the company grows, Newco's top management would have to articulate a *leadership philosophy* that would ensure appropriate replication of their vision in the company's many sites.

MATCHING THE THREE OPPORTUNITIES AND SEVEN SKILLS

Successful new health care ventures share two characteristics: They focus clearly on one of the three opportunities and they tailor the seven skills to match the managerial requirements of that opportunity. Ventures that attempt to take advantage of more than one of the three opportunities usually fail, because each of the opportunities requires a different kind of implementation of the seven skills.

For example, like many new ventures, Newco could be categorized as responding to either of two opportunities: It could be conceived of as a vehicle for lowering health care costs or as a vehicle for producing high-quality, convenient services for new consumers. Which is it? The answer is important, because the two purposes cannot be achieved simultaneously—they are as different as hamburgers prepared at McDonald's and at the Ritz. The differences in the implementation of the seven skills appropriate for each of these two opportunities are shown in Table 1-1.

Newco As a Cost-Reducing Organization

Organizations whose main purpose is to reduce costs must achieve and market low-cost health care services. Their target markets will consist of those to whom low costs are important: primarily governments, health insurance companies, employers who pay for health care, and, possibly, moderate income people who pay for their health care out of their own pocket. *Marketing* aimed at these buyers must persuade them that costs are lowered while satisfactory quality levels are maintained. This is a tricky sale: Lower costs frequently signal lower quality of health care. The sales staff must be given a clear explanation of how lower costs are achieved without lowering quality.

How are costs lowered? Most frequently, through economies of scale. For example, Pearle Vision Centers advertises that it can keep the cost for eyeglasses down because it is such a large company. The message is clear. Our eyeglasses are low cost, not low quality. To achieve these economies, the venture must be large, which in turn requires substantial amounts of capital. Newco's individual health care centers will not necessarily be large, but it will achieve economies by having a large number of centers.

With its large purchasing power, a chain can decrease costs and improve the terms of its purchases. It can also spread administrative expenses over a larger base. For example, Newco can afford to develop a top-notch billing and collection system because its costs will ultimately be paid for by many centers rather than one. Astute *financing* skills are needed to acquire the substantial capital that will achieve

Table 1-1 Matching Opportunities with Managerial Skills for Newco

	New Opportunity	
Seven Skills	*Cost-Reducing Services*	*New Consumer Services*
Marketing	Low-price, low-cost services marketed to insurance companies and employers; sales people are key	Medium-price, convenient services marketed to consumers; direct mail, public relations, and word-of-mouth are key
Finance	To finance lower cost through the economies of scale achieved by acquiring many centers and sharing administrative systems	To finance convenience thorough large capacity and ample staffing per center
Human Resource Management	Cross-training to increase staffing flexibility; medium turnover tolerated	Training to focus on patient satisfaction; low turnover policies
Operations Management	Tight staffing and physical capacity	Luxurious capacity and ample staffing
Managerial Control Systems	Cost-focused; frequent cost reports; quality measures focus on clinical care	Quality-focused; quality measures are focused on patient satisfaction as well as clinical care
Regulatory Management	To prevent regulation initiated by hospitals and health care professionals	To prevent regulation initiated by competing physicians
Leadership Philosophy	Centralized	Decentralized

these economies. Financing will provide the money necessary for creating a chain; buying supplies, inventory, and furnishings; negotiating real estate purchases or rentals; and providing working capital.

Costs can also be lowered through careful *human resource management*. Staff members can be cross-trained to perform different functions: The nurse at each center can be trained to take x-rays and both the nurse and radiological technician can be trained to fill in as occasional receptionists. *Operations management* can lower costs by ensuring that the capacity of the individual unit is not so large as to waste space, equipment, and personnel but not so small that customers are kept waiting for long periods. Additionally, operations management must ensure that capacity is balanced. For

example, highly paid physicians may needlessly remain idle at times if operations management has not provided a sufficient number of nurses and receptionists to prepare waiting patients for them.

Last, *managerial control systems* will ensure that costs are kept in line with the budget. In cost-controlling organizations, managers would be held responsible for expenses and would be rewarded on the basis of their ability to control expenses. Quality control systems would also be designed to ensure that quality remains at an acceptable level. In this version of Newco, quality measures would focus almost exclusively on the medical attributes of the services provided.

Cost-reducing ventures are vulnerable to regulatory requirements instigated by competitors who fear absorption into the chain and by health care professionals concerned about the loss of autonomy inherent in cross-training and tight cost control. For example, if Newco were to become a competitor of the neighborhood hospital's outpatient department, the hospital might lobby local politicians to introduce legislation requiring Newco to adhere to expensive construction guidelines. Similarly, the radiological technicians' lobby might request legislation to protect their members from being required to act as receptionists occasionally. *Management of regulation* would provide some protection against such challenges through presentation of the positive side of the Newco story—its provision of low-cost health care services.

Newco As an Organization Designed for New Consumers

If, on the other hand, Newco were conceived as an organization whose purpose was to serve new health care consumers—the working people and health care activists who cannot access the health care system at convenient times—its implementation of the seven skills would change significantly.

To begin with, the organization's *marketing* strategy would be primarily to target consumers who would be attracted to the health centers' convenient locations and hours and the high quality of the services. Low cost would not be a primary attraction for these consumers. While employers and health insurance companies would still constitute a target market, the marketing message would be different. Newco would emphasize that it provided convenient sites for occupational injuries and employment physicals. Marketing techniques for reaching consumers would include public relations, direct mail, and local advertising (which would reinforce Newco's image as an integral part of the local community).

Newco would now have to be managed to deliver convenient, high-quality services. How could this be achieved? *Human resource management* would focus on selecting practitioners who enjoy providing routine patient care rather than heroic emergency or specialist medicine. The employees would be trained in new ways of demonstrating their concern for the patients; for example, they would be asked to call patients after their visits to inquire about their progress. The employees would be rewarded for longevity with the firm so that patients would be assured of continuity of care and for demonstrated excellence in patient services.

Skilled *operations management* would provide sufficient capacity to ensure that patients have quick access to a practitioner even if they walk in without an appointment. The individual centers would be staffed to meet peak demand rather than average levels of demand. For example, if the peak demand is five patients an hour and the average demand is two patients an hour, the center would be staffed to meet the five patients an hour level of demand. *Managerial control systems* would focus on quality with measures that relate primarily to the patients' notions of quality. Managers would be rewarded on the basis of profits and for nonfinancial criteria such as customer satisfaction, facility cleanliness, and the rate of employee turnover. Length of patient wait would be a critical evaluation factor.

If Newco's goal were to attract new consumers rather than reduce costs, it would require substantially more capital per center. The higher staffing levels, the larger size of the centers, and the higher salaries for more experienced personnel will inevitably push the break-even point upward. *Financing* would be required to meet the increased expenses of each center until each reached its break-even point, as well as the capital requirements of building a chain. Because Newco would now be more likely to compete directly with physicians for patients, the physicians might well marshal their considerable political muscle to outlaw the entire concept. Again, *management of regulation* is needed to make known the benefits of the high-quality, convenient care this venture would provide.

The *leadership philosophy* of the two versions of Newco would vary as well. If the company were conceived of as a cost-reducing organization, economies of scale would be key to its success. These are best achieved with centralized management. After all, the economies of shared administrative systems cannot be realized if individual centers are permitted to develop their own systems. On the other hand, if Newco were conceived of as a consumer-responsive organization, it would achieve the highest quality of care by decentralizing and by giving individual center managers the authority to respond to local conditions. In both cases, an articulate *leadership philosophy* would be essential to success.

THE THREE NEW OPPORTUNITIES AND SEVEN SKILLS REVISITED

Some of the prior readers of this book have stated, "There are at least four opportunities, not just three. What about the opportunity to serve the elderly? Or the large new numbers of chronically ill? Or. . . .)" But these are new *markets*, not new *opportunities*. New markets require new ways of marketing existing products or services, whereas new opportunities require entirely novel ways of creating services or products. For example, serving the elderly *market* requires marketing an expanded version of existing models for providing nursing home, hospice, and home health services, but responding to the *opportunity* presented by elderly health care activists requires development of wholly new services or products to fulfill their need for mastery and control.

Some other of my prior readers have identified an eighth skill—one whose nature varies with the background of its originator. To scientists, it is the management of research and development (R & D); to management consultants, it is strategic thinking; to service managers, it is customer service; to computer experts, it is an information systems strategy; and so on. But all these are encompassed by the seven skills and the three opportunities. Strategic thinking is the development of the opportunity. Management of R & D is encompassed under the skills of operations and human resource management, as is customer service.

And the development of an information systems strategy is subsumed under the skill of managerial control. Although an eighth managerial skill may well exist, the seven skills as defined are sufficiently elastic to incorporate all those that have been suggested to date.

Some of my readers have also wondered whether a successful new venture must focus on only one of the three opportunities. Some companies say, "We provide low-cost services to the activist consumer" or "We offer high-technology services that lower cost and satisfy new consumers." But these companies, if successful, have focused on only one opportunity. A company developing a high-technology device that may lower health care costs must concentrate either on the opportunity to develop a new technology or on the opportunity to lower health care costs. As in the Newco example above, each opportunity requires a different implementation of the seven skills. New ventures that try to do too much usually wind up accomplishing too little.

Finally, some prior readers have questioned the fundamental premise that the seven skills are central to success. "It is all in the hands of the managers," they contend. "Good ones, with health care experience, succeed and poor ones do not." I do not agree. Although some managers, like some athletes, possess great native talent that requires little training, most good managers, like most good athletes, are the products of considerable coaching. And a Ph.D in biology is no more assured of success than a seasoned graduate of the school of hard knocks. Rather, success results from thoughtful managerial practices sedulously implemented. The winners are turtles, not hares. Successful health care entrepreneurs share no characteristic other than their devotion to good management.

HEALTH CARE INNOVATORS

The backgrounds of people drawn into the health care industry are as varied as the ventures they created. Some fit the stereotype of an engineer who creates a business in a dusty garage or laboratory; one even describes himself as a "grown-up techno-nerd." Others are business people whose experiences in accounting, finance, and law in other industries are then creatively applied to the health care arena. Yet others are health care service professionals with a vision.

The founders of two of the largest U.S. hospital chains typify these differences. Humana, a chain of 86 hospitals, was created by David Jones and the late Wendell Cherry, two Louisville, Kentucky lawyers. The partners began with a mobile home venture, WenDave; moved on to a nursing home chain, Extendicare; and then seized the opportunity to apply the lessons learned in their prior ventures to the hospital sector.

But for an unfortunate taste in corporate names, these two had the classic attributes of successful business people. They knew a bargain when they saw it and they managed their operations scrupulously. Humana hospitals were usually purchased at rock-bottom prices and operated at low costs. The bargain-spotting ability was not limited to health care. In 1989, Wendell Cherry sold *Yo Picasso*, a self-portrait of the artist, for a record $48 million, thereby earning a profit of more than $35 million.

In contrast, the Hospital Corporation of America (HCA) was formed by a father-and-son physician team. Dr. Thomas Frist, Sr., was a distinguished physician at the Vanderbilt Medical School, and his son and cofounder, Dr. Thomas Frist, Jr., was also a physician. Their medical focus was complemented by the business vision of the third founder, Jack Massey. Before HCA, Massey had created another hugely successful chain—Kentucky Fried Chicken. This seemingly incongruous pair of companies was united by a shared vision—by a commitment to a multiple site company that offered high-quality, convenient products.

The melding of the medical and business perspectives of HCA's founders produced a company substantially different in strategy and management from Humana. HCA was physician-friendly: Its aim was to "keep its docs happy." Humana was management-oriented: Its aim was to run a low-cost, high-

productivity hospital. HCA's data systems centered on quality. For example, its recently pioneered customer judgment system asks patients, physicians, employees, and members of the community to rank the quality of the local HCA hospital. Humana's systems were productivity-focused. Its large industrial engineering staff developed thousands of cost standards for every hospital function. And whereas Humana motivated efficiency by awarding its hospital administrators a bonus whose size was proportionate to the profitability of their hospital, HCA avoided incentive compensation because of the concern that it might motivate its administrators to cut expenses for items that physicians want.

HCA's physician orientation prevented it from diversifying into health care businesses that employ physicians as salaried workers rather than independent professionals and that require physicians to discount their fees, as in a health maintenance organization (HMO). Humana, on the other hand, readily employed salaried physicians to staff the medical offices that were central to the HMO it created (see the Humana, Inc., case study for additional details). While HCA avoided competing with its physicians, Humana pursued the efficiencies that employment of physicians could create.

The businessmen who founded Humana ran it on lean fuel, with tightly centralized management systems emanating from the company headquarters in Louisville. The physicians who founded HCA ran it as a decentralized company in which individual hospital administrators were free to implement the management systems they considered most appropriate for their local community.

Both companies were immensely successful—both provided high-quality care at lower cost than many stand-alone hospitals. But despite the apparent likenesses of the companies, the different backgrounds and values of their founders led them to manage their businesses in entirely different ways. The only commonality? The founders of each company paid attention to the details of management.

Not all successful entrepreneurs create entirely new companies; some succeed in recreating existing ones. For example, President Ben Lytle led the turnaround of the $2 billion Associated Insurance Companies, Inc., whose largest operation was Blue Cross and Blue Shield of Indiana, from an organization losing customers and employee confidence in the early 1980s to a diversified financial services organization and one of the largest health insurers in the United States. The new Associated gets high marks from industry observers for its marketing savvy and robust financial results. Reversing the fortunes of this massive organization was a notable accomplishment, akin to turning a battleship around in a small lake. The company's achievements are reminiscent of Lytle's own Horatio Alger career; he began as a computer systems specialist, an unusual background for the top manager of a health insurance company.

How did Lytle do it? He had a strategic vision of what his company could be and a belief that the people in the company could realize this vision if empowered to do so. Lytle's strategic vision was to decentralize operations, then use entrepreneurial units to diversify the geographic and product reach of the Midwest-based company into the South, Southwest, and West. He began with 5 strategic business units in 1983, breaking them down into 18 units by 1988 and into over 40 by 1991. The vanguard of decentralization consisted of marketing companies, each designed to provide a full line of employee benefits and insurance products to targeted business segments like the construction industry, schools, and local government entities.

The new companies were small, usually employing fewer than 200 people. Lytle explains the impact of small operating companies on employee morale:

> One of our employees told me of the change in her attitude. In the past, she worked in a large centralized claims department with about 500 other employees. She felt like "a cog in a very big wheel," who could skip a day of work without anyone really missing her. Today she works in a company of 65 employees, selling and servicing products to a unique set of customers. "They need me," she says. "And I can see the result of my work directly on customers and the company's profits."

"The world didn't change," notes Lytle. "But her new ability to see the impact of her work on customers, co-workers, and profitability changed her."

Lytle himself practices the decentralization he preaches. He dramatically downsized the headquarters' staff, selling the imposing skyscraper in which the company was housed and relocating its employees to a much smaller leased space. As Lytle admits, "Decentralization runs against management theories of economies of scale. But in service businesses, customers often get lost in the bureaucracy and the perceived economies of scale, most of which exist only in a cost-accountant's mind anyway. Our decentralized operations concentrate on profitability and increased service by focusing on a niche market and unique customer needs."

As can be seen, health care innovators have flocked to the industry from diverse prior occupations and with different visions. Even those in the same niche have found different ways of providing services: Witness the difference between HCA and Humana. All the innovators share the qualities of insight, discipline, and energy, but they have used these qualities to create many different kinds of enterprises. Predicting who they would be and what they would do is simply not possible. Their collective activities compose the foundation of any free market worthy of the name. But they all share one characteristic: They pay attention to the smallest managerial tasks. To them, God is in the details.

WHY SOME INNOVATORS SUCCEEDED

The Three Key Managerial Skills

In each type of business opportunity, three of the seven skills have proved critical. Successful new ventures implemented these three skills flawlessly; failed ones did not. As indicated in

Exhibit 1-1, the three managerial skills most critical to success differ with the nature of the opportunity.

Ventures intended to control health care costs depend most critically on the skills of financing and managerial control and the development of an appropriate leadership philosophy. Cost-controlling organizations frequently call on extraordinary financing skill to secure their large capital needs. They also require excellent managerial control systems to monitor and motivate efficient, effective production of health care and a clear, articulate leadership philosophy about the centralization or decentralization of authority and responsibility.

Organizations intended to serve new health care consumers should emphasize different managerial skills. They must create the convenient health care services that working families demand and the high-mastery services that health activists want. For these organizations, the skills of operations management and marketing are essential. Also important is the implementation of thoughtful human resource management to ensure that those producing the new products are committed to the vision of timely, high-quality, patient-responsive output.

Ventures that develop new health care technologies have found marketing skills essential for persuading new consumers of the virtues of a novel technology whose advantages may not

be readily apparent. Equally important is management of the regulatory function to convince the government agencies that regulate new medical devices and drugs to license the product, to persuade the insurance companies and the government to pay for yet another health care product, and to cause the Patent Office to grant the monopoly that may enable the developers of the technology to recoup their research and development investment. Finally, finance once again proves to be a key skill, because some new technologies require the investment of enormous sums. For example, in 1989, an average of $125 million was required to bring only *one* new drug to the market.

The relative importance of these functions is also manifested in the organizational visibility and compensation of those responsible for their attainment. In a new technology company, for example, the regulatory manager should play a pivotal role, and be placed in close proximity to the chief executive officer (CEO). In a new consumer venture, on the other hand, regulatory responsibility will frequently rest with an outside lawyer who is consulted as needed. And while human resource management is always an important function, the human resource manager will play a pivotal role in companies that provide new consumers with health care services and a lesser role in cost-controlling and new technology ventures.

The key role played by these skills is illustrated by the successful innovations described below.

Exhibit 1-1 Matching Opportunities with Managerial Skills: The Three Most Important Skills for Each Opportunity

Cost Control Finance Managerial Control Managerial Philosophy
New Consumers Operations Management Marketing Human Resource Management
New Technologies Marketing Management of Regulations Finance

New Cost-Reducing Ventures

Successful cost-reducing ventures implement powerful cost control mechanisms, devise innovative financing vehicles to lower expenses, and articulate persuasive leadership philosophies. Humana, for example, employs a large staff at its Louisville headquarters whose sole purpose is to figure out the most efficient ways to manage a hospital. No part of the hospital escapes their attention—the laundry and housekeeping departments are studied as closely as the operating rooms. Humana's widely hailed managerial control systems use the thousands of standards of performance they develop as benchmarks against which the actual performance of each Humana hospital is compared monthly. (See Case Study 9 for a fuller description of these systems.)

Abe Gosman created many innovations in the course of financing Mediplex, his nursing home chain (see Case Study 12). He first demonstrated that nursing homes can prosper despite being financed with large amounts of debt. At one time, Mediplex was over 80 percent debt financed, a rate unmatched by most other publicly held companies. To lower the cost of debt, he pioneered a financing vehicle that enabled the nursing home sector to use cheap tax-exempt financing that it otherwise could not access. These financing innovations enabled Mediplex to grow faster, at a lower cost, and in a more sure-footed way than many other entrepreneurial firms at that time.

The vehicle Gosman pioneered was a real estate investment trust (REIT), which he named Meditrust. It was legally exempted from paying income taxes. The tax exemption enabled it to obtain equity capital relatively cheaply. Stockholders wanted to own shares in Meditrust because the dividend income it earned for them arrived untaxed by Uncle Sam. Gosman then used Meditrust's cheap capital to buy Mediplex's assets; in effect, he transferred Meditrust's tax-exempt capital to Mediplex, thereby lowering its financing expenses considerably.

Ben Lytle greatly reduced costs with his leadership philosophy of decentralization. When he carved up his massive insurance behemoth into many small companies, he designated each as a profit center. The managers of each company are now held accountable for their company's revenues and expenses, and earn a sizable part of their income from a bonus directly related to their profits. To qualify, they must pass three hurdles. In addition to producing a sizable profit, they must secure the approval of their local board; pass a detailed financial and managerial audit; and receive high ratings from a survey of customers, community leaders, and employees. The new

small companies may buy their health insurance product from any vendor. They are not required to buy from Blue Cross-Blue Shield of Indiana. Since the core business is not guaranteed sales from its own companies, it too stays on its competitive toes.

New Health Care Consumer Ventures

Creators of successful health care ventures that serve working and activist consumers also have fashioned a number of managerial innovations. Their key challenge has been to motivate health service providers to respond to their patients' desire for fast, convenient, and personalized services. Implementing the necessary human resource and operations management skills is not simple. Most health care professionals are steeped in the mores of their profession rather than trained to respond appropriately to individual patient needs. Physicians, for example, are trained to excel in diagnosis and therapy, not in efficiency or "bedside manner." Not surprisingly, some physicians refer to their patients by the name of procedures, not by their own names. When Ms. Jones, who is in room 308 and has heart disease, is referred to as the 308 CABG (pronounced "cabbage"), the acronym for a coronary artery bypass graft procedure, she is being viewed as a medical problem, rather than as a human being. Such physicians are not callous; their behavior merely reflects the somewhat depersonalized medical practices they were taught.

The Shouldice Hospital in Toronto increased patient satisfaction by means of a radical departure from traditional operational and human resource management (see Case Study 15). The difference? It delivers only one service, a hernia operation. As a result, Shouldice doctors and nurses have become highly efficient in providing the service. In addition, the hospital can more readily measure the quality of its only product and act on the results. In the Shouldice system, the surgeons receive feedback about their failures and successes. For example, if a hernia operation fails and a recurrence takes place, the patient is referred back to the original surgeon and treated for free. The hospital's service providers are selected not only for their medical skills but also for their ability to thrive in this unusual environment. They see every hernia operation as a new challenge rather than as a duplicate of many others.

Shouldice also innovated in operational management by permitting patients active involvement in the hernia operation. Patients diagnose their health status and pinpoint the hernia's location before admission; shave and clean the site of the surgery before the operation; and are encouraged to walk off the operating table soon after the procedure ends. Further patient exercise is encouraged by the physical design of the hospital. Its few stairs are small and its lawns are gently sloped so that patients recovering from a hernia operation can walk without undue strain. Also, its central dining room is the sole source of food so that patients must walk there for meals. The results of this patient involvement? Lower costs, since patients perform some of the services normally provided by nurses, aides, and orderlies; greatly enhanced patient satisfaction, since activist patients gain the control they seek; and low complication rates.

These innovations in human resource and operational management greatly simplify Shouldice's marketing. The thousands of "alumni" who attend the hospital's annual reunion are but a few of the satisfied clients who provide the word-of-mouth referrals that are the key to Shouldice's success.

New Technology Ventures

Entrepreneurs who created successful technology-based companies pulled off another difficult-to-achieve feat: they balanced their proximity to the technology with proximity to the market. Often technology-based companies offer products that only a "techie" could love or else so dilute the technology in a vain effort to make it palatable to a nontechnical buyer that it quickly becomes obsolete or loses its technological edge.

Nellcor, a California manufacturer of medical devices, exemplifies successful marketing. Unlike most providers of medical technology, Nellcor first defined the market and then designed products to meet its needs. For example, only after surveying hospitals and physicians and determining the need, did Nellcor's engineers design a blood gas analyzer that measures the level of oxygen in the blood without invading the patient's body. Although the product incorporated many existing technologies, these technologies had never before been packaged in such a useful way. Anesthesiologists eagerly bought the analyzer to lower the risk to the patient of oxygen deprivation under anesthesia.

Nellcor's management of the regulatory process was also exemplary. It used the regulatory mechanism to help the marketing function. Rather than resisting regulation, Nellcor actively supported the development of standards of practice for anesthesiologists and standards of patient safety. The standards eventually published by anesthesiologists recommended the use of noninvasive blood gas analyzers. Nellcor's proactive regulatory approach reaped handsome marketing rewards.

Its success at marketing and the management of regulation greatly eased Nellcor's financing burdens. Its stock offering was widely supported, and Nellcor gained access to the extensive equity financing it required to support its growth.

WHY SOME INNOVATORS FAILED

But for every entrepreneur who has succeeded, there are many more who have not. The industry's landscape is littered with failed health care ventures. Maxicare, at one time the country's largest publicly held HMO, filed for reorganization under bankruptcy protection, and other HMOs lost millions of dollars. Many of the ventures created to institute new methods of delivering health care have been found wanting. For example, most home health service organizations have experienced huge losses and great difficulties in providing satisfactory services. And technology-based companies all too frequently have found a surprisingly small market for their products or have been unable to deliver on the brilliant promise of their science.

Impact of Reimbursement on Innovation

Understandably, the founders of failed ventures prefer to blame a hostile reimbursement environment rather than their own shortcomings. And they are partially correct. Health insurance coverage for a product or a service can indeed make or break a company.

The rise and fall of New York City's Visiting Nurses Association (VNA) illustrates the crucial role played by health insurance payments. When New York State decreed that the indigent patients who qualify for the state's health insurance program would now be eligible for home health services, the VNA, a truly charitable organization, happily increased its staff to serve this poor and needy patient population. The agency nearly quintupled in size. But when the state suddenly cut back health insurance funding for the poor, the VNA was stuck with an increased staff and no sources of funds for its indigent patients.

Success or failure in obtaining insurance coverage dramatically impacts technology-based health care ventures as well. For example, 3M (Minnesota Mining and Manufacturing), one of the world's most innovative technology-based companies, spent nearly $30 million developing a device that would enable the deaf to hear. The marvelous technological instrument could accomplish a miracle—it restored one of the five senses. But when the federal government failed to provide full compensation for its cost in the Medicare health insurance program for the elderly, surgeons virtually stopped implanting the device and 3M dropped further development of the product.

The products of many technology-based firms have substantial potential to improve health. An inability to secure health insurance can result in grave losses to society as a whole. But sometimes health insurance coverage can accomplish just the opposite: It can help to secure new ventures that are basically ill conceived.

For example, the diversification of many nonprofit hospitals into other health-related ventures was motivated primarily by two characteristics of health insurance. First, when Medicare began to reimburse hospitals at a fixed price per procedure, hospitals feared a decline in their profits; but, because they were confident of their ability to secure insurance coverage for other types of health care ventures, they rushed to provide services other than in-patient care (abetted by lawyers and accountants who saw a gold mine in the "corporate reorganization" that would ensue). Newly reorganized nonprofit hospitals secured insurance coverage for the provision of home and ambulatory health care services, among other diversifications.

Unfortunately, hospital managers frequently lacked experience with the skills needed to manage these new businesses. Despite the extension of health insurance coverage, these managerial deficiencies caused many of the ventures to falter. For example, one hospital's diversification into the provision of birth center services created adverse publicity when it failed to deal appropriately with human resource management issues that arose between its staff and those of the birth center. (See Case Study 13 for additional discussion.)

The Three Key Managerial Skills

Most of the managerial problems encountered are obvious—in retrospect. For example, some of the new ventures whose purpose was to lower health care costs implemented few managerial control systems. One HMO that committed itself to a fixed-price provision of health care services lacked the cost-accounting systems that would enable it to determine whether its costs were higher or lower than the fixed price. Others did not articulate the leadership philosophy that they needed in order to guide their growth. While Maxicare tripled in size in its quest to become a national HMO, its founders kept a tightly centralized control system in the company's California headquarters. Some claim that Maxicare's centralized management could not keep pace with its explosive growth. Maxicare wanted rapid growth, but its managers were reluctant to decentralize the power and authority to local areas that such growth required.

The combination of inappropriate managerial control and an inappropriate leadership philosophy may have created ultimately devastating financing problems for Maxicare. When it failed to pay its physicians in a timely and accurate fashion, some of them dropped out as Maxicare providers and sued the company. The loss of the patient revenues these physicians generated was a critical factor in the company's subsequent bankruptcy. Then, too, Maxicare's acquisition of another HMO company in its drive to create a national firm was widely criticized as an overvalued transaction.[13] Its failure to implement the three skills critical to the success of a cost-controlling new health care venture—managerial control, leadership philosophy, and finance—may well have sealed Maxicare's unhappy fate.

The lack of success of technology-based companies has been caused by managerial problems different from Maxicare's. Most frequently, managers of technology-based companies acted as if the breakthroughs they sought were just around the corner. Many were so dazzled by their scientific quest that they forgot to evaluate whether the technologies had sizeable market potential.

For example, one seasoned executive founded a firm to develop a totally automated clinical laboratory instrument for use by physicians in their offices. It was intended to provide cheaper and better analyses than could be attained by sending samples to laboratories. The instrument's design required mechanical arms to manipulate blood samples contained in miniature test tubes. Their mechanical grip had to be firm enough that the test tubes would not slip and yet delicate enough that they would not

shatter. Such complicated engineering specifications cost tens of millions of development dollars. The company ran out of money before it completed the device. But even if the engineering had succeeded, the high cost of the resulting instrument would have been beyond the financial reach of the physicians who constituted its intended market.

Larger and more successful medical technology firms have also failed to achieve their aims because of difficulties in the implementation of the three key managerial skills of marketing, management of regulation, and finance. Genentech, the widely hailed California biotechnology company that commercializes highly innovative technology, has not achieved the level of sales predicted for its first major product, the blood clot-dissolving drug tissue plasminogen activator (TPA). For one thing, Genentech assumed that physicians would immediately embrace this product (it dissolves the deadly clots that can clog up the blood vessels around the heart). But physicians proved more resistant to adoption than predicted, and thus far TPA's annual sales have fallen far short of the billion-dollar level first predicted. Then, too, Genentech was stunned when federal government regulators initially refused marketing rights and then refused reimbursement for this powerful drug. Genetech failed to demonstrate the medical effectiveness and cost-effectiveness of the drug to the regulatory establishment's satisfaction. Although Genentech attempted to correct these difficulties in marketing and management of regulation, the cure may have come too late. Early stumbles caused Genentech to abandon its aim of becoming a major independent firm and to sell a controlling interest to an established pharmaceutical company to generate the financing it required.

Similar marketing mirages appeared to the managers of new consumer health service companies who became so convinced of the efficacy of their approach that they neglected to check if potential clients shared their enthusiasm. For example, although some health clubs wonder why they cannot retain clients, the answer is clear: Classes are staffed by instructors who have 19-inch necks or waists, and clearly practice what they preach, but who are ineffective communicators.

These health clubs provide little training for their instructors, many of whom are lifelong jocks who cannot comprehend how their students permitted their bodies to become flaccid and who may even privately joke about their students' physical shortcomings. Absent training and empathy, the instructors can neither effect change nor instill client loyalty. This failure in human resource management is linked to the health clubs' marketing failures. Those most in need of their services are out having a coffee break, driven from the class by the instructors' inability to motivate and guide them appropriately.

The absence of operational management skills has also hampered the success of some health clubs. Because many of their activist clients are working people who use the facilities before or after work or on weekends, the health clubs experience relatively low attendance during the weekday but high attendance at other times. Nevertheless, all too few clubs have designed an operational management system that matches this pattern of demand. Instead, during pre- and postwork hours they are crowded or require people to wait for unduly long periods of time for access to equipment or services. Such waits undermine the very feeling of mastery and convenience their clients crave. These shortcomings in operations and human resource management are central to the health clubs' lack of financial success.

WHAT LIES AHEAD?

Parts II and III detail the three opportunities and the seven skills of management needed for their successful implementation. Their purpose is to extract the lessons from past failures and successes to create the roadmap for the much-needed new health care industry.

NOTES

1. Alan Jay Lerner, *Gigi* (Winona, Minn.: Hal Leonard Publishing Corporation, n.d.), 44.

2. U. S. Department of Health and Human Services, *Health United States 1989* (Hyattsville, Md.: U.S. Government Printing Office, 1989), 226.

3. George J. Schreiber and Jean-Pierre Poullier, "Overview of International Comparisons of Health Care Expenditures," *Health Care Financing Review; annual suppl.* (1989): 6.

4. Harvard Community Health Plan, *Annual Report, 1990* (Boston: Harvard Community Health Plan, 1991), 9.

5. *Prevention Index 1987* (Emmaus, Pa.: Rodale Press, 1987), 21.

6. McDougall Associates, *Medical Health Center Study: An Initial Summary Report* (Peabody, Mass.: McDougall Associates, 1990), 1.

7 . The Conference Board, "Which Provides More for Your Money?" New York City: The Conference Board, press release no. 3786, June 7, 1990, 3.

8. "Consumer Price Index, Third Quarter, 1989," *Medical Benefits*, November 15, 1989, 4.

9. U.S. Department of Health and Human Services, *Health United States 1989* (Hyattsville, Md.: U.S. Government Printing Office, 1989), 215.

10. U.S. Department of Health and Human Services, *Health United States 1989* (Hyattsville, Md.: U.S. Government Printing Office, 1989), 215, 232.

11. Alan B. Cohen, Joel C. Cantor, Dianne C. Barker, and Robert G. Hughes, "Young Physicians and the Medical Profession," *Health Affairs*, Winter 1990, 144.

12. Joyce Jensen, "Health Care Alternatives," *American Demographics*, March 1986, 37.

13. "What Happened? Maxicare Execs 'Got What They Deserved,'" *Managed Care Outlook*; special report, March 31, 1989.

Part II

Three New Opportunities
for Health Care Ventures

This part of the book documents the demographic, social, economic, and technological changes that created the opportunities for health care organizations that reduce costs, serve new health care consumers, and develop new medical technologies. Chapters 2 through 4 describe these opportunities, calibrate the size of the changes that created them, and discuss new companies that explore them. Chapter 4 concludes with a prediction of the likely future of each of the three opportunities.

Many new ideas are consonant with more than one of the three opportunities. Many activist consumer products also lower health care costs because consumers perform some of the services once provided by expensive professionals. The reverse is also true: Many cost-lowering health care products, like ambulatory health services, also appeal to working and activist consumers. And many technological innovations simultaneously appeal to activist

consumers and lower health care costs, like the home diagnostic tests based on monoclonal antibody technology that enable consumers to control the timing and site of diagnostic procedures that otherwise would have to be performed in expensive laboratories.

But companies that focus on more than one of the three opportunities rarely succeed. Why? Because the seven skills should be implemented in different ways for products designed to respond to each of the three and should receive different degrees of emphasis. A new technological product, for example, requires an emphasis on management of regulation that is uncalled for in the case of new consumer products. Few companies can balance the different emphases and different ways of implementing the seven skills that are required if more than one opportunity is explored simultaneously.

2

Ventures To Control Health Care Costs

The most obvious way to change the health care system is to control its costs. The challenge of controlling costs caught the attention of many business people who thought their skills would enable them to meet this challenge without sacrificing health care quality. They developed three new ways to control health care costs: vertical and horizontal integration, shifts in the continuum of care, and utilization review.

INTEGRATION FOR COST CONTROL

Some found the cost-reducing solution they sought when they observed that the health care industry was essentially a cottage industry, consisting of tens of thousands of stand-alone sites, including the many hospitals and nursing homes. They reasoned, "It will be a piece of cake to reduce these costs. All we have to do is buy a bunch of these stand-alone facilities and merge them into a sleek, efficient chain."

Horizontal Integration

The efficiencies they envisioned, which occur in any business as its size expands, are termed *economies of scale.* For example, consider a hospital's information systems department. In a stand-alone, 200-bed hospital, the department might have direct costs of $600,000, which equates to an annual cost per bed of $3,000. But in a chain of 30 such hospitals, the department's costs might grow to $6 million, which means that the cost per bed nosedives to only $1,000. Such economies are achieved through *horizontal integration*, the melding of many individual enterprises into one. They account for the success of businesses as diverse as the McDonald's fast-food restaurants, which benefit from the economies of shared marketing and purchasing, and the Hyatt hotel chain, in which architectural and service concepts are shared. (Case Studies 10 and 12 describe companies that attempted horizontal integration.)

Vertical Integration

Economies of scale are also obtained with *vertical integration,* which links the production function with the sales function. Vertical integration is usually found in companies whose manufacturing costs vary only a little as the volume of production changes; for example, a chemical company whose large factory will cost nearly the same to operate no matter what quantity of chemicals is produced. In high fixed-cost companies, a sales and distribution force is created to ensure that all the quantity that can be produced is sold. Because total costs will remain virtually the same regardless of sales volume, profits will increase rapidly with increased sales. Every additional sales dollar results in an almost identical increase in profit. For this reason, pharmaceutical companies with huge plants usually employ their own sales force, while other companies, whose costs can be more easily adjusted with changes in volume, are content to permit distributors or other outside marketing agents to sell their products.

Because many health service providers required large fixed costs, they appeared to be prime candidates for vertical integration. Hospital costs, for example, are largely fixed. Regardless of the number of patients a hospital treats, its depreciation, interest, space, and administration costs will remain virtually the same. These account for over half the costs of many hospitals. Though nursing and other direct patient costs will change with the volume of patients treated, such changes occur only with a large change in patient volume. No hospital would fire or hire a nurse because of a minor variance in patient volume. Indeed, in the short term, the only hospital costs to vary directly with patient volume are those of food, laundry, and drugs. These account for less than 15 percent of the costs of many hospitals.

Combining hospitals and physicians with a sales function to ensure full utilization of their fixed costs made sense. The sales force could generate volume in a number of ways. For example, it could offer large buyers, such as companies with many employees, a substantial price discount in return for buyers' directing their employees to the hospitals and doctors it represents. The health services would be sold in the context of a health insurance policy.

These new vertically integrated organizations were baptized with various unfelicitous names: Health maintenance organizations (HMOs), in-

dependent practitioner associations (IPAs), and preferred provider organizations (PPOs). Whatever their names and structural characteristics, all of them shared one common theme: They integrated the producers of health care services, physicians and hospitals, with the health insurance policies that sold the producers' services.

Jokes about the resulting health care alphabet soup were rife. But the jokes and initials masked important structural differences. One difference was in the method of provider compensation. Some of the organizations, called *staff HMOs*, employed only salaried physicians and sometimes owned their own hospitals; others paid independent physicians and hospitals a fixed price for providing each patient's health services (known as *capitation*); and yet others paid discounted fees for every physician service and hospital day. A second difference was in the organizational form chosen by the physicians. Some contracted only with independent physicians working in their own offices, others contracted only with groups of physicians, and yet others were indifferent to the physicians' organizational form. The third major difference was in the physicians' freedom to see patients other than those provided by the organization. In a *closed panel* organization, the physicians were limited to seeing the patients insured by the organization, whereas in an *open panel* organization, physicians were free to see any patients regardless of their source of payment. The fourth major difference was in the patients' ability to choose physicians. Patients who belonged to staff HMOs generally had the smallest choice, while those who belonged to PPOs were fully insured if they saw the "preferred providers" but were insured for a smaller percentage of their expenses, frequently 80 percent, if they saw other providers.

Different combinations of structural characteristics resulted in different types of organizations. The cost-controlling power of each type depended on its particular combination of characteristics. Staff HMOs, closed panel organizations with salaried providers, demonstrated the best cost-control record, but because they were the most expensive to initiate and offered patients only a limited choice of providers, they had the slowest rate of growth—only 1.2 percent from 1988 to 1989—and high disenrollment rates.[1] PPOs gave patients a larger choice of physicians and hospitals but achieved less control over total costs, perhaps because providers could compensate for their discounted fees by increasing the number of services they rendered.[2] Insurance companies that paid capitated fees found enrolling physicians to be more difficult than other forms of insurance companies because many physicians rejected the risk imposed by having to provide all of the services a patient might need for a prearranged set price. (See Case Study 19 for a description of a capitated-fee venture.)

Horizontal integration and vertical integration were not limited to the health service industry. The pharmaceutical and medical supply distribution industry also became increasingly consolidated, as illustrated by Baxter's acquisition of American Hospital Supply. And some middlemen were eliminated in new vertically integrated ventures. For example, the billion-dollar drug distribution company Medco Containment Services eliminated the drug store by sending pharmaceuticals directly to patients by mail. It claims impressive economies, with average savings of 20–30 percent over alternatives.[3]

The health industry innovators who dreamed of reducing costs by means of integration in some ways succeeded beyond their wildest dreams. For example, by 1989, HMOs had enrolled 14 percent of the U.S. population,[4] and PPOs had enrolled nearly 126 million employees and 60 million eligible family members.[5] The integrated ventures included the Hospital Corporation of America, which earned in its heyday annual revenues of over $4 billion and had more than 400 affiliated hospitals; Maxicare, one of a number of multi-billion-dollar chains of HMOs, IPAs, and PPOs; and hundreds of chains of nursing homes, psychiatric hospitals, drug addiction treatment centers, drug stores, medical supply and pharmaceutical distributors, and home health care providers. (The leading HMOs and PPOs and hospital and

nursing home chains are listed in Tables 2-1, 2-2, and 2-3.) They all shared one common managerial characteristic: A hub of core management intended to create the efficient administrative systems that all chain members could share.

REARRANGING THE CONTINUUM OF CARE

Integration was not the only cost-reducing solution attempted. Some saw a completely different way to reduce costs. They focused on the facilities for providing health care services. "If we can get patients out of inpatient facilities and into ambulatory ones or even to their own homes, we are bound to lower costs," they reasoned. (Inpatient facilities have beds in which patients sleep while recuperating; ambulatory facilities enable patients to "ambulate" or walk back to the beds in their own homes.) They wanted to rearrange the distribution of patients in the "continuum of care." In terms of the continuum as represented in Table 2-4, they wanted to move patients as far as possible, because at this end of the continuum housing and medical resources were less expensive.

These innovators focused primarily on the hospital, the most expensive provider of health care services. In 1989, hospitals accounted for 39 percent of all health care service expenses but served only 8 percent of the population.[6] Innovators reasoned, "Costs can clearly be reduced by providing services at a site other than the hospital—one with lower fixed costs." Would quality of care be sacrificed by using alternative sites? In many cases the answer was no. Indeed, in many instances quality of care was improved because the patients were not exposed to other health care risks as they would be in the hospital.

Three factors enabled the movement of health services out of the hospital. First, consumers wanted care that was convenient and controllable. Activist consumers bridled at the passivity implicit in lying on a hospital bed or operating table. Nearly 80 percent preferred same day ambulatory surgery to an overnight hospital stay.[7] They jumped at the chance to be

Table 2-1 Leading Chains and General Service HMOs

	Potential Enrollees	Tax Status
General Service HMOs		
1. Kaiser Permanente	5,600,000	Nonprofit
2. Blue Cross and Blue Shield	4,800,000	Varies
3. CIGNA Healthplan	2,000,000	For-profit
4. AETNA Life Insurance/PARTNERS	1,200,000	Varies
5. U.S. Healthcare, Inc.	1,100,000	For-profit
6. Health Insurance Plan of Greater New York	830,000	Nonprofit
7. PruCare (Prudential)	743,000	For-profit
8. Healthnet	566,000	Nonprofit
9. FHP	566,000	For-profit
10. Pacificare Health Systems, Inc.	540,000	For-profit
General Service PPOs		
1. Blue Cross and Blue Shield	11,800,000	Varies
2. USA Healthnet	4,700,000	For-profit
3. MetLife Network	2,900,000	For-profit
4. Affordable Health Care Concepts	2,700,000	For-profit
5. Admar Corp.	2,700,000	For-profit
6. Beech St., Inc.	1,900,000	For-profit
7. PruCare/Pru Net	1,600,000	For-profit
8. Travelers Preferred	1,400,000	For-profit
9. Private Healthcare Systems, Ltd.	1,300,000	For-profit
10. Aetna Life Insurance Co.	1,300,000	For-profit

Source: Reprinted from *Business Insurance,* December 1990, p. 1, with permission of Crain Communications, Inc., © 1990.

Table 2-2 Leading Investor-owned Hospital Chains (Ranked by Number of Beds, 1989)

Company	1989 Revenues (in billions of dollars)	1989 Profits (in billions of dollars)	Number of Beds
1. Hospital Corporation of America	$ 4.28	$ .8	24,767
2. Quorum Health Resources	NA	NA	21,067
3. Humana	4.09	.3	17,584
4. American Medical International	2.75	(.12)	14,888
5. Health Trust	1.77	NA	12,788
6. Charter Medical	1.18	(.37)	10,283
7. National Medical Enterprises	3.67	(.19)	7,670
8. Hospital Management Professionals	NA	NA	7,232
9. Paracelsus Healthcare Corporation	NA	NA	7,149
10. Psychiatric Institutes of America	3.67	(.19)	5,653

Source: Reprinted from *HealthWeek,* September 24, 1990, DR-8, with permission of HealthWeek Publications, Inc., © 1990.

Table 2-3 Leading Investor-owned Nursing Home Chains (Ranked by Number of Beds, 1988)

System	Number of Beds (1988)	Number of Units (1988)
1. Beverly Enterprises	109,951	1,000
2. ARA Living Centers	27,578	251
3. National Heritage	25,000	223
4. Manor Care	20,760	160
5. Health Care & Retirement Corporation	16,439	130
6. UniCare Health Facilities	15,277	134
7. National HealthCorp	8,515	70
8. Diversified Health Services	7,810	31
9. Angeli Group	6,908	55
10. Horizon Health Corporation	6,343	57
11. Meritcare	5,687	57
12. Meridian Healthcare	4,990	34
13. Britthave	4,560	47
14. Geriatrics & Medical Centers	4,494	22
15. American Medical Services	4,392	28

Source: Reprinted from *Standard and Poor's Industry Surveys: Health Care,* Vol. 157, No. 28, Sec. 1, pp. 28–29, with permission of Standard and Poor's Corporation, © 1988.

ambulatory patients. Not surprisingly, the volume of ambulatory surgical procedures increased enormously in the past decade.

Technological developments also made it possible to provide surgical and other care outside the hospital. "Smart" pumps enabled infusion therapy to be provided in the home because they limited snarls and blockages in the lines and thus reduced the need for continuous medical supervision. Small tubes with optic fibers (endoscopes), lasers, and miniature instruments and cameras enabled surgery to be performed using only small incisions and natural body openings. They reduced the need for the large surgical incisions that require long periods to heal and intensive nursing care. Surgeons can now insert an endoscope through a small opening, carefully place a camera inside to monitor progress, and sometimes use a laser as the main surgical instrument. The result? Many surgical procedures are performed on an ambulatory basis, including cataract removals, tonsillectomies, dilation and curettages (D & Cs), and knee repairs. Furthermore, the procedures tend to be of higher quality, because the

smaller incisions and use of lasers reduce the chance of infection, decrease trauma, and promote rapid healing.

The third factor was perhaps the most important. Many services were provided in hospitals for reasons that no longer apply. For example, although victims of head trauma injuries require intensive physical and speech therapy, they do not need the extensive laboratory, radiology, and physician resources of the average hospital. Nevertheless, many head trauma victims, after receiving their initial care in the hospital, remained there for the duration of their lengthy recovery periods.

"Niched" Facilities

Entrepreneurs carved out those hospital services that could be delivered in nonhospital sites in a process called "niching." The economies they achieved were stunning. For example, an average day in a rehabilitation center costs 25–50 percent less than a day in a hospital.

Table 2-4 The Continuum of Care

		Home Care			
	Child and Family Care	Chronic Long-Term Care/Hospice	Acute Care/ Rehabilitation	High-Tech Level Life Support	Physicians' Offices
Types of Services	Social services; nursing; education	Homemaker chores; activities of daily living; support	Skilled nursing; rehabilitation therapy; medical social services; homemaker chores	Kidney dialysis; intravenous therapy; respiratory therapy	All health care services that do not require a hospital stay
Providers	Social workers; nutritionists, educators	Unskilled aides for care; skilled nurses for hospice	Skilled nursing; therapists; unskilled aides	Specialty skilled nursing; drugs and supplies; equipment	430,000 patient care MDs (solo practitioners, 35%; employed, 25%; HMO participants, 32%; office-based, 76%; hospital-based, 24%)
Estimated Market Size	Title XX = $800 million in 1981	N/A	Medicare = $2.4 billion; private—N/A	Infusion services = $2 billion; total home health = $8.6 billion	$133 billion
Cost per Unit and Duration	N/A	$50 per visit; indefinite	$100 per visit; 1–3 months	$185 per day; 6–9 months	Surgical visit = $51; medical visit = $31

	Free-Standing Ambulatory Care Centers	Nursing Homes	Specialty Hospitals	Acute Care Hospitals
Types of Services	General medicine; ambulatory surgery; outpatient cancer therapy; kidney dialysis; diagnostic imaging; mental health; rehabilitation therapy	Post–acute hospital; skilled nursing facility; intermediate nursing home; lower level nursing home	Psychiatric hospitals; rehabilitation hospitals	Private, nonprofit community hospitals; teaching hospitals; state, county, and municipal government hospitals
Providers	Rehabilitation, 190 centers; outpatient mental health, 1,800 centers	116,000 nursing homes, over 25 beds	Psychiatric, 684 hospitals; rehabilitation, 135 hospitals	Community, 5,611 hospitals; teaching, 912 hospitals; government, 1,524 hospitals
Estimated Market Size	Rehabilitation = $1.1 billion; psychiatric = $3.0 billion; for others, number is unknown	Nursing homes = $54 billion	Psychiatric = $7.0 billion; rehabilitation = $5.47 billion	Hospitals = $250 billion
Cost per Unit and Duration	General medicine cost per visit = $80; others = 20% to 50% lower than hospital care (e.g., rehabilitation costs, $100 per visit)	Cost per day = $50–$100; average duration = 450 days	Psychiatric = $294–$613 per day ($7,500 to $10,000 per stay); Rehabilitation = $400 per day; 6-month stay	Cost per day = $500; cost per stay = $3,500–$4,000

Note: Data categories are not mutually exclusive and may overlap.

Sources: Laura Summer and Regina E. Herzlinger, "Note on Home Health Services" (Boston: Harvard University, 1988); American Medical Association, *Socioeconomic Characteristics of Physicians* and *Physician Characteristics and Distribution* (Chicago: American Medical Association, various years); Dorothy E. Ryan and Cheryl L. Alexander, "The Rehabilitation Industry" (San Francisco: Robertson, Stephens and Co, March 9, 1990), 3–6; Sherrie Epstein and Regina E. Herzlinger, "Note on Psychiatric Services" (Boston: Harvard University, 1988); "Cost Utilization Trends in Psych. Drug Abuse," *Medical Benefits*, March 30, 1990, 4; Joyce Lallman, Sherrie Epstein, and Regina E. Herzlinger, "Note on Long Term Care" (Boston: Harvard University, 1989); American Hospital Association, *Hospital Statistics* (Chicago: American Hospital Association, various years).

Niched health facilities reduced costs in two ways. First, they lowered fixed costs. The showcase head trauma rehabilitation center of the Greenery, for example, is located in a residential area rather than in an expensive downtown building, and it uses far fewer radiology, laboratory, and medical facilities than a hospital. Second, and more importantly, the founders of these new organizations focused their considerable talents and energies solely on the provision of one type of care. They thus developed an expertise that more general purpose health care providers were hard pressed to match. (Case Study 13 describes a niched health facility.)

Employers supported niched facilities. For example, 42 percent of them offered better health insurance coverage for patients selecting outpatient surgery and 15 percent required it.[8] No wonder niched health service providers proliferated: Technology made them feasible, consumers made them desirable, and employers made them affordable. In 1990, they included companies that provided ambulatory surgical services, like Medical Care International; companies that provided home health care services, like Critical Care America; head trauma rehabilitation firms, like the Greenery; and providers of post–acute hospital care, like Vencor. Their individual growth was stunning, too. Ambulatory surgical procedures have increased to over 40 percent of all surgeries. All the niched facilities shared one characteristic: 20 years ago their patients would have been hospitalized.

UTILIZATION REVIEW

The last major strategy to reduce health care costs emerged from observations that health utilization and resource patterns varied widely across the country. For example, Medicare enrollees living in the Pacific region had nearly 50 percent fewer hospital discharges than those in the East South Central area.[9] And while Massachusetts hospitals employed 6 people per average daily patient in 1986, South Dakota employed only 3.3 and South Dakota's health care ranking was higher than that of Massachusetts.[10,11] These variations seemed to offer an opportunity to business innovators: "Suppose we review the use of hospitals and physicians and insist that they follow our prescribed pattern of utilization. Imagine the cost reduction if Massachusetts used resources like South Dakota."

A new industry was spawned to provide the services necessary for utilization reviews. The review system included many mechanisms for reducing costs. For example, before admission to a hospital, an insured patient, in many cases, must now be certified by a utilization reviewer—a physician's say no longer guarantees admission. Once admitted, the patient's length of stay is monitored, and after discharge yet another reviewer supplies an opinion about whether the hospital-based surgical or diagnostic procedure was justified. These reviews are referred to as perspective, concurrent, and retrospective utilization reviews, respectively.

Quality Reviews

Concern about the effect of cost cutting on the quality of care created yet another industry whose purpose is to measure and manage the process of creating high-quality services. Unlike the utilization reviewers, who primarily evaluated hospital admissions and lengths of stay, the quality reviewers measured the quality of the care the patients received and that the hospitals and physicians provided. Firms like MediQual Systems delineated actual and predicted sickness and death rates adjusted for the severity of illness of the patients. In many cases, MediQual's data indicated no correlation between high prices and quality. The reverse pattern frequently prevailed—hospitals with higher quality charged lower prices.

Desperate employers seized this apparent opportunity to control their runaway health care costs. Virtually all large employers required some form of utilization review as part of their employees' health benefit plan. The number of new ventures providing utilization review services soared from 8 in the early 1970s to 38 by 1988.[12] By then, they reviewed the health

Table 2-5 Ten Largest General Service Utilization Review Firms, 1988

Company (Ownership)	Lives Serviced	Full-Time Staff			
		Total	Physicians	Registered Nurses	Physicians on Retainer
Intracorp (CIGNA Corp.)	11,500,000	600	NA	NA	NA
Corporate Health Strategies (Metropolitan Life Insurance Co.)	6,200,000	243	6	228	7
HealthCare COMPARE Corp. (independent)	5,000,000	433	27	300	NA
Peer Review Analysis Inc. (privately held)	4,000,000	45	7	16	65
Corporate Health Care Management (EQUICOR Inc.)	3,750,000	236	9	93	23
Cost Care Inc. (independent)	2,900,000	268	19	136	6
Value Health Inc. (privately held)	2,800,000	119	5	9	7
The Sunderbruch Corp. (privately held)	2,683,000	293	2	89	0
Western Medical Review (nonprofit corporation)	2,000,000	40	1	22	50
August International Corp. (privately held)	1,979,750	230	3	48	45

Source: Reprinted from *Business Insurance,* February 20, 1989, p. 1, with permission of Crain Communications, Inc., © 1989.

utilization patterns of over 40 million people (Table 2-5).

THE RESULTS

Health care costs remained recalcitrant despite these efforts to control them. Health industry apologists claimed the growth in costs was caused by factors beyond their control, like growth in the population and in the intensity of the services received. But a comparative economic analysis belies these claims. The four-country comparison in Figure 2-1 shows health inflation as a significant factor in the growth of health care costs even after adjust-ments for growth in population, general inflation, and intensity.

American employers suffered greatly. Health plan costs per employee rose from $1,724 in 1985 to $2,748 in 1989.[13] By 1988, employers' health costs equaled their net profits and were growing more rapidly than any other expense.[14] Employers soured on HMOs: 65 percent said that HMOs were not successful in cost-control.[15] General Motors found its 1988 PPO accruals higher than its traditional health plan.[16] HMO enrollment growth slowed dramatically and some HMOs suffered continued financial losses.[17] Utilization reviews were frequently seen as ineffective,[18] and the growth in hospital costs continued unabated.[19] (See Case Study 18

Annual Compound Rate of Growth

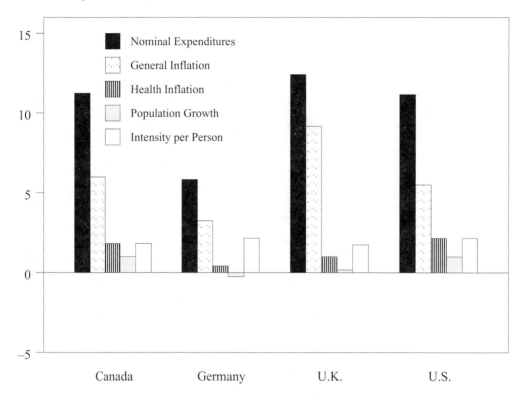

Figure 2-1 Factors Affecting Health Cost Increases—Decomposition of the Expenditure Increases, 1975–1987. *Source*: Robert B. Helms, "Investing in Our Future," Conference on Investing in Our Future, Clark University, Worcester, Mass., December 5, 1990, based on George J. Schieber and Jean-Pierre Poullier, "Overview of International Comparisons of Health Care Expenditures," *Health Care Financing Review*, 1989 Annual Supplement, Table 4, p. 6.

for a description of one employer's approach to the problem.)

As the 1990s began health care cost control was an opportunity still waiting to be fulfilled.

NOTES

1. "National Directory of HMOs 1990," *Medical Benefits*, December 15, 1990, 8.

2. Cynthia B. Sullivan and Thomas Rice, "Data Watch," *Health Affairs,* Summer 1991, 108.

3. *Medco Annual Report* (Fair Lawn, N.J.: Medco Containment Services, 1989), 8.

4. "Marion Merrell Dow Managed Care Digest," *Medical Benefits,* February 15, 1991, 5.

5. U.S. Department of Commerce, *U.S. Industrial Outlook, 1991—Health and Medical Services* (Washington, D.C.: U.S. Department of Commerce, 1991), 44-1.

6. National Center for Health Statistics, *National Health Interview Survey* (Hyattsville, Md.: National Center for Health Statistics, 1989).

7. Joyce Jensen, "Health Care Alternatives," *American Demographics,* March 1986, 36-39.

8. "Ambulatory Surgery Growing," *The BBI Newsletter*, September 18, 1989, 133.

9. U.S. Department of Health and Human Services, *Health United States 1988* (Hyattsville, Md.: U.S. Government Printing Office, 1988), 176.

10. U.S. Department of Health and Human Services, *Health United States 1988* (Hyattsville, Md.: U.S. Government Printing Office, 1988), 146.

11. "1989 NWNL State Health Rankings," *Medical Benefits*, November 15, 1989, 11.

12. Christine Woolsey, "UR Vendors Push Product over Price," *Business Insurance*, February 18, 1990, 3.

13. "Recent Steep Rise in Employers Health Costs Continued in 1990," *HealthWeek*, February 12, 1990, 4.

14. Katherine R. Levit, Mark S. Freeland, and Daniel R. Waldo, "Health Spending and Ability to Pay," *Health Care Financing Review* (Spring 1989): 9; "Meeting the Health Care Crisis," *Medical Benefits*, June 30, 1989, 1.

15. Sue Shellenbarger, "As HMO Premiums Soar, Employers Sour on the Plans and Check Out Alternatives," *Wall Street Journal*, February 27, 1990, B1.

16. "GM, Disappointed in its PPOs, Develops Specs to Guide Cutbacks," *Medical Benefits,* November 15, 1989, 8.

17. U.S. Department of Commerce, *U.S. Industrial Outlook, 1991—Health*, 44-3; Judy Greenwald, "Health Profits Improve," *Business Insurance*, March 26, 1990, 35.

18. "UR Industry Needs to Shape Up," *Managed Healthcare*, January 8, 1990, 23.

19. U.S. Department of Commerce, *U.S. Industrial Outlook, 1991—Health and Medical Services.*

3

Ventures To Develop
New Technologies

The second opportunity was perhaps the most dazzling. It held the promise of revolutionizing the provision of health care by creating organizations to develop new medical technologies.

THE OPPORTUNITIES OF NEW MEDICAL TECHNOLOGIES

Three technologies held the greatest potential. One was *computer technology*, whose increasing cost-effectiveness produced the lasers, cameras, sensors, and radios that provide the innards for powerful new medical devices. These devices can peer into the human body and dissolve tumors and arterial plaque without incisions, shatter kidney stones and gallstones with sound, replicate some of the five senses, and control faulty bodily mechanisms with greater accuracy and less pain than ever before possible.

Another promising opportunity was *biomaterials technology*, the development and use of materials that could be inserted in the body without triggering the massive counterattack it normally mounts against foreign invaders. These biomaterials may ultimately create the bionic person—replete with artificially implanted joints, heart, skin, liver, bones, veins, and arteries. When coupled with computer-based devices, they could regulate an erratic heart; accurately aim time-released doses of powerful drugs, hormones, and enzymes at the intended sites; and provide precise diagnostic sensors.

Perhaps most enthralling was *biotechnology*, the potential use of living organisms and biological processes to manufacture useful natural products. Though we have long used biotechnology to make bread, brew beer, and ferment soy sauce, its power was enormously magnified by the discovery of the structure of genes. With this discovery, it was possible to diagnose and correct genetic defects and to direct the genes to grow large quantities of useful, naturally occurring enzymes and other substances.

All three technologies have one thing in common: the potential to increase vastly the quality of health care—to reverse crippling genetic defects and to enable people to see, hear, and walk better and conduct lives freed of pain. No long complicated tale needs to be spun about their possible impact. It is immediately and stunningly apparent.

Economic opportunities drove innovation as well. For one thing, the markets for drugs and devices are enormous. The cardiovascular drug market for U.S. manufacturers alone accounted for nearly $5 billion in revenues in 1989. Even syringes and needles, which might seem to be minor products, represent a half-billion-dollar market (see Tables 3-1 to 3-4 for market size data). One successful drug could potentially command a billion dollars in annual revenues. No wonder many of the entrepreneurs who entered the pharmaceutical industry set as their goal the development of a billion-dollar company. It seemed entirely feasible.

RISKS OF DEVELOPING NEW TECHNOLOGY

Economic Risks

But the economic picture had its dark side. The patents on many established pharmaceuticals were expiring. (A patent grants an inventor a monopoly on the use of the invention for a certain period of time.) By 1990, half of Eli Lilly's patented drug sales producers went "off patent," as did 47 percent of Merck's and nearly 40 percent of Bristol-Myers', American Home Products', Johnson & Johnson's, Upjohn's, Pfizer's, and SmithKline's.[1] The generic market, in which off-patent drugs are sold primarily on the basis of price competition, was heating up. In 1 year, generic revenues climbed by $600 million to a record $4 billion in 1989; they are expected to climb to $13.2 billion by 1995, increasing from 12.5 percent of the ethical drug market in 1988 to 26.9 percent by 1995.[2] (Ethical drugs can be sold only with a doctor's prescription. Patented ethical drugs can be sold only by the companies that hold the patents. Off-patent ethical drugs can be sold by any licensed manufacturer.) Furthermore, governments are increasing the pressure to lower the prices of drugs and technology.

Worldwide competitors understood the opportunities thus created. American pharmaceutical companies earn substantial revenues abroad and the Japanese drug companies, among others, entered overseas markets.

Takeda, one of the largest Japanese pharmaceuticals, aimed to quadruple its international sales as a percentage of its revenues by the mid-1990s. MITI, Japan's juggernaut Ministry of International Trade and Industry, focused on biotechnology as a major target. The Japanese were willing to spend massive sums of money to realize their goals through large investments in U.S. biotechnology firms and even larger acquisitions. Chugai, a $900-million Japanese pharmaceutical, for example, paid $100 million for Gen-Probe; entered into a marketing agreement with Upjohn for EPO, a potential biotechnology blockbuster drug; and invested in Genetics Institute, a Cambridge, Massachusetts, biotechnology firm.[3]

Research Risks

The threats created by the loss of patent protection and global competition were dwarfed by the intrinsic difficulties of creating and producing innovative technological products.

For example, development of the plastic blood bag that is so widely used for the collection, storage, and infusion of blood required 12 years and scores of scientists and engineers skilled in plastics, production and tooling methodology, sealing and sterilization techniques, paper technology, anticoagulator stability, red cell preservation, and blood bank practices. Dr. Carl Walter, the inventor of the blood bag, enumerated the daunting technological breakthroughs needed for this seemingly simple product: plastic strong enough to be sterilized, flexible enough to withstand freezing, and impervious to bacterial growth; a steam sterilizing process that would not burst the bags, discolor the blood, or collapse the tubes; and a needle that could be safely and easily used to collect blood.

Dr. Walter founded the immensely successful blood company Fenwal to develop the product. Ultimately, despite his vision and persistence, luck played almost as large a part in its development as skill. The 12-year search for a suitable plastic ended with a chance conversation on an airplane between two strangers: One

Table 3-1 U.S. Pharmaceutical Market

Therapeutic Category	1989 U.S. Shipments		1988 Price Index (1982=100)	1988 Revenues Worldwide (millions $)
	millions $	%		
Central Nervous System	$ 6,498	20%	NA	$ 14,080
Anti-infectives	5,131	16	134.2	15,820
Cardiovasculars	4,826	15	185.8	22,350
Respiratory Therapy	3,637	11	NA	10,500
Neoplasms and Endocrine	2,388	8	126.6 [a]	10,760
Vitamins and Nutrients	2,618	8	120.1 [b]	NA
Dermatologicals	1,430	5	148.3	5,890
Digestive and Genitourinary[c]	4,335	14	—	27,480
Others	1,070	3	—	21,230
Total	$31,933	100%		128,110

[a]Price index is for endocrine only.
[b]Price index is for vitamins only.
[c]Dollar data are for gastrointestinal products only. Price index for laxatives is 135.4; for antacids, 143.5.

Sources: Standard and Poor's, *Industry Surveys: Health Care*, November 8, 1990, and July 13, 1989; *Scrip*, February 14, 1990, p. 29.

Table 3-2 U.S. Pharmaceutical Companies

Company	1990 Sales (billions $)		Percentage of U.S. Ethical Sales Off-Patent Drugs*
	Worldwide	U.S.	
American Home Products	$ 6.8	$ 4.6	87%
Bristol-Myers Squibb	10.3	7.0	26
Glaxo Holdings	5.4	2.1	20
Eli Lilly	5.2	3.3	44
Marion Merrell Dow	2.5	1.8	100
Merck	7.7	4.1	20
Pfizer	6.4	3.5	78
Schering-Plough	3.3	1.9	66
SmithKline Beecham	8.7	3.9	74
Syntex	1.7	1.2	90
Upjohn	3.0	1.8	91
Warner-Lambert	4.7	2.4	100

*Percent U.S. ethical drug sales off-patent 1987–94 vs. 1989 U.S. ethical drug sales.

Source: Excerpted from *Forbes,* April 15, 1991, p. 52, with permission of Forbes Publications, Inc., © 1991.

Table 3-3 Top-Selling Drugs in 1989

Name of Drug	Company	Treatment Category	Estimated Revenues (millions $)*
Zantac	Glaxo	Gastrointestinal	2,373 [1]
Capoten	Bristol-Myers Squibb	Hypertension	1,267
Vasotec	Merck	Hypertension	1,195
Tagamet	SmithKline Beecham	Gastrointestinal	1,030
Tenormin	ICI	Hypertension	1,020
Voltaren	Ciba-Geigy	Arthritis	975
Adalat	Bayer, Takeda	Hypertension	850 [2]
Ceclor	Eli Lilly	Anti-infection	696
Cardizem	Marion	Hypertension	658
Naprosyn	Syntex	Arthritis	645
Omnipaque	Sterling, Daiichi, Schering AG, Hafslund Nycomed	Imaging	620
Rocephin	Hoffman-La Roche	Anti-infection	597
Feldene	Pfizer	Arthritis	585
Mevacor	Merck	High cholesterol	556
Ventolin	Glaxo	Asthma	555
Zovirax	Wellcome	Viral infections	537
Augmentin	SmithKline Beecham	Anti-infection	497
Zaditen	Sandoz, Sankyo	Asthma	484 [3]
Ortho-Novum	Johnson & Johnson	Pregnancy prevention	450
Procardia	Pfizer	Hypertension	440

*Excludes bulk sales to [1]Sankyo, [2]Takeda, [3]Sankyo

Source: Reprinted from *Scrip-World Pharmaceutical News,* Review Issue 1989, p. 12, with permission of PJB Publications Ltd., © 1989. Based on a Barclays de Zoete Wedd investment report.

Table 3-4 Medical Devices Market

Market	1988 (millions $)	1989E (millions $)	1990E (millions $)	Compound Growth Rate (%)
Worldwide	$ 56,100	$ 60,000	$ 64,200	7%
United States	23,600	26,000	28,600	10
Surgical Appliances	9,100	10,000	11,000	10
Medical Instruments	7,200	7,800	8,500	9
Electromedical Equipment	3,400	3,500	3,600	3
X-Ray Equipment	1,750	1,800	1,850	2
Other	2,150	2,900	3,650	—

Note: E = estimate

Source: Reprinted from *Medical and Healthcare Marketplace Guide,* by R.C. Smith, Jr., pp. II–60, with permission of MLR Publishing Company, © 1991.

a Fenwal engineer and the other an inventor of a new plastic that possessed all the desired properties.[4]

Development Risks

These difficulties characterize the development of drugs and devices as well. The U.S. drug product development process, for example, requires proof of the structure of each drug's active ingredient and the formulation of each drug in ways that allow testing of its safety and efficacy. Even this seemingly simple step is laden with stumbling blocks. For example, testing a solid oral form of the drug frequently requires the addition of bulk and color to the active ingredient to achieve desired properties of stability, lubrication, and dissolution rate. The additives and the drug container may adversely affect its chemical and physical properties. These difficulties are amplified as a result of the many forms a drug can take. It can be formulated as a solid tablet, a capsule, time-released granules, a powder, and a liquid. It can also be formulated as a dermatological product, a nasal solution, a substance for inhalation or injection, a suppository, a transdermal device, an aerosol, and an opthalmologic mixture, among others.[5]*

Newly formulated U.S. drugs must then go through the extensive testing protocols described in Chapter 6. Small wonder that a new drug requires from $60 million to $200 million before it comes to market. It begins with a process governed by chance discoveries and trial and error as much as science and ends with 1 out of 3,000 drugs being commercialized.[6]

Manufacturing Risks

Last but not least, production poses a major risk for medical technology companies. For example, the biotechnology production process, in which large numbers of organisms are grown in vats full of rich nutrients to produce a desired product, is laden with pitfalls. If *Escherichia coli* bacteria are used as the host, the process causes them to produce large amounts of a foreign protein, one that is of no natural use to them. This leads to instability and the chance that the altered genes of the bacteria will mutate back to a more natural state. And because *E. coli* bacteria retain their proteins, rather than secreting them as antibiotic cells do, they must be broken apart through complicated separation procedures. Not surprisingly, the yield from these procedures can be very low. An alternative process uses mammalian cells or yeast cells, which secrete their product, but the

genetic processing is much more complicated and difficult to control and the cells require more carefully controlled environments to survive.

Even the manufacturer of conventional drugs or devices faces the risk of not passing the U.S. Food and Drug Administration's (FDA's) good-manufacturing practices (GMP) hurdle. The LyphoMed company is an example. LyphoMed produced generic electrolytes, vitamins, anti-infectives, cardiovascular drugs, and other injectables under private label for hospitals and pharmacies. Overall sales grew from $6 million in 1981 to $68 million in 1985, with profits at 10 percent. Alex Brown, an investment bank, predicted LyphoMed would become a $500-million company by 1990 and cited its reputation for product quality. New products were said to be the cornerstone of its growth, with some 40 new products already in the regulatory pipeline in 1986.

One year later, the company found itself in serious trouble with the FDA. Although the FDA relaxed testing requirements for approval of generic drugs in 1984, it insisted on compliance with the GMP regulations for production and quality control. It periodically audits firms for GMP compliance. In November 1987, the FDA's routine inspection found GMP deficiencies at one of LyphoMed's plants and subsequently reported 40 violations in follow-up inspections. In the summer of 1988, FDA inspectors cited the company for bacterial contamination of an intravenous drug solution. LypoMed inventories were seized and production facilities closed, to the acute discomfort of the firm and its clients (but of course to the benefit of the public).[7]

AN EXAMPLE OF OPPORTUNITIES AND RISKS: THE GENENTECH STORY**

The saga of Genentech, the fabled California biotechnology company, and its highly touted

---

*With thanks to F. Richard Nichol of IBRD in Irvine, Calif. for his assistance.

**This section was prepared with the research assistance of Sherrie Epstein.

clot-dissolving biotechnology drug tissue plasminogen activator (TPA) illustrates both the opportunities and risks of the new medical technologies.

Pharmaceuticals are probably the riskiest technologies because so little is known about the roles chemicals play in creating health. Until recently, most drug research was conducted by searching the earth for naturally occurring substances that showed chemical activity. Discoveries were made empirically, by trial and error. The relatively recent discovery of deoxyribonucleic acid (DNA) in 1944 made possible more methodical research by delineating the structure of genes. But the location of all genes, their functions, and their composition are still unknown. Defining these parameters will require many years and billions of dollars.

To compensate for the high risks of research, drug discoverers receive a patent that grants them a monopoly on the economic benefits to be derived from the invention. But the road between a patent and fame and fortune is a tortuous one. To be sold in the U.S. market, the world's largest, the drug must receive approval from the FDA. Then, if it is very expensive, the major insurers must agree to pay for its use. Then, the technology for producing it must be perfected. Finally, physicians and consumers must be convinced of the drug's desirability. Every one of these steps contains substantial pitfalls.

Genentech's TPA, called Activase, illustrates virtually all the risks of this process. The drug dissolves the clots thought to be the main cause of heart attack damage. Although other clot solvents existed, they were regarded as the pharmaceutical equivalent of Drano, potent chemicals that dissolved everything in their path, including the clots that stop brains from hemorrhaging. Activase, in contrast, was intended to be a much more specific solvent, a magic bullet that would target only the clots blocking the coronary blood vessels.

Genentech spent $200 million in developing Activase, competing furiously against some 20 to 30 other companies also developing TPA. In 1980, Genentech went public, at a price of $35 for each of a million shares. Its prospects were

so highly regarded that, despite the absence of any marketed products, its stock price was bid up to $89 a share.[8]

Genentech applied for a patent. As commonly occurs, the application was challenged on the grounds that the product was "obvious to those knowledgeable in the field." Wellcome of Britain was the first of many challengers.

In 1984, Genentech began clinical trials, and in the spring of 1987, an FDA advisory committee panel composed of scientists knowledgeable in the field, consumer and industry representatives, and biostatisticians reviewed applications from Hoechst for streptokinase—a bacterial enzyme not made through genetic engineering—and from Genentech for Activase. The streptokinase studies were judged to have been more complete. They showed substantial improvement of survival for 1 year after a heart attack on a large number of patients. Genentech's studies were faulted because the company had changed the form and dose of the drug during the trials and had used several different lengths of time for therapy. Most serious, at a 150-mg dose, unacceptable bleeding had occurred, and tests of a reduced dose were not complete.

The committee recommended postponement of approval until the FDA could review results of ongoing clinical trials. It was vigorously attacked by physicians for denying the public a valuable treatment and by financial analysts who believed Activase superior to other clot-dissolving agents.[9] Genentech's stock price fell from $48.25 to $36.75.

Eventually, some 6 months after the initial turndown, Genentech did get FDA approval, but two new controversies immediately surrounded it.

First, TPA was not proven clearly superior to two other clot dissolvers. Studies comparing each solvent to a control group did not show marked differences in efficacy among them. Because no horse race had been conducted—a head-to-head comparison of all three clot dissolvers was not part of the FDA process—physicians were confused about TPA's relative merits. Second, because it was much more expensive than the other two—$2,200 per treatment versus $1,700 for Beecham's Eminase and $200 for Hoechst's streptokinase—Medicare refused to cover it, arguing that it was not more cost-effective than the others. Genentech finally responded to public discontent about its high price by making the drug available for free to some low-income people.

To compound Genentech's problems, Activase did not sell as well as had been predicted by the company, although sales reached some $196 million in 1989. Other clot-dissolving drugs were not clearly better than Activase but were cheaper, and streptokinase had a third of the market.[10] Apparently, clot-dissolving therapy was "accepted widely but used infrequently," according to a Gallup and Duke University poll of physicians. Only 17 percent of the respondents administered these drugs to over 50 percent of their patients.[11]

Meanwhile, Genentech's competitors were closing in with their versions of TPA. To resolve doubts about which drugs were most efficacious, a head-to-head comparison of TPA and streptokinase was conducted. It was intended to resolve all doubt about TPA.

But when the landmark study of 28,000 patients in 13 countries was released—it showed equal death rates for streptokinase and TPA—critics immediately assailed it for allowing belated administration of the blood anticoagulant heparin, which is now recommended immediately after administration of TPA, and for its failure to answer the question of how long heart attack patients lived after being treated with one or the other.[12] A huge study published in 1991 showed streptokinase to be the most cost-effective of the three.[13]

Battered by challenges on patents, cost-effectiveness, and marketing, Genentech did not wait for the 1991 study results. In February 1990, Roche Holding, the Swiss parent of the pharmaceutical company Hoffmann-La Roche, paid $2.1 billion for 60 percent of Genentech.

THE THREE TECHNOLOGIES

The following sections describe the progress that has occurred in each of the three areas of medical technology—medical devices, biomaterials, and biotechnology—and assess the impact of each area.

Computer-Based Medical Devices*

The medical device industry had about $60 billion in worldwide sales in 1989.[14] Although its products fall under some 160 Standard Industrial Classification codes, most of the production in the industry can be categorized in four major segments: X-ray equipment, electromedical equipment, surgical and medical instruments, and surgical appliances and supplies. Many of these devices are computer-based. (Case Study 16 describes a company that manufactures medical devices.)

Profits measured as return on assets are higher than the average for total manufacturing over the past 20 years. In 1989 the percent return on assets for medical devices (Internal Revenue Service data) was 12.7 percent, compared with 10.5 percent for total manufacturing. And while employment in total manufacturing grew at an annual rate of 0. 5 percent over the 20-year period from 1963 to 1982, the employment growth in five medical device segments was 5.6 percent. Devices were manufactured by about 3,000 companies (3,400 plants). In 1982, nearly three-fourths of them were small establishments of fewer than 20 employees. Overall some 225,000 people were employed, 70 percent more than 10 years earlier. As in other industries, however, a few companies dominated the field. Baxter-Travenol, for example, was among the 8 leading companies in each of 28 products sold to hospitals.[15]

As with other aspects of health care, the cost of medical devices has been increasingly questioned. But the payments for devices have produced considerable benefits. For example, if Medicare did not cover kidney dialysis for all who needed it, the expansion of the kidney

---

*This section was adapted from "Note on Medical Technology," written by Sherrie Epstein under the supervision of Professor Regina E. Herzlinger (Boston: Harvard Business School, 1988), 19–25.

dialysis industry and the improvement in related devices would probably not have occurred. Although revocation of Medicare payment would undoubtedly have reduced costs, it would also have reduced the survival time of many of the 100,000 people on dialysis in the 1980s. Nearly 10,000 people per year died before 1972 when coverage was instituted, because of a lack of dialysis facilities. Similarly, the introduction of expensive computer-assisted tomography (CT) scanners was questioned by state planners in the 1970s, but scanners reduce the need for painful and dangerous invasive surgical procedures, and their use had become widespread in the 1980s.

The industry as a whole has been marked by innovation. There have been vast changes, for example, in the speed and accuracy of clinical laboratory results due to automation; in devices for ophthalmology, such as better suturing needles, disposable sharp blades for corneal surgery, and lasers; in imaging devices, which often obviate surgery; in the devices that wash out the blood after kidney failure; and in pacemakers to control the heart. Exhibit 3-1 lists some of the most important new and improved devices.

Two vivid examples of this innovation are the changes in clinical testing and retinal surgery since the 1950s. In the past, professional medical technologists completed blood tests by hand, perhaps six per hour. In 1983, they supervised a computerized machine that performed 1,800 individual tests per hour. No capital equipment was required in the 1950s, but the equipment to do the vastly increased number of tests in the 1980s cost about $400,000. The machines can do a dozen different kind of tests at once, and there are usually no savings in ordering only one kind of test. A blood sugar test for diabetes in the 1950s was performed by a skilled lab technician; tests on ten patients took about 3 hours to complete. In the 1980s, some 150 tests per hour can be done by a trained high school graduate. The cost per test in 1950 was $5 or more, but it is only pennies today.

Laser surgery to seal tears in the retina is now performed in a doctor's office, which enables patients often to avoid the more serious hospitalization and serious surgery to repair detached retinas. The laser surgery requires only a few minutes and is much less traumatic for the patient. Although lasers have been used mostly in ophthalmology, it is expected that presently experimental applications in cardiovascular and orthopedic surgery and dentistry will increase. Ear, nose, and throat specialists, gynecologists, gastroenterologists, and dermatologists are now using laser surgery. The price of lasers is expected to decline substantially as their use increases.

In addition to the medical devices already mentioned, the following are likely to be of significance in coming years.

Imaging Equipment

The growth of x-ray and electromedical equipment is expected to continue. The market for imaging equipment is predicted to reach $5 billion in 1994, up 51 percent from its 1989 level of $3.2 billion.[16] About $1 billion of this is attributed to the market for MRI, a noninvasive diagnostic technique that employs machines costing roughly a million dollars each. MRI produces clear, striking images of the soft brain and neurological tissues missed by bone scanning x-ray devices. It shows the damage much more exactly than was possible with other, prior devices and thus allows the surgeon a better chance of restoring function to the patient.

Cardiovascular Devices

Willem Kolff at the University of Utah pioneered the artificial heart, beginning its development in 1957. Although permanent use of the heart was attempted in some patients, too many problems—especially resistant infections, clotting, and rejection—emerged to make permanent use practical in the 1980s. However, partial artificial hearts are being used in thousands of patients annually to assist the pumping of blood in damaged hearts for short periods, up to a month. They take over the heart's function until the patient recovers from an acute illness or can be readied for a transplant.

Exhibit 3-1 Major New Medical Devices Used in Clinical Practice in the 1980s

Interventional medicine
- Angioplasty, arthrectomy, lasers
- Percutaneous drainage
- Percutaneous extractions (biopsies)
- Intravascular electrocoagulation

Oncology
- Photodynamic therapy
- Hyperthermia (ultrasound, RF)
- Patient-controlled analgesia
- Prefilled chemotherapy pumps

Dental care
- Lingual brackets
  Periodontal analysis
- TMJ diagnosis
- CAD/CAM crown or inlay
  manufacturing

Diagnostic imaging and radiology
- Doppler color ultrasound
- Paramagnetic image enhancement
- Transesophageal ultrasound
- Magnetic resonance imaging (MRI)
- Intraluminal ultrasound
- Angioscopy

Urology
- Lithotriptors (extracorporeal; laser)
- Laparoscopic gallstone removal

Neurosurgery
- Epilepsy pacemakers
- Percutaneous diskectomy
- High power YAG lasers

Critical care
- Continuous cardiac output
- Electronic charts
- Closed-loop fluid delivery
- Sensor technology for bedside blood gases

Opthalmology
- Refractive laser implants
- Glaucoma implants
- Electro-ocular implants
- YAG lasers for capsulotomies

Orthopedics
- Customized implants
- Bone growth stimulation
- Bone strength analyzers

Source: Based on "Healthcare Technology Developed in the 1990's," *Biomedical Business International*, January 24, 1990:4.

The number of heart transplants increased from about 50 in 1981 to over 1,500 in 1989.

Surgeons increasingly employ a balloon technique called angioplasty to avoid complicated coronary artery surgery. Angioplasty can be used to keep arteries open in the heart and elsewhere in the body, especially in the legs. It compacts the scar tissue and calcium from disease that build up and clog the arteries. The surgeon threads a balloon along a guide wire inside a long, narrow catheter (or tube), which enters the arterial system via the femoral artery in the thigh. The physician views the balloon through a fluoroscope and guides it into position, where it is then inflated to open the artery by compacting the plaque along its walls. Angioplasty was performed some 300,000 times in 1989, compared with about 250,000 open-heart operations. Hot and cold lasers were being combined with angioplasty to vaporize or compact the plaque that forms around arteries, thus potentially improving the success rates of

the operations. Atherectomy devices that shave off interior plaque deposits also show promise.

The ambulatory Holter electrocardiography monitor is widely used. This computer-based device automatically monitors and diagnoses patients with arrhythmias (arrhythmic heart beats thought to be associated with sudden cardiac death). It can be used to follow a patient's progress at home, thus often enabling patients to go home from the hospital earlier.

Pacemakers and defibrillators can be implanted in people who survive a heart attack due to arrhythmia. Pacemakers that electrically pace the heart's rhythm have become almost routine, with some 250,000 insertions performed in 1984. Defibrillators and other devices that shock a stalled heart back into action can presently be installed only in hospitals with catheterization and electrophysiology laboratories. Some 20,000 to 30,000 such operations were performed annually in the 1980s.

Kidney Disease Devices

Lithotripsy, which employs shock waves to destroy kidney stones, has improved patient recovery time and reduced suffering. It also seems likely to have applications in the treatment of other stones, such as gallstones, and foreign bodies. Up to 85 percent of patients with stones could be cured by this method rather than by surgery. The machines use ultrasonic energy to direct shock waves at the stones, dissolving them into a paste that can be excreted. The treatment lasts for about an hour, and the patient requires anesthesia. (Its relationship to high blood pressure is now being investigated.)

Biomaterials

The $10-billion biomaterials industry provides the materials that are used in applications ranging from false teeth to artificial organs (Exhibit 3-2). Biomaterials include nondegradable polymers, tissue adhesives, ceramics, glass, carbon, surface modifiers, metals, and biologically derived materials, such as porcine (pig) heart valves.

Although biomaterials have evolved enormously in the past 20 years, significant challenges remain. Many materials cause deadly blood clots and interfere with the functioning of drugs. Producing stable materials that do not disintegrate with use and that can be manufactured consistently is yet another challenge. (Degraded biomaterials can deposit toxic waste within the body.) As one indication of the long road ahead, the industry has yet to develop standardized measures for many material characteristics. (See Table 3-5 for future needs.)

The use of ceramics illustrates both the opportunities and risks of the biomaterials industry. Ceramics are attractive for use as implants within the body because they can fuse with bones to form very strong bonds, but they have a serious flaw—they can shatter in a small but significant number of cases. Process technology for manufacturing ceramics is more an art than a science, involving hundreds of variables. An imperfection in the ceramic surface appears to increase the probability of shattering. Yet the potential strength of ceramics presents an enormously attractive opportunity, particularly with an aging population and its attendant bone and joint deterioration problems.

As with many materials, the applications for ceramics will not be entirely clear until ceramic materials are developed. Many American manufacturers have shied away from what one labeled "agnostic marketing": they will not invest in a technology whose applications cannot be readily researched. But, in a classic case of catch 22, the applications of a material are often inspired by the material.

The founder of Kyocera, a $2-billion ceramics company, has a different attitude. He is more willing to bet that the development of a material will generate many applications. He placed one such bet when he acceded to Fairchild's request that he develop a new way to encapsulate integrated circuits in ceramic. When Fairchild turned to Kyocera, then a tiny Japanese firm, its request had been rejected by all American ceramics manufacturers. The resulting product now provides Kyocera with a billion dollars worth of business. And as a bonus for its willingness to take a risk, the company has become enormously skilled in the complex process of manufacturing ceramics, a skill it successfully applies to many other products, including medical ones.

Biotechnology*

The Biotechnology Revolution

The biotechnology revolution—the use of biological processes to produce natural products—began a century ago with Mendel's classic experiments in genetics and slowly progressed as a result of the work of many researchers, including Oswald Avery who demonstrated in 1944 that genes were made of

---

*This section is partially adapted from "Note on Medical Technology," written by Sherrie Epstein under the supervision of Regina E. Herzlinger (Boston: Harvard Business School, 1988).

Exhibit 3-2 Present Uses of Biomaterials

Artificial organs
- Artificial pancreas
- Artificial kidney–extracorporeal membrane oxygenators

Biosensors
- *In vivo/in vitro* blood and urine chemistries

Biotechnology
- Process/purification membranes
- Enzyme or cellular immobilization substrates
- Cell culture systems (hollow fibers, microencapsulation)
- Fermentation polymers

Cardiovascular
- Vascular grafts
- Heart valves
- Artificial hearts

Commodities and disposables
- Catheters (angioplasty)
- Syringes
- Gowns and gloves

Drug delivery/hybrid artificial organs
- *In vivo* controlled sustained release (ocular, uterine)
- Transdermal release
- Insulin pumps
- Artificial pancreas
- Extracorporeal therapy
- Synthetic oxygen carriers

Maxillofacial; dental; ear, nose, and throat; cranial
- Artificial teeth

- Soft tissue
- Mandibular augmentaton
- Ossicular replacement and reconstruction
- Intracochlear and extracochlear prosthesis for the profoundly deaf

Opthalmology
- Contact lenses
- Intraocular lenses
- Artificial corneas/intraocular implants
- Vitreous implants
- Bioadhesives

Orthopedics
- Artificial joints (hip, knee)
- Artificial bone
- Fixation plates/screws
- Fixation cements
- Spinal fusion
- Tendon prosthesis
- Artificial ligaments

Packaging
- Personal care/hygiene (sanitary napkins, tampons, comdoms)
- Diapers
- Enviornmentally degradable polymers
- Parenterals

Wound management
- Sutures
- Bioadhesives
- Dressings
- Staples
- Artificial skin
- Burn dressings

Source: Reprinted from *Medical Device and Diagnostic Industry*, Vol. 12, No. 3, p. 86, with permission of Canon Communications, Inc., © 1990.

DNA. In the next decade, James Watson and Francis Crick described the double helix on which the DNA molecules are strung. They showed that the variable sequence of the chemical units in the DNA molecule directs reproduction of living cells. Scientists were then able to understand the role of DNA in manufacturing protein and regulating synthesis (building up proteins one molecule at a time).

Protein molecules shape the body's form and function and determine health or illness. By 1975, further research enabled scientists to manipulate or engineer genetic material to manufacture proteins and to design genetic characteristics. Genes from one species could be recombined with those of another to reproduce rapidly.

Monoclonal antibodies are clones of natural protein molecules that fight off foreign substances (antigens) in the body. They can be produced by growing the cells that produce an antibody to a single specific antigen. When these cells are combined with malignant tumor cells (hybridomas), they reproduce interminably. Since 1975, monoclonal antibodies have been used to detect pregnancy, ovulation,

Table 3-5 Future Needs for Biomaterials

End-Use Application	Materials Needed
Burn/Wound Coverings	Grafts for epithelium cell regeneration
	Release of antibacterials
Cardiovascular Implants	Clot-resistant surfaces
	Small-diameter vascular grafts for coronary artery replacement
Catheters, Cardiovascular	Thromboresistant surfaces
Catheters, Urinary	Infection-resistant surfaces
Controlled-release Devices (for drugs)	Bioadhesives for skin and mucosal tissue
	Bioerodible polymers
	Protein delivery matrix materials
Dental Implants	Tooth implants with a stable perigingival junction
Diabetes-related Implants	Hybrid artificial organs
Ear, Nose, Throat Devices	Multichannel extracochlear prostheses
Extracorporeal Blood Treatment Equipment	Immobilized chemotherapeutic agents and enzymes for chemotherapy and detoxification
Neural Devices	Polymers that induce nerve regeneration
Opthalmologic Devices	Artificial corneas
	Vitreous implants
Soft-Tissue Reconstructive Surgery Products	Resorbable biodegradable polymers with concurrent release of bioactive agents to control wound healing
Wound Closures	Tissue adhesives
	Laser-weldable polymers that adhere to tissue

Source: Reprinted from *Medical Device and Diagnostic Industry*, Vol. 12, No. 3, p. 87, with permission of Canon Communications, Inc., © 1990.

---

hereditary diseases, infections, and some cancers. They have also been used as imaging agents that carry radioisotopes to cancerous cells and thus enable x-ray pictures to be taken, and as therapeutic agents that carry drugs to the cells. They may greatly reduce the number of deaths from septic shock, now the 13th leading cause of death. They may play yet another role as blockers of the body's natural defenses against other helpful biotechnology products.

Diagnostics are used on substances outside the body. Tissue, blood, or urine are exposed to a diagnostic test reagent to see whether the monoclonal antibodies or DNA probes (manufactured to imitate an organism to be targeted) attach themselves to a specific antigen. A "marker" reaction, which is initiated by the bound antibody, can be detected as a change in light absorbance, color, or reactivity with other reagents. Because the tests are performed outside the body, FDA approval might take only a few months rather than the customary years required for clinical testing of substances that must be ingested or injected.

Recombinant DNA technology has resulted in a number of drugs, (see Appendix 3-A), including EPO (erythropoietin), for treatment of anemia; CSF granulocyte, for the effects of chemotherapy and transplants; human insulin (human insulin causes fewer allergies than animal-derived insulin); human growth hormone; alpha interferon, for leukemia and hepatitis B; and, of course, TPA, the fast-acting, anticlotting drug used for heart attack patients.

Growth hormone, first assumed useful only to people with pituitary dwarfing conditions, is now being used for wound healing and investigated for use in helping obese people to lose fat rather than muscle when dieting, and for retarding wrinkles and the fat distribution characteristic of aging. Recombinant DNA techniques are now used to produce large quantities of the hormone. The limited supplies of growth hormone extracted from humans in the past were tainted when a few patients who had received the hormone developed a disease caused by a slow virus that results in dementia. Genetically engineered, uncontaminated growth hormone was therefore welcome, even though the initial cost was as high as the cost of the human extract.

Gene therapy is the introduction of a normal gene into patients whose illness is caused by the absence or malformation of that gene. In 1990, its use was approved for "bubble children" who must live in a plastic bubble because of genetic disorders that destroy their immune system. Although the approval was but one of many needed and the technology—which involves transplanting a mouse virus into a human being—is fraught with problems, the potential for gene therapy is substantial. It can help those with cystic fibrosis, hemophilia, cholesterol disorders, metabolic liver deficiencies, and other genetic diseases.[17] The first gene therapy was performed in 1990 at the U.S. government's National Institutes of Health.[18]

Lymphokines, among them interleukins and interferons, are proteins that act on the lymphocyte cells that regulate the immune system. Long recognized by scientists as having the potential to activate the body's antibody production against cancers and immune disorders, there were insufficient quantities of the substances for adequate testing before genetic engineering techniques became available.

It is hoped that employing the body's own defenses against disease will be more effective than surgery, radiation, and chemical drugs that poison the cancer but also damage healthy tissue. Biotechnology and pharmaceutical companies were outspending the National Cancer Institute in research on anticancer biologicals. The pharmaceutical companies were interested in a biotechnology approach because traditional research in chemotherapy had slowed. Most of the 30 or so drugs in use in the 1980s had been developed before 1965, and their response rates were low—15 percent was expected for treatment for some common cancers. Bristol Myers' anticancer research director said, "We've reached a plateau in what chemotherapy can accomplish."[19]

Biotechnology Companies

The biotechnology industry grew rapidly in the early 1980s, attracting a great deal of venture capital. Some 300 small companies had been formed, most by university scientists who were knowledgeable about the new techniques. Although the industry had reached the multi-billion-dollar level by 1989 and billions had been raised through stock offerings since 1980, products were still mostly in the "promise" stage and development capital was harder to attract than it had been earlier. Many predicted future acquisitions and mergers among the remaining companies. (See Table 3-6 for the major companies and their interests.)

Large pharmaceutical houses provide much of the capital investment in biotechnology. Merck and Eli Lilly and chemical companies like Monsanto were especially active, but all the major pharmaceutical companies were attempting to keep up. They anticipated competition domestically and also from international sources, especially in Japan and West Germany; firms in both countries had made substantial investments in U.S. biotechnology companies.

Most of the small companies do not expect to become major drug houses. They either have forged alliances through joint ventures with companies that are adept at dealing with the manufacturing, FDA, and Patent Office approval processes and have the necessary marketing experience or have acted as research sources and licensed their discoveries to larger companies. Two biotechnology companies were purchased by large pharmaceutical companies (Lilly and Bristol-Myers) for approximately $300 million each because their research efforts matched the needs of the purchasing companies and because the purchasing

Table 3-6 Major Biotechnology Companies and Their Major Products, 1989

Product	Company	Estimated 1989 U.S. Sales (millions $)
Human Insulin	Eli Lilly	$ 210
TPA	Genentech	196
Human Growth Hormone	Eli Lilly Genentech	145
EPO GCSF (Neupogen)	Amgen	95 40
Alpha Interferon	Schering-Plough Hoffman LaRoche	80
Hepatitis B Vaccine	Merck	65
OKT3	Johnson & Johnson	30

Source: Courtesy of Michael Gordon, analyst, Fidelity Investments, Boston, Massachusetts, and Maria I. Marmarinos, Brigham and Women's Hospital, Boston, Massachusetts.

companies had confidence in the scientists who would become part of the corporation.

Survival is a critical issue for most biotechnology companies. Many were formed with important scientists but too little management. A good case is Biogen, headed originally by a Nobel Prize winner and associated with other famous researchers in the United States and Europe. The company's research was uncoordinated and spread too thin. It planned to research all areas of biotechnology—medical, veterinary, agricultural, and environmental—simultaneously. Also, projects were undertaken that did not have clear commercial viability. Ultimately, the company dropped all but its medical projects, its scientific founder resigned, and new management came in. The company now has several important products.

THE RESULTS

The drug technology developments described above required huge research expenditures. The pharmaceutical companies alone spent over $9 billion on research in 1989.[20]

So, what happened? In the opinion of the Senate Committee on Aging, not much. It charged that

> the bulk of the research and development by the pharmaceutical companies produced magnificent new compounds that add little or nothing to drug therapies already marketed. Eighty-four percent of the new drugs brought to market by the 25 largest U.S. companies between 1981 and 1988 were "C" rated, having "little or no" potential for therapeutic gain. Just 12 important new drugs were introduced in the eight years.[21]

Other reports are equally sobering. Japan introduces three times the number of biomedical products as the United States, which is sixth among countries obtaining scientific patents. The U.S. spends more on life sciences research, but fewer commercial products emerge.

NOTES

1. "High-Tech Generics," *In Vivo*, January-February 1990,

12.

2. "Short and Long-Term Views of Generic Market," *Health Industry Today*, April 1990, 10.

3. "Japan's Next Battleground: The Medicine Chest," *Business Week*, March 12, 1990, 68–72.

4. Carl W. Walter, "Invention and Development of the Blood Bag," in *Milestones in Blood Transfusion and Immunohematology* (Basel: S. Kayer, AG, 1984), 318–24.

5. Lester Chafetz and Theodore I. Fand, "Product Development," in *The Clinical Research Process in the Pharmaceutical Industry*, edited by Gary M. Matoren (New York: Marcel Dekker, 1984), 308, 311.

6. Sherrie Epstein, "Note on Medical Technology" (Boston: Harvard Business School, 1988), 11.

7. Gail DeGeorge, "Has LymphoMed Moved to the Recovery Room?," *Business Week*, July 18, 1988, 118.

8. Natalie Angier, "The Selling of DNA," *New York Times*, October 29, 1989, Book Review section, 26.

9. Peter R. Kowey, "The TPA Controversy," *Journal of the American Medical Association,* 260 (1988), 2250–52.

10. Marilyn Chase, "Battle of Heart Attack Drugs Heats Up," *Wall Street Journal*, March 8, 1990, B1.

11. "The Drug Wars at AHA," *In Vivo*, January-February 1990, 9.

12. Marilyn Chase, "Old Heart Drug Works as Well as Costly TPA in Study," *Wall Street Journal*, March 9, 1990, B1.

13. Lawrence K. Altman, "Cheapest Anti-Clot Drug Is Found to Be Best," *New York Times*, March 4, 1991, B9.

14. *Medical and Healthcare Marketplace Guide* (Miami, Fla.: International Biomedical Information Service, 1990), II-60.

15. IMS America, unpublished data, 1983.

16. "Diagnostic Imaging Update, Part I," *BBI Newsletter*, January 24, 1990, 5.

17. Natalie Angier, "Gene Implant Therapy Is Backed for Children with Rare Disease," *New York Times*, March 8, 1990, 1.

18. "Gene Therapy Era Commences," *BBI Newsletter*, October 18, 1990, 196.

19. Joan O'C Hamilton, "Biotech's First Superstar" *Business Week*, April 14, 1986, 68–72; idem, "The Gene Doctors," *Business Week*, April 14, 1986, 76.

20. National Institutes of Health, *NIH Data Book, 1989* (Washington, D.C.: U.S. Government Printing Office, 1990), 2.

21. Senate Committee on Aging, *Prescription Drug Prices* (Washington D.C.: U.S. Government Printing Office, 1989), 5, 7.

Appendix 3-A

Leading Biotechnology Products
and Companies, January 1991

Product	Company	Estimated Potential Market Size*	Purpose
Atrial Natriuretic Factor	California Biotechnology, Merck	$50–$100 million	Natural blood pressure regulator for kidney disease; unimpressive results to date. Now being targeted as renal protective factor.
Calcitonin	Rorer, Sandoz, Ciba-Geigy, Unigene	$250–$300 million	Postmenopausal osteoporosis treatment if convenient delivery system can be developed.
CD4-Soluble T4 Receptor	Genentech, Biogen, Progenics	NA	AIDS virus receptor; unimpressive results to date. Genentech's focus is solely on pediatric use.
CSF Granulocyte	Amgen, Immunex, Chugai, Genetics Institute, Immunex, Glaxo (Biogen), Cetus	$1.5 billion	Combats effects of chemotherapy (Amgen) and aids bone marrow transplants (Immunex).
EPO (Erythropoietin)	Amgen, Chugai, Genetics Institute	$1.5–$2 billion	Stimulates red blood cell growth for treatment of anemia and kidney dialysis patients, and AIDS, cancer, and surgery to reduce need for blood transfusions.***
Factor VIII-C	Genentech, Genetics Institute, Chiron, Rorer	$800 million	For hemophilia with 20,000 to 30,000 victims worldwide, more than 80% estimated to have been exposed to AIDS.
Growth Factors for Wound Healing	Synergen, California Biotechnology, Chiron, Amgen, Merck, and many others	$1 billion**	To help nonhealing wounds like burns and diabetic ulcers to heal eventually.

Note: Products are ranked according to stage of development. Company lists do not include all companies.

*Market size estimates by Michael Gordon, as of March 1990

**Market size estimates by Weisbrod and McGann, as of January 1991

***Data provided by Maria I. Marmarinos, Brigham and Women's Hospital, Venture Group, Boston, Massachusetts.

47

Product	Company	Estimated Potential Market Size*	Purpose
Human Growth Hormone	Genentech, Lilly, Serono, Biotechnology General, Nordisk	Genentech—$157.1 million Lilly—$52.0 million	Genentech and Lilly have Orphan Drug Status until 1993 and 1994.
Immune Therapeutic Monoclonal Antibodies	Johnson & Johnson, XOMA, Immunex, ImmunoGen, Centocor (Tocor)	$575 million	For use against autoimmune diseases, like arthritis and lupus, and rejection of transplants.
Interferon	Biogen, Schering-Plough, Genentech, Interferon Sciences, Wellcome, Cetus, Toray/Daiichi, Amgen, Hoffman La Roche, many others	Alpha—$600 million to $1 billion Beta—$200 million Gamma—$500 million	Kaposi's sarcoma, hairy cell leukemia, carcinoma, arthritis, hepatitis.
Interleukin-1	Immunex, Cistron Tech., Hoffman La Roche, SmithKline Beecham, Immunex	$250 million	Wound and burn healing and protection against chemo- and radiotherapy damage.
Interleukin-2	Cetus, Immunex, Amgen, Cel-Sci Corp., Cellular Products, Immuno Therapeutics, Biogen	$250 million	Cancer. Disappointing results as a stand-alone, but results of combination with alpha-interferon look promising.
Interleukin-3	Immunex, Genetics Institute	$300 million	Aplastic anemia and cancer.
Interleukin-4, -6, -7	Immunex, Schering-Plough, Genetics Institute	Too early	Tumors and bacterial and viral infections.
Interleukin Inhibitors	Synergen, Schering-Plough, Immunex	Too early	Autoimmune disease and inflammatory conditions, such as septic shock and emphysema.
Lung Surfactant	Abbott, Burroughs Wellcome, California Biotechnology, Genetics Institute***	$250–$400 million	Neonatal respiratory disease.***
Monoclonal Antibody Imaging—Cancer	Centocor, NeoRx, Immunomedics, Cytogen, Hybritech (Lilly)	$200 million	Antibodies that carry radioisotopes to cancer cells for x-rays.
Monoclonal Antibody Imaging—Cardiovascular	Centocor, Cytogen	$50 to $100 million	Likely to be substituted with MRI and ultrasound imaging techniques.

Product	Company	Estimated Potential Market Size*	Purpose
Monoclonal Antibody Therapeutics—Cancer	Cytogen, Immunomedics, Centocor, NeoRx, XOMA, Lilly	$500 million in mid-1990s**	In 1991, Cytogen's products looked promising.
Breast Cancer	Bristol-Myers Squibb, Cytogen, ImmunoGen, Genentech		For use against metastasis of cancer cells and drug delivery.
Colorectal Cancer (ADCC)	ImmunoGen, NeoRx, Bristol-Myers Squibb, Centocor, XOMA, Immunomedics, Lilly (Hybritech), Cytogen, ImmunoGen		
Gastrointestinal Cancer	Cytogen, Genetic Systems		
Lung Cancer	Bristol-Myers Squibb, Lilly, NeoRx, ImmunoGen		
Lymphoma	Techniclone, Immunomedics, ImmunoGen, DEC Pharmaceuticals***		
Melanoma	XOMA		
Ovarian Cancer	Bristol-Myers Squibb, Centocor, NeoRx, Cytogen, XOMA, Genentech		
Septicemia Monoclonals	XOMA, Centocor, Cetus, Chiron, Immunex	$500 million	For use against septic shock. Currently, Centcor's product appears better than XOMA's. Synergen's Interleukin-1 Inhibitor may prove the most effective.
Superoxide Dismutase	Chiron, Enzon, Biotechnology General, DDI Pharaceuticals, T Cell Sciences	$150 million	Disappointing clinical results have slowed development; it is used to prevent damage caused by free radicals produced when oxygen-rich blood enters oxygen-deprived tissues; may prevent tissue damage during a heart attack or in organ transplantation.

Product	Company	Estimated Potential Market Size*	Purpose
Thrombolytics and Antithrombotics	Genentech, SmithKline Beecham, American Home Products, Abbot Labs, Centocor, Miles (Bayer), Biogen, Monsanto, Rorer, Cytogen, Ciba-Geigy, Marion- Merrell Dow, Bristol- Myers Squibb, Lilly, CytRx	Eminase—$250– $400 million TPA—$600–$800 million Activase—$210 million (Genentech)**	To prevent blood clots; used after a heart attack, angioplasty, and for unstable angina.
Tumor Necrosis Factor	Genentech, Abbott, Biogen	$0 to $25 million	A natural cancer-killing molecule. Side effects are considerable.
Vaccines			
AIDS Vaccine	MicroGeneSys, Bristol-Myers Squibb (Oncogene), Immune Response, Repligen, Cambridge Bioscience, Chiron (Biocine), British Biotechnology, Genentech, Hoechst	AIDS—unknown	Immune Response and MicroGeneSys appear to have led in an uphill battle.
Hepatitis A Vaccine	SmithKline Beecham, Chiron, Merck, Genelabs	Hepatitis—$350 million	
Hepatitis B Vaccine	Genzyme***, Merck (Chiron), SmithKline Beecham, Amgen, Genentech, Biogen	Merck and SmithKline Beecham—$180 million. Biogen receives royalties from both.	
Hepatitis C Vaccine	Chiron, Genelabs		
Hepatitis E Vaccine	Genelabs		
Malaria Vaccine	SmithKline Beecham, Hoffman La Roche, MicroGeneSys, Chiron***, Biogen	NA	
Herpes Vaccine	Chiron, Lederle, ImClone***	NA	
Influenza Vaccine	Chiron, Lederle, ImClone***	NA	
Pertussis Vaccine	Amgen	NA	
CMV Vaccine	Chiron	NA	
Melanoma	Oncogen (Bristol-Myers Squibb)	NA	

4

Ventures To Serve
New Health Care Consumers

A newspaper headline nicely encapsulates this opportunity: "Lessons of the 80's: Emphasize Health, Eliminate Hassles."[1] Health care activists wanted mastery over their health status. Working health care consumers craved convenient services. One group wanted health; the other, no hassles.

The following two sections discuss the characteristics of each group and of the new health care ventures created to meet their needs. (Case Studies 6, 13, and 15 describe three such ventures.)

HEALTH ACTIVISTS

A large segment of today's American health care consumers are health activists who take responsibility for their own health. Though they greatly respect physicians, they are not blindly obedient to medical advice. To the contrary, they credit themselves for their good health status. Most of today's American health care consumers no longer agree with the once widely held tenet that "the doctor knows best, for reasons that we cannot possibly understand." Instead, they want to create their own health in concert with the physician. One survey found

39 percent of the American public were health activists, another 40 percent were willing to share their decision-making power with physicians, and only 21 percent were following the traditionally complaisant patient model.[2]

Although health activists are popularly depicted as narcissists, like the bone-thin, aerobicized, idle ladies who lunch (or rather nibble), they are, instead, part of a broader transformation in social values. A polling firm characterizes today's Americans as valuing pragmatic, strategic, cost-effective relationships that allow them to be self-reliant and remain in control.[3] Information enables them to achieve such mastery and competence. Their values manifest themselves in events as diverse as the emergence of financial advisers, who were once restricted to the very wealthy but are now widely available to provide much cherished information to the middle class, and in the election of President George Bush, valued for his pragmatism and experience.

The next generation is likely to be an activist one too. Children in the 4th through 12th grades overwhelmingly cited their own personal experience as "the most believable authority in matters of truth." Their confidence in themselves vastly exceeded the credence they were willing to grant teachers, science, the church, scripture, and the media.[4]

One of the most telling indications of the value placed on self-reliance is the increasing degree of self-service in retailing. Americans are now willing to pump their own gas, compose their own salads, order by mail from a catalogue, and select their shoes from boxes massed on the store floor. Few of these self-services are offered at reduced prices. Americans buy them not to reduce costs but because they value the mastery that self-service allows.[5]

Manifestations of self-reliance abound in health care. Sixty percent of Americans say they work hard at staying healthy, even to the extent of changing their life styles if necessary.[6] Health activism has caused a precipitous decline in the incidence of many harmful personal habits. Many Americans have stopped smoking, reduced the amount of alcohol they drink, brought their serum cholesterol levels under control, and increased safety precautions and diagnostic testing substantially (Table 4-1). Health activism runs deep in American society: It is not solely, or even primarily, a "yuppie" phenomenon. In many instances, low-income people engage in health-promoting activities as much as high-income people. Indeed, low-income people are even more likely to abstain from drinking, avoid drinking and driving, and conduct breast self-examinations than those with annual incomes exceeding $50,000.

Health activists do not shy away from more direct involvement in health care services. Increasingly, hospitalized patients administer narcotic painkillers themselves. Rather than waiting for a nurse to give them an injection or tablet, they push a button that activates the release of the analgesic into an intravenous line inserted in their veins. This process, called PCA (patient-controlled analgesia), has worked miracles. Patients administer less analgesia and achieve better pain relief and quicker recovery rates.[7] Some activists order their own laboratory tests for pregnancy, cholesterol, anemia, and diabetes in a drug store rather than a doctor's office. The costs are low—from $5 to $22—and the results are usually available within ten minutes.[8]

Entrepreneurial Responses

Entrepreneurial responses to the needs of the health activists have been varied and plentiful. The widespread availability of health information is one response to their desire for control. A *Wall Street Journal* tally revealed that its 1989 coverage of medical aspects of the heart exceeded its coverage of George Bush, Donald Trump, or Michael Milken.[9] Only a third of those under 35 rely on their physician for information.[10] Instead, they use the media. No wonder *Reader's Digest*, the world's most widely read magazine, recently paid $29.1 million for *American Health*, a publication squarely targeted at the activists.[11] Some of the information even simulates medical training. For example, a video game called "Life & Death" allows the user to play the role of a surgeon who orders laboratory tests, diagnoses the patient, and decides when and where to operate.[12] Fitness tapes, how-to health books and magazines, health clubs, and home exercise devices are also aimed at the activist market.

The health activist has caused traditional consumer retailing companies to redefine themselves. Many food, clothing, cosmetics, and over-the-counter drug companies have repositioned themselves as health companies. Billion-dollar sports shoe companies, like Reebok, grew almost overnight to service the needs of health activists with injury-reducing and performance-enhancing shoes. And new powerful drugs may enable cosmetic companies to claim, for once correctly, that they can create a youthful, healthy appearance by filling out wrinkles or regrowing hair.

The American food industry discovered this group's interest in eating healthful food. As one result, Pringle's potato chips, which are made by frying a reconstituted dehydrated potato mix in deep fat, have been supplemented by a "light" version. When the cholesterol-reducing properties of oatmeal were discovered, Quaker Oats repositioned its oatmeal as a health food rather than merely a food. The category of nutritious prepared food was also created. Healthy Choice, a line of frozen foods, achieved an astonishing $150 million in sales

Table 4-1 Percentage of the Population Using Safety Precautions, Controlling Risk Factors, and Diagnostic Testing

Safety Precautions, Risk Factors, and Diagnostic Testing	Percentage of the Entire Population (%)		Percentage of Those with Income Under $15,000 (%)	Percentage of Those with Income Over $50,000 (%)
	1983	*1987*		
Current Smokers (over 20 years old)				
Male	35.4%	31.5%		
Female	29.9	27.0		
	1971–1974	*1976–1980*		
High-Risk Serum				
Cholesterol Level (Ages 25–74)	23.2%	21.9%		
	1983	*1987*		
Safety Precautions				
Steps To Avoid Accidents at Home	72.0%	84.0%	84.0%	77.0%
Smoke Detector at Home	67.0	81.0	74.0	84.0
No Drinking and Driving	68.0	78.0	86.0	68.0
Wearing Seatbelts in Front Seat of Car	19.0	60.0	56.0	77.0
Diagnostic Testing				
Yearly Blood Pressure Reading	82.0	83.0	84.0	82.0
Biannual Pap Exam for Women	75.0	79.0	73.0	90.0
Monthly Breast Self-examination	37.0	42.0	56.0	41.0
Yearly Dental Checkup	71.0	75.0	58.0	84.0
Abstain from Consuming Alcohol	40.0	35.0	54.0	24.0

Sources: Health United States, 1988, Tables 51, 53, 56; *Prevention in America*, (Emmaus, Pa.: Rodale Press, 1988), Tables 5-1, 5-2, 5-5, 7-3, 8-2, 8-4.

after only five months of national distribution. Its secret? A face-off comparison of its nutritional merits with those of its competitors. Said Mike Harper, the chief executive officer of the company, "It's food for people who want to stay healthy, not just for old goats who have some kind of problem." He not only believes in the health activist consumer, he is one. Harper developed the food product line after recovering from a heart attack.[13]

Drug marketers also acknowledged the health activists by abandoning long-held beliefs that American consumers were confused by multipurpose drugs. Simplistic ads about "TUMS for the tummy" that hailed the virtues of this venerable remedy for an upset stomach were replaced with complex messages about TUMS' efficacy in preventing osteoporosis, a bone loss disease, as well as gastrointestinal problems.[14]

TUMS' sales boomed—a happy result, because TUMS appeared to provide the most cost-effective osteoporosis prevention then available.[15] Federal government officials supported this consumer activism. Noted one, "Six out of every 10 medicines [purchased] are nonprescription products. Yet total spending for self-medication products adds up to less than two cents of the U.S. health-care dollar. Self-care is the largest component of our health care system and the least costly."[16]

Doctors also recognized the existence of the health activist, albeit somewhat grudgingly. A Vancouver, Canada, doctor humorously explained the radar signals that enable him to identify patients from California: "They come with check lists of recommended tests and want me to sign a contract before providing care." In "Why I Let Patients Tell Me What Treatment

They Need," one physician ruefully details the questions he needs to ask his activist patients: "What magazines do you read? Who's your favorite TV medical reporter? Have you come with your own diagnosis? Do you know what treatment you need?"[17]

Eighty percent of family practitioners agree with his analysis of the activist patient population. They feel that medical decisions must be jointly reached by fully informed patients and their doctors.[18]

Health maintenance organizations (HMOs) provide information as a way of keeping their health activist patients from straying. Lack of choice of physicians is a major complaint of HMO members. To remedy it, two new HMOs are providing extensive information about their physicians—everything from specialties to hobbies—on a computerized data base that patients can use themselves.[19] They hope that availability of this information will enable activists to have some of the control they want.

Women constitute a major activist force. They are key targets because, as indicated in Table 4-2, they use substantially more physician and hospital resources than men. And their longer life span doubles their use of nursing homes as compared to men. One group claims that women account for over 65 percent of all health care purchases.[20]

Programs aimed at activist women health care consumers range from birth centers to mammography units. Birth centers offer a low-technology alternative for women who do not want anesthesia and forceps to intrude on the birthing process. These mothers-to-be want control over their birthing experience and are not willing to cede it to physicians in an impersonal, technology-dominated procedure. They are assisted by nurse-midwives who share their views of what an appropriate birthing experience should be like. (Giving birth in a birth center for normal risk cases carries no additional risk for either the baby or the mother.)[21]

Mammography centers, which use radiological techniques to diagnose breast cancer, were transformed in order to respond to the needs of activist women. In the past, they had that spe-cial institutional look—hospital beige paint and steel chairs. The source of the disturbing rumbling noises emanating from the mammography machine as a camera rotated within it was left unexplained. The transformed mammography centers are beautifully decorated and have an antique or modern look tailored to their clients' tastes. More importantly, they provide the information and control their clients seek. The mammography process is carefully explained and the results are discussed in a follow-up letter. To enhance the patients feelings of mastery, many mammography centers added demonstrations on breast self-examination techniques and the effect of nutrition on breast cancer.

Other health services have also clearly focused on the health care activist. For example, the Shouldice Hospital in Toronto, Canada, which performs only hernia surgical procedures, is renowned for its low costs and high quality of care. Its secret? Dr. Shouldice founded his hospital with two then-radical beliefs: he thought that patient involvement promotes recovery and that patients should walk as soon as possible after their operations. (Dr. Shouldice also believed the hernia incision is best sutured by stitching overlapping layers of tissue rather than by sewing all layers together, as in a seam.)

Dr. Shouldice incorporated these beliefs into his hospital. Its activist patients are highly involved in their care. They determine their own time of admission, assess their condition before being admitted, shave and clean the skin of the hernia area before the operation, and, if possible, literally walk away from the operating table. Soon after the operation, they are encouraged to participate in an exercise class. Finally, because neither meals nor a telephone are provided in the patients' rooms, they must walk to a central service area.

As a result of such patient involvement, the Shouldice Hospital claims faster recuperation and lower costs and "redo" rates than are typical. The patients' satisfaction is enormously enhanced by their involvement in the process. Thousands of them throng the annual alumni reunion.

Table 4-2 Male and Female Utilization of Health Services

	Annual Physician Contacts (1987)	Date Since Last Physician Contact (1987)		
		Less Than 1 Year	*1–2 Years*	*2 Years or More*
Female	6.0	81%	10%	9%
Male	4.6	72	12	16

	Hospital Use (1987; per 1,000 population)		Nursing Home Residents (1985; per 1,000 population)
	Operations	*Days of Care*	
Female	118.3	831.1	47.7
Male	76.4	789.2	29.0

Sources: Health United States 1988, pp. 106, 107, 112, 118, 123.

Results to Date

Despite these innovations, the overall results in satisfying activist health care consumers are disappointing. As indicated in Table 4-3, only 30 percent of Americans rated their health care system as correctly balanced. Overwhelmingly they want a greater emphasis on prevention of illness. This desire crosses all socioeconomic boundaries. It is strongest among college-educated people and those earning over $50,000 a year and weakest among those who are 65 or over, those who have an annual income under $15,000, and those who lack a high school degree. But, even among these latter groups, at least one out of every three wanted more emphasis on prevention. Americans want to control their health status, not merely to treat their diseases.

WORKING PEOPLE

While activist health care consumers sought greater mastery, the huge group of working consumers—over 120 million strong in 1987—sought convenience. As a *Business Week* poll noted, "Shoppers are a dwindling species."[22] Three factors shaped their increased need for convenient health care services. (I provide extensive statistical documentation here to help entrepreneurs measure the size of various potential opportunities for serving this group.)

First, because an increasingly large fraction of Americans work, fewer people remain at home to handle the logistics of receiving health care services—making appointments, picking up x-ray films and laboratory test results, and buying drugs and devices. The need for convenience also increased because many people work odd hours and have inflexible schedules. The 16 percent of the 1985 workers who work shifts and the 80 percent with inflexible work schedules were sure to increase as a percentage of the labor force, because these work schedules were most prevalent among the fast-growing service occupations (Table 4-4).

Changing demographic patterns also increased the need for convenient health care services. Fewer family units consisted of two adults who could provide back-up for each other. In one-third of all households, no

Table 4-3 Attitudes about Increased Treatment or Prevention in Health Care

	Balance Is Right	More Emphasis Should Be Given to:	
		Treatment	Prevention
Total Adults, 1983	18%	12%	52%
Total Adults, 1984	23	10	52
Total Adults, 1985	24	14	51
Total Adults, 1986	28	8	43
Urbanism			
Central City	25	11	46
Rest of Metropolitan Area	31	7	45
Outside Metropolitan Area	30	7	37
Sex			
Male	27	8	45
Female	31	9	42
Age			
18–29 Years	31	11	46
30–39 Years	32	9	42
40–49 Years	26	6	51
50–64 Years	24	8	40
65 Years and Over	29	6	37
Education			
Not High School Graduate	25	15	30
High School Graduate	27	9	42
Some College	31	9	44
Four-Year College Graduate	31	3	52
Household Income			
$7,500 or Less	18	14	37
$7,501–15,000	31	10	37
$15,001–25,000	27	8	48
$25,001–35,000	30	8	43
$35,001–50,000	34	7	48
$50,001 and Over	28	4	54
Usual Occopation of Head of Household			
Blue-Collar Labor, Service	27	9	42
Clerical or Sales	32	10	44
Professional Manager or Proprietor	30	6	48

Source: Reprinted from *Prevention Index 87*, p. 21, with permission of Rodale Press, © 1987.

household member is present to care for other members if they ever needed continuous care.[23] Single-head-of-household families with children under 18 increased to 8 percent of all households in 1987. One of every four children under 18 lived with only one parent then,

almost double the 1970 percentage.[24] And 24 percent of all households consisted of people living alone, as shown in Table 4-5.

The aging and increasingly female labor force (Table 4-6) also affected the need for convenient health care services. The rate of use

Table 4-4 Work Schedules (1985)

	Total Employed (thousands)	Shift Workers (%)	Workers with Flexible Schedules (%)
Total	73,395	15.9	12.3
Husbands	29,201	16.4	13.0
With Children under 18	18,101	17.1	NA
Wives	15,432	10.0	10.3
With Children under 18	7,831	10.7	NA
Women With Other Marital Status	6,828	16.3	11.8
With Children under 18	2,921	16.5	NA
Men With Other Marital Status	4,410	19.2	15.0
With Children under 18	614	18.7	NA
By Occupation			
Managerial and Professional	18,944	8.6	18.2
Technical, Sales, Administrative	21,961	11.7	14.6
Service Occupations	7,268	38.4	8.5
Precision Productions	10,477	13.0	6.8
Operators, Fabricators, and Laborers	13,326	23.7	6.4
Farming, Forestry, and Fisheries	1,418	10.1	15.1

Source: Statistical Abstract 1988, Washington, D.C., U.S. Government Printing Office, 1989, Tables 631, 632 and *Statistical Abstract 1990*, Table 643.

Table 4-5 Households by Type and Presence of Children

Type of Household	1980[a]	1987[b]
Family Households	73.7%	72.1%
With Children under 18	38.4	35.6
Married Couples with Own Children under 18	30.9	27.5
Male without Spouse and Own Children under 18	0.8	1.1
Female without Spouse and Own Children under 18	6.7	7.0
Nonfamily Households	26.3	27.9
Living Alone	22.7	23.6

[a]Total number of households in 1980 was 80,776,000.
[b]Total number of households in 1987 was 89,479,000.

Source: Statistical Abstract 1989, p. 48.

of health care services increased after age 15 (Table 4-7), and women used more health care services than men.

The diminished health that accompanies aging has other profound effects on working people. Twenty-two percent of those over 65 and 58 percent of those over 84 have some dis-ability. The assistance they require in activities of daily living most frequently is provided by family members, 31 percent of whom had another job and 9 percent of whom had quit work to become a caregiver.[25] As shown in Table 4-8, few of the disabled elderly were in nursing homes. Most were in the community.

Table 4-6 Labor Force Composition by Age and Sex (Numbers in Millions)

	1970 (millions)	1987 (millions)	2000 (projected) (millions)
Male			
Total Male	51.2	66.2	73.1
16–19 Years	4.0	4.1	4.5
20–24 Years	5.7	7.8	7.0
25–34 Years	11.3	19.7	16.6
35–44 Years	10.5	15.6	20.1
45–54 Years	10.4	10.2	16.3
55–64 Years	7.1	6.9	7.2
65 Years and Over	2.2	1.9	1.4
Female			
Total Female	31.5	53.7	65.6
16–19 Years	3.2	3.9	4.4
20–24 Years	4.9	7.1	6.7
25–34 Years	5.7	15.6	15.1
35–44 Years	6.0	12.9	18.4
45–54 Years	6.5	8.0	14.2
55–64 Years	4.2	4.9	5.7
65 Years and Over	1.1	1.2	1.0
Total Labor Force	82.8	119.9	138.8

Source: Statistical Abstract 1989, p. 376, Table 621.

Working people's need for a source of care for their elderly relatives will intensify in the future. As shown in Table 4-9, the most rapid population growth rate among the elderly has been for those 85 years and older—the very group that needs the greatest assistance in daily life. Their children are frequently elderly themselves and usually middle aged.

Entrepreneurial Responses

Responses to the desires of working people for services delivered in convenient locations and at convenient times include televised shop-at-home services, mail order shopping catalogues, fast-food restaurants, and Domino's Pizza (which guarantees a 30-minute delivery). The desire for convenience is the key to the development of superstores for office, computer, and home supplies and shopping malls. It is also the impetus for narrow-niche retail outlets, like clothing boutiques, in which customers can quickly find the precise type or class of merchandise they seek.

The responses to working people's need for convenient health care services were of three types. Entrepreneurial firms provided health care services (1) at convenient times, like Domino's Pizza; (2) in convenient locations, like shopping malls; or (3) through convenient packages, like clothing boutiques.

Ambulatory health service centers like those of WelMed, a Newton, Massachusetts, company, were designed to provide health services at convenient times (up to 24 hours a day, seven days a week) and in convenient locations, for example, malls and suburban neighborhoods. Seventy percent of their users cite convenience as the lure. For younger consumers, convenience meant "no appointment," whereas for older ones it meant proximity to home. Nearly 80 percent preferred ambulatory health service centers to hospital emergency rooms.[26]

Table 4-7 Health Service Use by Age Group (1987)

| | Annual Average Physician Visits | Interval Since Last Visit to Physician | | Days of Hospital Care per 1,000 |
		Less Than 1 Year	More Than 2 Years	
Under 5 Years	6.7	93%	7%	489
5–14 Years	3.3	76	10	144
15–44 Years	4.6	72	16	407
45–64 Years	6.4	75	16	988
65 Years and Over	8.9	85	10	2,111
Total	5.4	77	13	645

Source: Health United States 1988, Tables 61, 62, 66.

Worksite provision of health care was aimed at the same goal. Mammography tests, for example, were increasingly performed in mobile vans that came to the employees' worksite. What could be more convenient? Explains Dr. Nina Ellenbogen, the founder of a company that performs mammograms in a 36-foot mobile van parked in an employer's lot, "We're pushing more toward corporations because [our patient] is a woman that has no time."[27]

Some of the new health services combined all three convenience factors by offering a clearly focused product delivered in a convenient site and at a convenient time. Salick Health Care centers, for example, provide cancer therapy services at outpatient sites that are open 24 hours a day. Their emphasis on convenience is immediately apparent. While a valet greets cancer patients and parks their cars at the Salick centers at no charge, hospital cancer patients must struggle to find a parking space in the crowded hospital garage.

Salick centers were created when Dr. Bernard Salick's young daughter contracted bone cancer. The inconvenient hospital care process his family experienced in her case inspired him to form an organization that would ease the cancer therapy process for patients and their families. The resulting cancer centers are compact, eliminating the long trek between the hospital's radiology unit—usually buried deep in the recesses of the hospital—and the other sources of care. Yet, their chemotherapy rooms are spacious so that family members can stay with patients while they receive slow intravenous infusions of chemicals that destroy cancerous cells, and they are also cheery, filled with every type of media outlet and with artwork. Free food and beverages are always available. Finally, therapists are on call to support both patients and their families as they valiantly struggle with the dreadful disease.

The eyeglasses stores that dot shopping malls share the same concept of a neatly packaged service offered at convenient times and locations. They make it easy to buy eyeglasses by telescoping the cumbersome traditional process in which patients received a prescription from a physician or optometrist in one site, chose a suitable style in another, and then waited weeks until the lenses arrived. The new stores provide both the diagnosis and the lenses at one site, and some even guarantee a 1-hour wait for glasses.

Working people's need for health care services for their elderly relatives was a primary cause of the explosion in the number and type of nursing homes and home health care providers. From 1965 to 1988, spending on nursing homes increased from $2 billion to $54 billion, and from 1982 to 1990, home health care spending increased from $6 billion to $18 billion.

Table 4-8 Selected Characteristics of Nursing Home and Community Residents 65 Years and Older

Subject	Living in Nursing Homes (1985)	Living in Community (1984)
Total 65 Years and Over		
Number	1,316,000	26,343,000
Percentage	100.0%	100.0%
Age (Percentage Disabled)		
65–74 Years	16.1 (1.3)	61.7 (12.3)
75–84 Years	38.7 (5.6)	30.7 (22.1)
85 Years and Over	45.2 (22.1)	7.6 (36.1)
Total Disabled as Percentage of All Elderly	4.6	17.3
Sex		
Male	25.4	40.8
Female	74.6	59.2
Race		
White	93.1	90.4
Black	6.2	8.3
Other	0.7	1.3
Marital Status[a]		
Widowed	64.2	34.1
Married	16.4	54.7
Never Married	13.5	4.4
Divorced or Separated	5.9	6.3
With Living Children	63.1	81.3
Requires Assistance in:		
Bathing	91.2	6.0
Dressing	77.7	4.3
Using Toilet Room	63.3	2.2
Transferring[b]	62.7	2.8
Eating	40.4	1.1
Difficulty with Bowel and/or Bladder Control	54.5	NA[c]
Disorientation or Memory Impairment	62.6	NA
Senile Dementia or Chronic Control Brain Syndrome	47.0	NA
Number of Activities of Daily Living Dependencies[d]		
Fewer than Three	28.5	67.0
Three or More	71.5	33.2

[a]For nursing home residents, marital status at time of admission.
[b]Getting in or out of bed or chair.
[c]Although comparable data are not available, the 1984 *National Health Interview* found that 6 percent of the community-resident older population had difficulty with urinary control or had urinary catheters.
[d]Alice M. Rivlin and Joshua M. Weiner, *Caring for the Disabled Elderly* (Washington, D.C., The Brookings Institution, 1988), p. 6.

Source: National Center for Health Statistics. Data from the *National Health Interview Survey, Supplement on Aging*, 1984, and the 1985 *National Nursing Home Survey,* Advance Data Nos. 115, 121, 133, and 135; and unpublished data.

Table 4-9 U.S. Population by Age and Sex (1960–2040)

	1960 (thousands)	1980 (thousands)	2000 (projected thousands)	2020 (projected thousands)	2040 (projected thousands)
Total Population					
All Ages	183,216	232,669	273,949	306,931	328,503
Under 20 Years	70,828	74,045	77,001	80,376	84,234
20–44 Years	59,216	97,145	98,261	97,345	102,160
45–64 Years	36,466	45,587	62,435	76,557	74,853
65 Years and Over	16,706	25,892	36,252	52,653	67,256
65–74 Years	11,094	15,627	18,334	30,093	29,425
75–84 Years	4,671	7,688	12,496	14,909	24,565
85 Years and Over	941	2,577	5,422	7,651	13,266
Male Population					
All Ages	90,513	114,069	133,798	149,538	158,833
Under 20 Years	35,957	37,807	39,334	41,067	43,045
20–44 Years	29,126	43,754	49,424	49,063	51,513
45–64 Years	17,852	22,086	30,592	37,616	36,935
65 Years and Over	7,578	10,422	14,448	21,792	27,340
65–74 Years	5,168	6,819	8,250	13,779	13,559
75–84 Years	2,043	2,838	4,741	5,907	9,865
85 Years and Over	367	765	1,457	2,106	3,886
Female Population					
All Ages	92,703	118,600	140,151	157,393	169,670
Under 20 Years	34,871	36,238	37,667	39,309	41,189
20–44 Years	30,090	43,391	48,837	48,282	41,189
45–64 Years	18,614	23,501	31,843	38,941	37,918
65 Years and Over	9,128	15,470	21,804	30,861	39,916
65–74 Years	5,926	8,808	10,084	16,314	15,866
75–84 Years	2,628	4,850	7,755	9,002	14,670
85 Years and Over	574	1,812	3,965	5,545	9,380

Source: Social Security Administration, Office of the Actuary, *Actuarial Study No. 85*, July 1981.

These financial changes were accompanied by structural ones. Between 1950 and 1980, the public sector's share of nursing home patients fell from almost 40 percent to about 3 percent, while the private sector's share rose from 37 percent to 86 percent. Nearly 70 percent of nursing home beds were owned by businesses by 1986. The business segment of the nursing home industry became increasingly consolidated in the early 1980s as large, publicly owned chains acquired smaller operations.[28]

Similar changes occurred in the home health care sector. Entrepreneurial businesses supplied a large fraction of home infusion services and durable medical equipment sales and rentals. The business sector accounted for only approximately 35 percent of all home health service providers, early in the 1980s, but this percentage was growing rapidly.[29]

Results to Date

The results, however, indicate that the convenience needs of Americans are not being fully satisfied. Patients complain of unduly long waits for appointments and the receipt of services. Millions of elderly people and their caregiving families are left unserved even though nursing homes are operating at nearly full capacity. And many services are still delivered at inconvenient hospital sites, rather than at community health centers. For example, while the number of ambulatory surgeries has grown enormously, they still total less than half of all surgeries.

Bundling health care services in creative ways is yet another opportunity waiting to be explored. Patients plagued with ubiquitous health care problems, like "bad backs," headaches, sore feet, and chronic pain, must spend considerable time seeking appropriate sources of care. There are all too few "back centers" or other problem-focused centers that provide a multidisciplinary team to diagnose and treat such problems. Instead, patients themselves must create a network of providers, shuttling back and forth among many types of physicians, therapists, and purveyors of support devices.

For these patients, the present health care system appears to be organized to meet the needs of its providers, not its patients. While an orthopedic surgeon undoubtedly benefits from the peer support and administrative economies gained by joining a group of other orthopods, patients want groups organized around their medical needs, not by medical specialty.

Today's health care system is like an inconveniently located restaurant to which a patron must bring bread, meat, produce, baked products, and beverages before enjoying a meal. Harried working consumers are looking for better ways to meet their health care needs.

FUTURE OPPORTUNITIES

Many opportunities thus remain in the health care industry. Below I describe those most likely to occur and those most desired. (Although I am brave enough to present these predictions, I am not so brave as to attach dates to them.)

Cost-Controlling Opportunities

The main target of cost control will remain the 39 percent of personal health care expenses spent in hospitals. These costs will be controlled in two ways: many more hospital services will be performed at other sites, primarily ambulatory ones, and hospitals will increasingly become part of a vertically integrated system of health care services.

For example, Dr. John Simon, a visionary Arizona surgeon, is planning a vertically integrated health care system in which many services will be offered in hotels. His reasoning? Many hospital procedures do not require the extensive nursing care and equipment that hospitals provide; they can be performed more cheaply and with higher patient satisfaction in a setting more like a hotel. Dr. Simon estimates that the bulk of hospital care can be provided in hotel-like units that cost $80,000 to $95,000 per bed rather than $350,000 per bed, which is the construction cost for units in high-technology hospitals. In his words, "We got infatuated with concrete and metal." In Simon's system, many services will be offered in specialized facilities like birth centers or hernia hospitals. Specialized multidisciplinary teams will be available for specific problems, such as injured backs, heads, knees, feet, digestive systems, and for specific groups of people, such as athletes and women. Already a similar group of California "recovery hotels" charge $593 a day for care that costs $1,590 a day in a hospital.[30]

Further efficiencies will be obtained through greater vertical integration of health care service providers. High-technology hospitals will be linked to community hospitals, nursing homes, and other providers of inpatient and ambulatory care so that each patient can be readily transferred to the most cost-effective setting. Multimodality diagnostic centers will be part of the system, but diagnostic procedures will increasingly be performed outside the hospital.

Vertically integrated systems will be operated at local, state, and regional levels, rather than the national level, because health care needs vary dramatically from one local area to another. Some of the benefits of horizontal integration will be obtained through the formation of buyers groups for drugs, supplies, and equipment. Vendors that offer cheaper or better products will be the only ones to succeed in this market. Distributors and manufacturers of drugs, supplies, equipment, and information systems will increasingly consolidate to achieve the necessary efficiencies and high quality levels.

In the future, services will be squeezed out of "concrete" installations—hospitals, nursing homes, and specialized sites such as inpatient units for drug addiction or head trauma recovery. They will also be squeezed out of the home, which is an inefficient site for delivering care. For example, the nurses who care for home-infusion patients spend at least half their time traveling. If the patients came to the nurses, the nurses could use the extra time for patient services.

The costs of hospital, nursing home, and home health care services will increasingly be controlled with services delivered at convenient ambulatory sites. Patients needing infusion and other types of long-term care, like diabetes care, will be serviced at such sites. Ambulatory settings will also provide care for patients recovering from major surgical procedures, who are presently treated either at nursing homes or at home. For example, people recovering from hip implants or fractures will be transported to an ambulatory site with a special day treatment program. Many of these settings will be owned or managed by entrepreneurial physicians, because they are the most knowledgeable providers of ambulatory care.

Managed care organizations will, in the near term, substantially increase their penetration of the insurance market. In 1990, many large American cities—such as New York, Philadelphia, and Miami—had less than 21 percent of their population in HMOs.[31]

Technology will also reduce the costs of health care. Service providers will increasingly depend on technology as the availability of low-paid, talented, educated workers decreases. For example, whirlpool baths and conveyor belts or robots to deliver drugs and food will be increasingly utilized as substitutes for nurses. And because nurses spend a large portion of their day recording data, health care informa-

tion systems will become better integrated. A universal patient identifier will enable a patient's medical record to be easily compiled from many sources. Also, patients might typically carry their records with them from one health care site to the next. In some cases, they might even enter data directly on their own medical records, using the information stored in the medical instruments they own.

New Consumer Opportunities

As health care service delivery moves out of the hospital setting, working Americans will be able to receive more convenient care. Increasingly, diagnosis, therapy, and monitoring will be performed at the worksite. Companies will permit employees to take off the time required for examinations performed at their worksite by mobile medical units. For example, employees will be permitted the time required to undergo a dental checkup in a well-equipped van parked in the company's lot.

The working consumer market will also inspire the creation of at-home shopping for routine health care items, like drugs and medical supplies, or big-ticket items, like a wheelchair. At-home diagnostic kits will become more prevalent. And day-care centers for impaired relatives, like those with Alzheimer's, will ease the load of the harried working health care consumer. Intergenerational day-care centers in which the elderly help to care for the young are likely to become much more common at worksites.[32] Finally, bundled, focused health services for those plagued with chronic problems with backs, feet, pain, and so on, will be readily available.

Health activists will be served in many ways. Food with attractive nutritive qualities will become increasingly available. The line between cosmetics and drugs will blur. Health care activists will have access to cosmetics that create internal changes, like reversing wrinkles or growing hair, rather than mere superficial changes in appearance. Dermatologists at cosmetics counters in department stores may present activist consumers with both "cosmetics" and "pharmaceuticals" to improve their appearance, ranging from a powerful medication to reverse wrinkles and scars to a medication that induces long-lasting changes in nail or hair color. (Cosmaceuticals is the awkward name presently given to these cosmetic-pharmaceutical hybrids.)

Health services will appeal to health activists who wish to be involved in the health therapy process. Planetree, a California company, encourages patients and their families to provide health care services normally delivered by hospital professionals. The result? Lower cost, higher satisfaction, and increased quality. Health technology will cater to them as well. Activist patients and their companions will not shy away from using powerful devices like at-home defibrillator paddles for reviving stalled hearts if they have the medical conditions that require such devices. They will also increasingly own medical devices that monitor health status, such as a complete cardiac or lung-function unit. These devices will use well-designed computer programs to interpret the information gathered from the patient and sound an alarm when medical intervention is warranted because an abnormal state has been detected.

Health promotion services will become much more readily available to enable health activists to take charge of their health status. Smoking cessation programs, mental health and addiction counseling, and weight-loss activities will become as prevalent at worksites as fitness programs are now.

The availability of health information will explode. Health activists will be able to learn about new providers, drugs, devices, and "cosmaceuticals." The information may appear on computer programs, like Prodigy, jointly created by IBM and Sears to provide activists with self-help quizzes, polls, and clubs whose members have similar interests. The computer programs will be interactive and individualized. For example, they might calibrate an individual's response in relation to those of other respondents.

Clones of *Consumer Reports* to rate new providers will appear. The clones will use the *Con-sumer Reports* procedures for evaluating multiple attributes and will contain surveys of consumer satisfaction. A nursing home issue might, for example, follow the format of the annual *Consumer Reports* car issue. While the car issue discusses "How to Shop Smart for a New Car," "Which Options to Choose?" "How *CU* Tests and Rates Cars," and "Summary Judgments of the 1989 Cars," its nursing home clone might contain the following: "How to Shop Smart for a Nursing Home" (price and insurance information); "Which Options to Choose?" (a discussion of the merits of various nursing home options such as room types, meal packages, and transportation); "How *CU* Tests and Rates Nursing Homes" (details of the independent audits, readership surveys, and governmental and licensing data used to arrive at the ratings); "Summary Judgments of the Nursing Homes" (a consumer's guide to the "best buys," the nursing homes with the best quality and price combinations).

For reasons discussed elsewhere, health insurance policies will increasingly be sold directly to the public rather than to large buying groups such as employers.[33] Three kinds of policies will be offered: catastrophic coverage policies with high-cost-sharing characteristics; comprehensive policies with broad coverage; and various HMO-like products. Heavy users of health care services will choose either the comprehensive or the HMO options. The former will be costly but permit free choice of providers; the latter will cost less, offer a wide choice of benefits, but limit access to providers. Infrequent users of health care will opt for catastrophic coverage. The costs of such policies will be relatively low because of their large enrollments and the relative rarity of catastrophically expensive medical events.

The policies will be sold by a distribution network like the one that presently sells automobile, home, and life insurance policies directly to consumers. Health insurance will be integrated into the financial planning services many of them already offer. The insurance companies that dropped out of the group health market may return. And some of the Blue Cross-Blue Shield plans that suffered losses of over $3 billion in 1987 and 1988 may merge with other insurance companies that offer a full range of products and are experienced in selling directly to consumers.

New Technologies

The prospects of new technologies are no less dazzling. Most exciting is the advent of the bionic person replete with artificial bones, joints, organs, and sensory devices. New computerized implantable medical devices will monitor the functioning of internal organs, such as the heart, kidney, or brain, and jolt them into action, or supersede them should they fail. They will help victims of stroke and of heart, neurological, and kidney disease by monitoring and simulating the body's own electrochemical regulatory system. Ever smaller endoscopes will enable repair of impaired tiny blood vessels deep in the body. Smaller, smarter computer-based devices will be used to outfit transport vehicles so that the therapeutic process can begin as soon as the vehicles arrive on the scene. And devices to repair or create neurological pathways will enable the blind to see, the deaf to hear, and the crippled to walk. Finally, electromagnetic, light, and ultrasonic devices will improve the healing process.

Technology will have yet another important effect on the health care system. Advanced voice-activated and optical recognition computer systems will provide simple methods for entering and storing health information. These systems promise to revolutionize the flow, quantity, and accuracy of health care data. Their first likely application is in the offices of consulting physicians, such as radiologists, who must record a great deal of information for the benefit of other physicians. They will then spread to the hospital for use by nurses, who record voluminous data about their patients, and to the practices of office-based physicians, who will use the systems for managerial purposes, such as billing and writing letters, and medical purposes, such as entering data on a patient's medical record.

New biomaterials will enable the development of implantable drug delivery systems that provide therapeutic doses at the right time and place. For example, an implant of the powerful chemicals used to treat cancerous cells near the tumor site will release the proper dose directly at the site that needs to be treated. These drug delivery systems will range from biocompatible polymers or fatty tissues that disintegrate at known rates to adhesive bandages or "watches" that release drugs through the skin at a controlled pace. New biomaterials will also be combined with computerized devices to create continual sensors that can, for example, diagnose a person's health from urine and fecal matter in the toilet.

Developments in biomaterials will also enable the growth of organs composed of human tissues. A functioning liver has already been grown, on a scaffolding of body-compatible biomaterial, from scrapings of a rat's liver cells by Neomorphics, a New York firm. Better materials will strengthen reconstruction of bones and perhaps even other tissues, such as cartilage or muscle. Artificial joints for arthritis victims with degenerated finger, feet, and other joints will equal the effectiveness of the already hugely successful artificial knee and hip joints. Biodegradable staples will ease the surgical healing process. (A list of such products was presented in Table 3-5.)

Biotechnology will assist in the organ growth process, producing compatible blood vessels and skin that do not trigger the body's defense system against them because they are grown from the patient's own cells. New drugs will stimulate the internal production of the powerful natural substances needed to fight disease or strengthen the body. EPO, for example, a drug produced by Amgen in California and Genetics Institute in Massachusetts, stimulates the growth of red blood cells and thus reduces the need for transfused blood for anemia victims. New biotechnology processes will also produce human red blood cells and purified and stabilized red blood cells from animals. In addition, gene therapy will correct tragic genetic defects. Finally, new substances will avert some of the damage we do to ourselves by blocking the pleasure obtained from illicit drugs. Discovery of the site of the cocaine receptor in the brain, for example, will facilitate the discovery of a substance to block the action of the receptor, thus eliminating cocaine's effect and desirability.

NOTES

1. Kathleen Deveny, "Lessons of the 80's: Emphasize Health, Eliminate Hassles," *Wall Street Journal*, November 28, 1989, B1.

2. American Board of Family Practice, *Rights and Responsibilities* (Lexington, Ky.: American Board of Family Practice, 1987), 38.

3. American Board of Family Practice, *Rights and Responsibilities*, 4.

4. Robert Coles, *Girl Scouts Survey on the Beliefs and Moral Values of America's Children* (New York City: Girl Scouts of the USA, 1990), p. 25, Table 2-1.

5. "The Push for Self Service," *New York Times*, April 9, 1989, Business section, 1, 15.

6. American Board of Family Practice, *Rights and Responsibilities*, 8.

7. "Gain, No Pain," *In Vivo*, January–February 1988, 33–34.

8. "Newsflash Medical," *Self*, March 1990, 233.

9. "Bigger Than Bush," *Wall Street Journal*, May 11, 1990, R4.

10. Richard K. Thomas and William F. Sehnert, "The Dual Health Care Market," *American Demographics*, April 1989, 46–47.

11. Randall Rothenberg, "Some Tough Lessons from Near-Death," *New York Times*, March 27, 1990, D25.

12. "Outliers," *Modern Healthcare*, April 23, 1990, 48.

13. Steve Warner, "How Josie's Chili Won the Day," *Forbes*, February 5, 1990, 57–61.

14. Richard L. Benedict and Regina E. Herzlinger, "The GI Wars: TUMS vs. Rolaids," 9-189-118 (Boston: Harvard Business School, 1989).

15. "The Truth about Calcium," *Consumer Reports*, May 1988, 291.

16. Nadine Brozan, "More People Seek a Pill for Every Ill," *New York Times*, March 12, 1988, 56.

17. John R. Egerton, "Why I Let Patients Tell Me What Treatment They Need," *Medical Economics*, January 22, 1990, 129.

18. American Board of Family Practice, *Rights and Responsibilities*, 65.

19. David Sussman, "History of HMO Doctors," *Health-Week*, March 26, 1990, 38.

20. "Women's Services as a Diversification Strategy," *Briefing*, Washington, D.C.: Arthur Young, April 9, 1989, 1.

21. "Birthing Centers Offer Safe Hospital Alternative," *Modern Healthcare*, January 8, 1990, 16.

22. "Shoppers Are a Dwindling Species," *Business Week*, November 29, 1990, 144.

23. Joyce Jensen, "Health Care Alternatives," *American Demographics*, March 1986, 37.

24. *Statistical Abstract, 1988* (Washington, D.C.: U.S. Government Printing Office, 1990), p. 52, Table 71.

25. Robyn Stone, Gail Lee Cafferata, and Judith Sangle, *Caregivers of the Frail Elderly: A National Profile* (Washington, D.C.: U.S. National Center for Health Services Research, 1987), 17.

26. Jensen, "Health Care Alternatives," 37.

27. Julie Waresh, "A Modern-Day Crusader," *South Florida Business Journal*, March 20, 1989, 12.

28. Joyce Lallman, Sherrie Epstein, and Regina E. Herzlinger, "Note on Long-Term Care," 9-186-186 (Boston: Harvard Business School, 1986), 4.

29. Laura Summer and Regina E. Herzlinger, "Note on the Home Health Industry," 9-186-214 (Boston: Harvard Business School, 1986), 14.

30. Sandra Blakeslee, "Recovery Hotel," *New York Times*, January 24, 1991, B10.

31. "HMO Market Penetration," *Medical Benefits*, January 30, 1991, 11.

32. Kathleen Teltsch, "For Younger and Older, Workplace Day Care," *New York Times*, March 10, 1990, 1.

33. Regina E. Herzlinger, "Healthy Competition," *The Atlantic Monthly*, August 1991, 69–83.

DATA SOURCES

Bibliographies

Literature Search. *National Library of Medicine.* Bethesda, Md.: National Library of Medicine, yearly.

Rees, Alan M., and Catherine Hoffman. *The Consumer Health Information Source Book.* 3d. ed. Phoenix: Oryx Press, 1990.

Audiovisual Materials

National Medical Audio-Visual Center Catalog. Bethesda, Md.: National Library of Medicine, yearly.

Indexes

Cumulative Index of Hospital Literature. Chicago: American Hospital Association, quarterly.

Index Medicus. Bethesda, Md.: National Library of Medicine, monthly.

Quarterly Cumulative Index to Index Medicus. Chicago: American Medical Association, quarterly.

Journal Abstracts

Abstracts of Health Care Management Studies. Ann Arbor, Mich.: Health Administration Press, quarterly.

Handbooks

American Heart Association. *Heartbook.* New York: Dutton, 1980.

The American Medical Association Family Medical Guide. New York: Random House, 1987.

Clark, Randolph Lee, and Russell W. Cumley. *The Book of Health.* New York: Van Nostrand Reinhold, 1973.

Facts at Your Fingertips, Hyattsville, Md.: U.S. Department of Health and Human Services, biennial.

Journals

Cost Control

Business & Health

Business Insurance

Healthcare Financial Management

Medical Benefits

Modern Healthcare

Topics in Health Care Financing

New Consumers

American Demographics

American Health

Monthly Labor Review

Public Opinion

Self

New Technologies

Drug Topics

Journal of the American Dental Association

Journal of the American Medical Association

Medical Devices and Diagnostic Industry

Science

The New England Journal of Medicine

Transactions: American Society of Artificial Internal Organs

Industry Notes

(All are available from the Case Publishing House at the Harvard Business School, Boston, MA 02108.)

Decker, Susan, and Regina E. Herzlinger. "Note on Health Maintenance Organizations." 9-187-158.

Epstein, Sherrie, and Regina E. Herzlinger. "Note on Financing the Health Care Industry." 9-186-170.

———"Note on the Health Care Industry." 9-186-169.

———"Note on Psychiatric Services." 9-187-087.

———"Note on Substance Abuse Treatment." 9-187-094.

———"Note on Medical Technology." 9-187-110.

———"Note on the Health Care Industry." 9-186-189.

Fradd, Brandon, and Regina E. Herzlinger. "Note on the Pharmaceutical Industry." 9-189-076.

Herzlinger, Regina E. "Note on the Hospital Information Systems Industry." 9-187-092.

Lallman, Joyce, Sherrie Epstein, and Regina E. Herzlinger. "Note on the Long-Term Care Industry." 9-187-093.

Summer, Laura, and Regina E. Herzlinger. "Note on the Home Health Industry." 9-186-214.

Part III

The Seven Skills of Management

The seven skills discussed in this part of the book can make the difference between success and failure. Yet they are often only barely discussed, as if acknowledgment of the need for these skills was sufficient for their implementation or as if they could simply be delegated to others. The following is an all too frequent comment: "Right, marketing. I will get a marketing person. There are thousands of them out there."

But life is not so simple. Many experienced new venture managers count themselves lucky to find one "right" marketing person. Yes, hundreds of thousands of people have had some marketing responsibilities. And, of these, some thousands may even have health care backgrounds. But new ventures are innovative. Past experiences are unlikely to be totally relevant. The right person is the one who can implement the particular skill for a novel idea. Founders themselves must know enough about the skill to guide, motivate, and evaluate their managers. Merely hiring the right person to implement a skill about which the top management knows little is a sure recipe for disaster.

The next six chapters discuss the seven skills in depth: marketing, management of regulation, finance, managerial control, human resource management, operations management, and leadership philosophy. Each is discussed in sufficient detail to allow an understanding of the skill and the key issues of its implementation. While some readers may find that the discussions merely scratch the surface, others may find them overwhelmingly complex. To help guide the latter, Exhibit III-1 contains a checklist of the seven skills and the activities central to their successful implementation. Each chapter concludes with suggestions for further readings.

Chapters 5 through 7 discuss the skills needed for a new venture to market its product, finance its creation and growth, and manage the regulatory environment around it. I have grouped these skills together because they are more technical and impersonal than the others. They require knowledge of facts, like the regulatory hurdles that U.S. health care ventures must clear, and techniques, like those of analyzing investment proposals. I present these facts and techniques only because they are critical for successful implementation of these skills. For example, financial evaluations cannot be implemented without an understanding of the techniques of discounting and financial analysis.

Exhibit III-1 The Seven Skills

Marketing
Positioning the Product
Choosing an Appropriate Sales and Marketing
    Strategy

Management of Regulation
Managing Reimbursement Regulations
Managing Conflict-of-Interest Regulations
Managing Technology Regulations
Managing Personnel Regulations
Managing Facility Regulations

Finance
Finding Sources of Capital
Deciding on Uses of Capital
Matching Sources and Uses of Capital

Managerial Control
Planning
Measuring Actual Results
Analyzing the Differences between Planned and
    Actual Results
Evaluating and Motivating

Human Resource Management
Creating an Organizational Structure
Recruiting, Training, and Developing Personnel
Recognizing and Rewarding Personnel

Operations Management
Delineating the Production Process
Sizing
"Make or Buy" Decision Making

Leadership Philosophy
Centralizing versus Decentralizing Authority and
    Responsibility

5

Marketing

The marketing function in new health care organizations consists of first positioning the product by matching its characteristics with the needs of intended customers and then identifying the sales and marketing techniques best suited for reaching those customers. These two steps are discussed in greater detail below. (Case Studies 3 and 4 illustrate some of the main issues.)

POSITIONING THE PRODUCT

Nellcor, a California medical device company, provides an excellent example of product positioning. The company developed a noninvasive process to measure the levels of gases in an anesthetized patient's blood. The development of this process was important for two reasons. First, patients under anesthesia are in a state not far removed from death. Complications in blood gases, such as a shortage of oxygen, may kill them. Second, the traditional system of measuring a patient's blood for oxygen saturation was invasive, slow, and cumbersome. For example, in the interval between the time that a surgeon first noticed an anesthetized patient's blood turning blue from

lack of oxygen to the time that a confirming lab report could be issued, the patient might suffer serious damage. Nellcor estimated that such problems caused approximately 10,000 patients a year to die under anesthesia. Malpractice insurance costs of anesthesiologists were soaring.

Enter Bill New, an anesthesiologist with a Ph.D. in Electrical Engineering, and Jack Lloyd, a successful entrepreneur. They recognized the problem and applied existing technology to solve it. They developed a version of a high-tech BAND AID brand adhesive bandage that is wrapped around an anesthesized patient's finger. The bandage has light-emitting diodes on one end and a photodetector on the other. Blood gas levels affect the amount of light the bandage detects in the finger. A computer analyzes the amount of light and rapidly signals any deficiency of oxygen in the blood to the anesthesiologist.

Nellcor positioned the noninvasive device as a new technology that increased patient safety. Had the company focused on patient management, anesthesiologists might have responded defensively, but because it focused on patient safety, potential defensiveness was defused and sales soared. Nellcor buttressed its product positioning by supporting the creation of the Institute for Patient Safety, which eventually became part of the accrediting body for anesthesiologists. Nellcor's technology thus became an established part of the profession's protocols.

The company's claims of increased safety proved to be correct. Studies at two major hospitals demonstrated a marked reduction in preventable anesthesia-related deaths and complications after the introduction of devices like Nellcor's.[1]

Did the company live happily ever after? Not exactly. Nellcor's great success—sales soared by $115 million in a 4-year period—attracted competitors. Its patent position was not strong enough to prevent others from invading its turf. Prices are expected to drop from $4,000 a unit in 1987 to $2,400 in 1993.[2] After much soul searching, the company came back, this time stressing superlative customer service and capitalizing on its low production costs. The same technology is now being used in the intensive care unit. There it is positioned differently—as a way of lowering health care costs by substituting technology for labor in monitoring patients.

As time went on, Nellcor accomplished the remarkable job of successfully repositioning its device from a new technology focus to a cost-controlling focus. In both cases, it clearly tied the product characteristics to the needs of users.

Delineating the Product Characteristics

Replicating Nellcor's marketing success in positioning its products is not easy. Like Nellcor's products, most of the new medical innovations that fulfill one of three purposes—lowering health care costs, serving new customers, or providing powerful new medical technologies—can be positioned to fulfill more than one of these purposes. For example, at-home diagnostic tests are simultaneously new technologies and innovations that serve health activist consumers. Similarly, cost-lowering services, like birthing centers, can simultaneously serve new consumers.

Clear delineation of which of the three purposes a new venture serves is important, be-cause different managerial skills must be emphasized for each. For example, the skills needed to reduce costs are different from those needed to satisfy activist or working consumers. Thus, although Humana's massive advertising campaign to attract patients to its ambulatory facilities met with some degree of initial success, it attracted all too few repeat customers. Why? Because the cost-controlling Humana facilities did not provide patients with the convenience they craved. Humana's traditional style of managing its hospitals emphasized managerial control of costs rather than operational control of services designed to meet the needs of retail customers.

Marketing can help clarify which one of the three purposes the products should be positioned to fulfill by delineating the size of the prospective market and the ease of reaching it.

Identifying the Buyer

The six major buyers of health care products and services include (1) new consumers who want convenience, mastery, and lower costs; (2) hospitals; (3) physicians; (4) other major providers of health care services, such as nursing homes; (5) employers, who buy health insurance and some health care products; and (6) insurance companies, which decide whether or not to include a new product or service among the items they cover.

The different interests these buyers have in the three new types of products are detailed in Table 5-1. Hospitals are interested in lowering their costs, particularly for patients whose care is paid at fixed prices, like Medicare patients, or sharply discounted rates, like Medicaid patients. They also want to enlarge profits by leveraging their names and patient lists. Finally, hospitals want to remain competitive with other hospitals through access to the best physicians and latest medical technology. If a hospital's best doctors consider an MRI reading essential to their practice of medicine, the hospital will buy an MRI system. If it does not, a competing hospital will do so and lure the

Table 5-1 Potential Interest of Buyers in Three Types of New Health Care Products or Services

Buyers	*Cost-Controlling Innovations*	*Innovations That Serve New Consumers*	*New Technologies*
Consumers	Products not covered by health insurance (e.g., drugs, home health, and nursing home services)	Products that increase convenience (e.g., 24-hour care at a convenient site) or mastery (e.g., health information, health promotion, powerful drugs, and devices)	Products that clearly improve health status
Hospitals, Physicians, Nursing Homes, Other Health Care Providers	Products that reduce the cost of caring for insured patients whose insurance pays only a flat or discounted payment, or uninsured patients (e.g., non-hospital sites for quicker discharge of Medicare patients)	Products that attract activist consumers (e.g., birth centers) or working consumers (e.g., ambulatory surgical centers)	Products that increase the ability to compete with other providers (e.g., new diagnostic techniques)
Employers	Health insurance and other services that reduce cost (e.g., HMOs and utilization review mechanisms)	Products that enhance the ability to recruit and retain activist and harried employees (e.g., mobile health units and on-site fitness centers)	Products that clearly improve employees' health status (e.g., a device that reduces jet lag effect for pilots)
Health Insurers	Products or services that reduce the costs of health insurance (e.g., sites that provide services outside the hospital)	Products that attract insured people who are healthy	Products or services that clearly improve health status (e.g., new diagnostic techniques)

doctors to it. Physicians and other health providers have interests similar to the hospitals. They too want to lower their costs, leverage their names, and compete through the use of new technology.

Employers are primarily interested in lowering their health care costs and providing their employees with competitive health insurance policies. They may also be intrigued with the prospects of health care services or products that help recruit or retain employees in a tight labor market. Insurance companies want to offer employers attractive health insurance policies at competitive prices.

The buyers play different roles with respect to different products, sometimes acting as decision makers, sometimes as end users, and sometimes as both. For example, although the decision maker for the purchase of an expensive new diagnostic machine is the hospital, the end users are the physicians who refer their patients and the patients themselves. Similarly, while the decision maker for the purchase of hospital services is the payer, most likely an insurance company, the end users are the patient and the physician. The marketing analysis should distinguish which role the buyer is playing and ensure that both the decision maker and the end user are informed about the product.[3]

Each buyer has different degrees of interest in the three types of health care innovations. Because insurance companies paid 95 percent of hospital care expenses and consumers only 5 percent in 1989, insurers are more likely to be interested in innovations that reduce hospital expenses than consumers (Table 5-2). But because consumers paid 45 percent of nursing home expenses and 73 percent of pharmaceutical expenses in 1989, their degree of interest in reducing costs in these two categories is likely to be very high.[4] The 37 million American consumers who do not have health insurance for some portion of the year will be interested in cost-lowering innovations in all categories.

Many submarkets exist within each of the six markets. For example, heart disease, the most prevalent cause of death, is treated most frequently by cardiac surgeons and cardiologists. The cardiologists cannot treat heart disease surgically: Their therapeutic arsenal is limited to noninvasive techniques such as drugs and office monitoring and testing. Meanwhile, cardiac surgeons performed 270,000 coronary artery bypass operations in 1988 to unclog arteries choked with plaque. (These operations are commonly referred to as "open-heart surgery" because they require sawing open the chest.)

Within these dry statistics lies the success of angioplasty. This technique unclogs arteries, just like coronary artery bypass surgery, but it can be performed nonsurgically by threading a balloon into the arteries through a small incision and inflating it to compact arterial plaque. Angioplasty expanded substantially the cardiologists' therapeutic arsenal. Small wonder that the number of procedures increased to about 300,000 in 1988.

The companies producing angioplasty catheters and balloons segmented the market appropriately by targeting cardiologists. Had they limited the market and targeted only cardiac surgeons, adoption of angioplasty would likely have proceeded at a slower pace.

Reaching the Markets

The six markets are reached in different ways. Consumers are traditionally approached using the marketing techniques enumerated in Exhibit 5-1. They include advertising, public relations, product promotions and discounts, and sales. The consumer sales force in the health care industry includes physicians, hospitals, and other health care providers who act as the patient's advisors and agents. The five other health care buyers are reached with unusual marketing techniques like joint ventures and by employing lobbyists and financial intermediaries (see Exhibit 5-1).

Consumer marketing techniques should be used in all cases in which the consumer is the end user. For example, although the primary buyer of HMO insurance policies is the employer, HMOs must nevertheless use consumer marketing techniques to inform

---

Exhibit 5-1 Most Frequently Used Marketing and Sales Techniques for the Six Buyers of Health Care

Consumers	Hospitals, Physicians, Other Health Care Providers, Employers, and Insurance Companies
Direct Mail	Trade Shows
Telemarketing	Trade Journals
Public Relations	Sales Force
Community Activities	Research
Advertising	Financial Intermediaries
Discounts, Coupons, Premiums, Incentives	Joint Ventures
Promotions	Consultants and Other Advisors

Table 5-2 National Health Expenditures by Source of Funds and Type of Expenditure (billions of dollars)

Year and Type of Expenditure	All Sources	Private Consumer					Government		
		All Private Funds	Total	Direct	Private Insurance	Other	Total	Federal	State and Local
1987									
National Health Expenditures	496.6	294.8	282.6	127.9	154.7	12.3	201.7	142.7	59.0
Health Services and Supplies	479.3	288.7	282.6	127.9	154.7	6.1	190.6	133.8	56.8
Personal Health Care	438.9	269.3	263.9	127.9	136.0	5.5	169.6	128.8	40.9
Hospital Care	192.6	94.8	92.4	20.5	71.9	2.3	97.9	77.7	20.2
Physicians' Services	101.4	70.7	70.6	28.2	42.5	0.1	30.7	25.3	5.4
Dentists' Services	32.4	31.7	31.7	20.8	10.9	—	0.7	0.4	0.3
Other Professional Services	16.2	11.5	11.4	7.1	4.3	0.1	4.7	3.5	1.2
Drugs and Medical Sundries	32.8	29.3	29.3	24.4	4.9	—	3.5	1.9	1.6
Eyeglasses and Appliances	8.8	6.9	6.9	5.9	1.1	—	1.9	1.8	0.1
Nursing Home Care	41.6	21.8	21.5	21.1	0.4	0.3	19.8	11.1	8.8
Other Personal Health Care	13.1	2.6	—	—	—	2.6	10.4	7.1	3.3
Program Administration and Net Cost of Private Health Insurance	25.9	19.4	18.7	—	18.7	0.7	6.6	3.6	2.9
Government and Public Health Activities	14.4	—	—	—	—	—	14.4	1.4	13.0
Research and Construction of Medical Facilities	17.3	6.1	—	—	—	6.1	11.1	8.9	2.3
Noncommercial Research	9.0	0.4	—	—	—	0.4	8.6	7.9	0.7
Construction	8.3	5.7	—	—	—	5.7	2.5	1.0	1.5

continues

Table 5-2 continued

Year and Type of Expenditure	All Sources	All Private Funds	Private Consumer				Government		
			Total	Direct	Private Insurance	Other	Total	Federal	State and Local
1990									
National Health Expenditures	647.3	378.2	363.4	162.0	201.4	14.8	269.0	195.5	73.6
Health Services and Supplies	626.5	371.5	363.4	162.0	201.4	8.1	255.0	184.0	71.0
Personal Health Care	573.5	344.6	337.4	162.0	175.4	7.3	228.9	178.2	50.7
Hospital Care	250.4	118.9	115.9	24.6	91.3	3.0	131.5	107.7	23.8
Physicians' Services	132.6	89.9	89.9	35.1	54.7	0.1	42.7	35.8	6.9
Dentists' Services	41.8	41.1	41.1	26.8	14.2	—	0.8	0.4	0.4
Other Professional Services	22.9	16.2	16.0	9.7	6.3	0.2	6.7	4.9	1.8
Drugs and Medical Sundries	42.1	37.4	37.4	30.7	6.7	—	4.7	2.5	2.1
Eyeglasses and Appliances	11.2	8.4	8.4	7.0	1.5	—	2.7	2.6	0.1
Nursing Home Care	54.5	29.1	28.7	28.0	0.7	0.4	25.4	14.3	11.1
Other Personal Health Care	18.0	3.5	—	—	—	3.5	14.4	9.8	4.6
Program Administration and Net Cost of Private Health Insurance	34.6	26.9	26.0	—	26.0	0.9	7.7	4.2	3.5
Government and Public Health Activities	18.5	—	—	—	—	—	18.5	1.6	16.8
Research and Construction of Medical Facilities	20.7	6.7	—	—	—	6.7	14.0	11.5	2.5
Noncommercial Research	11.5	0.4	—	—	—	0.4	11.0	10.2	0.8
Construction	9.3	6.3	—	—	—	6.3	3.0	1.3	1.7

Source: Health Care Financing Administration, Office of the Actuary, 1987, Division of Cost Estimates.

employees about their services. And although the primary buyer of high-technology equipment is the provider of health care services, manufacturers should use public relations techniques to inform customers about their products, so that the customers ask their providers to use the products.

Positioning a product requires clearly defining the product's main purpose and the mechanisms for reaching the six types of potential buyers. For example, marketing a birth center positioned to serve activist women involves consumer marketing techniques, while marketing a birth center positioned to reduce costs involves targeting insurance companies and employers. The size of each market depends on the characteristics of the geographic area in which the new product or service is to be offered. For example, some parts of the country may have greater interest in cost control than in health activism. If it is less costly to market to employers and insurers than to consumers in those areas, the founders of a birth center chain can serve a larger, easier-to-reach market by positioning the chain as a cost-controlling mechanism rather than a service for activist women. (The data and industry background provided in Part II and Appendixes A, B, and C should prove useful for analyzing the size of alternative markets.)

CHOOSING AN APPROPRIATE SALES AND MARKETING STRATEGY

The importance of an appropriate sales and marketing strategy is underscored by the saga of PET (positron emissions tomography) scanners. PET scans for screening heart disease are more reliable than thallium scans and less invasive than coronary angiography, whose use involves weaving catheters through plaque-clogged arteries. And PET scans are cheaper to boot. Yet, although the technology has been available for decades, there are only 50 scanners in the United States.

What is the problem? According to the *Wall Street Journal*, "many cardiologists resist PET tests because they stand to lose economically if the test supplants stress testing. That's because PET tests would probably be done at major medical centers—in contrast to stress tests, which can be done in the doctors' offices."[5]

A market analysis would have indicated to PET scanner manufacturers that the number of office-based cardiologists is far greater than the number of hospital-based ones. An analysis of alternative ways of reaching office-based physicians would have identified starting joint ventures and using financial intermediaries as highly effective methods. These marketing methods are discussed in greater detail below.

Obtaining Health Insurance Coverage

Health insurance coverage should be the foremost concern for virtually all new health care products and services. Because health insurance insulates the consumer from the cost of an innovation, obtaining insurance coverage for the innovation will boost sales. If health insurance policies do not include payment for the innovation, consumers must pay for it entirely out of their own pockets. When the new product or service is very costly, they may be unwilling to pay for it and will tend to prefer similar products or services that are insured, even if the uninsured new product is better.[6] (I find the importance of insurance coverage a deplorable aspect of the American health care system. It is, nevertheless, an important business reality. New ventures that succeed in obtaining coverage prosper; those that do not generally fail.)

For example, a company offering an effective diet therapy for people so overweight that they are called "morbidly obese" was unable to secure insurance coverage for its services. The insurance companies decided that "weight loss" was not a "medical service," although many illnesses, like diabetes and heart disease, are clearly linked to gross obesity. Insurers further objected to the provision of the therapy in a community center rather than a hospital. The intensive therapy cost $2,000, a price most potential patients could not afford. The company folded. (See Case Study 3.)

A similar therapy was subsequently offered by another company. The new version was wildly successful. The secret of its success? The company joint-ventured its programs with hospitals, thus negating the insurance companies' concerns about the location and the "medical" nature of the service. Once insurance coverage was approved, patients appeared in record numbers. (Ironically, the new company's services cost more than its predecessor's because the new company added the hospital's overhead and fees to its own expenses.)

Factors important for favorable reimbursement coverage include the following:

- Joint ventures with hospitals. These are especially important for service-providing companies. Blue Cross, the nation's largest health insurer, was formed by hospitals, and many Blue Cross plans still favor services provided by or in conjunction with hospitals. Other insurers feel more comfortable with the quality of care delivered in a hospital than in newer health care service sites.
- A clear demonstration of cost savings and quality for services provided outside the hospital setting and for technology used in the hospital. Affiliation with well-known, highly regarded physicians is helpful.
- Scientific evidence demonstrating the safety and efficacy of new technology. These demonstrations require long and costly research.
- Active public concern regarding the problem being treated (e.g., AIDS therapy and fertility treatments).

Because insurance companies are hesitant to extend coverage, some innovators completely bypass them. Instead, they head to a friendly state legislature and lobby for legislation that requires companies offering health insurance policies to include certain services in their coverage. Many states, for example, have passed regulations that require the inclusion of drug and alcohol therapy in all employer health insurance policies. Such "mandates" usually result from intense lobbying by providers. Florida therapists, for example, provided free massage services to legislators to persuade them of the need to mandate health insurance coverage for their services.[7]

Techniques for Consumer Marketing

Consumer marketing and sales techniques are used by virtually all new health care ventures but especially by ventures directed at new consumers or at controlling costs. Unfortunately, consumer marketing in health care has not had many conspicuous successes. Indeed, some new ventures are so dubious of their ability to reach consumers directly that they opt to disseminate their products through agents. For example, although many at-home diagnostic tests were created to provide convenience and increase the mastery of new consumers, they require a physician's prescription or interpretation of the results. Although the physician's involvement reduces convenience and the consumer's sense of mastery, it considerably simplifies the marketing process. In effect, the physician sells the product to the patient.

Direct mail and telemarketing are among the few successful health care consumer marketing techniques. With a well-designed data base, they can be used to send personalized messages to likely consumers. For example, when the Marriott Corporation decided to sell life-care condominiums to affluent elders in Washington, D.C., it sent a direct mail offer to a carefully selected group. For a $1,000 deposit, they would get first pick at the condos described in the package—luxuriously appointed, with a pool, maid service, a health club, and various degrees of nursing care. Nearly 2,000 deposits flooded in.[8]

Public relations techniques are also successful. When consumers become aware of medical research that demonstrates the efficacy of a new technique or product, they tend to request it. One surgeon noted that his patients asked that a laser be used in their surgery rather than a scalpel because they wanted the latest in high-tech medicine. The provision of research information through seemingly objective media (e.g., magazine, journal, and newspaper articles and radio and television news programs) increases a product's credibility.

The media readily broadcast news of medical innovations because of the great public interest they arouse. One of the ten most watched video news releases of 1989 was SmithKline Beecham's description of its new cardiovascular drug Eminase; an estimated 27 million people watched it. Not surprisingly 15–20 percent of all video news releases deal with health and drugs.

Of course, these techniques must be used responsibly. The public should be aware, for example, that the source of the information is the company supplying the new product or service, and the information must be accurate. SmithKline's protocol for its Eminase video is a good model. SmithKline requested FDA review of the script and included a warning of contraindications for its use in the video and its accompanying press kit.[9]

Participation in community activities provides a useful marketing technique for health care service ventures. Personal letters from physicians to community residents, notices in local supermarkets and community centers, discreet billboards, and participation in local fairs all raise awareness of and comfort with a new service. *Point-of-sale material* is also useful. For example, employees cited the primary reason for their selection of an HMO as the brochure describing its services that was distributed to them by their employer.

Other *traditional consumer marketing techniques* (e.g., discounts, coupons, premiums, and incentives) are less successful or of unproven efficacy. These techniques risk "cheapening" the service or product offered because of their traditional association with low-cost merchandise, but they may prove useful in promoting cost-controlling innovations. Not surprisingly, some HMOs use coupons to attract enrollees. Promotions, such as a free cholesterol screening clinic, may be effective in attracting potential patients, but their efficacy in attracting steady users is not well documented. They should be carefully implemented. A sullen, disheveled representative at a promotion conveys a poor image of the service or product.

Advertising is rarely cited by patients as a major factor in their decision to try a new health care service provider. In a private HMO survey, only 37 percent of the respondents cited advertising as the prime reason for joining the HMO and fewer than 10 percent could recall any advertising, despite the HMO's substantial media budget.

Nevertheless, advertising is frequently used, sometimes in an innovative fashion. For example, an ad for a provider of addiction recovery services offered the following candid assessment of the low likelihood of a quick cure: "Lately, it seems like a lot of treatment programs are using speed—but, if your life is handcuffed by drugs and alcohol, over-night recovery sales pitches get old real fast."[10] Others are notable for their crispness. A punchy yellow pages telephone directory ad with the heading "Real Help for Tough Problems" at least doubled the number of people calling the psychologist who placed it.[11]

Advertising may be effective in promoting over-the-counter pharmaceuticals. It is extensively used, at any rate. Such advertising is frequently based on market research about the characteristics of consumers and their use of the product. Research helps to shape the advertising message and the media in which it is disseminated. For example, when the calcium-based antacid tablet TUMS was found to help prevent osteoporosis, a bone-loss disease affecting people who do not ingest sufficient calcium in their normal diets, a marketing issue surfaced: Should TUMS' traditional advertising message ("TUMS for the Tummy") be expanded to note its efficacy in preventing osteoporosis or should a separate campaign be designed for TUMS as a disease preventative?

A comparison of the demographic characteristics of antacid and calcium tablet buyers (Table 5-3) indicated that some segmentation was warranted. Indigestion aids were much more widely used than vitamin and calcium tablets in the South and by older people and those with incomes under $15,000 a year. Women used calcium tablets much more than men, whereas indigestion aids were more often

Table 5-3 Socioeconomic Characteristics of Users of Indigestion Aids and Vitamin and Calcium Tablets (1986)

	Indigestion Aids		Vitamin and Calcium Tablets	
	Percentage of All Buyers[a]	Users as Percentage of Adult Population[b]	Percentage of All Buyers[c]	Users as Percentage of Adult Population
Sex				
Men	46.2	48.6	39.4	34.1
Women	53.8	51.5	60.6	47.8
Education				
Graduated College	15.5	44.5	20.4	48.2
Some College	16.9	46.8	19.4	44.0
Graduated High School	40.1	51.6	38.1	40.4
Less Than High School	27.5	54.1	22.1	35.9
Age				
18–24	13.9	44.0	13.8	36.0
25–34	22.2	46.5	23.2	40.1
35–44	17.7	48.3	17.3	38.9
45–54	13.5	51.7	14.1	44.3
55–64	14.7	56.7	14.0	44.2
65+	17.9	57.0	17.6	46.2
Household Income				
$50,001+	18.6	44.6	23.8	46.9
$40,000–50,000	13.3	47.6	14.8	43.5
$35,001–40,000	8.0	48.4	8.3	41.3
$25,001–35,000	19.7	52.7	17.8	39.2
$15,001–25,000	19.4	52.3	17.9	39.9
Less Than $15,000	21.1	54.1	17.4	36.9
Region				
Northeast	20.2	47.1	22.7	43.5
North Central	25.0	50.6	25.2	41.8
South	37.7	55.0	31.4	37.7
West	17.1	44.3	20.8	44.5

[a]Total buyers of indigestion aids = 86,713,000.
[b]Total adult population = 172,957,000.
[c]Total buyers of vitamin and calcium tablets = 71,387,000.

Source: Reprinted from Richard L. Benedict and Regina E. Herzlinger, "The GI Wars: TUMS vs. Rolaids," Case no. 9-189-118, Boston, Harvard Business School, pp. 11, 14.

purchased by men than women. This research indicated that TUMS positioned as an osteoporosis aid should be marketed in media with an upscale women's audience, and that TUMS positioned as an indigestion aid should be targeted at lower-income consumers and at certain areas of the country, especially the South.

Some new ventures base their consumer advertising strategy completely on medical

research. For example, a full page ad in the *New York Times* trumpeted the awards for allergy and immunology research established by a company manufacturing a device that purports to kill cold viruses with inhaled heat. When the product was first introduced, the company's claims for its device were challenged by *Consumer Reports.* The firm fought back by taking its research case to the public. This ad, the latest in a series, linked the device to distinguished researchers in the field by citing, for example, the Nobel Prize winner who designed it. It also listed innovators whose contributions were wrongfully scorned in their lifetimes. Its prize was named after one, Sir Hiram Maxim, whose invention of the machine gun was applauded but whose development of a steam inhaler to ease his chronic bronchitis was dismissed by the medical establishment. The ad ended with this rueful quote from Sir Maxim: "From the foregoing it will be seen as a very creditable thing to invent a killing machine, and nothing less than a disgrace to invent an apparatus to prevent human suffering."[12]

Although this strategy can succeed, relying on medical research evidence as the basis for advertising may also backfire. For example, although a 1988 American study appeared to establish that women who broke their hips had consumed less calcium than those who did not, a 1989 British study reached the opposite conclusion. It showed no evidence that fractures increase with declining calcium intake.[13] By 1991, the effect of the hormone estrogen in preventing bone loss in postmenopausal women appeared to be well established, but the role of calcium remained unclear. In addition, calcium had negative effects on people with a tendency to form calcium-containing stones in their urinary tracts, and it could even interfere with the absorption of iron and phosphates.[14] An advertising strategy based solely on the wonders of calcium—or any other medical breakthrough—could well boomerang if subsequent evidence disputes the original findings, a not uncommon event.

Techniques for Marketing to Hospitals and Other Providers and Payers

Marketing to buyers other than consumers includes many traditional techniques.

Advertising at trade shows and in trade journals can be effective and efficient. For example, when Spacelabs introduced a prototype ambulatory blood pressure monitor at a cardiologists' convention, it immediately received a substantial number of orders. Most frequently, trade shows are useful for identifying potential buyers who should then be contacted subsequently.

A sales force is a conventional marketing technique, but health care salespeople tend to have unusual backgrounds. Many of them have health or medical training. Genentech uses registered nurses as salespeople for its product TPA. Some pharmaceutical "detail men" are medical school dropouts or once worked in a hospital, and many health insurance salespeople have work experience in the human resource department of a corporation. U.S. Surgical created a whole new sales category of "stapling technicians" who received substantial training in the appropriate use of surgical staples. Some salespeople have even been the recipients of the services they now sell. For example, drug addiction therapy services are frequently sold by recovering addicts.

Such unusual backgrounds help salespeople function as effective educators about novel technologies or services rather than as mere order takers. For example, the sales representatives of Medtronic, a leading pacemaker company, are expected to be in the operating room to watch implant procedures and to support the physicians either as team players or partners. Medtronic targets small community hospitals that do not have the extensive back-up staff of larger hospitals. Its salespeople provide that back-up.[15] Some surgeons may think so highly of the sales representatives' knowledge of the details of inserting the pacemaker that they rely heavily on their advice in performing implants.

To support them in these challenging roles, health care salespeople should receive extensive training. At Medtronic, they participate in three training programs over a 1-year period. The subjects range from selling techniques to product knowledge. The salespeople also serve internships and do role-playing as part of their training. Some salespeople are trained to identify changes in market characteristics. For example, the salespeople at Intermedics, another pacemaker company, helped identify the changing role of surgeons. While surgeons were once solely responsible for the selection of most products, the Intermedics salespeople felt that product selection has come to be shared by the "surgeon [who] does the cutting and the cardiologist [who] positions the electrodes."[16] Salespeople should be trained to identify changes in the market because they have the closest contact with the market.

But salespeople cannot work miracles. They must be armed with the good points about their product. If it is cost reducing, they must provide evidence of cost reductions achieved. If it enhances convenience or mastery, evidence of these enhancements must be clear. If it is a new technology, evidence must demonstrate it is a clearly dominant technology that vastly improves the quality of care or reduces side effects.

Research is an important marketing tool used by the new technology-based or service ventures. Journal articles that demonstrate the efficacy of a new technology or service are key to its acceptability. Demonstrations of the relative cost-effectiveness of the products are also increasingly important. For example, Genentech was asked to demonstrate not only that TPA dissolved blood clots within the body but also that it was more cost-effective than other cheaper clot solvents.

Surprisingly, indeterminate or even negative research results do not necessarily adversely affect sales. For example, because angioplasty patients may experience reformation of the blockage, researchers hoped that a laser beam used in combination with balloon angioplasty would reduce the incidence of blockage reformation. Research results did not support their reasoning, but the sale of laser-based devices held steady.[17] Why? Because practicing physicians became comfortable with the device; patients enjoyed the use of high-tech lasers; the new device was no worse than the old one; and, most fundamentally, the physicians probably did not trust the research conclusions. They had witnessed many research conclusions flip-flop in the past and may have suspected that the conclusion about the efficacy of lasers might add to the number.

This is not to deprecate the value of research for marketing purposes. It helps to legitimize important innovations and secure insurance payments for new services or technologies. One addiction services company, for example, created a research foundation to evaluate the efficacy of its treatments. The company's bankers were aghast when the foundation was first proposed. "What will you do if the research finds your therapy is ineffective?" the chagrined bankers asked. The company's president replied,

> We will revise our approach and announce the fact to our users. Our new approach will put us a step ahead of our competitors, who will be using a treatment proved ineffective. But if the researchers find our treatment to be effective, we can use that finding to our favor as well. After all, the fact that we were not afraid to be evaluated indicates our interest in providing the very best services.

Lobbying is yet another key technique in marketing to nonconsumer buyers. It is most frequently used to secure insurance reimbursement for an innovation or to clear regulatory impediments. State and federal governments increasingly mandate that certain technologies, services, or groups of people be covered by employer health insurance. Lobbyists have also been effective in securing congressional funding for medical research. Mary Lasker, who was married to an innovator in modern advertising, used his techniques and her natural ability to help expand the budget of the National Cancer Institute from $18.9 million in 1950 to $1 billion in 1990. When she was awarded the prestigious Gold Key Award, the announcement noted, "Mary Lasker, in her way, is probably responsible more than any other person for the National Institutes of Health."[18]

Interest groups can help with lobbying. The elderly are a large and well-organized interest group whose assistance can smooth the passage of relevant legislation and funding. Groups affiliated with various diseases and medical problems can also be of help. AIDS activists, for example, continually lobby for greater funding for AIDS research and more rapid

FDA evaluation of new therapies. If interest groups are not involved, they can do irreparable harm. One company was stunned when representatives of the deaf community failed to support a hearing device the company had spent $30 million in developing. These deaf persons felt that deafness is a natural condition and that attempts to "heal" it demean them and make deafness appear to be an "illness."

Benefit consultants and other professionals hired as advisors to buyers, such as accountants, lawyers, and third-party administrators, are influential in purchasing decisions.

Financial intermediaries can be useful in marketing by spreading out the cost of expensive medical technology such as radiological diagnostic equipment, which can carry a price tag of over $1 million and require installation costs of equal magnitude. Many of the buyers interested in using the new technology might not be able to find the resources to pay for it. Financial intermediaries may lower the effective price.

Some intermediaries offer leasing contracts that enable health facilities to rent rather than purchase equipment. Many manufacturers and leasing companies, like the Linc Group, supply these leases. Other intermediaries purchase the equipment and charge the user a flat rate per use. For example, MRI devices are purchased and installed by an intermediary group that then charges the hospital or physician that orders an MRI reading a flat rate. These companies are usually owned by physicians (e.g., radiologists of an MRI center). The use of many diagnostic and laboratory devices has been greatly enhanced through these intermediaries. New health care ventures can facilitate their creation. (See Case Study 5 for a description of one such intermediary.)

Joint ventures are often useful for marketing purposes. The new health care venture can form an affiliation with employers, insurers, physicians, hospitals, or other providers of health care services. The partner hopes that the joint venture will increase its profits and enable it to better serve patients, while the new health care venture hopes that its partner will provide a market for its innovation or lower its costs.

Joint ventures between physicians and hospitals are traditional. Physicians refer their patients to the hospital in exchange for free or low-cost space and administrative support. Hospitals even give physicians bonuses for agreeing to practice there and frequently guarantee the first years of a physician's income in a hospital-based practice. In 1987, 88 percent of U.S. hospitals reimbursed physicians for relocation expenses and provided them with practice start-up assistance, 52 percent provided free office space, and 36 percent granted interest-free loans.[19] The cost of these physican-bonding programs is high. Large hospitals spent $1.2 million on them in 1990, and the average hospital spent $565,000.[20]

All three types of new health care companies have used joint ventures for marketing. Cost-controlling enterprises sometimes form joint ventures with employers, health care providers, and insurers. Many HMO and PPO companies enter into joint ventures with hospitals and physicians, who agree to discount their prices in exchange for new patients. Both partners gain: The HMOs and PPOs lower their costs and the providers find new patients. Yet each party maintains its independence and focus. The PPOs and HMOs concentrate on lowering administrative costs and acting as gatekeepers and the providers concentrate on providing high-quality services.

Organizations that provide ambulatory services have also formed joint ventures with hospitals or physicians. For example, Caremark, a Baxter subsidiary that offers home infusion services, has a number of hospital joint ventures. From Caremark's perspective, the joint ventures provide it with a patient base, while from the hospitals' perspective, the arrangement has three advantages. First, because hospitals are increasingly paid a fixed rate per procedure, they have an incentive to discharge patients to another provider of care. When Medicare pays a flat rate of, say, $6,000 for the care of a coagulation disorder victim, the hospital is motivated to lower its costs by discharging the patient as soon as possible. Second, hospitals have lost a great deal of money as a result of bungled diversifications

Table 5-4 Key Product Characteristics of Health Care Innovations

	Innovations That Reduce Costs	Innovations That Increase Mastery	Innovations That Increase Convenience	Technological Marvels
Key Focus	Low costs	Self-help	Convenient to use	Powerful new technology
Primary Target Markets	Health insurers, employers, consumers	Health activists	Working people	Physicians, health facilities
Price	Low	Competitive	Competitive	High
Most Common Channels of Distribution	Health insurance companies	Self-help sites (e.g., health clubs); high-choice sites (e.g., gourmet supermarkets)	Easily accessible sites (e.g., at work or at a shopping mall)	Established distributors; joint ventures with health care providers
Key Marketing Techniques	For consumers: popular media, coupons, discounts, advertising; for employers and insurers: discounts via sales force	Public relations, advertising in self-help media (e.g., *American Health*), direct mail, point-of-sale material	Public relations, early morning and late evening media, direct mail, point-of-sale material	Research publications, public relations campaigns that focus on medical qualities, salespeople with special training, joint ventures

into nonhospital health care ventures. Hospitals that once dreamed of creating their own sources of nonhospital care are now painfully aware of the advantages of a partner with a track record in managing these new sources of care. Third, most hospitals do not have enough patients to justify creating a business of their own. For example, in 1987, the average hospital had fewer than 100 patients a year who might qualify for home infusion therapy (see Case Study 13). Their patient base was simply not large enough to sustain a home infusion business. But when a new venture combines the patients from a number of hospitals, the large, merged patient base substantially increases the new venture's viability.

Some cost-controlling innovators have entered into joint ventures with employers. CIGNA, a large insurance company, for example, joint-ventured with Allied-Signal, a large corporation that chose CIGNA to replace all its other HMOs and PPOs. CIGNA, in return, agreed to provide services while increasing health insurance costs only 10 percent per year for 3 years; if medical care cost increases exceed the 10 percent mark, CIGNA must absorb the difference. CIGNA hopes to gain economies of scale through the effort—43,000 employees are enrolled—while Allied-Signal hopes to achieve cost control.[21]

Organizations that target new consumers also form joint ventures with other providers. Health Stop, an ambulatory physician services firm in Newton, Massachusetts, for example, formed joint ventures with hospitals. Health Stop refers patients who needed hospitalization to the hospitals, while the hospitals lend Health Stop their names and provide a fee (see Case Study 6). A new technology venture that uses physicians as the primary referral source for patients may forge an agreement for physicians to refer patients to the new venture in exchange for a share of the ownership. For example, many laboratory and high-technology diagnostic centers are partially owned by the physicians who refer their patients there.

Such arrangements are coming under increased scrutiny as concern mounts about the incentives for abuse and overutilization they create. Joint ventures may motivate hospitals to discharge patients prematurely and limit inappropriately the patient care they provide, and they may also cause physicians to recommend excessive diagnostic testing. On the other hand, many joint ventures are more efficiently managed than alternative organizations. (These regulations are discussed in Chapter 6.) In all cases, full disclosure of the providers' interest is important. For example, the hospital discharge planner who refers patients to a home health agency in which the hospital is a partner should disclose that fact and provide patients with other sources of home health care services.

The product characteristics, buyers, and key marketing techniques that accompany them are summarized in Table 5-4. The art of marketing is in carefully tailoring all of these techniques to a clearly identified buyer.

Last, a word of caution. Many professionals in the health care sector regard marketing with distaste, viewing it as a tool to manipulate the public. It should never be used in this way. Instead, marketing should be viewed and used as a service that enables the public to be informed of new valuable products or services. Marketing is the key to the information that enables a free market.

NOTES

1. "Oximetry Reduces Complications," *BBI Newsletter*, November 16, 1990, 217.

2. Ibid.

3. Steve Diamond, of the Management Analysis Center, Cambridge, Massachusetts, is responsible for this insight.

4. Health Care Financing Administration, "Sources of Funds for Personal Health Care in 1989, " *HHS News*, December 20, 1990.

5. John Koten and Thomas M. Burton, "Telltale Heart," *Wall Street Journal*, May 11, 1990, 9.

6. Milt Freudenheim, "Will Hospitals Buy Yet Another Costly Technology?" *New York Times*, September 9, 1990, 5.

7. Susan B. Garland, "How Less Could Be More in Insurance," *Business Week,* May 21, 1990, 47.

8. Janet Novack, "Tea, Sympathy, and Direct Mail," *Forbes*, September 18, 1989, 210–11.

9. Joanne Lipman, "News Videos That Pitch Drugs Provoke Outcry for Regulations," *Wall Street Journal*, February 8, 1990, B6.

10. "Comprehensive Care Ads Don't Promise Easy Cures," *Modern Healthcare*, January 7, 1991, 49.

11. "Therapists Seek Help in Advertising," *Insight*, February 11, 1991, 40–43 .

12. "Announcing the 1990 Sir Hiram Maxim Awards," *New York Times*, May 5, 1990, 7.

13. "Calcium May Not Prevent Hip Fractures in the Elderly," *BBI Newsletter*, November 17, 1989, 176.

14. "Calcium Supplements," *The Medical Letter on Drugs and Therapeutics*, November 17, 1989, 101–103.

15. Debra Matei, "Pacemaker Leaders Set New Market Strategy," *Health Industry Today* 54, no. 4 (1990): 6.

16 "Pacemaker Leaders," 7.

17. Charles R. Appelby, "'Cool Laser' Won't Replace Balloon Angioplasty," *HealthWeek*, April 9, 1990, 31.

18. *Archives of Physical and Medical Rehabilitation*, March 1976, 148.

19. "Healthcare's Hidden Costs," *Medical Benefits*, February 15, 1990, 4.

20. "Cost of Wooing Physicians Skyrocketing," *Modern Healthcare*, May 7, 1990, 39.

21. Jerry Geisel, "Allied-Signal Reaps Savings," *Business Insurance*, March 19, 1990, 1, 38.

SUGGESTED READING

Marketing

Aaker, David A. *Advertising Management.* 3d ed. Englewood Cliffs, N.J.: Prentice-Hall, 1987.

Alsop, Ronald. *The Wall Street Journal on Marketing.* Homewood, Ill.: Dow Jones-Irwin, 1986.

Bonoma, Thomas V. *Segmenting the Industrial Market.* San Diego, Calif.: Lexington Books, 1983.

Cady, John F. *Strategic Marketing.* Boston: Little, Brown, 1986.

Coffman Larry L. *Public Sector Marketing.* New York: Wiley, 1986.

Corey, E. Raymond. *Industrial Marketing.* 3d ed. Englewood Cliffs, N.J.: Prentice-Hall,1983.

Cravens, David W. *Strategic Marketing Cases and Applications.* 2d ed. Homewood, Ill.: R.D. Irwin, 1986.

Cundiff, Edward W. *Fundamentals of Modern Marketing.* 4th ed. Englewood Cliffs, N.J.: Prentice-Hall, 1985.

Davis, Kenneth Rexton. *Marketing Management.* 5th ed. New York: Wiley, 1985.

Day, George S. *Analysis for Strategic Market Decisions.* St. Paul, Minn.: West Publishing, 1986.

Fogg, C. Davis. *Diagnostic Marketing.* Reading, Mass.: Addison-Wesley, 1985.

Ford, Neil M. *Sales Force Performance.* San Diego, Calif.: Lexington Books, 1985.

Frankel, Bud. *Your Advertising's Great—How's Business?* Homewood, Ill.: Dow Jones-Irwin, 1986.

Haas, Robert W. *Industrial Marketing Management.* 4th ed. Boston: PWS-Kent Publishing, 1989.

Handbook of Modern Marketing. 2d ed. New York: McGraw-Hill, 1986.

Hutt, Michael D. *Business Marketing Management.* 3d ed. Chicago, Ill.: Dryden Press, 1989.

Jain, Subhash C. *Marketing Planning and Strategy.* 3d ed. Cincinnati, Oh.: South-Western, 1990.

Johnson, Eugene M. *Profitable Service Marketing.* Homewood, Ill.: Dow Jones-Irwin, 1986.

Kinnear, Thomas C. *Principles of Marketing.* 2d ed. Glenview, Ill.: Scott, Foresman, 1986.

Kotler, Philip. *Principles of Marketing.* Englewood Cliffs, N.J.: Prentice-Hall, 1989.

———.*Marketing Management.* 6th ed. Englewood Cliffs, N.J.: Prentice-Hall, 1988.

———. *Marketing Professional Services.* Englewood Cliffs, N.J.: Prentice-Hall, 1984.

———. *Principles of Marketing.* 4th ed. Englewood Cliffs, N.J.: Prentice-Hall, 1989.

Lovelock, Christopher H. *Marketing for Public and Nonprofit Managers.* New York: Wiley, 1984.

———.*Public and Nonprofit Marketing.* 2d ed. Redwood City, Calif.: Scientific Press, 1989.

———. *Services Marketing.* Englewood Cliffs, N.J.: Prentice-Hall, 1984.

Marketing Handbook. Homewood, Ill.: Dow Jones-Irwin, 1985.

Nagle, Thomas T. *The Strategy and Tactics of Pricing.* Englewood Cliffs, N.J.: Prentice-Hall, 1987.

Nash, Edward L. *Direct Marketing.* 2d ed. New York: McGraw-Hill, 1986.

Ries, Al. *Marketing Warfare.* New York: McGraw-Hill, 1986.

Seglin, Jeffrey L. *America's New Breed of Enterpreneurs.* Reston, Va.: Acropolis Books, 1985.

Shapiro, Benson P. *Marketing Management.* Homewood, Ill.: R.D. Irwin, 1985.

Still, Richard Ralph. *Essentials of Marketing.* 3d ed. Englewood Cliffs, N.J.: Prentice-Hall, 1986.

Terpstra, Vern, *International Dimensions of Marketing.* 2d ed. Boston: PWS-Kent Publishing, 1988.

Weinstein, Art. *Market Segmentation.* Chicago: Probus Publishing, 1987.

Yoshino, Michael Y. *Marketing in Japan.* Wesport, Ct.: Praeger, 1975.

Market Research

Aaker, David A. *Marketing Research.* 4th ed. New York: Wiley, 1990.

Boyd, Harper W. *Marketing Research.* 7th ed. Homewood, Ill.: R.D. Irwin, 1989.

Chisnall, Peter M. *Marketing Research.* 3d ed. New York: McGraw-Hill, 1986.

Churchill, Gilbert A. *Marketing Research.* 5th ed. Chicago, Ill.: Dryden Press, 1991.

Crimp, Margaret. *The Marketing Research Process.* 2d ed. Englewood Cliffs, N.J.: Prentice-Hall, 1985.

DeBruicker, Stewart. *Cases in Consumer Behavior.* 2d ed. Englewood Cliffs, N.J.: Prentice-Hall, 1986.

Honomichl, Jack L. *Honomichl on Marketing Research.* Lincolnwood, Ill.: NTC Business Books, 1986.

Kinnear, Thomas C. *Marketing Research.* 3d ed. New York: McGraw-Hill, 1987.

Lee, Donald D. *Industrial Marketing Research.* 2d ed. New York: Van Nostrand Reinhold, 1984.

Luck, David Johnston. *Marketing Research.* 7th ed. Englewood Cliffs, N.J.: Prentice-Hall, 1987.

Marketing Information Systems: Selected Readings. American Marketing Association, 1976.

O'Shaughnessy, John. *Why People Buy.* Oxford, England: Oxford University Press, 1987.

Zikmund, William G. *Business Research Methods.* 3d ed. Chicago, Ill.: Dryden Press, 1991.

6

Management of Regulation

REGULATORY REQUIREMENTS

Governments regulate five aspects of health care organizations: Reimbursement, conflict of interest, facilities and operations, personnel, and technology. (See Table 6-1 for examples of government regulations.) Although some managers may bemoan the onus of regulation, it is a social necessity for services and products as complex, costly, and potentially harmful as those in health care. Astute managers instead use regulation to their advantage, viewing it as a competitive weapon that eliminates or discourages potential new entrants to their markets or that affirms their quality. For example, one home infusion company noted in an ad, "We are one of the first companies to voluntarily participate in a quality review process—a fact that few, if any, other infusion companies can match."*

Many regulatory decisions effectively create barriers to competition. A company that receives a patent for a new drug is granted a long-lived monopoly to the economic benefits

---

*With thanks to tpc Inc. of California for sending this advertisement.

that will accrue from the sales of the drug. And a firm that receives a government certificate attesting to the need for its proposed new health care facility will cause its competitors to think long and hard before applying for a certificate in the same geographical area. Some new companies seek out regulatory protection. For example, Nellcor, a company that produces noninvasive anesthesia devices, quietly lobbied for the creation of patient safety standards in anesthesia. Not surprisingly, Nellcor's products were key to meeting the standards once they were developed.

Is management of the regulatory process ethical or is it a sleazy activity, besmirching those who attempt to do it? In one sense, it is as ethical as stealing a base in a baseball game. After all, a good player scores the most runs within the rules of the game. But, in a larger sense, if the regulatory rules run counter to the long-run interests of our society, managers should search their consciences before using them for their own interests. For example, lobbying U.S. federal and state governments to impose "mandated" items that employers must include in their employees' health insurance coverage is intrinsically unethical. It is a hidden corporate tax that has substantially increased

Table 6-1 Examples of Federal and State Government Regulations

Purpose	Type of Regulation
Providing Protection	Quarantines for contagion Establishment of Public Health Service (1912) Licensing of physicians Pure Food and Drug Act (1906) Building codes and safety standards for hospitals Accreditation of medical education
Expanding Access Before 1940	Long-term care for mentally ill and tubercular patients Health care for armed services Health care for mothers and children
After 1940	Hill-Burton Act, which was intended to build hospitals and provide free care for the poor (1946) Regional medical programs designed to improve delivery and quality of medical care (1965) Family planning (1970) Health professions acts designed to expand manpower (1956–76) Medicare and Medicaid (1965), which were intended to give health benefits to the elderly and poor COBRA, which was intended to extend health insurance benefits to terminated or unqualified employees
Planning Advisory	Comprehensive Health Planning Law (1966) Partnership for Health (1967) Public Health Service Amendments (1970) National Health Planning Act (1974)
Regulatory	State certificate-of-need laws to restrict capital expansion; laws resulted from requirements in Social Security Amendments (1972) Economic Stabilization Program (1971–74), which set caps on rates for hospitals Prospective payment by Medicare (1983), which established diagnosis-related groups (DRGs) to contain costs State rate-setting programs designed to control hospital prices (1975–85)
Ensuring Quality	Professional Standards Review Organizations (1972) Food and Drug Act Amendments (1971, 1976) PROs (Professional Review Organizations) for Medicare (1983) Research, especially support of the National Institutes of Health

the cost of U.S. health insurance. If voters were asked if they wanted to pay taxes for the mandated items—one state requires that health insurance must pay the cost of wigs for bald men—they would likely say no. Yet legislators go along with mandating because it appears to provide extra benefits with no extra taxes.

I do not mean to suggest, however, that management of regulation is so intrinsically unethical that thoughtful managers should disdain it. To the contrary, it is an important function that enables valuable innovations to be implemented. New ventures that bungle the regulatory process may find it impossible to realize their dreams. Even as seasoned a company as 3M was forced to abandon an innovative product because of its inability to obtain the government reimbursement needed to sell the product.

In what follows I describe each of the five types of regulation and illustrate how a private organization can help create favorable regulatory outcomes. The discussion begins with the two types of regulations that affect all new health care ventures: Reimbursement and conflict of interest. It then proceeds to the regulatory activities with less widespread influence: The facility and personnel regulations that primarily affect cost-controlling and new consumer ventures and the technology regulations that play a crucial role for new technology enterprises.

This chapter discusses only those key regulations that affect U.S. health care organizations. The many other government regulations of private firms are discussed in the books and articles listed as suggested readings at the end of the chapter.

REIMBURSEMENT REGULATION

The U.S. federal government regulates the rates of payment for health services and products used by the elderly under the Medicare health insurance program. State governments perform the same function for the medically indigent insured by the Medicaid program.

The impact of these regulations differs by sector. Although Medicare payments accounted for 19 percent of all personal health care expenses in 1989, their influence was much more pronounced in the hospital sector, where they paid for 27 percent of the expenses. Similarly, although Medicaid accounts for only 11 percent of the total pie, it is responsible for 43 percent of nursing home payments.[1] And because nursing homes, physicians, and hospitals represent the bulk of Medicaid's and Medicare's expenses, the government devotes considerable effort to regulating the reimbursement of these providers.

Reimbursement Determinations

Private health insurance companies judge how to reimburse a new procedure by considering the following three questions:

1. Is the new procedure covered by existing health insurance policies?
2. Is is demonstrably safe and effective?
3. Would employers be prepared to pay for it if it were included in future health insurance policies?

These questions are answered through extensive consultation with employers and health care providers who are expert about the new procedure. Note that neither the cost of the procedure nor its cost-effectiveness are presently considered. Nevertheless, these issues are likely eventually to play a role in the reimbursement approval process. For example, a recent evaluation of three blood clot-dissolving drugs reviewed not only their medical efficacy but also their price. The *New York Times* headline for its report on this research was prophetic: "Cheapest Anti-Clot Drug Is Found To Be the Safest."[2]

Medicare pays hospitals a flat price rate per DRG (diagnosis-related group). The DRG is assigned to patients on the basis of their primary diagnosis, and is adjusted for sex, age, and complications. For example, in one Massachusetts hospital in 1990, DRG 399 paid $2,501.47 for patients with a coagulation disorder and no complications; patients with complications were in DRG 398, which were paid a flat rate of $4,447.66. Although basic DRG prices are uniform across the country, they are adjusted for hospitals in exceedingly large or small urban or rural areas and take into account teaching status and the severity of illness. In 1991, Medicare paid separately for hospitals' capital costs and medical education expenses. All the other hospital expenses incurred by Medicare patients must be paid for with the DRG prices.

DRG prices are determined by the Health Care Financing Administration (HCFA), which is within the Department of Health and Human Services. HCFA is advised by ProPAC, the Prospective Payment Assessment Commission, whose purpose is to ensure that the DRG payment rates do not prohibit useful technological innovations.

The DRG payment method is being extended to ambulatory care facilities (they are paid a flat rate per procedure) and to physicians (they will be paid on the basis of a fee schedule with the acronym RBRVS, short for resource-based relative-value scale). The method has also been applied to HMOs, which receive a flat rate per Medicare enrollee. In addition, HCFA is proposing a new prospective payment system for hospital capital.

Although some states experimented with regulating the prices paid by all insurers, these attempts are waning in influence. In 1991, only Maryland still used this "all-payer" system. *Medicaid* payment rates differ by state. They are generally low.

The impact of Medicare and private insurance reimbursement can be substantial. Because HCFA is reluctant to create new DRG categories, the developers of new technologies to be used in hospitals must try to ensure that they are assigned to the DRG category that provides the most favorable payment rate. Providers of products or services to physicians will find them more or less eager to buy once the new RBRVS goes into effect. In 1990, it was predicted to increase payments for family practice physicians by 37 percent but to reduce fees to radiologists and surgeons by 3–21 percent. Changes in their income will inevitably affect these physicians' interest in buying support services and products.

3M provides a vivid illustration of the impact of Medicare reimbursement. President Reagan congratulated the company when the U.S. Food and Drug Administration (FDA) approved its design for a cochlear implant (a device that enables some deaf people to hear). But when HCFA classified the implant in a DRG that covered only 70 percent of its costs, the rate of implantation was reduced so dramatically that 3M ultimately dropped the product. Conversely, when angioplasty treatment received a favorable DRG classification, its use boomed.[3]

Managing the Reimbursement Process

The pharmaceutical company Merck presents an excellent example of astute management of this process. When the state of California, which accounts for 10 percent of the U.S. prescription drug market, threatened to limit its Medicaid recipients to a small list of low-cost drugs, Merck responded aggressively. It offered to cut the prices it charged Medicaid to as low a level as the prices it offers its lowest-paying customers.

The move demonstrated smart politics and smart business. Politically, Merck presented itself as a responsible corporate citizen. It also forestalled attempts to remove Merck's expensive but powerful drugs from the Medicaid list. And Merck's offer put considerable economic pressure on its competitors, because they customarily grant their lowest-paying customers much larger discounts than does Merck. Matching Merck's offer will cost them much more than it does Merck, but if they do not match it, they may lose their Medicaid business.[4] Merck's response was institutionalized in 1990 congressional legislation that required drug manufacturers to give Medicaid a rebate on drug purchases.[5]

3M's handling of the cochlear implant regulation is instructive as well. 3M reportedly did not sufficiently involve the Office of Technology Assessment and the National Institutes of Health in the design of its new medical device. The scientists in these government organizations are extensively consulted by HCFA on reimbursement issues, especially if the technology being evaluated threatens to increase costs, as did the cochlear implant. Many of the government's scientists favored a different design from the one presented by 3M. The company paid the price of failing to heed their advice.[6]

Successful management of the reimbursement process requires a proactive strategy: Managers must seize the offensive, present their side of the story, and involve influential professional and interest groups.

CONFLICT-OF-INTEREST REGULATION

Conflicts of Interest

The Harvard Medical School was rocked by reports that one of its faculty members withheld adverse research results about a medical innovation produced by a company in which he held substantial financial interest. He was accused of waiting to release the results until after he had sold his stock—at a substantial profit. The charge? Conflict of interest. That charge was also levied against a University of Pennsylvania professor who, the university charged, colluded with a corporation to deprive the university of its rightful share in their patent for a wrinkle-removing drug, Retin-A.[7]

The bifurcation in a researcher's interests as a professional and a stockholder represents one type of potential conflict of interest. Conflicts of interest may be quite widespread. In 1991, many college and university academics are simultaneously owners, employees, consultants, and stockholders of companies. Scientists who were to evaluate the clinical efficacy of a new technology frequently owned sizable stock holdings in the company manufacturing it. One survey found that 25 percent of faculty members had worked as paid consultants to industry in the past 2 years. Some became vastly enriched by their dual roles. Professor Herbert Boyer, a founder of Genentech, held stock worth $80 million when the company went public.[8]

Conflict-of-interest concerns are not limited to academics, however. Critics also charge that physicians who invest in laboratories and other sources of care perform many more services than those who do not invest and that they may also receive kickbacks from hospitals and others for patient referrals. Indeed, the 1987 amendments to the Medicare and Medicaid fraud and abuse statutes (the so-called anti-kickback provisions) prohibit any form of remuneration that creates patient referrals. "Safe harbor" rules defining legitimate joint ventures between physicians and providers cover the following areas: investments, space rental, equipment rental, personal services and management contracts, sale of practice, referral services, warranties, discounts, employees, and group purchasing organizations.

The interpretation of Medicare fraud and abuse regulations was still murky in 1991. An administrative law judge clarified them somewhat in ruling that offers that explicitly pay physicians for referrals are illegal but that those "intended to influence provider choice, as opposed to [those] which foreclosed provider choice are not."[9] The case involved dividends paid to physicians who invested in clinical laboratories. The government argued that the dividends paid by the laboratories to their physician investors were unusually large in order to encourage the physicians to send their patients to the labs. The labs argued that they did not require referrals as a condition for the physicians' earning a return on capital they invested in the labs.[10]

U.S. Representative Ted Weiss is among the many legislators considering conflict-of-interest regulation. His bill would require scientists who conduct research with federal funds to verify the absence of a financial interest in the outcome. Representative "Pete" Stark filed similar legislation that would prohibit physicians from owning companies to which they refer their patients. His 1989 bill included penalties for self-referral that ranged from a $15,000 fine to expulsion from Medicare reimbursement.

But there is another side to the conflict-of-interest story. For one thing, the migration of science out of academia and into industry can work economic miracles. A Massachusetts Institute of Technology (MIT) study showed that the 636 Massachusetts businesses founded by MIT affiliates had 1988 sales of nearly $40 billion and employed 200,000 people. If the academics had been prohibited from having any financial interests in these companies, some part of this impressive record might not have been achieved.

Then, too, teaching and research activities benefit from the involvement of academics in real-world enterprises. As a Yale professor of finance noted, "It's difficult to teach finance unless you do some finance."[11] Finally, the physicians who own laboratories and other diagnostic facilities are likely to run them more efficiently than hospitals. Why? Because ownership increases efficiency, especially when it is clearly focused on one service, and because physicians generally own facilities whose services they are expert in delivering.

Conflict-of-interest legislation could prove harmful to companies in which researchers and physicians play major roles; for example, the firms in which academics are founders, key researchers, designers of clinical trials, and board members. It could also force many to choose between their affiliation with a company and their affiliation (or job) with a hospital or academic institution.

Managing Conflict-of-Interest Regulation

Because of the murkiness of the regulation, disclosure of a potential conflict of interest to investors and other interested parties is advisable. Disclosure achieves the best of both worlds: the benefit of continuing a valuable relationship and the forthright revelation of the conflict this relationship potentially raises. (Speaking of full disclosure, my favorable citation of the MIT study may be colored by my being an MIT graduate.) To minimize fraud, a company can also issue restricted stock, whose rights lapse with evidence of fraud and abuse on the part of the scientist or physician to whom it was issued. Fraud can be minimized with carefully designed clinical research experiments whose results cannot be easily manipulated. For example, a drug efficacy experiment in which a patient receives either a placebo or an active drug without the researcher's being aware of which one is being administered provides substantial fraud protection.

What about physicians who refer patients for excessive laboratory tests or other procedures in labs in which they own an interest? Here too the physicians should disclose their financial interest in the laboratory to their patients. But the real solution to excessive utilization lies with the patient, not the doctor. In normal circumstances, buyers do not overconsume merely because the seller tells them to do so. For example, most people do not use excessive amounts of legal services even if their lawyers advise it. Why the difference? Health care patients, unlike legal clients, do not pay directly for many services. A better solution to the problems of overuse of health care services may be to involve the patients more closely with payment for costs rather than barring physicians from providing them.

TECHNOLOGY REGULATION

In the United States, the medical technology embodied in new drugs or devices is regulated in at least three ways:

1. The U.S. Patent Office grants inventors exclusive rights to the economic benefits resulting from their inventions for a limited period of time. Patents can be enormously valuable for new technology ventures.
2. An FDA license is needed to market drugs and medical devices. Related manufacturing practices and promotional materials also require FDA approval.
3. The U.S. Congress regulates technology in various ways. For example, the Orphan Drug Act grants a company a 7-year monopoly in the case of a drug that has only a limited market.

These regulators, their impact on new technology companies, and management of the regulatory process are separately discussed below.*

Patents

American patent laws were developed in the late 1700s to encourage innovation by protecting the commercial rights of inventors. Patents are granted by the Patent and Trademark Office of the Department of Commerce. A patent allows the persons who receive it to exclude others from making, using, or selling their invention for 17 years. The patent can be assigned or inherited. The discovery of any "new and useful process, machine, manufacture, composition of matter, or new and useful improvements" may be patented, which effectively includes "everything made by man and the processes for making them." "Useful" is defined as able to operate for the intended

---

* Dr. Brandon Fradd, in "Note on the Pharmaceutical Industry" (9-189-076), and Sherrie Epstein, in "Note on Medical Technology" (9-187-110), provided some of the description of the technology regulation process. Both notes were written under the supervision of Regina E. Herzlinger and are available from the Harvard Business School.

purpose. Methods of doing business and printed matter have been excluded by the courts from patenting. The idea alone for something new is not patentable; a complete description must be included.[12]

Inventions must be novel in order to be patentable. Neither the inventors nor anyone else can apply for a patent more than 1 year after the invention has been described in print, used publicly, or placed on sale. Small differences in an invention that would be obvious to anyone knowledgeable about the product or process cannot be patented. The written description of the invention must be complete enough that anyone "skilled in the art" can make and use it. The inventors must present clearly their "claims" about unique aspects of the invention. The claims will be referred to if questions of infringement arise. Patent experts in a given field will know about claims that have not been upheld.

Patent attorneys or agents search the Patent Office Library in Arlington, Virginia, to be sure that no prior patent exists before an application is made. The large number of Patent Office examiners will conduct a more complete search, and only they may review pending patents. As a result, applications are frequently refused despite the initial search by attorneys.

Some 100,000 patent applications are processed each year, with the decision process averaging 2 years. If a decision by the examiners is negative, it can be appealed first to the Patent Office Board of Appeals. There may be several exchanges of arguments as the inventors try to convince the examiner of the patent application's worth. Appeals against negative decisions are usual and can be taken to the Court of Customs and Patent Appeals or to the Federal District Court for the District of Columbia.

Once a patent is granted, a variable initial fee is charged for issuing it. A fee must be paid in each of the 17 years if the patent is to remain in force.

A critical patent issue is effective life. A product may be marked "patent pending" as soon as a patent is filed. Several years may pass before the Patent Office is able to examine the patent and decide on approval. Once approved, the patent's life begins. However, with pharmaceuticals, the product must be tested extensively before it can be marketed. Thus, the patent's effective life is much shorter than the patent's actual life. As regulation has forced longer periods of research and development, the effective lives of patents have begun to shorten. In 1984, the Waxman-Hatch Act allowed companies to extend the lives of their patents for up to 5 years under certain circumstances.

The average number of drug patents is 2,233 a year. In 1989, 935 patents were issued for health care biotechnology.[13] These patents differ in some ways from other drug patents. For one thing, the Patent Office is reportedly understaffed in biotechnology. As of August 1987, there was a backlog of 7,800 patent applications, and the average time between first reading and final decision was 25.3 months. Biotechnology patents are much more complicated than typical pharmaceutical patents. The molecules are much bigger and not as well understood; the procedure for synthesizing them is much more complicated and may even require depositing a sample of an altered life form in lieu of a written description; and questions of equivalence among competing versions of the same molecule are more ambiguous. These complications require the claims of a biotechnology patent to be carefully stated, and there is a greater likelihood of suits disputing those claims. Suits are particularly likely for important well-known biotechnology molecules targeted by many companies, each wanting the most exclusive patent possible.

Many court cases are still pending, and only a few clear settlements can serve as guidelines for the future. One guide is the Supreme Court's ruling that life forms are patentable. Another is that a natural substance can be patented if human intervention alters the form of the substance as it occurs in nature (for example, by purifying it). Most cases, however, are settled on a case-by-case basis and without clear indications for future judgments.

The legal battle over patent rights for erythropoietin (EPO), an antianemia drug produced commercially through biotechnology, illustrates the problems. Initially, the Boston Federal District Court ruled that the Massachusetts company Genetics Institute's patent covered EPO. Its patent was on the EPO molecule that the company had purified from human urine. The court ordered Amgen, a California company which isolated the human gene for EPO and developed the genetically engineered process for producing it, to enter into a cross-licensing agreement with its rival.[14]

These findings were reversed in a federal appeals court decision that ruled Amgen's patents as valid and dismissed Genetics Institute's claims that it was the first to conceive the nature of the gene that creates EPO. Genetics Institute stock lost nearly a third of its value when the decision was announced. Despite the reversal in rulings, the new decision still leaves a key issue unresolved: While traditional patents cover novel compounds no matter how they are produced, for biotechnology products the key novelty may lie in the production process rather than the compound.[15] How much importance a new process will have in securing a patent for a biotechnology drug was not clear in 1991.

Even when granted, patent protection may be limited. Patents are frequently characterized as invitations to a lawsuit. If they are not carefully worded, their protection is nil. The inventor of magnetic resonance imaging (MRI), for example, earns no royalties from the many companies manufacturing MRI equipment, despite the patent he holds. After spending $2.2 million in failed patent lawsuits, he has given up. "Patents don't work," he said. What's the problem? Faulty language in his original patent. The patent claimed that MRI would detect cancers by comparing signals from malignant and healthy tissue, but clever MRI equipment companies circumvented his patent by searching the images produced by the technique rather than comparing signals. This legalism enabled them to waltz into the lucrative market without paying the inventor any royalties.[16]

When a patent is upheld, it is, nevertheless, a powerful barrier to competition. When American Home Products won a preliminary patent decision against Johnson & Johnson regarding a new birth control pill, it almost eliminated a rival that hoped to take a $200 million bite out of the market.[17] Similarly, Wellcome gave up its $80 million investment in tissue plasminogen activator (TPA) after a court ruling that, along with Genetics Institute, it had infringed on Genentech's patents.[18]

Managing the Patent Process

Patents require the involvement of superlative lawyers who are masters of both patent law and the technology involved. But excellent "lawyering" probably will not avoid biotechnology patent disputes. Because of the present novelty of the science, increased experience will be necessary before biotechnology patents become more tightly written. Substantial legal expenses will be part and parcel of the commercialization of biotechnology.

The patent issue should neither begin nor end with lawyers. Managers can resolve patent disputes by cross-licensing their technology. Genentech, for example, resolved a patent dispute with another company over the drug Interferon by cross-licensing the technology. And when Xoma sued its rival, Centocor, for patent infringement regarding a valuable septic shock drug, an observer noted that the lawsuit would be settled because the CEOs of both companies "are deal makers, not terminal litigators."[19]

FDA Regulation of Drugs

In 1938, the Food, Drug and Cosmetics Act gave the FDA authority to regulate drug safety. The FDA divided drugs into prescription drugs and over-the-counter drugs. The FDA approves both kinds of drugs and their labels. Doctors are required to instruct patients in the use of prescribed drugs; those sold over-the-counter must have printed instructions on the label. Further amendments required manufacturers to prove the "efficacy" as well as safety of their products. The amendments were passed in the wake of the publicity about thalidomide, a sleeping pill, which was responsible for severe birth deformities among the children of women who had taken the drug while pregnant. The damage caused by thalidomide convinced Congress that further regulation was important.

The FDA monitors biologic and synthetic drugs. Biologics are substances found in the human body and synthetics are anything else. The two FDA monitoring groups operate independently and may have separate policies for approval of drugs that could have very similar effects. For example, TPA is processed as a biologic and streptokinase as a synthetic, even though both clot-dissolving drugs have similar mechanisms of action and similar effects.

FDA testing requirements proceed along well-defined stages. Once a new chemical entity (NCE) has been discovered, it must be tested in animals to determine its desirable and undesirable effects. When an NCE has been deemed promising, the company files for an investigational new drug (IND) exemption from the FDA to test in human beings. The testing proceeds in three phases: (1) Healthy volunteers are used to examine safety and dosage; (2) a small group of people who need the intended treatment are tested to determine the drug's therapeutic value; and (3) diseased and normal people are tested to establish that the therapeutic effects seen in phase 2 are indeed associated with the drug. Testing can stop at any point for reasons of safety or efficacy.

Once the company has completed satisfactory testing, it files for a new drug application (NDA). If the FDA feels that the drug is safe and effective, it approves marketing. Otherwise, the application is turned down. At this point, the company may decide to continue testing the compound or abandon it. The FDA usually rejects compounds either because of safety concerns or because the clinical trials were deemed inadequate for confirming that the desired effects were associated with the compound.

The FDA process from discovery to approval requires an average of 8.2 years—32.3 months for NCEs, 2.6 years for NDAs, and 5.6 years for the IND process. Only 7 percent of the INDs filed from 1977 to 1987 resulted in approvals.[20] In 1990, the FDA approved 23 new drugs, with 27.7 months average time for approval, the shortest time in the past decade.[21]

The FDA introduced two significant approval modifications in the 1970s. First, the abbreviated NDA (ANDA) for generics required a company to demonstrate only that the generic drug has the same chemical properties inside the body as the original drug and that the company adhered to good manufacturing practices. The generic company could cite published data in lieu of clinical testing to support claims of safety and effectiveness. Second, treatment INDs are applied to drugs that are not yet FDA-approved but that represent treatments for diseases listed as serious or life-threatening by the FDA. It allows the company to distribute its product after only limited demonstration of safety and efficacy rather than after full clinical trials. The company may recover its costs but may not make a profit. The most likely beneficiaries of treatment INDs will be start-up companies with limited funds, and its greatest effect will be for diseases such as acquired immune deficiency syndrome (AIDS).

Approval for new drugs is much quicker in most foreign countries, reflecting less stringent regulation and more cooperative regulatory boards. Various proposals have been made to alter the nature of the FDA, and the suggestion has even been made to abolish it, with companies assuming legal liability for toxic drugs.

The FDA in 1966 implemented more rigid requirements for the advertising of drugs. Advertisements were required to indicate side effects, necessary precautions, and effectiveness. Promotional terms had to be cleared with the FDA.

Because over-the-counter drugs present less serious problems than prescription drugs, the FDA's supervision of them was scanty until the 1960s. In 1966 the agency rated the efficacy of 400 over-the-counter products and found only one-fourth of them to be effective. Since at the time there were some 100,000 over-the-counter products, it was thought that FDA regulation was unlikely to threaten production, but the

FDA examined products by class rather than individually.

FDA Regulation of Medical Devices

Regulation of the testing and marketing of medical devices by the FDA was greatly expanded under the 1976 Medical Device Amendments to the Food and Drug Act in the wake of concerns about increasingly complicated medical devices. Some devices had caused injuries and death, especially pacemakers, intrauterine devices, and heart valves. Government supervision of the many medical products developed for direct use by consumers in the home also was seen as necessary. The FDA allows exemptions from many of the requirements of the 1976 amendments for firms that make devices that present no significant risk (Class I devices). Class II devices in theory can be shown to be safe and effective through performance standards; but in practice many of their performance standards have yet to be completed. With so many devices to attend to, attention has focused on Class III devices, those that present significant risk.

The Class III applicants frequently choose to use the so-called 510K process in which the FDA determines whether the device is substantially equivalent to a device that existed before enactment of the 1976 law. If it is judged not to be substantially equivalent, the Class III new device's manufacturer must receive FDA's premarket approval (PMA) before selling it. Until it is obtained, the FDA may grant an investigational device exemption (IDE) that permits manufacture of the new device solely for purposes of conducting the clinical studies of its safety and efficacy that may be needed for the PMA.[22]

The approval process is hardly *pro forma*. For example, two companies' applications to market gallstone lithotripsy devices were rejected by the FDA for the following reasons: The difficulty of treatment, the questionableness of any advance over gallstone surgery, unanswered questions about the needs for retreatment, and the use of a drug in the clinical trials that had not been approved for use in the United States. One applicant was also faulted for lack of clarity in presentation.[23]

Only a small number of products have gone through a full approval process, because those that are only modifications of existing products can go through the quicker 510K review. In 1987, there were 224 IDE and 46 PMA filings and approvals as compared with 4,992 510Ks. IDEs required 69 days and PMAs 337 days of processing in 1987. Since 1980, a quarter of the IDEs filed have received PMA approval.[24]

Device manufacturers and initial distributors are also required to file a medical device reports (MDR) with the FDA when they become aware that a device may have contributed to a death or serious injury. A 1990 law expanded this requirement to health care providers. It also directs the FDA to develop procedures for tracking medical devices so that unsafe ones can be quickly recalled. It empowered the FDA with new mandatory recall rights.[25] The FDA sends out "safety alert" letters to medical personnel when serious hazards in medical devices are discovered. Recent examples include warnings about faulty anesthesia breathing tube connectors and defibrillator batteries.

FDA Regulation of Manufacturing

The FDA also regulates the manufacture of drugs and devices to ensure their quality. Manufacturers must prepare a detailed description of their production and distribution procedure and are spot audited to verify their adherence to these procedures.. Producers that fail the audit may appeal the FDA's filings. The FDA can close factories and seize the inventories of manufacturers that failed to adhere to the so-called good manufacturing practice specifications.

Managing the FDA Regulatory Process

FDA regulation of drugs and devices is very much influenced by the quality of the associated science, as it should be. To assure that the appearance matches the reality, many ventures try to affiliate themselves with respected scientists, physicians, and teaching hospitals. Such affiliations inevitably enhance an organization's credibility. Distinguished scientists and physicians may participate on the company's scientific advisory committee, conduct research on the company's new products, and design the clinical trials the FDA uses to test the safety and efficacy of the technology.

The advice of former technology regulators is also invaluable, whether they served in the FDA, the Patent Office, or the National Institutes of Health. Political involvement may be helpful. The support of an important member of Congress may speed the technology-regulating process. Although government regulators are professionals, a political appeal usually helps to underscore the importance of the technology. For example, when the two California senators asked for a special FDA review of a new drug that was potentially competitive with one produced by a California biotechnology company, in an apparent attempt to slow down its approval, the FDA quickly complied.[26] The FDA is also sensitive to the constraints of small businesses.

A strong, well-funded FDA may well be in the best interest of technology ventures. Why? Because a strong FDA can allay fears about venal, corrupt manufacturers by detecting and eliminating the few who fail to follow the FDA's testing, reporting, and manufacturing guidelines. In 1991, the FDA was generally regarded as underfunded. The absence of sufficient personnel may have contributed to the scandalous behavior of Bolar and Vitarine, generic drug companies that falsified their ANDA, by substituting ethical drugs for their own generic equivalents, and other documents. A number of FDA officials were accused of taking bribes to speed some companies through the ANDA process. The FDA commissioner was relieved of his position as a result of these events.[27]

Underfunding of the FDA has caused Congress to threaten even greater regulation of drugs and devices. For example, after a child

died because of the failure of a device that monitors infants at risk for sudden infant death syndrome, a U.S. representative and a U.S. senator immediately held a press conference featuring the child's distraught parents. The politicians promised even greater FDA power.[28] However, the tragedy might have been averted if the FDA had merely implemented its present authority.

Orphan Drug Regulation

In 1983 Congress passed the Orphan Drug Act to encourage development of drugs with limited markets. The act grants a 7-year monopoly for drugs that would be of use to fewer than 200,000 people in the United States. It has stimulated the development of drugs such as human growth hormone, which is used to treat children with a rare pituitary deficiency, and EPO, an antianemia drug. It has had unforeseen negative consequences, however. Though meant to recover only research and development costs and provide a reasonable profit, sales of growth hormone and EPO place them among the top 36 drugs in the whole industry, with annual revenues in excess of $100 million. A proposed 1990 amendment would permit exclusivity only if the market remained below 200,000.[29]

Managing Orphan Drug Regulation

In a sense, orphan drug regulation is merely an extension of patent legislation. Trade associations are key for protecting this legislation. For example, the companies Genetech and Amgen, both beneficiaries of the legislation, have convinced the biotechnology trade association to support the Orphan Drug Act and other extensions of patent protection. Although some other biotechnology companies quit the association in a huff, claiming that it was being manipulated,[30] the companies that leave trade associations lose the political clout and leverage that such associations can provide.

Trade associations representing medical technology ventures can potentially fulfill important missions. For example, they could lobby Congress to form a no-fault insurance fund to compensate victims of rare, severe complications resulting from medical technologies. Alleged victims of adverse effects would bring their complaints to a federal committee that would decide appropriate compensation. The proposal has not been funded yet, and in 1987 the Wyeth Company was successfully sued for $15 million in damages related to severe adverse effects from diphtheria vaccine. Companies that belong to and lead trade associations enormously amplify their own power to help push through legislation that serves both their interests and the interests of society.

SERVICE PERSONNEL REGULATION

Regulation of health service personnel is achieved through the licensing activities of many health care professional organizations. Physicians who specialize in different fields of medicine are certified by various professional societies. Their licenses are frequently supported by additional state examinations and requirements for continuing professional education. Nurses, technicians, dentists, pharmacists, and other health service personnel also fall under the jurisdiction of different licensing authorities and face similar examination and continuing education rules.

Health care scientists and engineers are generally not subject to licensing requirements. Indeed, some of the most creative did not graduate from high school or college. But they are the exceptions. Most health service personnel are subject to rigorous licensing requirements, that must be continually updated.

Companies that depend on changing the role played by the health professional in order to achieve cost control should lobby their state legislatures to ensure that their point of view is understood. Otherwise, they may find that state licensing boards have acted to prohibit the very

changes they seek. For example, office-based dentists may convince the dental licensing board to prohibit the practice of dentistry in a mobile van that comes to the patient's worksite. Although arguments based on considerations of quality are often used to justify such licensing restrictions, frequently the restrictions are primarily motivated by the desire of one group to protect itself from competition by others or from change.

OPERATIONS AND FACILITY REGULATION

The certificate of need process determines the amount and type of capital that a health service organization can deploy. This process enables a state government to determine whether a facility's plans for expansion of its building or equipment meet the needs of the community. In practice, few certificate of need applications are denied, but the organization may not operate without it, and some insurers, most notably Medicare, will not reimburse for provided services if a certificate is lacking. (See Appendix B for additional discussion of this subject.)

Obtaining a certificate of need requires the development of a plan to justify the construction. As explained in the Case Study 12, approval is usually based on an analysis of the following community factors:

- the composition of the population and its need for the service being offered
- the present availability of facilities to meet this need
- the economic base of the potential market and its ability to sustain the proposed facility
- the availability of staff to attract patients and provide services in the facility
- the accessibility of the proposed site to potential clients and staff

The plan is presented to the regulators of the certificate of need process, usually a board comprising citizens, health care professionals, and state regulatory officials. The companies that succeed in winning approval are careful about the applications they file. They do not file those likely to be rejected because they are so transparently unnecessary, nor those likely to lead to a major battle with a community or with a strongly entrenched alternative provider.

Another type of regulation is provided by the Joint Commission on Accreditation of Healthcare Organizations (Joint Commission), which monitors quality of health care services. The seal of approval of this nonprofit, independent organization is widely valued in the industry. It has been extended to 5,400 hospitals and 3,200 other health care organizations.

The Joint Commission's method of monitoring quality is to send a team of inspectors into a health facility to evaluate many aspects of its functioning. The review subjects range from evaluation of the organization's monitoring of its medical staff to the administrative procedures used in the lab. The Joint Commission is itself under continual review, as providers and users voice their displeasure with the process. For example, a meeting between hospital representatives and the director of the Joint Commission resulted in his promising to control the costs and increase the turnaround time of the process.[31]

The Joint Commission recently made public its accreditation decisions and the major deficiencies it observed after public complaints of its undue secretiveness. The revelations were startling. For example, less than half the hospitals surveyed complied with the requirements for surgical case reviews. These revelations and other indications of quality lapses will likely bring about a sixth regulatory requirement about quality in health service organizations in the near future.[32]

NOTES

1. Health Care Financing Administration, *HHS News*, December 30, 1990, Table 3.

2. Lawrence K. Altman, "Cheapest Anti-Clot Drug Is Found To Be the Safest," *New York Times*, March 4, 1991, B9.

3. Nancy M. Kane and Paul D. Manoukian, "The Effect of

the Medicare Prospective Payment System on the Adoption of New Technology," *New England Journal of Medicine* 321 (1989): 1378–83.

4. Ron Winslow, "Merck Plans Medicaid Price Cut," *Wall Street Journal*, April 23, 1990, B1.

5. Standard and Poor's, *Health Care,* November 9, 1990, 2.

6. Kane and Manoukian, "The Effect of the Medicare Prospective Payment System."

7. "Penn Charges Retin-A Inventor with Conflict," *Science*, March 22, 1990, 1028.

8. "Million Dollar Professors," *Business Week*, August 21, 1989, 91.

9. Merit C. Kimball, "IG's Doc-Investor Stance Hammered by HHS Judge," *HealthWeek*, March 11, 1991, 1.

10. David Burda and Sandy Lutz, "M.D. Referrals Clarified," *Modern Healthcare*, March 11, 1991, 2.

11. "Million Dollar Professors," 91.

12. U.S. Department of Commerce, *General Information Concerning Patents* (Washington, D.C.: Patent and Trademark Office, February 1982).

13. "Biotech/Drug Development," *BBI Newsletter*, June 14, 1990, 109.

14. Edmund L. Andrews, "Amgen Wins Fight over Drug," *New York Times*, March 7, 1991, D1.

15. Edmund L. Andrews, "Patents," *New York Times*, March 9, 1991, Business section, 2.

16. Edmund L. Andrews, "Hall of Fame for Inventor of Imaging," *New York Times*, December 4, 1989, 34.

17. "A Bitter Pill for J & J," *Business Week*, March 12, 1990, 43.

18. Joann S. Lublin, "Wellcome Halts Six-Year Effort on Heart Drug," *Wall Street Journal*, May 11, 1990, B1.

19. Richard Koening, "Xoma Sues Archrival Centocor: Patent Violation on Drug Alleged," *Wall Street Journal*, April 18, 1990, B9.

20. J. Leighton Read and Paul M. Campbell, "Health Care Innovation," *Health Affairs*, Summer 1988, 183.

21. "Drug Industry Sees 12% Revenue Hike in '91," *Modern Healthcare*, February 4, 1991, 19.

22. U.S. Department of Health and Human Services, *Regulatory Requirements for Medical Devices* (Washington, D.C.: U.S. Government Printing Office, May 1989).

23. "Gallstone Lithotripy Suffers FDA Setback," *HealthWeek*, December 14, 1989, 25.

24. Read and Campbell, "Health Care Innovation," 183.

25. Jonathan S. Kahan, Howard Holstein, and Rodney Munsey, "The Implications of the Safe Medical Devices Act of 1990," *Medical Device and Diagnostic Industry*, February 1991, 44.

26. "Genentech: A David That Comes on Like Goliath," *Business Week*, October 30, 1989, 165.

27. "Has the Generic Drug Ban Really Gone Bust?" *In Vivo*, February 1990, 9, 10.

28. Henry A. Waxman, *Congressman Henry A. Waxman News*, November 3, 1989.

29. Standard and Poor's, *Health Care*, November 9, 1990, 4.

30. Andrew Pollack, "Group Split over Law on Drugs," *New York Times*, March 28, 1990, D3.

31. Dean Mayer, "Hospitals Air Complaints with JCAHO President," *HealthWeek*, January 22, 1990, l.

32. "Hospital Accreditation Statistics," *Medical Benefits*, December 15, 1990, 6.

SUGGESTED READING

Breyer, Stephen G. *Regulation and Its Reform*. Cambridge, Mass.: Harvard University Press, 1982.

Buchanan, James M. *The Demand and Supply of Public Goods*. Chicago: Rand McNally, 1968.

Demsetz, Harold. "Why Regulate Utilities?" *Bell Journal of Economics and Management Science* 8 (1977): xi–22.

Derthick, Martha, and Paul J. Quirk. *The Politics of Deregulation*. Washington, D.C.: Brookings Institution, 1985.

Fainsod, Merle. "Some Reflections on the Nature of the Regulatory Process." In *Public Policy*, edited by C.J. Friedrich and E. Mason, 297–323. Cambridge, Mass.: Harvard University Press, 1940.

Horowitz, Robert. *The Irony of Regulatory Reform*. Oxford, England: Oxford University Press, 1989.

Kahn, Alfred E. *Economics of Regulation*. 2d ed. Cambridge, Mass.: MIT Press, 1988.

Kolko, Gabriel. *The Triumph of Conservatism*. New York: The Free Press, 1963.

McConnell, Grant. *Private Power and American Democracy*. New York: Knopf, 1966.

McCraw, Thomas. *Prophets of Regulation*. Cambridge, Mass.: Harvard University Press, 1984.

Peltzman, Sam. "Toward a More General Theory of Regulation," *Journal of Law and Economics* 19 (1976): 211-40.

Scherer, Frederick. *Industrial Market Structure and Economic Performance*. 3d ed. New York: Houghton Mifflin, 1990.

Stigler, George. "The Theory of Economic Regulation," *Bell Journal of Economics* 2 (1971): 3–21.

Tirole, Jean. *The Theory of Industrial Organization*. Cambridge, Mass.: MIT Press, 1988.

Vietor, Richard H.K. *Strategic Management in the Regulatory Environment*. Englewood Cliffs, N.J.: Prentice-Hall, 1989.

U.S. Department of Health of Human Services, "Medicare and State Health Care Programs: O/G Anti-Kickback Provisions," 42 CFR, part 1001, 1990.

7

Finance

Financing new health care ventures involves three different activities: finding sources of capital, delineating appropriate uses of the capital, and crafting an appropriate match between sources and uses of the capital.

FINDING SOURCES OF CAPITAL

Money can be raised in three ways: It can be earned through profitable operations, borrowed, or raised by selling ownership rights in the company. Nonprofit organizations, legally barred from having owners, cannot raise money by selling ownership rights but can raise money through donations, gifts, and grants.

Equity

Equity sources of capital require the founders to transfer some of their ownership rights to venture capitalists or other investors. These investors purchase some of the company's shares of stock, or equity, in exchange for providing it with money. Venture capitalists typically provide some of the initial financing for a new venture and receive a sizable percentage of the

ownership of the company in return—from 10 percent to as much as 80 percent. Their capital is considered to carry a high cost because they receive a large chunk of the ownership in exchange for providing relatively small sums of money. But venture capital is invested in companies with little or no track record. The investment is therefore very risky. The high cost of the capital may be justified by the venture capitalists' assumption of high risks.

Investment bankers typically sell part of the ownership of a company that has a fairly well-established track record—usually a company that has been in existence for 3 or more years—to the public, other financial institutions, or wealthy private individuals. Investment bankers' fees are usually a function of the size of the sale. The fees range from 3 percent to 8 percent or more of the total value of the stock offering. For example, if the company sells $200 million worth of equity in the stock markets, investment bankers might earn a fee of 4 percent of $200 million, or $8 million.

Other companies or individuals may also invest directly in a new venture, usually because it is synergistic with their interests or competencies. A large pharmaceutical company may invest in a new biotechnology venture whose products are consistent with its own. For example, Bristol-Myers was an early stage investor in Oncogene because of their shared focus on cancer drugs. Other reasons for investment include related diversifications: for example, a hospital's or large insurance company's investment in a new HMO or utilization review company. Individual investors have similar motives. Thus, a real estate developer might invest in a nursing home company because his or her construction experience can help the new venture to succeed.

The three sources of equity capital dilute the ownership rights of the firm's initial founders and key staff members, but they also provide a source of liquidity, or cash. Frequently, founders sell some of their stock once the company is publicly traded, thus converting their "sweat equity" into cash. ("Sweat equity" refers to the investment made by founders in the form of hard work, low income, and "sweat.")

Debts

Lenders are the second source of capital. They provide financing in exchange for an IOU that commits the firm to repay the money along with interest on the outstanding loan and whatever other fees are associated with it.

Loans can be obtained on a short- or long-term basis. Some loans must be repaid within 30 days, whereas others can be repaid within 15–30 years, like those secured by the real estate and other tangible assets of the company. The *term* of the loan—that is, the length of time before repayment—is usually related to the purpose of the financing. For example, loans incurred to build a new building clearly require a much longer term than loans incurred to finance the company's inventories.

The *covenants* on most debt agreements require the company to maintain acceptable legal and financial performance standards, such as a maximum debt to equity ratio. If these covenants are violated, the debt may go into default, thus enabling lenders to file for the legal bankruptcy protection that would help secure repayment of the loans.

The sources of debt capital range from commercial banks, which provide a full array of loans, to investment banks, which sell long-term debt on the public markets or place it with other financial institutions. The company's suppliers also provide a form of debt capital. When a supplier ships drugs to a pharmacy without requiring payment until 30 days have elapsed, it is effectively granting the company a 30-day loan with which to buy the drugs. Frequently, manufacturers of capital equipment also provide attractive financing arrangements. For example, General Electric, which sells expensive medical diagnostic equipment, can provide its own financing for buyers.

A REIT loan is a loan obtained from a *r*eal *e*state *i*nvestment *t*rust. It generally carries a higher interest rate than a bank loan and can only be used to purchase real estate. REIT loans are granted for riskier ventures than the norm.

Ventures whose assets are heavily invested in real estate sometimes form their own REITs. For example, the nursing home company Mediplex formed the REIT Meditrust. The company sells its assets or borrows against them through the REIT. It thus converts its real estate assets into cash at fair market values. Because the company's top managers usually act as the advisors to the REIT and one or more of them may be included among the directors, the company can maintain some control over its real estate. For example, when Mediplex was sold to Avon, the leases and the mortgages on its nursing homes were held by Meditrust. The founder of Mediplex was the advisor to and a director of the REIT. When Avon subsequently tried to sell Mediplex to another company, the REIT sued, claiming that the proposed sale placed its assets in jeopardy. Avon ultimately sold Mediplex back to its original founder.

The costs of debt capital are usually lower than the costs of equity capital. They consist primarily of interest expenses, which range from 6 percent to 15 percent of the outstanding amount of the loan. Because interest expenses can be deducted from revenues in computing income taxes, their after-tax cost is even lower. For example, a corporation in a 30 percent tax bracket has an after-tax cost for a 10 percent interest expense of only 7 percent [.10 − (.30)(.10) = .07].

Nonprofit organizations that qualify for municipal bond financing also have access to low-interest expense financing. The buyers of municipal bonds do not have to pay federal income taxes on the bond interest they earn. Because of this tax provision, they are willing to buy a bond that pays a lower interest rate than a taxable bond. Typically, tax-exempt debt carries interest rates 25–30 percent lower than the interest rates of taxable debt.

Although nonprofit organizations that issue tax-exempt debt pay lower interest rates and can receive donations that are tax deductible to the donors, nonprofit status has a major financial disadvantage: These organizations cannot access the equity markets because they do not have owners.

Profits

Profitable operations generally are not a source of capital for new ventures. Health service ventures rarely break even until 3 or more years have passed. Technology-based companies can generate more immediate revenues by selling their technology in exchange for royalties and fees, but this source of capital is an expensive one. They may be selling the very seed corn from which they had hoped to grow. Contracting to perform research for large pharmaceutical companies is yet another source of cash. But research contracts may distract the company's scientists from the research efforts that are key to the company's success.

As an example consider the Immunex Corporation, which had 1989 revenues of $28 million and a loss of $4.5 million. It revised its strategy in 1988 after realizing that it could not achieve its goal of selling its own products before 1995 because its "efforts had been devoted to licensees' products." Its new strategy was to acquire products—a goal the company found "best met" by reacquiring rights to its own products from its licensees.[1]

Perspectives of Suppliers of Capital

The perspective of those lending money differs from the perspective of investors. Lenders are primarily concerned with the venture's ability to repay the loan and the associated interest as measured by the critical "coverage" ratio—the relationship between the cash flow from operations and the interest expenses. A low ratio significantly increases the interest charged. A moderate chance that the loan will not be repaid usually eliminates loan prospects.

Lenders' earnings accrue as a percentage of the loan. They thus favor large capital-intensive ventures that require substantial capital and relatively mature ventures that have reasonable assurances of generating the cash flow needed to pay interest. Lenders provide most of the capital for horizontally integrated health care ventures. These organizations can attract low-cost debt capital because they are amalgams of presently existing businesses whose past credit history provides lenders with some comfort about their ability to repay the loan. Because horizontally integrated ventures are very capital-intensive, they use sizable amounts of loan capital. For example, the Hospital Corporation of America's (HCA's) loans amounted to a staggering 69 percent of its total capital in 1980.

The financing of new, innovative companies generally originates from their founders' "sweat equity" and from venture capital. As a new venture prospers, the amount of financing it can secure increases and the cost of its money decreases, because venture investors are more confident of the success of the investment. The stages of investment range from seed financing ($25,000 to $300,000), to start-up financing, to first- and second-stage financing ($3 million to $50 million) for a currently operating business. Sometimes bridge financing is used to carry a venture from one financial stage to another. Initial venture capital investment levels range from $500,000 to $5 million in exchange for as much as 40 percent or more of the firm's ownership. Subsequent rounds of venture financing can raise invested capital to $50 million, with the founders' ownership share slipping by 20–50 percent.

Venture capital–backed companies include those providing innovative health services; breaking into the new consumer markets; and developing original pharmaceuticals, computer-based devices, and materials. Venture capitalists generally prefer technology ventures to health service ones, because they perceive technology ventures as more proprietary, especially if they have patents, and less dependent on management skills for success.

Risks Associated with Capital Sources

The risks of the different sources of capital vary. Because equity capital sources place a large emphasis on growth, equity-financed firms must maintain sizable increases in earnings. If they fail to do so, they will not be able to secure new equity capital and may even lose their autonomy. The pharmaceutical companies that lost their independence through mergers with other companies, like SmithKline Beecham, or were acquired, like Sterling Drug, are examples of firms unable to generate sufficient earnings growth to maintain their access to the stock markets at acceptable prices. On the other hand, companies with large debt loads face the threat of bankruptcy if they cannot generate enough cash to cover their sizable interest payments. Maxicare, at one time the nation's largest public HMO, went bankrupt in part because it was 55 percent debt financed and was unable to meet its heavy load of interest payments.

Of the three sources of money, debt capital is usually the cheapest but may also be the riskiest. If a company cannot meet its debt covenants, its debt holders can throw it into bankruptcy. On the other hand, equity capital funded by external investors dilutes the ownership and control of the company's founders. The financing decision must thus balance the lower costs associated with debt capital and the risk of bankrupting the company that it carries against the higher costs of raising money and the loss of control that equity financing entails.

DECIDING ON USES OF CAPITAL

Uses of Capital

Money can be used to sustain unprofitable operations; to invest in short-term assets, like inventory or receivables, or long-term assets, like real estate, research, or large equipment and buildings; to repay existing debt; or to buy back shares of the stock the company has sold to the public. Health care ventures use capital for all four purposes.

If they can afford it, health care ventures use capital to *finance their strategies*. Abe Gosman, for example, foresaw the demand for upscale drug addiction therapy facilities. At one time, most addicts were treated in bleak, barracklike environments. Gosman observed that addiction was becoming more prevalent among middle- and upper-income Americans, and he sought to establish a chain of comfortable centers in which to treat them. But the market was a long time in coming. At times, his model treatment center, with the capacity to treat 100 or so patients, had only a handful of patients. Gosman did not reduce his staff. He maintained a nearly full complement of employees so that the facility would always look busy no matter how small the number of patients.

This strategy was expensive, but Gosman won the day. The facility has 220 beds, is now always nearly full, and is the model for many others like it.

The investment in *short-term assets* can also be considerable, particularly for accounts receivable (bills sent out for services or products received by the customers for which no payment been made). Health service organizations generally can expect very slow turnover of receivables. It is not unusual for them to wait from 3 to 9 months before the bills they send out are converted into cash. Also, payments for new types of services or technologies may require considerable explanation before they are forthcoming. For example, the home health company, New England Critical Care's receivables average 130 days before they are converted into cash. In many industries, this rate would be appallingly high; but in the home health care industry it is stellar. This remarkable record was accomplished by a collection staff of 70 people (for $50 million in revenues) and a 6-person team devoted to explaining the company's services to insurers.

Fixed asset investments constitute a large percentage of total cash outflows for organizations whose purpose is to affect control of health care costs through vertical or horizontal integration. These organizations spend millions of dollars on buildings and equipment to achieve their sought-after economies of scale.

Health care organizations also use money to *buy back their publicly held stock*. For example, the Hospital Corporation of America borrowed money to buy back its existing publicly traded stock. It then formed a new privately held organization. Sometimes companies buy back outstanding debt, especially if the debt was issued when interest rates were abnormally high.

Some large pharmaceutical companies have an unusual problem—they cannot find enough uses for their capital because they have not generated sufficient internal research projects to consume the cash their profitable operations generate. What to do with the cash? If it is left sitting idle, the companies are not acting to maximize the value of their stock. Sometimes, the companies use their cash to buy back stock. The remaining stockholders benefit as a result. Another use of their cash is to purchase fledgling health care technology firms. Eli Lilly, for example, acquired a biotechnology company for $300 million and a host of cardiovascular device companies at a total price tag approaching $1 billion.

Capital Budgeting

The capital budgeting process is the framework in which decisions about using capital are made. It should contain the following elements:

1. Potential investments should be sorted into categories by purpose, such as the following: new business investments; employee safety and health investments;

and investments needed to maintain the business. These categories permit similar investments to be compared with each other and eliminate nonsensical comparisons, such as a comparison between an investment to remove a boiler's asbestos lining and an investment to expand the ambulatory health service business.

2. Separate criteria should be delineated for each category. For example, the rate of return expected for a new business venture should be higher than the rate of return expected for expansion of an existing business. Why? Because the new venture is much riskier. Thus, a proposal to add new beds in a hospital will probably be accepted even if it earns less than an investment to start a new hospital-based business, such as home health care services.

3. The returns and costs of each investment should be delineated. This step requires clear articulation of the cash that will be generated and used by a new project over its lifetime. The assumptions underlying the projections should be scrupulously checked. In some requests for capital, cash outflows are underestimated, inflows overestimated, and project lifetimes misestimated.

4. Cash flows should be discounted to their present value. The interest rate used for discounting should reflect the company's cost of raising money. For example, in a company that pays 20 percent before taxes for its money, the net present value of an investment costing $10 million and generating the cash flows shown in Table 7-1 is a negative $668,000. This project is infeasible. It must be rethought or scrapped.

5. The projects with the highest present values or highest ratios of discounted returns to costs should be given funding precedence in each category. (Additional explanation of capital budgeting criteria is contained in Appendix 7-A.)

The capital budgeting process ultimately depends on the thoroughness of the underlying

Table 7-1 Example of Discounted Cash Flow Computation

Beginning of Year	Cash Outflow (thousands)	Cash Inflow (thousands)	Discount Rate at 20%	Discounted Cash Flow[a] (thousands)
1	$10,000	0	1.00	$(10,000)
2	0	$1,000	.83	830
3	0	1,500	.69	1,042
4	0	2,000	.58	1,160
5	0	4,000	.48	1,920
6	0	5,000	.40	2,000
7	0	7,000[b]	.34	2,380
Total Present Value				($668)

[a]Discounted cash flows equal cash inflows and outflows multiplied by the discount rate.
[b]The project is sold for $7,000,000 at the beginning of year 7.

analysis. The three most common errors in implementing the process are these:

1. *Focusing on revenues and expenses instead of cash inflows and outflows.* Cash is the lifeblood of a company.
2. *Using an arbitrary project lifetime rather than one geared to the lifetime of the investment.* If a computer is likely to become obsolete in 4 years, then the right project lifetime for considering its purchase is 4 years. If a building will last for 40 years, the right lifetime for analyzing its value is 40 years. Frequently one lifetime is used for all types of investments.
3. *Using an inappropriate framework for analysis.* The returns credited to an investment should include only those that result from the investment. Further, the costs of the investment should be only those incurred because the project is undertaken. Cash inflows and outflows that will occur whether or not the project is undertaken are not relevant and should be omitted from the analysis.

MATCHING SOURCES AND USES OF CAPITAL

The third financing function is that of matching the sources and uses of funds from an economic and a strategic perspective. (Case Study 8 describes one such match.)

Economic Considerations

Short-term capital is perhaps the easiest and least costly form of financing to obtain. Lenders feel comfortable in extending short-term financing because they can quickly learn if the company is capable of repaying it. On the other hand, if they extend credit for long periods of time, they may have to wait 10, 15, or even 20 years before they learn whether the company can repay its debts.

As a result, long-term capital is usually more expensive and difficult to obtain than short-term capital. But, most new ventures need long-term sources of financing. Companies that create new technologies, for example, usually require a minimum of 5 years to bring new drugs, materials, or medical devices to the market. Similarly, a venture that intends to combine existing organizations to control the costs of health care may require massive long-term sources of money to purchase the facilities it plans to consolidate into a sleek horizontally or vertically integrated chain. Even vertically integrated HMOs require funds while they are building up their market.

In some cases, lenders are willing to provide long-term financing, particularly for the cost-controlling health care ventures that combine and reorganize existing facilities. The lenders often feel they understand existing facilities—the hospitals, nursing homes, and so on—and thus are more willing to take the risk of extending credit for a 15- to 30-year period of time. In most instances, however, new ventures confront an understandable reluctance on the part of the sources of capital to provide them with the long-term financing they need.

Companies trying to develop a new technology or appeal to a new consumer segment generally find lenders leery of providing debt capital, and they must rely either on the equity markets for long-term capital or use short-term financing to meet long-term funding needs. Thus, most biotechnology companies are funded by the sale of their equity to the public, venture capitalists, or private investors. They also rely on short-term contracts with pharmaceutical companies to fund their research. Such contracts are risky. If the biotechnology company does not develop a product in a short period of time, the pharmaceutical company may well cancel the contract. But the biotechnology companies may have no alternative sources of financing available—except in countries whose government provides substantial amounts of long-term funding, like Japan. Some U.S. biotechnology firms have sold out to large pharmaceutical companies, abandoning their dreams of creating billion-dollar companies in the face of these grim financial realities.

Strategic Considerations

The strategic match between sources and uses of funds is at least as important as the economic one. A venture capitalist with experience in areas related to the new venture and in taking a company public or selling it to a large investor is generally preferable to one that does not have this background. This experienced venture capitalist can bring more than money to the new venture. A large company that is in a related line of business is a better strategic partner. It can benefit a new venture as a result of its knowledge of the relevant regulatory mechanisms, its sales force, and its marketing skills. It will also value the new venture more highly because it already has the infrastructure needed for developing the new product.

Sometimes the ideal corporate partner can even provide complementary technology. For example, Amgen's manufacturing process for its antianemia drug erythropoietin (EPO) used roller bottles to feed cells. Many questioned Amgen's ability to apply this process to large-scale production. Enter the Kirin Brewery Company. An unlikely partner? Not really, because, as Amgen's former CEO noted, "Kirin knows bottles."[2] With Kirin as a partner, Amgen's EPO production process worked more smoothly.

Investors with "deep pockets" are preferred to others. Venture capitalists who control relatively small funds may rush to "cash out" their investments so that they can demonstrate their acumen to the next round of investors in their funds. Their new ventures may find themselves sold to other investors or going public prematurely. They will then need to devote precious managerial resources to developing these new relationships rather than to growing.

THE FINANCING PROCESS

Mechanics of Financing

The mechanics of the financing process are relatively straightforward. The venture documents its plans for using the capital and its ability to repay it or increase its value. The document bears different names: Venture capitalists call it a "business plan" and investment bankers and bond financiers call it a "prospectus."

The expectations of the different financing sources vary. Because venture capitalists take the biggest risk, as the first to invest in an unproven venture, they demand the largest reward. Their standard expectation is for a 50 percent annual return and the ability to sell the company in 5 years to the public or another owner. To put this expectation in perspective, they figure a $1 million investment will grow to the breathtaking level of $7.6 million in 5 years.

Investment bankers resell the equity of a venture in the stock market in a process called "going public," thus converting some of the founders' investment into cash. The equity is usually priced as some multiple of the company's earnings. When the stock markets are booming, health care equities can reach dazzling multiples. For example, Genentech stock increased eightfold from late 1984 to mid-1987, when it was valued at $65 per share of stock.[3] But, when the stock markets are depressed, health care companies find it difficult to attract attention. Genentech stock was decimated in the October 1987 stock market crash and traded at about $21 a share in late 1989. By 1990, it sold 60 percent of its ownership to a Swiss pharmaceutical company.

Investment bankers will take the venture public only if they think it can sustain an attractive rate of growth, usually 20–40 percent a year. Although this growth is enormously larger than other types of investments, it is lower than that expected by venture capitalists. Why? Because the investment bankers' participation comes at a later stage, when the company has already demonstrated some staying ability. Both capital sources earn their income as a fraction of the value placed on the company: The greater the growth, the greater their income.

Valuation Analysis

The valuation of the investment is determined as the present value of its future cash flows as discounted by the investor's cost of capital. Sometimes, the cash flows of three scenarios are projected: success, marginal success, and complete failure. These are multiplied by the probability of their occurrence (typically 25 percent, 50 percent, and 25 percent, respectively) to obtain an average value for the investment.[4]

Valuation analysis should also reflect the different perspectives of potential investors. A firm that already has the marketing or production facilities needed by the new venture will value an investment in that venture more highly than an investor that does not. For example, a new firm with a novel cardiovascular product is worth more to Bristol-Myers Squibb or Merck, companies with a substantial number of cardiology products, than to a pharmaceutical company that lacks presence in the cardiology market. The latter will have to create the needed sales and production resources from scratch.

Private investors may value the proposal more highly than venture capitalists. For example, the stock market slump of late 1990, coupled with the still unfulfilled promise of some public biotechnology companies, made it more difficult for biotechnology firms to go public. As a result, venture capitalists' interest in such investments cooled, and they demanded larger ownership shares for their investments. But private investors remained interested. Thus, Athena Neurosciences, after three rounds of venture capital financing, raised $13.3 million from private investors in 1991. Its CEO noted that the private placement price was "certainly a better price than we would have gotten from the venture-capital market."[5]

Dividing up the value among the investors requires assessments of present versus future value. Venture capitalists try to increase the value of their share through convertible preferred stock. This class of securities enables venture capitalists to have their cake and eat it too. It requires the firm to pay out regular cash dividends (unlike common stock, which carries no requirements for dividend payment) if the firm is profitable but not attractive enough to be acquired or go public, and it can also be converted to common stock. Venture capitalists may also want options to purchase future shares of stock at a prespecified price.

The use of such preferred stock and options may lower the value for other investors. An option granted now to buy stock at some future time may carry enormous opportunity costs. For example, if the venture capitalists can exercise an option to buy stock at $2 when the stock is selling to others at $12 a share, they pocket the difference of $10 (for a share purchased at $2 and sold at $12). However, their gain is the firm's loss—it receives only $2 rather than $12 for every share of its stock sold to the venture capitalists.

Valuation of Licenses

Similar considerations apply when a firm transfers some of its knowledge to others in exchange for payments of up-front fees and future royalties. Usually, the royalty payments are structured as a percentage of net revenues. A future royalty is essentially an option to buy a share of the company's revenues at some future price. Traditionally, royalty percentages decrease with the size of the revenues. For example, they may be 12 percent of the first $5 million and decrease to 10 percent after $20 million of revenues. But if future royalties are viewed as an option on future success, they should increase as a percentage with increasing sales revenue; the company's sales success should yield more value, not less. Up-front fees increase present cash flow but usually reduce the percentage of royalties to be paid in the future. Like the dividend on preferred stock, they decrease risk but at a cost of future values to be received.

Royalties range from 2 percent to 12 percent, with 6 percent very common. In theory, they can be immensely profitable: A 6 percent royalty on a billion-dollar drug amounts to $60 million a year in profits, for example. The amount of the up-front fee depends on the readiness of the product, the size of the ultimate market, and the company's need for the product. For example, a pharmaceutical company whose star product is a fading cardiovascular drug may well pay millions of dollars in fees for a potential replacement. But the same cardiovascular product will be worth much less to a pharmaceutical company that specializes in gastrointestinal products, because its sales force does not sell to the cardiologists who would buy the drug. Similarly, a drug that enables a pharmaceutical company to differentiate itself from competitors who offer "me too" products will also command a sizable fee.

In the past, biotechnology companies preferred to "take the money and run" through a greater up-front fee and lower royalties, whereas pharmaceutical companies preferred the reverse arrangement, which ties the compensation more closely to the product's ultimate value.

More recently, some biotechnology companies have been able to arrange better deals with established pharmaceutical companies that entitle them to far greater up-front payments, joint marketing, and a share of the profits. Immunex, in a deal with Eastman Kodak, for example, received $20 million and the right to market the products it develops in the enormous U.S. market. Kodak, in return, received the benefits of Immunex's ability to characterize certain proteins, 6–9 percent of Immunex's ownership, and marketing rights outside the U.S. SmithKline and Nova struck a deal involving the investment of $50 million by SmithKline in a venture that permits Nova to act as a partner with respect to any resulting products. These rich deals were arranged with pharmaceutical companies whose reportedly dry product pipelines forced them into structuring more attractive technology transfer offers.[6]

Warranties should be sought regarding the reality of the value. Financial audits or reviews by independent third parties, such as certified public accountants, provide verification of the systems for internal control in the firm and thus offer some protection against financial fraud. For transfers of technology, the following questions should be asked: Is the technology "fit for use"? Is "know-how" being transferred along with a patent or a prototype? Will the technology be held confidential? Who is indemnified in the event of a product liability suit? Who owns "future improvements"? Can the technology be used in different applications from those initially envisioned?[7]

Negotiating Process

Three aspects of the process of negotiating an investment deserve careful consideration. First, the bidding process can be opened to all comers or limited to a few selected parties. An open process creates a larger pool of options from which the firm can choose, but a limited process ensures a short list of serious bidders so that the firm does not waste its time in evaluating hopelessly inappropriate bids. The bidding can even be limited to only one investor if it dominates all others. A second consideration is whether to establish a cutoff date for the negotiations. Because the process can drag on and on, as various bids are reconfigured and adjusted, a cutoff date can be useful. (However, cutoff dates are rarely observed in practice.)

The third and most important consideration is of the characteristics being sought in potential investors. The willingness to pay a good price is, of course, an important characteristic, and the firm should consider the price it seeks for the investment before it begins the process. But price is hardly the only criterion for selecting a winning bidder. Others include the form and timing of the payment (some investors structure investments so that the level of investment is contingent on future performance); the prior investment history of the bidder; and whether the bidder seeks a seat on the company's board. It is helpful to find out how the investors have behaved with failing companies as well as with successful ones. Some are quick to pull the plug in cases of failure, whereas others are remarkable caregivers, who can nurse an ailing venture back to health.

the firm. To ensure that all bidders are financially competent, firms sometimes require sizable up-front deposits before the bidding process begins.

A typical agreement will cover the different phases of the project, such as research and development, product license, and manufacture, and also specify management of the collaboration for the research and development phase. The following issues are typically considered in the R & D phase: the period of time, up-front fees and payment schedules, budgets, the responsibility for regulatory filings, patent ownership and filing costs, legal defense costs, prohibition from competitive activity, publications, and the title to technology.

For the licensing phase, the following are considered: the holder of the license, the territory, the royalty rate, sublicense rights, the term of license, the minimum royalty, and accounting for royalties. For the manufacturing phase, the following are considered: the manufacturer identification, product characteristics, the territory, the payment basis, procurement shipments and financing terms, the right to abrogate the contract, and the responsibility for product liability. Finally, the agreement should specify how the venture will be managed, the frequency of the meetings, "buyout" options, and how disagreements will be worked out. (Case Studies 14 and 17 discuss such licensing issues.)

Contractual Terms

All negotiations should also contain clauses to ensure that the winning bidder will fulfill the promises that have been made. They should include minimum performance clauses that stipulate the level of performance required within a given amount of time. The clauses may require the bidder to pay a fee if the performance target has not been met. They may also abrogate the contract (known as a "drop dead" provision) if minimal performance persists over a period of time, and they may specify that all value transferred is returned to

NOTES

1. Immunex Corporation, *1989 Annual Report* (Seattle: Immunex Corporation, 1989), 3.

2. "Can Amgen Follow Its Own Tough Act?" *Business Week*, March 11, 1991, 95.

3. Teena L. Lerner, "Health Care—2000" (New York: Shearson Lehman Hutton, February 12, 1990), 5–6.

4. Daniel R. Scherlis and William A. Sahlman, "A Method for Valuing High-Risk, Long-Term Investments," 9-288-006 (Boston: Harvard Business School, 1989).

5. "Talking Deals," *New York Times*, February 14, 1991, D2.

6. Roger Longman, "Equal Partners," *In Vivo*, September–October 1988, 25–29.

7. Lita L. Nelsen, "Intellectual Property and the University," in *Albany Law School Annual Conference of Intellectual Property*, Vol. 2 (New York: Matthew Bender and Company, 1988), 3-1– 3-19.

SUGGESTED READING

Finance

Brigham, Eugene F. *Fundamentals of Financial Management*. 5th ed. Hinsdale, Ill.: Dryden Press, 1989.

Gotthilf, Daniel L. *Treasurer's and Controller's Desk Book*. Englewood Cliffs, N.J.: Prentice-Hall, 1977.

Hallman, G. Victor. *Personal Financial Planning*. 4th ed. New York: McGraw-Hill, 1987.

The Handbook of Economic and Financial Measures. Homewood, Ill.: Dow Jones-Irwin, 1984.

Kaufman, George G. *The U.S. Financial System*. 4th ed. Englewood Cliffs, N.J.: Prentice-Hall, 1989.

Meyer, Paul Anthony. *Monetary Economics and Financial Markets*. Homewood, Ill.: Richard D. Irwin, 1982.

Roden, Peyton Foster. *Finance: Environment and Decisions*. 4th ed. New York: Harper & Row, 1986.

Schwarz, Edward W. *Financial Futures*. Homewood, Ill.: Richard D. Irwin, 1986.

Sloane, Leonard. *The New York Times Book of Personal Finance*. New York: New York Times Books, 1985.

Stillman, Richard Joseph. *Guide to Personal Finance*. 5th ed. Englewood Cliffs, N.J.: Prentice-Hall, 1988.

Train, John. *Famous Financial Fiascos*. New York: Crown Publishers, 1985.

Van Horne, James C. *Financial Market Rates and Flows*. 3d ed. Englewood Cliffs, N.J.: Prentice-Hall, 1990.

Public Finance

Bell, Daniel. *The Deficits*. New York: New York University Press, 1985.

Hay, Leon Edwards. *Accounting for Governmental and Nonprofit Entities*. 8th ed. Homewood, Ill.: Richard D. Irwin, 1989.

Herzlinger Regina E., and Denise Nitterhouse. *Financial Accounting and Managerial Control for Nonprofit Organizations*. Cincinnati: South-Western Publishing, 1991.

Appendix 7-A

Capital Budgeting Criteria

A typical investment proposal involves the outlay of a large amount of money at the present time that will generate a stream of income some time in the future; for example, such a proposal might involve substituting a toll-booth guard with a machine that accepts tolls, sounds alarms if needed, provides change, and keeps count of the total revenues. If the machine costs $54,000, requires annual maintenance, operating, and insurance expenses of $2,000, and replaces a guard whose salary and fringe expenses are $20,000 a year, is it a good investment?

Payback. A simplistic answer to this question is provided by the calculation of the number of years required to "pay back" the initial investment. Every year the machine is in place, it saves $20,000—the expense of the guard—and costs $2,000, thereby generating net cash savings of $18,000 a year. The number of years required to *pay back* the initial investment of $54,000 can be calculated as:

$$\text{Payback years} = \frac{\text{initial investment}}{\text{annual net cash savings}}$$

$$= \frac{\$54,000}{\$18,000} = 3 \text{ years}$$

If the machine is expected to last less than 3 years, the payback criterion indicates that the investment is not worthwhile. If the machine's expected lifetime is more than 3 years, however, then the investment is worthwhile because the machine will have paid for itself by the third year. After that point, the net cash flows will be pure gravy.

Net Present Value. The payback analysis assumes that a cash flow of $18,000 in year 2 is equivalent in value to a cash flow of $18,000 in any other year. But is it? If somebody offered to give you $18,000 2 years from now in exchange for your giving up $18,000 right now, you should reject the proposal. Why? Because having $18,000 right now is worth more than $18,000 some time in the future. This is the (admittedly slippery) concept of the time value of money.

To answer the question of whether this machine is a good investment, we must compute the present value of its cash savings of $18,000 a year and compare the savings to the cost of the machine. For example, if the machine lasts for 4 years, the present value of the savings of $18,000 that it generates, when valued at 8 percent, is $59,616 [($18,000 a year)(3.312)].* This sum is larger than the

Source: Adapted from *Financial Accounting and Managerial Control for Nonprofit Organizations* by R.E. Herzlinger and D. Nitterhouse, with permission of South-Western Publishing Co., © 1991.

amount needed to purchase the machine. To put it another way, we spend $54,000 to create savings worth $59,616 when we buy the machine. It appears to be a wise investment.

Internal Rate of Return. Is 8 percent the right interest rate with which to compute the net present value? Because the task of picking the "right" interest rate is complex, some people avoid it by computing the internal rate of return of the project. The internal rate of return is the interest rate that equates the net present value of the cash inflows and outflows associated with the project.

What is the internal rate of return of the project above? To calculate it we will do the following:

1. Divide the investment by the annual net cash inflow. This is

$$\frac{\$54,000}{\$18,000} = 3$$

2. Look across the 4-year row in an annuity table† to find the number closest to 3. It occurs at an interest rate between 12 and 13 percent. It tells us that this project has an internal earning rate between 12 or 13 percent. If we earn less than this rate on alternative projects, this project is clearly desirable as an investment.

Unfortunately, although the internal rate of return is probably the simplest criterion for answering the question of what and how much to buy, it is frequently an erroneous one. To return to our example, suppose that we can invest $54,000 either in this machine or in a certificate of deposit that will pay 10 percent interest every year for 4 years. Suppose also that the best interest rate that we can obtain for investing the $18,000 a year of savings the machine generates is 5 percent. Which is the best option for investment of the $54,000—the four year 10 percent certificate or the machine?

It might appear that the machine investment is the preferred investment because it yields an internal rate of return higher than 10 percent. But this analysis ignores the interest rate at which the savings from the machine can be invested. When this rate is included in the anlysis, the certificate is the better investment. As shown in Table 7-A-1, the certificate investment is worth $79,061 at the end of 4 years, while the machine investment is worth only $77,583. Why? Because the certificate option re-invests yearly interest at 10 percent, while the machine option does so only at a 5 percent rate.

The internal rate of return cannot serve as the sole criterion for decision making. It must be complemented by consideration of the rates of return that can be earned by the cash generated from the investment.

---

* 3.312 is the present value of $1 a year for 4 years at 8 percent interest. To put it another way, if $3.31 are deposited right now in an account that pays 8 percent annual interest, the depositor will be able to draw out $1 a year for 4 years. If we invest $59,619 right now in an investment that pays 8 percent interest, we will be able to draw out $18,000 a year, for 4 years.

† An annuity table defines the present value of $1 for different periods of time and interest rates.

Table 7–A–1 Illustration of the Use of Internal Rate of Return As a Criterion for an Investment

	Option A: Buy a bond that yields 10% a year for 4 years.		Option B: Buy a machine that generates savings of $18,000 a year for 4 years. Each year's savings can be invested at a 5% rate.
End of Year	End of Year Value = Beginning of Year Value Plus Interest at 10%	End of Year	End of Year Value = $18,000 per Year and Interest at 5% on Last Year's Value
1	$59,400 = ($54,000 + $5,400)	1	$18,000 = ($18,000)
2	$65,340 = ($59,400 + $5,940)	2	$36,900 = ($18,000 + $900 + $18,000)
3	$71,874 = ($65,340 + $6,534)	3	$56,745 = ($36,900 + $1,845 + $18,000)
4	$79,061 = ($71,874 + $7,187)	4	$77,583 = ($56,745 + $2,838 + $18,000)

8

Managerial Control Systems

Managerial control systems help companies plan the results they want to attain, measure whether these results have occurred, analyze the causes of the differences between planned and actual results, and motivate employees to close the gap. They are the organizational equivalent of a thermostat: Like this device, they are set at a prespecified level, measure whether the desired level has been attained, and, if it has not, activate another mechanism to attain it.

Until recently, managerial control systems were rarely implemented in the U.S. health care industry. When payment for health care services or technology was on a cost-plus basis, as it was in the good old days, there was little need for such systems. But the great concern about increasing health care costs and the emergence of newly cost-conscious consumers has changed all that. Managerial control systems are essential to many new health care ventures. Unfortunately, their importance is equaled by the difficulty of implementing them in this industry.

Planning is difficult because few standards exist to specify desirable outputs. The "right" number of doctors per 100,000 people is as

unknown as the "right" amount of money to spend for developing a new biotechnology product. Of course, standards are notably absent in many other industries, but health care is based on the youngest of sciences, medicine, and thus has fewer scientific laws to rely on than other industries that can apply the laws of physical and chemical sciences.

The absence of a history of management control enormously complicates the *measurement* process. Many health service providers sputter along with antiquated accounting systems designed to generate bills and pay employees. Health care measurement systems have traditionally focused on measuring inputs, how much was spent, and not outputs, what was accomplished by spending the money. It is difficult to recast these systems for managerial purposes, like measurements of whether the plans of the hospital have been attained.

To get a sense of the sheer magnitude of the measurement task in many health service organizations consider the following. A large 750-bed hospital opens 70,000 medical records for new patients each year and has over 1,000,000 records in active storage. Each record contains tens of thousands of pieces of information about the patient's social and demographic status and the diagnostic and treatment procedures received in the hospital. These data generate millions of billable items, whose payment status must be carefully monitored. The $300 million the hospital spends is accounted for in the general ledger and then presented in different formats to conform to the reporting requirements of the hundreds of different outside parties who receive cost-accounting data from the hospital, including information on how the hospital spent $40 million in outside research grants and over $10 million in restricted donations.

Motivating health care employees to close the gap between planned and actual results presents yet another substantial problem in implementing managerial control systems. Many health care workers are professionals. To them, doing a good job means acting in accordance with professional norms when performing a diagnosis, interpreting an x-ray film, providing nursing care, and so on. Many of them do not identify with corporate norms. They believe that acting in accordance with professional norms inevitably leads to corporate success. "If I am a good doctor, the company is bound to succeed, unless they mess up," says the typical professional. Who are "they"? The faceless managers whose corporate goals many professionals neither understand nor share.

Lower-level nonprofessional employees also feel distanced from corporate goals, but for a different reason. Many health care organizations are rigidly hierarchical, and there is an uneasy coexistence between professional and managerial spheres of influence. Lower-level nonprofessional employees are at the very bottom rung of this hierarchy. Yet these lower-level employees are often the very ones with whom the patient has the greatest contact (one hospital CEO noted the average hospital patient sees the room maid more than any other employee) and whose work is absolutely essential for the organization's survival (dirty public bathrooms or production facilities can cause a health care facility to be shut down). Their job titles are a good indication of their misper-

ceived organizational status: They are aides, maids, and technicians.

Managerial control systems are thus essential for many new health care ventures and yet, difficult to implement. Each part of a managerial control system is discussed below.

PLANNING

The heart of good management is the realization of carefully considered plans. Unanticipated results, whether positive or negative, are the *bete noir* of a professional manager. One CEO, for example, was dismayed to find at year's end millions of dollars of unexpected profits. Although the news was good—it was, after all, a profit—he would have preferred to have predicted it in his projections for that year. To that CEO, good managers create the profits they project; they are not merely the beneficiaries of good fortune.

However, in many organizations planning is neglected. Mechanistic planning prevails: Next year's plan equals last year's actual results plus inflation. Or managers are prodded to deliver meaningless corporate goals. "Can you do 14 percent more next year?" prods the CEO. "Uh-huh," responds the manager. Neither has any idea how this 14 percent increase will be generated. Such offhand goals are rarely achieved.

Good planning should be carefully implemented. It must reflect simultaneously top management's goals for growth and the predictions of line managers about the results they can attain. In planning terminology, the plan must reconcile "top-down" views (e.g., views about the earnings increases needed to attract investors) with "bottom-up" perceptions (e.g., the minimum budget needed for research and development). A professional planner can be helpful in presenting analyses of the industry and competitors, compiling inflation projections and regulatory trends, suggesting alternative scenarios, and managing the flow of paper in the process. But planners can become impediments if they are allowed to usurp managerial prerogatives and create the plan rather than to facilitate its creation.

The planning process requires considerable time and effort. Many companies start next year's planning process 6 months before the end of the current year. They involve virtually all layers of management in defining the plan. The process is iterative: The plan is continually honed before the final document emerges.

The final plan can take many forms, although every plan should be based on a consistent set of projections about the future. The plan can encompass a 10-year or a 1-year time horizon. It can be presented as an operating budget, a cash budget, a multiyear capital budget; or a headcount or personnel budget.

Plans can be expressed in geographical and site terms (e.g., "We will penetrate the New England region with 32 new sites" or "Next year we will sell to hospitals in Florida with fewer than 200 beds"). Plans can also specify quality goals (e.g., an average patient wait of less than 20 minutes in a chain of ambulatory service offices). In technology-based firms, planned attainments are phrased in yet different terms. 3M, the highly innovative technology-based company, reportedly charges its managers with deriving the bulk of their revenues from entirely new products every 5 years.

Plans generate the goals against which actual results are measured. They state the targets the organization hopes to achieve. But they can provide much more. The interactive process of planning can breed commitment to the goals specified in each plan. Managers and professionals buy into corporate objectives. The planning process also forces participants to look beyond their own sphere of responsibility and examine the impact of their activities on the rest of the organization. Finally, the planning process can be an excellent management training tool. One professional told me,

> I did not understand management until I was given the responsibility for developing my department's budget. Doing the budget caused me to think about marketing and its effect on revenues; production and its effects on expenses; and finance and its effect on the money we have available. I saw the forest instead of the trees. When I

started doing the budget, I was a professional. When I finished, I was a manager.

MEASURING ACTUAL RESULTS

In the second part of the managerial control process, the actual results are measured against the plans, and the variances between actual and planned results are identified. Because the measurement process can easily drown in details, it should focus on only those few items that are critical to the success of the organization. For cost-controlling organizations, a focus on costs is critical. In new consumer organizations, measures of patient satisfaction or feelings of control are key. And in new technology organizations, progress in developing the medical technology is the central measurement issue.

Measuring Outcomes

Organizational outcomes should be measured in financial and nonfinancial terms. Revenues, the financial value of sales delivered in the period, are of critical importance. Although managerial control systems frequently lack formal measures of clinical quality, these are at least as important as financial measurements. For example, MediQual Systems, a Massachusetts company, has a system for measuring the morbidity and mortality rates of different physicians within a hospital. Three years of measurement and feedback seemed to have influenced a decline in the rates of patient morbidity associated with some physicians (Table 8-1).

Operational characteristics should also be measured, such as the cleanliness of the facility and the length of time patients wait before being seen. For example, a hospital whose public bathrooms are to be cleaned every hour might use a worksheet that cleaners must sign after completing their work. The bathrooms' cleanliness should be audited on a random basis to ensure that the work was done. New England Critical Care, a home infusion company,

Table 8-1 Effect of Feedback on Incidence of Illness after Treatment for Heart Attacks and Shock

Physician	1985	1986	1987
a	7%	4%	5%
b	22	10	7
c	21	17	12
d	12	10	8
e	15	12	2
f	9	10	9
g	18	2	1
h	12	10	5
i	11	1	1
j	11	11	12

Source: Courtesy of MediQual Systems, Inc., Westborough, Massachusetts.

developed a detailed outcome measurement system that focused on quality, the company's distinctive attribute. Included in the quality measures were patient ratings of the nurses' punctuality and their ability to painlessly and accurately insert a needle in a vein, as well as assessments of the cleanliness of the vans used by the company to deliver infusion solutions and of the van drivers' neatness, friendliness, and punctuality.

Increasingly, those who pay for or certify health service providers are requiring standardized measures of outcomes. For example, Blue Cross/Blue Shield of Minnesota will pay hospitals for illnesses that are classified by the expected risk of adverse outcomes. Excess hospital costs caused by exceeding the predicted outcome rates will not be reimbursed.[1]

Measuring Inputs

Expenses, or the costs of the resources consumed to achieve the outcomes, must also be carefully measured. These costs can be measured along two dimensions: They can be direct or full costs and they can be process or product costs.

Direct costs are the costs of those resources whose use can be unambiguously traced to a certain outcome. The direct costs of a visit to a physician's office include the value of the time spent by the physician, nurse, and other service provider with the patient and the value of any drugs supplied or diagnostic tests administered. But the physician's office also has many indirect costs, including space and capital depreciation expenses and the costs of the accountant and lawyer hired by the physician. These indirect costs are allocated to the outcome in a full cost system.

Full costs include all the resources used to provide the patient visit. In that sense, they provide a good measure of inputs. But full costs include many allocated costs that result from somebody's judgment about how to spread out the indirect costs across outcomes. The measurement of direct costs, on the other hand, is much less subjective.

Exhibit 8-1 illustrates the alternative cost computations. As illustrated, the full costs of a physician visit can vary from $80 to $120 per visit, depending on whether the indirect costs of $100,000 are allocated on the basis of the number of visits or on the basis of physician hours. Either method of allocation is perfectly acceptable to accountants, as are many others.

The other dimension of cost accounting measures costs on a process or a product basis. A *process measure* accounts for the costs of providing a product or service, while a *product measure* uses time sheets and supply requisition forms to trace exactly how much

Exhibit 8-1 Comparison of Full and Direct Costs per Visit to a Physician's Office

---

Given:

Visit required 1 hour of physician's time and 1.5 hours of registered nurse's time.
Physician salary = $80,000 for 2,000 hours, or $40 an hour.
Nurse salary = $40,000 for 2,000 hours, or $20 an hour.
Rent, administrative, and equipment costs = $100,000.
Visits for the year = 10,000.

Direct Cost of Visit:

Value of 1 hour of physician's time + 1.5 hours of registered nurse's time =

$$(1 \text{ hour}) \times (\$40) + (1.5 \text{ hours}) \times (\$20) = \$70$$

Full Cost of Visit:

Direct cost + allocated indirect costs =

$$\$70 + \frac{\$100,000}{10,000 \text{ visits}} = \$80$$

Note: In this example, the indirect cost is allocated at $10 per visit. But it can be allocated in many other ways. For example, allocation on the basis of the use of the physician's time would be perfectly acceptable. In that case, the allocation to this visit would equal $50 ($100,000 ÷ 2,000 hours) and the full cost of the visit would rise to $120 ($70 + $50).

---

time and supplies were spent on every product or service. For the physician's office described above, process costing would measure the cost per day or average visit, whereas product costing would measure the costs of every different type of procedure, like a physical. The expenses of implementing a process accounting system are much lower than for a product accounting system.

Most health service organizations use a full-cost, process accounting system. For example, the typical physician's office will compute its cost per patient visit in the following manner: It will divide its total costs by total hours to measure the full cost per hour for the process of delivering health care. Then it will compute the cost per patient visit by multiplying this hourly cost by the number of hours of care the patient received. Thus, if the full cost per hour is $80 and the patient required 2 hours of care, the cost of the visit will be $160.

But in many circumstances, use of product and/or direct costs is desirable. Organizations that control costs or that serve new consumers should have a product costing system that

measures the costs of providing these new products or services. For example, this information could have helped some now-defunct HMOs to determine if their premium prices were lower than their costs.

Direct-cost information is particularly important for a fixed-cost organization that operates at less than full capacity. In these circumstances, it may be willing to sell some of its outputs at prices lower than full cost. Because some of the expenses will remain the same no matter what the volume of sales, like the cost of space, any contribution to coverage of those costs is welcome. But a full-cost system creates the false impression that a sale transacted at a price less then full cost is generating a loss (Table 8-2). A direct-cost system would not create this incorrect impression.

As Table 8-2 shows, whereas the full-cost system indicates a loss of $5 for a $75 visit, the direct cost system more correctly identifies that the $75 visit contributes $5 toward the physician's indirect expenses. The direct-cost system more closely approximates the natural economic distinction between *fixed* and *vari-*

Table 8-2 Profit and Loss under Full and Direct Costing

	Full Cost	Direct Cost
Price	$75/visit	$75/visit
– Cost	$80/visit	$70/visit
Profit (Loss)	$ (5)	$ 5

able costs. Variable costs, those that change with the volume of output, are likely to be direct ones, whereas fixed costs, which remain the same at every level of output, are frequently closely approximated by indirect costs. In the case under discussion, the physician's office has fixed costs of $100,000. Every $75 visit will contribute $5 toward the coverage of those costs. But a full-cost system may cause that contribution to appear to be undesirable.

ANALYZING THE DIFFERENCES BETWEEN PLANNED AND ACTUAL RESULTS

Variance Analysis

Variance analysis isolates the causes for the differences between planned goals and actual results. It separates the events that can be controlled by managers from those that cannot. It also separates the effect of factors controlled by different managers. Variance analysis is thus useful for evaluating managerial performance. It can be applied to explain the differences between the planned and actual performance of any financial measure, such as revenues, expenses, and profits.

Variance analysis is most frequently used in manufacturing firms, where it generally distinguishes variances from the plan caused by changes in the volume of sales activity from those caused by changes in the efficiency of production. These two variances are referred to as *volume variances* and *efficiency variances*. Why are these variances measured? Because they are controlled by two different managers

(volume changes are controlled by the marketing staff and efficiency changes are usually the responsibility of those in the production area) and because they are usually the primary causes of differences between planned and actual results.

The analytic process of variance analysis is comparable to taking partial derivatives in calculus. It is the process of analyzing the effect of one variable on the system by holding everything but the variable of interest constant. Thus, a "volume" variance analysis holds everything constant except those things affected by a change in volume, and an "efficiency" variance analysis does the same for changes in efficiency.

An Example of Variance Analysis

The variance analysis illustrated in Exhibit 8-2 explains why actual hospital costs were $70 million higher than planned. Although hospital managers explained that the increase occurred because the actual volume of hospital days of 300,000 was much higher than the 200,000 planned, the analysis does not confirm their explanation. Yes, the increased volume of 100,000 days caused a cost increase of $40 million, but the total cost increase was $70 million, not $40 million. The remaining variance was caused by a $30 million negative efficiency variance—hospital costs rose from $400 to $500 per day. Had the hospital maintained its actual costs at the planned level of $400 a day, its total costs would have been at least $30 million lower. The components of the $70 million in negative cost variances were thus increased volume ($40 million impact) and decreased efficiency ($30 million impact).

Variance analysis separated the cost impact of increased volume from the cost impact of decreased efficiency. It can do the same for revenues, separating the impact of volume and price on revenues. For example, if the planned price per day were $600 and the actual price were $550, the price variance would be $15 million [($600 planned price per day – $550 actual price per day) × (300,000 days)] and the

Exhibit 8-2 Graphic Depiction of Cost Variance Analysis

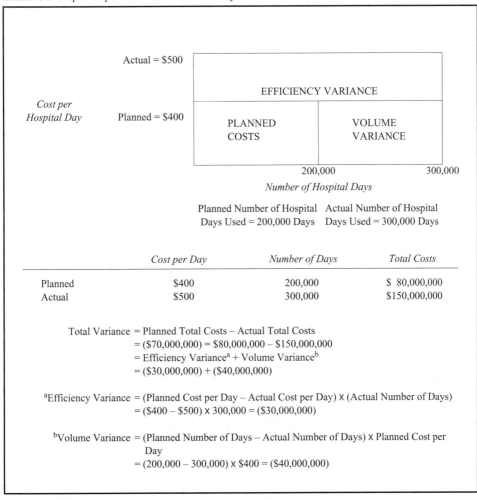

	Cost per Day	Number of Days	Total Costs
Planned	$400	200,000	$ 80,000,000
Actual	$500	300,000	$150,000,000

Total Variance = Planned Total Costs – Actual Total Costs
= ($70,000,000) = $80,000,000 – $150,000,000
= Efficiency Variance[a] + Volume Variance[b]
= ($30,000,000) + ($40,000,000)

[a]Efficiency Variance = (Planned Cost per Day – Actual Cost per Day) × (Actual Number of Days)
= ($400 – $500) × 300,000 = ($30,000,000)

[b]Volume Variance = (Planned Number of Days – Actual Number of Days) × Planned Cost per Day
= (200,000 – 300,000) × $400 = ($40,000,000)

volume variance would be a negative $60 million ($600 per day × 100,000 days). (Negative revenue variances represent positive news because actual revenues are greater than those planned.) The joint effect of the volume and price variances is a negative $45 million. Revenues were planned at $120 million ($600 per day × 200,000 days), whereas actual revenues were $165 million ($550 per day × 300,000 days). Had prices been held at their planned levels, revenues would have increased $60 million over those planned because of the great increase in volume.

Revenue and cost variances can be combined to perform a *profit variance analysis* that explains why actual profits differed from planned ones. In this example, profits were planned at $40 million ($120 million in revenues – $80 million in costs), whereas actual profits were $15 million ($165 million – $150 million). Profits were $25 million lower than planned. Why? Decreased efficiency reduced profits by $30 million and decreased prices by $15 million. The negative impact on profit of the reduction in efficiency and prices was offset by a volume variance whose net effect on profits was a positive $20 million.

This computation is depicted in Table 8-3. If you are having difficulty in following the analysis, rest assured that you are not alone. It is a difficult subject. I include it with full awareness of both its difficulty and its importance.

Table 8-3 Profit Variance Analysis

(millions of dollars)

	Planned	–	Actual	=	Total Variance	=	Volume Variance	+	Price Variance	+	Efficiency Variance
Revenues	$120	–	$165	=	$(45)	=	+$(60)[a]	+	$15[b]	+	NA
– Costs	$ 80	–	$150	=	– $(70)[c]	=	– $(40)[c]	–	NA	–	$(30)[c]
Profits	$ 40	–	$ 15	=	$ 25	=	$(20)	+	$15	+	$30

[a]Volume Variance = (Planned Number of Days – Actual Number of Days) x Planned Price per Day
= (200,000 – 300,000) x ($600) = ($60,000,000)

[b]Price Variance = (Planned Price per Day – Actual Price per Day) x Actual Number of Days
= ($600 – $550) x 300,000 = $15,000,000

[c]Cost Variances were computed in Table 8-2.

EVALUATION AND MOTIVATION

The measurement system should be coupled to an incentive compensation process that holds managers responsible for certain results and rewards them in accordance with their ability to achieve the desired results. In the case discussed above, those responsible for efficiency would likely receive negative evaluations. The evaluation of marketing managers' performance is more complex. If the marketing people reduced prices in order to gain volume, the net effect of their move was a positive one. Volume variances increased profits by $20 million, whereas price variances decreased them by only $15 million. On the other hand, if the large volume increase caused efficiency to plummet, a claim those responsible for efficiency would surely make, then the overall effect of cutting prices to increase volume was negative.

A financial outcome for which managers are held accountable is labeled a *responsibility center.* If managers are held responsible for profits, their responsibility center is said to be a *profit center;* if costs, it is an *expense center;* if revenues, it is a *revenue center;* and if total returns, it is an *investment center,* whose revenues, expenses, and level of invested capital are all measured.

In some large organizations, managers of responsibility centers may be required to conduct business transactions with each other. For example, the Humana case study (Case Study 10) indicates that the company's health insurance and hospital units dealt with each other as if they were two separate companies. When the internal responsibility centers buy and sell to each other, as when the hospital unit sells hospital days to the health insurance unit, the sales price is labeled a *transfer price.* Because the purpose of transfer pricing is to impose market discipline on transactions between two parts of the same firm, the transfer price should equal the market price.

For example, in a vertically integrated health insurance company like Humana, the health insurance division wants the prices of the services provided by its own internal hospitals to be at least as low as those charged by hospitals that the company does not own. If its hospitals' division's costs are lower than the market-based transfer price, the hospital division's efficiency will be indicated by the high profits it will earn, as shown in Exhibit 8-3. But if the hospital division's costs are higher than the market price, the inefficiency will be clearly documented by losses.

The financial responsibility given to a manager should be commensurate with the

Exhibit 8-3 Use of Transfer Pricing To Evaluate Efficiency of Internal Production

Given:
Market price for a hospital day is $500, so internal hospital gets paid for its services to the company's health insurance division at $500/day.

Results:

Efficient Hospital Division		Inefficient Hospital Division	
Revenues	$500/day	Revenues	$500/day
Cost	– $400/day	Cost	– $700/day
Profit (Loss)	$100/day	Profit (Loss)	($200/day)

manager's authority. The director of a hospital pharmacy should be held accountable for its costs and inventory levels but not for the entire hospital's revenues or profits. After all, the pharmacy director lacks control over total hospital performance. Salespeople can be held responsible for their level of sales, for selling expenses, and for the prices they are able to obtain on sales, but they cannot be held responsible for the costs of the product they sell.

Health care managers should also be responsible for nonfinancial outcomes such as the quality of clinical care, operational characteristics, and the quality and rate of turnover of the staff. For example, one HMO regularly monitors the following events to ensure it provides the highest quality of care:

1. undesirable occurrences (e.g., all patients hospitalized after minor surgery)
2. patient advocacy notes (clinical care complaints referred by the patient advocate or by others)
3. quality assurance and risk management committee minutes
4. minutes of safety, disaster, and maintenance committee
5. incident reports (reports involving clinical issues referred by executive director)
6. other screens already in place for reviews mandated by the Board of Registration in Medicine
7. potential or actual claims (referred by loss control coordinator)

Managers should be rewarded with financial and other incentives in accordance with their ability to achieve specified goals. They may receive a share of the profits they have earned, granted in cash or stock options, or a bonus. Many companies have other forms of recognition, such as a club whose membership comprises only those with exceptional organizational achievements or awards for the employee of the month or the year. The Riverside Methodist Hospital in Columbus, Ohio, holds a yearly employee celebration modeled in scope and grandeur after Hollywood's Academy Awards presentation. Winning employees are brought to the festivities in a horse-drawn carriage and enter the large ballroom in which the ceremony is conducted on a red carpet. The event is recorded on a videotape presented as a momento to the winning employee and broadcast on the hospital's internal television system.

Financial incentives are frequently structured to motivate employees to maintain a long-term connection with the firm. In these cases, incentive compensation is paid on a *time-vested* basis, which means that employees can receive their incentive payment only after a certain amount of time with the organization. (The incentive compensation funds are invested by the organization until they vest.) Incentive pay may also be *performance vested*, which means that it is paid out only if the organization as a whole reaches prespecified financial or other goals. In this way, employees are motivated to consider the effect of their performance on the organization as a whole rather than to focus solely on their own niche. For example, in a performance-vested system, the manager of a drug factory that is a cost center will be motivated to consider whether reduction in the expenses for which he or she is held responsible will cause such a reduction in quality that the company's total performance will be reduced.

MANAGERIAL CONTROL OF COST-CONTROLLING AND NEW CONSUMER ORGANIZATIONS

Managerial control systems are critical for organizations whose purpose is to control health care costs. To achieve their goals, they must carefully plan their costs; continually monitor actual results against plans; and motivate their employees to adhere to planned cost levels. All this must be accomplished with acceptable quality levels. The organization should have tangible measures of quality, as well, to reassure itself and its customers that costs are not being controlled through sacrifices in quality.

Measuring Actual Costs

Measuring costs presents a great challenge. In the past cost-plus reimbursement environment, accounting systems were focused on maximizing reimbursement. A great deal of effort was expended on allocating costs to those payers whose cost-plus reimbursement formulas would provide the greatest profits. This orientation is very different from that required to constrain costs. When the federal government declared that it would no longer reimburse hospitals for their costs but instead would pay a fixed price for each DRG (diagnostic-related group), and when beleaguered corporations began to examine closely health care bills that in the past they paid, without question, accounting systems of many health service organizations needed to be reconfigured to focus on measuring costs accurately.

Most organizations did not know their costs for different DRGs or procedures with any degree of accuracy. Their cost accounting systems measured the average cost of an hour of ambulatory care or a day of hospital care. They then estimated the cost of a procedure by multiplying the cost per time unit by an estimate of the time the procedure required. Thus, if the cost per hospital day was $500 and the average delivery of a baby required a 3-day hospital stay, then the cost of a birth was estimated at $1,500.

This kind of cost accounting assumes that the process of care is identical for all services. For example, it assumes that the costs of caring for a burn victim and a healthy mother are the same—$500 a day. But the assumption is clearly wrong. The burn victim requires a great deal more nursing care, diagnostic testing, and therapy than a healthy mother and her baby. New cost accounting systems were needed to focus on the products, not the process, of health care.

The process of measuring product costs in cost-controlling organizations involves development of a *standard* or planned cost per output and measurement of actual costs against this standard. It is detailed in Case Study 11. Product costs require extensive records. All service-providing personnel must maintain immaculate time sheets that record the amount of time they spent in providing different types of service. Requisition forms for expensive drugs and supplies must also tie their use to a particular service. And costs jointly shared by all, like those of administration and space, must be thoughtfully allocated to particular services.

Developing Standards

Measuring actual costs requires meticulous, extensive documentation. It is an onerous task but a feasible one. Developing standards for costs is even more difficult, because few standards exist. The most frequent standards are those provided by an organization's own past experience. Thus, if its average cost for a birth last year was $2,000, a hospital might well adopt the $2,000 cost as a standard for next year. This approach ensures that standards are realistic and acceptable. It does not, however, ensure efficiency. The $2,000 birth may represent wildly inefficient use of resources. If so, it is a poor goal to choose to replicate.

Humana solves the problem of developing standards by using a team of industrial engineers who develop standards of optimum resource use for different activities (see Case Study 9). Using engineers to design standards increases their accuracy but is much more expensive than using average performance.

The absence of standards in delivering health care has been widely observed. For example, North Dakota has significantly better health status than Michigan (see Table 8-4). Yet its use of health care resources is lower than Michigan's. The table dramatizes the absence of a standard relationship between resources expended and outcomes achieved.

A Dartmouth Medical School physician observed the absence of standards with the following dramatic example.

> There is a city in Maine where the surgical procedure of hysterectomy (removal of the uterus) was done so frequently in the past decade that, if the rate persists, 70 percent of the women there will have had the

operation by the time they reach the age of 75. In a city less than 20 miles away, the rate of hysterectomy is so much lower that, if it persists, only 25 percent of the women will have lost their uterus by age 75. What could account for the disparity? The most important factor in determining the rate of hysterectomy seems to be the style of medical practice of the physicians in the two cities. In one city surgeons appear to be enthusiastic about hysterectomy; in the other they appear to be skeptical of its value.[2]

To support research that compares different treatments and technologies and identifies those producing the best results, Congress passed the Outcomes Assessment Research Act in 1989, and appropriated $568 million over the following 5 years to fund it. HMOs and other managed medical care organizations are independently pursuing similar research. Only 8 percent remained uninvolved in such efforts in 1989. Hospitals are also participating. Five New York State hospitals are contributing to a $2.25 million pool that will eventually be redistributed on the basis of measures of the hospitals' quality of care.[3] St. Vincent Hospital in Portland, Oregon, developed a new quality program for total hip replacement patients. Its new quality standards reduce the average hospital stay by 3.5 days yet maintain quality.[4]

Table 8-4 An Example Showing the Lack of a Standard Relationship between Resources Used and Health Outcomes Achieved

	North Dakota	*Michigan*
1989 State Health Rank	2.0	48.0
Low Birth Weight Babies per 100 Live Births	4.9	6.9
Cancer per 100,000 Population	408.0	454.0
Number of MDs per 100,000 population (1986)	15.7	20.8
Number of Employees per 100 Hospital Patients (1986)	335.0	554.0

Sources: "1989 NWNL State Health Rankings," *Medical Benefits*, November 15, 1989, p. 10; *Health United States 1988*, pp. 130, 146.

The Cleveland medical community and business community have jointly embarked on a brave new venture. After the hospitals and doctors specify measures of the progress patients should have after a hospital stay, the hospitals will be ranked on the basis of these measures in fields like cardiology and urology. Participating businesses will then subsidize their employees' selection of the higher-quality facilities.[5]

MediQual Systems, a Massachusetts company, has a well-developed system for measuring the predicted and actual rates of hospital illness and death associated with a given diagnosis (adjusted for the severity of the patients' illness). As shown in Table 8-5, many of the Western Pennsylvania hospitals with the highest prices also experienced higher than expected morbidity and mortality rates. Although these data are sparse, and were collected over only a short period of time, additional data of this kind will ultimately prove illuminating. For example, if the patterns shown in Table 8-5 persist, both patients and physicians will grow leery of hospitals with high price and high morbidity and mortality rates.

Organizations serving new consumers should translate consumer wishes into measurable standards. For example, an organization that provides convenient care must articulate the standards with which convenience will be measured, like the length of wait before a patient is seen. Consumer surveys are invaluable sources of this information. Johns Hopkins Health System in Baltimore, Maryland, is polling 500 inpatients and 2,700 outpatients about their satisfaction with services and personnel at the hospital.[6] Savvy organizations find that market surveys can do double duty because they also enable competitive comparisons. One HMO, for example, discovered that its disenrollment rate—the quit rate of its enrollees—was 25 percent, which compared poorly with 11 percent for a traditional insurance plan and 18 percent for comparable HMOs in its market. Its consumer surveys revealed the reason: The HMO scored lower on the key dimensions of choice, control, and convenience than most of its competitors.

Motivation

Motivating personnel to reduce health care costs is difficult. Some health care firms utilize mechanistic but nevertheless effective motivational devices. U.S. Health Care, for example, pays its primary physicians a fixed price per patient. If their actual expenses are below this fixed price, they share in the resulting profits; if above, they share in the loss. Small wonder that U.S. Health Care has very low costs. But these devices have two drawbacks. Some physicians are understandably reluctant to see U.S. Health Care patients, and some patients are concerned about the level of care they receive with such a motivational system in force. To compensate, the company has installed measures to ensure that its physicians and hospitals do not withhold needed care.

Herb Paris, CEO of Mid-Coast Health Services in Brunswick, Maine, motivated his employees through education. Paris's explanation of why the hospital had to become the lowest-cost provider in the area proved so persuasive that his staff was motivated to achieve this goal. When he asked for their help in lowering costs, employees came up with an idea: They would use their vacation days when the hospital had low occupancy rather than on a set schedule. The hospital's staffing thus varies directly with its occupancy, reducing the need to hire costly part-time people as well as the expense of idle staff.

Paris achieved a remarkable change; he converted fixed costs to variable ones. The change was accomplished by convincing employees that their activities contributed directly to the greater good of the hospital. Paris overcame the traditional divergence between "them" and "us." To reinforce this feeling, Paris provides liberal employee benefits. His reason? "In this way, I show that I care about each one of them as a whole person, not just as an employee."

NOTES

1. "Minnesota Blue Cross First To Link Outcomes to Payments," *Report on Medical Guidelines & Outcomes Research*, November 1, 1990, 1.

Table 8-5 Actual and Expected Bacteria in Blood for 17 Hospitals over 6 Months in the Harrisburg, Pennsylvania, Area

Hospital	Number of Patients	Average Stay (Days)	Average Admission Severity Score	Age 65 and Over (%)	Deaths		Medically Unstable during First Week (Major Morbidity)		Averge Charge ($)
					Actual Number	Expected Number	Actual Number	Expected Number	
Carlisle Hospital	39	7.8	2.5	82.1	8	8.97	1	2.39	$ 5,899
Chambersburg Hospital	39	9.4	2.4	69.2	5	7.30	1	2.15	5,203
Community Gen Osteo	48	8.8	2.7	79.2	18	13.61	5	3.38	8,756
Community Hosp. of Lancaster	9	6.3	2.3	55.6	1	1.88	1	0.41	5,289
Ephrata Community Hospital	14	9.1	2.8	100.0	2	3.98	0	1.18	5,968
Gettysburg Hospital	34	9.8	2.5	76.5	3	6.74	3	1.95	6,436
Good Samaritan Hosp./Lebanon	46	8.6	2.6	87.0	15	12.78	1	2.81	7,878
Hanover General Hospital	32	8.5	2.2	65.6	5	4.44	2	1.32	4,330
Harrisburg Hospital	66	10.3	2.6	84.8	21	16.15	9	4.42	10,655
Holy Spirit Hospital	78	10.3	2.4	71.8	15	15.66	7	4.80	7,339
JC Blair Memorial Hospital	23	7.6	2.1	60.9	3	3.61	1	0.95	5,826
Lancaster General Hospital	76	9.1	2.5	73.7	18	15.77	2	4.42	6,279
Memorial Hospital of York	26	7.9	2.6	53.8	4	6.12	1	1.55	7,791
Polyclinic Medical Center	45	7.7	2.5	80.0	10	9.75	4	2.67	7,413
Saint Joseph's of Lancaster	46	10.3	2.6	65.2	6	8.88	3	2.94	9,061
University Hosp. of Hershey	46	8.8	2.7	43.5	9	10.00	5	2.88	9,093
York Hospital	90	9.5	2.4	70.0	12	16.45	6	4.87	5,759
REGION 5	757	9.1	2.5						7,205

Sources: Reprinted with permission from *Hospital Effectiveness Report* by Pennsylvania Health Care Cost Containment Council, p. 73, © 1991.

2. John Wennberg and Alan Gittelsohn, "Variations in the Medical Care among Small Areas," *Scientific American*, April 1982, 120.

3. Ernst and Young, "NY Hospitals Gamble with Quality Incentive Pool," *Health Care Briefing*, January 1990, 11, 12.

4. Sharon McEachern, "All Eyes on Medical Outcomes," *HealthWeek*, February 26, 1990, 28, 33.

5. Ron Winslow, "Cleveland Hospitals To Get Quality Checkup," *Wall Street Journal*, December 8, 1989, B1.

6. Ernest and Young, "Satisfaction Data," *Health Care Briefing*, January 1990, 11.

SUGGESTED READING

Managerial Control

Financial Management Handbook. 3d ed. Brookfield, Vt.: Gower, 1988.

Gotthilf, Daniel L. *Treasurer's and Controller's Desk Book*. Englewood Cliffs, N.J.: Prentice-Hall, 1977.

Herzlinger, Regina E., and Denise Nitterhouse. *Financial Accounting and Managerial Control in Nonprofit Organizations*. Cincinnati, Ohio: South-Western Publishing, 1991.

Merchant, Kenneth A. *Control in Business Organizations*. Boston: Pitman, 1985.

Sathe, Vijay. *Controller Involvement in Management*. Englewood Cliffs, N.J.: Prentice-Hall, 1982.

Vancil, Richard F. *Financial Executive's Handbook*. Homewood, Ill.: Dow Jones-Irwin, 1970.

Van Horne, James C. *Fundamentals of Financial Management*. 7th ed. Englewood Cliffs, N.J.: Prentice-Hall, 1989.

Accounting Handbooks

Ameiss, A.P., and N.A. Kargas. *Accountant's Desk Handbook*. 3d ed. Englewood Cliffs, N.J.: Prentice-Hall, 1988.

Arkin, H. *Handbook of Sampling for Auditing and Accounting*. 3d ed. New York: McGraw-Hill, 1984.

Black, H.A., and J.D. Edwards. *The Managerial and Cost Accountant's Handbook*. Homewood, Ill.: Dow Jones-Irwin, 1979.

Blensly, D.L., and T.M. Plank. *Accounting Desk Book*. 9th ed. Englewood Cliffs, N.J.: Prentice-Hall, 1989.

Bullock, J., eds. *Accountants' Cost Handbook: A Guide to Management Accounting*. 3d ed. New York: Wiley, 1983.

Kay, R.S., and D.G. Searfoss. *Handbook of Accounting and Auditing*. Boston: Warren, Gorham and Lamont, 1989. (See also the annual cumulative supplement *Update*.)

Pescow, J.K., ed. *Accountant's Encyclopedia, Revised*. 2 vols. Englewood Cliffs, N.J.: Prentice-Hall, 1981.

9

Human Resource Mangement

Human resource management involves recruiting and developing appropriate staff, recognizing and rewarding their efforts, and creating an organizational structure consistent with the purposes of the venture and the needs of its employees.

Human resource management is most important and challenging in organizations that cater to new health care consumers. In such ventures, health care professionals trained in providing traditional therapy must learn to provide health promotion for activist health care consumers; professionals trained to service a passive, horizontal patient must be reoriented to deal with the needs of the vertical, mobile one; and medical personnel trained to provide the highest quality medical care as defined by their profession must learn to be responsive to their patients' definition of quality as well.

Human resource management issues are important in new technology organizations as well. The main challenge is to generate original, useful research by recruiting visionary scientists and providing the organizational structure, recognition, and rewards that motivate stellar performance. This challenge is immense. Pharmaceutical company research spending surged to over $19 billion in 1990, spurred by the need to replace the large number of drugs that were losing patent protection. However, in the opinion of the Senate Special Committee on Aging, "the bulk of research and development produces insignificant new compounds that add little or nothing to drug therapies already marketed."[1]

ORGANIZATIONAL STRUCTURE

Most health care ventures are organized by the functional specialties of the relevant professionals rather than by customer needs. Hospitals, for example, are organized into departments of surgery, medicine, radiology, physical therapy, and a laboratory. No one of these departments can meet the needs of the patient with a problem like back pain. Instead, the patient must integrate the services of the surgeon to be found in the department of surgery; the neurologist to be found in the medical department; the radiologist (who will take films of the patient's back); the laboratory, (which will analyze bodily tissues and fluids); and various sources of physical therapy.

Organizations that cater to new consumers should provide a different kind of organizational structure—one focused on the patient, the user of the services, rather than on the supplier.

Some health service–providing organizations have already fashioned this structure. For example, the Shouldice Hospital in Toronto is devoted solely to providing hernial surgery. It does so in order to provide the highest quality of care. The Shouldice Hospital is organized by the needs of its patients rather than by the needs of its professionals.

Pharmaceutical companies have also experimented with a host of organizational structures to foster the creativity they need. Merck, one of the most successful, is organized by departments that are divided into various subgroups, such as chemistry or microbiology, and project teams with specific product development goals. One of these project teams created Mevacor, a radical new drug to lower cholesterol.

Merck's project teams have no budget or direct authority. Instead, money and time are granted by the different subgroups whose members make up the project team. This system encourages collegiality and unity of purpose, creating product champions among the project's sponsors. As a product is developed, the project team meets changing needs by adding more people or people from new departments. Informal or underground projects are tolerated, even encouraged.[2]

Abbott, another large pharmaceutical company, has taken a similar approach, designating "venture heads" with complete responsibility for a project's success or failure. As the manager of its pharmaceutical division explained,

> One of the industry challenges is R & D productivity. Traditionally, companies have taken a functional approach so no one person is responsible for the product. With no product "ownership" you have a relay race in the dark. You run the race very fast and hard and hope someone comes along and picks up the baton. But you never know for sure when or how long it takes for that baton to be picked up. There's no sense that "this is mine and I'm going to make it happen."
>
> We had the functional system and our products were taking too long. We didn't find many people who were very excited about the individual projects. So we evolved the venture system—we picked some of our best people and made them venture heads with complete responsibility for everything that happens [in a particular product line].
>
> They have their own budget and people report directly to them. Since we installed [the system] in January 1987, we've found that it's brought a real rejuvenation of the entrepreneurial spirit with R & D.
>
> As an example, we filed NDAs for clarithromycin and temafloxacin [two new antibiotics]. Temafloxacin went through clinical trials in 23 months. We feel that's tangible evidence of a highly successful system.[3]

Johnson & Johnson presents yet another model of organizational structure. Widely hailed for its excellent record of acquisition in the period 1950 to 1986, Johnson & Johnson entered 77 new businesses, mostly by acquisition, 18 of which were in entirely new fields. Of acquisitions made by 1980, only 17 percent had been divested by 1986, giving it one of the best retention records among all companies.[4]

This remarkable record owes a great deal to Johnson & Johnson's organizational structure. In 1988 it was a conglomerate of more than 150 companies worldwide devoted mostly to health care. While the parent company's 1986 sales exceeded $7 billion, many of its units had sales of less than $100 million. Each is run as a semi-independent unit with a complete functional staff: There are 25 chief financial officers in the United States alone. This decentralization is central to Johnson & Johnson's philosophy. It allows each unit to focus on the needs of its own end users and prevents senior staff from making decisions about areas in which they have no experience.

RECRUITING

The Shouldice Hospital reinforces its patient focus by recruiting surgeons who are excited, not bored, by the prospect of performing the same operation over and over again. These surgeons are like expert violin makers—they are challenged to achieve perfection in the process of building the same instrument again and again. The Shouldice surgeons find their work continually interesting. "Each hernia is different," they say. They aim for consistency. "Excellent is the enemy of good," notes one. Shouldice wisely recruits surgeons who are not only medically competent but also psychologically attuned to the purposes of the hospital.

The psychological traits of employees should be consistent with the needs of the job. Because its patients primarily interact with the drivers who deliver their solutions, New England Critical Care takes care to recruit only smiling, extroverted people for the job. Dr. Art Stratton, chief executive officer (CEO) of Mariner Health Care of Massachusetts, looks for one key piece of evidence when he recruits nursing home administrators: "I want people who will take it personal." Stratton selects people who identify so closely with the company's goals that, if they fail to achieve them, they blame themselves for the failure.

Stratton seeks other traits as well for his decentralized company. For example, he recruits only experienced managers to run his nursing homes.

> Health care is a local business, dependent on a local network. Somebody who is just out of school does not have this network. My local administrator is the key to my success. The traditional model of putting new graduates in charge of nursing homes and helping them with a superlative corporate staff is not for me. My superlative people are placed in charge of nursing homes, not in the corporate office.

How are superlative employees found? Recruiting ingenuity is important. For example, some people are happy to work off-peak hours because family or other responsibilities keep them at home during regular working hours. Others with heavy family responsibilities will select companies that offer convenient access to day care and shopping resources. An outstanding physician recruiter notes that "the

spouse is key." One CEO placed a single mother with two children in charge of delineating the criteria for new locations. He thought that she could specify better than most the characteristics of a location that could draw people like her to work for his company. As a reward, he appointed her as the manager of a new location.

TRAINING AND DEVELOPMENT

Some managers feel that if they recruit the "right" person, everything else will take care of itself. This feeling is most frequently evidenced in companies with substantial middle management turnover. In them, hapless middle managers are all-too-often blamed for the failures of top management. Although recruiting is important, it must be complemented by many other skills, including training and development.

Mission

The single most important objective of training is to cause employees to share top management's vision of the purpose of the new venture. After all, the venture was begun as a departure from traditional ways of doing things. Employees should understand how and why this venture differs from others.

Preparing a mission statement is useful (Exhibit 9-1). Explaining to employees what the mission statement means is also important. Mariner Health Care devotes at least one day a year for review of the mission in each of its nursing homes. Says its CEO,

> I want every employee, from the top to the bottom of the organization, to be able to tell me what the mission of the organization is. Only when they understand it, and believe it, will we be able to accomplish it.

Exhibit 9-1 Sample Mission Statement

Mariner Health Care
is committed to being the best provider of health care services in the Northeast. We will achieve this goal because we understand and are dedicated to the fundamental concept of health care: ONE PERSON CARING FOR ANOTHER.

Mariner believes that providing exceptional health care is a complex endeavor involving individual caregivers, families, professionals, educators, regulators, and business people. Mariner believes this endeavor requires our:

Commitment to Employees
Our employees are the direct providers of care. To provide exceptional health care, we realize a stable group of motivated, well-trained people is required.
—Mariner is committed to educating, retaining, and supporting employees.
—Mariner is devoted to creating an environment of openness that fosters communication among all employees.
—Mariner is committed to promoting teamwork and to recognizing and rewarding individual achievement.

Innovation in Health Care
Health care needs are constantly changing. We continuously seek better ways to provide health care services.
—Mariner is committed to education in the health care industry; for our employees and all health care professionals.
—Mariner is dedicated to redefining the health care system to improve the delivery of services to society.
—Mariner is devoted to encouraging employees to seek creative solutions in all aspects of their work.

Leadership in the Community
Health care is delivered by a network of local providers. To provide exceptional health care, we take a leadership role in each community we serve.
—Mariner is dedicated to being a key member of the local health care network.
—Mariner is committed to working closely with all members of the community in order to enhance our services.
—Mariner is dedicated to serving the community by being an active resource for health care information and guidance.

Source: Courtesy of Mariner Health Care.

Training

The absence of appropriate training can be devastating. Many health clubs, for example, suffer from an inability to retain a sufficient number of customers. The reason is simple: Although the instructors may be Adonises with 19-inch necks or Venuses with 19-inch waists, they have rarely been trained to empathize with and motivate their flaccid students. Without such training, they cannot change their students' behavior—other than to motivate them to walk out the door.

Training should focus on the substance and process of the job. For example, a nursing home that provides care for patients who are more seriously sick than the norm trains its nurses in the care appropriate to the patients' needs. The training accomplishes two goals. It not only prepares the nurses to provide excellent care for medically challenging patients but also renews their intellectual interest in what can otherwise be perceived as a dull, repetitive job. Health Stop, a company with a number of ambulatory physician service centers, achieves the same results by inviting specialists to discuss their specialties or new treatments for common problems. The Health Stop physicians welcome these training sessions. They provide a forum for sharing observations, problems, and solutions. And because provision of training is a service that traditional stand-alone physician practices cannot emulate, it enhances the physicians' bond to the company.

New consumer companies find role-playing to be an effective training technique—one that causes providers to empathize with their patients. The reasons for lack of empathy are not always immediately apparent. One psychiatric hospital company, for example, encountered unexplained difficulty in treating women who had been sexually abused as children. The reason for the difficulty was discovered through a role-playing exercise, which revealed that the hospital's empathetic therapists were so repelled by the horrific experiences of their patients that they practiced classic avoidance behavior: They refused to hear what the patients were saying. Training and support of these staff members enabled them to better serve their clients.

Training should focus on work interactions as well as on the content of individual jobs. These interactions are central to the success of organizations that serve new health care consumers. Yet they may pose difficulties for health care professionals who are unfamiliar with and uncomfortable with these new relationships.

One new program was nearly undermined by strained work relationships. A birth center in Massachusetts was created to serve mothers who wanted to deliver their babies in a birth center rather than in a hospital. Although it was only a short distance away from a hospital, its parent organization, a deep personal chasm developed between the birth center and the hospital. The birth center was managed by a team of nurse-midwives who wanted a flat, egalitarian organizational structure, whereas the hospital wanted them to have a traditional hierarchical organizational structure, with one person clearly in charge of others. The hospital's request was antithetical to the nurse-

midwives' values. Their belief in personal empowerment permeated their thinking. It was as central to the birthing process they enabled as it was to their view of the appropriate organizational structure. An authoritarian organization in which some nurses supervised others was inconsistent with this belief.

The strain in the relationship between the hospital's management and the nurse-midwives caused difficulties. Bad feelings hardened. Finally, one of the birth center's founders and guiding spirits resigned and discussed her problems with the local newspapers. The resulting negative publicity might have been avoided with training that enabled each side to better understand the other's point of view.

Training and development can also help cost-controlling ventures. In the past, health service costs were constrained by paying poor wages and creating lower-responsibility, lower-salary positions. For example, as the wages of registered nurses rose, they were supplemented by licensed practical nurses, who in turn were supplemented by aides. But this technique is no longer feasible because of the changing role of women in the economy. The women who traditionally provided the bulk of the labor force in health service organizations—as nurses, technicians, dietitians, aides, housekeepers, and, increasingly, physicians—no longer feel constrained to work in the health service field, just as they no longer feel limited to a career as a teacher or secretary. The wide choice of career opportunities now available to women means that reducing costs by paying low wages is no longer feasible.

Nurses, for example, want significantly higher wages and working hours that are more convenient. They no longer readily accept assignment to the 3:00 P.M. to 11:00 P.M. shift or to the dreaded 11:00 P.M. to 7:00 A.M. shift. Although nurses recognize that these hours must be covered, they will refuse to make the sacrifice if they feel that they are stuck in a job with no career prospects, treated as second-class citizens, and paid low wages. Most other health service workers share these feelings: They insist that their work be valued both financially and managerially. If it is not, they will turn to other occupations. Increasingly, nurses are enrolled in my MBA class at the Harvard Business School; their presence there would have been unthinkable 20 years ago.

Some organizations deal with this situation openly and sincerely. Others may attempt to smother the problem in public relations. One hospital, for example, widely publicized a program that gave nurses primary responsibility for patient care and options for careers in nursing administration or research. As a tangible sign of its changed attitude, nurses are encouraged to enter their observations of a patient's condition alongside the physician's in the patient's medical record. In the past, nurses' observations were relegated, with appropriate symbolism, to the back of the record.

However, the program may lack substance. One physician seemed to miss the point completely when he complained about the nurses' entries in the medical record: "They write and write and write. They take up so much space and say so little."

Many hospitals have more straightforward responses. For example, when the nurses in one hospital's neonatal intensive care unit voiced concern about having to tie down the limbs of premature infants so that they would not dislodge the feeding and ventilating tubes that kept them alive, management listened and responded. It provided a research budget to enable the nurses to develop an environment in which the infants could thrive without the discomfort of being tied down. The nurses designed a new type of incubator, similar to a womb, in which the infants rested so comfortably that they no longer were inclined to thrash around. As a result, their limbs could be left untied without the danger of their dislodging the vital tubes.

Mariner Health Care developed an interesting approach toward recruiting and training nurses to work with the elderly. Some nursing students view work in long-term care facilities as requiring minimal skills and providing little satisfaction because elderly patients rarely get well. Mariner designed a unique training program that exposes nursing students to the wide variety of skills needed to provide long-term care. The training takes place in a new long-term care community in which nurses interact with healthy as well as sick elderly people. The nursing center is located on an elderly housing campus, close to the town's senior center, so students can work with the well elderly. Through these linkages, students come to understand the varied and ever-changing needs of the elderly, how to coordinate care as patient needs change, and the continuum of services available to the elderly.[5]

Training Program Participants

Participation in training programs is sometimes limited to managerial and professional employees. But in service-providing organizations, every employee in contact with a patient plays a major role and should be trained to fulfill it.

A company that provides chronic care to head trauma victims learned a dramatic lesson about the important role played by low-level employees. The company spends about $300 a day on rehabilitative services for patients with cognitive, emotional, and physical disabilities incurred through head injuries. One of their patients was a normal young boy who appeared to be mildly retarded as he was recovering from a head injury sustained while diving. The boy was occasionally taken home on weekends by a company driver. On one trip, the driver could not find the boy's home. When the boy pointed out the correct way, the exasperated driver replied, "You do not know anything. You are too stupid." After the child finally arrived home and told his concerned mother about the incident, she promptly withdrew him from the center.

The center's director feared that the boy's rehabilitation would be severely compromised by this change. He called the mother and asked her if she wanted to be present when he fired the driver on Monday morning. He also invited her to the new training program he had implemented for the company's drivers. She not only came to these sessions but also re-enrolled her child in the rehabilitation center.

Mentorship

Mentorship plays an important role in the creation of new organizations. It is particularly important in organizations with rigid hierarchies and a well-established routine. In these organizations, administrative or professional innovators may find a cold reception for new ideas. Indeed, some of the scientists who left academic institutions to create new technology companies did so with a sigh of relief; they were glad to escape what they perceived as bureaucratic, political, and sometimes professionally destructive environments. Well-established mentors can help upstart innovators wend their way through this jungle.

(Do not misunderstand my point here. This is not a pop psychology discourse on the wonders of mentorship but a realistic appraisal of the difficulties of creating new ventures in bureaucratic organizations. While mentors are important, as I will shortly illustrate, they do not guarantee success.)

Carl Walter, an eminent surgeon who cofounded the famed Fenwal blood products company, writes touchingly of his mentor, "Coach" Zollinger, and of the important role he played in the career of the iconoclastic Dr. Walter. In one case, when young Walter discovered that a hospital's drinking water system and sewage system were linked, his discovery fell on deaf ears. He dramatized the point by placing blue dye in the container into which bed pan contents were emptied. When the blue dye showed up in the water fountains, Dr. Walter had demonstrated his case—but too vividly. The hospital's top staff was outraged. The source of the outrage? Dr. Walter's all-too-public demonstration of the problem. Fortunately, Coach Zollinger saved the messenger who brought the bad news. Without his intervention, Dr. Walter's subsequently brilliant career in the same hospital could well have come to a premature end.[6]

RECOGNITION AND REWARD

Recognizing and rewarding outstanding employees is key to the success of all new health care ventures. But this is easier said than done.

Top managers in large or decentralized organizations find it difficult to recognize the contribution of many employees because their work is so far removed from the purview of top management. To remedy this problem, Erie Chapman, the creative CEO of the Riverside Methodist Hospital in Columbus, Ohio, spends one day a month in the role of a staff member of the hospital, such as an orderly or an x-ray technician. Although he does not practice medicine while role-playing, he does discover what the job consists of and the frustrations and rewards encountered. (Among other observations, Chapman noted the profound effects of a uniform on relationships. Some of his colleagues did not recognize him when he was dressed in an orderly's garb.) After he has finished role-playing, Chapman shares his discoveries with the other staff members of the hospital and, with their participation, begins to remedy any problems he observed.

Texas Instruments recognizes scientific contributions as well as managerial ones. Its scientists may choose to pursue a scientific or a managerial career. Both are equally honored. Texas Instruments' chief scientist is on par with the company's top management. To recognize scientific work and to ensure that it is pragmatic, Merck grants its scientists stock option when they meet certain drug development deadlines.

Rewards can take many forms. The most successful are those that are clearly tied to the individual's accomplishments and that are granted in a way that develops a sense of ownership. Health Stop "sold" some centers to the physicians practicing there and provided the financing. In many of the "owned" practices, productivity and patient satisfaction increased substantially. Physicians who are "owners" do not need to be urged to delegate their work or to check on how their patients are faring. Ownership provided them with the impetus to do so automatically. These newly configured Health Stop offices benefit from a clear division of responsibility. Headquarters provides administrative support (it performs the billing, collection, quality control, hiring, and legal functions) and the local health care practitioners do what they are most capable of doing: Providing high-quality yet efficient health care services.

Medical Care International, a Texas-based company that runs ambulatory surgical care centers, rewards the nurses who serve as the centers' administrators with bonuses as large as 50 percent of their salaries. The administrator's time- and performance-vested bonus is based on the center's operating income. No wonder the company enjoys high profits, growth, and quality. It also has one of the best collection rates in the industry. Its secret? Collections are done at each local office rather than centrally, and the quicker the collections, the higher the administrator's bonus.

But designing an effective and fair compensation system is often not easy. The range of factors to be considered is illustrated by Boston Sobriety Development's design of an incentive system to motivate the sales-people who marketed its substance abuse therapy services. One requirement was the need to differentiate the sales potential of the different regions in which the company operated. Salespeople who worked in easy areas, in which the concept of addiction recovery was well accepted and little competition existed, were to be rewarded differently from those in tough-to-sell areas with low acceptance of the need for treatment of addiction or with fierce competition. A good system would recognize that the high-volume salesperson in the first area had an easier job than the high-volume salesperson in the second.

Another consideration was of motivating the salespeople to spend enough in selling expenses so they were certain of getting sales but not so much that they dissipated the company's profit from the sales they generated. A third factor involved the rate at which the incentive compensation was paid to the salesperson: The company needed a "payout" rate that would motivate the salespeople to remain with the company by deferring payment to future years but yet would also provide them with a reasonable cash flow. Finally, the amount of incentive compensation had to be sufficiently large so that no other organization would easily match it but not unnecessarily large.

Complicating the design of the system was the fact that the salespeople in this organization were all recovering drug addicts. (See Case Study 2 for further discussion.)

New England Critical Care provides a good example of recognition and reward with resources other than money. Although the company's salaries are competitive, the true rewards are psychic ones. Explains CEO Patrick Smith,

> People who want to work in health care are altruistic. If you create the right environment for them, they will kill themselves for the company. The right environment recognizes and rewards their effort. For example, we have an "entrepreneur of the year" contest for the employee with the most innovative ideas. I send a note or a gift even to the losers. We have an entrepreneurial climate here. Naysayers have a low profile. Only the risk-takers get our rewards. As a result, I have a constant flow of good ideas for improving our services.

NOTES

1. Senate Special Committee on Aging, *Prescription Drug Prices*, Serial No. 101-D (Washington, D.C.: U.S. Government Printing Office, August 1989), 5.

2. Brandon Fradd and Regina E. Herzlinger, "Note on the Pharmaceutical Industry," 9-189-076 (Boston: Harvard University, 1989), 30.

3. Karen Southwick, "Paul Clark, Insider Interview," *HealthWeek*, February 26, 1990, 20.

4. Fradd and Herzlinger, "Note on the Pharmaceutical Industry," 33.

5. Sandra Lawson, Vice President, Mariner Health Care, "Mansfield Nursing and Rehabilitation Center Project Summary," private correspondence, 114–15.

6. Carl W. Walter, "Coach Zollinger," *American Journal of Surgery* (1986): 730–32.

SUGGESTED READING

Argyris, Chris. *Strategy, Change, and Defensive Routines.* Boston: Pittman, 1985.

Bernstein, Paula. *Family Ties, Corporate Bonds*. New York: Doubleday, 1985.

Block, Peter. *The Empowered Manager*. San Francisco: Jossey-Bass, 1987.

Bowditch, James L. *A Primer on Organizational Behavior*. 2d ed. New York: Wiley, 1990.

Child, John. *Organization: A Guide to Problems and Practice*. 2d ed. New York: Harper & Row, 1984.

Davis, Keith. *Human Behavior at Work*. 8th ed. New York: McGraw-Hill, 1989.

Hampton, David R. *Organizational Behavior and the Practice of Management*. 5th ed. Glenview, Ill.: Scott, Foresman, 1987.

Handbook of Organizational Behavior. Englewood Cliffs, N.J.: Prentice-Hall, 1987.

Handbook of Organizational Behavior Management. New York: Wiley, 1982.

Huse, Edgar F. *Organization Development and Change*. 3d ed. Minneapolis, Minn.: West Publishing Company, 1985.

Kets De Vries, Manfred F.R. *The Neurotic Organization*. San Francisco: Jossey-Bass, 1984.

Kotter, John P. *Organization*. 2d ed. Homewood, Ill.: Richard D. Irwin, 1986.

Lau, James Brownlee. *Behavior in Organizations*. 4th ed. Homewood, Ill.: Richard D. Irwin, 1988.

Lauffer, Armand. *Careers, Colleagues, and Conflicts*. Beverly Hills: Sage Publications, 1985.

Lawrence, Paul Roger, and Jay William Lorsch, *Organization and Environment*. Rev. ed. Boston: Harvard Business School Press, 1986.

Lee, Robert Arthur. *Organizational Behaviour*. Brookfield, Vt.: Brookfield Publishing Company, 1985.

Lewis, Phillip V. *Organizational Communication: The Essence of Effective Management*. 3d ed. New York: Wiley, 1987.

Luthans, Fred. *Organizational Behavior Modification and Beyond*. Glenview, Ill.: Scott, Foresman, 1985.

McGregor, Douglas Murray. *The Professional Manager*. New York: McGraw-Hill, 1967.

Mangham, I.L. *Power and Performance in Organizations*. New York: Blackwell, 1986.

Mills, Daniel Quinn. *Labor-Management Relations*. 4th ed. New York: McGraw-Hill, 1989.

Organ, Dennis W. *Organizational Behavior*. 3d ed. Plano, Tx.: Business Publications, 1986.

Perrow, Charles. *Complex Organizations*. 3d ed. New York: Random House, 1986.

Ritti, Richard R. *The Ropes To Skip and the Ropes To Know: Studies in Organizational Behavior*. 3d ed. New York: Wiley, 1987.

Roethlisberger, Fritz Jules. *Man-In-Organization*. Cambridge, Mass.: Harvard University Press, 1968.

Sims, Henry P. *The Thinking Organization*. San Francisco: Jossey-Bass, 1986.

Wexley, Kenneth N. *Organizational Behavior and Personnel Psychology*. Rev ed. Homewood, Ill.: Richard D. Irwin, 1984.

Zaleznik, Abraham. *The Motivation, Productivity and Satisfaction of Workers*. Boston: Harvard University, Graduate School of Business Administration, 1958.

10

Operations Management and Leadership Philosophy

OPERATIONS MANAGEMENT

Operations management creates the services and products promised by a new venture. Although it is important for all kinds of new ventures, it is crucial for those that aim to serve new health care consumers. Excellent operations management can transform these ventures from pedestrian businesses to worldclass competitors—or so argue Richard B. Chase and Robert H. Hayes in a provocative article.[1]

Chase and Hayes delineate four stages in the life of a service organization. In the first stage, the organization survives by its mere presence and location, like a corner clothing store. In the second, value is added by a chain operation, like a department store chain. In the third, strengths in operations management create great customer values, like the department store Nordstrom's, which is reknowned for the excellence of its customer service. In the fourth stage, operations management enables the firm to become a worldclass competitor. How is this transformation managed? Chase and Hayes provide an outline of the process (Table 10-1). Firms that understand their customers and use both workers and managers to satisfy these customer needs reach the lauded stage 4.

How do health care providers presently rate? For hospitals, the ratings are not high. Consumers rate hospitals as one of the worst values for the money, ranked even below lawyers or automobile repair fees.[2] The excerpt below, which describes the experiences of W. Edwards Deming, widely considered to be the leading authority on quality, during a 1987 hospital stay, helps to explain why:

> Well here I am, flat on my back literally and in other ways, right ankle resting on three pillows.
>
> My nurse of the moment (RN [registered nurse]) came in at about one o'clock to wrap my leg from the knee down in a hot towel and insulator. As a first step, she turned on the hot water in the wash bowl, as she needed hot water for the towel; departed. "I'll be right back...." Anyway, a social worker dropped in about a half hour later. I asked her if she would mind turning off the hot water to avoid more waste of water and energy. She did. In about half an hour, the nurse came back to put on the towel, but she needed hot water, therefore turned on the hot water. This time she actually returned and completed the task.

Table 10-1 Four Stages of Service Firm Competitiveness

Stage	Customer	Work Force	First-Line Management
1	Satisfy an unspecified customer at minimum cost	Negative constraint	Controls workers
2	A market segment whose basic needs are understood	Efficient resource; disciplined (follows procedures)	Controls the process
3	A collection of individuals whose variation in needs is understood	Adaptive—permitted to select among alternative procedures	Listens to customers; coach and facilitator for workers
4	A source of stimulation, ideas, and opportunity	Innovators—create procedures	Listened to by top management as a source of new ideas; mentors workers to enhance their career growth

Source: Richard B. Chase and Robert H. Hays, "Operations Strategy for Service Firms," Boston, Mass., Harvard Business School, Working Paper, abridged version of Exhibit 3, p. 19.

Dr. Sch. ordered from the drug store (in the hospital) a paste for the itch that had set in in Minneapolis. The drug store was out of one of the ingredients: must order it from the wholesaler, and cannot make it up till Monday, as this is Saturday, no delivery from the wholesaler till Monday. I need it tonight. On prodding from Dr. Sch. the drug store sent someone out to another drug store to fetch the missing ingredient. The paste came up that evening.

Unbelievable: the same scenario took place some days later. My nurse of the afternoon ordered from the drug store a refill for the paste for itch. No problem, except that there would be a delay, as (again) the drug store would have to order from the wholesaler one of the ingredients. Tomorrow will be Saturday, next day Sunday; Monday they would have it. I hope to be on the way out by then. Meanwhile, they would send up a substitute which would be in the form of a lotion, not paste. Actually, I'd prefer the lotion, but the paste came too, same evening. The drug store had again, on Dr.

Sch.'s prodding, sent out for the missing ingredient.

On another day, my nurse of the moment (RN) came in three times between 8:30 and 10:00 to say that she would be right back to make my bed. I offered to get out of it so that she could make it up straightaway, but she may not have heard me. Each time, "I'll be right back." Anyhow, near noon she came and actually did the job. Of course, I'll live, bed made or no.

I wonder why is a registered nurse making beds? It seems to me that making beds is not good use of her time. Her education and skill could be put to better use, so it seems to me. Are there not helpers to do this kind of work? Maybe there are good reasons for what I don't understand.

All the while, nurses are on a dog-trot, panting for breath, working at top speed, losing time, not for start-up, but for no start.

The man that designed the shower had obviously never used one. The shower head, when not held by the hand, can only dangle and flood the floor. There is a tiny shelf in the shower only big enough to hold a wafer of soap. There is only one bar to hold on to. Use of this shower would be a risky business without a friend close by for rescue. Somebody sold somebody a bill of goods.

Intravenous diffusion due at 6:00. The nurse came at 5:05 to insert the needle into the more or less permanent spigot in my left arm, known as a Heparin Lock, departed. The infusion would run around 90 minutes. Meanwhile, some time after she left, in reaching for something on the shelf, I reached too far and pulled the needle out of the Heparin Lock. The nurse, when she came in around 6:00 saw what had happened; was startled, but said not a word; merely carried everything away, liquid and tube. I supposed that she would return and start over. Time went on; no return.

At 8:30 I reported to Meg, head nurse in charge on the shift, that the intravenous diffusion due at 6:00 had not been given. It was important to me, and important to Dr. D., else why bother with it? Her first impulse was to call (at home and maybe asleep) the nurse that left the job undone. It seemed to me I told her, that it matters not what the nurse might say: I know what happened, and what did not. I called Dr. Sch. His secretary said that she would notify him at once and that he would call Dr. D.

The infusion came straightaway. The head nurse returned to say that the nurse that was to give the infusion at 6:00 had recorded the infusion as given. It is possible that she recorded it in advance, with the intention to give it, and did not correct the record. Is this the regular procedure, to record intention? Who would know?

An unsuspecting physician, looking at the record for his patient, would assume that the infusion had been given, and could draw wrong inferences about how the patient has been doing on the drug. In my case, as it turned out, no harm. But how would he know? A nurse, a physician, has a right to suppose that the medication was delivered as ordered and as recorded.

Dr. Sch. assured me that he is running down this lapse in every detail, and that nothing like it will ever happen again here—the usual supposition, actual only working on a defect, not its cause.

Is it regular procedure in a hospital for a nurse to indicate on her record before she does it, that she has done it? Would she go back and change the record if she did not do it? Why should she? Who would know?

What is the purpose of the record? To inform the physician about intentions, or to tell him what happened?

A little figuring told me that insertion of the needle at 5:05 for infusion to start at 6:00 (if she came back on time) would tie the patient in bed for over $2^1/_2$ hours, the first hour tied in bed, then $1^1/_2$ hours for the infusion, plus time added for the nurse to come to take the needle out of the Heparin Lock, and take the whole thing away. This long time in bed, with $^3/_4$ cup of liquid infused, could create great discomfort for a patient.

My nurse of the moment put on a hot towel this afternoon. "I'll be back in 20 minutes, and if I don't come, please ring." Sixty-five minutes later I pressed the button. A helper came in; explained to me that this was not her kind of job, so she canceled the light for the nurse, and went off. Thirty minutes later I rang again for the nurse. The same helper came and observed again that the job was not in her line of duty, so again she canceled the light and went off. The solution was simple, for me, merely discard the towel and insulation myself, with the rules or against the rules. The same event recurred another day.

This experience leads to questions. Why should an aide, unable to perform the task, cancel the light? The nurse on duty for that night would not know that her patient needed a nurse. What if a nurse were suddenly vital to a patient? If he were in a single room, he would be left stranded. His nurse would not know that he had rung for her. In a room with two patients, the other one might be able to fetch a nurse. Moral, if you are acutely ill, don't go into a private room unless you have your own private nurse on duty at all times.

Shirley, a registered nurse, came to see me as a friend. She made the remark that a Heparin Lock ought to be examined at the end of 48 hours and maybe changed. It had now been in eight days. I asked later one of the nurses how long it should stay in one place. A nurse came and changed it from left arm to right arm.

What is the moral of all this? What have we learned? One answer: The Superintendent of the hospital needs to learn something about supervision. Only he can make the changes in procedure and responsibility that are required.

Talks between physicians and nurses, even with the head nurse, accomplish nothing. The same problems that I have noted will continue. A physician cannot change the system. A head nurse cannot change the system. Meanwhile who would know? To work harder will not solve the problem. The nurses couldn't work any harder.[3]

How can operations management improve these kinds of problems? The following four steps are key, according to Joe Flower:

1. Define quality from the customers' point of view.
2. Discover how you compare to your competitors in these measures of quality.
3. Define the changes needed in operations management so that the desired quality can be achieved.
4. Form teams to ensure that the desired changes are implemented.[4]

What are the unique tools of operations management that enable these changes to be implemented? There are three. Operations management depends on designing a *production process* that delivers high-quality, low-cost goods and services; deciding on the *size* of the production system; and delineating whether production will be conducted in house or purchased (the so-called *make or buy* decision). (These are illustrated in Case Study 7).

DESIGNING A PRODUCTION PROCESS

Patient Involvement

Designing a production process for a new venture requires considerable ingenuity, as is illustrated by Dr. Shouldice's design for his hernia hospital. The doctor wanted to serve activist health care consumers with efficient, high-quality care. He accomplished his goal by means of a unique twist: Shouldice patients are part of the healing process rather than passive recipients of services. The patient prepares himself or herself for surgery by shaving the hair off the skin that is to be operated on; the patient steps off the operating table and is assisted in walking back to the room; and he or she eats meals and makes telephone calls in a central area because Shouldice provides neither meals nor phones in patient rooms.

The hospital's physical design enables all of these activities. It has very few stairs so that newly recovered patients can walk easily, and its grounds are gently sloped and beautifully landscaped to attract walkers. The result? Activist patients are satisfied, the operation heals more quickly, and costs are lowered because patients perform some of the work that is usually performed by paid personnel.

Other new ventures designed for health activists have also integrated patients as a key source of care in the production process. For example, the Planetree philosophy, as implemented in two California hospitals, encourages the education of patients, including providing access to their medical records; the involvement of patients, who are allowed, for example, to schedule their own meals and tests; and the leveraging of the nurses' efforts with those of family members or loved ones who live with the patients.[5]

The New York University Medical Center's Cooperative Care System has reduced the cost of hospital care and decreased the rate of rehospitalization with a variant of this self-care theme. Each of its 104 homelike rooms contains two beds—one for the patient, the other for a family member or friend. Both the patient and the roommate are trained by a multidisciplinary professional team.

Since the medical center's inception in 1981, it has treated 6,000 patients. Its patients are severely ill: 20 percent of the patient days are from those who have AIDS and another 20 percent who have cancer. Despite this, in 1988–1989 the unit had 43 percent fewer organizational personnel and a 38 percent lower operating budget than the usual hospital. The most telling indication of this program's success is that the rate of admission directly to the unit is much greater than predicted. Activist patients seek it out. Currently, 9 of every 10 of its patients have been admitted directly; 70 percent of them spend their entire hospital stay there.[6]

Production processes can be designed to increase the satisfaction of patients by involving them in more subtle ways. Even the best-designed process will, occasionally, cause patients to wait for services. Managing the wait so that it is perceived as tolerable is an operations management challenge. Some health care firms involve patients by keeping them informed of the length of the wait: Activist patients respond positively to information. Others use technology: They give the patients beepers that buzz when the service provider or product is ready. Shopping mall eyeglass stores that advertise immediate service have the best of two worlds when they give their customers beepers: more time in which to produce the eyeglasses and happier customers who have gained the convenience and mastery over time that they seek. Still other health care firms provide activist patients with the opportunity to obtain information and self-assessments of their health by providing them with interactive video systems that they can use while they wait.

Health care firms try to reinforce the positive impact of their services. A follow-up letter, a record of the patient's health status, a written reminder of the time for an annual physical, or even written information on recent research findings all serve to recall and make tangible the patient's feelings of having received excellent services.

Architectural Design

Sometimes the architectural design of a firm can also reinforce the operations management message. For example, the Comprehensive Cancer Center at Cedars-Sinai Hospital in Los Angeles is housed in a sleek and starkly modern building. The architecture is highly functional—simultaneously communal, with shared public spaces, and private, with private rooms in which chemotherapy is administered located directly off the communal space.[7] The purpose of this no-frills, functional architecture is to instill in patients confidence in their own ability to fight the disease, rather than to convey the false impression that the hospital is a cozy, sheltering environment.

Quality Control

Maintaining high-quality services is a critical component of operations management. The Allegheny General Hospital in Pittsburgh presents a good example of a well-balanced quality control system. The hospital's expenses are budgeted to increase by no more than the consumer price index, a rate of increase substantially below that of most hospitals. If actual expenses are less than those budgeted, the savings are shared half by employees and half by the community in the form of reduced charges. In the fiscal years 1987–1989, actual expenses were substantially below those budgeted. To forestall the possibility of quality sacrifices, these savings are not shared unless quality assurance guidelines are also met. Some of its measures of quality are presented in Table 10-2.

The quality of production is also critically important to medical technology firms. Production quality flaws occur in large and small companies alike. Abbott, a pharmaceutical giant, was prohibited from selling to federal agencies certain drugs manufactured in its North Chicago plant. The reason? "Serious violations" of the Food and Drug Administration's (FDA's) manufacturing quality standards.[8] The results can be devastating. After the FDA

Table 10-2 Allegheny General Hospital Quality Assurance Summary Report—Radiology Department

	11/89 to 1/90 (% compliance)	*2/90 to 4/90 (% compliance)*	*5/90 to 7/90 (% compliance)*
1. Eliminate unacceptable outcomes	99.07	98.90	99.54
2. Eliminate unacceptable excessive waiting time (15 minutes for general diagnostics and 20 minutes elsewhere)	91.03	88.18	85.12
3. Establish repeat rate of 5% or less	99.00	95.38	95.16
4. Compare and correlate findings of barium enemas with gastrointestinal studies and/or surgical pathology	100.00	100.00	100.00
5. Diagnostic report will be available within 28 hours of examination completion	81.60	94.83	81.00

Source: Reprinted with permission of Allegheny General Hospital.

closed three of its plants and seized its products for poor manufacturing quality, most major purchasers refused to buy LyphoMed's products. "Substandard product is a sin that pharmacists don't forget easily," noted one. LyphoMed staged an almost miraculous recovery. Its remedy? Hiring a manager who is legendary as an FDA fix-it person.[9]

DECIDING ON SIZE

Sizing is the awkward name given to the second important operations management activity—choosing the size of the proposed venture. If the size—as defined by the physical, human, and financial resources invested—is excessively large, resources will be wasted; if it is too small, customers will be turned away or kept waiting needlessly.

Although the size of the new venture usually depends on anticipated demand and supply, some organizations willingly forgo fulfillment of all the potential demand for their services if they feel that quality will be compromised. The Shouldice Hospital has refrained from expanding or franchising its operations because

Dr. Shouldice felt that he could not exercise sufficient quality control if the organization grew substantially larger.

In other cases, technology is a key consideration in the sizing decision. For example, the founders of a diagnostic center that uses a number of expensive radiology machines must decide how large each machine should be. In reaching their decision, they need to consider not only demand but also the dates and prices of the likely successors to the present machines. If an imminent new technology will render obsolete a presently available unit, then a small unit should be purchased now, because it will have to be scrapped when the new technology debuts. Similarly, if an existing technology is likely to become much cheaper in the future because of increased competition or production efficiency, a unit purchased now should be as small as possible.

The balance among different inputs to the production process is also an important factor in the sizing decision. For example, a decision about the size of an ambulatory physician center must be shaped by the fact that the doctors spend an average of 20 minutes with each patient whereas staff members spend 10 minutes.

In production terms, these resources are unbalanced. For every two patients seen by the doctor, the staff will be idle for 20 minutes. Over an 8-hour period, each doctor can see 24 patients, but the staff can handle twice this many. The sizing solution seems obvious: Either double the number of doctors or halve the staff. But if the center has been built with only one examination room, doubling the number of doctors is not possible. And if the staff consists of one nurse, halving his or her time is not feasible either.

What to do? In some unbalanced production processes, a mobile unit is helpful, since it can temporarily increase capacity. In others, the idle resource can be employed in meeting other responsibilities. For example, if the physicians can comfortably delegate some of their work to the nurses, a more balanced system will result.

"Scaling up" from one size of operations to the next is another sizing issue. It is particularly pertinent in companies that manufacture biotechnology and biomaterial products. Their production technology is very subtle—dependent on just the right mixture of nutrients, hosts, temperature, and atmosphere. Scaling up the production process may upset this subtle balance in ways difficult to predict. In these firms, the scaling up process must be treated as experimental so that large investments are not made in a process that does not work. Alternatively, the risk of scaling up can be contracted out to other companies whose sole purpose is the manufacture of biological substances.

INTERNAL PRODUCTION VERSUS EXTERNAL PURCHASING

Make versus buy, the issue of whether to produce in house or to buy products from outsiders, is the third critical operations management activity.

Making versus Buying from a Few Outside Suppliers

Buying products that are available from only a few outside suppliers may leave the buyer in an undesirably dependent position, excessively at the mercy of the supplier. On the other hand, such suppliers may have expertise that the buyer would find hard to replicate. In these cases, the buyer either acquires the supplier or makes a large investment in the supplier's firm, if possible, or else structures a multiyear purchase contract. These arrangements ensure continuing availability of the purchased product.

Maxicare, a health maintenance organization (HMO), discovered the importance of such considerations when its largest supplier severed its relationship with the company. The supplier was a large physician group that delivered many of Maxicare's health services. Maxicare had not secured the group's long-term commitment to the company. The physician group felt its relationship with Maxicare to be unbalanced—it was giving too much and receiving too little in return. Its departure was a key factor in the ultimate downfall of the HMO.

Making versus Buying from Many Outside Suppliers

For products with many outside suppliers, the make-versus-buy decision is more straightforward, and involves consideration only of the costs of each alternative source.

Such suppliers usually compete aggressively with each other, seeking to distinguish themselves with the excellence of their product or service or their competitive pricing. For example, in the ferociously competitive $15-billion hospital supplies market, distributors work hard to meet the needs of hospitals. Baxter International, the leading distributor, has enabled some hospitals to close expensive warehouses and to reduce their inventories with a system it calls "stockless inventory." It delivers small orders "just in time" directly to the hospital's departments rather than to the hospital loading dock. The savings can be considerable—an estimated one dollar's worth of handling saved for every dollar's worth of supplies purchased in the hospital.[10]

Many companies are unduly optimistic about the costs of "making," underestimating the difficulty of production timing, quality, and costs. Health service companies have increasingly turned to outside suppliers of services they once produced themselves, such as data processing or laundry, in belated recognition of the virtues of buying rather than making. These purchase contracts must be continually evaluated to ensure that purchase price and quality are at competitive levels.

LEADERSHIP PHILOSOPHY

Most small, new health care ventures aspire to become large, well-established organizations. A clear philosophy about how tightly or loosely to manage a venture during its growth phase is essential to achieving this goal. The usual route to large growth is with the delegation of considerable power and authority to local managers. They can rapidly expand the business by exploiting their knowledge of the local environment and the opportunities it presents. But such delegation entails considerable loss of control by the company's top management. Many founders cannot let go, because of temperament or fear of the consequences. They may want simultaneously to exercise tight centralized control and to achieve rapid growth; but frequently, the two goals are incompatible.

What Is Decentralization?

Northwestern Mutual Life provides an excellent example of how a decentralized organization operates. Here is a selection from its statement of performance:

> Many life insurance companies employ salaried managers to run their branch offices. Agents, sometimes salaried, have many of their expenses borne by their home office. Many home offices provide trips and vacations as prizes for their sales contests. Not the Northwestern.
>
> Each general agent, who has the franchise for a territory, is an independent business person. He or she decides when

and where to open satellite district offices, and cultivates agent career paths, so a strong district agency system also develops. The general agent must fund a clerical staff, pay rent, buy or lease computers, and run his or her own show. He or she recruits, trains and supervises agents and is encouraged to send them to the home office, after they have proven themselves, for further educational schools and seminars—all this largely at his or her own expense. The Northwestern general agent does not operate at the expense of the Northwestern policyholder.

> In turn, the Northwestern sales force is comprised of independent salespeople who also pay their own way. They rent their office space, hire and fund their own staff, pay their own phone bills, buy their own computers, and, in short, operate as any other self-supporting business. They develop their own clientele and select their own marketplaces. The general agent, the district agent, and the sales agent earn their dollars through commissions. All must manage their businesses well to become and stay successful. All pay their own way to our Annual Association of Agents meeting. No subsidies, no bureaucracy, no sheltered environments are provided for the work force.
>
> What, in turn, does the company provide? (1) The lowest net cost life insurance product available; (2) an exclusive franchise to market the products; (3) legal, accounting, and educational support encouraging professional growth and development.
>
> Northwestern Mutual agents on their own have achieved excellence in the industry: 32 percent have won the National Quality award, the industry's top citation, versus the top 20 company average of 6 percent. Thirty-five percent have earned the industry's educational Blue Ribbon, the CLU designation, compared with 14 percent of the competition. Twenty-five percent have won honors in the coveted Million Dollar Round Table, compared to an average of only 4 percent for the top companies.
>
> The distribution system works. Many expenses and costs that other life insurance

companies absorb, the Northwestern instead passes on to all agents who effectively deal with them as the inevitable costs incurred by independent business people. The agents excel in the industry, the company benefits by keeping management and attendant costs out of the home office, and the policy owner wins: low expenses combined with low mortality keep investable dollars within the Northwestern for the welfare of the policy-owners.

General Robert Wood Johnson, who was largely responsible for Johnson & Johnson's becoming a major health care company, was one of the earliest advocates of decentralization in health care organizations. He noted, "The value of splitting up huge centralized, concentrated operations is principally the restoration of human values which were submerged.... when....all...operations [were put] under one roof." [11] The loss of creative ideas and people in overly centralized firms can be devastating. One of the many top scientists who left a large pharmaceutical firm explained his departure by saying, "It's hard to be entrepreneurial there."[12]

Bristol-Myers presents yet another good example of the benefits of decentralization. This pharmaceutical company's successful growth over the years was fueled by its acquisitions. Bristol-Myers bought companies carefully selected for their excellent management, charged them with results to be obtained, and then left them alone. When the company bought Genetic Systems, a start-up biotechnology company for a startling $300-million price tag, the market value of its stock increased by more than $300 million. Wall Street analysts felt at the time that Bristol-Myers' decentralized management would make this acquisition work.

More recently, the merger of Bristol-Myers with Squibb was hailed as a success, whereas Eastman Kodak's purchase of Sterling Drug was viewed as a failure.[13] Bristol-Myers and Squibb smoothly merged, but virtually all of Sterling's top management left after the acquisition by Kodak. The reasons are many, but

Bristol-Myers management philosophy is key. It holds excellent managers responsible for results and then grants them the freedom to attain them.

Managers of decentralized units should behave as if they owned their own company rather than rely on the well-filled coffers of the parent company to cushion their path. Although they usually compete aggressively with other similar companies, sometimes the competition is heightened by the creation of competitive companies within the same firm. For example, Dr. Roy Vagelos, the chief executive officer (CEO) of Merck, entered into a joint venture with DuPont that competes directly with Merck in both research and sales.[14]

Management Style

The decision about whether a company will be managed in a decentralized or a tightly centralized fashion also depends, to a surprisingly large extent, on the styles and preferences of its management. Some top managers are overwhelmed by the copious data produced by centralized companies. They want to see the forest, not all the little trees. Others thrive on numbers. Patrick Haggerty, the late CEO of Texas Instruments, was legendary for the ability to condense a slew of numbers into meaningful statistics. "He can walk through a huge factory and tell you its income at the end of his tour," an admirer told me in testimony to Haggerty's remarkable ability to synthesize data.

Humana's founders and top managers also control the company by the numbers. They exercise tight, detailed control of the financial events in every one of their hospitals and HMOs. Their preference is not surprising. Its founders were trained as certified public accountants and lawyers—people who thrive on detail. It is difficult to grow such a company rapidly, a fact Humana's management painfully discovered when it tried and failed to grow quickly to a national scale. Humana is now highly profitable and efficient but smaller than originally planned. The Hospital Corporation of

America, on the other hand, grew rapidly in part because its top management consisted of two physicians who felt comfortable delegating authority and responsibility to their local managers.

Articulating a Leadership Philosophy

Many new health care ventures would like to have their cake and eat it too. They would like to maintain tight centralized control and to grow rapidly. Some new ventures have floundered on the shoals of this desire. Maxicare, for example, failed in part because it did not decentralize control during a period of national expansion. With boxes of data from all over the United States waiting to be opened in Maxicare's California headquarters, the operations of the company understandably faltered. Many of the remaining HMOs reduced their market and geographic scope in response to Maxicare's experiences, opting for tight control of their operations and sacrificing the growth they might otherwise have had.

A leadership philosophy must be explicitly articulated by the company before growth begins. Some firms find it helpful to have a veteran of such growth on the board of directors. Others hire professional managers who are comfortable with decentralized, rapidly growing environments. One firm even has a plan for replacing its founding CEO with an experienced operating manager. The founder, in this case, readily acknowledges his inability to manage growth. He views himself as a visionary, a creator of new ideas for multibillion-dollar firms. He is the architect, not the builder.

All of these approaches share one characteristic: The development of a leadership philosophy before growth occurred. The process of developing a philosophy is not an easy one. It requires difficult choices about rates of growth and painful evaluations of the ability of the firm's founders to lead it during successive stages. Most firms understandably prefer to avoid making these choices, but their reluctance bears a price. When such a firm

starts to grow, it is like a rudderless ship in a storm. All too often, it becomes the victim of growth rather than its beneficiary.

Medical Care International, a Texas-based ambulatory surgery company, demonstrates the importance of such a philosophy. In its early days, the company grew rapidly but failed to maintain profitability. The reason? The company lacked a philosophy about how to manage its growth. But it recovered. From 1984 to 1989, while its revenues increased nearly fivefold, a loss of $14 million was replaced by a profit of $16 million.

This turnaround was accomplished by devising a clear philosophy about managing growth. Medical Care International is a decentralized company. The managers of each of its centers have both the responsibility for achieving certain goals and the concomitant authority. Who are the managers? They are primarily nurses, who can earn hefty salaries and bonuses up to 50 percent of their salaries for achieving the desired goals.[15]

The results achieved by this and other clearly articulated leadership philosophies are impressive.

NOTES

1. Richard B. Chase and Robert H. Hayes, "Operations Strategy for Service Firms," Working Paper Series 90-045 (Boston: Division of Research, Harvard Business School, 1990).

2. Regina E. Herzlinger, "Healthy Competition," *Atlantic Monthly*, August 1991, 69–83.

3. W. Edwards Deming. "Observations and Comments," *Society for Health Systems Journal*, Spring 1990, 74–77. Reprinted with permission.

4. Joe Flower, "Managing Quality," *Healthcare Forum Journal*, September-October 1990, 65–68.

5. Clark W. Bell, "Personalized Patient-Care System Should Be Explored," *Modern Healthcare*, November 24, 1989, 14.

6. Anthony J. Grieco, Shirley A. Garnet, Kimberly S. Glassman, Patricia L. Valoon, and Margaret L. McLure, "New York University Medical Center's Cooperative Care Unit," *Patient Education and Counseling* 15, no. 1 (1990): 3–15.

7. Paul Goldberger, "A Tough Building Helps Patients Fight Disease," *New York Times*, February 24, 1991, H28.

8. "FDA Bans Drug Purchases from Abbott," *HealthWeek*, March 26, 1990, 2.

9. Julia Flynn Siler, "LyphoMed's Vital Signs Are Stabilizing," *Business Week*, July 3, 1989, 46.

10. Milt Freudenheim, "Removing the Warehouse from Cost-Conscious Hospitals," *New York Times*, March 3, 1991, F5.

11. "Robert Wood Johnson," *Modern Healthcare*, September 10, 1990, 61.

12. "Merck Needs More Gold from the White Coats," *Business Week*, March 18, 1991, 103.

13. Karen Southwick, "Dust Still Settling in the Wake of Recent Drug Mergers," *HealthWeek*, March 26, 1990, 4.

14. Ibid., 103.

15. Sandy Lutz, "Medical Care International's Strategy for Success," *Modern Healthcare*, January 8, 1990, 66.

SUGGESTED READING

Operations Management

Articles

Barry, L. , V. Zeithaml, and A. Parasuraman. "Quality Counts in Services, Too," *Business Horizons*, May-June 1985.

Bowen, D.E. "Managing Customers as Human Resources in Service Organizations," *Human Resources Management* 25 (1986): 371–83.

Chase, R.B. "The Customer Contact Approach to Services: Theoretical Bases and Practical Extensions," *Operations Research* 29 (1981): 698–706.

———. "The 10 Commandments of Service Management," *Interfaces* 15, no. 3 (1985): 68–70.

———. "Where Does the Customer Fit in a Service Operation?" *Harvard Business Review*, November-December 1978, 137–41.

Chew, W.B. "No-Nonsense Guide to Measuring Productivity," *Harvard Business Review*, January-February 1988, 3–8.

Hart, C. "The Power of Unconditional Service Guarantees," *Harvard Business Review*, July-August 1988, 54–62.

Luthans, F. "Service Human Resource Management: Results of a Behavioral Approach," in *Service Management Effectiveness*, ed. D. Bowen, R. Chase, and T. Cummings (San Francisco: Jossey-Bass, 1989).

Maister, D.H. "Balancing the Professional Service Firm," *Sloan Management Review* 23 (Summer 1982): 19–23.

———."The Psychology of Waiting Lines," in *Managing Services*, ed. C.H. Lovelock (Englewood Cliffs, N.J.: Prentice-Hall, 1988).

Metzger, R.O., and S. Dey. "Affluent Customers: What Do They Really Value?" *Journal of Retail Banking* 8, no. 3 (1986): 25–35.

Pollock, A.J. "Banking: Time to Unbundle the Services?" *Long Range Planning* 18, no. 1 (1985): 36–41.

Quinn, J.B., and C.E. Gagnon. "Will Services Follow Manufacturing into Decline?," *Harvard Business Review*, November-December 1986, 95–103.

Sasser, W.E. "Managing Supply and Demand in Service Industries," *Harvard Business Review*, November-December 1976, 133–40.

Schmenner, R.W. "How Can Service Business Survive and Prosper?" *Sloan Management Review,* Spring 1986, 21–32.

Schneider, B. "The Service Organizations: Climate Is Crucial," *Organizational Dynamics*, Autumn 1980, 52–65.

Shostack, G.L. "Designing Services That Deliver," *Harvard Business Review*, March-April 1984, 133–39.

Thomas, K.H. "Framework for Branch Performance Evaluation," *Journal of Retail Banking* 1, no. 4 (1982): 24–34.

Wind, J., et al. "Courtyard by Marriott: Designing a Hotel Facility with Consumer-based Marketing Models," *Interfaces* 19, no. 1, (1989): 25–47.

Books

Albrecht, K., and R. Zemke. *Service America!* Homewood, Ill.: Dow Jones-Irwin, 1985.

Bateson, J. *Managing Services Marketing: Text and Readings*. Hinsdale, Ill.: Dryden, 1989.

Carlzon, J. *Moments of Truth*. New York: Perennial Library, 1989.

Heskett, J.L. *Managing in the Service Economy*. Boston: Harvard Business School Press, 1986.

Lovelock, C.H. *Managing Services*. Englewood Cliffs, N.J.: Prentice-Hall, 1988.

Operations Research

Buffa, Elwood Spencer. *Essentials of Management Science*. New York: Wiley, 1978.

———. *Management Science/Operations Research*. 2d ed. New York: Wiley, 1981.

Handbook of Operations Research. 2 vols. New York: Van Nostrand Reinhold, 1978.

Hillier, Frederick S. *Introduction to Operations Research*. 4th ed. Oakland, Calif.: Holden-Day, 1986.

Lapin, Lawrence L. *Quantitative Methods for Business Decisions*. 4th ed. San Diego: Harcourt Brace Jovanovich, 1988.

Levin, Richard I. *Quantitative Approaches to Management*. 7th ed. New York: McGraw-Hill, 1987.

Leadership Philosophy

Albanese, Robert. *Managing—Toward Accountability for Performance.* 3d ed. Georgetown, Ontario: Irwin-Dorsey, 1981.

Bennis, Warren G. *Organization Development.* Reading, Mass.: Addison-Wesley, 1969.

Business Policy and Strategy: Concepts and Readings. 3d ed. Homewood Ill.: Richard D. Irwin, 1983.

Caplow, Theodore. *Managing an Organization.* 2d ed. New York: Holt, Rinehart and Winston, 1983.

Drucker, Peter. *Managing the Nonprofit Organization.* New York: HarperCollins Publishers, 1990.

———. *The Efficient Executive.* New York: Harper & Row, 1967.

Part IV

Creating New Health Care Ventures

11

The New Venture Evaluation Process

The three new opportunities in the health care sector and the seven managerial skills critical to the success of new ventures have now been introduced. But what is the process for evaluating the viability of a new venture? For separating the losers from the winners? This is a key question in creating new health care ventures. This chapter details the process for answering it (Exhibit 11-1).

The first three steps of the evaluation process are crucial: Begin with a market assessment, continue with an analysis of the venture's financial viability, and conclude with a financial valuation of the venture. If the venture cannot leap the hurdles of an easily attained break-even volume and financial valuation greater or equal to the level of investment required, it is not viable. But these are merely preliminary hurdles. In addition, the process must consider (1) the fit between the opportunity and the managerial resources assembled to take advantage of it, (2) the sustainability of the venture, and (3) its financial and technological risks. The process should conclude with an assessment of the impact of the venture on society.

CAVEATS

Throughout, the evaluation process must be informed by three *caveats*: Life is not literature, basic is beautiful, and beware of true believers. These three caveats are associated with any venture analysis.

Life is not literature. A witty venture capitalist once observed that just as literature is "all romance and no children" and life is "just the reverse," in his experience all business plans were "literature" whereas business reality was "life." In other words, while the plans provide the very rosiest picture of what will happen, reality is likely to require much more work because of higher costs, lower prices, and tighter schedules than those planned.

Basic is beautiful. Market projections should be tied to basic data about the health care system (some of the key U.S. data are presented in Table 11-1). Thus, a proposal to acquire a community hospital must be linked to the hospital demand and supply in the area, a proposal to build a diagnostic facility should be tied to the need for diagnostic testing, and a proposal to develop a new artificial heart

Exhibit 11-1 Checklist for Evaluating New Ventures

1. Caveats
  Life Is Not Literature
  Basic Is Beautiful
  Beware of True Believers
2. Market Assessment
  Converting an Opportunity into a Marketing Plan
  Competitive Analysis
  Evaluating the Marketing Plan
  Sales to Whom?
3. Financial Viability
  Break-even Volume: Price x Volume = (Fixed Costs) + (Variable Costs) x (Volume)
  Market Share Analysis
4. Valuation Analysis
  Cash Flows
  Required Rates of Return
  Terminal Value
5. Sustainability
  Revenues
  Market Share
  Costs
  Management
6. Financial Risk Assessment
  Red Flags
  Accounting Considerations
7. Managerial Assessment
  Fit of Managerial Skills and Opportunity
  "Wannabes" versus "Experienced" Managers
8. Societal Impact
9. Technological Risk Assessment
  Understanding the "Black Box"
  Production, Financial, Regulatory, and Patent Considerations
  Peer Review and Its Limits

should be supported with an estimate of the number of people likely to need it and of the market share of competitors.

Sounds obvious, no? But in many new venture proposals, such data are notable for their absence. The founders either assume that they will achieve the same market size as their competitors or, more frequently, merely assert that some fraction of the total market will be theirs.

Beware of true believers. The problems mentioned above most frequently occur in the case of true believers—zealots who have devoted much time to the proposed venture. True believers convince themselves of the venture's viability and labor mightily to make it a reality. The first two *caveats* are imperative for evaluating the work of true believers. Although true believers do not purposely misrepresent facts, they are not always credible sources of information.

MARKET ASSESSMENT

Converting an Opportunity into a Marketing Plan

Real life is not neat and tidy. New ideas do not appear with labels identifying the kind of opportunity they represent and the managerial skills needed to implement them. Ventures are created because someone has an idea and a

Table 11-1 Basic Characteristics of U.S. Health

Health Care Categories

Health Status	1970	1987
Live Births (in thousands)	3,731.0	3,809.0
Life Expectancy at Birth (in years)	70.9	75.0
Male	67.1	71.3
Female	74.8	78.4
Death Rates (per 100,000 population)	714.3	535.5
Heart Disease	253.6	169.6
Stroke Related	66.3	30.3
Cancer	129.8	132.9
Lung Disease	13.2	18.7
Pneumonia and Flu	22.1	13.1
Liver Disease	14.7	9.1
Diabetes	14.1	9.8
Accidents	53.7	34.6
Suicide	11.8	11.7
Homicide	9.1	8.6
AIDS (number of cases)	NA	106,270.0 (1989)

Health Resource Use	1980	1988
Hospital Discharges (per 1,000 population)	159.1	117.8
Hospital Days of Care (per 1,000 population)	1,136.5	754.8
Average Hospital Length of Stay (in days)	7.1	6.4
Nursing Home Residents 65 or Older (per 1,000 population)	47.1 (1977)	46.2 (1985)
Mental Health Admissions (per 1,000 population)	7.4 (1975)	7.6 (1986)
HMO Enrollees (in thousands)	9,078 (1980)	31,883 (1989)

Hospital Discharges (in thousands)	1980	1988
Female	22,686	18,504
Delivery of Child	3,762	3,781
Heart Disease	1,513	1,686
Cancer	954	898
Fracture	580	508
Pneumonia	368	452
Male	15,145	12,642
Heart Disease	1,688	1,955
Cancer	875	772
Fracture	582	506
Pneumonia	414	472
Stroke Related	371	336
Inguinal Hernia	458	232

Diagnostic Procedures (in thousands)	1980	1988
Female	3,532	6,902
Ultrasound	204	963
CAT Scan	154	838
Radioisotope Scan	289	390
Endoscopy of Small Intestine	164	279
Laparoscopy	235	133

continues

Table 11-1 continued

Health Care Categories

Diagnostic Procedures (in thousands)	1970	1987
Male	3,386	6,665
CAT Scan	152	775
Ultrasound	114	599
Cystoscopy	543	399
Angiocardiography	174	749
Radioisotope Scan	236	315
Arteriography	180	246

Health Care Resources	1970	1987
Active Physicians (in thousands)	311	521
Office-based Practice, Nonfederal	189	337
General and Family	50	55
Cardiovascular	4	10
Internal Medicine	23	56
Pediatrics	10	23
General Surgery	18	24
Obstetrics and Gynecology	14	24
Opthalmology	8	13
Orthopedic Surgery	7	14
Psychiatry	10	19
Hospital-based Practice, Nonfederal	66	116
Interns and Residents	46	80
Hospital Staff, Full Time	20	36
Registered Nurses (in thousands)	750	1,627
Dentists (in thousands)	96	140
Short-Stay Hospitals	6,193	5,967
Hospital Beds (in thousands)	936	1,046
Nursing Homes	14,133 (1976)	16,033 (1986)
HMOs	175 (1976)	647 (1989)

Health Care Expenditures	1980	1987
Personal Health Care (in billions)	$219.7	$442.6
Amount per Capita	$934.0	$1,758.0
Percentage of Total National Health Expenses		
Hospitals	37%	39%
Physicians	19%	21%
Dentists	6%	7%
Nursing Homes	6%	8%
Hospital Inpatient Expenses, per Patient Day	$244.0	$537.0
Medicare Funds (in billions)	$36.8	$82.0
Medicaid Vendor Payments (in billions)	$23.3	$45.0
Health Research and Development Funds (in billions)	$7.9	$18.7

Source: U.S. Department of Health and Human Services, *Health United States, 1989* (Washington, D.C.: U.S. Government Printing Office, 1990). Health Status (Tables 2, 14, 23, 42), Health Resource Use (Tables 70, 79, 123), Hospital Discharges (Table 73), Diagnostic Procedures (Table 75), Health Care Resources (Tables 86, 87, 93, 99, 123), Health Care Expenditures (Tables 102, 108, 110, 114, 124, 127).

scheme for putting it into practice. Both idea and scheme are usually ill defined. The challenge is to translate this messy reality into a clear statement of the relevant opportunity and then into a marketing plan. How to do it? Research and elbow grease are essential—research to determine how consumers respond to the new product or service and elbow grease to convert their responses into a marketing plan that positions the product.

Market research serves two purposes. It delineates how to position the product and then establishes whether a market exists and, if so, estimates its size. Market research is critical for any new venture. Entrepreneurial ideas may be either visionary or crackpot. Only a thin line separates the two. The line? Many consumers follow visionaries; few follow crackpots. Market research is critical for distinguishing between the two. The research process is simple. It describes the product, its purpose, and its costs. It then asks potential consumers if they would buy it and why.

The process for obtaining this information is a dry sell, a procedure in which a product or service is described to potential consumers, who are then queried about whether they would buy it, at what price, and how rapidly. The sell cycle—the amount of time needed to close the sale—is a critical price of information. Many health care products require a sell cycle of several years. The dry sell also ascertains potential consumers' responses to the attributes of the product. For example, one dry sell discovered a strong preference for the IBM PC as the platform for a proposed new management information system among the hospital chief financial officers who were its intended clients. The discovery was fortunate, because the system was initially designed to run on another brand of computer.

Strangely, many new ventures are created without any market research. One company spent $10 million in product development before it discovered that physicians simply would not spend a few hundred thousand dollars for the management information system it was producing. In this firm, as in many others, managers felt that market research was not needed. Their product was obviously wonderful—to them.

Before consumers are contacted, it is important to clarify whether the purpose of the product is to lower costs, appeal to new consumers, or exploit some dazzling new technology. The answers are frequently surprising. Take the case of a computer program that searches the voluminous medical literature for research that provides answers to questions such as this: What conclusions have been reached by clinical research evaluating the efficacy of pacemakers? The program was designed by a professor of medicine to simplify his frequent quests for relevant research data. It is exceptionally user-friendly, requiring only minimal training for its mastery. (This description of the venture is based on the computer program called Paper Chase, developed by Professor Howard Bleich of the Harvard Medical School. The usage, cost, and revenue data presented have been disguised. The entrepreneur discussed herein is entirely the figment of my imagination. Dr. Bleich is such a good entrepreneur that I was forced to create a poor one for pedagogical purposes.)

The product is a new technology, right? Not so. New technologies are dazzling pieces of creative science. They alter the power of medicine, dramatically increasing its diagnostic or therapeutic abilities. The literature search program is not sufficiently innovative to qualify for this league. If potential consumers were asked why they might consider using the program, it is not likely to score high on this dimension.

What kind of opportunity is it then? It may potentially lower costs, but the connection between searching the medical literature and lowering health care costs is a bit far-fetched.

Only one category is left. The new computer program, if it is to be marketable, must appeal to new consumers. One group of new consumers consists of health activists who want to read the medical literature directly. Any other group? Sure. Physicians who want to access research results directly, either to improve patient care or for their own research. The physicians most likely to use computers to update their knowledge are those who grew comfortable with them in their own training and to whom thorough knowledge of research findings is very important. They are likely to be under 55 years old and to be high-technology specialists. Where can they be found? These are the sort of doctors who are affiliated with teaching hospitals.

Should the program be marketed to the health activist, the physician, or both? Because the entrepreneur in this case is himself a research physician, he feels more comfortable with marketing to his fellow doctors. He wishes to defer the examination of the health activist market. For the purposes of exposition here, we will honor his request, but in real life we would evaluate the health activist market as well as the physician market.

Translating Research Findings into a Market Size Estimate

Armed with research that positions the product in one of the three opportunities, and of the likely buyers in this segment, the next step is to estimate the size of the market. Establishing market size is essential to the evaluation of the opportunity's financial attractiveness. Usually the larger the market, the more financially appealing the opportunity. Ventures for small markets find it hard to attract financing interest unless they are extraordinarily profitable.

A clear understanding of the marketing potential of the product is key for estimating market size. In the example of the literature search program, we have determined the likely buyers. These doctors are located in the 972 teaching hospitals in the United States with more than 200 beds.[1] One such hospital used it for an average of 8,400 searches in a year-long market test. Thus, the market size can be as large as 8,164,800 searches a year (8,400 searches x 972 centers). If the average literature search costs $6, the financial size of the market would be $48,988,800 (8,164,800 searches x $6 each). However, the test hospital was very large, so the average hospital would

probably use fewer searches. The market size is likely closer to half of the estimate above, or roughly $25 million. Although most venture capitalists would turn their noses up at such a small market size, it may be a perfect size for a small, private business.

What about the market size of an ambulatory health service company, like Health Stop? In contrast, its market size is enormous. With Health Stop positioned to appeal to the health activists who make up 40 percent of the U.S. adult population, the market size is well over 40 million adults. If each health activist visits a doctor four times a year and pays $50 per visit, the financial value of this market can be estimated at $8 billion. With Health Stop positioned as a cost-reducing company, the market is even larger, because interest in cost reduction applies to virtually every patient rather than only the 40 million activists.

As in the examples above, estimates of market size should be linked to basic characteristics of the American health care system. Yet, sometimes, new ventures' claims about a certain market size are not verified. For example, the size of the artificial blood market was estimated by one new venture at $2 billion and by another at $8 billion. Neither offered the verification of their estimates that could have been provided with an explanation of the current uses of blood, by purpose, and how artificial blood products can substitute for existing natural ones. (Some of the fundamental data useful for delineating market size for U.S. health services are contained in Table 11-1. Additional data about U.S. activist and working health care consumers and the industry, its technology, and its financing can be found in Part II and the Appendixes.)

Competitive Analysis

An analysis of the competition is a critical part of the market size estimate. If competitors do not presently exist, they are likely to be attracted when the new venture proves viable. Founders should explain the competitive barriers they will create to protect their market.

If competitors are already present, the new venture must clarify its competitive advantage.

First Movers

In some cases, the first-mover advantages accruing to the first company to offer the product may be significant, because many consumers are loyal to providers or do not want to be troubled to find another source. For example, many patients are loath to switch physicians and health professionals are reluctant to switch medical supplies or instruments with which they are comfortable. In other cases, the first-mover advantage may be negligible. For example, consumers may readily switch antacid medication brands, and the company must struggle to create brand loyalty. In yet others, the first mover may be at a disadvantage. For example, the firm manufacturing the first cochlear implant abandoned it due to unanticipated regulatory difficulties. Other companies learned from its difficulties in managing the regulatory process and succeeded where the first mover failed.

Legal Barriers to Entry

In technology-based companies, the regulatory process may create barriers to entry. Although obtaining patents and FDA approvals is a costly and time-consuming process, it prevents casual competitors from entering the business. Patents do not guarantee lack of competition, however. A patent may not be broad enough to prohibit a competitor. Or it may focus on a new substance while the competitor patents a new use. In the biotechnology field, the novelty of the science to both examiners and applicants inevitably creates chinks that will be discovered in future patent litigation.

Even a perfect patent provides no assurance of lack of competition. If the market is large enough, competitors with deep pockets will be attracted to it and might even risk patent infringement suits to enter the market. Small companies may lack the financial war chest needed to fight a competitor armed with tens of millions of dollars to spend on a legal battle. Even if they might have eventually prevailed in the courts, some ventures settle or sell out to competitors for smaller sums than they could have earned if they were armed with the financial resources to enforce their patents. Others persist in defending their patents—but these ventures risk losing their identity as operating companies and becoming more like law firms devoted to winning legal battles.

Legal barriers to entry are weaker for other types of health care ventures. Licenses and trademarks are virtually the sole legal barriers to entry that can be erected by firms that reduce costs or serve new health care consumers. (Certificates of need and other regulatory requirements generally can also be met by competitors.) Excellence of management is the major barrier to competition that is available to these companies. Managerial excellence explains McDonald's remarkable ability to withstand the ferocious competition by others lured by the large size of the fast-food market and the ease of entering the business.

Managerial Barriers

Health care companies with excellent management need not fear competition. Companies that cater to new health care consumers can sustain a high degree of customer satisfaction if they conscientiously implement the critical management skills of operations management, human resource management, and marketing. Companies that reduce health care costs can also maintain their edge with good management. Humana, for example, steadily maintained excellent profits in its hospital division. The secret? Sustained, careful attention to its three key management skills: finance, managerial control, and an articulate leadership philosophy.

Sustainability of Prices

I was concerned when a friend told me of his plans to offer dental services to indigent nursing home patients whose health care costs are paid by Medicaid health insurance.

Although he assured me that profits would be high, I was uncomfortable with a venture that earned high profits for services provided to the poor, and I also feared that, sooner or later, those high margins would attract Medicaid's attention. At that point, Medicaid reimbursement would, inevitably, be reduced. The disastrous financial condition of nursing homes, which receive their primary funding from Medicaid and which had a razor-thin median profit margin of 1.2 percent in 1988, vividly demonstrates this problem.[2]

Ventures like my friend's, which depend on only one or a few revenue sources, are vulnerable to the reduction or withdrawal of their revenues. For example, changes in Medicare's payments for cataract surgery performed in ambulatory surgery centers are estimated to have reduced the centers' revenues by $50 million in 1991. The centers were vulnerable to such a substantial impact from a change in one payer's rates for only one procedure because cataract surgery accounted for 27 percent of all their procedures and 50 percent of their Medicare cases.[3] New technologies for the elderly—such as heart devices—are similarly dependent on Medicare payments and vulnerable to changes in the payment scheme.

The more dispersed the sources of revenues, the lower the venture's exposure to changes in any one of them. Some revenue sources are more sustainable than others because of their intrinsic characteristics, as detailed below.

Medicaid, health insurance for the poor, offers low rates of reimbursement and slow payment of bills. It is financed in part by state governments that sometimes squeeze Medicaid payments when they get into fiscal difficulties. Few powerful political pressures exist to increase Medicaid payments. The primary Medicaid constituency consists of the poor—unfortunately, they are not strong politically. Medicaid vendors can easily be portrayed as venal exploiters of the poor if they insist on prompt and full payment. Although Medicaid providers are legally entitled to payment, they may be political sitting ducks if the government chooses to delay, withhold, or withdraw payment promises.

Medicare rates of payment are generally fair, in my opinion, and sustainable. Medicare is funded by the federal government and backed by the elderly—an enormously powerful political group. The government has had little success in controlling Medicare costs to date, and Congress is continually pressured for extension of Medicare benefits. Nevertheless, more stringent controls are inevitable because of the growth in the number of the elderly and Medicare's drain on the national economy.

Managed care organizations, such as HMOs and PPOs, are highly cognizant of their costs and try to negotiate low prices. On the other hand, they are unlikely to change vendors, because their patients want to have consistent services and are concerned about the quality of their care. As a result, revenues from managed care organizations are likely to be sustainable but not highly profitable. Because some managed care organizations are financially vulnerable, evaluation of their financial condition must be an integral part of an analysis of the sustainability of revenues (see "Financial Risk Assessment" below).

Insurance companies like Blue Cross-Blue Shield and CIGNA traditionally offer the best reimbursement rates. But because these payers currently suspect that they are the victims of a "cost shift" in which they are overcharged to compensate for underpayments by Medicaid and others, they may become more stringent payers in the future.

Self-payments are revenues paid directly by the recipients rather than their insurance companies. The quality and sustainability of so-called self-pay revenues depend on the credit of the service recipients. Although some hospitals obtain low yields on self-pay revenues because many of the uninsured users of hospital services are poor, other new health care ventures, such as eyeglass providers, have excellent payment experiences. They use cash or credit card payments. The self-pay category is, of course, highly price conscious and susceptible to price competition.

In general, ventures that provide services to reduce cost can attract reimbursement from insurers more readily than new technology ventures. Insurers are leery of new technologies—they view them as potential bottomless pits. Insurers traditionally have had little interest in paying for the services or products that serve new consumers. These are generally paid for directly by their users.

Evaluating a Marketing Plan

The marketing plan should answer the following questions about the new product or service: To whom will it be sold? Why would they buy it? How many will be sold? When and where will it be sold? And how much will it cost? Vague or global answers to these questions should sound an alarm: A plan that specifies all hospitals, doctors, and patients as potential customers is one that did not benefit from much critical thought. The clear and detailed story is the one that should inspire confidence in the viability of the venture.

But the mere presence of voluminous data does not necessarily indicate a penetrating market analysis. The data presented must be clearly relevant to the market being discussed. Sometimes they are not. For example, the plan for commercializing the literature search computer program came complete with many charts and graphs showing the explosion in the artificial intelligence market. Superficially, it looked good for the venture—all boats rise in a rising sea. But on closer inspection, the connection between the artificial intelligence market and the literature search program was obscure. Artificial intelligence products are purchased by those who want to automate simple, repetitive factory or clerical tasks. These are not likely to be customers for a program that searches the medical literature.

The probable market for the literature search program consists of researchers and clinical providers of medicine located at some 900 academic medical centers. They would buy the search routine to help them in their research or teaching activities. For example, they might search the medical literature for the citations of the latest findings about management of high blood pressure to present in lectures to their interns. Research doctors under age 55 would probably feel comfortable using a computer to do this work, but older physicians or hospital administrators would likely resist it.

How would the program be sold? If the market consists of medical academics, then the easiest sales tactic is to demonstrate the accessibility and speed of the program to its potential users by employing a direct sales force, by exhibiting the program at conferences for research and advanced clinical physicians, and, if possible, by publishing articles about the program in the journals they read. If they are interested in buying it, they can buy the program without great delay because they have sufficient political muscle and funding sources, via their research grants, to buy the program themselves, without much further approval.

Are there any competitors? There happen to be three, including the federal government itself and a large well-financed company with a great track record for selling a similar search program to lawyers. Why then would anybody buy the program? Because the founder is himself a professor of medicine and thus understands his market better than his competitors. His program is unusually user-friendly.

At this point, the merits of the program as compared with the merits of its competitors can be weighed by testing it with potential users. But even if they validate the program's superiority, the analysis has barely begun. For example, we have yet to determine if it is financially viable.

FINANCIAL VIABILITY

Determining financial viability is basically simple although not necessarily easy. It involves calculating the volume of sales at which the venture covers its costs, or "breaks even," and assessing whether attainment of that volume level is viable. In the search program example, the break-even level is the number of paid searches whose combined revenues would equal the costs of the new venture. The break-even level is then compared to the total market and to the competitors' market share, to determine if it can be attained. For example, if the break-even level is attained only if sales have been made to 70 percent of the market, the literature search program is unlikely to be financially viable given the strength of its competitors.

Like many things worth doing, computing the break-even level is easier said than done. First, it requires assignment of a price to each unit to be sold, say $6 per search or $36 per hour. (The average search requires 10 minutes.) Is this price a reasonable one? In this case, we happen to know our competitors' prices; but do not be misled by their availability. For most new ventures, market prices are not available, either because no competitors exist or, if they are present, because the new venture may not want to adopt their prices.

Break-even analysis next requires delineation of the fixed and variable costs of running the venture; that is, those costs that remain the same regardless of the level of activity (fixed) and those that change with volume (variable). These data are hard to come by. Further, their assignment of costs to fixed and variable categories is usually ambiguous. After all, over an infinite time all costs are variable, and in the short term, all costs are fixed.

In this case, cost data for the new venture are available, (see Exhibit 11-2). When classified as fixed and variable, they indicate a fixed cost of $250,240 and a variable cost of $8 per hour. These costs would be covered by the revenues generated from 53,623 searches or 8,937 hours of computer time. (To check, multiply $36 an hour by 8,937 hours. The answer should approximately equal the fixed cost of $250,240 plus the variable costs of $8 an hour times 8,937 hours.)

Can the program attract 53,623 paid searches? To answer this question, we must estimate the size of the total market. Market research at a local academic medical center showed that it conducted 8,400 searches last year. If we extrapolate these results to all medical centers, the maximum market consists of 8,164,800 searches (8,400 searches × 972 medical centers). If we approximate the likely market as half the maximum one, the break-even volume for the proposed venture requires about 1 percent of the market (53,623 ÷ 4,082,400), a very low level. After it is attained, every additional search hour will bring in $36 of revenue and require only $8 of costs, thus contributing $28 to profits.

VALUATION ANALYSIS

So far, we can conclude that this venture is viable in the sense that it requires attainment of only a small market share to break even. But how much is it worth to a potential investor?

The answer depends on three factors: (1) The rate of return that investors in the venture expect to earn; (2) the maximum market share the venture can attain; and (3) the amount of money that someone is likely to pay for the venture at the end of 5 years, the so-called terminal value.

For simplicity, suppose this venture can ultimately capture 20 percent of its specific market and that no additional expenses will be required to enable it to grow to that size. Also, assume that there are three potential investors.

Exhibit 11-2 Revenues and Costs of Literature Search Program

Average Price:	Per hour, $36; per search, $6.
Fixed Costs:	1 supervisor; 1 programmer; 1.5 secretaries; 3 medical librarians; 3 computer operators; travel, overhead, and benefits = $250,240.
Variable Costs:	Computer use = $4 per hour; royalty to database = $4 per hour
Capacity:	Present level of operations can handle ten times more activity.

The first is a venture capitalist who expects a 50 percent return per year on funds invested, the second is a private investor who expects a 25 percent annual return, and the third is a nonprofit foundation that is considering buying the program from the entrepreneur so that it can be made more widely available. The foundation wants to earn the same return on this investment as it currently earns on its endowment, 15 percent.

The cash flows are projected, by estimating the annual revenues that can be attained with a 20 percent market share and subtracting from them the fixed costs of $250,240 and the associated total variable costs (Exhibit 11-3). The terminal value is frequently projected by multiplying the cash flow in the past year by the *multiple*. The multiple is usually derived from the amount recently paid for the acquisition of a similar type of business. For example, if a health information system company that generated $1,000,000 in cash flow a year was recently purchased for $10,000,000, the multiple is 10 ($10,000,000 ÷ $1,000,000).

Applying the multiple of 10 to the $3,560,000 of annual cash flow this project generates in year 5 yields a terminal value of $35,600,000.

The cash flows and terminal value are discounted to their net present value—the amount of money that if invested right now at the specified rates of return would generate the same cash flows and terminal value as the project (see Exhibit 11-3). The figures indicate that the highest net present value of the project is assigned by the foundation. In other words, if the entrepreneur wants to sell his business, the foundation will likely pay the most for it.

This computation can also be used to calculate the fraction of the new venture's ownership a founder must sell to others in order to acquire needed capital. Suppose that in this case the entrepreneur will need $1 million in initial investment and will reinvest the $3,560,000 generated each year in the venture. He intends to sell it at the end of 5 years. How much of the venture's ownership should he give up right now to acquire $1 million in investment funds?

Exhibit 11-3 Steps in Valuation Analysis

A. Compute Likely Market Size:
    1. Total market size = 8,164,800 searches or 1,360,800 hours.
    2. Likely market size = 1,360,800 hours ÷ 2 = 680,400 hours.
    3. Twenty percent of likely market = 136,080 hours.
B. Compute Annual Cash Flows at that Market Size:
    1. Annual cash flow at 20 percent of market = ($36 x 136,080 hours)
      − ($8 x 136,080 hours) − $250,240 = $3,560,000.
C. Compute Present Value of Annual Cash Flows:
    1. Present value of annual cash flow for 5 years discounted at:
      50% annually = $6,182,000
      25% annually = $9,574,000
      15% annually = $11,934,000
D. Compute Present Value of Terminal Value:
    1. Present value of terminal value at year 5 of $35,600,000 discounted at:
      50% = $4,688,000
      25% = $11,665,000
      15% = $17,700,000
E. Valuation - Present Value of Terminal Value and Annual Cash Flows:
    1. Total present value (sum of C and D) when discounted at:
      50% = $10,870,000
      25% = $21,239,000
      15% = $29,634,000

Note: Numbers are rounded to nearest thousand so that they do not convey an unwarranted air of precise accuracy. They are the product of many estimates about market size, prices, costs, and the life of the product.

If the investor is a venture capitalist, he or she will expect the $1 million to grow to $7,593,750 in year 5 ($7,593,750 = $1 million compounded for 5 years at the required 50 percent rate of return). Assuming that the company is then sold for $35,600,000, the venture capitalists will earn the 50 percent return they seek if they are given 21.3 percent ownership of the venture ($7,593,750 ÷ $35,600,000).

Exit Strategy

A critical component of the valuation process is the strategy for liquidating the investment in the business. Three options exist: The venture can be sold, it can continue as a private venture that generates cash, or it can be taken public.

The exit strategy of selling the venture to another company is frequently cited and may lead to the highest valuation. A new venture that is complementary to the product line of an existing business will generally be worth more to that business than to any other party, because the business can use its existing infrastructure to support the new venture while others must spend considerable sums to create the same infrastructure.

For example, a company that sells information to physicians, such as a publishing firm, would be interested in a new venture complementary to its product line and would be willing to value it at a high price. After all, the new venture will provide the publishing company's existing sales and distribution network with one more product to sell. Other buyers or the new venture itself must expend considerable sums to replicate the sales, distribution, production, and other managerial resources that the publishing company already has in place. To put it another way, an exit strategy that involves the sale of the new venture to an existing business with complementary product lines will reduce the costs of the new venture to the acquirer and therefore increase its value.

On the other hand, in some cases the sale of a new venture to an existing business may sound its death knell, because the corporate environment may smother the new venture's entrepreneurial instincts. Sometimes a new venture may be purchased solely for the purpose of eliminating it as a competitor. In cases where no suitable partner can be found, the strategies of going public or remaining a private firm are more desirable and will lead to a higher valuation.

Most valuation analysis is just as simple. It compares the cash flows the project will generate with the returns that investors want to earn on their capital. If the present value of the cash flow is lower than the level of investment required, the project is not viable. It must be abandoned or reconfigured in a way that makes it more financially attractive. For example, if the present value of the cash flows that will be generated by a new drug is $40 million and the project requires $50 million of investment, the project is not viable. It must be abandoned or rethought in a way that makes it financially viable.

Valuation Rules of Thumb

Sometimes valuation analysts use rules of thumb, such as a dollar value per bed or per member. For example, one rule-of-thumb market value for a bed in a drug and alcohol addiction treatment facility was $100,000 in 1986. But such rule-of-thumb values result from particular industry conditions. They are not valid when these conditions change. Some found, to their dismay, that the bed they had purchased for $100,000 in 1986 was selling for $30,000 by 1990. Why? Because the basic dynamics of the industry had changed. The high profits earned in 1986 for addiction therapy services attracted not only many new suppliers but also the attention of the insurance companies. The insurers reduced their rates of reimbursement, a reduction the many new suppliers in the industry had no choice but to accept. The consequent downward spiral in profitability reduced valuation.

This inevitable result of industry dynamics came as a surprise to those who used valuation shortcuts and rules of thumb. The initial overvaluation would have been apparent with careful "basic is beautiful" analysis. Rules of thumb may be a good way for measuring thumbs, but they are surely worthless for financial valuation.

SUSTAINABILITY

The valuation analysis illustrated above assumed that the venture could maintain a 20 percent market share, a $36 per hour search fee, and its initial costs. The sustainability of all these assumptions must be evaluated.

Market Share Sustainability

In the example under discussion, users will be reluctant to switch to another computer program that requires them to learn yet another new operating system. Thus, market share is probably sustainable if the company delivers a good product at a competitive price.

In many cases, however, switching costs are not high. It is easy for a consumer to buy Rolaids instead of TUMS, for example. In these cases, the founders must demonstrate how they will protect their market from erosion by a competitor.

Revenue Sustainability

A few considerations are relevant to predicting revenues. First, the possibility of a price war usually exists. A competitor may decide to reduce prices to force the new venture out of the market. In many cases, established competitors can survive a price war much better than a new venture. It simply does not have the cash reserves needed to continue if prices are greatly reduced.

A price war is unlikely to occur among companies offering literature search programs. After all, the physicians who use the search programs do not pay for them. They pass their costs on to the hospital or their research grants. They are unlikely to notice or care about a price reduction, and therefore a price war would be pointless.

The second consideration in revenue sustainability is the stability of the revenue sources themselves. Some revenue sources are more stable than others. For example, a venture funded primarily by Medicaid payments is much less stable than one funded by private insurance payments, because Medicaid is an erratic source of revenues. In the case at hand, the revenue sources—the hospital itself and the research grants—are stable. They are unlikely to deny or reduce their commitment to pay for searches of the medical literature.

Cost Sustainability

Ventures that rely on only a few key individuals or suppliers are highly vulnerable to increases in the costs of those key resources. One company, for example, was dependent on one salesperson for 30 percent of its sales. She held the company hostage by demanding substantial compensation increases. The company had no option but to accede. Similarly, St. Jude Medical, a successful manufacturer of heart valves, was held hostage by the supplier of the carbon used in the valve. It cut off St. Jude's supply when it heard that St. Jude was researching its own carbon.[4]

Key supplier costs are clearly not sustainable; they are likely to inflate greatly unless the venture has "locked them in" with long-term purchase agreements. But costs may inflate for other reasons. They sometimes grow because initial cost estimates are inconsistent with the product the company is creating. For example, a company purporting to offer high-quality nursing home services budgeted for only 2 nurses per 40 patients. Its staffing pattern was typical of low-cost nursing homes, and was inadequate for the kind of luxury facility it claimed to be. Growth of its costs was inevitable. Many business plans project unrealistically modest cost increases. Construction and research and development costs are generally underestimated, as are their completion schedules. It is worthwhile to ensure that all plans embody realistic inflation factors. (I usually double the estimates of the cost and time required, thus violating my own injunction against using rules of thumb.)

Sustainability of Management

Sometimes the management team that develops a small venture is not well suited to operating it during the next stage of its development. In some cases, the founders have difficulty in letting go or in implementing an orderly plan for the company's growth. The telltale signs of this situation include high turnover rates in top management, the absence of clear, time-phased plans, and the dreaded financial condition known as "a loss."

Some advocate firing the founders at this phase. (Venture capitalists are sometimes called "vulture capitalists" because of their supposed predilection for firing founders and feasting on their corpses.) But this solution is traumatic and eliminates a prime source of continued innovation.

There are no easy solutions to this problem. The presence of experienced executives on the board, preferably ones who have participated in building other companies, is useful. These executives not only enlarge the founders' perspectives but also, if warranted, may step in to manage the firm itself.

A clear management development plan for the founders may also be helpful. For example, the executive education programs at a well-known Eastern graduate school of business administration provide senior managers of small firms with functional training, with a broad business perspective, and with a group of peers undergoing the same transformation. Nominating founders for the boards of directors of other organizations, preferably large ones, is yet another method of broadening their managerial exposure.

Wise founders anticipate this issue and prepare a plan for addressing it. A scientist who founded a company to develop his exciting technological innovation but whose work experience was limited to middle management positions, reassured early stage investors in his firm with his honesty: "We will hire a chief executive officer as soon as we can afford it. I will be on the board and serve as the chief scientist. I do not have the talent, experience, or inclination to play a major managerial role." He and his board reached this decision very early in the life of the company, thus reducing the likelihood of the wrenching turmoil many new ventures experience when they must make managerial changes at a later stage in their growth.

FINANCIAL RISK ASSESSMENT

Financial risk consists of three components, each of which is discussed as follows.

One component of financial risk is related to the nature of the business in which the company is engaged. A company trying to find a cure for AIDS is engaged in a very risky venture. Its chance of success is low. On the other hand, a firm with a certificate of need to provide hospital services is not burdened with as much risk, although it too has a significant chance of failure.

The second risk component is caused by the economy as a whole. All boats rise in a rising sea and must sink when the tide goes out. A strong booming economy will help most nascent companies; a recession will hurt them.

The third element of risk is caused by the company's financial structure. The following signals are relevant to assessing this element of financial risk:

1. Small cash reserves relative to the cash needs of the company indicate a potential *liquidity* problem.
2. Large amounts of debt financing as a percentage of total capital indicate a possible *solvency* problem, particularly if the debt must be repaid rapidly.
3. Low or nonexistent cash flow from the operations of the company indicates a *profitability* problem. Revenues that are excessively concentrated in one payer category, particularly if the revenues and

costs do not match up well, also indicate a profitability problem. For example, as shown in Table 11-2, the financial reversal suffered by XYZ Hospital can be attributed almost entirely to its increasing proportion of Medicare patients and their increasing average length of stay. Because Medicare pays at a flat rate regardless of the length of the stay, the long stays caused severe losses.

4. Assets that are tied up for long periods of time before being used in the company's operations or converted into cash indicate an asset *turnover* problem.

5. A large fraction of fixed costs creates a potential *financing* problem. For example, a venture that insists on hiring its own sales force for distribution and sales rather than using a distributor or manufacturing representatives is saddling itself with a large fixed cost.

Quality of Accounting

Financial risk analysis relies primarily on a firm's financial statements. But accounting can be very flexible. The results presented on the financial statements can be made to appear very different with a different interpretation of accounting principles. The three financial items whose value can change materially with different interpretations of accounting principles are discussed below.

Accounts receivable are assets that reflect the value of bills that have not been collected in cash. Their value is dependent on managerial estimates of the percentage of the bills that will be collected. Few organizations ever collect all of their bills. Sometimes managers estimate a much higher collection rate than that experienced by other comparable organizations, or, in a growing organization, they may estimate that collection rates will improve. Both kinds of estimates should raise red flags. Rapid growth is usually accompanied by decreased collection rates, and a company must explain how it will attain better collection rates than its peers.

Substantial revenues from long-term contracts, such as a 4- or 5-year contract to develop a new health service facility, should raise yet another red flag. The annual profits earned from these contracts are frequently shown in the financial statements on the basis of managerial estimates of the percentage of the work that has been completed. If these estimates lead to unusually high profit margins and the work is far from complete, a red flag should be raised about the realism of the profit predictions.

The reserves estimated by health insurance companies for the year-end magnitude of the health expenses incurred by their enrollees that have not as yet been reported should be examined carefully. (These reserves are booked because the bills for medical expenses incurred by enrollees in December will probably not be received by the insurance company until

Table 11-2 Effect of Revenue Concentration on Financial Risk

XYZ Hospital; 1988 = profitable; 1989 = $5 million loss

	Payers' Share of Patient Day Revenues		Average Length of Stay (days)	
	1988	1989	1988	1989
Medicare	49.9%	58.2%	11.3	12.8
Blue Cross	17.4	14.8	4.3	4.1
Commercial Insurers	20.3	16.1	3.9	3.0
Self-pay	5.5	3.4	5.6	4.9
Medicaid	6.1	6.0	11.0	10.3
Other Sources	.7	1.6	NA	NA

January or February; but if its fiscal year ends in December, the company must estimate the amount of expenses incurred by its enrollees in December regardless of when the bills are received.) Sometimes the estimates for expenses incurred but not yet received are very low. If the balance sheet reserve account for the amount of these expenses decreases as a percentage of total capital over time, a red flag should be raised.

Nonprofit Organization Accounting

Assessing financial risk in nonprofit organizations is complicated by their unique accounting practices. The following factors must be additionally considered for them.

Nonprofit organizations frequently reorganize themselves into a holding company with a number of subsidiaries. Evaluation of their financial condition should be based on statements that account for the whole of the organization and not merely some of its parts.

Nonprofit organizations frequently categorize their resources as restricted or unrestricted. Technically, legally restricted resources are limited to the uses specified by their donors. Restricted resources are relevant to a risk analysis because they cannot be employed at management's discretion. For example, the capital in an endowment fund generally cannot be used—only the income earned on the capital may be spent. Misinterpretation of the nature of the endowment fund assets may thus mask an underlying liquidity problem.

On the other hand, some nonprofit organizations attempt to disguise their wealth by labeling unrestricted resources with confusing terms like "quasi-restricted" or "board-restricted." These resources may be freely used for operating purposes and are thus relevant to a liquidity analysis despite their misleading titles.

Governmental organizations use a modified form of accrual accounting. They recognize revenues only when cash is collected and recognize expenses as soon as a purchase order authorizing the expense is issued. Their bottom line (the difference between revenues and expenses) is thus not comparable to the bottom line in other organizations. Generally, their version of accrual accounting will lead to a lower profit than other versions of accounting.

Conversely, nonprofit organizations, particularly government organizations, are not diligent in recognizing their long-term liabilities for pensions and other retirement benefits. Thus, liabilities, a major factor in solvency analysis, may well be understated in these organizations.

MANAGERIAL ASSESSMENT

Many new ventures are long on vision and short on management. Even with financial viability relatively assured, an evaluation of the managerial skills necessary for successful implementation is imperative.

The most straightforward way to conduct this assessment is to evaluate the fit between the key managerial skills and the opportunity being pursued. The computer search program, for example, is a new consumer innovation catering to a new generation of academic physicians. The managerial skills most critical to its success are operations management, human resource management, and marketing.

Has the entrepreneur highlighted these? Well, he does plan to hire some medical librarians to do marketing. What of operations and human resource management? The entrepreneur predicts no operational problems. He has no plans for the development of his staff. What about managerial control? Management of regulations? (Is there a liability associated with the program?) Leadership philosophy? Not a word. In most cases, a two-alarm bell would now be ringing, but in a venture of such small size the founder's personal involvement may provide sufficient guarantee of adequate management of these areas. His presence and interest alone may be sufficient to control the organization, manage its employees, and market the product. But he must provide assurance of his continued willingness to manage in the long term.

More usually, review of the work histories of key personnel is an important part of the managerial assessment process. An organizational chart filled with "wannabes"—people who "want to be" president, chief financial officer, or product developer—is a chilling sight. On the other hand, prior experience provides no guarantee of success. For example, the founder of a new consumer computer company staffed his organization with people previously employed by a large, highly respected computer company. Was their background relevant? Only if their prior employer catered to new consumers and offered user-friendly software. However, if like many computer companies, it sold products to engineers, who do not need user-friendly programs, the employees' seemingly relevant computer experience is useless. And although their big company experience might help avoid big failures, it would not necessarily help them create a big success, particularly in a venture serving activist consumers.

How about "health care" experience? If the experience was in selling intravenous solutions to hospital pharmacies, its applicability to this venture is dubious. Health care is a multibillion dollar industry comprising many subareas. Mere work experience in some niche of the industry does not ensure a good managerial fit.

SOCIETAL IMPACT

So where are we in evaluating the medical literature search venture? If we follow the checklist in Exhibit 11-1, we have ascertained the following facts: (1) We understand the market (it is small but sustainable); (2) the venture is financially viable; (3) venture capitalists are less likely to invest in it than private investors or institutions; and (4) although little thought has been given to managerial issues, the venture, because of its small size, may not require much management. The founder appears well suited to managing this company. The production risks also appear to be minor.

All in all, a solid venture—but not the next Genentech. However, our evaluation is not complete. The most important item has yet to be discussed: The impact of the venture on society.

For ethical and business reasons, a venture that will have a negative or neutral social impact should not be pursued. Ethically, it is immoral to prey on the weak or poor or to increase our monstrous health care costs without providing a positive return to society. And it is bad business too, because sooner or later worthless ventures are exposed, reviled, and eliminated from the health care system. For example, "Medicaid mills," nursing homes, and HMOs that maltreated their poor patients were drummed out of business through exposure in the media and regulatory action. Even less blatant infractions are closely watched. For example, Genentech was forced to roll back the prices of its drugs to Medicaid patients because of public outrage at the multithousand-dollar price tag the company was demanding from the poor.

What is a socially "worthless" venture? It is one that offers no benefits to those who use the product or service. Is the sale of copper bracelets as an arthritis cure a worthless venture? Of course. Copper bracelets will not relieve arthritis, and their sale merely puts money in the pockets of the seller.

But many ventures are not so clearly worthless. Their social utility depends on the perspective of the evaluator. Frequently, potential users applaud them, while existing providers revile them. For example, from the perspective of many mothers, a birthing center represents a lower-cost alternative to a hospital delivery and enables health activists to exercise far greater control over the birthing process. Sound great? Hospitals do not think so. To the contrary, they claim that birthing centers steal away their healthiest patients and thus raise the costs of the complicated births that remain in the hospital. Further, they claim a birthing center is a riskier environment in which to have a baby because it does not have all the standby emergency equipment that a hospital has available.

Who is right? The argument based on cost is clearly wrong. The costs of a complicated delivery are not affected by other births in the hospital. If a complex delivery costs $200,000, its costs will remain the same whether the hospital performs 1,000 normal births or no normal births. Hospitals muddy the cost waters with this false argument. The quality argument is better grounded. Although the latest research indicates equal risk levels to a healthy mother in either setting, the birthing center is undoubtedly a riskier birthing environment than a fully equipped hospital. But the hospital also costs substantially more, up to three times as much, and entails substantial loss of control by the mother.

What to do? Because birthing centers are aimed at health activists, women who are eager and competent to manage their own health care, it seems clear to me that the ethical solution is to permit the clients to make the decision. Health activists should be informed of the full range of alternative birthing environments and their pros and cons. To deny them that freedom of choice seems to be the unethical alternative.

A similar societal dilemma accompanied the creation of ambulatory physician offices in shopping malls and downtown office buildings: Patients loved them, hospitals did not. From the patients' point of view, the innovation is a boon. Says one Manhattan resident, "When I moved here, I didn't have a private doctor, so this has been great." Physicians like them too. "I get to see a whole spectrum of patients here," says one physician who would otherwise be restricted to hospital patients. But the hospitals do not like them. "They take away our best customers, those who take up the least amount of time and who are able to pay," says the president-elect of the New York Chapter of the American College of Emergency Physicians. And the offices are inevitably accused of providing lower-quality or unneeded care.[5]

These examples are similar to many other ethical dilemmas seemingly presented by the creation of new ventures. Although they purportedly represent unfair competition to existing providers, I do not see this as a good argument against their existence. All ventures that successfully respond to one of the three opportunities—lowering health care costs, increasing consumer satisfaction, and developing medical technology—are unquestionably desirable. Of course, fraudulent new ventures

are despicable, as are those that knowingly prey on the weak, infirm, or ignorant. But ventures that offer innovations that improve the health care system should not be cast aside merely because they compete with existing health care providers. We must encourage innovation, not suppress it.

TECHNOLOGICAL RISK ASSESSMENT

The emperor's new clothes syndrome is not unknown in technology-based ventures. The technology promised by an enthusiastic and seemingly competent scientist never materializes. As Gertrude Stein reportedly said of one American city, there is no there there. Although few of us have the scientific training necessary to evaluate the viability of the technologies being presented, fewer still have the confidence to admit our lack of knowledge. Thus, technological risk is usually ignored or poorly assessed, sometimes with disastrous results.

The eight steps in Table 11-3 are helpful in assessing the risk of a new technology. They will be discussed in the context of the two technological proposals presented below. (To my knowledge, these ventures do not exist. I have created them for illustrative purposes only, and resemblance to real ventures is accidental.)

Case A: Burn Management Technique

A new technique has been developed for improving the healing of burn wounds.

When the technique was tried on a rat, the burn wounds healed faster and with fewer infections than burn wounds conventionally treated. The effect on scarring was not measured, because a method for measuring the characteristics of scar tissue does not presently exist.

The technique uses commonly available items. It may, however, be patentable as a new use for these common items. Their cost is low.

The researcher has published five articles on this subject in highly respected journals. No market size data were presented.

Table 11-3 Issues in Technological Risk Assessment and Sample Applications

Issues	Burn Technology	Sleep Technology
1. Understanding the Black Box	Virtually none	Little
2. Depth of Research	Some	A great deal
3. Downside Risks	Some	A little
4. Financial Considerations:		
Market Acceptability	Good	Likely
Product Pipeline	Some	One
Market Size	Large	Medium
5. Regulatory Issues:		
Seriousness of Problem	Very serious	Serious
6. Potential Competition from Other Technologies	Some	Some
7. Likelihood of a Patent	Unknown	Unknown
8. Production Considerations	No problems	No problems

The researcher believes this technique may also be useful for healing other wounds, such as those created by surgery, accidents, or diseases. It may also be a new method for drug delivery, using the skin as the point of entry for drugs rather than the mouth or a needle. No experiments have tested these ideas as yet.

Case B: Sleep Deprivation Technique

A new technique has been developed for remedying the effects of sleep deprivation on travelers and night shift workers. It does not involve any chemical, surgical, or mechanical manipulation of the body.

The technique has been extensively tested on animals and humans. The location of the part of the body affected by the technique is known. The technique is very successful in restoring normal body functions to the sleep-deprived. Its long-term effects are unknown.

The researcher has worked in this area for 20 years and published over 50 papers in well-respected journals.

The technique involves a new use for commonly available items. It thus may receive a new use type of patent. It has fairly low costs. No market size data were presented.

Understanding the Black Box

The first step in the assessment of technological risk is to determine whether the scientific mechanisms underlying the technique

are understood. This process is commonly referred to as understanding the internal mechanisms of the "black box." In Case A, the burn wound technique, the black box remains sealed—the reasons for its efficacy are not understood. Wound healing is a process of growth. Its mysteries are as profound as the mysteries of human growth. Many research questions remain unanswered.

Case B fares a little better. The researcher knows the location of the cells affected by his technique and has studied its impact on them. But here too the black box has not been cracked wide open. The biochemistry and mechanisms of sleep are complex; much remains to be learned about them and their response to the technique.

Many of the technological advances in use fail this black box test. For example, although mechanical and chemical techniques are widely used to reduce the plaque deposits that block the flow of blood in arteries, there is little understanding of why these plaque deposits form. The possible effects of these techniques on the re-formation of plaque deposits thus cannot be predicted. Nevertheless, drugs or devices to reduce arterial plaque formations are used to treat millions of people.

Depth of Research

Because the black box test is frequently failed, the assessment of technological risk must instead consider the amount and quality of the research underlying the technology as a surrogate for the understanding of its causal mechanisms. In Case B, the researcher has studied the technique for many years, published the results widely, and experimented on many animals and human beings. The researcher in Case A, in contrast, has published far fewer articles, researched the problem for a shorter amount of time, and experimented only with rats.

Case A raises a number of red flags. Because of its shorter history, this research has not been subjected to much peer review. Other scientists have not yet had their say about the technique's efficacy. The use of rats as the only test animals is also of concern. Rat skin is different from human skin, and rats are otherwise not ideal analogues to human burn victims. The researcher must use other animals and ultimately humans to test the efficacy of the technique.

Case A may ultimately turn out to be a wonderful technique. But at present it is riskier than Case B because of the paucity of animal trials and published research and the absence of data about its effect on humans.

Downside Risks

The long-term effects of both techniques are unknown, as is true of many other technologies. Many drugs and devices are adopted after only a few years of experimentation. By permitting early adoption, government regulators explicitly accept the risks of the unknown in order to allow the therapeutic benefit that can be gained with more immediate use and the benefits of learning more about its long-term consequences.

All medical interventions cause some negative long-term consequences, because they interfere with our normal body rhythms. The human body is a beautifully balanced mechanism. Intervention with any one part will inevitably upset it elsewhere. Even aspirin, among the best-known and most benign of drugs, was found to cause, occasionally, a serious children's disease.

Technological risk assessment must consider the probability of discovering problems with the technique in the long-term. In both Case A and Case B, problems are inevitable, but they appear to be more likely in Case A. The therapy in Case A invades the body and may alter an important bodily function. Because the therapy in Case B is noninvasive, it has a lower probability of causing harm.

Financial Considerations

A critical issue in the analysis of a technological innovation is whether it is acceptable to the market. Physicians are reluctant to switch from familiar products that work well to new products with which they have no experience and whose efficacy is not yet completely proven. Technologies that are excessively innovative encounter difficulty in gaining market acceptance, particularly if they are invasive. Although the technologies in Cases A and B are both innovative, the lower invasiveness of the sleep deprivation therapy may make it more acceptable. On the other hand, the financial risk of A is lowered because it can be used in familiar hospital settings, whereas the appropriate setting for the use of B is unknown.

From a financial perspective, technologies that can create a "product pipeline" because of their potential application in many new products are preferable to those that can be used for only one product.[6] Market size data would be helpful, but they are unavailable for the sleep deprivation therapy. The size of the market for a wound-healing therapy is indicated by the following data: 3.5 million people have skin ulcers, pressure sores affect 7 percent of acute care hospital patients, over 100,000 people are hospitalized for burns annually,[7] and more than 25 million surgeries are performed yearly. Despite the absence of market data, both technologies clearly serve large potential markets. Because the technology in Case A deals with both wounds and burns, it has greater product pipeline potential than the other technology, which appears to have only one application.

Regulatory Issues

Regulatory problems multiply when the black box is tightly shut, the science is a mile wide and an inch deep, and the downside risks are substantial. Also affecting the likelihood of difficulty in the regulatory process are the availability of alternative technologies and the seriousness of the underlying problem. Technologies that can be "grandfathered" because they relate to a predecessor technology are generally more quickly cleared by the FDA. And while burns, wounds, and sleep disorders are all serious problems, regulatory hurdles are likely to be more quickly overcome for a drug that promises to treat life-threatening diseases like AIDS than for either of these two technologies. Indeed, the FDA is presently considering modifying its clinical trials requirements, and switching to "surrogate markers" that test changes in the patient's biochemistry instead of waiting for longer periods to test the efficacy of AIDS drugs.[8]

Potential Competition from Other Technologies

Biotechnology may render the wound-healing technique in Case A obsolete through the development of an effective, controllable human growth hormone that promotes wound healing or the development of cheap, effective methods of growing and grafting human skin onto wounds. As for Case B, a drug may be discovered that safely and effectively regulates the sleep cycle. At the present time, the technologies competing with the wound-healing technique are at more advanced stages of development than the potential technological competitors to the sleep deprivation therapy. Indeed, a salve from China is now said to provide miraculous regeneration of burned tissues.[9] However, none of the competitive technologies appears to be at an advanced stage.

Consideration of potentially competitive technologies should embrace a broad range of alternatives. Although competitors are fre-

quently defined as similar technologies, competition often emanates from products that use entirely different technologies from the one being evaluated. For example, the disease of endometriosis, in which excess tissue in the uterus causes infertility and other problems, was first treated with a major surgical procedure. The invention of new medical devices made much less invasive procedures for curing the disease possible because they enabled surgery through small incisions in the navel. But surgery will ultimately prove unnecessary because of a drug that promises to eliminate the problem. Thus, the technological modalities used to treat the disease ranged from a scalpel and operating room equipment, to a new medical device, to a biochemical compound. Sometimes, even a new service may provide competition to the technology being considered. For example, widespread improvement in sanitation and personal hygiene would likely reduce the need for technologies that treat medical problems caused by lack of sanitation, such as hepatitis.

Likelihood of a Patent

The presence of a lawyer who specializes in patent law and is knowledgeable about the technology is invaluable. Does an MIT-trained chemical engineer with a law degree meet these specifications? Although such a lawyer might seem qualified, he or she is not suitable if the product requires an understanding of electrical engineering principles. Experience in filing for patents and patent infringement suits is another key legal asset.

Production Considerations

Considerable difficulties frequently occur in the production of many medical technologies. Quality control problems in manufacturing drugs and devices, difficulties in producing a consistent and stable material in biomaterials production, and a variety of complications in scaling up the production of biotechnology products from the laboratory to a large factory have all occurred. Production difficulties are relevant in assessing technological risk.

The technologies in Cases A and B are unlikely to have major production problems because they are composed of readily available items. In many other technologies, production considerations are more substantial. The key issues are these: Do manufacturing procedures already exist? Is sufficient manufacturing capacity already present? Has the scaling up of the technology's manufacturing process been demonstrated? Do the existing manufacturers have clean records with regulatory authorities about the quality of their manufacturing process? An answer of no to any of these questions should raise concerns about potential production problems.

The Limits of Peer Review

Scientists often urge "peer review" as a surrogate for independent, outside verification of their work. But although the judgment of knowledgeable peers is certainly important, it is hardly infallible and may well be obstructive. Some important medical discoveries have been actively opposed by the inventors' peers. For example, the promoter of the use of ether as an anesthetic was so reviled by his peers that he committed suicide. They ignored his immensely important suggestion, which subsequently greatly reduced the pain of surgery and ultimately, but belatedly, enabled the development of many surgical procedures.

Medicine is a relatively young science. Unlike the physical sciences, medicine has few universally valid and proven laws. Although the science of biology became enormously more powerful as a result of the discovery of DNA's structure, much still remains to be learned. Consequently, medical research is more subject to fads and peer pressure than other, better-established areas of scientific research.

It is unwise to rely solely on peer review for purposes of technology assessment. To the extent possible, investors and managers must inform themselves about the technology, its potential, and its limitations. Scientists should clearly explain the technology to investors. Scientists who are unable to do so may well be indicating their own lack of clarity about the underlying mechanisms. As in any profession, an unclear or incoherent explanation is often a better indicator of the presenter's fundamental lack of understanding of the subject, than of the listener's lack of intelligence.

THE WELL-MANAGED HEALTH CARE VENTURE

Now that we have examined the process of evaluating new ventures, what are the characteristics of a well-managed venture ? The turnaround of International Medication Systems, a once faltering California firm that in one year increased sales by 38 percent and profits by 20 percent, illustrates the impact of management on a new venture.

When the company was purchased in 1988, it had a broad line of medical products. The first thing its new management did was to focus on one of the three opportunities. It lopped off 30 percent of the products and zoomed in on one with great promise—a patented needle called Stick-Guard. The needle's plastic sheath protected users from accidental punctures. Although it was potentially a great boon for health care workers who feared AIDS or hepatitis infections from an accidental needle prick, it had been languishing on the company's "to do" list for almost 4 years.

The needle was positioned as a new technology that substantially increased the quality of care. It was considerably more expensive than other needles; but hospitals heeded the message. A large financial settlement reached between a hospital and a doctor who contracted AIDS through an accidental needle prick reinforced the need for this new technology.

Regulatory management issues were moot because the needle had already been patented, but marketing issues remained. The company had only 29 sales representatives, too few to cover the many thousands of hospitals and clinics in its market. The solution? Direct mail to 6,700 hospitals and clinics. The first mailing for this important, yet easy-to-understand technological innovation yielded an extraordinarily high 13 percent response rate. Also, the marketing staff and marketing expenses were increased. As a result, customers noted greater responsiveness to their needs. Past difficulties in filling orders were remedied with the investment in substantial back-up inventories and a larger manufacturing facility.

The new management also invested in considerable training. An extensive bilingual family of videotapes was developed for training production workers. They were required to pass a test after training. Defects dropped in half. Salespeople also attended mandatory sessions to become familiar with the company's complex product line. Policies and procedures were clearly delineated, and employees were held accountable for their performance. New rewards were implemented. The company instituted a profit sharing plan and vested all employees immediately after its creation. "They told me it was crazy to vest them so soon," notes CEO Randall J. Wall, "but I wanted to show that we cared about our employees." Financing these changes required an investment of $10 million, provided by a letter of credit. Many other small changes were made. For example, the company provided volleyball courts for its employees. The attention to detail paid off: Turnover dropped substantially.

No wonder International Medication Systems succeeded. It developed a clear focus on a new technology and implemented the marketing and finance skills most needed to translate that focus into success. It did not neglect the other skills: Managerial control was used to pare the product line; operations management to size the organization appropriately; and human resource management to train and motivate employees. And International Medication Systems had a

clear leadership philosophy. Its new managers, experienced in large corporate environments, had little doubt about the value they could add with centralized management. "It was time to take our corporate experience and put it into something entrepreneurial," said Mr. Wall.

The resulting success story applauds his insight.[10] Replicating the success of this company requires replication of the techniques it used: a clear focus on the market opportunities, a balanced implementation of the seven skills, and the knowledge that successful management requires not only bold strokes and broad visions but attention to detail.

Take a deep breath. We have come a long way. But, as was said of Gigi, the best is yet to come. The new health care system is waiting to be created.

NOTES

1. Association of American Medical Colleges, *Teaching Hospitals* (Washington, D.C.: Association of American Medical Colleges, July 1989), 15.

2. Fred Bazzdi, "Nursing Homes Operating at a Loss," *Modern HealthCare*, November 12, 1990, 37.

3. Tinker Ready, "HCFA Caps Lens Payments," *Health-Week*, February 26, 1990, 8.

4. Patricia Kelly, "King of Hearts," *Corporate Report, Minnesota*, April 1988, 42–48.

5. Howard W. French, "Walk-in Doctor's Offices," *New York Times*, February 11, 1990, 25.

6. John T. Preston, "Creating New Companies and Business Units within Existing Companies via University Licensing Agreements," working paper (Cambridge, Mass.: Massachusetts Institute of Technology, 1989).

7. "Wound Healing Update," *The BBI Newsletter*, December 7, 1989, 183.

8. "Cutting the Red Tape on AIDS Drugs," *Business Week*, February 25, 1991, 63.

9. "A Simpler Way to Save Lives," *Newsweek*, May 7, 1990, 68–69.

10. David J. Jefferson, "Corporate Experience Bolsters Small Firm in Big Way," *Wall Street Journal*, May 22, 1990, B2.

Part V

Case Studies

What follows are 20 case studies, 19 describing new health care ventures and one the economic environment that motivates their creation. The cases all depict real-life ventures, usually from the perspective of their founders or chief executive officers. They collectively describe the three opportunities (indeed, virtually all of the major sectors in the U.S. health care system) and the seven skills as shown in Table V-l.

These cases represent neither success nor failure, do not indicate right answers or wrong ones. Rather, they enable the reader to learn how others managed the opportunities in the sector and to decide whether the strategies used and the managerial skills implemented were appropriate. They provide a window from which to observe this new world.

LEARNING FROM A CASE STUDY

No doubt, some might prefer that the window encompassed a much smaller view. "Why are these cases so long?" is a query I have encountered more than a few times. My answer may seem surprising: From my perspective as a teacher, most of these case studies are too short, not too long. After all, the purpose of a case is to duplicate for its readers the situation that real managers encounter, the maelstrom of relevant and irrelevant factors, most of them ambiguously presented, for which they must prepare and implement appropriate responses. "Short" case studies artificially edit this reality, planting heavy clues so that the reader can quickly discover the relevant issues. In the interest of conserving the reader's time, they may sacrifice much of the important process of learning how to sort out the managerial wheat from the chaff, to pluck the important issues out from the welter of details that surround them. Then, too, it is the sum of many seemingly small details that creates the difference between success and failure.

The case studies included here are the result of repeated but reluctant condensations. They are designed, even after shortening, to help the reader duplicate the reality facing managers, to examine the details that make the difference. It is important, when confronting a data-filled exhibit or a lengthy narrative description of some managerial action, not to quickly flip the page. Those details are there for a good reason.

The managerial skills that create successful new ventures are eternal verities. The skills

Table V-1 Case Study Subjects

Case Study Title	Sector	Major Topics
Beverly Hospital	Nonprofit hospital services	Creating new ventures to reduce cost and to serve new consumers
Boston Sobriety Development, Inc.	Alcohol and drug abuse rehabilitation	Implementing a compensation system for sales personnel
Center for Nutritional Research	Health promotion	Marketing a new venture
Computers in Medicine, Inc.	Management and clinical information	Marketing a new venture
Diagnostic Imaging, Inc.	Free-standing diagnostic centers	Financing a new venture
Health Stop: Strategy	Ambulatory service centers	Creating a new venture
Health Stop: Production Process	Ambulatory service centers	Operational management
Hospital Corporation of America and McLean Hospital	Mental health services	Valuing a new venture and human resource management
The Hospital Replacement Decision	For-profit hospital services	Leadership philosophy and managerial control systems
Humana, Inc.	For-profit hospital and HMO services	Creating a new venture
Hyatt Hill Health Center	Health services for the poor	Managerial control systems
Mediplex Group, Inc.	Long-term care services	Creating a new venture to control costs
New England Critical Care, Inc.	Home health services	Creating a new venture: What is the opportunity?
North Shore Birth Center	Maternity services	Human resource management
Novel Combination of Two Drugs	Phamaceuticals	Financing research and development through joint ventures
Shouldice Hospital Limited	Single-purpose hospitals	Operations and human resource management
Spacelabs	Medical devices	Marketing a new medical device
Technology Transfer	Biotechnology	Financing research and development through joint ventures
Trinity University	Health insurance	Controlling health care costs
United States Health Care Systems, Inc.	HMOs	Managerial control

used long ago by Alfred Sloan to forge the initial great success of General Motors are still relevant today. Similarly, the managerial techniques used to launch a new health care venture continue to be worthy of study long after the venture has failed or succeeded. For example, the issue of how to design a managerial control system, which is discussed in the Hyatt Hill Center case, is as important today as it was in 1971 when I wrote the case. Although some of the other case study subjects may have changed their direction, the changes are not relevant. The purpose of a case study is to illuminate managerial skills rather than to describe the current state of an organization.

WHERE IS THE RIGHT ANSWER?

At the end of my classes, I am sometimes asked for the "right" answer that would prescribe what should have been done in a given situation. I wish I could provide it, both for my students' satisfaction and my own. We all crave certainty, I no less than others, and we all hope to find the golden formulas that will guarantee success in our ambiguous world.

But I cannot provide the "right" answer, nor an appraisal of what "really" happened. It would be dishonest to do so. Every business situation can be handled in many different ways, each no more right than the others. And what really happened depends on the vantage point of the observer: A camera pointed at a face produces a different picture from one directed at the hand.

A case study should allow the reader to see the many ways that a good answer can be achieved and to more quickly eliminate the bad answers. Although I provide below a brief update on each case as of mid-1991, please do not think that these updates condemn or justify the managerial actions depicted in the cases. It is up to the reader to decide whether the successful venture could have been even more successful with different applications of the seven skills and whether the managers of failed ventures nevertheless did the best that they could do in difficult circumstances.

CASE UPDATES

Beverly Hospital gained market share in its competitive market, ultimately taking over a neighboring hospital.

Boston Sobriety Development, Inc., implemented a sales compensation system but went out of business, as did the *Center for Nutritional Research; Computers in Medicine, Inc.; and Diagnostic Imaging Inc.*

Health Stop continues in operation, with current revenues of approximately $70 million and over 60 centers.

The *Hospital Corporation of America* did not acquire McLean Hospital. Instead, McLean entered into a more limited joint venture with another hospital corporation. This joint venture was dissolved in 1990.

Humana, Inc., has refocused its HMO business and continues to manage hospitals successfully.

The *Hyatt Hill Health Center* remains in operation but has not been widely replicated.

Mediplex Group, Inc., continues in operation. It went public and then was purchased by Avon shortly after the case. It was repurchased by its founder in 1990.

New England Critical Care, Inc., is now a publicly owned corporation, the second largest in the field.

The *North Shore Birth Center* continues in operation, although some changes in management personnel have occurred.

The *Novel Combination of Two Drugs* proved to be technologically infeasible.

The *Shouldice Hospital Limited* continues in successful operation.

Spacelabs was spun off from Squibb and continues to operate as a successful company.

The *Technology Transfer* was consummated with different agreements from those described.

United States Health Care Systems, Inc. continues in successful operation.

Case Studies

Table of Contents

Case Study 1

Beverly Hospital

On a mild April weekend, Northeast Health Systems Inc./Beverly Hospital was about to hold its board retreat. In its CEO's view, attendees should "come away from our retreat with a clear vision of the strategic initiatives that must be pursued to preserve our provision of high-quality patient care services and financial integrity." In his opinion, the following were the key to the hospital's survival:

1. the need to anticipate and preempt any loss of patient volume resulting from the increasingly competitive health care environment
2. the plan for expansion of services to outlying north suburban areas
3. the development of closer relationships with nearby hospitals

BACKGROUND OF BEVERLY HOSPITAL

Founded in 1888, Beverly Hospital was a 238-bed acute care nonprofit community institution, serving primarily the North Shore area of metropolitan Boston, including the city of Beverly and eleven other municipalities (Exhibit 1.1). The hospital was located on a 38-acre site in the city of Beverly, a coastal community approximately 20 miles northeast of Boston. Route 128, the major circumferential highway serving the greater Boston area,

Note: This case was prepared by Professor Regina E. Herzlinger. Case Study 14, North Shore Birth Center, describes one of the Beverly Hospital's subsidiaries.

Copyright ©1991 by the President and Fellows of Harvard College. Harvard Business School Case No. 1-187-091.

was a quarter-mile to the north of the hospital and the hospital owned a licensed heliport on its property. The service area had a good employer base, with 123 firms employing over 100 people each.

The four most significant demographic factors affecting the Beverly Hospital/NHSI were:

1. a stable, no-growth total population
2. an increase in the elderly population, especially in the over-75 age group. The North Shore had a greater proportion of elderly than the nation as a whole (14% vs. 11.5%)
3. low growth in the number of children in the area
4. higher-than-average income and asset levels in Beverly's primary and secondary service areas, particularly for the older age groups

Modern facilities were available in the hospital's maternity and pediatric floor and the emergency, physical, speech and occupational therapy, surgery, renal dialysis, audiology, ancillary, and outpatient departments. But in 1986, 116 of its medical-surgical beds were still in outmoded four-room suites and the psychiatric beds were on the third floor of a building constructed in 1927. To renovate these areas, add 3 maternity beds, and buy a full-body scanner to replace the head scanner, the hospital filed CON applications.

The hospital's occupancy and lengths of stay had remained stable since 1981, unlike some of its competitors (see Table 1.1). (The hospital's description of its competitors is in Exhibit 1.2.)

Exhibit 1.1 Beverly Hospital's Service Area

	Population			% of Beverly Hospital's Discharges	
	1970	*1985*	*1990*	*1982*	*1984*
Beverly	38,348	37,880	38,380	42.9	43.0
Hamilton	6,373	6,900	6,850	5.2	5.5
Manchester	5,151	5,390	5,370	4.2	4.8
Salem	40,556	37,300	35,980	3.5	3.6
Danvers	26,151	23,320	22,590	4.4	4.0
Gloucester	27,941	28,200	28,540	4.9	5.7
Ipswich	10,750	11,300	11,370	10.6	8.5
Wenham	3,849	3,870	3,840	2.5	2.9
Topsfield	5,225	5,780	5,840	1.7	1.7
Essex	2,670	3,040	2,110	2.7	2.4
Boxford	4,032	5,610	5,840	.8	.8
Rowley	3,040	4,100	4,380	.9	1.1
Total Primary Service Area	174,086	172,690	171,090	84.3	84.0
Total Secondary Service Area	NA	NA	NA	15.7	16.0

MASSACHUSETTS HEALTH SERVICE AREA VI

Table 1.1 Beverly Hospital: Summary of Historical Operating Statistics for Service Area Hospitals, 1980 and 1984

(patient statistics exclude newborns)

	Discharges	Patient Days*	Length of Stay (days)	Occupancy (%)	Number of Beds					
					MED/ SURG	ICU/CCU	Obstetric	Pediatric	Psychiatric	Total
Beverly Hospital										
1980	7,965	68,334	8.6	78.50	173	19	14	16	16	238
1984	7,895	69,028	8.7	80.90	173	19	14	11	16	238
Hunt Memorial Hospital										
1980	5,590	42,027	7.5	83.00	107	8	10	13	0	138
1984	5,217	40,461	7.8	76.00	115	8	10	11	0	144
Addison Gilbert Hospital										
1980	4,694	37,941	8.1	80.80	97	10	8	14	0	129
1984	4,560	39,754	8.7	80.50	102	8	8	5	12	135
Lynn Hospital										
1980	11,273	103,008	9.1	93.20	232	14	31	28	0	305
1984	8,649	74,431	8.6	67.60	232	14	30	25	0	301
Union Hospital										
1980	2,425	21,843	9.0	51.50	84	5	0	0	27	116
1984	6,509	54,567	8.4	72.70	174	12	0	0	24	210
Salem Hospital										
1980	10,902	118,106	10.8	85.10	304	23	17	0	35	379
1984	12,097	108,143	8.9	78.00	304	23	17	0	35	379

*Patient days are not precisely equal to the product of discharges and length of stay because of rounding errors.

Exhibit 1.2 Beverly Hospital: Competitive Hospitals

The other short-term acute care hospitals providing health care services to residents of Beverly Hospital's primary and secondary service areas include Hunt Memorial Hospital, Addison Gilbert Hospital, Salem Hospital, North Shore Children's Hospital, and AtlantiCare Corporation. A summary of management's information regarding these organizations follows.

Hunt Memorial Hospital

The hospital is owned by the Town of Danvers and is the only hospital that shares the primary service area of Beverly Hospital. Hunt has recently renovated its ICU, increased its bed complement by eight, and obtained a head computerized tomography scanner. Recently, Hunt supported the establishment of a physician in the Town of Middletown and opened a walk-in urgent care center adjacent to a shopping mall in Danvers. A proprietary urgent care chain has also opened a facility across from the same shopping mall. Hunt has announced plans to extensively renovate its labor, delivery, and day surgery areas. Hunt has also discussed a possible management contract with Hospital Corporation of America officials. Hunt is unaffiliated with most HMOs in the area, with some small exceptions.

Addison Gilbert Hospital

The hospital is a 135-bed acute care general hospital located in Gloucester, approximately 12 miles northeast of Beverly. A recent renovation project improved several ancillary departments and established the psychiatric service. Addison Gilbert has limited HMO affiliations to one IPA. Addison Gilbert plans to construct a skilled nursing facility. No long-term care beds are available in the current bed need formula, published by the Massachusetts Department of Public Health, for the Gloucester area.

Salem Hospital

The hospital is located in Salem, approximately five miles from Beverly Hospital. Salem provides several specialized services, including radiation therapy and cardiac catheterization. Salem plans to modernize its emergency and ambulatory care departments, maternity suites, and to replace its power plant at a total cost of about $26,000,000. Salem is affiliated with many HMOs. It has also indicated an interest in long-term care with possible plans for a home and/or durable medical equipment venture. Salem and Beverly Hospital are currently discussing the feasibility of a joint venture. Salem now has a management contract for a 35-bed hospital in Marblehead, six miles from Beverly, and a contract for selected services for a 99-bed municipal hospital in Peabody, six miles from Beverly.

North Shore Children's Hospital

The hospital is a 50-bed pediatric hospital adjacent to Salem Hospital. It has a teaching affiliation with Tufts/New England Medical Center, Boston, and a number of shared service arrangements with Salem Hospital. North Shore Children's maintains an eight-bed inpatient pediatric physiatric service and operates a number of specialized outpatient clinics and human service counseling programs. It opened a satellite outpatient facility in Peabody that provides a range of therapeutic day care and counseling services, along with some preventive medical services. Other satellites are planned. North Shore Children's is discussing with Beverly Hospital a psychiatric outpatient joint venture in Beverly. North Shore Children's is the only pediatric hospital north of Boston and provides most of its in-patient services to patients who reside in Lynn, Salem, and Peabody.

AtlantiCare Corporation

This is the corporate holding company for Lynn Hospital and Union Hospital, both located in Lynn, about 15 miles southwest of Beverly. Lynn Hospital, a 301-bed acute care facility, is located in the center of the city. Union Hospital, with 210 beds, is located in the north suburban area. In September 1985, AtlantiCare submitted a $59,000,000 Determination of Need application to consolidate Lynn Hospital operations at the Union Hospital site with a reduction of 130 beds from a total bed complement of 511. Although both Lynn and Union Hospitals are in the secondary service area of the hospital, they are considered competitors because of the growing importance of HMOs on the North Shore.

The number of physicians affiliated with the hospital had grown by 44 from 1980 to 205 MDs and 20 dentists by 1985. Twenty practiced full time with the hospital; all others were in private practice, mostly in the primary service area. The 10 MDs who accounted for 27% of the hospital's 1984 discharges all had their principal offices in one of the hospital's two condominium medical office buildings. Total discharges by department and physician, by age, are in Table 1.2.

THE CHANGING HEALTH CARE ENVIRONMENT

The changes detailed below in the 1980s health care system affected all hospitals, including Beverly.

Reimbursement Changes

Hospital finances were dramatically affected because both government and private insurance companies focused on cost savings. Medicare destroyed the cost-plus mentality of hospital management when it initiated prospective pricing schedules in the fall of 1983. The private insurance industry, prodded by corporate America, was also forcing hospitals to be competitive and reviewing their utilization. In 1981, Massachusetts Blue Cross began to set the prospective annual level of allowable costs on the basis of 1981 costs adjusted forward for inflation, changes in volume and case mix, and exceptions for costs associated with a CON. For 1985, Beverly Hospital's Blue Cross reimbursement was 9.1% below the amount it would have received prior to the prospective payment system.

These changes caused reductions in hospital occupancy, as the lengths of patient stays and admission rates declined sharply.

New Entrants Competing for a Hospital's Patient Base

New competitors in Massachusetts' health care delivery sector included HMOs and PPOs, free-standing urgi- and surgi-centers, and home health care.

The HMOs' and PPOs' growth affected hospital utilization in two ways: (1) They had an economic incentive to minimize inpatient hospitalization and to encourage alternative outpatient health care for members, and (2) utilization for certain hospitals was increased because members could use only those hospitals with which they had an affiliation agreement. Free standing urgi-centers and surgi-centers also provided a challenge. They were operated by private physicians who often banded together to raise the capital outlay needed, and increasingly by for-profit chains such as Health Stop. Those institutions, run on a high-volume, low-overhead basis, had begun to make inroads into hospital emergency rooms (which account for 15–30% of inpatient admissions) and surgical visits.

The large home health care market was considered both a benefit and problem for hospitals. On the one hand, with the availability of home care, hospitals could more easily reduce the length of stay. On the other, the home health market was becoming more sophisticated and some routine hospital procedures such as kidney dialysis could shift completely to the home.

PRODUCT LINE MANAGEMENT

In 1984, Beverly Hospital established 16 product lines. These "centers of excellence" were structured into four groups, each independently responsible to a strategy review board of senior management representatives. The product line groups, for example, included one comprising Emergency Room, Respiratory/Pulmonary, Psychiatry, and General Surgery services.

The product line process began with intensive training of all managers in marketing and strategic problem-solving. The product line team leader presented the product strategies for the coming year to the review board, which then prioritized each product line for the coming year. Although only one product line for each team was reviewed per year, the plan-

Table 1.2 Beverly Hospital: Analysis of Physician Age and Discharges by Specialty, Fiscal Year Ended September 30, 1984*

Active Staff	Number of Physicians	Total Discharges 1984	Age 30–44		Age 45–54		Age 55–64		Age over 65	
			Physician	Discharge	Physician	Discharge	Physician	Discharge	Physician	Discharge
Anesthesia	4	0	2	0	1	0	0	0	1	0
Emergency and Outpatient	5	5	2	0	2	0	1	5	0	0
Family Practice	11	1,055	7	865	1	89	1	65	2	36
Internal Medicine	38	3,145	23	1,348	14	1,517	1	280	0	0
Obstetrics and Gynecology	9	1,278	4	420	3	526	2	332	0	0
Pathology	2	0	0	0	1	0	1	0	0	0
Pediatrics	15	969	8	480	3	170	3	258	1	61
Psychiatry	8	178	5	178	1	0	1	0	1	0
Radiology	5	0	1	0	3	0	1	0	0	0
Surgery	29	1,888	8	268	15	1,296	4	100	2	224
Total Active Staff	126	8,518	60	3,559	44	3,598	15	1,040	7	321
Cumulative Active Staff Discharges by Age Group		8,518		3,559		3,598		1,040		321
Cumulative Active Staff Discharges as a % of Total Discharges		96.65 %		40.38 %		40.83 %		11.80 %		3.64 %
Total Associate, Courtesy, and Consulting Staff	86	295								
Total All Physicians	212	8,813								

Note: Active staff includes provisional physicians.

*Total number of discharges accounts separately for each physician involved with a discharge.

ning process was thought to be beneficial for those more comfortable with operations.

Beverly Hospital's current marketing slogans resulted from the first year of product line management. To reposition itself and communicate its new role in the North Shore community, Beverly adopted as a marketing logo, "More than a Hospital…a Family Centered Health Care System." This concept provided the basis for advertising several of the product lines, with "high-tech" ads, stressing medical qualities, and "high-touch" ads, stressing warmth.

One product, women's health, resulted from a number of focus groups, marketing studies, surveys, and brainstorming sessions. Marketing data indicated that although most health care services were purchased by women, services were not geared to fulfill their need for a place with a "comfort zone" and for providers who delivered specialized care. The studies also found that North Shore women wanted "someone to talk with who will listen to my needs." As a result, Beverly's Women's Health Connection was established as a referral line staffed by volunteers and specialized professionals. The project team described the connection as a place "where your search for information ends." Additional plans for the Women's Health Connection include a women's library, an off-site mammography unit, and specialized women's health care services.

Another product line resulted from the nurse manager of the general surgery group observing the problems the surgical staff and patients experienced in admission time and surgical scheduling. In the past, surgical patients were admitted the day before their operations to give the nursing staff ample time to make the patients comfortable, order and receive results for all appropriate tests, and answer questions. As HMO admissions began to represent a more significant percentage of Beverly's patient load, this comfortable process changed and patients came to the hospital the day of surgery as "AM admits." Tests performed outside the hospital (usually at the HMO) caused problems in recordkeeping. At times, patients did not receive adequate preparation for their operation.

As day surgery increased, Beverly Hospital found alternative ways to educate patients before admission. A videotape was produced and shown in the hospital and community. A volunteer program enabled patients to come into the hospital a few days prior to their procedure, have their tests performed, ask questions, and tour the facility. Comfortable "living rooms" were set aside for patients and their families to use. Patients were to be treated as guests in a hotel, rather than admits in a hospital; for example, where once patients who entered the outpatient area were given a dressing room and a garbage bag for their clothing, they were now assigned a locker.

The current product line strategy was to create a pre-admission testing center for central control of all testing and information, so that physicians and their staff could retrieve test information from one point.

HMO AFFILIATIONS

In 1986, HMOs accounted for 15% of admissions in medical/surgical, 32.4% in obstetrical, 38.4% in pediatric, and 12.7% in pychiatric. By 1987, Beverly Hospital's affiliations with seven major HMOs and PPOs were critical to its future (see Exhibit 1.3).

In 1982, a hospital Subcommittee on Alternative Delivery Systems was established to educate the hospital staff about HMO affiliations and to review opportunities. Its original members were six physicians, the CEO, six board members, and two management representatives. The first meeting consisted of a presentation of the benefits of HMO affiliations to physicians as well as the hospital.

One significant proposal emerged when the committee learned that the largest Massachusetts HMO was negotiating with the competitor, Salem Hospital, for services to the HMO's North Shore health center. Beverly made an aggressive attempt to capture the HMO's interest before it had an opportunity to solidify this relationship. After reviewing a lengthy

Exhibit 1.3 Beverly Hospital: HMO/PPO Affiliations

Beverly has hospital service agreements with five area HMOs. In 1985, approximately 13% of all hospital admissions were members of an HMO, a percentage expected to increase in the future.

In May 1984, the hospital entered into a five-year hospital service agreement with a 213,000-member closed-panel HMO. Beverly Hospital is currently its sole provider for its Peabody Center for all hospital services, except for psychiatric services and tertiary level services not provided at the hospital. It also has a three-year hospital service agreement with a group practice HMO with 57,863 members. Beverly and Hunt Hospitals are currently its only providers of hospital services on the North Shore. The hospital has an agreement with an IPA whose enrollment is currently 120,000 members, the second largest HMO in Massachusetts. The IPA currently has agreements with all of the hospitals within Beverly Hospital's competitive area.

In May 1985, the hospital entered into an agreement with a Blue Cross IPA. Each subscriber elects a primary care physician and a primary hospital upon enrollment. Both hospital and physician are then paid a fixed sum per enrollee each month for providing all services to patients. The hospital's limited experience with this plan precludes prediction of its eventual impact. However, there are risk-sharing arrangements between primary care physician providers, the hospital, and specialist providers. As of August 1, 1985, 500 of the plan's 1,055 members chose Beverly Hospital as their primary hospital.

In 1984, the hospital entered into an agreement with a closed panel HMO sponsored by Blue Cross which operates a medical center located in Peabody, a five-minute drive from the hospital. The HMO has an enrollment of 3,602 as of August 11, 1985, and also has agreements with Salem Hospital and the two AtlantiCare Corporation hospitals to provide similar services.

In 1984, the hospital entered in an agreement with John Hancock Mutual Life Insurance Company to participate as a network hospital in John Hancock's SelectCare, a preferred provider organization (PPO) which began operations in the fall of 1984 and had an enrollment of approximately 20,000 members as of January 1, 1985.

document stressing Beverly's lower length of stay, the HMO chose Beverly Hospital as its primary acute care facility for North Shore members.

ORGANIZATIONAL CHARACTERISTICS

In 1983, Beverly Hospital established Northeast Health Systems Inc./Beverly Hospital, a vertically integrated system providing all levels of health care services, including acute, long-term, and home care; medically assisted housing; and ambulatory care. Its principal assets were 12 acres of prime land in the city of Peabody, five miles to the south of Beverly. The land was to house (1) a magnetic resonance imaging center in cooperation with Beverly Hospital and four other area hospitals; (2) a free-standing ambulatory surgical center; (3) a 142-bed nursing home; and (4) a medical office building. Its principal subsidiaries were as follows:

MedQuest Corporation was to arrange for services provided by new health care organizations. MedQuest was constructing and operating a 122-bed long-term care facility on the grounds of Beverly Hospital, as an equal partner with a subsidiary of National Medical Enterprises, a for-profit California-based health services firm. It also filed CON applications to construct and operate a Peabody nursing home and a free-standing kidney dialysis center with nine stations in Lynn, Massachusetts, as a jointly owned venture between MedQuest and Massachusetts General Hospital, a large Harvard University teaching hospital. Its subsidiary, Northeast Medical Management Services, Inc., was a for-profit company that provided management services to ambulatory medical providers.

NHS Properties, Inc. was a nonprofit real estate holding company.

Cable Housing and Health Services Corporation was established to develop the hospital's Ipswich property. The hospital also owned another 10-acre site in Ipswich on which it ran an emergency room and medical office building.

SurgiQuest was established to construct and operate an ambulatory surgical center on the Peabody property along with Medical Care International (a publicly traded corporation). A CON application for construction of a surgery center had been approved.

PHYSICIAN RELATIONS

Dr. William Otto was the elected president of the medical staff. Dr. Otto recalled the "tremendous rupture" occurring between the primary care physicians (Internal Medicine, Pediatrics, Family Practice, and Ob/Gyn) and the specialists when HMOs came in. "Capitated" HMOs placed the primary care physician in control of all fees so as to serve as the patient's care manager or "gatekeeper." Under the old system, the specialists were in the catbird seat, with few checks on their cost and/or reimbursement structure.

About 50 of Beverly's physicians incorporated as the Beverly Doctors' Association so that they could respond to financial opportunities that might not be obtainable without a formal structure. The primary care physicians controlled this organization. Dr. Otto stated that one of the most significant issues facing Beverly's physician group was "who will be in control? If it is not the primary care physician, the primary care physicians will not join the alternative delivery system model. Without the primary care physicians, the capitated plans cannot survive."

EMPLOYEES

For fiscal year 1984, Beverly Hospital employed an average of 881 full-time equivalent employees or approximately 3.2 full-time equivalent employees per adjusted occupied bed. Of this staff, 269 were nurses, 112 were administrative and supervisory personnel, and 159 were professionals, including laboratory, pharmacy, radiology, therapy, and social workers. The hospital was eager to preserve its non-union status.

FINANCIAL DATA

See Tables 1.3 to 1.9 and Exhibit 1.4 for Beverly Hospital's financial performance during the early 1980s.

POINTS TO PONDER

1. Assess the hospital's competitive position in the North Shore area. What opportunity is the Beverly Hospital seeking to fulfill with its product line management, joint ventures with other hospitals, reorganization, and HMO initiatives?
2. Will the hospital be successful in these ventures and why?

Table 1.3 Beverly Hospital: Income Statement

	Years Ended September 30,					Ten-Month Period Ended July 31,	
	1980	1981	1982	1983	1984	1984	1985
Patient Service Revenue	$26,144,960	$30,486,975	$35,865,886	$37,577,571	$41,705,412	$35,281,500	$36,550,923
Deductions from Revenue	3,396,581	3,962,713	5,280,612	4,444,378	6,255,825	5,704,200	4,621,818
Net Patient Service Revenue	22,748,379	26,524,262	30,585,274	33,133,193	35,449,587	29,577,300	31,929,105
Other Operating Revenue	304,760	314,074	385,572	383,723	612,596	568,813	468,281
Total Operating Revenue	23,053,139	26,838,336	30,970,846	33,516,916	36,062,183	30,146,113	32,397,386
Total Operating Expenses	22,575,908	26,825,438	31,808,511	33,191,214	35,698,984	29,861,063	31,364,788
Income (Loss) from Operations	477,231	12,898	(837,665)	325,702	363,139	285,050	1,032,598
Total Nonoperating Revenue—Net	1,072,909	3,010,577	1,837,865	1,691,757	1,845,444	1,434,993	1,560,886
Excess of Revenues over Expenses	$1,550,140	$3,023,475	$1,000,200	$2,017,459	$2,208,573	$1,720,043	$2,593,484

Table 1.4 Beverly Hospital: Comparative Charges

	Beverly Hospital	Salem Hospital	Hunt Hospital	Addison Gilbert Hospital	Lynn Hospital	Union Hospital
Average Semi-Private Room Rates						
Medical/Surgical	$195	$260	$220	$260	$192	$395
Maternity	170	200	200	260	250	NA
Psychiatric	235	260	NA	325	NA	395
Pediatric	170	NA	201	254	247	NA
ICU/CCU	340	700	450	550	480	699
Newborn	130	185	140	164	225	NA

Table 1.5 Beverly Hospital: Balance Sheets

	September 30,	
Assets	*1984*	*1983*
UNRESTRICTED FUNDS		
CURRENT		
Cash	$ 1,173,888	$ 1,396,585
Patient Receivables, Less Allowance for Uncollectible		
Accounts of $475,000 in 1984 and $450,000 in 1983	5,406,542	4,551,940
Other Receivables	873,212	703,038
Due from Third-Party Payers	—	278,160
Funds Held by Trustees	434,488	449,307
Inventories	787,310	784,723
Prepaid Expenses	190,857	130,307
Account Receivable—Affiliate	275,307	69,680
TOTAL CURRENT ASSETS	$ 9,141,604	$ 8,363,740
OTHER		
Cash and Cash Equivalents	231,072	793,921
Investments	11,876,563	9,354,285
Funds Held by Trustees	1,854,314	1,981,190
Unamortized Financing Costs and Bond Discounts	594,429	626,004
Other Assets	27,716	4,206
TOTAL OTHER ASSETS	$ 14,584,094	$ 12,759,606
PROPERTY, PLANT, AND EQUIPMENT—NET	23,995,340	23,795,416
TOTAL UNRESTRICTED FUNDS	$ 47,721,038	$ 44,918,762
RESTRICTED FUNDS		
SPECIFIC PURPOSE FUNDS		
Investments	$ 104,519	$ 96,358
Due from Unrestricted Funds	338,266	265,208
TOTAL SPECIFIC PURPOSE FUNDS	$ 442,785	$ 361,566
PLANT EXPANSION FUNDS		
Pledges Receivable, Less Allowance for Uncollectible		
Pledges of $48,000 in 1984 and $87,000 in 1983	$ 238,013	$ 436,441
TOTAL PLANT EXPANSION FUNDS	$ 238,013	$ 436,441
ENDOWMENT FUNDS		
Cash	$ —	$ 1,817
Investments	3,723,529	3,536,678
TOTAL ENDOWMENT FUNDS	$ 3,723,529	$ 3,538,495

Note: See notes to financial statements (Exhibit 1.4).

continues

Table 1.5 continued

Liabilities and Fund Balance	September 30, 1984	September 30, 1983
UNRESTRICTED FUNDS		
CURRENT		
Notes Payable to Bank	$ 167,977	$ 407,907
Accounts Payable	876,743	999,282
Construction Costs Payable	—	52,150
Accrued Vacation Pay	886,619	781,518
Accrued Expenses	822,530	454,673
Accrued Interest Expense	352,561	354,943
Advances from Third-Party Payers	128,767	227,110
Due to Third-Party Payers	1,062,146	—
Current Installments on Long-Term Debt	327,783	316,916
Due to Restricted Funds	304,163	246,437
TOTAL CURRENT LIABILITIES	$ 4,929,289	$ 3,840,936
LONG-TERM DEBT		
Bonds Payable—Series A	2,780,000	3,000,000
—Series B	10,485,000	10,545,000
Mortgage Notes Payable	—	—
Capital Lease Obligation	7,202	31,290
Installment Loan Payable	347,267	311,750
TOTAL LONG-TERM DEBT	$ 13,619,469	$ 13,888,040
FUND BALANCES		
Operating	29,172,280	27,189,786
TOTAL UNRESTRICTED FUNDS	$ 47,721,038	$ 44, 918,762
RESTRICTED FUNDS		
SPECIFIC PURPOSE FUNDS		
Fund Balance	$ 442,785	$ 361,566
TOTAL SPECIFIC PURPOSE FUNDS	$ 442,785	$361,566
PLANT EXPANSION FUNDS		
Due to Unrestricted Funds	$22,993	$ 7,661
Fund Balance	215,020	428,780
TOTAL PLANT EXPANSION FUNDS	$ 238,013	$ 436,441
ENDOWMENT FUNDS		
Due to Unrestricted Funds	$ 11,110	$ 11,110
Fund Balance	3,712,419	3,527,385
TOTAL ENDOWMENT FUNDS	$ 3,723,529	$ 3,538,495

Table 1.6 Beverly Hospital: Statements of Revenues and Expenses—Unrestricted Funds

	Years Ended September 30,	
	1984	*1983*
PATIENT SERVICE REVENUE	$ 41,705,412	$ 37,577,571
Less Allowances and Uncollectible Accounts	6,255,825	4,444,378
NET PATIENT SERVICE REVENUE	$ 35,449,587	$ 33,133,193
OTHER OPERATING REVENUE	612,596	383,723
TOTAL OPERATING REVENUE	$ 36,062,183	$ 33,516,916
OPERATING EXPENSES		
Salaries and Wages	17,825,650	16,776,748
Physician Salaries and Fees	1,645,066	1,573,566
Fringe Benefits	2,941,074	2,546,863
Supplies and Contracted Services	10,123,782	9,412,659
Depreciation	1,701,716	1,495,460
Interest	1,461,696	1,385,918
TOTAL OPERATING EXPENSES	$35,698,984	$ 33,191,214
INCOME FROM OPERATIONS	$ 363,199	$ 325,702
NONOPERATING REVENUE (EXPENSE)		
Unrestricted Gifts and Bequests	186,627	218,235
Unrestricted Income from Endowment and		
Board-Designated Funds	1,610,074	1,449,180
Gain on Sale of Securities	144,962	75,668
Net Loss from Rental Properties	(87,417)	(87,873)
Other Nonoperating Revenues (Expenses)—Net	(8,802)	36,547
TOTAL NONOPERATING REVENUE—NET	$ 1,845,444	$ 1,691,757
EXCESS OF REVENUES OVER EXPENSES	$ 2,208,573	$ 2,017,459

Note: See notes to financial statements (Exhibit 1.4).

Table 1.7 Beverly Hospital: Statements of Changes in Fund Balances

	Unrestricted Funds	Restricted Funds		
		Specific Purpose	Plant Expansion	Endowment
BALANCES—October 1, 1982	$24,694,932	$301,899	$833,335	$3,347,777
Excess of Revenues over Expenses	2,017,459	——	——	——
Contributions	——	43,082	70,480	——
Restricted Investment Income and Gains	——	29,084	——	179,608
Transfers to:				
Unrestricted Funds Included in				
Revenues and Expenses	——	(4,080)	(6,059)	——
Finance Property, Plant, and				
Equipment	477,395	(8,419)	(468,976)	——
BALANCES—September 30, 1983	$27,189,786	$361,566	$428,780	$3,527,385
Excess of Revenues over Expenses	2,208,573	——	——	——
Contributions	——	63,248	8,788	——
Restricted Investment Income and Gains	——	31,655	——	185,034
Decrease in Allowance for Uncollectible				
Pledges	——	——	39,000	——
Transfer of Net Assets to Northeast				
Health Systems, Inc.	(483,973)	——	——	——
Transfers to:				
Unrestricted Funds Included in				
Revenues and Expenses	——	(2,006)	(15,332)	——
Finance Property, Plant, and				
Equipment	257,894	(11,678)	(246,216)	——
BALANCES—September 30, 1984	$29,172,280	$442,785	$215,020	$3,712,419

Note: See notes to financial statements (Exhibit 1.4).

Table 1.8 Beverly Hospital: Gross Patient Service Revenue, by Service, Year Ending September 30, 1984

Service	Routine	Ancillary	Total
Inpatient			
Medical-Surgical	$9,304,837	$10,616,861	$19,921,698
Pediatric	468,892	559,616	1,028,508
Obstetrics	740,807	859,332	1,600,139
Psychiatry	1,194,313	149,504	1,343,817
ICU	1,772,976	3,021,428	4,794,404
Newborn	493,950	65,240	559,190
Subtotal Inpatient	13,975,775	15,271,981	29,247,756
Outpatient			
Emergency	1,947,755	1,039,674	2,987,429
Clinic	539,742	2,930,415	3,470,157
Satellite Clinic	0	2,786,660	2,786,660
Surgery	219,976	1,148,021	1,367,997
Ambulatory Dialysis	0	1,845,407	1,845,407
Subtotal Outpatient	2,707,473	9,750,177	12,457,650
Total Patient Care	$16,683,248	$25,022,158	$41,705,406

Table 1.9 Beverly Hospital: Ancillary Expenses, by Service (dollars in thousands)

Service	Total	Direct	Allocated
Inpatient			
Medical-Surgical	$ 6,593	$ 4,256	$ 2,337
Pediatric	367	239	128
Obstetrics	869	565	304
Psychiatry	90	59	31
ICU	1,740	1,131	609
Newborn	187	122	65
Subtotal Inpatient	$ 9,846	$ 6,372	$ 3,474
Outpatient			
Emergency	$ 874	$ 568	$ 306
Clinic	2,277	1,480	797
Satellite Clinic	2,315	1,505	810
Surgery	658	428	230
Ambulatory Dialysis	1,642	1,067	575
Subtotal Outpatient	$ 7,766	$ 5,048	$ 2,718
Total Expenses	$ 17,612	$ 11,420	$ 6,192

Exhibit 1.4 Beverly Hospital: Edited Notes to Financial Statements, Years Ended September 30, 1984 and 1983

A. Summary of Significant Accounting Policies: Investments

Investments are recorded at cost or quoted market on the date of the gift. Allowances are provided for permanent declines in value. Investment income and net gains and losses on security sales of unrestricted funds, as well as unrestricted investment income on endowment funds, are included in nonoperating revenue in the statements of revenues and expenses. Investment income on specific purpose funds, restricted investment income on endowment funds, and the net gains and losses on security sales of specific-purpose funds and endowment funds are included in the statements of changes in fund balances of the restricted funds.

B. Corporate Restructuring

Effective January 1983, the Beverly Hospital Corporation's Board of Trustees approved certain resolutions in connection with a corporate restructuring of the Hospital. The restructuring provided, among other things, the establishment of a new corporation, Northeast Health Systems, Inc., which will function as a parent holding company for Beverly Hospital Corporation and several other newly formed organizations. As part of the restructuring, the Hospital transferred $483,973 of unrestricted cash to Northeast Health Systems, Inc. during 1984. This transfer was accounted for as a reduction in unrestricted fund balance and is included in the statement of changes in fund balances.

Case Study 2

Boston Sobriety Development, Inc.

INTRODUCTION

Lou Brown's marketing system for Boston Sobriety Development, Inc. (BSD), had worked so well in the developing days of inpatient drug and alcohol treatment facilities that his facilities always had the highest occupancy rates in the industry. But this year the system was coming apart and Lou wondered what he should do next.

BSD marketed through salespeople assigned to local and national accounts. The local sales force of "community relations representatives" called on local agencies, therapists, physicians, and detoxification centers, informed them of BSD's programs, and offered facility tours. The usual representative was a recovering alcoholic or drug addict without sales experience. One facility's marketing manager described his ideal rep as a former drug addict who had been "clean" (without drugs) for two years and was so broke that he or she didn't even have a credit card. The national sales office, located 150 miles from the corporate office and 100 miles from the nearest facility, was created to accommodate Jim Flimm, a star marketer with a proven ability to sign up high-volume national union accounts.

Although the national office contributed a significant share of BSD's overall census, some senior managers were concerned about the

Note: This case was prepared by Ellen Ratner under the supervision of Professor Regina E. Herzlinger. The identity of the company described has been disguised.

company's dependence on one marketer and his high costs of doing business.

Lou asked his vice president of marketing to design a system to increase local facility-based marketing (see Exhibit 2.1), but it was not yet implemented. Although the reps were accustomed to the point system shown in Exhibit 2.1, their bonuses were not very significant.

In February of this year, Jim Flimm accepted an offer from a competitor and left BSD with all of his staff, taking 90 percent of his accounts with him (see Table 2.1). Lou wanted to motivate the local reps to compensate for his departure with a system that would provide them with good income and motivate them to manage their expenses and fulfill long- and short-term sales goals.

BSD COMPANY HISTORY

BSD was one of the three companies of Optimal Health Inc. (OHI), whose strategy was to turn around existing health care facilities, both economically and professionally. BSD was to buy free-standing (nonhospital) alcohol and drug facilities and use its management expertise to provide for a profitable and professional turnaround.

Three years ago, OHI decided to liquidate, selling the HMO which was its largest asset because of the negative changes in that industry. BSD was sold to its management in a leveraged buyout (LBO) financed by some of OHI's original venture capital companies, with back-up financing from a large insurance company.

Exhibit 2.1 Boston Sobriety Development, Inc.: Incentive Compensation Program Plan

MEMORANDUM

TO: Lou Brown, President, BSD

FROM: Vice President of Marketing

DATE: January 29, this year

RE: *Incentive Compensation Program—Marketing Representatives*

Introduction

   The Marketing Representatives' Incentive Program is based on the
following assumptions:

1. Our goal is to increase revenue by increasing local facility census on a profitable basis.
2. A key objective is to attract and retain highly qualified, productive local marketing personnel.
3. Further expansion and penetration of existing and new markets is essential to BSD's long-term success.

Key Elements

1. Minimum production (i.e., census) standards based on paying admissions.
2. The four factors for determining a marketing representative's total monthly incentive compensation include:
   —Total number of admissions
   —Number of new referral sources
   —Referrals to special emphasis programs commensurate with corporate objectives
   —Reimbursement value of each admission
3. Bonus payments to marketing representatives will be made in full during the month following the admission. Adjustments may be made retroactively if actual circumstances and factors of an admission differ from those first reported.
4. A sales expense factor will not be included in the formula. Adherence to existing written guidelines is a condition of employment and management of the marketing representatives with respect to expenses is the responsibility of the marketing director.
5. The program will be uniform at all facilities. It will reward equally for intra-facility admissions.
6. Special Emphasis Programs will be determined and approved by the appropriate management committees on an *ad hoc* basis. Frequent (quarterly) review of the weight placed on a special program will take place.

Components

1. *Admission*

Category		Weight
A	First admission for a new referral	2.0
B	Admissions to gay and lesbian program	1.5
C	Special Emphasis Program	Various
D	Any combination of A, B, or C	(.6 x combined weight)
E	All other inter- or intra-facility admissions	1.0

2. *Reimbursement*

Percentage	Factor
100% of charges	1.1
90% of charges	1.0
80% of charges	.9
70% of charges	.6
60% of charges	.4
Less than 60% of charges	0.0

Exhibit 2.1 continued

3. *Formula to Determine Cumulative Points*

Total of:

Each Admission Weight x Reimbursement Factor = Number of Points

4. *Point Value*

Cumulative Points	Value
0–9	$0
10–12	$40 for each point beginning at #10
13–15	$120 for each point beginning at #13
16–18	$160 for each point beginning at #16
19–21	$200 for each point beginning at #19
22 Plus	$240 for each point beginning at #22

Top management, including Jim Flimm, held 20 percent of the company. Lou Brown, BSD's president, retained his position after the LBO.

BSD

BSD provided treatment to patients through seven inpatient facilities and two outpatient clinics. It provided a continuum of services, ranging from assessment to inpatient and continuing care. BSD's treatment philosophy was formulated in the early 1980s when inpatient treatment was considered the most effective modality in treating drug and alcohol addictions. BSD's clinical rationale for inpatient treatment was that other life issues such as abuse, incest, and family alcoholism required intensive care that could be offered only in an inpatient facility. With it, early traumatic and family experiences could be addressed and relapse prevented.

The negative past work experiences of BSD's top management with large bureaucracies caused them to decentralize BSD from its inception. Most managerial decisions were

Table 2.1 Boston Sobriety Development, Inc.: Patients, by Source and Type of Admissions, March, Last Year, and This Year

	A	B	C	D	E	F	Total
Total Patients, This Year, March	56	37	67	33	106	85	384
Local Census	48	26	67	26	73	58	
National Census	8	9	0	7	33	27	
Source of Patients, March							
New Admits	12.5%	5.6%	NA	39.1%	8.7%	6.3%	
"House" Admits[a]	12.5%	44.4%	NA	17.4%	4.3%	31.3%	
Other Admits	75.0%	50.0%	NA	43.5%	87.0%	62.4%	
Total Patients, Last Year, March	54	66	58	26	121	79	404

[a]A new patient who walks in without a referral from an agency or employee assistance program that was contacted by the local representative.

made at the facility level. BSD's top management included a president, chief financial officer, chief operating officer, vice presidents of marketing and clinical programs, and two vice presidents of operations, each of whom was responsible for certain facilities. Control of the facilities included regular visits by the operations vice presidents and frequent visits by the clinical, marketing, and finance vice presidents. The entire management team met monthly with each facility executive director for a facility review including finance, operations, marketing, and clinical issues.

BSD hoped to differentiate itself by providing special programs for problems such as cocaine addiction and chronic relapse and for underserved groups like law enforcement officers. Its inpatient center for lesbians and gay men was the first in the country. BSD programs were recognized for their innovativeness.

ADDICTION TREATMENT

Addiction (also referred to as chemical dependency) can be defined as the compulsive consumption of a mood altering substance that affects a person's emotional, psychological, and work life. Addiction treatment addresses both physical addiction and psychological dependency. Theories abound about the origin of chemical dependency, with most focusing on a combination of genetic predisposition, environment, early childhood experiences, and the addictive potential of certain substances.

Treatment for alcoholism consisted primarily of detoxification until the early 1940s. Then, spurred by the growth of Alcoholics Anonymous (AA), several "dry out" centers began which combined detoxification with help from other AA members or psychiatrists (see Exhibit 2.2). Official recognition of alcohol and drug addiction began with the establishment of the government's National Institute of Alcohol Abuse and Alcoholism in 1971 and the National Institute of Drug Abuse shortly thereafter. A credentialing system for alcohol and drug counselors was developed in the late 1970s.

With increased availability of insurance reimbursement for treatment in the 1980s, centers for alcoholism offered a standardized 28-day rehabilitation program, consisting of group therapy, lectures, AA meetings, and family involvement. Although several experiments have raised the possibility of alcoholics returning to "normal" social drinking, treatment programs in the United States have maintained lifetime abstinence "one day at a time" as their goal.

Simultaneously, therapeutic communities developed for the treatment of drug addicts. They were confrontational, long-term (6 months to 3 years) self-help models, run primarily by recovering drug addicts. Narcotics and Cocaine Anonymous Programs based on the AA model began to proliferate, and treatment of drug addiction was incorporated into the 28-day format under the more generalized name of chemical dependency treatment.

REIMBURSEMENT

Insurance reimbursement, from the late 1960s until the mid-1980s, focused on inpatient, 28-day treatment programs for alcohol diagnosis and drug addiction. Insurance coverage for inpatient alcohol and drug treatment was mandated in approximately two-thirds of the states, and approximately 65% of insured employees had alcohol and drug coverage in 1989. Corporate employee assistance programs (EAPs), which enabled confidential referrals for treatment, grew from fewer than 500 in 1973 to over 10,000 in 1986. The EAPs performed a gatekeeper function, selecting the treatment modalities appropriate to corporate employees' needs and referring them to services at centers that the EAPs designated.

Average costs for alcoholism services per insured employee rose sharply, from $118 in 1984 to $169 in 1987. As a result, HMOs usually paid for only 5 to 10 days of inpatient detoxification, followed by outpatient services. Some insurance reimbursers approved inpatient

Exhibit 2.2 Boston Sobriety Development, Inc.: The Twelve Suggested Steps

1. We admit we were powerless over alcohol—that our lives have become unmanageable.

2. Came to believe that a Power greater than ourselves can restore us to sanity.

3. Made a decision to turn our will and our lives over to the care of God as we understood Him.

4. Made a searching and fearless moral inventory of ourselves.

5. Admitted to God, ourselves, and to another human being the exact nature of our wrongs.

6. Were entirely ready to have God remove all these defects of character.

7. Humbly asked Him to remove our shortcomings.

8. Made a list of all persons we have harmed, and became willing to make amends to them all.

9. Made direct amends to such people wherever possible, except when to do so would injure them or others.

10. Continued to take personal inventory and when we were wrong, promptly admitted it.

11. Sought through prayer and meditation to improve our conscious contact with God as we understood Him, praying only for knowledge of His will for us and the power to carry that out.

12. Having had a spiritual awakening as the result of these steps, we tried to carry this message to alcoholics and to practice these principles in all our affairs.

Source: Courtesy of Alcoholics Anonymous.

treatment only after two outpatient failures. Pre-certification (prior approval for treatment) at BSD facilities was required for almost 80% of patients at some facilities. Treatment centers were also subjected to increasing concurrent reviews, postdischarge record review, longer waits for reimbursement, and pressures to reduce the length of stay.

BSD MARKETING

BSD's services were historically purchased by EAPs in corporations and large unions. A small, but significant, portion of patients were referred by alumni of the treatment programs. Some patients just walked into the facility, drawn to it by advertising, word of mouth, or a friend's advice.

Most payment came from the patient's insurance company, although some union accounts were paid from Taft-Hartley Health and Welfare funds. BSD did not accept military personnel's insurance, Medicare, or Medicaid reimbursement. The level of Blue Cross/Blue Shield reimbursement varied by facility. In all facilities, commercial insurance, like CIGNA, paid significantly higher rates than Blue Cross. Although most insurance plans required patients to pay between 10–20% of the cost out of their own pockets, this was often waived or discounted. Combinations of discounts, transportation, and posttreatment follow-up (continuing care) were frequently used to obtain a large account. BSD's attempts to obtain HMOs' and PPOs' business had not been successful.

Local marketing strategy was developed at the facility level with consultation from the corporate management team. Each facility's marketing plan used different combinations of community relations representatives, regional advertising, and alumni referrals. Community relations representatives were usually hired for their contacts or knowledge of the recovering community. Until recently, BSD had no formalized training program for them; they were trained by observing other marketers and participating in sales calls with the facility marketing director.

In the past, community relations representatives were paid to place patients in BSD's inpatient beds, with little emphasis on the amount of reimbursement. Some placed patients with reimbursement as low as 60% of BSD's prices. Most of the reps worked from their homes. They were encouraged to refer to other facilities if their customers needed a specialized program, including BSD's lesbian and gay men's facility. The reps reported weekly to the facility marketing directors.

THE ISSUE

Lou wanted his incentive system to motivate the reps to increase the census, improve the re-imbursement, and control their sales expenses. He wondered if and how the system should reflect differences in the market potential and economic structure of each center (Table 2.2), as well as the difference among the performances of the representatives (Table 2.3). He also wanted a plan and timetable for implementing the system. He thought that the system suggested by his vice president of marketing was the right idea, but it needed refinement.

POINTS TO PONDER

1. What opportunity is BSD fulfilling?
2. Identify all the variables that should be included in the incentive system and specify how they should be incorporated.
3. Specify a plan for implementation of the incentive system.

Table 2.2 Boston Sobriety Development, Inc.: Consolidated Statement of Income for the Month Ended April 30, This Year

	Facilities						Day Treatment	Corporate
	A	B	C	D	E	F		
FTEs	7.5	65	95	40	127	93		
EPOB[a]	1.4	2.2	1.4	1.2	1.2	1.2		
Average Gross Census	41	21	67	32	106	64		
Average Net Census	38	21	64	31	102	61		
Licensed Beds	92	85	70	36	138	82		
Net Patient Days	1,140	630	1,920	930	3,060	1,830		
Revenues								
Gross Revenues	$461,051	$298,095	$920,810	$455,615	$1,099,439	$847,792	$18,600	$2,308
Less: Contractual Allowances	65,223	14,784	13,828	11,763	302,864	160,779	2,698	0
Administrative Allowances	33,165	28,944	43,827	9,191	103,084	55,327	0	0
Bad Debt Allowance	27,778	71,539	55,774	40,100	43,987	51,445	735	0
Total Allowance	126,166	115,267	113,429	61,054	449,935	267,551	3,433	0
Net Revenues	334,885	182,828	807,381	394,561	649,504	580,241	15,167	2,308
Other Income	0	1,376	9,391	4,417	0	0	0	4,590
Total Net Revenues	334,885	184,204	816,772	398,978	649,504	580,241	15,167	6,898
Operating Expenses								
Direct Patient Care								
Salaries and Fringe Benefits	84,594	79,443	116,326	75,277	154,170	112,267	6,305	6,095
Other Costs	54,107	49,079	50,907	49,277	75,171	66,024	400	6,095
Total Direct Care	138,701	128,522	167,233	124,554	229,341	178,291	6,705	6,095
Related Patient Care								
Salaries and Fringe Benefits	30,244	25,766	53,441	7,853	58,376	42,236	0	
Food and Food Supplies	12,856	6,962	18,749	19,001	33,599	30,649	0	
Occupancy Expense	13,414	60,539	23,341	35,501	20,903	46,829	5,091	5,665
Other Costs	476	850	0	476	1,626	476	0	0
Total Related Care	$ 56,990	$ 94,117	$95,531	$ 62,831	$ 114,504	$120,190	$ 5,091	$ 5,665

[a]EPOB = employee per occupied bed.

continues

Table 2.2 continued

	Facilities						Day Treatment	Corporate
	A	B	C	D	E	F		
Operating Expenses								
Marketing Expenses								
Salaries and Fringe Benefits	$ 18,161	$ 17,102	$ 0	$ 7,587	$ 30,495	$ 21,001	$ 0	$ 47,296
Commissions and Bonuses	0	0		0	3,145	(731)	0	5,000
Travel and Entertainment	10,744	2,034		6,207	4,104	5,518	0	16,561
Marketing and Advertising	39,917	9,687	15,549	20,571	44,980	4,116	0	12,926
Other Costs	4,844	7,995	476	7,619	10,296	3,886	(1,000)	(3,989)
Total Marketing Expenses	73,666	36,818	16,025	41,984	93,650	33,790	(1,000)	77,794
General and Administrative	$115,422	$ 96,534	$162,872	$ 77,651	$ 87,662	$139,870	$ 10,364	$240,168
Operating Expense	384,779	355,991	467,120	307,020	524,527	473,041	21,161	329,724
Operating Profit (Loss)	(49,894)	(171,787)	349,652	91,958	115,977	107,200	(5,994)	(322,826)
Total Nonoperating Expense	(90,095)	(53,573)	(111,431)	(36,666)	(85,471)	(150,726)	0	(5,252)
Profit (Loss) before Intercompany Charges	(139,989)	(225,360)	238,221	55,292	30,506	(43,526)	(5,994)	(328,076)
Total Intercompany Charges	(27,317)	(13,992)	(44,641)	(21,321)	(70,626)	(102,051)	(828)	261,587
Profit (Loss) before Taxes	(167,306)	(239,352)	193,580	33,971	(40,120)	(145,577)	(6,822)	(66,489)
Income Tax Expense	(3,000)	—	—	(1,000)	0	3,000		
Profit (Loss) after Taxes	(170,306)	(239,352)	193,580	32,971	(40,120)	(148,577)	(6,822)	(66,489)

Table 2.3 Boston Sobriety Development, Inc.: Average Salary and Expenses, Referrals, February, This Year, by Facility and Representative

Facility	Representative	Salary and Monthly Expenses	Total Referrals	Referral Average Cost
A	1	$ 984	12	$ 82
	2	844	2	422
	3	847	2	423
	4	1,056	1	1,056
	5	1,448	1	1,448
	6	983	0	—
	Average Annual Salary/Representative	26,000		
B	1	897	13	69
	2	1,068	3	356
	3	278	2	139
	4	458	1	458
	Average Annual Salary/Representative	30,000		
C	No Individual Representatives	448	56	8
D	No Individual Representatives	16,500	33	500
E	1	1,943	29	67
	2	1,024	16	64
	3	871	13	67
	4	1,062	6	177
	5	403	1	403
	Average Annual Salary/Representative	28,000		
F	1	616	14	44
	2	378	6	63
	3	413	7	59
	4	924	6	154
	5	1,195	5	239
	6	175	1	175
	Average Annual Salary/Representative	30,000		

Case Study 3

Center for Nutritional Research

Michael Kenyon, a health care consultant, completed his evaluation of the Center for Nutritional Research at Boston's New England Deaconess Hospital. It treated morbidly obese patients through a combination of exercise, behavioral counseling, and a special nutritional regimen developed over a 10-year period. George L. Blackburn, M.D., the Center's founder, had just received an offer from a company that wanted to buy his treatment concept. He contacted a friend, Peter Phildius, for some advice, who had referred him to Mr. Kenyon (see Exhibit 3.1 for their professional backgrounds).

As Mr. Kenyon reviewed his findings, he wondered, "The market for this type of program is substantial, and I'm not aware of any other program that has been as successful at treating obesity as Dr. Blackburn's. But how could this program be made into a business?"

OBESITY

Obesity and overweight are prevalent in the American population. In common usage, "obesity" is used for overweight, but the two conditions are not necessarily simultaneous. Obesity is an excess of body fat, while overweight is an excess of weight relative to standards for height. Obesity is usually measured

by the amount of fat tissue; overweight reflects all body tissues, bone, muscle, and fat. At the 85th percentile of the weight-height distribution, in the male population 23% are overweight (this includes athletes) and 19% are obese; for women, the percentages are 30% overweight and 28% obese. The incidence of these factors varies by age as well as by sex. (See Exhibit 3.2 for conditions thought to be associated with morbid obesity.) Noted Dr. Blackburn,

> Patients who weigh more than twice their ideal body weights based on height, frame, and activity level are considered to be morbidly obese. Those who weigh between 30% and 100% above their ideal weights have medically significant obesity. This obesity is an especially life-threatening condition requiring medical attention. Much evidence has been accumulated linking obesity and an increased frequency of chronic disease.[1]

Because of the increased incidence of medical problems among the obese, they use more health care resources than their proportion of the population. Extra weight complicates surgery in a number of ways: physical access through a thick fat layer is difficult; fat tissue preferentially absorbs anesthetics; the pulmonary problems common among obese persons pose additional anesthesia-related risk; and excess weight often causes organ compression and a shifting of organs. Surgeons can expect a longer operation and recovery and a higher frequency of complications in obese patients.

Note: This case was prepared by Joyce Lallman and James Angel under the supervision of Professor Regina E. Herzlinger.

Exhibit 3.1 Center for Nutritional Research: Professional Backgrounds of Michael H. Kenyon, George L. Blackburn, M.D., and Peter P. Phildius

> MICHAEL H. KENYON is a principal in Blue-Kenyon Associates, a consulting firm specializing in marketing and strategic planning in the health care industry. Following 5 years of increasing management responsibility as an officer in the Naval Nuclear Power Program, Mr. Kenyon earned an MBA with High Distinction from the Harvard Business School where he was a Baker Scholar and compiled a perfect grade point average. From 1976 to 1979 Mr. Kenyon held a series of marketing positions with Baxter Travenol Laboratories, Inc., including marketing responsibility for all four major product groups in the company's largest division.
>
> GEORGE L. BLACKBURN, M.D., Ph.D., is an associate professor of surgery at the Harvard Medical School and director of the Nutrition Metabolism Laboratory at the New England Deaconess Hospital. Dr. Blackburn is one of the leading authorities on the medical and surgical treatment of obesity as well as on the broader subject of nutrition, including parenteral and enteral feeding, and nutrition in cancer patients. Dr. Blackburn has published several hundred articles, papers, monographs, and books on his technical specialties. Through the Center for Nutritional Research, Dr. Blackburn has accumulated 10 years of clinical investigation involving over 2,000 patients regarding the appropriate multidisciplinary treatment of obesity.
>
> PETER P. PHILDIUS is president and chief operating officer of National Medical Care. He has had 21 years of experience with health care businesses, including 18 at Baxter Travenol. At Baxter Travenol he had operating responsibility for five different operating divisions, including Parenterals, Artificial Organs, and Fenwal.

Causes

The causes of obesity are thought to include metabolic predisposition, psychological factors, behavioral factors, and changes in activity level. These factors often interact, producing a vicious cycle of behavioral, medical, and physical problems. According to the Massachusetts Department of Public Health, whose weight survey results are in Table 3.1,

> The years between 45 and 64 seem to be the most vulnerable period for overweight; well over half this group had reached the 110% level or above, including over a quarter at the 130% mark. Respondents who did not complete high school had the greatest relative prevalences of overweight and severe overweight.[2]

Explanations of obesity fall into several general categories:

- *Psychological.* Studies of obese people who were not seeking psychiatric help reveal few psychological differences from control populations.[3]
- *Biological.* Animals regulate both body size and the oxygen level of their blood with little consciousness; thus, a biological mechanism may govern body size and obesity may result from some disorder in this mechanism. Although the precise mechanism has not yet been determined, much research is being done in the field.

Exhibit 3.2 Conditions Associated with Morbid Obesity

> Increased risk of death of person 60% overweight.
>
> Diabetes mellitus (10 × normal)
> Hypertension (3 × normal)
> Coronary heart disease (3 × normal)
> Congestive heart failure (NA)
> Restrictive lung disease (NA)
> Degenerative arthritis (NA)
> Gallbladder disease (5 × normal)
> Infertility (NA)
> Psychosocial incapacity (NA)
> Cancer (2 × normal)
>
> *Source*: George L. Blackburn

Table 3.1 Center for Nutritional Research: Commonwealth of Massachusetts, Percentages of Respondents Overweight and Underweight, According to Sex

Percentage of Ideal Weight	Men (%)	Women (%)
<90	6.6	10.6
Normal (91–109)	46.2	49.1
110–119	23.2	14.3
120–129	11.9	7.1
130–139	4.9	5.6
>140	7.2	13.2

Source: Reprinted from *New England Journal of Medicine*, April 29, 1982, pp. 1048–1051, with permission of the Massachusetts Medical Society, © 1982.

The "setpoint" theory argues that people have a natural setpoint at which their bodies will try to maintain themselves and that it is extraordinarily difficult to maintain a different weight. In support of this, researchers find a variety of abnormalities in obese people, even after they have lost weight.[4]

The biological model is also supported by studies of genetically obese rats who when left to themselves will become highly obese. Obesity can be created in laboratory animals by creating lesions in certain parts of their brain.[5]

Richard Wurtman et al. at MIT discovered that several nutrients in food affect the chemistry of various neurotransmitters in the brain. They proposed a plausible mechanism to explain the carbohydrate craving experienced by many overeaters.[6] Other researchers have focused on the level of heat generated by the body, known as thermogenesis, thinking that the body will, among other things, vary the rate of heat generation to match energy intake and expenditure.

The number of fat cells in the body may also be involved in some way. These do not change as an obese person loses weight, but the cells may merely shrink and give off chemical signals that the brain interprets as signs of starvation.

- *Chemical Addiction.* The behavior of many overeaters resembles that of drug addicts and alcoholics. Faced with evidence of the damage caused by further abuse, they nevertheless continue to overeat. As one formerly obese person put it,

> I don't really know the meaning of full or the meaning of hungry. All I know is that food tastes good and that I want more of it. Left to my own devices I could easily spend 24 hours a day eating. I was never really amazed at the fact that once I got started I couldn't stop eating. What I couldn't figure out is how other people could stop (Overeaters Anonymous meeting).

Although addiction treatment methods have advanced remarkably over the past few decades with the advent of drug and alcohol rehabilitation centers and the success of the Alcoholics Anonymous program, much remains to be learned. Moreover, while an alcoholic can survive without alcohol, an overeater cannot live without food, so that the applicability of drug and alcohol withdrawal principles to food is not clear.

- *Food Sensitivity/Allergy.* Another theory holds that some people are so sensitive to certain foods or substances found in foods that continued consumption of these foods distorts the person's appetite.

- *Cultural.* Some theories propose a cultural explanation of obesity. Some claim that eating disorders seem to strike women more often than men in reaction to a male-dominated society that makes unrealistic fashion demands on women's bodies. However, these theories have not undergone scientific testing. Others have found inverse correlations between obesity and social class for women.[7]

Treatment

Treatment for obesity is offered by physicians and other health professionals, governmental agencies and nonprofit groups, and many commercial enterprises. Treatment methods include medication, diets, support groups and/or exercise programs. In 1981, two of the leading commercial weight loss programs were Weight Watchers International, Inc., and Nutri/System, Inc. The Weight Watchers weight loss program was taught by trained lecturers who were former members. It was open to people who had at least ten pounds to lose and helped them to adhere to an eating regimen developed by the company. Weight Watchers International, Inc., was acquired by the H.J. Heinz Company in 1978. Prior to its acquisition, Weight Watchers operated company-owned programs in 7 states in the United States and in 18 foreign countries and had franchised programs in many other states in the United States and 7 foreign countries. Of the $39.2 million in Weight Watchers' 1977 revenues, 16% came from fees from company-operated domestic classes, 43% from company-operated foreign classes, 17% from domestic franchise commissions, and 3% from foreign franchise commissions. The company's 1977 net income was $8.6 million, and it employed 6,300 people.

Nutri/Systems, Inc., another network of company-owned and franchised weight loss centers, was started in 1971 and went public in 1981. Its target clients were middle-income families over 30 years of age who lived within 5 miles of 1 of its centers. The typical client was more than 30 pounds overweight. The program included individual supervision, diet, behavior education, nutritional counseling,

mild exercise, and maintenance. Nutri/Systems also sold packaged, premeasured foods to its clients. The company's centers were of two types: medical, which offered blood tests and electrocardiograms upon entry into the program; and nonmedical, which offered more behavioral education, more exercise, and a higher calorie diet than the medical centers. The average fee per client in 1981 was $300, and, for clients of medical centers, $90 more for the initial medical exam. In addition, clients paid $30 per week, on average, for food items. In 1981, there were 350 franchised and 58 company-owned centers. Of the $49.2 million in 1981 revenues, 30% was from company-owned centers and 57% was from franchised centers (13% was from sales of franchises and other sources). Net income in 1981 was $9.2 million. By September 1, 1981, Nutri/Systems had centers in 45 states and 613 employees.

Diet Workshop (DW) was founded by Lois Lindauer in 1965 after she lost "one third of herself" and started helping friends. Four major products were offered:

1. Regular classes met weekly and ran indefinitely; members could start or stop at any time. The fee was $15 to register and $7 per week. Members who reached goal weight became, for $28, "Lifetime Members," entitling them to free class attendance for the rest of their lives if they did not exceed their goal by 2 pounds or miss classes for more than a month.
2. A "Quick Loss" program cost $65 up front and lasted for 6 weeks. It was held several times per year.
3. A workplace program equivalent to the Quick Loss program was sold through corporations to employees for $48; the companies provided the space and the scales.
4. A "person to person" program provided individual counseling. The fee was $150 for 8 weeks; $250 for 12 weeks; or $325 for 24 weeks.

Although Diet Workshop's market consisted of those who want to lose weight, 97% of the group members were female. (There are more men, however, at the workplace programs and in the individual counseling.) Of their members, 60–70% were white, 50% married, and 50% employed full time. The average age was from 30 to 55, and they generally needed to lose from 20 to 50 pounds; 15–20% maintained their weight loss. Approximately 50% of the members were retreads.

Diet Workshop had 40 franchises in 23 states and was strongest in the New England and East Coast area. DW no longer sold franchises. It claimed approximately 1 million "attendances" per year at 2,000 to 2,500 groups per week. (An attendance is a visit to a Diet Workshop lecture.) Gross sales were about $10 million, including optional portion-controlled food items such as vitamin supplements, diet salad dressings, and dried soups sold at its meetings, but not in supermarkets. These items accounted for approximately 10–15% of sales.

Overeaters Anonymous (OA) is a nonprofit fellowship of those who seek to help each other to recover from the disease of compulsive overeating. Patterned after the highly successful Alcoholics Anonymous program, it is a voluntary organization that imposes no dues or fees on its members. OA supports itself from member contributions. There are 6,000 groups with over 100,000 members.

Because each local OA group is autonomous, there are wide variations in the size and nature of meetings. Newcomers are told to try several different meetings to see whether or not they like the program. Meetings are held wherever convenient and inexpensive space can be found. In a typical meeting, which lasts $1^1/_2$ hours, group members recount their recovery from compulsive overeating.

CENTER FOR NUTRITIONAL RESEARCH

The Center for Nutritional Research at Boston's New England Deaconess Hospital was founded by George L. Blackburn, M.D., Ph.D., Associate Professor of Surgery at the Harvard Medical School. Dr. Blackburn

explained how he became interested in the field of nutrition:

In the business world, entrepreneurship means engaging in a business activity for reasons of self-interest. My definition of entrepreneurship is fighting the *status quo* to make things better, in line with the Hippocratic oath.

My original research focused on iatrogenic disease (diseases brought about by the hospital stay). One of the most serious iatrogenic problems is malnutrition. Food is not appetizing to patients who have other diseases or are recovering from surgery, so I tried to solve the problem of overcoming starvation and feeding them.

To conduct my research, I needed subjects to enter a "controlled starvation" program where I could simulate the malnutrition state. I placed ads in the newspaper in order to attract people who wanted to lose weight, and I found that many of the people who replied were desperate to find a program that worked.

Through experiments conducted during the period from 1971 to 1973, I found that the combination of weight loss and my nutritional program helped people with diabetes, heart disease, hypertension, and other medical problems. While I was in the Ph.D. program at MIT, I learned about nutrition, almost in spite of myself. (Medical school training in nutrition essentially disappeared in 1923.) My postdoctoral work was in nutritional biochemistry.

It is often difficult to motivate high-risk patients to accept some type of intervention or treatment because they may be shy and withdrawn. I look for help from prepaid health plans in this area because they have an incentive to intervene in the life-style of the high-risk individual to reduce the demands that the "high-risk" person could place on their medical services. Employers also have an incentive to intervene for employees who are at high risk or who have high-risk family members to care for at home.

My treatment program for obesity has four main elements (1) diet, based on physiologic biochemistry and endocrinology; (2) exercise, with a program developed by my partner, an exercise physiologist; (3) behavioral counseling, with a program developed by a behavioral therapist; and (4) life-style education, with group support activities and lectures on nutrition, stress reduction, and exercise. The modified fast "physiology" shuts off a patient's appetite, and he or she becomes "nonhungry" within 72 hours. We've spent ten years researching which nutrients allow a patient's body to retain lean tissue while burning off the fat. When patients enroll in the program, the origin of their obesity is determined. Then they are offered a program tailored to their individual needs.

Our treatment program is distinguished from others by at least three factors:

a. Originality. I invented the protein sparing modified fast. Consumers would prefer to be treated by the founders of the technique rather than imitators.

b. Reputation. There is a credibility factor here. There is no doubt that investment in research and adherence to an ethical line attract patients. People are willing to pay a premium price for professional service.

c. Entry costs. It would take at least a year and several million dollars to duplicate my program, and two or three years to break even.

Although my Center for Nutritional Research is located at the New England Deaconess Hospital, the hospital cannot provide capital support of my work, and the nutritional field of obesity is low on its list of priorities. While grants from the National Institutes of Health (NIH) for the basic research exist, NIH does not support applied therapy research. The medical establishment is not focused on nutrition as a therapy. Involvement with a commercial venture seems to be the only avenue for continuing my development of this clinical program. By the way, I don't share the alarm over for-profit care expressed by some of my colleagues. Both nonprofit and profit services need guidelines, monitoring, and ongoing evaluation.

I've been approached by a company that wants to buy my treatment concept and the right to base their services on my research. I'm not sure if I should sell it or start my own business. My research shows that this therapy can delay the onset of disease. This is very important to individuals, but from an economic standpoint, will insurers or employers be interested in paying for these medical nutritional services?

The Opportunity

Michael Kenyon was hired by Dr. Blackburn to advise him on the prospective sale of his treatment methodology to an outside firm. He explained the situation as he saw it:

The company that approached Dr. Blackburn has offered to pay him $500,000 for his treatment concept and the right to base their services on his research. Dr. Blackburn would be required to do some consulting for them and be their scientific spokesperson, but would continue his academic research. The company would manage the marketing, financing, and other business aspects of the service.

Dr. Blackburn spent ten years of his life developing his treatment program. He feels the technology would be difficult to reproduce, and would like an equity arrangement or a royalty. The company feels that Dr. Blackburn's technology is not proprietary, and refuses to offer royalties or equity.

I have spent a week studying Dr. Blackburn's program, and I feel he has a very effective treatment technology. The norm for other programs treating obesity is a 1% success rate. Dr. Blackburn's success rate is 40%, and he has good, long-term studies to base it on. I also feel his technology is proprietary, and can be made more so with more management. There must be a difference in technology if his program results are so much better than the others.

One of Dr. Blackburn's inventions is the "protein sparing modified fast," which prevents cannibalization of the body's own protein. His nutritional regimen is not something a person can do on his or her own. It must be carefully monitored to avoid risks. The caloric load in this regimen is under a level that is safe to follow without medical supervision. Many of his patients have serious medical problems in addition to obesity. The nutritional regimen has to be sustained over 20 to 30 weeks, because under this regimen patients lose weight at the steady rate of $2^{1}/_{2}$ pounds per week. It is difficult to sustain this regimen over such a long period of time, especially with people who aren't well medically; the dosage of protein is critical. In order to monitor compliance with the program, Dr. Blackburn uses a breath test to measure the level of ketones produced as a result of the fast (ketones are a byproduct of fat metabolism). Weight loss without ketone production indicates a loss of water and muscle mass, which can be dangerous. The presence of ketones indicates that fat is being metabolized and the program is having the desired effect. Hardly anyone else uses this nutritional regimen, which uses real food instead of protein supplements.

The behavioral aspects of Dr. Blackburn's program have evolved over a period of ten years. His program does not treat obesity as a psychiatric disorder, and therefore does not involve "getting into people's heads." His view is that obesity results from a genetic predisposition and behavior traps, and his program attempts to unwind patients' food behaviors from the other aspects of their lives. The behavioral component of the program is based on a 300-page manual that has gone through three evolutions in the last ten years. Each week, patients are asked to read a specific chapter of the manual and complete a homework assignment. The manual provides instruction on such topics as cognitive restructuring, time and stress management, nutrition, and ways to measure and record food intake. For example, a person suffering from job stress and poor eating patterns who normally rushes home after work to prepare dinner may be directed to take a one-hour walk after work instead.

I believe that the market for Dr. Blackburn's program is very large: by extrapolating regional data to the United States, I estimate that approximately 16% of the adults in the United States are over 130% of ideal body weight. At a price for treatment of $1,000, this equals a multi-billion-dollar market. Dr. Blackburn is providing tertiary care on an outpatient basis for a problem the medical community isn't treating.

This program isn't adding to the total cost of the health care system by adding free-standing facilities that duplicate what hospitals do. His program is moving with the tide toward cost-effective care, by getting people out of the hospital and preventing future hospitalization.

I've spent some time looking at the operations aspects of Dr. Blackburn's Center for Nutritional Research. It occupies two office suites (about 2,200 square feet in total) on the seventh floor of the New England Deaconess Hospital, and it is absolute pandemonium!

During an average week approximately 130 people came through the clinic, but this is just a guess. Some people didn't sign in; others who signed in didn't stay for the complete program. There were no recordkeeping systems and no written protocols. Even with all this confusion, Dr. Blackburn's program has had outstanding clinical results, which makes me think it must be a fantastic program.

The staffing of Dr. Blackburn's program includes people with a variety of skills. I looked at the client characteristics, program operations, program costs, and pricing and reported my conclusions to Dr. Blackburn [see Exhibit 3.3]. I also sketched out a plan for setting this up as a business.

Although the current staffing of Dr. Blackburn's program appears sufficient for a research clinic, if it is to be run as a business, the staffing needs to be upgraded (for example, nurse's aides should be replaced by nurses). Also, all patients should get the same level of professional care.

Exhibit 3.3 Center for Nutritional Research: Analysis Summary

George L. Blackburn, M.D., Ph.D.
Associate Professor of Surgery
Harvard Medical School
New England Deaconess Hospital
Boston, MA 02215

Dear George:

To supplement our meeting on October 22, I've prepared the following outline of the points discussed.

Findings
The 26-week program is the basic CNR program. It represents half your existing patient load.

Program	Number of Current Patients	Percentage of Total
13 week	28	12
26 week	115	50
52 week	52	23
Fee for service	35	15
(predominantly maintenance)		

Patients come to CNR from three main sources, but doctor referral is the largest, and it is rising. Over one-third of current patients were themselves former patients (restarts) or were referred by a patient. This is remarkable word-of-mouth support.

Source of Referral	Number of Patients	Percentage of Total
Doctor	75	33
Patient	56	24
Media	51	22
Restart	25	11
Friend	12	5
Other	11	5

CNR patients tend to be high risk. You are getting the more difficult patients.

Risk	Number of Patients	Percentage of Total
Low risk	78	37
Average risk	105	50
High risk	27	13

Since pricing is based on minimum necessary service less a discount, a substantial number of patients overrun their paid-in fees. Roughly 37% can be classified as overruns.

Even though the literature sent to the patient emphasizes a payment schedule heavily loaded to the front end of the program, deferred payment is now the major method used, and it is gaining ground.

Payment Method	Number of Patients	Percentage of Total
Regular	107	47
Deferred[a]	121	52
Third Party	2	1

[a]The deferred payment schedule is a 25% down payment, with the remaining fee paid in five equal monthly payments.

continues

Exhibit 3.3 continued

Conclusions

Pricing is too low across the board, for these reasons:

- Gross margins are 10% or less, on a "true cost" basis.
- Prices per week are less than half those of the major competition.
- Product/service quality is above anything else available.

Pricing is too low also for problem patients, who constitute a high percentage of CNR patients.

- Pricing is figured on the ideal patient, with no allowance for overruns.
- 63% of CNR patients are moderate or high health risks.
- 37% of existing patients show cost overruns.

Current pricing practices do not reflect the "holistic" nature of the program. Seminars, lectures, materials, and the notion of immersing a patient in the program experience are important and valuable in achieving results, but are not reflected in patient charges.

Even though third-party payers reimburse only a small fraction of program costs, CNR billing practices have been driven by what is acceptable to the insurance companies. This limits your ability to recover costs and to make an adequate profit.

CNR lacks both a budget and an operating report. Because no data are prepared, it is difficult to monitor expenses, operating level, cash flow, or other parameters.

The program for developing new patients has been largely passive, rather than being a managed activity designed to achieve certain objectives. CNR has been extremely successful at gaining new patients, but much less so than is possible, given the quality and uniqueness of the program.

- Materials sent to the paient are not as informative as they could be.
- Emphasis on up-front payments can be discouraging.

The secretarial/administrative workload is too heavy for the resources available. Some examples:

- Patient records do not meet CNR standards.
- Routine patient audits are delayed.
- Physician contact letters (very important) are delayed.
- Program improvements are not developed as rapidly as desired.
- Maintenance activities such as editing, update meetings, etc., are not done.

At least some excess capacity exists. There are no obvious reasons why 20 to 30 patients per week, in addition to current levels, could not be handled with existing staffing levels and facilities.

A review of the current compensation levels at CNR indicates that they are adequate for current responsibilities, but some concerns need to be raised.

Although the talent/interest/dedication is present in the existing staff, CNR is currently undermanaged.

- You do not have the time or inclination to manage it.
- The administrative workload interferes with the handling of broader issues. . . .

Regards,

Michael H. Kenyon
Blue-Kenyon Associates

My projections are that a basic free-standing program could be operated for a minimum of $16,000 per month, not including charges for marketing or corporate overhead [see Tables 3.2 and 3.3]. This is based on getting about $30,000 in free time from Dr. Blackburn. At this level of staffing, a free-standing clinic could serve about 125 patients per month. If the clinic added another full-time nurse and full-time counselor, and corresponding physician and psychologist services, it could serve approximately 250 patients per month. It might be wise to also add a full-time exercise therapist, because exercise is an important component of the program, and a part-time nutritionist, for a couple of hours a week.

Currently Dr. Blackburn is charging an up-front flat rate of $995 per patient for a 26-week program of whatever level of services is necessary. His program is running at about two-thirds capacity, and he's losing money. He has a fair number of free-care patients and some patients require very intensive services. He uses the flat pricing arrangement because he doesn't want patients to misread his motives if they need more treatment than the average patient.

The average patient comes in three weeks out of four. The standard weekly visit involves seeing a nurse for 10 minutes, then a counselor for 20 minutes, and then a physician, nutritionist, or educational lecture (depending upon the needs of the patient and where he or she is in the program). The educational lectures are usually presented by guest lecturers, although Dr. Blackburn has begun using videotapes which patients can view at their convenience. A patient sees a physician for 45 minutes to 1 hour four times in a six-month period. I believe nurses can handle about 100 patient visits per week, and counselors can handle about 75 visits per week.

The average patient lives within 30 minutes of Dr. Blackburn's clinic, with an occasional patient living 45 minutes away. Travel time is an issue, because participation in the program involves weekly visits. Right now patients have to pay $3 for parking each time they visit, and there are constant complaints over congestion in the Deaconess area.

The Risks

There are so many unknowns to this business. If this program were to expand to new sites, all staff would have to have a very high skill level to deal with the extremely sophisticated and difficult patients this program serves. It would be important to standardize the treatment and the training, but without stifling it or regimenting it.

Other risks are that there is no system for ensuring quality (and patients won't pay their bills if they don't receive quality service), this treatment isn't reimbursed by third party payers, and there is no known marketing of this type of service. I'm not sure if it should be marketed to physicians, to corporations, or to the general public.

POINTS TO PONDER

1. Dr. Blackburn has developed an effective, proprietary treatment program, but what kind of business opportunity is it?
2. What are the managerial skills critical for his program's transformation into a business? Specify how marketing should be planned and implemented.

Table 3.2 Center for Nutritional Research: Budget Required to Replicate the Center for Nutritional Research

Expenses	Annual Budget
1 Office Manager	$ 16,000
1 Nurse	18,000
1 Nurse's Aide	12,000
1 Master's-level Social Worker	15,000
1 Bachelor of Arts-level Counselor	13,000
1 Part-time Bookkeeper	8,000
Physician Time	60,000
Psychologist Time	15,000
Lecturer's Fees	5,000
Rent and Utilities	20,000
Miscellaneous	22,000
Total	$204,000

Note: This budget assumes $30,000 in free time from Dr. Blackburn. Marketing and corporate overhead expenses are not included.

Table 3.3 Center for Nutritional Research: Minimum Budget for Free-Standing Nutritional Clinic

Expenses	Annual Budget
1 Office Manager	$ 25,000
1 Nurse	22,000
1 Counselor	17,000
1 Secretary	17,000
Physician Time (4 hours per week)	20,800
Psychologist Time (2 hours per week)	7,800
Rent (3,000 sq. ft. @ $18/sq. ft.)	54,000
Miscellaneous	28,000
Total	$191,600

Note: Projected patient load is 125 patients per month.

NOTES

1. George L. Blackburn, M.D., and Elizabeth St. Lezin, B.S., "Obesity," *Conn's Current Therapy*, 1983, 444–49.

2. Craig A. Lambert, Ph.D., David R. Netherton, M.S., Lorenz J. Finison, Ph.D., James N. Hyde, M.S., and Sharon J. Spaight, B.A., "Risk Factors and Life Style: A Statewide Health-Interview Survey," *The New England Journal of Medicine*, April 29, 1982, 1048–51.

3. William T. Reynolds, "Toward a Psychology of Obesity: Review of Research on the Role of Personality and Level of Adjustment," *International Journal of Eating Disorders*, 2, no. 1(1982):54.

4. Gina Kolata, "Why Do People Get Fat?" *Science*, March 15, 1985, 1327.

5. Ibid.

6. Richard Wurtman, "Nutrients That Modify Brain Function," *Scientific American*, 246(1982): 50.

7. Catherine E. Ross and John Mirowsky, "Social Epidemiology of Overweight: A Substantive and Methodological Investigation," *Journal of Health and Social Behavior*, 24 (September 1983): 228–298.

Computers in Medicine, Inc.

In a lawyer's office overlooking Boston harbor, on a hot afternoon in July, Wendy Vittori signed the documents that would officially launch Computers in Medicine, Inc. (CMI). The president and chief executive officer of the fledgling company felt a sense of exhilaration. CMI's innovative computer system for medical group practices would, for the first time, enable doctors to take full advantage of the revolution in information technology.

For Dr. Julian Fisher, executive vice president, it was also a moment of great personal satisfaction. Fewer than 18 months ago he learned that his mother's fatal heart attack from complications following surgery might have been avoided if her doctors had seen the results of an EKG conducted the previous day that placed her in a high-risk category for this type of surgery. An expert in medical computer applications, he was convinced that more timely access to this vital information could have saved his mother's life.

THE CONCEPT

CMI was founded by a group of technical and medical professionals who shared a common interest in developing a comprehensive, integrated information management

system for group medical practices. With initial equity funding of $1.2 million from 40 private investors, CMI began operation in August.

CMI sought to meet the total information management requirements of a group practice with a single, integrated, easy-to-use turnkey system that would cost no more than the cost of billing alone. Its PULSE system incorporated four key areas of information management: Patient Care, Practice Management, Office Automation, and Billing and Accounting. The Patient Care module presented patients' medical histories on a touch-screen terminal showing vital signs, lab test results, and responses to medications, thus enabling the physician to track illnesses and evaluate treatments rapidly. Touch-screen technology, which had become available at a reasonable cost by mid-1983, allowed access to a computer without requiring the user to type on a keyboard. The Practice Management module offered reports on the financial performance of the practice to facilitate future planning and business decision making. Office Automation techniques such as appointment scheduling, word processing, and electronic mail were incorporated to enhance productivity and efficiency in the day-to-day running of the office. An Accounting module provided billing and accounts receivable capabilities with tracking of payments by item for each visit, automatic filing of claims, and third-party reimbursement.

Taking advantage of state-of-the-art technologies, the PULSE system offered an optional voice synthesis feature for remote access that enabled authorized physicians to retrieve vital patient information from their office records over the telephone. The device was designed to function 24 hours a day, even in an empty office.

PULSE included a sophisticated database search capability to provide immediate access to information on drugs and drug interactions. Updates were routinely incorporated so that the database reflected the latest drug interaction information available. The system could produce personalized drug education sheets for patient use, covering areas such as precautions, guidelines for proper use of prescribed medications, and potential side effects. The system also provided access to public information services and databases, with automatic dialing of subscriber codes.

A typical PULSE multi-user configuration—priced at $70,000— included a Digital PDP-11 minicomputer, a Rainbow 100 personal computer, a video display terminal with touch screen, color graphics, and a printer.

THE MARKET

Recently, the medical group practice market had grown in the number and size of practices. The advantages of shared overhead costs and ability to offer a greater range of medical services contributed to this growth. Group practice physicians, who represented only 1.2% of the medical profession in 1940 and 12.8% in 1969, accounted for well over 25% of all doctors in active practice by the beginning of 1984. CMI decided to focus its efforts on the "mid-range" groups, consisting of five to twenty-five physicians, the fastest growing segment of the market (see Tables 4.1 and 4.2).

Stiff competition from alternatives such as health maintenance organizations and Medicare and Medicaid limits on physician fees greatly changed the environment in which doctors operated. Traditionally, medicine was on a "cost-plus" basis, with increased costs passed along to the health care consumer. As cost containment became a serious issue, the physician's need for sophisticated management tools became more pressing. Yet medical groups were slower than most businesses to adopt information technology, as indicated by the

slow turnover of their receivables (see Table 4.3) and the low percentage of expenditures spent on computer services and equipment.

Selling computers to most doctors was difficult, according to Wendy Vittori. "They are skittish when it comes to technology." Regarded by society as ultimate experts, they could feel threatened by areas of expertise outside their realm. Besides, "they think in terms of what it costs to open the door—user cost is not a priority concept for them," she explained. With PULSE, CMI set out to reach the physician who already appreciated this kind of sophisticated information technology and who would not balk at the up-front cost. "We set out to appeal to the buyer who liked the best," explained Wendy Vittori, "the one who buys a Mercedes." CMI management positioned their PULSE product as the Mercedes of medical computer systems—the original sales promotional material was modeled on a Porsche brochure.

Because many unique features of the PULSE system—such as touch-screen access, voice synthesis, and drug interaction search—were expressly developed for the physician as end user, CMI decided to direct its marketing efforts directly to the physician. Their competitors' marketing programs had routinely been directed at the group administrator within a practice. Sales cycles were extended by the need to first convince the administrator, only to have the physician/owner come up with a final, different choice.

Sales of medical group computer systems and services were projected to exceed $300 million in 1983, and by 1985, when annual expenditures were expected to reach $450 million, the average group practice would be spending $75,000 per year on computer systems and services (see Table 4.4).

THE TECHNOLOGY

The underlying design philosophy of the PULSE computer system was to enhance the functionality of existing products while matching existing prices. "We felt that we

Table 4.1 Computers in Medicine, Inc.: Number of Medical Group Practices, 1975–1985

Practice Size by Physician Number	1975	1980	1985 (Estimated)	Compound Annual Growth Rate 1980–85
3–4	4,437	5,956	9,450	9.7%
5–7	2,282	2,725	4,642	11.2
8–15	1,145	1,312	2,884	17.1
16–25	332	390	695	12.3
Over 25	297	379	667	12.1
Total Groups	8,493	10,762	18,338	11.5%
Number of Group Physicians	66,842	88,290	140,392[a]	
Number of Physicians	409,000	487,000	520,000[a]	

[a] 1984 data.

Sources: Estimates based on "Forecasts of Physician Supply and Requirements," Office of Technology Assessment of the Congress of the United States, 1980.

Table 4.2 Computers in Medicine, Inc.: Medical Group Practice Growth, 1969–1980

Type of Practice	1969			1980		
	Groups	Physicians	Average Size	Groups	Physicians	Average Size
Single Specialty	3,169	13,053	4.1	6,156	29,456	4.8
Multi-specialty	2,418	24,349	10.1	3,552	54,122	15.2
Family Practice	784	2,691	3.4	1,054	4,712	4.5
	6,371	40,093	6.3	10,762	88,290	8.2

Source: American Medical Association.

would differentiate the product by saying, 'Yes, you can have one that does billing, but for the same price you can have one that does more,'" explained Wendy Vittori.

CMI management chose a Digital (DEC) PDP-11 minicomputer for the PULSE system. This series had been the world's largest-selling family of minicomputers for 15 years, with over 300,000 installed by mid-1983. Despite cost considerations, a minicomputer was selected over a microcomputer configuration because "the PC was not up to the sophistication of the product when CMI started," according to Wendy Vittori. "The game plan was to have its capabilities be the hallmark of PULSE. Then, as hardware became less expensive, or PCs became more capable and network technology more advanced, we could expand

Table 4.3 Computers in Medicine, Inc.: Medical Group Management Association Mean Income and Expense per Physician, 1981

Multi-Specialty Groups (number of physician FTEs[a] in group)

	All Sizes		3–6		7–15		16–25		26–35		36–50		Over 50	
	$	%	$	%	$	%	$	%	$	%	$	%	$	%
Gross Fee-for-Service Charges	234900		253400		214900		232300		262100		240800		259900	
Adjustments	13100		16200		11000		12800		12500		14000		18400	
Adjusted Fee-for-Service Charges	224500		243300		206500		222000		251000		229400		243900	
Bad Debts and Write-offs	9300		10000		8700		9100		11700		9700		7900	
Prepaid Contract Charges	62000		—		76700		111000		23200		39900		53300	
Fee-for-Service Collections	215700		274400		200100		205800		236600		215000		231300	
Prepaid Contract Revenue	50600		—		61500		110600		19200		29300		39600	
Other Revenue	5000		3100		2800		8600		2800		5500		6000	
Total Cash Collections	226200	100.0	223800	100.0	209800	100.0	229400	100.0	242800	100.0	233900	100.0	253500	100.0
All Nonphysician Salaries	46700	21.1	46200	23.7	42900	20.7	48300	21.2	48700	20.4	48100	20.8	53300	20.9
Group Practice Executive Staff	4100	1.8	5900	2.1	4900	2.4	4000	1.7	3400	1.4	3600	1.6	3200	1.3
Business Office Personnel	6400	2.9	10300	4.2	6900	3.5	6300	2.8	6600	2.7	5800	2.6	4200	1.7
Data Processing Personnel	1800	.8	2900	1.2	2000	.9	1900	.8	1500	.6	1600	.6	1600	.6
Other Administrative Personnel	2200	.9	—	—	3100	1.5	2700	1.1	1000	.5	1800	.7	1900	.8
Registered Nurses	6900	3.0	9700	3.7	7100	3.4	6900	2.9	7200	3.0	6200	2.6	6100	2.4
LPNs[b] and Aides	7500	3.3	7400	2.9	7500	3.8	8100	3.4	7100	3.0	7300	3.2	7200	2.8
Medical Receptionists	5000	2.2	5400	1.8	4600	2.2	5100	2.2	5600	2.3	5100	2.2	5300	2.1
Medical Secretaries/ Transcribers	2800	1.2	4000	1.2	2200	1.0	2300	1.1	3700	1.5	2900	1.3	3600	1.4
Medical Records Personnel	3100	1.4	1900	.7	2900	1.4	3600	1.6	3300	1.4	3200	1.3	2800	1.1
Physician Extenders	2900	1.3	3700	1.3	3400	1.7	2500	1.0	1700	.7	3800	1.7	2500	1.0
Laboratory Personnel	4500	2.0	4900	2.0	3800	1.9	4900	2.2	4600	1.9	4000	1.8	5600	2.1
Radiology Personnel	3100	1.3	11200	3.2	2400	1.2	2400	1.1	3000	1.2	2300	1.0	3800	1.5
Physical Therapy Personnel	1400	.6	—	—	1000	.5	2100	.9	1400	.6	950	.4	1000	.4
Optical Personnel	1200	.5	—	—	2800	.7	1600	.6	1100	.5	950	.4	650	.3
Housekeeping, Maintenance and Security Personnel	1900	.8	1100	.4	1800	.8	1800	.8	2000	.8	1800	.8	2300	.9
Other Support Personnel	4600	1.7	4000	1.3	5200	1.4	6300	2.3	3400	1.3	1900	.9	6600	2.4

Single Specialty Groups (type of specialty)

	Anesthesia		Ophthalmology		Pediatrics		General Surgery		Urology		Psychiatry		Neurosurgery	
	$	%	$	%	$	%	$	%	$	%	$	%	$	%
Gross Fee-for-Service Charges	268800		410000		170400		342700		334900		161400		351500	
Adjustments	18700		33100		7700		20300		23700		6700		25700	
Adjusted Fee-for-Service Charges	256300		386800		162700		329100		314500		154600		325700	
Bad Debts and Write-offs	3100		6400		8400		23700		8300		12900		18100	
Prepaid Contract Charges	—	—	—	—	—	—	—	—	—	—	—	—	—	—
Fee-for-Service Collections	221100		413000		—		296400		401600		141700		328000	
Prepaid Contract Revenue	—	—	—	—	—	—	—	—	—	—	11700	—	—	—
Other Revenue	—	—	2000	—	—	—	1800	—	—	—	—	—	—	—
Total Cash Collections	252900	100.0	374300	100.0	156100	100.0	306500	100.0	308700	100.0	154900	100.0	310500	100.0
All Nonphysician Salaries	53100	18.2	94100	23.5	33800	21.4	35300	11.8	38600	13.3	17900	12.0	38700	12.4
Group Practice Executive Staff	—	—	6600	1.7	—	—	4400	1.5	5600	1.6	2800	1.9	7600	2.5
Business Office Personnel	—	—	5800	1.4	—	—	3700	1.3	5500	1.3	2500	1.9	—	—
Data Processing Personnel	—	—	—	—	—	—	—	—	3500	1.1	—	—	—	—
Other Administrative Personnel	—	—	—	—	—	—	—	—	—	—	—	—	—	—
Registered Nurses	—	—	—	—	—	—	5600	2.0	—	—	—	—	7200	2.0
LPNs[b] and Aides	—	—	13600	3.0	—	—	—	—	9100	2.9	—	—	—	—
Medical Receptionists	—	—	7400	1.8	—	—	5700	2.1	6400	2.1	2400	1.7	—	—
Medical Secretaries/Transcribers	—	—	6200	1.4	—	—	7000	2.3	—	—	1600	1.3	11400	3.4
Medical Records Personnel	—	—	—	—	—	—	1700	.7	3200	.8	—	—	—	—
Physician Extenders	—	—	—	—	—	—	—	—	—	—	—	—	—	—
Laboratory Personnel	—	—	—	—	—	—	—	—	—	—	—	—	—	—
Radiology Personnel	—	—	—	—	—	—	—	—	2800	.9	—	—	—	—
Physical Therapy Personnel	—	—	—	—	—	—	—	—	—	—	—	—	—	—
Optical Personnel	—	—	—	—	—	—	—	—	—	—	—	—	—	—
Housekeeping, Maintenance and Security Personnel	—	—	—	—	—	—	—	—	—	—	—	—	—	—
Other Support Personnel	—	—	4600	1.2	—	—	2000	.6	—	—	—	—	—	—

continues

Table 4.3 continued

Multi-Specialty Groups (number of physician FTEs[a] in group)

	All Sizes		3–6		7–15		16–25		26–35		36–50		Over 50	
	$	%	$	%	$	%	$	%	$	%	$	%	$	%
All Computer Expenses	3500	1.6	3600	1.6	3600	1.8	3500	1.6	3700	1.5	2900	1.2	3400	1.3
Computer Service Bureau Fees	3000	1.4	4500	1.7	3400	1.7	3200	1.5	3100	1.3	2300	1.0	2200	.9
Computer Equipment Rental/Depreciation	1400	.6	1600	.6	1500	.7	1600	.7	800	.3	1200	.5	1500	.6
Computer Equipment Maintenance Expenses	550	.3	900	.3	800	.4	500	.2	500	.2	350	.2	300	.1
Computer Supplies	550	.3	600	.2	800	.4	650	.3	550	.2	350	.2	400	.2
Other Computer Expenses	550	.3	450	.2	850	.4	350	.1	—	—	550	.2	200	.1
Total Accounts Receivable	72100	100.0	73100	100.0	65000	100.0	74500	100.0	81200	100.0	68000	100.0	79000	100.0
Accounts Receivable <30 days		27.8		28.3		31.0		26.8		25.6		25.3		26.7
Accounts Receivable 31–60 Days		19.0		26.8		17.3		19.0		18.6		21.4		19.4
Accounts Receivable 61–90 days		11.2		14.0		10.4		11.2		11.6		11.5		11.9
Accounts Receivable 91–120 days		8.7		12.3		9.6		8.3		8.3		7.7		7.9
Accounts Receivable >120 days		33.2		18.6		31.7		34.7		36.0		34.2		34.2

Single Specialty Groups (type of specialty)

	Anesthesia		Ophthalmology		Pediatrics		General Surgery		Urology		Psychiatry		Neurosurgery	
	$	%	$	%	$	%	$	%	$	%	$	%	$	%
All Computer Expenses	4000	1.4	4700	1.4	4200	2.6	3500	1.2	5100	1.6	4000	2.3	—	—
Computer Service Bureau Fees	—	—	—	—	—	—	—	—	—	—	—	—	—	—
Computer Equipment Rental/Depreciation	—	—	2400	.6	—	—	—	—	—	—	—	—	—	—
Computer Equipment Maintenance Expenses	—	—	—	—	—	—	—	—	—	—	—	—	—	—
Computer Supplies	—	—	—	—	—	—	—	—	1200	.3	—	—	—	—
Other Computer Expenses	—	—	—	—	—	—	—	—	—	—	—	—	—	—
Total Accounts Receivable	61500	100.0	89400	100.0	—	—	82900	100.0	143600	100.0	45300	100.0	102400	100.0
Accounts Receivable <30 days		31.5		32.3		—		—		24.6		29.8		35.5
Accounts Receivable 31–60 Days		19.1		24.2		—		—		17.1		14.2		19.0
Accounts Receivable 61–90 days		12.0		10.3		—		—		8.5		12.7		12.9
Accounts Receivable 91–120 days		9.0		14.1		—		—		9.3		15.8		7.4
Accounts Receivable >120 days		28.6		19.1		—		—		40.6		26.8		25.2

[a]FTEs = full-time equivalent employees.
[b]LPNs = licensed practical nurses.

Source: Medical Group Practice Management Association: *Cost and Production Survey Report*, 1982 report based on 1981 data.

Table 4.4 Computers in Medicine, Inc.: Estimated Annual Expenditures for Medical Group Computer Systems and Services, 1980–85 (dollars in millions)

Practice Size	1980	1981	1982	1983	1984	1985	Compound Growth (%)
3–4 Physicians							
Expenditures	$ 34.8	$ 40.2	$ 51.8	$ 63.5	$ 77.2	$ 84.1	19.3
Installed Base	838	976	1,140	1,326	1,545	1,800	16.5
5–7 Physicians							
Expenditures	$ 49.7	$ 59.4	$ 74.1	$ 88.0	$103.6	$121.5	19.6
Installed Base	820	975	1,160	1,375	1,635	1,940	18.8
8–15 Physicians							
Expenditures	$ 47.2	$ 58.4	$ 78.2	$ 89.4	$111.6	$128.1	22.1
Installed Base	705	831	980	1,153	1,358	1,600	17.8
16–25 Physicians							
Expenditures	$ 30.5	$ 35.8	$ 43.0	$ 52.3	$ 57.9	$ 66.0	16.7
Installed Base	240	280	322	373	432	500	15.8
26–49 Physicians							
Expenditures	$ 21.6	$ 24.3	$ 28.4	$ 32.8	$ 34.7	$ 39.0	12.5
Installed Base	95	106	115	130	140	153	10.0
50+ Physicians							
Expenditures	$ 4.2	$ 5.0	$ 5.9	$ 7.1	$ 8.4	$ 10.0	18.9
Installed Base	14	14	14	16	20	24	11.4
Total							
Expenditures	$188.0	$223.1	$281.4	$333.1	$393.4	$448.7	
Installations	$2,712	$3,181	$3,731	$4,373	$5,130	$6,017	

Source: Business plan for Computers in Medicine, Inc., 1983.

our market penetration by taking advantage of these trends." Personal computers were incorporated as an integral part of the system, however, to implement word processing and business management spreadsheet functions

With its superior technology, DEC dominated the minicomputer market in the early 1980s, but did not compare with IBM in the personal computer market. With the introduction of its Microsoft Disk Operating System-based PC in 1981, IBM had set the standard for future personal computer software applications, leaving competitors such as DEC, who still used the traditional operating system, at a disadvantage. An engineering-driven manufacturer, Digital's strength had always

been at the higher end of the market, with products designed for the large, sophisticated end user, including original equipment manufacturers. IBM, though never a leader technologically, used its superior marketing expertise to capture the retail market, forcing other manufacturers to follow suit with compatible products. (The PULSE Digital Rainbow PC configuration was subsequently replaced with an IBM PC.)

"CMI incorporated off-the-shelf software packages into PULSE in addition to integrating over 500 programs developed by the company's own staff," according to Wendy Vittori. The Accounting subsystem was based on the product specifications of a physician information and billing system (PIBS), which had been installed in over 60 medical group practices at the time. By utilizing a proven package, CMI hoped to shorten the development cycle, avoid product specification errors, and leverage the PIBS installed base to generate PULSE reference sites and system sales. Features of several other off-the-shelf software packages were incorporated into aspects of the PIBS product for the Office Automation module. Lotus 1-2-3, a nationally recognized spreadsheet system, was used to implement various financial analyses in the Practice Management module.

"The PULSE system was competitive with existing products appealing to mid-range group practices," according to Tom Bergan, vice president for marketing. Competitive in-house systems ranged in price from $25,000 to over $200,000. "PULSE was not competitive for smaller groups, but we were less interested in the low end of the market, which was very price conscious," he added. A configuration supporting up to 20 users was priced at $70,000 to $100,000, depending on options, while a high-end configuration with up to 40 users was priced from $120,000 to $200,000. The system could also be leased for approximately $2,400–$3,700 per month.

The original production schedule for PULSE was accelerated by 3 months as a result of rapid engineering staff-up at CMI and the PIBS agreement. Product development began in earnest in January 1984 and the product was to be ready by June. July and August would be devoted to final documentation production and product packaging in anticipation of the first customer shipments in September 1984. Early test-site placements and initial sales were vital to ensure adequate demonstration opportunities and referrals.

THE COMPETITION

Over 200 companies offered some type of group practice computer system. CyCare, the largest, with revenues of $30 million, commanded less than 10% of the total market. CMI faced competition from service bureaus, other turnkey systems and, to a lesser extent, individual purchases of hardware and off-the-shelf software by physicians.

The medical group computing market had remained relatively unchanged over the previous 5 years. Product differentiation was achieved largely through price and service, with the small local companies that offered high levels of service at relatively low prices competing effectively with larger, nationwide firms. Details about the larger competitors follow.

CyCare entered the group practice market in 1968 and by 1982 held the largest market share, with 400 installations in the United States and Canada. A public corporation since 1981, CyCare offered batch, shared service, distributed processing, and in-house turnkey systems.

Science Dynamics Corporation, a privately held company headquartered in California, had 1980 revenues of $15 million and an installed customer base of 325 clients in all 50 states. The company tended to focus on the shared system approach.

Interpretive Data Systems (IDS), founded in 1974, marketed both turnkey systems and shared services. The company focused on the large, hospital-based groups and had achieved a significant penetration in this market. IDS generated revenues of $8 million in 1982, operating sales offices in Chicago, San Francisco, and Dallas. IDS turnkey systems ran on Digital computers.

Shared Medical Systems (SMS), founded in 1969, provided information processing services to both hospitals and physician groups. SMS reported revenues of $160 million in 1982, with physician system revenues estimated at $7 million. Considered one of the strongest companies in the health care computing market, SMS's success in the hospital environment had not been equaled in the medical group market.

IBM's $6 million in revenues in the medical group market came through system houses such as Management Systems of Wausau and Burlington Data Processing and through the direct sale of turnkey products, ranging in price from $25,000 to over $100,000. IBM had been particularly successful among smaller practices, selling the low end of its product family, especially the Datamaster Physician Management System. Although the increasing popularity of personal computers promised to open up new market opportunities for the IBM PC, competing with the specialized customer support staff of the system houses and service bureaus was seen as a factor that might limit the company's market share.

Management Systems of Wausau, Inc., was one of the oldest of the service bureau companies. By the early 1980s, it had also introduced turnkey systems servicing approximately 250 groups in 30 states.

Service bureaus dominated the market in the early 1970s by offering cost-effective billing and accounts receivable services on mainframe computers. The service bureaus processed transaction logs submitted for data entry by the group practices. By the mid-1970s, when the availability of lower cost mini- and microcomputer systems and the ease of use of on-line data entry eroded some service bureau business, they provided computer terminals at the practices with on-line access to their central databases. Their fees ranged from 5% to 15% of collections, depending on type of services performed, specialty and size of group practice,

and type of client. Services ranged from billing functions only to collections and appointment scheduling; for example, Boston-based Medical Practice Management, Inc., offered an in-depth knowledge of third-party collecting and the latest changes in codes and regulations, in addition to accounts receivable management and appointment scheduling (see Table 4.5).

Personal computer purchases were increasingly common among physicians and CMI also faced competition from the many software packages that targeted the medical market. "For $15,000 or lower, you could put together a personal computer and billing system software package," explained Dr. Julian Fisher, "but I question if even the most sophisticated PC could meet the total information management needs of a mid-range medical group." Nonetheless, CMI was competing with "the perception on the part of the physician" that a PC could do the job. According to Fisher, "one-quarter of the software package manufacturers go out of business every year."

MARKETING STRATEGY

CMI management sought to differentiate PULSE by marketing directly to the physician

---

Table 4.5 Computers in Medicine, Inc.: Medical Practice Mangement, Inc., Fees and Services

Pricing Schedule

1. Accounts receivable management: percentage of net collections except as otherwise indicated.

	Patient Visits (thousands)			
Adjusted Gross Billing ($)[a]	0–5	5–10	10–20	20+
0–75,000	$10,500	$14,500	N/A	N/A
75,000–150,000	$12,500	$16,500	N/A	N/A
150,000–300,000	9.9%	10.4%	11.0%	11.7%
300,000–500,000	9.7%	9.9%	10.4%	11.0%
500,000–750,000	8.5%	8.8%	9.2%	9.7%
750,000–1,000,000	7.6%	7.8%	8.0%	8.4%
1,000,000–2,000,000	6.9%	7.0%	7.2%	7.5%
2,000,000+	6.8%	6.9%	7.1%	7.4%

[a]Adjusted gross billing = gross billing less third-party disallowances.

2. Appointment scheduling/account inquiry: $65.00 per month per practitioner.

and using advertising and public relations much more aggressively than other suppliers of medical computing products. An extensive marketing campaign was mapped out to ensure initial product awareness and generate qualified sales leads on an ongoing basis.

CMI retained a Boston-based public relations group well known for its successful introduction of the Lotus Development Corporation. A press conference was to announce the product in Boston and to gain editorial coverage for CMI in leading business and medical journals. Plans were also formulated to collaborate with the Instructional Division of the American Medical Association on a documentary film explaining the use of computers in clinical care. CMI products would be shown to illustrate the range of nonaccounting uses of information technology available to physicians.

Advertising and sales promotion materials were handled by a Boston advertising agency specializing in the medical field. Educational seminars by industry experts and members of CMI's staff were planned for major metropolitan areas throughout the country, with locations chosen to meet the needs of CMI's sales programs. This series would focus on the role of information technology in medicine, with attendance on a prepaid basis to ensure good quality attendees. The direct-mail program was initially to promote the PULSE products and subsequently to advertise the seminar series. A number of key trade shows were attended, and a newsletter planned for CMI customers and targeted prospects, on a periodic basis. By highlighting new product features, the newsletter would be a primary marketing vehicle for the company's installed base.

CMI's own direct sales force consisted of people with a minimum of 10 years' experience in direct sales to physicians. Although a background in computer sales was a plus, this was considered less important than credibility within the physician community. Field offices would be opened to coincide with projected growth in sales, but initially the salesperson worked from his or her home. There were to be 8 in 1985, growing to 22 in 1988.

Because of the sensitivity of users to downtime, customer service played a key role. CMI's own service organization would ensure direct telephone support by trained staff members familiar with both PULSE hardware and software. This support would be provided initially from corporate headquarters, with additional field offices established as volume increased. Initial hardware maintenance would be provided by Digital at customer locations in the field; but as volume grew, CMI hoped to provide hardware support at the customer site, with backup support by Digital at CMI offices. Customer training would be provided by a CMI team at the time of system installation, and CMI staff would assist in the integration of the system into the office environment. Post-installation support services were provided at no additional cost during a 90-day warranty period, at the end of which a service contract would provide for ongoing, full-support services, at an annual cost of 10% of the initial system price.

MANAGEMENT AND FUTURE PLANS

CMI's major operating officers included the four original founders of the company, a vice president for marketing, and a finance director. An organization of approximately 20 was anticipated by the first year of operations, growing to 40 by the end of the second year.

President and CEO Wendy Vittori came from a marketing background at Digital, where she had headed up DEC's Medical Systems Group, responsible for strategic planning and sales. DEC's customer base comprised OEMs and end users, with direct sales predominantly focused on hospitals and government agencies. One of 18 product groups at Digital, the Medical Systems Group generated annual sales of over $50 million.

Chairman of the Board David Friend had 15 years' experience in establishing and running start-up companies and was a recognized authority in computer graphics. A previous business venture, Computer Pictures Corporation, had been acquired by Cullinet Software, Inc., for $14 million.

Executive Vice President Julian Fisher, M.D., was a practicing neurologist at Boston's Beth Israel Hospital and a member of the Harvard Medical Center faculty, where he had devoted considerable effort to the improvement of medical care through computer technology.

Vice President for Development Dirk Brinkman had extensive experience in the design and implementation of medical information systems in a variety of medical areas. Prior

to joining CMI, he directed new software product development in the Medical Systems Group at Digital.

Vice President for Marketing Tom Bergan had directed all marketing and software development programs in the Occupational Health area at Digital before coming to CMI.

Finance and Administration Director Joseph Grimm was previously finance manager of the Medical Systems Group at Digital, responsible for financial reporting, budgeting, and planning for worldwide operations. See Table 4.6 for 1984 plans to raise additional equity financing.

Table 4.6 Computers in Medicine, Inc.: Income Statement ($ in thousands)

	Projected Income Statement (5-year period ending 9/30/88)				
	FY1984	FY1985	FY1986	FY1987	FY1988
Number of Units Sold	5	42	82	140	220
SALES	$ 500	$ 4,080	$ 8,485	$14,450	$22,650
System Sales	0	65	415	750	1,350
Upgrade Sales	0	155	700	1,800	3,000
Service Revenue	$ 500	$ 4,300	$ 9,600	$17,000	$27,000
Total					
COST OF SALES					
Equipment	$ 234	$ 1,738	$ 3,402	$ 5,630	$ 8,500
Royalties	6	49	102	173	272
Warranty & Service	67	462	953	1,716	2,613
Total	$ 307	$ 2,249	$ 4,457	$ 7,519	$11,385
GROSS MARGIN	$ 193	$ 2,051	$ 5,143	$ 9,481	$15,615
OPERATING EXPENSES					
R & D	$ 614	$ 522	$ 838	$ 1,136	$ 1,524
Marketing	756	1,256	1,337	1,677	2,038
Selling	370	992	1,417	2,282	3,361
Administrative & Financial	461	786	1,057	1,305	1,804
Service Start-up	69	0	0	0	0
Total	$ 2,270	$ 3,556	$ 4,649	$ 6,400	$ 8,727
OPERATING INCOME	($ 2,077)	($ 1,505)	$ 494	$ 3,081	$ 6,888
Interest Income	157	76	32	85	252
Interest (Exp)	0	(14)	(108)	(64)	0
PRETAX INCOME	($ 1,920)	($ 1,443)	$ 418	$ 3,102	$ 7,140
Taxes	0	0	0	44	2,957
AFTER-TAX INCOME	($ 1,920)	($ 1,443)	$ 418	$ 3,058	$ 4,183

POINTS TO PONDER

1. What opportunity does this product represent? Is the product well suited to the opportunity?

2. What managerial skills are critical for its success?

3. Evaluate CMI's implementation of each of these skills. If your evaluation is negative, specify the reasons and the changes needed.

Case Study 5

Diagnostic Imaging, Inc.

BUSINESS PLAN: THE COMPANY

Diagnostic Imaging, Inc., is a start-up company whose goal is to create a nationwide network of free-standing diagnostic centers using nuclear magnetic resonance (MR) technology. The company proposes to create 10 to 20 centers in its first three years of operation.

Diagnostic Imaging, Inc., has operated the first free-standing MR center in the United States, in Belleville, Illinois, for approximately eight months, at approximately a break-even level. It was built for $2 million in about three months. It is a resource for the development of medical and technological protocols, business procedures, and training materials. The successful track record in Belleville is considered to be a major competitive advantage for the company.

The principals of the company are the three physicians who originally conceived and supervised the development of the Belleville center and a management team with extensive experience in financial consulting, business start-ups, and health care management.

The primary business risks are technological and regulatory.

TECHNOLOGICAL RISKS

MR technology is rapidly evolving, and there are a number of alternative feasible approaches.

Note: This case was prepared by Dr. James Rhea and edited by Professor Regina E. Herzlinger.

The obsolescence rate of early equipment purchases will be high, although there should be a strong secondary market for used equipment in the early years of the industry. The Technicare equipment chosen by Diagnostic Imaging for the Belleville center has proven to be competitively priced, reliable, and well supported by the manufacturer, a division of Johnson & Johnson. Although the company plans to use the same equipment in additional centers, it is exploring the capabilities of other manufacturers. By developing a relationship with a major manufacturer in what is developing as an intensely competitive industry, the company should gain significant price, delivery, and support concessions.

The technical risk of obsolescence is partially offset by impending technical developments in MR software support that should greatly reduce imaging time and increase the profitability of existing equipment.

ENVIRONMENTAL AND REGULATORY CONSIDERATIONS

Because cost containment has become today's fundamental health regulatory issue, hospitals will find increased difficulty in paying for expensive medical equipment.

FDA Approval of MR Equipment

MR equipment is covered by Food and Drug Administration (FDA) regulations requiring the manufacturer to establish that the device is safe by placing it at investigational sites and collecting data. At the present time, only 2 of the 20 companies manufacturing MR equipment have FDA approval.

Certificate of Need

The federal government reimburses states for payments through the Medicare and Medicaid program. A Certificate of Need (CON) must be secured by hospitals that plan to establish a new type of service or expend significant capital on new equipment. Obtaining it can be an obstacle to hospitals in acquiring new technology, because they must prove that equipment is needed and that it does not duplicate other technology. Possession of a CON is essential because a provider cannot be reimbursed by Medicare or Medicaid without it. Blue Cross/Blue Shield and a few private insurance companies may also require approval before payment.

States vary in the administration of the CON process. A few have placed one-year moratoria on all Certificates of Need. In others, the moratorium applies only to particular kinds of services such as those for the mentally retarded or alcoholics. In general, the northeastern states are much more stringently regulated than those in the Southeast and West. In many states, Certificate of Need regulations do not apply to nonhospital capital expenditures.

Equipment Acquisition by Hospitals

Obstacles to the acquisition of MR equipment by hospitals include the novelty of the technology, clinical uncertainties, regulatory constraints, and economic uncertainties. Many hospitals are waiting for official guidelines to CON and reimbursements before investing in MR devices. These obstacles provide an opportunity for the development of outpatient MR diagnostic centers.

Diagnostic-Related Group Reimbursement

Medicare's prospective payment system, called "diagnostic-related group" (or DRG) reimbursement, is being considered for adoption by Blue Cross/Blue Shield and other insurers.

The DRG system gives hospitals an incentive to control costs. If a hospital spends less than the DRG rate on a patient, the hospital may keep the extra amount. However, it must absorb the cost itself if it spends more. DRGs do not change the fee-for-service method of physician payment. Since total hospital cost will decrease with the patient's length of stay, DRGs create an incentive for diagnoses in outpatient diagnostic centers rather than in a hospital.

MAGNETIC RESONANCE IMAGING TECHNOLOGY

History

The theoretical basis for magnetic resonance imaging was the finding that components of the nuclei of atoms, protons and neutrons, have magnetic properties. Later, experimental work demonstrating the possibility of revealing the composition of materials using magnetic resonance won the Nobel Prize for its researchers.

Magnetic resonance was first used to create *in vivo* images in 1973. By 1980, production prototypes could image an entire human body. By the end of 1983, at least 75 MR units had been installed worldwide, and 160 to 200 units are expected to be installed by the end of 1984.

General Principles of Magnetic Resonance Imaging

Magnetic resonance imaging utilizes the fact that the nuclei of certain elements, when placed in a strong magnetic field, will absorb radio waves at specific frequencies, called resonance frequencies. Each element has a unique resonance frequency for any given magnetic field strength.

When the external source of radio waves is turned off, the elements that absorbed radio frequency energy emit radio signals at their resonance frequencies. These return signals are analyzed using sophisticated computer programs. In the human body, hydrogen, phosphorus, and sodium emit signals strong enough to be easily detected and are present in sufficient concentration to generate an image.

There are several uncertainties about the technology. The use of chemicals to enhance the diagnostic information available is still experimental. There is considerable debate about the optimal magnetic field strength for hydrogen imaging. While higher field strengths result in better images, they also cause the resonance frequency of the hydrogen atoms to increase and the tissues of the body to absorb proportionately more of the energy of the radio signal released by the atoms, which makes detection more difficult. Attempting to overcome this by using a higher beam strength raises the danger of excessive heating of the patient's tissues. The FDA has approved imaging units with field strengths of 0.5 to 0.6 Tesla. (Magnetic fields are measured in gauss or in Tesla; the earth's magnetic field is about .5 Tesla.)

To image elements other than hydrogen, a field strength of 1.5–2.0 Tesla appears to be necessary. Machines of this strength were introduced in 1984. Spectroscopic analysis can require field strength as high as 15 Tesla. When such high field strength machines will be available is uncertain, and their clinical usefulness has not been established.

Equipment Used in Magnetic Resonance Imaging

There are three main components to an MRI system: field magnets; radio transmitter/receiver and antenna; and computers controlling data acquisition, storage, processing, and display.

Magnetic Types

There are three different magnetic designs: resistive magnets, permanent magnets, and superconducting magnets.

Resistive magnets account for approximately 30% of MR units in use. They consume large amounts of energy and are constructed with ordinary copper windings. While the magnet itself is relatively inexpensive, resistive magnets are limited to a field strength of about .3 Tesla.

Permanent magnets, accounting for 5% of all current installations, are very large, weighing up to 100 tons. They do not require any energy to maintain their magnetic fields, nor extensive shielding.

Superconducting magnets currently are used in 65% of installations. Production prototypes have been constructed with field strengths as high as 2 Tesla. They operate at a low temperature, which causes the wire coils to lose all electrical resistance. As a result, the electric current that establishes the magnetic field will circulate for years without significant decay.

Superconducting magnets are expensive, accounting for one-third the cost of the whole system. The liquid helium used to cool them is expensive and difficult to handle. They are sensitive to metal and to electric fields in nearby areas, and thus require more expensive shielding. However, it would appear that they will be the magnets chosen because of the higher field strengths possible.

Radio Equipment

Radio equipment consists of a tunable radio frequency generator that broadcasts a signal through a coil antenna surrounding the patient and located inside the field magnets. Shielding is necessary against outside radio transmissions.

Data Processing Equipment

Computer hardware and software handle three different tasks: control of the test scan, including the variation in strength of the magnetic field and the generation and reception of radio frequency generator signals; data acquisition and storage; and image processing enhancement and display.

The software controlling test protocols is the area in magnetic resonance (MR) technology most subject to change and obsolescence as physicians learn which tests are most appropriate for a given purpose.

THE MARKET FOR MAGNETIC RESONANCE IMAGING

Although estimates of MR's eventual market vary widely, there is little doubt that it will be the most rapidly growing diagnostic technology, displacing computed tomography (CT) scanning as the primary diagnostic technique for many brain and central nervous system disorders by 1987. The technique's application to imaging of other areas of the body is expected to grow as research continues.

Lessons from Other Technologies

A number of insights can be gained from reviewing the history of another dramatic innovation in diagnostic medicine—the CT scanner. When it was introduced, it also was the most expensive equipment to have been developed for the medical field and offered dramatic improvements over existing technology.

In its early years, few companies had equipment available for sale. Similarly, only Technicare and Diasonics have had their MR devices approved by the FDA. After a few years, both supply and demand grew rapidly. Price competition began and companies supplying CT scanners continuously upgraded their devices in an attempt to maintain market share.

CT technology underwent four distinct generations in its first ten years. Most of the changes in the technology were not retrofittable, and hospitals were faced with the choice of keeping obsolete technology or selling it to generate revenue toward the purchase of a new device. Larger hospitals sold their older devices to smaller hospitals. There was a rapid escalation of expenditures on CT scanners; regulators began to set strict limits on future acquisitions, and sales of CT technology declined dramatically.

The CT scanner experience is likely to dissuade many hospital administrators from investing in the first wave of MR technology. Hospitals and regulators will assume that it will become obsolete in the next two to three years. Most hospitals will probably wait a year or two before purchasing the equipment, but then will attempt to establish an MR center in the hospital or in an outpatient center through a partnership with a local physician group.

To take advantage of the probable delay in hospitals' acquiring MR equipment, Diagnostic Imaging, Inc., must establish its centers quickly. The first MR center in a local area will capture a significant share of the market. Regulators will be resistant to add centers in the same area.

Market Estimates

In 14 hospitals with MR investigational centers, the number of patients screened ranged from 1 to 189 per month, with a mean of 74.6.[1] Patients received MR diagnostic tests for Hodgkin's disease (42%), 68% for lymphosarcoma, 42% for malignant neoplasm, and 48% for hemangioma.[2] These data could be used to project utilization of MR by applying them to the number of patients with each disease.

Another study predicted that MR equipment sales will grow at a rate of 15% per annum through 1987 and will displace 66% of the market previously occupied by CT scanning by that time.[3] Yet another source projects equipment sales of $700 million in 1987. At an average cost of $1.5 million per device, this would represent the purchase of 466 units in 1987 alone.[4]

Although these estimates vary, there is consensus among industry observers that MR will grow very rapidly and will be the predominant imaging technique in the next ten years.

End User Markets

Buyers of MR equipment include hospitals, hospital chains, and outpatient diagnostic centers. The following analyzes the potential of each of these segments as markets for Diagnostic Imaging, Inc.

Tertiary Hospitals

Tertiary hospitals are large, sophisticated institutions; they include teaching hospitals and specialty clinics such as the Lahey and Mayo Clinics. They deal with complex cases and usually have specialty centers, such as burn and trauma centers. Although their costs are high, they have not had significant budgetary problems, as they are supported by large endowments and/or federal research and teaching grants. Their powerful and prestigious boards of directors help them to win most regulatory battles. In 1982, 836 of these hospitals had medical school affiliation.

It is likely that most tertiary hospitals will acquire magnetic resonance imaging equipment within the next two years. The leading institutions already have them and most of the others are in the process of acquiring them.

Secondary Hospitals

Secondary hospitals, numbering about 5,000, include suburban and public hospitals that have a few hundred beds and treat the general public for routine illnesses. They have active emergency rooms and OB and general surgery departments. They have faced serious fiscal and regulatory constraints during the last few years, and it is highly unlikely they will be able to purchase magnetic resonance imaging equipment.

Secondary hospitals have cut back on management personnel. The project management and operational assistance offered by Diagnostic Imaging, Inc., should be valuable to them. Most secondary hospitals cannot generate funds for large capital acquisitions and could use the assistance of Diagnostic Imaging, Inc., in developing limited partnerships with local physicians. The association of a secondary hospital with an outpatient MR diagnostic center will keep the hospital in the mainstream of technological change without requiring a major capital investment.

Physician Groups

Groups of physicians are not likely to purchase and manage MR centers independently. Their nonhospital status allows them to avoid many of the regulatory obstacles faced by hospitals. Established physicians and group practices are eager to access MR technology for diagnosis, and those who admit patients to secondary hospitals realize that it is unlikely that their hospitals will be acquiring it.

Physician groups and smaller secondary hospitals are considered to be the primary market for Diagnostic Imaging, Inc., The following methods were used to select target geographic markets.

THE SELECTION OF TARGET MARKETS

Because it is important for Diagnostic Imaging, Inc., to establish its centers quickly, states whose regulators would prevent rapid implementation were not included in this market analysis; these were New York, Connecticut, New Jersey, Massachusetts, New Hampshire, Vermont, Maine, California, and Maryland.

Criteria relating to the nature of the health care system and sociopolitical and economic characteristics were applied to the Standard Metropolitan Statistical Areas (SMSAs) in the remaining states (Table 5.1) to select the most likely markets.

Average per Capita Income

The 1980 census identified the top 100 SMSAs in average per capita income. There is a high correlation between number of practicing specialty physicians and per capita income; thus, the income measure identifies communities with resident specialists, physicians who are potential limited partners.

Because it must be anticipated that each center will experience some early delay in collecting revenue from Medicare and some private insurers, the ability of the patient to pay for the service may be important to its success. Residents of high-income areas are likely to have private insurance and be able to self-pay.

Table 5.1 Diagnostic Imaging, Inc.: Market Analysis

State	SMSA	Income Total (millions)	Income Per Capita (thousands)	Medicare Expenditures (millions)	Number of Physicians	Hospitals Number	Hospitals Beds	Regulatory Status	AMI Sites	AMI Beds	HCA Sites	HCA Beds
				FIRST-LEVEL SITES								
Georgia	Atlanta	$17,469	$22.2	$54.6	3,402	54	10,296	Open	0	0	2	499
Idaho	Boise City	1,489	21.1	3.5	252	4	700	Open	0	0	0	0
Iowa	Cedar Rapids	1,680	22.1	4.1	188	2	1,099	Open	0	0	0	0
	Des Moines	3,324	22.0	10.9	495	7	2,504		0	0	1	118
	Sioux City	1,017	18.8	3.8	154	2	888		0	0	0	0
Kansas	Topeka	1,723	20.0	6.5	370	8	2,625	Open	0	0	0	0
	Wichita	3,907	21.4	69.8	731	8	2,693		0	0	0	0
Louisiana	Lafayette	1,361	19.6	3.3	221	5	775	Open	0	0	1	60
	New Orleans	9,869	19.8	32.7	2,762	27	8,264		0	0	1	271
Minnesota	Rochester	869	22.5	4.5	1,378	4	2,458	Open	0	0	0	0
Missouri	Kansas City	12,683	21.8	49.8	2,526	37	8,150	Open	0	0	0	0
	St. Louis	21,986	21.4	75.7	4,293	50	17,306		0	0	1	64
Nebraska	Lincoln	1,692	20.1	4.7	288	7	1,612	Open	0	0	0	0
	Omaha	4,990	20.9	16.9	1,362	16	5,234		0	0	0	0
Nevada	Las Vegas	4,043	21.8	17.8	456	10	1,750	Open	0	0	0	0
	Reno	2,116	23.6	6.4	354	4	1,169		0	0	1	95
Washington	Bremerton	1,254	21.1	3.7	149	2	288	Open	0	0	0	0
	Olympia	1,112	20.7	2.9	158	1	206		0	0	0	0
	Richland	1,345	23.5	2.4	139	4	332		0	0	0	0
	Seattle	16,489	23.9	44.1	3,666	34	5,533		0	0	0	0
West Virginia	Charleston	2,382	20.2	7.9	473	8	1,674	Open	0	0	0	0
Wyoming	Casper	853	25.8	1.1	96	1	282	Open	0	0	0	0

continues

Table 5.1 continued

State	SMSA	Income Total (millions)	Income Per Capita (thousands)	Medicare Expenditures (millions)	Number of Physicians	Hospitals Number	Hospitals Beds	Regulatory Status
Arizona	Phoenix	$12,492	$21.2	$62.4	2,589	29	6,732	Moderate
				SECOND-LEVEL SITES				
Florida	Daytona	1,731	16.0	16.6	286	8	1,381	Moderate
	Fort Lauderdale	9,296	20.9	104.2	1,564	25	6,591	
	Gainesville	964	16.6	4.1	783	5	1,441	
	Miami	14,249	20.7	165.1	4,433	40	10,612	
	Sarasota	1,922	19.2	20.9	365	4	1,101	
	West Palm Beach	5,400	22.0	70.4	865	14	2,537	
Illinois	Chicago	73,245	24.2	223.4	14,604	127	42,322	Moderate
	Davenport	3,660	22.4	9.2	383	10	2,343	
	Decatur	1,172	21.3	3.0	170	3	937	
	Kankakee	872	19.7	3.5	110	4	1,596	
	Peoria	3,681	22.9	10.0	556	7	2,091	
	Rockford	2,596	22.1	6.8	402	6	1,438	
	Springfield	1,779	18.9	6.1	445	4	1,685	
Oklahoma	Enid	573	20.3	1.6	76	3	478	Moderate
	Oklahoma	7,391	20.3	22.6	1,643	26	5,779	
	Tulsa	6,000	20.7	21.1	876	20	3,396	
Oregon	Eugene	2,167	17.4	19.2	362	6	679	Moderate
	Portland	11,914	21.5	38.4	2,578	28	5,997	
Pennsylvania	Harrisburg	3,963	20.3	14.2	914	10	2,861	Moderate
	Philadelphia	42,791	21.2	241.1	10,520	118	31	
	Pittsburgh	20,825	20.9	86.6	4,159	38	16,087	
	Reading	2,752	19.8	11.9	460	6	1,886	
Texas	Amarillo	1,529	20.7	5.0	236	6	1,209	Moderate
	Dallas	27,883	22.7	90.9	4,487	90	15,045	
	Houston	28,828	25.0	71.9	5,083	67	15,138	

THIRD-LEVEL SITES

State	City							
	Midland	903	$28.1	1.7	73	2	235	
	Odessa	1,005	22.0	2.1	86	2	412	
	Tyler	1,081	19.7	4.4	200	5	969	
	Wichita Falls	1,185	21.4	23.6	168	7	1,551	
Colorado	Denver	15,860	23.4	43.4	3,753	34	8,333	Stringent
	Fort Collins	1,976	20.2	2.8	188	4	315	
Indiana	Evansville	2,673	19.7	10.3	422	9	2,603	Stringent
	Fort Wayne	3,467	21.4	9.7	483	8	2,235	
	Gary	6,017	23.4	15.2	642	8	2,973	
	Indianapolis	10,856	21.5	32.4	2,406	23	7,375	
	Kokoma	982	21.3	2.6	84	3	576	
Michigan	Detroit	45,782	24.3	199.7	6,975	83	22,755	Stringent
	Flint	5,018	22.8	19.5	560	8	2,477	
	Kalamazoo	2,415	20.5	9.1	505	6	2,054	
	Lansing	4,153	21.6	11.1	596	10	1,564	
	Saginaw	2,090	21.5	6.4	251	6	1,706	
Ohio	Cincinnati	12,548	20.9	42.3	2,711	26	8,030	Stringent
	Cleveland	19,558	22.1	71.8	4,311	42	12,090	
	Toledo	6,895	20.3	29.4	1,193	14	4,185	
Virginia	Richmond	6,045	21.9	20.5	1,598	17	4,699	Stringent
Wisconsin	Kenosha	1,154	22.0	3.9	98	2	539	Stringent
	Milwaukee	13,934	22.9	50.0	2,736	35	9,041	
	Minneapolis	21,017	23.7	61.6	4,284	41	12,235	
	Racine	1,633	23.1	5.2	147	4	618	
	Sheboygan	904	20.8	2.5	84	3	500	

Medicare Expenditures

The top 100 SMSAs in Medicare expenditures were identified. Although Diagnostic Imaging, Inc., will not rely upon income from Medicare to generate revenue, this criterion is a good measure of the overall level of activity in the health care system. A high rate of Medicare expenditure is usually matched by high rates of expenditure by other payers.

Physician:Population Ratio

The SMSAs with the highest rate of physicians per 100,000 population were identified to supplement the Medicare criterion as an indicator of the size of the local medical community.

The SMSAs identified by these criteria were matched to develop a list of cities with high rates on all of them. Cities that scored in the upper levels of one criterion but low on the the other two were not included in the target market. The resulting list contains 73 SMSAs that are good potential markets.

They are separated into first-, second-, and third-level markets, based on the stringency of health regulations toward outpatient centers. First-level markets are those 22 with open health regulatory systems that do not require CONs for outpatient clinics and generally have favorable regulations. Second-level markets include 30 that have moderate regulatory environments. Third-level markets are the 21 sites located in states that have very stringent regulations. Several of the states in this category have imposed moratoriums on CONs.

Further Analysis of First-Level Markets

Further analysis of the 22 first-level markets was conducted to identify the first effort target markets for Diagnostic Imaging, Inc., centers.

Number of Hospitals

The number of nontertiary hospitals indicates the potential for a Diagnostic Imaging, Inc., center formed through a coalition of local hospitals and physicians. Areas with a large number of hospitals are likely to be open to the development of shared services.

Location of Private Health Care Companies

The presence of these businesses in a community is an indication that the political and regulatory system is not opposed to the establishment of health care programs by outside companies and that demand in the area is sufficient to support high-quality health care.

Other Indicators

Other information collected included total population, trends in population, and the presence of larger tertiary hospitals and other diagnostic centers.

Physician/Hospital Groups Identified

A number of physician and hospital groups have contacted the Belleville center and asked for assistance developing MR centers. They became aware of the Belleville center through Technicare or through other physicians who know the Belleville physician group.

COMPETITION

The MR diagnostic center industry is in its early development stage. Competitors are a number of small, newly-developed formed companies and spin-offs of larger companies in related businesses. At present, the barriers to entry are relatively low. The firms that have entered are evenly balanced in terms of financial backing and management capability, with no firm having a dominant position. During the early growth phase of the industry's development, competition will focus on establishing centers and capturing positions in the most desirable markets.

After some time, as industry growth levels off and local markets have sufficient MRI capacity, competition is likely to focus on pricing.

Direct Competition

NMR Centers, Inc. NMR Centers is a private, closely held company founded in 1982 solely to provide hospitals and private groups with capital, management, and marketing services for establishing outpatient MR facilities. Elscint, an MR equipment manufacturer, is one of the larger shareholders in NMR Centers, Inc. The company has raised $6 million through private placements and has $6 million in the offering stage. It plans to raise $15 million by the fall of 1984 and $50–$60 million by November 1985.

The company hopes to be a leader in the industry and intends to establish 30 centers within the next 12 to 18 months. NMR acts as general partner and hospitals, physicians, or other profit-making corporations are sought as investors. The company has contracts with Technicare, Diasonics, Siemens, GE, and Fonar, allowing NMR to purchase equipment at lower costs and provide their centers with excellent delivery, service, upgradeability, and training packages.

NMR places a full-time manager on site at each center, who handles all administrative tasks. The technologists in the center are employed and trained by NMR Centers, Inc., and seminars are conducted for affiliated physicians. The company also handles public relations and local marketing.

As of September 1984, NMR Centers has one center in operation, in Urbana, Illinois (located about 100 miles from ours). Three other centers are "in the closing stage."

NMR bases patient fees on seven separate procedures and charges from $650 to $1,185 for the technical fee. The physician interpretation fee is 25% of the technical fee. The company projects an 85% collection rate. The company's rate of growth was achieved without major resources in marketing or advertising.

International Imaging, Inc. International Imaging, Inc., is a subsidiary of Adventist Health Systems, the largest nonprofit hospital chain in the United States. Adventist Health Systems owns 75 hospitals nationwide and also operates a number of billing, consulting, and other professional services for physicians and hospitals.

International Imaging considers itself a "diagnostic imaging partner," entering into limited partnerships with physicians or hospitals for the establishment of MR centers.

The company currently operates two outpatient CT clinics and does not have any operational MR centers. They are constructing a center in California in association with Harbor UCLA.

International Imaging's president was formerly the manager of strategic planning for General Electric. He has 15 years' experience in medical technology and diagnostic services.

The financing of the center depends on the partnership model selected. If the physicians or hospital choose to be general partners with International Imaging, Inc., they receive an equal share of all tax benefits and profits. If the physicians choose to be limited partners, they receive a share of profits proportional to their investment.

Medical Resources, Inc. Medical Resources, Inc., of Englewood, New Jersey, was founded and is chartered by Ernest DeSalvo, M.D., who practiced medicine until founding his company in 1981. The company is opening free-standing imaging centers for magnetic resonance and other imaging modalities. The centers are owned by limited partnerships and developed in joint ventures with hospitals.

Medical Resources, Inc., expects to operate 100 diagnostic centers by 1989. The firm currently operates five free-standing centers, none with MRI. It will begin selling partnerships in four more centers this year and have one-year options to organize fifteen more centers. The new centers will be multiple-modality centers with ultrasound, CT, and nuclear medicine scanners, as well as magnetic resonance.

Medical Resources, Inc., was established five years ago. After establishing two centers, the company won the backing of Concord, a venture capital subsidiary of Dillon Read and Co., which put up $1 million in return for 20% of the stock in the company. Medical Resources, Inc., is currently offering about 25% more of its stock to venture capitalists in return for $3–$3.5 million in financing. The company expects to realize $2.5 million in revenues from its management contracts in 1984, and $15 million in 1985. The company projects pretax profits at 40% of revenues.

Hospital Corporation of America (HCA). To avoid conflict with its own physicians, HCA has not built outpatient imaging centers. However, the company is planning slowly to develop MR facilities in its hospitals.

American Medical International (AMI). In July of 1983, AMI established a Diagnostic Centers Division of free-standing imaging centers. The centers are intended to offer multiple-modality imaging services, including MR, CT, and other diagnostic techniques. Groundbreaking for the first occurred in April 1984. The company plans to have 50 centers in operation by the end of 1985.

Humana, Inc. Humana currently has a Certificate of Need for installation of an MR unit at one hospital, but construction has not yet begun. It does not expect to install more than four units by the middle of 1985.

Calumet Coach. Calumet Coach has been in business since 1946, manufacturing mobile units of special design. Its primary customer, until 1967, was the military, when it began to develop a line of coaches for medical purposes.

Currently, the company has over 140 mobile CT units in the field and employs 65 people. It has been working on the design for a mobile MR unit for the past year.

DESCRIPTION OF THE BELLEVILLE CENTER

Development of the Center

Approximately four months elapsed from initial planning to operation. The group selected Technicare (a Johnson & Johnson subsidiary) as equipment supplier and paid a deposit of $100,000 in October 1983 for delivery of a system within four months. The Project Development Construction Company

(PDC) was hired to manage the design and construction of the facility. PDC is one of the few companies with experience in constructing a turnkey building for magnetic resonance equipment.

In December, the MR equipment arrived and was installed while the building was still under construction. (For the development of future sites, equipment installation should follow the completion of the building because dust from construction can damage the equipment.)

The group obtained industrial revenue bond financing and began to arrange for letters of agreement with local hospitals for referral of outpatients. The principals identified physicians who would refer patients and become limited partners and formed a corporation, Magnetic Imaging of Belleville, in January 1983.

The center received an exemption from CON from the state agency. By the middle of January, the computer software was delivered, and Technicare specialists were training technicians. Patients were imaged at the facility in the second week of January 1984.

Utilization Rates

During the first month, the center processed an average of four procedures per day. By the end of February, an average of six patients a day were being screened. Management decided to keep the procedure rate at a modest level so that sufficient time was available to perfect clinical and operating procedures. No effort was made to publicize the center, and only the physicians who were limited partners and their colleagues knew of its availability. The utilization rate increased during June and July to a level of eight patients per day after eight months through various marketing and development efforts.

Fully operational centers will handle 10 to 12 procedures per day. Of these, approximately 30% will be images of the head; the rest will be spine and full-body images. Once the modality becomes more widely used, the demand for whole-body imaging is likely to grow.

Downtime and Repair

There have been fifteen down days since the opening of the Belleville center. Three down days were caused by software problems. Replacement software arrived each time late in the afternoon of the same day. A week was lost when a worker accidentally dropped a wrench into the machine. The wrench was pulled into the head coil and caused extensive damage. An additional two days of downtime resulted while staff members worked to refine operating procedures. During July, the center was closed for seven days for installation of Technicare's new software program, which speeded up procedure time.

Billing and Collections

To date, the Belleville center has collected only from patients and private insurance companies. Medicare or Medicaid have not established rates for MR, but are expected to do so in the next year.

Most private insurance companies pay MR claims within 30–60 days. The current collection rate is 65%.

A computerized billing system will be installed in late September.

Relationship with Technicare

The center has had a good experience with Technicare as its equipment supplier. Technicare perceives the center as one of its showcase installations and has provided several pieces of equipment at no charge, including upgrading of the camera used in acquiring images, additional memory capacity in the computer, new software, and a camera for taking Polaroid pictures of images.

Diagnostic Imaging, Inc., expects to receive favorable treatment from Technicare, including price reductions on equipment and service contracts. Both managerial and technical personnel at Belleville recommend Technicare as supplier for all of the Diagnostic Imaging, Inc., centers.

DESCRIPTION OF A PROTOTYPE CENTER

Ownership

Each center will be jointly owned by Diagnostic Imaging, Inc., as general partner and individual physicians, hospitals, or other investors as limited partners. As general partner, Diagnostic Imaging, Inc., will own 60% of the equity of each center; limited partners will own 40%. The operation of the management company will be supported from the 60% share of the revenue allocated to Diagnostic Imaging, Inc.

Limited partners' investment will be used to subsidize the start-up capital and cash needs of each center. It is anticipated that approximately $500,000 will be supplied by the limited partner investors (25 investors at $20,000 each). The majority of the capital required for facility construction and the purchase of equipment will be provided by mortgages on the building and equipment.

Limited partnership offerings will be made approximately two months prior to the operation of the center; however, Diagnostic Imaging, Inc., will ensure the likely participation of local investors prior to deciding to establish the site. Limited partners and the management company will share tax loss benefits and income from the center proportionately to their investment.

Management of the Center

The center will be managed by Diagnostic Imaging, Inc., under a management contract with the local partnership. The local physician investors will form the nucleus of a physicians' advisory board. Diagnostic Imaging, Inc., will have full responsibility for planning and supervising the construction of the facility, for center operations, and for its financial performance.

Diagnostic Imaging, Inc., will establish billing procedures, new personnel orientation, and licensure and regulatory approval. General supervision will be provided by a diagnostic imaging site manager, who will have up to three centers under his management purview. The Diagnostic Imaging, Inc., controller will receive weekly financial and operation statistics reports.

The center will staffed by one full-time technician, a secretary/receptionist, and a manager-technician. The manager-technician will spend approximately 15 hours per week on administrative duties and the remainder conducting patient procedures. As utilization of the center increases, additional staff will be hired.

Relationships with the Local Medical Community

The center will establish links to the local medical community through the local physician management group, other investors, and their colleagues. However, establishment of formal relationships with other medical practitioners will be an important part of the implementation of a center.

Relationships with local hospitals are particularly important. The center will establish formal written agreements with hospitals in its area. They will normally receive a discount on procedures for all patients they refer to the center and often will bill and collect fees from patients they refer. In hospital-billed cases, the hospital will be expected to guarantee payment to the center within 30 days of billing.

Referral and Scheduling of Patients

Patients will be referred to the center by their physicians whose offices will make appointments for the patients, specify the area of the body to be scanned, and give a preliminary diagnosis. The center will require that a patient's history and other test results be forwarded prior to the imaging procedure.

The aim is to schedule a minimum of ten procedures per day during the 7:00 A.M. to 6:00 P.M. working hours. Appointments will be overlapped to account for lateness and no-shows.

Optimal Utilization Rates

Normally, utilization rates at a center will be low during the first month of operation, averaging about three to six procedures per day. As clinical personnel become more familiar with MR technology and marketing efforts are undertaken, the number of procedures will increase. By the end of the first year, the center should be handling 12 procedures per ten-hour day.

Maintenance and Supply Costs

Technicare will provide maintenance on the equipment. During the first year of operation, the equipment is fully warranted, and there are no maintenance charges. After the first year, the service contract will cost approximately $112,000. It will include a full-time, on-site Technicare specialist who will have sole access to the machine approximately half of one day each week, scheduled during regular operating hours.

Maintenance on the building will be handled by a local building and grounds service company, at an annual cost of $4,000-$5,000. Consumable supplies will cost approximately $17 per patient, including drugs, emergency equipment, and clerical supplies.

Start-Up Capital Requirements

The start-up capital requirements assumed in the models are based on the experience in Belleville. Estimated equipment cost of $1,500,000 is included based on the assumption that the cost per machine will be lower for Diagnostic Imaging, Inc., as a purchaser of a number of units. The building and land costs are not expected to vary significantly among sites.

Start-up capital will be required three to five months before the operation of a clinic for items such as land purchases, down payment on equipment, etc. For illustration purposes, we have shown these costs as a net "pre-opening" line on the cash flow statements (Tables 5.2 and 5.3).

The projections assume a mortgage on the building, land, and equipment at approximately 85% of the original purchase price, at 13% interest expense for seven years. Additional start-up capital will be provided by investors' contributions and venture capital.

Operating Cash Flow Assumptions

The following assumptions are based on the experience of the Belleville center and equipment suppliers' projections:

- Number of procedures: 10 to 15 per day at full capacity.
- Phase in of 3 to 6 per day for the first three months, 6 to 12 per day for the next nine months, and further increases based on improved protocols and software.
- Number of working days: Average of 21 per month.
- Price: Current charges plus 10% inflation per year.
- Collection rate: Based on experience in Belleville and in outpatient CT centers.
- Service costs: Current charges by suppliers.
- Maintenance and insurance costs: Belleville experience.
- Manager-technician: Annual salary of $30,000.
- Other staff: Technician at annual salary of $25,000, secretary at annual salary at $12,000.
- Staffing requirements: One manager-technician; one technician per 10 procedures and one secretary per 12 procedures per day.
- Supplies: Based on Belleville experience: $17 per procedure with 10% annual inflation.
- Depreciation: Tax standards of 5 years on equipment and 15 years for building.
- Investor shares: 40% for limited partners and 60% for general partners.
- Tax benefits and costs are assumed at the 50% bracket.
- Investment tax credit: $150,000 for purchase of equipment.

During the start-up phase of the company, corporate staff will consist of a president and CEO, a director of development, and a controller. Consultants will be used as necessary.

Additional staff will be added as the pace of center development dictates. Key additional hires will include:

- Every three sites: One full-time site manager ($40,000) to provide consistent oversight for local center staff.
- At six centers: A director of operations ($60,000) supervising site managers and all center staffs.
- At ten centers: A director of marketing responsible for new market development, the coordination of promotional campaigns, and oversight of local public relations efforts.

The following assumptions are used for management company costs:

- Personnel: Chairman ($50,000), president ($100,000), vice president-development ($40,000), senior secretary/office manager/bookkeeper ($27,000).
- Rent: Approximately 1,000 sq. ft. at a cost of $25/sq. ft.
- Telephone: Approximately $1,000 per month with an initial equipment purchase of $600.
- Equipment: Copying machine, computer, dictaphone, miscellaneous supplies for start-up.
- Travel: Travel will vary depending on the number of start-up clinics during the year and the frequency of management visits to the sites. The current assumptions are for four to six trips per start-up and regular travel to establish centers.

The projected financials (Table 5.4) assume an absolutely regular schedule of center start-ups. Making due allowances for contingencies and start-up scheduling congestion, $1.5 million in initial capital is required to launch the venture.

Table 5.2 Diagnostic Imaging, Inc.: Model Diagnostic Center Pro Forma Cash Flow Statement—Year Number One Receipts Minus Disbursements

	Preopening	1	2	3	4	5
ASSUMPTIONS						
Number of Working Days per Month		21	21	21	21	21
Procedures per Day		4	4	4	6	6
Price per Procedure		$ 500	$ 500	$ 500	$ 500	$ 500
Collection Rate		0.5	0.5	0.5	0.5	0.5
MONTHLY CASH RECEIPTS						
Amount Billed		$ 42,000	$ 42,000	$ 42,000	$ 63,000	$ 63,000
Amount Collected		6,930	20,790	20,790	24,255	31,185
Billing Service Revenue		630	630	630	945	945
Limited Partner Proceeds		500,000				
TOTAL RECEIPTS	$ 0	$ 507,560	$ 21,420	$ 21,420	$ 25,200	$ 32,130
CASH DISBURSEMENTS						
Manager-Technician		$ 2,500	$ 2,500	$ 2,500	$ 2,500	$ 2,500
Technician		2,083	2,083	2,083	2,083	2,083
Clerical		1,000	1,000	1,000	1,000	1,000
Fringe Benefits		1,675	1,675	1,675	1,675	1,675
Utilities		800	800	800	800	800
Supplies		1,260	1,260	1,260	1,890	1,890
Service Agreement		0	0	0	0	0
Maintenance		250	250	250	250	250
Insurance		600	600	600	600	600
Legal and Audit		135	135	135	135	135
Cryogen		3,400	3,400	3,400	3,400	3,400
Loan—Principal $1,555,714		11,448	11,572	11,812	11,991	12,168
—Interest 13%		16,854	16,730	16,490	16,311	16,134
Real Estate Taxes		0	0	0	0	0
Miscellaneous		1,000	1,000	1,000	1,000	1,000
Management Company G & A		2,206	2,206	2,206	2,300	2,300
Nonmortgaged Expenditures	$ 349,289					
TOTAL CASH DISBURSED	$ 349,289	$ 45,211	$ 45,211	$ 45,211	$ 45,935	$ 45,935

continues

Table 5.2 continued

	6	7	8	9	10	11	12	Total 1st Year
	21	21	21	21	21	21	21	
	6	6	6	8	8	8	8	
$	500	500	500	500	500	500	500	
	0.5	0.75	0.75	0.75	0.75	0.75	0.75	
$	63,000	63,000	63,000	84,000	84,000	84,000	84,000	$ 777,000
	31,185	36,382	46,777	51,975	62,370	62,370	62,370	457,380
	945	1,418	1,418	1,890	1,890	1,890	1,830	15,120
								500,000
$	32,130	37,800	48,195	53,865	64,260	64,260	64,200	$ 972,500
$	2,500	2,500	2,500	2,500	2,500	2,500	2,500	$ 30,000
	2,083	2,083	2,083	2,083	2,083	2,083	2,083	25,000
	1,000	1,000	1,000	1,000	1,000	1,000	1,000	12,000
	1,675	1,675	1,675	1,675	1,675	1,675	1,675	20,100
	800	800	800	800	800	800	800	9,600
	1,890	1,890	1,890	2,520	2,520	2,520	2,520	23,310
	0	0	0	0	0	0	0	0
	250	250	250	250	250	250	250	3,000
	600	600	600	600	600	600	600	7,200
	135	135	135	135	135	135	135	1,620
	3,400	3,400	3,400	3,400	3,400	3,400	3,400	40,800
	12,342	12,515	12,686	12,855	13,023	13,188	13,352	148,952
	15,960	15,787	15,616	15,447	15,279	15,114	14,950	190,672
	0	0	0	0	0	0	0	0
	1,000	1,000	1,000	1,000	1,000	1,000	1,000	12,000
	2,300	2,300	2,300	2,395	2,395	2,395	2,395	27,698
$	45,935	45,935	45,935	46,660	46,660	46,660	46,660	$ 551,948

continues

Table 5.2 continued

	Preopening	1	2	3	4	5
NET OPERATING RECEIPTS (DISBURSEMENTS)		(37,651)	$ (23,791)	$ (23,791)	$ (20,735)	$ (13,805)
CUMULATIVE CASH FLOW	$ (349,289)	113,060	$ 89,269	$ 65,478	$ 44,743	$ 30,938
RECEIPTS MINUS DISBURSEMENTS (ADJUSTED)	$ 0	(37,651)	$ (23,791)	$ (23,791)	$ (20,735)	$ (13,805)
Add: Principal Payments		11,448	11,572	11,812	11,991	12, 168
Profit before Depreciation		(26,202)	$ (12,218)	$ (11,979)	$ (8,744)	$ (1,637)
Less: Depreciation		19,815	19,815	19,815	19,815	19,815
TAXABLE INCOME (OR LOSS)		(46,017)	$ (32,033)	$ (31,793)	$ (28,559)	$ (21,452)

Tax @ 50%
Tax Savings @ 50%
Investment Tax Credit

AFTER TAX BENEFITS

PER UNIT AFTER TAX BENEFITS

LIMITED PARTNER SHARE @ 40%

MANAGEMENT COMPANY SHARE @ 60%

continues

Table 5.2 continued

	6	7	8	9	10	11	12	Total 1st Year
	$ (13,805)	$ (8,135)	$ 2,260	$ 7,205	$ 17,600	$ 17,600	$ 17,600	$ (79,448)
	$ 17,136	$ 9,001	$ 11,261	$ 18,467	$ 36,067	$ 53,668	$ 71,269	$ 71,269
	$ (13,805)	$ (8,135)	$ 2,260	$ 7,205	$ 17,600	$ 17, 600	$ 17,600	$ (79,448)
	12,342	12,515	12,686	12,855	13,022	13,188	13,352	148,952
	$ 1,463	$ 4,380	$ 14,946	$ 20,060	$ 30,623	$ 30,788	$ 30,952	$ 69,507
	19,815	19,815	19,815	19,815	19,815	19,815	19,815	237,780
	$ (21,278)	$ (15,435)	$ (4,869)	$ 245	$ 10,808	$ 10,973	$ 11,137	$ (168,273)
								$ 0
								84,136
								150,000
								$ 234,136
								4,683
								$ 93,654
								$ 140,482

Table 5.3 Diagnostic Imaging, Inc.: Model Diagnostic Center Pro Forma Cash Flow Statement—Years Number Two, Three, Four

	Total 2nd Year	Total 3rd Year	Total 4th Year
ASSUMPTIONS			
Number of Working Days per Month	21	21	21
Procedures per Day	10	12	12
Price per Procedure	575	650	650
Collection Rate	0.75	0.75	0.75
Amount Billed	$ 1,449,000	$ 1,965,600	$ 1,965,600
Amount Collected	1,057,691	1,438,149	1,459,458
Billing Service Revenue	28,350	34,020	34,020
TOTAL RECEIPTS	$ 1,086,041	$ 1,472,169	$ 1,493,478
CASH DISBURSEMENTS			
Manager-Technician	$ 30,000	$ 33,000	$ 33,275
Technician	25,000	29,583	29,563
Clerical	12,000	13,300	13,200
Fringe Benefits	20,100	22,735	22,818
Utilities	9,600	9,600	9,600
Supplies	0	0	0
Service Agreement	112,500	112,500	112,500
Maintenance	3,000	3,000	3,000
Insurance	7,200	7,200	7,200
Legal and Audit	1,620	1,620	1,620
Cryogen	40,800	40,800	40,800
Loan–Principal	172,363	192,556	229,018
–Interest	167,255	146,762	112,600
Real Estate Taxes	5,004	5,024	5,024
Miscellaneous	12,000	12,000	12,000
Management Company G & A	41,824	43,717	41,590
TOTAL CASH DISBURSED	$ 660,266	$ 673,397	$ 673,808
NET OPERATING RECEIPTS (DISBURSEMENTS)	$ 425,776	$ 798,772	$ 819,670
Add: Principal Payments	$ 172,363	$ 192,856	$ 229,018
Profit before Depreciation	598,139	991,628	1,048,688
Less: Depreciation	342,778	327,778	327,776
TAXABLE INCOME (OR LOSS)	$ 255,361	$ 663,852	$ 720,912
Tax (Benefit) @ 50%	$ 127,680	$ 331,925	$ 360,455
Tax Savings @ 50%	0	0	0
Investment Tax Credit	0	0	0
AFTER TAX INCOME	$ 127,680	$ 331,925	$ 360,455
PER UNIT AFTER TAX INCOME	2,554	6,639	7,209
LIMITED PARTNER SHARE @ 40%	$ 51,072	$ 132,770	$ 144,182
MANAGEMENT COMPANY SHARE @ 60%	$ 76,606	$ 199,155	$ 216,273

Table 5.4 Diagnostic Imaging, Inc.: Managing Company *Pro Forma* Cash Flow for 1984–88

	1984	1985	1986	1987	1988
RECEIPTS					
Clinic Operating Receipts	$ 0	$ (351,051)	$ 89,582	$ 3,356,236	$ 6,738,686
Management Contract Fees	0	40,644	200,735	372,602	429,328
Limited Partnership Proceeds	0	1,500,000	3,000,000	500,000	0
TOTAL RECEIPTS	$ 0	$ 1,189,593	$ 3,290,317	$ 4,228,838	$ 7,168,014
SALARY EXPENSE					
Salaries	$ 36,667	$ 233,333	$ 372,500	$ 435,000	$ 435,000
Fringe Benefits	7,333	46,667	74,500	87,000	87,000
Total Salaries and Benefits	$ 44,000	$ 280,000	$ 447,000	$ 522,000	$ 522,000
OTHER CASH EXPENSES					
Equipment	$ 25,000	$ 0	$ 0	$ 0	$ 0
Supplies	2,200	13,200	14,520	15,972	17,569
Telephone	2,400	14,400	15,840	17,424	19,166
Travel	12,000	72,000	79,200	115,670	115,870
Promotional Materials	10,000	15,000	10,000	15,000	15,000
Rent	5,000	30,000	33,000	36,300	39,930
Legan and Accounting	5,000	24,000	24,000	24,000	24,000
Consultants	0	36,000	36,000	36,000	36,000
Miscellaneous	3,000	12,000	13,200	14,520	15,972
OTHER CASH EXPENSES	$ 64,600	$ 216,600	$ 225,760	$ 274,886	$ 283,507
PRE-OPENING NONMORT-GAGED EXPENDITURES	$ 0	$ 1,397,156	$ 2,095,734	$ 0	$ 0
CENTER INITIAL WORKING REQUIREMENTS	$ 0	$ 0	$ 0	$ 0	$ 0
CENTER, OTHER CASH DISBURSEMENTS	$ 108,600	$ 0	$ 244,551	$ 1,309,325	$ 2,695,474
CASH EXPENSES FOR COMPANY	$(108,600)	$(1,893,756)	$(3,013,045)	$(2,106,211)	$(3,500,981)
NET CASH FLOW (EACH YR)		$ (704,163)	$ 277,273	$ 2,122,627	$ 3,667,033
CUMULATIVE CASH FLOW (EACH YR)		$ (812,763)	$ (535,490)	$ 1,587,137	$ 5,254,170

POINTS TO PONDER

1. What kind of opportunity does this plan represent?
2. Do you think it is viable? If not, what changes would you recommend?

NOTES

1. *RNM Images*, April 1984.
2. These conditions represent tumors that are well visualized by MR.
3. *Diagnostic Imaging*, November 1983.
4. *RNM Images*, February 1984.

Health Stop: Strategy

Joseph Maloney, M.D., chief medical officer for Health Stop, said,

> In no other industry is the relationship between the consumer and the provider as unbalanced as in health care. You wait a week for an appointment, and, then, you wait for another hour in the doctor's office. If the office is closed, you go to the emergency room and wait until the life-and-death emergency cases are taken care of. Any dry cleaner that operated this way would be out of business.

Health Stop Medical Management, Inc. (HS), incorporated in April 1983, had become, by 1984, the largest operator of free-standing ambulatory care offices in New England and the second largest independent operator of such facilities in the country. The company had 19 walk-in medical offices, approximately half operated in affiliation with community hospitals. HS's objective was to become the most profitable national competitor in its business through a strategy of dominance of several regional markets.

OVERVIEW OF AMBULATORY CARE INDUSTRY

Ambulatory care refers to health care services that do not require hospitalization. Tra-

ditionally, such care was provided in physicians' offices or hospital emergency rooms and outpatient departments. Recently, several new types of organizations have entered the ambulatory care market: surgery centers; free-standing ambulatory care centers (FACs); and multiple-specialty group practices. FACs treated minor emergencies or other medical needs and patients who ordinarily used private physicians. They usually provided walk-in service with no appointment; extended hours, of between 12 and 24 per day, six to seven days a week; staffing by full-time physicians and other medically qualified personnel; and laboratory and x-ray facilities on the premises.

Frequently located in shopping malls, they were called "docs-in-the-box." Approximately 10% were owned and operated by hospitals and about 70% by private physicians or physician groups, with one to three centers per organization concentrated in a single metropolitan area. The remaining centers were owned by nonphysician investors or were part of larger multiple unit chains. The largest chain, MedFirst, was operated by Humana, Inc., with 81 centers in 12 states.

Market

The 82 million visits made in 1982 to the emergency rooms of community hospitals, at least 80% of them for a non-life-threatening problem, had grown for a decade at an annual rate of 3%. There were approximately 800 million patient visits to doctors' offices each year. An estimated 25% of the population did not have a regular family physician and some

Note: This case was prepared by Professor Regina E. Herzlinger, Joyce Lallman, and Assistant Professor Nancy Kane.

FACs reported that these patients represented a significant portion of their volume.

Average FAC 1982 charges for routine care were between $30 and $75 per patient visit, while the average charge for visiting a hospital emergency room was between $75 and $175. Many insurance policies were being changed to limit payment for hospital-based care and encourage ambulatory care settings.

A nationwide survey of users indicated convenience (11% of respondents); faster service (14%); proximity to home (10%); and no waiting (8%) or appointment (15%) as major factors in their use of FACs. Factors less frequently cited included that their physician was unavailable (7%) and lower expense (6%). The users were better educated than the average (35% were college educated); older (28% in the 34–44 age group); and wealthier (20% had household incomes over $50,000). Most preferred FACs to a visit to an emergency room.[1]

Regulation

FACs did not need facility licenses and the staffing or equipment expense associated with licensing requirements, because they qualified under state laws as physicians' offices rather than hospitals or clinics. If their physicians were licensed to practice medicine, they could avoid the "Certificate of Need" (CON) process requiring hospitals and other institutional providers (nursing homes, skilled nursing facilities, etc.) to show that their area needed a medical facility. FAC ancillary services, laboratory and x-ray, could also be provided more cheaply because they were not subject to licensing requirements; for instance, in some FACs, nurses ran the x-ray machines instead of certified technicians. There were, however, some regulatory efforts underway. The Massachusetts Hospital Association filed a bill that, if passed, would require FACs using the term "emergency" to obtain a CON and be licensed as a clinic. A Florida law prohibited x-ray technicians who held only a basic safety certificate from practicing radiologic technology in walk-in emergency centers.

However, other government actions increased the operating flexibility of FACs. A Supreme Court ruling allowing professionals to advertise prompted the growth of legal, dental, and medical retail outlets, FACs being among them.

Supply of Physicians

Another factor prompting FAC growth was a growing supply of doctors. Young physicians, finding it difficult to operate successful private practices in an increasingly competitive market, looked outside private practice. In Massachusetts, the physician "oversupply" was substantial: 285 M.D.s per 100,000 population versus 206 M.D.s per 100,000 population nationally. Physician supply in Massachusetts grew by 52.5% from 1970 to 1980, while the population grew by only 0.9%.

The average number of visits per week varied by practice type and employment status of the physician and was declining steadily. In 1975, the average physician had 139 visits a week; by 1984, this declined to 119. The group practice physician saw more patients a week than the solo physician—123 versus 116 in 1984. The self-employed physician saw 125 visits a week versus 108 for the employed. New England physicians saw only 108 visits a week versus a high of 150 visits weekly in the East South Central region.

HEALTH STOP

Health Stop (HS) offices were designed for people who did not have a regular physician or whose regular physician was unavailable, and new residents who had not yet established a relationship with a doctor. The centers were not equipped for patients with chronic problems, life-threatening emergencies, specialist care needs, or major surgery. In case of extreme emergency, Health Stop personnel stabilized patients and transferred them to a nearby hospital. Each center was equipped with emergency equipment as a precautionary measure. It was located in easy-to-reach locations, such as shopping centers, with convenient parking.

The Boston area offices extended as far west as Worcester, south to Hyannis, and north to New Hampshire. They were open from 8 A.M. to 8 P.M., 365 days a year. No appointments were necessary. Patients were to be greeted within 60 seconds after they walked through the door and seen by a doctor within 15 minutes. Staffing at each center consisted of two permanent full-time physicians and about ten full- or part-time nurses, medical assistants, technicians, and other personnel. (One M.D. was in the office at one time.)

The price of medical treatment was comparable to an average doctor's office visit, $25 to $45, and substantially lower than hospital emergency room fees of $45 to $160. Laboratory and x-ray services were provided on-site for additional charges. The centers accepted as full payment the amount Blue Shield or Medicare reimbursed for the services rather than billing the patient for any balance.

Health Stop's occupational medicine program accepted Worker's Compensation (payment for injuries to employees that were incurred at the work site) coverage and saw members' employees on a priority basis. The employer was called within one hour of the visit regarding the outcome and was mailed all necessary paperwork within 48 hours. Physical examination packages for executive, pre-employment, insurance, and return to work purposes were offered at discounted prices. As of 1984, more than 250 employers had joined this program, along with a major union group of 9,000 people.

Company Background

HS was founded by Kenneth Hachikian and Joseph Maloney, M.D. Mr. Hachikian, president and chief executive officer, graduated from Harvard College and its business school. He spent nine years at the Boston Consulting Group, Inc., and left his position there to manage a small company. He noted:

After looking at about one hundred businesses, I found one that epitomized the type I wanted to buy—a small, family-run company in Vermont that produced cutting tools for machines; however, this opportunity didn't materialize. Another business was Health Stop, an idea I got after hearing about a physician in Chicago who started four walk-in medical centers.

The criteria I used were that it could make a sustainable above-average return on equity and that it produced a product or service I could feel good about. Health Stop met these tests better than the other businesses I considered.

It was the only business I seriously considered that fell into the category of health care.

Mr. Hachikian spent the spring and summer of 1982 writing the business plan for Health Stop and then turned to the task of raising money:

On a one-to-ten scale of financing knowledge, I thought I was a six or a seven. I was really a two. I went through many dark moments during the 12 months I was trying to raise money. I believe, though, that the financing I finally got was better than the options that fell through.

Mr. Hachikian chose Boston as the location for the first Health Stop offices because of its competitive situation. He explained:

When Health Stop was started, there were 20 walk-in centers in existence in the market. The largest player had three centers and only three were in good locations. I saw that the Boston market was wide open and fragmented, with potential for growth.

Another important factor was the presence in Boston of Dr. Maloney, a physician-partner who was qualified and willing to recruit and manage physicians, "sell" hospitals, and "let the businessman run the show, except for the practice of medicine."

Joseph Maloney, M.D., served as chief medical officer of HS and the president of the professional corporation to which Health Stop provided management services, Ambulatory Health Associates (AHA). After Harvard Medical School, Dr. Maloney completed an internship in general medicine. He decided not to start a practice as an independent physician because, as he said, "I wanted to get more leverage on the system." He spent five years as a consultant to many regulatory authorities and as an emergency physician. In 1978, he started Atlantic Medical Associates, Inc., which provided emergency physicians on a contract basis to participating hospitals and medical offices. In 1982, Dr. Maloney joined Mr. Hachikian in the effort to secure financing for Health Stop.

Strategy

HS's strategy was to be the most significant factor in each of its markets—pre-empting the most desirable locations and establishing a strong brand image via significant scale in marketing.

Its management intended to develop a set of proprietary skills that, together with financial leverage, would enable it to become a leading national manager of free-standing ambulatory care offices. These skills included architectural planning, interior layout, administrative procedures, equipment and supply purchasing, staff training, quality control, site selection, and consumer and industrial marketing. Management believed that it could establish strong competitive barriers to entry through strong brand loyalty among both consumers and industry and extensive marketing and financial agreements with other health care providers—in particular, hospitals and HMOs.

Organizational Structure

Because of a Massachusetts law prohibiting business corporations from practicing medicine, two separate corporations were established to provide Health Stop services. HS conducted all business functions, such as operations, marketing, real estate, finance, billing, and nonphysician personnel services, and AHA provided physician services.

AHA assigned all of the revenues generated by the emergency contracts and Health Stop centers to HS. From this, HS met its contractual obligations to AHA, including the payment of physician salaries. All other center expenses (nurses, receptionists, leasing, supplies, etc.) were direct expenses of HS.

Strategy and policy decisions were made by a five-member committee of the vice presidents of marketing, operations, and finance; Dr. Maloney; and Mr. Hachikian, who retained final decision-making authority. Dr. Maloney had full control of the medical practice at Health Stop offices, including the authority to hire and terminate physicians and to design their compensation package.

Physican Recruitment and Medical Practice

AHA offered physicians a "competitive" compensation for start-up practices, a defined work schedule, and a sense of having their own practice. Physicians were paid a gross salary of $30–$32 per hour for an average of 40 hours per week. Other benefits were malpractice coverage and inclusion in a profit-sharing plan, which distributed 12% of HS profits. The benefits were vested to ensure employee retention. Including profit sharing, the full-time AHA physician could earn over $100,000 per year.

Dr. Maloney described Health Stop's appeal to physicians as follows:

> The regular schedule of 40 hours per week is attractive to physicians with child care responsibilities or to some of the younger physicians who really value their leisure time.
>
> The options for physicians just starting out are to accept a low-paying job with an institution, sign on with a partnership, or start their own practice. Doctors signing

on with partnerships may have to work 80 hours per week for an eventual annual income of $90,000 per year. This total salary doesn't look so good on an hourly basis. Starting your own practice is difficult in the Boston area, because of the competition and reluctance of bankers today to lend capital to start-up physicians.

We primarily attract younger physicians, but also some middle-aged or older physicians who are fed up with running their own practices. Their expenses keep rising, while their revenues drop with the decline in patient volume as HMOs and FACs cut into their practices. We do not seek physicians who are willing to work for less money.

Although we don't offer physicians the opportunity to provide full "continuity of care," because our physicians do not see patients in the hospital, they do follow the same patient for all of his/her ambulatory primary care needs. Most patients would see such services, in combination with the Health Stop physician's greater availability and accessibility, as greater continuity of care relative to most traditional practitioners.

Health Stop physicians were board-certified or board-eligible internists, family practitioners, or emergency room physicians. Although HS did not dictate to physicians how they should practice medicine, doctors were encouraged to make follow-up calls to patients after visits to answer any questions the patients may have forgotten to ask and to check on their well-being.

Quality assurance involved a standard review of patient records to ensure documentation of treatment. Each office had a quality assurance committee, which included the center's supervisor and medical director as well as Dr. Maloney and HS's manager of operations. Utilization review was conducted to detect under- and overutilization of resources by analyzing patient statistics such as the percentage receiving x-rays, laboratory services, or referrals to specialists, as normalized by case-mix and patient characteristics. These data showed if physicians were keeping patients in the system for the appropriate amount of time and if ancillary services were utilized appropriately. Dr. Maloney, as vice president of the Eastern Massachusetts PSRO, was thoroughly familiar with these review procedures. He felt the Health Stop's ancillary services per visit were underutilized in some centers because of an insufficient number of staff members.

To increase staff productivity, there were no specialized job assignments for the nonphysician staff. All staff members were trained to administer laboratory and x-ray tests, to take patient information, and to log patients in and out. All of the staff other than physicians were hired by HS, subject to the approval of the office's medical director.

Site Selection

Site selection was considered one of the most important variables in the success of a Health Stop center. Relevant selection variables included population density (at least 50,000 people within three miles); family size (greater than 2.5 per household to ensure the presence of children); per capita income (to avoid both low-income areas, with patients who could not afford to pay, and very high-income areas, where private practices proliferated); and proximity to small- and medium-size industry (to serve industrial accidents, pre-employment physicals, etc.); as well as accessibility and visibility of the site and the proximity of competition (no other center within a three-mile radius). (See Table 6.1 for examples of the market analysis.)

Because Health Stop preferred sites that offered the "least resistance to the customer," it tried to locate next door to products delivered on a convenience basis—near grocery stores, department stores, or fast-food restaurants. According to Dr. Maloney:

> When patients see a doctor on their own turf, they are likely to feel better about the care they're receiving. In addition, when patients perceive being on a more

Table 6.1 Health Stop: Market Analysis

Opportunity Area	Population	% Under Age 18	% Over Age 65	% Population Growth 1970–1980	Average Household Size	Average Household Income	Number of Physicians FP/GP	IM	Distance from Hospital
1. Weston/Wayland/ Sudbury	16,058	46.4	3.6		4.0	$29,084			Four miles from Waltham Hospital (44,410 ER visits) and Emerson Hospital (30,888 ER visits)
	13,711	40.8	6.0		3.7	29,715			
	12,068	35.0	7.6	7%	3.9	39,168			
2. Lexington	32,569	38.5	7.9	12	3.6	28,817	3	11	Four miles from Symmes Hospital (16,029 ER visits), Charles Choate Memorial (48,408 ER visits), and Emerson Hospital (30,888 ER visits)
3. Burlington/Wilmington	27,551	46.7	3.2	17	4.1	18,914			Four miles from Winthrop Community (14,893 ER visits) and six miles from Winchester Hospital (19,477 ER visits) and Symmes (16,029 ER visits)
	18,195	43.3	5.4		3.9	19,808			
4. Reading/Lynnfield	23,742	38.0	8.8		3.5	22,191			Six miles from Winchester Hospital (19,477 ER visits), New England Memorial (27,027 visits), and Josiah B. Thomas (19,610 ER visits)
	10,657	38.4	6.4		3.2	29,447			
5. Acton	24,479	43.2	4.3	12	3.6	25,316			Four miles from Emerson Hospital (30,888 ER visits)
6. Sharon/Canton/Foxboro	13,602	39.4	6.6	2	3.3	25,039			Four miles from Mass Correctional (7,189 ER visits), Norwood Hospital (50,350 ER visits), and Goddard Memorial Hospital (37,217 ER visits)
	18,257	40.1	7.2		3.4	22,157			
part of	15,625	38.4	8.7		3.4	19,180			
7. Braintree/Randolph/ Holbrook	30,053	38.5	7.1	11	3.3	18,558			Four miles from Milton Hospital (16,582 ER visits), Quincy City Hospital (34,414 ER visits), and Goddard Memorial Hospital (37,217 ER visits) and six miles from Cardinal Cushing General Hospital in Brockton (39,474 ER visits) and Brockton Hospital (43,653 ER visits)
	11,811	41.5	6.4		3.4	18,558			
8. Weymouth	5,099	36.6	9.9		3.1	14,294	0	1	Four miles from Quincy City Hospital (34,414 ER visits) and six miles from Milton Hospital (16,582 ER visits)
	26,812	39.7	7.4	29	3.2	14,202	2	1	
	15,509	37.3	8.2	16	3.1	18,442	4	2	

Note: ER = emergency room; FG/GP = family practitioner/general practitioner; IM = internal medicine.
Source: SMG Marketing Group, Inc.

equal footing, they are more likely to comply with treatment regimens.

Once a desirable area was selected, specific real estate sites were chosen. Health Stop either leased store fronts or purchased land and constructed facilities. The necessary leasehold improvements for any leased facility cost from $100,000 to $200,000 per location. Health Stop negotiated an exclusive ten-year agreement with a real estate developer to locate, build, own, finance, and subsequently lease back and maintain HS's property. The developer received a fixed monthly administrative fee, percentage commissions, and other fees for the services it provided.

Marketing Strategy

Craig Panther, vice president of marketing, uncovered a number of key characteristics of the primary care market in the process of marketing Humana's MedFirst chain. First, a surprisingly large number of the under-40 middle class (defined as the middle 60% of the income distribution and predominantly blue collar) had no established ties with doctors; even recently moved families with children had no pediatrician. Further, women chose doctors for the whole family, making 70% to 90% of all health care decisions, and women under age 45 had a significant preference for female doctors, perceiving them to be more caring and more appealing to children.

Mr. Panther described health care marketing as a creative and subjective activity that is still in the "research and development" stage:

> The product is still the doctor, and that particular doctor's quality of care; a marketing strategy can bring the patient in the door the first time, but only the physician can bring her back for repeat visits.

However, getting that first visit was an expensive proposition. According to Mr. Panther, "The market requires broadcast media to create awareness in consumers that there is a third alternative when they need medical attention." In his opinion, direct mail was necessary for consumer comprehension of a new and complicated product. Finally, brand name awareness was to be worked into the first two components. "We are still working on inducing the new patient; we're not even close to saturation. Another difficult aspect is to make that patient remember us when he or she needs us only three or four times a year."

With a hypothetical budget of $1 million, Mr. Panther would spend no less than 40% on television and radio; 30% on direct mail; a small portion on newspaper advertising; and the rest on outdoor and transit advertising for "maintenance" purposes, keeping the Health Stop name in front of the public between major advertising campaigns.

Health Stop used an aggressive marketing strategy in promoting each FAC, with a budget of approximately $70,000 for each office in its first year of operation and an ongoing annual budget of $50,000 per office. The consumer marketing program included direct mail; radio, newspaper, and transit advertising; television; community programs (PTA, school visits, Boy Scouts, Chamber of Commerce, etc.); promotional programs (free blood pressure tests, hearing tests, flu shots, etc.); and physician/nurse call-backs to all patients. Industrial marketing included calling on small- and medium-size companies to secure their industrial accidents, pre-employment physicals, OSHA testing requirements, etc.; promotion to industrial nurses via continuing medical education programs; and coordination in providing extended-hour coverage for HMOs. The effect of price competition was unclear.

Economies of scale were key to Health Stop's advertising strategy. As of October 1984, there were over five million people in the area covered by a television signal. With its 19 offices, Health Stop's potential market was two million people. As Mr. Panther stated, "the use of television advertising is possible for us because we are talking to two million people, while our competitors are trying to reach 50,000."

Patient satisfaction surveys (see Exhibit 6.1) were used not only for marketing, but also to assess medical competency, courtesy of staff, pricing, and operations (such as waiting time). The survey was mailed to patients, yielding a return rate prior to October 1984 of 10% to 20%, considered high for surveys of this type.

Financing

Health Stop raised $6.2 million in equity from venture capital and institutional investors during its first year of operation and a line of credit for $1.5 million.

The company expected to generate positive cash flow by the beginning of 1985 and to fully pay down any used portion of its credit line during the balance of the year. In anticipation of reaching break-even, the company and its investors decided to raise additional equity capital through another private placement to finance further growth into other markets. Health Stop's financial statements and unit profitability projections can be found in Table 6.2.

To reduce claim processing costs, payment by patients who were not insured was requested at the time of service. If an insurance company paid for a specific service, HS charged directly for it. Routine office visits were usually not insured but ancillary services, such as laboratory and x-ray, and procedures, such as sutures and eye flushing, usually were.

The major payers were Blue Shield, Medicare, Medicaid, the commercial insurance companies, Worker's Compensation, and corporate accounts for occupational medicine. Each of these payers varied in their requirements. Blue Shield, for example, maintained a profile of charges on each physician that was updated based on the physician's profile one and a half years previously. Blue Shield would pay 95% of an allowable amount which was the lower of the physician's profile or the average charge for a service made by all physicians in the area.

Medicare paid 80% of allowable charges, based on the same profile system used by Blue Shield. The administration of Medicare pay-

ments was performed by Blue Shield. The allowable charges had been frozen at the same level for the last two years.

Medicaid fees were determined by the Massachusetts Rate Setting Commission and updated periodically but not regularly. Present fees amounted to between 40% and 45% of charges. Worker's Compensation reimbursed physicians at Medicaid rates. The law required that physicians must bill Worker's Compensation even if the patients had other forms of insurance available.

Commercial insurance companies usually paid the full amount of the charge. The various commercial insurance companies had standardized their claim form in the Northeast, which simplified billing. However, because they had increased their deductible from $50 or $100 up to $250 or $500, the charge for most Health Stop patients was less than the deductible.

Occupational medicine payments were made on the basis of fee-for-service charges, with amounts about 15% below Health Stop's regular charges. Other groups who provided a large number of patients, such as a union's health benefit plan, received a similar discount.

Relationships with Other Health Care Providers

By 1984, eight Health Stop centers had agreements with local community hospitals; they included four general partnerships, one limited partnership, and three cooperative marketing agreements. Through them, HS raised $1.5 million in cash, lowered risk through sharing of operating losses, and used the hospitals' names in marketing the related centers. Health Stop believed that none of its competitors had raised as much capital from hospitals.

Regulatory constraints affected these agreements. Fee-splitting arrangements, in which the referring organization gets part of the fee charged by the organization that performs the service, were illegal. Also, a nonprofit hospital corporation could not directly invest in a Health Stop office.

Table 6.2 Health Stop: Unit Profitability Projections—Years 1–5, as of July 1984

Period	Year 1	Year 2	Year 3
Patients/Day	$ 24	$ 44	$ 50
Days/Period	365	365	365
Patients/Period	8,669	16,060	18,053
Average Charge	$43.90	$48.29	$51.19
Gross Revenue[a]	$ 380,543	$ 775,506	$ 934,133
Allowances	57,081	116,326	140,120
NET REVENUE	$ 323,461	$ 659,180	$ 794,013
GUARANTEES			
2 MD's Guarantee to PC	$ 140,160	$ 148,570	$ 157,484
Overreads[a]	4,334	8,511	10,253
Malpractice PC	4,800	5,088	5,393
Total Guarantee	$ 149,294	$ 162,169	$ 173,130
EXPENSES			
Staff (Receptionist $6/hr.; RN $15/hr.)	$ 89,529	$ 107,116	$ 136,451
Fringes	17,906	21,423	27,290
Reference Lab	6,935	13,619	16,405
Medical Supplies	17,337	34,047	41,011
Office Supplies	1,734	3,405	4,101
Malpractice Insurance	2,000	2,120	2,247
Billing/Support Services	21,672	40,150	45,625
Rent	41,000	36,000	36,000
Leasehold Depreciation	12,000	12,000	12,000
Equipment Depreciation	20,000	20,000	20,000
Utilities	6,000	6,360	6,742
Telephone	3,000	3,180	3,371
Facility Insurance	3,000	3,180	3,371
Maintenance	1,800	1,908	2,022
Marketing	70,000	50,000	50,000
Real Estate Commissions	10,000	—	—
Legal	2,000	—	—
Miscellaneous	13,000	12,720	13,483
TOTAL EXPENSES AND GUARANTEES	$ 488,207	$ 529,397	$ 593,249
PBIT & PROFIT SHARING	(164,746)	129,783	200,764
Profit Sharing to PC	845	15,574	24,092
Contribution to Management Company	(165,591)	114,209	176,672
Profit Sharing to Management Company	564	10,383	16,061
PBIT*	(166,154)	103,826	160,611
ACCUMULATED PBIT	(166,154)	(62,328)	98,283

[a]Gross Revenue is the product of the average charge and the patients in the period. The number does not exactly equal the product of the two because of rounding in the average charge number shown in this table.

*PBIT = Profit before interest and taxes.

continues

Table 6.2 continued

Year 4	Year 5	Comments
56	62	
365	365	
20,440	22,630	
$54.26	$57.51	Price increases in first 24 months reflect increasing mix of trauma, there-after prices increase 6%/year
1,109,002	1,301,493	
166,350	195,224	Assume 50% cash, 50% receivables with a 70% collection for a net allowance of 15%
942,652	1,106,269	
166,933	176,949	$32/hour for 12 hours/day
12,172	14,285	100% overread of x-rays and EKGs, averaging $.50/patient[†]
5,717	6,060	
$ 184,822	$ 197,294	
		Costs are generally based on actual experience and, except for rent, billing, depreciation and marketing, are increased at 6%/year
$ 164,697	$ 186,770	Staff levels increase with volume
32,939	37,154	Fringes 20% of wages
19,475	22,856	$.80/patient
48,689	56,140	$2.00/patient
4,869	5,714	$.20/patient
2,382	2,525	
51,100	56,575	Billing and support services are provided centrally; cost of $2.50/patient is not inflated because costs will decrease with volume
36,000	36,000	
12,000	12,000	Ten-year depreciation
20,000	20,000	Five-year depreciation
7,146	7,575	
3,573	3,787	
3,573	3,787	
2,144	2,272	
50,000	50,000	Expenditures are a function of management policy
—	—	
—	—	
14,292	15,150	
$ 657,702	$ 715,599	
284,950	390,670	Profit before interest, taxes (PBIT), and profit sharing
34,194	46,880	12% of PBIT to PC
250,756	343,790	
22,796	31,254	8% of PBIT to employees at each center
227,960	312,536	
326,243	638,779	

[†] "Overreads" refers to a quality assurance function whereby x-rays and EKGs interpreted by the physician on duty are reviewed by the radiologist and cardiologist, respectively.

Exhibit 6.1 Health Stop: Patient Opinion Survey, May 1984 (total patient responses = 688)

1. Was this your first visit to Health Stop?
  Yes = 80%   No = 20%

2. For which of the following reasons did you visit Health Stop?
  Routine illness   = 38%   Routine physical exam = 7%
  Sudden illness   = 14   Job-related injury   = 2
  Minor injury   = 17   Other   = 22

3. From the time of arrival, about how long did it take you to be seen by:
  A. The nurse or technician?   B. The physician?
    10 minutes or less   = 87%   10 minutes or less   = 53%
    10 to 20 minutes   = 10   10 to 20 minutes   = 38
    20 to 30 minutes   = 2   20 to 30 minutes   = 5
    Over 30 minutes   = 1   Over 30 minutes   = 4

4. Please give us your opinions of Health Stop in the following areas:

	E^a	VG^a	G^a	F^a	P^a
Courtesy & Professionalism of Staff	71%	24%	5%	0%	0%
Waiting Time	63	25	8	3	1
Doctor's Courtesy & Understanding	67	25	6	1	1
Clarity of Physician's Instructions	66	26	6	1	1
Nurse's Courtesy & Understanding	69	25	6	0	0
Fairness of Charges	36	27	24	9	4
Convenience of Health Stop Location	68	21	9	2	0
Overall Satisfaction	56	33	8	2	1

5. In the future, will you and your family use Halth Stop for:
  Most of your medical needs   = 23%   Medical care related to employment = 3%
  Some of your medical needs   = 35   When current family doctor is
  Treatment of sudden illness   unavailable   = 14
    or injury   = 23   Other   = 2

6. Does your family currently have a family doctor?
  Yes = 46%   No = 54%

7. Will you consider using your Health Stop physician as the family doctor?
  Yes = 65%   No = 35%

8. Please indicate how you first became aware of Health Stop. If more than one, please check all sources you remember.
  Newspaper   = 15%   Television   = 12%
  Direct mail   = 21   Billboard   = 6
  Friend or relative = 17   Other   = 19
  Radio   = 10

Please check here if you would like to serve on our Health Stop patient advisory board.
  13%

[a]E = excellent; VG = very good; G = good; F = fair; P = poor.

To further integrate itself into the health care delivery system, HS was contacting HMOs to provide after-hours medical services to its subscribers in lieu of hospital emergency rooms. Under such an arrangement, the HMO would provide a significant financial incentive to its subscribers to utilize Health Stop facilities.

Competition

There were approximately 45 FACs in the greater Boston market. HS's next largest competitor operated four and two competitors had three offices each. No other competitor had more than one office. Three competitive offices had closed in the previous six months. Of the 19 HS offices, only 4 had directly comparable competitors in their market areas. At each of its locations, however, the HS office competed against traditional physicians' offices and hospital emergency rooms.

As of October 1984, approximately 1,500 FACs operated in the United States, over 100 of them by two chains with substantially greater financial resources than HS. It was anticipated that other large corporations would decide to enter the field in the future and that competition would become increasingly intense.

THE FUTURE

HS's short-term plans included introducing specialist physicians such as gynecologists and general surgeons, who would see patients by appointment and would be compensated on a percentage basis, retaining 70% of charges at low volumes and 50% at higher ones. It was also adding mobile ultrasound capability in some offices to capture ancillary activity previously referred elsewhere.

Long-range goals included expanding into new regions of the country and growing through acquisitions and further development of partnerships with hospitals. It planned to either open or acquire another 35-40 FACs throughout the country in 1985 and 1986, in a pattern of regional concentration in metropolitan areas with populations of 500,000 to 3,000,000 people. Management had also considered working with public agencies to provide ambulatory services to the low-income community.

Mr. Hachikian offered his view of the future:

> The for-profit sector will continue to gain significant market share against the nonprofit sector, and it will be for the good. Health care was as mismanaged and poorly run as any regulated business.

Dr. Maloney spoke enthusiastically of the future:

> I expect Health Stop to emerge as the "class act" nationally. We will be able to attract capital and acquire other regionally dominant groups of centers. We can do this because of our board's positive attitude toward growth.
>
> The smaller chains can't afford to do the marketing or invest in high-quality executives; to pay for this, you need at least 20 centers in an area. This takes a lot of capital.

POINTS TO PONDER

1. What area of opportunity is Health Stop exploring?
2. What are the managerial skills critical to its success? Has the company paid sufficient attention to these skills? If not, what should it be doing in addition to its present managerial activities?
3. Is Health Stop a viable business?

NOTE

1. *Modern Healthcare*, May 24, 1984, pp. 32–34.

Health Stop: Production Process

Health Stop's primary business was that of operating a chain of physicians' offices. In October, the patient volume in the company's 20 offices was not sufficient to make it profitable (Table 7.1). The July cumulative deficit was $7.1 million.

The Braintree, Massachusetts, office experienced more operational problems than others (Exhibit 7.1), including discontented employers who received employees' physical examination results weeks late. One of the company's best physicians was transferred to Braintree and additional staff time was made available. After a few months, the transferred doctor stated, "Waiting time does not now appear to be a serious problem for the patients. When it is very busy, some will wait one, or one and one-half hours before I can see them, but maybe only one patient per week will leave without being seen."

Mr. Hachikian, chief executive officer, and Dr. Maloney, chief medical officer for Health Stop, wanted to review their office management practices to avoid recurrence of this problem and determine how office profits could be improved.

OFFICE OPERATIONS

Staffing

Operating a center required a physician, nurse, and an x-ray or laboratory technician,

each working 12-hour shifts for three or four days per week. Staffing for a week thus required two full-time equivalent physicians, nurses, and technicians. To accommodate sickness, vacation (10 days per year), and holidays (7 days per year), a floating pool of employees was guaranteed 36 or 40 hours per week and assigned as needed. Other employees agreed to a per diem compensation for voluntary coverage of a vacancy. Health Stop could staff as needed without incurring significant overtime costs.

All offices were open from 8:00 A.M. until 8:00 P.M. on weekdays; from noon until 6:00 P.M. on Sunday; and from 9:00 A.M. until 5:00 P.M. on Saturdays. When patient volume reached 25 patients per day, a receptionist was added for 20 hours per week. At 30 patients per day, 40 hours per week of receptionist time were budgeted.

The maximum number of patients one physician could see per day was about 75. When this volume was attained at the Hyannis office, one- to one-and-one-half-hour waiting times were frequent. More than 75 patients per day required a second physician or a physician's assistant.

Office Management

The nurse designated as the facility supervisor was responsible for scheduling the nonphysician staff, maintaining office inventory, ensuring preventive maintenance of equipment, and providing proper documentation in each patient chart and corporate reports. She reported to one of two nursing supervisors for all of the offices, who in turn

Note: This case was prepared by Dr. James Rhea and revised by Professor Regina E. Herzlinger.

Table 7.1 Health Stop: Consolidated Statement of Operations for Month Ended July 31

(in thousands)

	Actual		Budget	
	Month	*YTD*[a]	*Month*	*YTD*[a]
Management Fees	$ 827	$ 5,725	$1,190	$6,592
Less: Operating Expenses				
Office Expenses	1,104	6,944	989	6,803
General and Administrative Expenses	100	645	102	665
Total Operating Expenses	1,114	7,589	1,091	7,468
Operating Income (Loss)	(287)	(1,864)	99	(876)
Less: Minorities' Interest in Consolidated				
Joint Venture Losses	41	290	30	250
Interest Income (Expense)	(14)	(69)	(4)	(52)
Net Income (Loss)	$ (260)	$ (1,643)	$ 125	$ (678)
Corporate Expenses				
Payroll and Benefits	$ 54.1	$ 376.4	$ 55.4	$371.8
Rent, Utilities	17.5	79.9	17.5	86.5
Telephone	2.7	17.4	2.5	17.5
Legal, Consulting and Accounting	12.0	75.1	11.7	81.9
Other	13.8	96.0	15.4	107.8
Total Corporate Expenses	$100.1	$ 644.8	$102.5	$665.5

[a]YTD = Year-to-date: fiscal year began January 1.

reported to Mary Ann Tocio, the regional manager for all the offices. Ms. Tocio remarked, "We like to have the offices autonomous. Of course, the corporation is in charge of hiring and supervising the training of new personnel, but the facility supervisor is really in charge of the day-to-day operations within an office."

Training

All nonphysician staff were cross-trained for 80 hours to perform nursing, x-ray, laboratory, or administrative duties. The first day was spent in the business office to learn billing and insurance. Two days of laboratory training followed at one of the local offices under the supervision of the manager of laboratory services. Subsequently, two days were spent in x-ray and one in nursing training. The trainee was then assigned to an experienced employee in one of the offices. After three months, each employee was reviewed by the facility supervisor. If performance appeared substandard, the employee received additional training. Ms. Tocio stated:

> Because an employee with a nursing background will be more comfortable performing nursing duties than taking x-rays, we encourage employees to specialize in their area of previous training when it is busy. But so that they will become more comfortable with any of the jobs, we encourage employees to swap jobs when it is not busy.

Facility Quality Control

Quality control procedures included informal periodic visits to each office by corporate staff

Exhibit 7.1 Health Stop: Patient Opinion Survey

1. Was this your first visit to Health Stop?
   Yes = 73% (61%)[a]   No = 23% (37%)

2. For which of the following reasons did you visit Health Stop?

Routine illness	= 34% (33%)	Routine physical exam	=	10% (11%)
Sudden illness	= 16 (16%)	Job-related injury	=	2 (9%)
Minor injury	= 20 (12%)	Other	=	18 (19%)

3. From the time of arrival, about how long did it take you to be seen by:

A. The nurse or technician?		B. The physician?	
10 minutes or less	= 71% (29%)	10 minutes or less	= 41% (31%)
10 to 20 minutes	= 17 (29%)	10 to 20 minutes	= 29 (26%)
20 to 30 minutes	= 5 (16%)	20 to 30 minutes	= 9 (11%)
Over 30 minutes	= 4 (18%)	Over 30 minutes	= 16 (26%)

4. Please give us your opinions of Health Stop in the following areas:

	E[b]		*VG*[b]		*G*[b]		*F*[b]		*P*[b]	
				In Percent (%)						
Courtesy & Professionalism of Staff	66	(51)	25	(36)	6	(7)	2	(5)	1	(1)
Waiting Time	50	(17)	25	(26)	13	(18)	6	(20)	4	(15)
Doctor's Courtesy & Understanding	62	(45)	24	(34)	7	(11)	3	(3)	1	(3)
Clarity of Physician's Instructions	61	(51)	24	(30)	8	(9)	2	(3)	1	(3)
Nurse's Courtesy & Understanding	63	(54)	25	(31)	7	(12)	1	(1)	<1	(1)
Fairness of Charges	36	(29)	26	(23)	19	(18)	8	(12)	4	(7)
Convenience of Health Stop Location	63	(53)	23	(32)	10	(1)	2	(2)	<1	(1)
Overall Satisfaction	53	(32)	30	(42)	9	(14)	3	(7)	2	(3)

5. In the future, will you and your family use Health Stop for:

Most of your medical needs	= 42% (28%)	When current family doctor is	= 21% (12%)
Some of your medical needs	= 38 (39%)	unavailable	
Medical care related to		Treatment of sudden illness or injury	= 17 (34%)
employment	= 2 (4%)	Other	= 5 (3%)

6. Does your family currently have a family doctor?
   Yes = 54% (53%) No = 44% (45%)

7. Will you consider using your Health Stop physician as the family doctor?
   Yes = 53% (53%)   No = 36% (39%)

[a]Percentages inside parentheses are for Braintree office; other percentages are for all offices combined.
[b]E = excellent; VG = very good; G = good; F = fair; P = poor.
Note: Numbers do not add up to 100 because of nonresponse or multiple responses.

such as the managers of laboratory services, x-ray services, and operations and even Mr. Hachikian. Following them, an evaluation form was filled out and communicated to the facility supervisor.

A formal facilities audit was used for laboratory, x-ray, nursing, overall appearance, and operations. It reviewed the routine performance of controls for laboratory studies (this ensured the laboratory test was accurate), preventive maintenance, inventory levels, and documentation in the patients' medical records (checked by reviewing 15 randomly selected records). As an incentive bonus, $1,000 was awarded to the center with the best facility audit, to be divided among all its nonphysician employees. Follow-up audits were planned on a six-month or yearly basis to reassess the quality of the facility and determine whether problems had been successfully corrected. Employees' performance was also evaluated yearly with their superior.

PHYSICIANS

As chief medical officer at Health Stop, Dr. Maloney was ultimately responsible for the organization and management of the physicians. He commented:

> The effect of the corporation is felt through the Quality Assurance and Utilization Review committees and physicians cannot control the level of inventory and equipment. One physician wanted to purchase special equipment for the performance of ear, nose, and throat examinations. The Corporate Supply Committee, which consists of two physicians, two nurses, and the manager of purchasing, determined that such equipment existed in a different office and it was simply a matter of transferring it, rather than purchasing new equipment.

Physician Responsibility

The two full-time physicians at the office were responsible for scheduling physician time. Absent physicians were covered by on-call or part-time physicians. Each full-time physician was required to be on call for service at any office one day per month.

Medical practice problems were to be solved at a local level if possible. If not, the physician would report to Dr. Avrohm Melnick, the senior medical director, a full-time physician practicing in the Brookline office. Dr. Melnick stated, "It is our intention that all of the physicians feel autonomous and responsible for all decisions concerning the medical care of their patients."

Office physicians were responsible for coding each visit so that an appropriate charge would be made and for managing the flow of patients so that the practice could operate smoothly. Corporate policy urged them to delegate responsibilities to better accomplish these tasks, including patient triaging (determining which patient should be seen first), answering phone calls and calling back patients, and ordering clearly necessary laboratory and radiographic procedures, such as a urinalysis for a probable urinary tract infection or ankle films for an ankle injury. By delegating, the physician would have more time to see patients when it was busy. The physicians also referred patients to specialists and developed a list of physicians who would accept referrals. In an office affiliated with a hospital, the physicians typically used the hospital's medical staff.

Physician Compensation

Continued Dr. Maloney:

> In a private office, the physician knows that income will reflect the number of patients seen. Here at Health Stop we compensate our physicians with a base salary between $28 and $32 an hour. This results in greater income than most physicians earn in private practice. However, we do not want it to cause the physician to become lazy.
>
> Our initial profit-sharing plan turned out to be ineffective. In the period in which we are interested in having physicians build their practices, there are no profits typically. And to award physicians on the basis of overall profitability presents a motivational problem for physicians who do not tend to think like that.
>
> As a result, we changed the compensation package: Physicians will get the greater of either their base salary or a total amount which depends on the revenues they generate. For example, we now pay the physicians the greater of either the base salary or 24% of gross charges up to $24,000 in charges and 15% of gross charges after that. If a physician were seeing 50 patients a day with an average charge per patient of

about $52, our package would result in a very nice income. The physicians can understand it.

By the way, we pay on the basis of gross revenue and not net revenue to avoid discrimination against patients who receive substantial discounts from our charges, such as Medicaid patients.

Physician Training

Training of physicians began with their interviews. First, Dr. Melnick discussed his expectations and the advantages and disadvantages of practice at Health Stop. Next, Mr. Hachikian, Dr. Maloney, and Craig Panther, the vice president of marketing, interviewed them, voicing their expectations of physicians in a business setting. If offered a job, a half-day meeting introduced new physicians to corporate personnel. In August, 75% of the new physicians attended this meeting. They then accompanied Dr. Melnick in seeing patients and observing staff operations. Experienced physicians were paired with new ones. After visiting the new doctors at their offices to answer questions and offer suggestions, they sent memos to Dr. Melnick describing the results of their visits. As of October, Dr. Melnick had not yet received any memos, although the visits had occurred during the summer.

Continuing medical education was provided, bimonthly, in well-attended Saturday morning meetings that featured talks by inside and visiting speakers.

Dr. Melnick stated:

I sent a questionnaire to each of our physicians asking what types of medical problems they were uncomfortable treating; for example, a physician with a background in surgery might be uncomfortable treating a medical problem such as diabetes. We discuss these areas at our continuing medical education meetings on Saturdays. Also, we encourage any physician to call others who practice with Health Stop for consultation about a particular problem. I am developing a list of the physicians' subspecialty area of expertise to facilitate this interaction.

Dinners and informal cocktail parties for all physicians and corporate officers were held, according to Dr. Maloney, to "create the feeling that we really belong to a group and are not practicing in an isolated office alone. Communication among the physicians and corporate staff is very important, yet because of the geographic dispersion of our offices it can be difficult."

MONITORING QUALITY OF MEDICAL CARE

Although governmental regulations did not require a private doctor's office to formally assess quality in any way, Dr. Maloney stated:

We monitor the quality of our operations for our own purposes, despite the time and expense. From an ethical perspective, we want to provide high-quality care. From a corporate perspective, it should help us in marketing, in dealing with our competitors, and in reducing malpractice problems. The physicians who don't like to have their work reviewed by others are not the type we want. We don't want physicians to hide in their office and not be subject to review by their associates. There is a good self-selection process. The physicians know that we have this before they come to work with us and those who don't like it will find work somewhere else.

Two committees, comprising three senior physicians, monitored the quality of medical care. The Quality Assurance Committee identified areas to be investigated, such as the treatment of patients who complained of low back pain. It then developed an audit form (Exhibit 7.2) sent to each physician with patients who had that problem. The low back pain audit form was returned by approximately 70% of the physicians. The first such audit involved

Exhibit 7.2 Health Stop: Low Back Pain Audit

1. Definition

An adult presenting to Health Stop with acute or recurrent low back pain.

Please audit five charts of such patients for the following criteria and indicate the encounter form numbers of those charts audited below. This completed form must be returned by *each office no later than October 25.* We thank you for your attention to these audit forms.

Encounter form numbers: 1. _____
2. _____
3. _____
4. _____
5. _____

2. Criteria

All records of patients seen at Health Stop for low back pain should contain notation of the following:

		Noted	Not Noted
A) History	• Date, time, and manner of onset of symptoms	_____	_____
	• Description of quality and location of pain	_____	_____
	• Presence or absence of leg pain	_____	_____
	• History or trauma and/or activity at time of onset	_____	_____
	• Occupation and/or usual physical activity of patient	_____	_____
	• Work or not work related	_____	_____
B) PE	• Straight leg raising	_____	_____
	• Deep tendon relaxes of the lower extremities	_____	_____
	• Evaluation of sensory functions and motor strength in the lower extremities	_____	_____
C) Labs	• Lumbosacral spine film	_____	_____
D) Instructions	• Give instruction sheet, medication plan	_____	_____
E) Documentation	• Follow-up	_____	_____

Hopefully, the Ambulatory Health Associates physicians will strive for 100% documentation of the above criteria. The Quality Assurance Committee is aware that it is frequently impossible and/or not appropriate to document all of the items in every case. As an initial goal, we will set 70% compliance as a necessary level for satisfactory practice.

_____
Physician Name

_____
Physician Name

_____
Office

care given to patients with diseases that must be reported to the government. After finding that not all such patients were being reported, Dr. Melnick spoke to the nonreporting physicians and modified the facility audit to include routine assessment of whether reportable diseases were in fact being reported. The committee's protocols served as guidelines for the diagnosis and therapy of the most common illnesses. They were derived from standard material from the Academy of Family Practice and were included in the physician policy and procedures manual. Dr. Maloney noted, "While these protocols are to be used, the judgment of the individual physicians should dictate the care any given patient receives."

The second quality monitoring committee, the Utilization Review Committee, assessed factors such as each physician's over- and underutilization of laboratory and x-ray examinations or the frequency of narcotics prescriptions. Dr. Maloney stated, "We could fill the place up with patients in a hurry if we gave out narcotics right and left. However, we're not running a candy store. This is the sort of thing our quality control is intended to prevent."

A monthly report of all the physicians' utilization activity was sent to them (Table 7.2). If a physician were underutilizing or overutilizing certain examinations, Dr. Melnick or Dr. Maloney discussed the problem with the physician. Dr. Maloney noted:

> Although most of our physicians are responsive to such review, I have had to fire two who failed to meet minimum quality standards.
>
> I talked with one physician who rarely ordered x-rays in situations where they should have been ordered. This failure is harmful in many ways. If patients expect an x-ray, for example, and fail to receive one, they will probably go down the street to an emergency room and have one there at a much greater total cost. An x-ray can be very reassuring...part of the practice of medicine is to provide reassurance and comfort. It would be bad if a patient were to have an x-ray somewhere else and something was found that influenced our care.
>
> Overall, we x-ray about 17% of our patients. On average, across the country, patients with the diseases we see will receive x-rays approximately 20–25% of the time.

Patients' complaints were also recorded at the individual offices and reviewed by Dr. Melnick. If he felt it necessary, he would give the physicians involved a copy of the complaint and meet with them to discuss it. Operating policies were also designed and modified to control quality; for example, a log in which abnormal laboratory results were recorded was also used to track whether the patient had been informed of them. Dr. Maloney stated, "In a big hospital it is sometimes possible for abnormal results to fall through the cracks. We don't intend for that kind of thing to happen here."

To enhance the quality of radiographic examinations and electrocardiograms, they were interpreted twice: first by the physician in the office, then by a cardiologist or radiologist. If they disagreed with the initial interpretation, they would call the physician involved. Although the error rate of primary care physicians was low, it had been shown that one of the best ways to reduce it was a second interpretation.

PATIENT FLOW

In general, patients were seen by the receptionist first. If the physician delegated initial screening responsibility, they next saw a staff employee, who inquired about the problem and might order certain laboratory or x-ray examinations. They were then seen by the physician. Finally, they returned to the reception area to formalize future appointments and to take care of the bill. If the physician decided to see all patients initially, they were first seen by the receptionist, then the physician, and then had x-rays and laboratory examinations. They saw the physician again following the results of the x-ray or laboratory examination.

There was substantial variability in the time required for these steps. The encounter with the receptionist in which the patient stated the problem and provided insurance and personal information usually required 5 minutes. Initial inquiry about the patient's problem by the nurse or physician would consume 5 to 10 minutes. The corporate examination protocol suggested that a basic physical examination would generally take 15 minutes or less and a comprehensive physical examination was thought to take 30–45 minutes. A gynecological physical examination was thought to take 15–20 minutes or less, and a pediatric physical examination between 10 and 15 minutes. A

Table 7.2 Health Stop: August Report of Physician Activity

Physicians	Total No. of Patients	Fraction of Patients Receiving		Average Revenue per Visit ($)
		X-Rays (%)	Lab Tests (%)	
A	398	10	53	49.92
B	472	14	73	55.78
C [a]	450	20	49	56.70
D	342	15	51	52.59
E	547	12	43	45.79
F	382	09	79	51.79
G	367	16	49	51.28
H	258	12	84	53.27
I	356	05	48	48.16
J	356	10	48	47.87
K	840	17	70	54.29
L	352	14	74	52.20
M	383	11	86	53.63
N	585	09	88	55.44
O	344	16	70	54.96
P	376	13	69	52.95
Q	442	14	50	48.50
R	192	18	66	55.39
S	195	14	62	51.56
T	276	09	56	48.67
U	429	19	61	55.52
V	226	08	64	50.11
W	363	14	58	53.75
X	434	15	91	60.37
Y	463	16	45	52.13
Z	397	19	59	52.73
AA	370	15	86	55.20
BB	315	08	64	52.30
CC	331	25	76	64.23
DD	288	13	99	57.09
EE	465	12	49	49.28
FF	217	17	53	49.53
GG [a]	351	22	83	72.85
HH	363	11	52	49.44
II	160	09	58	48.82
Totals [b]	12,867	14	65	53.43

[a] Braintree physicians.
[b] Data for full-time physicians only.

physical examination was usually performed in case of illness (as opposed to injuries). The examination for an injury or follow-up visit was shorter, requiring 10 minutes or less.

X-ray and laboratory examinations were not performed on all patients. Radiographic examinations at Health Stop averaged approximately 12 minutes for each type of x-ray, with a range from approximately 5 to 15 minutes. The time to perform lab tests varied from 5 to 15 minutes. Blood tests not performed within the office laboratory were sent to a commercial laboratory for analysis. An electrocardiogram added 15 minutes to the visit.

Corporate examinations were typically more extensive; for example, one corporation required a complete history and physical examination, as well as x-rays of the spine and chest, urinalysis for the presence of drugs, blood tests, a pulmonary function test, and audiometry. Three of the Health Stop offices were equipped to perform such complete corporate examinations. At Braintree, for example, a separate examination room was present for both pulmonary function tests (tests of lung capacity) and audiometry (tests of hearing). Pulmonary function or audiometry tests required from 10 to 20 minutes each.

The final visit to discuss test results could last from 5 to 30 minutes. From 5% to 7% of the patients seen by Health Stop physicians were referred to specialists. The need for such a referral was explained to the patient, and the physician would call and write the specialist to whom the patient was being referred. Such referral activity could consume up to 30 minutes. The final encounter with the receptionist would take less than 5 minutes.

Patient volumes varied by hour and day (Tables 7.3 and 7.4). Walk-in patients could arrive at any time. If a follow-up visit were necessary, as it was for about 30% of the patients, the patient was scheduled to return on a particular day, although the hour was at the patient's discretion. Patients requiring occupational medicine physical examinations were asked to arrive on Tuesdays or Thursday.

PROFITABILITY

Mr. Hachikian said:

> When we started, the break-even volume in an office was 42 patients per day. It took us six months to get that down to our original projected break-even of 34 patients per day, and now that is down further to 27 patients per day. We have increased charges some but most important has been our focus on costs. For example, we closely control staffing levels and the amount of inventory. We reduced per office inventory costs from ten to five thousand dollars.
>
> Also we have worked on market share. We not only want to see more patients, but specifically patients who require repeat visits and patients who have more serious illnesses, requiring laboratory and x-ray services.

Physicians' Roles

Health Stop tried to increase volume by advertising and stressing physician responsibility for building volume. Physicians who were taking too long with the patients and not delegating were contacted by Dr. Melnick and encouraged to work more efficiently.

The director of operations felt that the primary cause of inadequate profits was the difficulty in managing physicians; for example, new patients who were drawn in by an

Table 7.3 Health Stop: Average Daily Volume of Patients (Mid-August–Mid-September)

	Sun	Mon	Tues	Wed	Thurs	Fri	Sat	Average
All Offices								
Week 1	16	38	34	33	33	33	23	30.2
Week 2	15	33	34	37	33	27	22	29.0
Week 3	12	13	35	34	31	28	27	26.0
Week 4	16	34	29	29	30	29	24	27.4
Braintree								
Week 1	17	51	42	50	44	43	35	40.3
Week 2	19	43	48	45	59	38	26	40.0
Week 3	11	23	43	50	47	21	35	32.5
Week 4	10	49	30	42	40	40	27	34.0

Table 7.4 Health Stop: Hourly Variation of Volume by Day for 1 Week in Braintree

	Sun	Mon	Tues	Wed	Thurs	Fri	Sat
8:00–9:00 A.M.	—	5	3	3	4	3	3
9:00–10:00	—	9	3	8	3	3	1
10:00–11:00	—	4	2	2	1	1	5
11:00–12:00	—	3	2	4	4	4	2
12:00–1:00	2	2	1	2	1	1	3
1:00–2:00	3	3	5	6	3	2	1
2:00–3:00	1	3	1	4	3	4	2
3:00–4:00	2	4	2	0	3	3	2
4:00–5:00	3	3	2	3	1	0	1
5:00–6:00	0	2	3	3	1	1	2
6:00–7:00	0	4	1	6	5	7	1
7:00–8:00	3	1	1	0	4	3	6

advertising campaign to increase volume encountered excessive waits for services. To reinforce the importance of physician productivity, Dr. Melnick used the list of revenue per patient generated by each physician (Table 7.2). The physicians at the bottom were called to discuss their performance. Physicians who remained at the bottom were flagged by Dr. Maloney.

Fees

Dr. Maloney pointed out that since Health Stop began operations, the charge for a basic visit had increased from $32 to $35 to $38:

> We have not noticed any adverse effects. The patients have not complained, even when they have to pay the amount themselves. We're still much less expensive than an emergency room and cost no more than most other private offices. Convenience is worth something to the patients and for most of our centers they don't have to pay for parking, which for many emergency rooms will cost six dollars.

Marion Zimmerman, the manager of billing, stated:

> Fees are based on three factors: volume, the charges of competitors, and marketing considerations; for example, on high-volume items we will try to increase our charges, while on low-volume items it doesn't matter as much.

To speed collections, twice a day couriers brought the patient encounter and daily check-out forms to the corporate office to be checked for accuracy. The information was then submitted to the third-party payers through the company's computers. The payers responded by tape, indicating the accounts paid and those rejected. As a result, Health Stop maintained one of the lowest accounts receivable levels in the industry, approximately 90 days.

THE FUTURE

Mr. Hachikian felt that Health Stop would soon be profitable. While no new offices were to open in the immediate future, Health Stop was developing the business of office management. One of its offices was sold to a physician, with Health Stop receiving a fee for managing the office. By the end of the year, he expected four or five additional offices to be sold to the physicians.

In thinking of the future, Mr. Hachikian said:

> There is a shift from inpatient to outpatient care in the industry and we should be in a position to take advantage of that. The fee-for-service market is declining and Medicare may not reimburse physicians on a fee-for-service basis in the future. Also there is a shift to "managed care" such as health maintenance organizations which receive a fixed amount annually for the care of patients. To take advantage of that, we will soon be affiliating with an HMO or developing our own.

POINTS TO PONDER

1. Outline the managerial skills employed at Health Stop, such as designing the organizational structure, and implementing the quality control, training and staffing, compensation, reporting, and operational management systems.
2. Evaluate the impact of these skills on the quality, volume, and efficiency of Health Stop's operations. Suggest specific improvements if you think they're warranted. Analyze specifically patient flow and physician capacity utilization.
3. What is the effect of the description of the management skills on your assessment of the company's viability?

Case Study 8

Hospital Corporation of America and McLean Hospital

Massachusetts General Hospital [MGH] is negotiating the sale of its prestigious, nonprofit psychiatric center, McLean Hospital, to Hospital Corporation of America (HCA), the largest commercial operator of hospitals in the United States.

Tracey Wood was surprised by the front page story. She began to consider its implications. As a security analyst, Ms. Wood followed the hospital management industry and knew the purchase of McLean would be a major step for HCA. But this proposal was of more than professional interest; as a resident of the Boston suburb of Belmont where McLean Hospital was located, she had a personal interest in the sale.

She began by identifying the important questions from both perspectives. Why would HCA want to purchase McLean? Was the rumored $60 million the right price? How would McLean fit in with HCA's operating philosophy and management control systems? From another point of view, should there be concern over patient selection, the use of excess McLean land in crowded Belmont, support for research and teaching, or simply having a for-profit Nashville-based hospital company as a major taxpayer and community member? Or, from a broader perspective, what were the implications of this sale for nonprofit health care in the Boston area, and how would the traditionally liberal government of the Commonwealth respond to it?

THE PROPOSED DEAL

The chairman of Massachusetts General's board commented:

> Underlying the move is the need to raise millions of dollars to upgrade both facilities. It's more than we can raise and more than we can properly borrow. For HCA, the acquisition of a mental hospital with the stature of McLean would help insure the quality of all their other mental hospitals. In no way is this a move on HCA's part to make a "fast buck." This is a prestige move for them. Rather, Hospital Corporation of America is committed to supporting teaching, research, and education, and would continue the affiliation with Harvard Medical School.
>
> The problem is that MGH's physical plant is now about 60 percent obsolete.... A $114-million fund drive for MGH's planned renovations represents only about half of what ultimately will be needed. What we need [for the whole] job may more than double the total capital improvement.
>
> Meanwhile, McLean recently had a $40-million renovation and construction plan approved. It's difficult to imagine where all that money could come from. HCA approached us right at the time when we were wondering what we could possibly do. From where I sit, they are a quality hospital enterprise.

Note: This case was prepared by Richard B. Siegrist, Jr., and Joyce Lallman, under the supervision of Professor Regina E. Herzlinger.

There may be some fussing about this. I think the great problem is that there are a great many people in academics who think that anything to do with the private sector is God-awful. But these discussions will never come to fruition without the complete agreement of Harvard Medical School.[1]

McLean's executive director explained the proposal to his staff and reassured them of HCA's interest in maintaining McLean's high quality and relieving the hospital of its financial burdens. The staff was concerned about their lack of involvement in the negotiations and dubious about HCA's sincerity. "We were left stunned," said one staff member. The staff organized itself and hired a leading law firm—one of seven applying for the *pro bono* job—to analyze their situation. HCA representatives met directly with the organizers as well as the MGH and McLean leadership. One psychiatrist, for example, was flown to HCA headquarters in Nashville to discuss his role in their adolescent psychiatry program. The terms of the sale are in Exhibit 8.1.

MCLEAN HOSPITAL

McLean Hospital, a 328-bed not-for-profit psychiatric hospital, was founded in 1811 as a sister institution to MGH. Until 1980, both McLean and MGH were independently operated divisions of one corporation; they became separate charitable corporations thereafter. McLean's board of trustees was also the board of General Hospital (which provided all medical services) and MGH (which provided financial and legal services to McLean and the General Hospital). Review of McLean's operations was conducted by a three-member subcommittee of the board, two trustees emeriti, and two community representatives.

Although the seven teaching hospitals affiliated with the Harvard Medical School all offered psychiatric services, McLean Hospital was the only solely psychiatric teaching hospital. Approximately 360 psychiatrists and psychologists held joint appointments at McLean and the medical school. Resident training and research were an important part of the hospital's mission.

Many of the present McLean buildings dated back to 1895, when it moved to its 240-acre site in Belmont, a 25,000-resident town contiguous to Cambridge and occupied primarily by Harvard and MIT employees. Land in Belmont was very scarce. In 1985, the average price of a one-family house was $300,000. McLean Hospital had received approval for construction of a new 44-bed building to replace existing beds; renovation of seven existing buildings; and construction of a dining hall and library. The construction plan resulted from a 5-year long-range planning process with considerable involvement of the McLean professional and administrative staff.

McLean was administered in a collegial, participatory fashion—consistent with the mores of its professional staff. Dr. Francis de Marneffe, the general director of McLean, was responsible for its operations and Dr. Shervert H. Frazier, McLean's psychiatrist-in-chief, directed the hospital's clinical, research, and teaching programs.

For 1983, McLean Hospital generated a surplus of $2.4 million on net revenues of $37.4 million, up from $1.0 million on net revenues of $33.0 million the previous year. During 1983, McLean provided $910,000 of free care and bad debt, representing 2.3% of gross revenues. Tables 8.1 through 8.5 and Exhibit 8.2 provide more detail on McLean's and MGH's financial status.

Patient Treatment and Research Activities

McLean tailored treatment programs to the individual needs of each patient, selecting from the most advanced, proved psychiatric methods known. Treatment methods included medication; individual psychotherapy; group and family therapy; behavior therapy; rehabilitation services (such as career planning, job training, and training in independent living skills); and electroconvulsive treatment (occasionally rec-

Exhibit 8.1 The Hospital Corporation of America and McLean Hospital: MGH Conditions for Sale of McLean Hospital to HCA

By Jean Dietz
Globe Staff

Massachusetts General Hospital [MGH] made public a list of conditions yesterday it said must be met by Hospital Corporation of America [HCA] before trustees will agree to the sale of McLean Hospital in Belmont to the business-for-profit hospital chain.

One condition requires the governing board of an HCA-owned McLean Hospital to have the majority of its members from Massachusetts General Hospital and Harvard Medical School.

Another condition requires that the professional staff at McLean be employed by a not-for-profit staff association consisting of faculty members of Harvard Medical School. The association would contract with the hospital to provide services, an arrangement similar to that at other teaching hospitals.

In addition, five Harvard Medical School professorships to be filled by McLean staff would be established and funded by HCA.

Both Burr and Martin said no purchase price has been discussed up to this point in the negotiations. The preliminary agreement calls for HCA to carry out and complete a McLean construction program authorized by the Public Health Council. Although the capital improvements for $35 million have been approved, hospital officials said that without a sale, improvements would cost the hospital $50 million if the money had to be borrowed.

Total capital improvement costs needed at McLean will run to about $200 million.*

Other provisions stipulated by the trustees include:

- Sufficient power to the board to insure quality of patient care, teaching, education and research;
- Continuing devotion of the current percentage of patient care revenues to free care;
- Protection of traditional academic freedom according to existing Harvard Medical School standards and procedures;
- Formal recognition by HCA of rights of McLean employees, including pension benefits;
- Transfer of corporate responsibility for research carried out by Harvard faculty at McLean to Harvard Medical School;
- Agreement by the corporation that MGH will have a right to repurchase the hospital "at a favorable price" should HCA wish to sell or cease operating McLean in the future.

*The *Globe* story is in error. The $200 million are required for MGH, not McLean (Regina Herzlinger).

Source: *Boston Globe*, September 20, 1983. Reprinted with permission.

ommended for severe depression). These were administered through a variety of service modalities: inpatient services, day service outpatient services, community residential services, patient education, and contractual services. McLean's staff also included internists, neurologists, pharmacologists, neuroscientists, educators, and clergy.

About 40% of the patients treated by McLean each year were hospitalized. Forty-four of the inpatient service beds were located at the Hall-Mercer Children's Center, and the remainder in 8 buildings with 15 treatment halls (see Tables 8.6 and 8.7 for utilization statistics). Each hall was served by a "hall team" made up of a psychiatrist or psychologist in charge (PIC), psychiatric residents (physicians training in psychiatry), nurses, clinical social workers, and rehabilitation therapists. The PIC managed the treatment program of every patient on the hall and coordinated the efforts of the hall team.

In fiscal year 1983, McLean treated 3,618 individuals in its inpatient, outpatient, and community residential services. Inpatient admissions totaled 1,171, up 10% from the prior year, and the inpatient occupancy rate

Table 8.1 The Hospital Corporation of America and McLean Hospital: The McLean Hospital Corporation, Balance Sheets (September 30)

Assets	1983	1982
UNRESTRICTED FUND		
CURRENT ASSETS		
Cash	$ 562,071	$ 286,574
Cash Equivalents	3,000,000	900,000
Accounts Receivable—Patients	7,126,114	6,498,668
Less Allowance for Doubtful Accounts	828,030	770,115
	6,298,084	5,728,553
Accounts Receivable—Other	850,795	580,997
Due from McLean Restricted Funds	6,227	135,473
Inventories—at Cost	368,797	357,675
Prepaid Expenses	111,464	85,136
Total Current Assets	11,197,438	8,074,408
NONCURRENT ASSETS		
Investments—at Cost (which approximates market value)	289,955	157,223
Construction in Progress	1,739,578	495,684
	2,029,533	652,907
PROPERTY, PLANT, AND EQUIPMENT—AT COST		
Buildings	17,126,382	16,541,041
Equipment	7,566,310	6,960,226
Land Improvements	612,763	577,375
	25,305,455	24,078,642
Less Accumulated Depreciation	12,401,991	11,355,976
	12,903,464	12,722,666
Land	521,784	521,784
	13,425,248	13,244,450
	$ 26,652,119	$ 21,971,765
RESTRICTED SPECIFIC-PURPOSE FUNDS		
Cash	$ 25,476	—
Due from Investment Pool[a]	220,756	$ 178,020
Investments—at Cost (quoted market value of $1,014,338 at September 30, 1983; and $1,297,262 at September 30, 1982)	1,014,259	1,322,896
	$ 1,260,491	$ 1,500,916

[a]See Exhibit 8.1, which is an integral part of this balance sheet.

continues

Table 8.1 continued

Liabilities and Fund Balances	1983	1982
UNRESTRICTED FUND		
CURRENT LIABILITIES		
Current Maturities of Long-Term Debt	$ 66,152	$ 64,334
Accounts Payable	1,453,419	678,090
Accrued Liabilities	2,837,980	2,348,139
Due to MGH	20,837	10,148
Current Financing—Blue Cross	1,678,495	1,278,374
Deferred Revenue	799,705	594,670
Due to Third-Party Payers	1,421,219	753,988
Other Fiduciary Exchanges	10,759	3,659
Total Current Liabilities	8,288,566	5,731,402
LONG-TERM DEBT (less current maturities)	1,679,513	1,745,666
LOANS PAYABLE TO INVESTMENT POOLS	161,000	187,000
DEFERRED COMPENSATION LIABILITY	286,784	154,052
COMMITMENTS AND CONTINGENCIES	—	—
FUND BALANCES		
General Fund	4,556,772	2,719,195
Plant Fund	11,679,584	11,434,450
	16,236,356	14,153,645
	$ 26,652,219	$ 21,971,765
RESTRICTED SPECIFIC-PURPOSE FUNDS		
Due to McLean Unrestricted Funds	$ 6,277	$ 135,473
Disability Self-Insurance Reserve	58,094	57,125
Equity in Undistributed Security Gains and (Losses) of Investment Pools	6,670	(4,797)
Fund Balances		
Temporary	924,647	1,099,894
Restricted Endowment Income	264,803	213,221
	1,189,450	1,313,115
	$ 1,260,491	$ 1,500,916

reached a record high of 93.5% in January 1983. Eighty percent of inpatient admissions were age 50 or under. Tables 8.8 and 8.9 contain other patient statistics; sources of payment for patient services can be found in Table 8.10.

Most of McLean's clinical staff were employees of the hospital, although some independent practitioners referred their patients there. Over 10 percent of McLean's operating budget was committed to basic and clinical research. McLean's research program had 118 principal investigators who researched brain systems, architecture, and neurochemistry and did clinical and/or laboratory studies of such

Table 8.2 The Hospital Corporation of America and McLean Hospital: The McLean Hospital Corporation, Statement of Revenues and Expenses, Year Ended September 30

	1983	1982
Patient Service Revenue	$ 39,188,539	$ 35,692,007
Deductions		
Free Care	310,189	633,859
Contractual Adjustments	895,667	1,469,406
Provision for Uncollectible Accounts	599,864	587,627
Total Deductions	1,805,720	2,690,892
Net Patient Service Revenue	37,382,819	33,001,115
Other Operating Revenue		
Transfers from Restricted Funds		
Research and Other Specific Purposes	3,544,273	3,517,106
Indirect Cost Recoveries	1,532,020	1,504,701
Revenue from Contract Services and Other	3,600,027	3,432,956
Total Other Operating Revenue	8,676,320	8,454,763
Total Operating Revenue	46,059,139	41,455,878
Operating Expenses		
Salaries and Wages	27,253,358	25,045,531
Employee Fringe Benefits	5,944,599	5,077,693
Supplies	2,012,001	1,973,925
Utilities	1,656,720	1,794,972
Outside Services	2,035,571	1,906,838
Taxes and Insurance	449,158	399,493
Depreciation	1,046,014	984,625
Interest	137,919	120,388
Total Operating Expenses	40,535,340	37,303,465
Research and Other Specific-Purpose Expenses	3,544,273	3,517,106
Total Expenses	44,079,613	40,820,571
Excess of Revenues over Expenses from Operations	1,979,526	635,307
Nonoperating Revenue		
Investment Income Received from the		
Massachusetts General Hospital	30,242	34,555
Investment Income Transferred from Restricted Funds	90,177	81,975
Investment and Other Income	315,644	211,010
Total Nonoperating Revenue	436,063	327,540
Excess of Revenues over Expenses	$ 2,415,589	$ 962,847

Table 8.3 The Hospital Corporation of America and McLean Hosptial: The General Hospital—Summary of Revenues and Expenses

(in thousands)

	Fiscal Year Ended September 30					Six Months Ended March 31	
	1978	1979	1980	1981	1982	1982	1983
Patient Service Revenue	$158,948	$182,534	$198,795	$228,908	$263,050	$127,562	$139,685
Deductions from Patient Service Revenue	16,597	24,063	22,415	28,531	33,790	14,888	19,172
Net Patient Service Revenue	142,351	158,471	176,380	200,377	229,260	112,674	120,513
Other Operating Revenue	55,612	61,708	68,465	79,499	97,194	48,186	52,300
Total Operating Revenue	197,963	220,179	244,845	279,876	326,454	160,860	172,813
Total Operating Expenses	200,114	219,895	246,304	283,019	329,337	163,445	174,409
Income (Loss) from Operations	(2,151)	284	(1,459)	(3,143)	(2,883)	(2,585)	(1,596)
Nonoperating Revenue	2,792	3,888	5,021	6,391	4,990	2,604	2,003
Extraordinary Item		(1,805)					
Accounting Change			(2,506)				
Excess (Shortage) of Revenues over Expenses	$ 641	$ 2,367	$ 1,056	$ 3,248	$ 2,107	$ 19	$ 407

Table 8.4   The Hospital Corporation of America and McLean Hospital: The General Hospital Corporation, Balance Sheets (September 30)

Assets	1982	1981
UNRESTRICTED FUND		
CURRENT ASSETS		
Accounts Receivable		
Patients	$ 47,589,810	$ 36,589,790
Other	3,739,275	3,223,541
	51,329,085	39,813,331
Less Allowance for Doubtful Accounts	3,847,686	2,961,775
	47,481,399	36,851,556
Due from Third-Party Payers		2,404,877
Due from the Massachusetts General Hospital	46,195	1,177,512
Due from the General Hospital Restricted Fund	216,425	——
Inventories	4,811,947	4,187,433
Prepaid Expenses and Deposits	1,905,589	1,576,205
Total Current Assets	54,461,555	46,197,583
NONCURRENT ASSETS		
Investments—at Cost (which approximates market value)	1,187,752	1,335,315
Due from Third-Party Payers—Deferred		305,420
Construction and Debt Service Assets	8,881,737	16,542,072
Construction in Progress	11,445,447	32,443,565
Land, Buildings, and Leasehold Improvements	171,017	1,477,443
Advance Payments	578,531	659,495
	22,264,484	52,763,310
PROPERTY, PLANT, AND EQUIPMENT—AT COST		
Buildings	150,876,858	117,104,516
Equipment	38,701,445	31,998,815
	189,578,303	149,103,331
Less Accumulated Depreciation	52,355,156	46,150,544
	137,223,147	102,952,787
Land	4,323,615	3,271,926
	141,546,762	106,224,713
	$ 218,272,801	$ 205,185,606
RESTRICTED SPECIFIC-PURPOSE FUNDS		
Cash	$ 4,890,699	$ 2,943,392
Due from the General Hospital Unrestricted Fund		3,591,446
Due from Investment Pool	4,520,840	——
Investments—at Cost (quoted market value of $46,254,724 and $29,766,824 in 1982 and 1981, respectively)	45,683,850	29,731,425
Construction in Progress	3,015,513	3,132,380
	$ 58,110,902	$ 39,398,643

continues

Table 8.4 continued

Liabilities and Balances	1982	1981
UNRESTRICTED FUND		
CURRENT LIABILITIES		
Current Maturities of Long-Term Debt	$ 297,554	$ 270,889
Loans Payable to Investment Pools	4,727,000	4,884,000
	5,024,554	5,154,889
Due to the General Hospital Restricted Fund	——	3,591,446
Due to Third-Party Payers	6,498,854	——
Accounts Payable	14,945,911	10,174,552
Accrued Liabilities	13,739,493	13,291,340
Total Current Liabilities	40,208,812	32,212,227
LONG-TERM DEBT, Less Current Maturities	61,139,847	62,142,401
COMMITMENTS AND CONTINGENCIES		
FUND BALANCES		
General Fund	20,703,412	24,410,999
Plant Fund	82,162,160	72,501,423
Depreciation Fund	14,058,570	13,918,556
	116,924,142	110,830,978
	$ 218,272,801	$ 205,185,606
RESTRICTED SPECIFIC-PURPOSE FUNDS		
Research Advances		$ 5,469,522
Due to the Massachusetts General Hospital		187,288
Due to the General Hospital Unrestricted Fund	216,425	
Deferred Compensation Liability	$ 6,415,356	$ 4,760,500
Reserves		
Worker's Compensation	782,587	715,978
Disability Insurance	714,940	515,825
Equity in Undistiributed Security Gains of Investment Pools	52,800	9,943
Fund Balances		
Restricted Endowment Income	8,135,527	6,340,502
Temporary	41,793,267	21,399,085
	49,928,794	27,739,587
	$ 58,110,902	$ 39,398,643

Table 8.5 The Hospital Corporation of America and McLean Hospital: The General Hospital Corporation, Statements of Revenues and Expenses, for the Year Ended September 30

	1982	1981
Patient Service Revenue	$ 263,050,333	$ 228,909,097
Deductions		
Allowances to Patients (net of Free Care Income of $1,117,255 and $990,637 for 1982 and 1981, respectively)	$ 11,377,165	$ 8,998,294
Contractual Adjustments	21,461,567	18,689,474
Provision for Uncollectible Accounts, Net of Recoveries	951,341	843,743
	33,790,073	28,531,511
NET PATIENT SERVICE REVENUE	229,260,260	200,377,586
Other Operating Revenue		
Transfers from Restricted Funds		
Research and Other Specific Purposes	73,163,299	59,786,427
Indirect Cost Recoveries	9,557,242	7,442,683
	82,720,541	67,229,110
Other	14,473,193	12,269,561
TOTAL OPERATING REVENUE	326,453,994	279,876,257
Operating Expenses		
Salaries and Wages	137,119,072	119,729,439
Supplies and Expenses	105,153,051	92,460,917
Depreciation	8,633,474	6,865,520
Interest	5,268,380	4,177,210
	256,173,977	223,233,086
Research and Other Specific-Purpose Direct Expenses	73,163,299	59,786,427
LOSS FROM OPERATIONS	329,337,276	283,019,513
	(2,883,282)	(3,143,256)
Nonoperating Revenue		
Investment Income Received from MGH	1,412,897	1,377,235
Investment Income Earned by Construction and Debt Service Assets—net	1,227,333	1,415,945
Investment Income Transferred from the General Hospital Restricted Funds	700,815	659,995
	3,341,045	3,453,175
EXCESS OF REVENUE OVER EXPENSE	$ 457,763	$ 309,919

Exhibit 8.2   The Hospital Corporation of America and McLean Hospital: Edited Note to the McLean Hospital Corporation Financial Statements, September 20, 1983 and 1982

INVESTMENTS

All investment securities owned by the Massachusetts General Hospital, the General Hospital Corporation and the McLean Hospital Corporation are held by custodians. . . the Hospital maintains substantially all of its investments in investment pools. Asset, liability, and capital balances of these pools at September 30, 1983 and 1982, were as follows:

	1983	1982
ASSETS		
Cash	$ 292,458	$ 1,072,370
Loans Receivable from Participating Corporations	4,603,000	4,914,000
Investments—at Cost (quoted market value of $124,020,049 and $119,581,782)	101,934,253	112,438,980
Total Assets	$106,829,711	$118,425,350
LIABILITIES AND CAPITAL		
Due to Specific-Purpose Funds of Participating Corporations	$ 5,810,854	$ 4,698,860
Undistributed Security Gains		
Net Gains Realized on Securities Sold	34,896,918	32,539,781
Less Amounts Distributed on Redemption of Units	(9,486,443)	(6,234,683)
	25,410,475	26,305,098
Pooled Capital*	75,608,382	87,421,392
Total Liabilities and Capital	$106,829,711	$118,425,350

*A summary of the pooled capital ownership follows:	1983	1982
The McLean Hospital Corporation	$ 949,346	$ 1,220,450
The Massachusetts General Hospital and the General Hospital Corporation	74,659,036	86,200,942
	$ 75,608,382	$ 87,421,392

diseases as Alzheimer's, Huntington's, and schizophrenia.

Management

Dr. Francis de Marneffe, general director, outlined the factors contributing to McLean's reputation:

Much of our reputation stems from historical factors. McLean was the third

psychiatric hospital to be founded in the United States. During the 19th century it was a leader in "moral treatment," whereby patients were treated humanely and with dignity. McLean was the first psychiatric hospital to open a school of nursing, a biochemical laboratory, or a psychological laboratory, all before the turn of the century. McLean's teaching and research activities have also contributed greatly to its reputation. Because of its affiliation with Harvard University, Harvard medical students

Table 8.6 The Hospital Corporation of America and McLean Hospital: McLean Hospital Utilization Statistics

	1978	1980	1982
Inpatient Statistics			
Average Available Beds	325	328	328
Patient Days	104,056	104,048	104,667
Admissions	1,412	1,184	1,232
Average Length of Stay (days)	74	88	85
Median Length of Stay (days)	49	45	43
Percent Occupancy	88%	87%	87%
Outpatient and Other Statistics			
Adult Outpatient Clinic Visits	19,642	18,361	16,026
Children's Outpatient Visits	4,485	4,264	4,126
Appleton Outpatient Visits	6,530	7,377	7,851
Community Residential and Treatment Services	9,941	14,819	17,678
Contract Division Revenue ($000)	$455	$1,055	$2,524

Table 8.7 The Hospital Corporation of America and McLean Hospital: Psychiatric Hospitals' Utilization Statistics

(days of care in thousands)

	1980	1981	1982	1983e	1984e
Days of Care					
General Hospitals	10,501	10,704	10, 953	11,236	11,368
Psychiatric Hospitals	6,374	6,922	7,351	7,830	8,231
Days/1,000 Persons	74.1	76.7	78.9	81.4	82.9
Psychiatric Beds					
General Hospitals	35,262	36,265	36,929	37,195	38,770
Psychiatric Hospitals	21,454	23,799	25,691	26,630	28,780

e = estimate.
Source: McLean Hospital

have rotated through McLean for 30 years. McLean receives more than $7 million in research grants each year, which gives it the largest research budget of any psychiatric hospital in the U.S. and the tenth largest research budget of any U.S. hospital.

Before I became general director in 1962, the hospital experienced a budget deficit which threatened its viability. My goals when I came on board were to balance the budget and to point McLean in the general direction where we wanted to move. I think I have accomplished these goals. While it is important to manage with a strong sense of fiscal responsibility, there are many *prima donnas* here whose contributions must be recognized. It may appear that the participatory way McLean is managed is less efficient, but in the long run it may be more efficient.

Members of the professional staff at McLean are responsible to the psychiatrist-in-chief. I don't interfere with the management of clinical, research, or teaching activities, but instead concern myself with questions of space,

Table 8.8 The Hospital Corporation of America and McLean Hospital: McLean Hospital Inpatient Admissions by Prior Hospitalization and Other Characteristics, October 1, 1982, to September 30, 1983

	1st to any Hospital (%)	*1st to McLean (%)*	*Readmission to McLean (%)*	*Total Admission McLean (%)*	*Total Other Hospitals (%)*	*U.S. Average (%)*
SOURCE						
Home	73	47	63	61	54	NA
General Hospital	12	9	6	10	10	
Mental Hospital	1	33	14	16	20	
Other and Not Determined	14	11	17	13	16	
Total (%)	100	100	100	100	100	
Number	450	447	274	1,171	NA	
DIAGNOSIS						
Disorders First Evident in Infancy, etc.	13	6	3	8		NA
Organic Mental Disorders	3	2	2	2		5
Alcoholism	26	10	9	16		19
Drug Dependence	15	8	5	11		27
Schizophrenia	1	5	5	4		25
Major Affective Disorders	29	53	64	46		
Other Psychoses	2	8	4	5		17
Neuroses	3	2	1	2		
Adjustment Disorders	4	2	1	2		
Personality Disorders	3	3	5	3		6
Other	1	1	0	1		1
Total	100	100	100	100		100
Number	450	447	274	1,171		NA
AGES						
3–13	8	2	0	4		
14–20	18	18	9	16		
21–30	30	28	30	29		
31–40	20	19	26	21		
41–50	11	11	13	11		
51–60	5	11	6	8		
61–70	3	7	8	6		
71–80	3	3	6	4		
81+	2	1	2	1		
Total	100	100	100	100		
Number	450	447	274	1,171		

Source: McLean Hospital

Table 8.9 The Hospital Corporation of America and McLean Hospital: Number of Patients, Place of Origin, and Delivery Site for McLean Hospital

	Number	Percentage	Total Patients
Boston	92	8.5	
Boston Suburbs	347	32.5	
Other Massachusetts Cities and Towns	466	43.0	
Out-of-State	180	16.0	
Total	1,085	100.0	
Inpatient			1,587
Outpatient			1,823
Partial Hospital			77
Community Residences			131

finances, general policy, and legal issues. On paper, the general director is ultimately in charge. However, in practice, all major decisions have joint approval from the psychiatrist-in-chief and me. We are both members of the McLean board of trustees, which meets once a month.

A great deal of input to management decisions comes from the various committees at McLean. For example, to involve more of the staff in budget decisions we created a 20-member budget committee. We start each fiscal year with a "bare bones" or "worst case" budget. If our revenues exceed our expectations, the budget committee sets spending priorities. Their recommendations are given to the 10-member resource management steering committee, which makes budget decisions throughout the year.

The key to managing people in this complex environment is listening; knowing what people are talking about. I let the staff know that I'm interested in both quality of care and fiscal issues. It helps that I am a psychiatrist and still see patients.

The McLean environment provides a variety of incentives for its professional staff members, including the freedom to fulfill their own ego ideals. There are opportunities for research and teaching, there are rewards in the form of Harvard appointments, and there is the sense of being affiliated with a prestigious institu-

tion. These incentives are more significant than financial incentives; McLean doesn't pay its professionals exceptionally well. If a professional staff member should fail to deliver what is expected, he or she will experience peer pressure to reform, as well as more formal reprimands in the utilization review process. With the current changes in the health care industry, we may have to find better ways to remunerate our professionals, and develop a more quantifiable control system for our staff. This will be difficult, because it runs counter to the existing environment.

For nonprofessional staff, McLean's pay scale is comparable to that of the local area. None of the staff is unionized. McLean is considered a nice place to work. There are no time clocks to punch, and the environment is one where there is much respect for people.

We are considering getting involved with a for-profit health care company for three reasons: (1) to gain access to capital, (2) to gain ongoing support for our research and education activities, and (3) to diminish the risks associated with borrowing capital and with the changes likely to come in reimbursement. We offer a for-profit company our brains, programs, creativity, and reputation. For example, we have developed specialty programs to treat alcoholism, eating disorders, and affective disorders. Our research activities have yielded more

Table 8.10 The Hospital Corporation of America and McLean Hospital: Payer Sources and Charges as of September 30, 1982

	The General Hospital			McLean Hospital			Licensed Number of Beds[a]	Average Semiprivate Room Rate[a]
	1980	1981	1982	1980	1981	1982		
Payers								
Medicare	34%	34%	34%	8%	8%	8%		
Blue Cross	26	26	26	31	32	30		
Medicaid	9	9	8	3	2	2		
Commercial Insurance, Worker's Compensation, and Self-Pay	31	31	32	58	58	60		
Total	100%	100%	100%	100%	100%	100%		
Hospitals								
McLean							328	1st 30 days—$297; thereafter—$280
Bournewood							80	$290
Westwood Lodge							75	$290
The Arbour							132	$264
Charles River							58	Adult—$220
Human Resources Institute							68	Adolescent—$255

[a]Numbers of bed and rates as of October 1, 1982.

Source: McLean Hospital

effective drugs and other products, such as better tests for detecting illicit drugs in blood and urine. These products may be appropriate for commercial development.

THE HCA PSYCHIATRIC COMPANY

HCA, headquartered in Nashville, Tennessee, was an investor-owned, for-profit corporation engaged in the ownership, management, and construction of acute care and psychiatric hospitals. HCA was by far the largest investor-owned hospital chain in the world in terms of revenues, profits, hospitals, beds, and employees.

HCA seriously entered the psychiatric care market in 1981 with the acquisition of 22 psychiatric hospitals. Those were combined with several previously acquired mental health facilities into a newly formed subsidiary, the HCA Psychiatric Company, the largest owner of psychiatric hospitals in the world. By 1984, HCA had more than 40 psychiatric hospitals.

With over 5,000 beds, 21 of HCA's owned general hospitals contained psychiatric or substance abuse facilities with 600 beds. HCA anticipated further growth in the psychiatric area, primarily through the construction of new facilities in communities lacking private psychiatric hospitals.

The psychiatric care market was attractive for several reasons. First, the former county-state-federal system of psychiatric hospitals was gradually being replaced by smaller, modern, private facilities. By 1982, approximately 60% of the nation's psychiatric hospitals were private, for-profit facilities. Second, demand for psychiatric care was increasing; industry, third-party insurers, and individuals in general were becoming more aware that problems such as stress, depression, anxiety, and substance abuse were widespread and, when left untreated, were causing a major human and financial drain. Third, the increased demand for psychiatric care was generally covered by private insurance or employer programs that paid the hospital at favorable rates.[2]

HCA was renowned for its decentralization and concern for quality of care.

POINTS TO PONDER

1. Is there good fit between McLean and HCA?
2. Is the $60 million price a correct value for the deal?
3. What will the impact be on the town of Belmont?
4. What will the impact be of a major for-profit taking over such a landmark non-profit organization?

NOTES

1. *Boston Globe*, August 2, 1983.

2. Additional details of HCA are provided in "Hospital Corporation of America," HBS Case Services #0-182-067, revised February 1988 (Boston: Harvard Business School, 1988).

Case Study 9

The Hospital Replacement Decision

Kelly Bolton, Humana's regional vice president of the Hospital Division for the Sunbelt, was reviewing a memo from corporate about his feasibility study for a replacement hospital (see Appendix 9-A). The memo questioned several of the key assumptions made in the study. With corporate's alternative assumptions, the internal rate of return for the replacement facility would fall from regional's 15% to 10%.

He wondered how to proceed. The initial proposal was submitted three years ago. The next step in the capital budgeting process would require the Hospital Division's president to present the project to the Management Committee of Humana. Should he defend the original assumptions or adopt corporate's alternative assumptions? Or should he simply withdraw the project proposal?

He realized that his decision could affect his region's budget performance, the incentive compensation of his hospital administrators, his relations with corporate, and morale within the region and the community where the replacement facility would be built. To help clarify the factors involved, Bolton decided to review the background of the replacement hospital proposal and the history, management style, organizational structure, and management control systems and policies of Humana. (His review of management systems was limited to the Hospital Division.)

MANAGEMENT STYLE

Humana had the same top management in 1988 as it did when it was founded in 1961: David Jones as chairman and CEO and Wendell Cherry as president. Their management philosophy permeated the organization. Commented Wendell Cherry,

> Our value added is from management. We don't tell the doctors how to practice medicine; but we do know how to manage an organization. We centralize our management systems to ensure that our know-how is shared with all of our institutions.

Centralized management included strong financial systems, measurement of performance against specific goals, standardization of policies and procedures, a highly leveraged compensation structure, and clear delineation of responsibility. Hospital administrator John Morse, an ex-naval officer and Wharton MBA, summarized Humana's management environment:

> The philosophy at Humana is very clear to all. The company is highly systems oriented and emphasizes standardization of policies and procedures. Humana, unlike some other hospital management companies, has a clear delineation of the responsibility of corporate versus the responsibility of the hospital; there are

Note: This case was prepared by Richard B. Siegrist, Jr., under the supervision of Professor Regina E. Herzlinger. Background material on Humana is provided in Humana, Inc., Case Study 10.

few gray areas. The hospital administrator and staff influence the hospital's direction but many decisions are made by corporate. But the administrative staff has a great deal of operational power. And we're prepared to move up the ladder because we understand Humana's policies so clearly.

ORGANIZATIONAL STRUCTURE

Humana's organizational structure was a traditional one. The president and chief operating officer, Wendell Cherry, as well as the heads of the corporate departments of Internal Audit, Legal, Finance and Administration, and Communications and Planning reported directly to David Jones, the chief executive officer, as did the hospital and group health division heads. Mr. Jones also served as chairman of the board of directors and chairman of the Management Committee, which developed corporate strategy and management policies, determined earnings goals, and reviewed major capital expenditure proposals.

The Hospital Division, the mainstay of Humana's operations, was divided into six geographic regions, each managed by regional vice presidents who reported to the president of the Hospital Division. Each region contained 15 to 20 individual hospitals. The regional vice presidents were responsible for growing the business of their regions.

The hospital administrators in a region reported to the regional vice president. Each hospital administrator was responsible for the operation and performance of his or her hospital and for supervising the various departments within the hospital itself. The management structure of a hospital varied with its number of beds, size, and revenues.

CAPITAL BUDGETING PROCESS

Humana's annual capital spending plan forecasted capital expenditures for the next three years. It classified capital expenditures into four areas: existing hospital operations, development (including the acquisition of hospitals and construction of new hospitals in new markets), Health Services Division (which encompassed expenditures for alternative health care delivery system projects), and other (such as new corporate offices and equipment, aircraft, computers, etc.). Existing operations outlays were classified by specific type: hospital replacements, expansion of existing hospital facilities, renovation or expansion of ancillary or outpatient services, equipment purchases, and non-revenue-producing construction (such as a new roof or air conditioning system).

Although the Corporate Budget Department performed a preliminary review of the budgets, the specific projects they included were formally reviewed and approved at a later time. To estimate total spending, the department attached probabilities of approval to the projects in the hospital capital budgets. While no specified limit was placed on the total capital spending, the Planning Department's five-year business plan, updated every six months, served as a backdrop to these decisions. Capital expenditures were assumed to be financed 25% from operations and 75% from new long-term debt.

Specific capital projects required formal approval. Hospital administrators could approve all projects within their limits ($6,000 typically); the regional vice president, projects less than $20,000; and the Capital Expenditure Request Committee, all projects greater than $20,000. Its recommendations were made to the vice president of administration, who, in turn, presented recommendations to the president of the Hospital Division. The president of the Hospital Division could approve projects under $1 million. All other projects were presented to the Management Committee for approval by the president of the Hospital Division and the regional vice president involved.

The hospital administrator prepared financial feasibility studies for all capital expenditure requests, containing 10-year *pro forma* income statements. The related balance sheet was prepared by the Hospital Division's budget department. An after-tax internal rate of return for the project over the 10-year period was computed, with 15 % being the usual minimum requirement. The Corporate Budget Department reviewed all feasibility studies and communicated reservations to the responsible regional official, typically the regional vice president. Outstanding issues were resolved prior to the presentation of any project to the Management Committee for approval.

In evaluating specific projects, the Management Committee did not apply a uniform required rate of return. Rather, it estimated the company's cost of capital and performed a discounted cash flow analysis based on the risks. Project approval decisions were not based solely on the numbers. Intangible considerations could have a significant influence on the approval or rejection of a capital project.

ANNUAL BUDGETING PROCESS

The budgeting process at Humana was a combination of a top-down and bottom-up approach. The Management Committee set an overall budget, by reviewing macroeconomic conditions and environmental factors to arrive at assumptions about the next year and budgeting an earnings per share (EPS) figure on the basis of Humana's past performance, Wall Street expectations, and intuition about what was attainable. It received a consolidated income statement and balance sheet (factoring in predicted capital expenditures) for the budget year, as prepared by the Planning Department. This budget was then broken down into four areas: hospital operations, development, Health Services Division, and other. The hospital operations budget was further divided into regional budgets. Pretax margin was the key figure in that budget.

Simultaneously, the hospital administrators built up budgets for their hospitals from the department level. The bottom-up budgets were summed by region and compared with the regional budget developed by the Management Committee. If a profit shortfall existed in a region, it was made up by reducing the individual budgets of the hospitals within that region. Each region stood on its own. The top-down regional budgets or the overall EPS target were rarely altered.

Approved capital expenditures were factored into the hospital and regional budget. The hospital was charged imputed interest of 14% on the total capital expenditure, including any additional working capital required, and received imputed interest of 8% on any free cash it provided to corporate. Capital expenditures did not change regional pretax margin targets. The hospital incurring a capital expenditure may receive a budget exception for its targeted pretax margin but the other hospitals in its region are expected to make up its shortfall in profit.

PERFORMANCE MEASUREMENT

Performance measurement at Humana used three primary systems: the general ledger, productivity management, and patient business systems.

- The general ledger system was centralized at corporate headquarters. Each hospital submitted monthly data via computer terminal to headquarters. Corporate processed the information and sent back a variety of reports. The key general ledger report was the hospital budget analysis (Table 9.1), which compared the current month and year-to-date income statements with their budget. No adjustment was made for differences between budget and actual in number of patient days or case mix. The report highlighted pretax margin, accounts receivable days outstanding, occupancy, and paid hours per patient day. If the hospital administrator could attain the targeted pretax margin figure, line item variances from budget were of lesser importance.

- As a complement to the financial orientation of the general ledger system, Humana used its productivity management system, which measured labor productivity for

Table 9.1 The Hospital Replacement Decision: General Ledger System

Hospital Division
Ingersoll Memorial Hospital[a]

HOSPITAL BUDGET ANALYSIS

	Budget			Actual (May)			Variance	
	Amount	%	$/P.D.[b]	Amount	%	$/P.D.[b]	Inc./Dec. - $	%
Routine Services	$ 977,787	35%	$ 181.27	$ 981,262	33%	$ 181.38	$ 3,475	—
Inpatient Ancillary Revenue	1,581,985	56	293.29	1,698,539	57	313.96	116,554	7
Total Inpatient Revenue	2,559,772 *	91	474.56	2,679,801 *	91	495.34	120,029 *	5
Outpatient Ancillary Revenue	261,818	9	48.54	275,727	9	50.97	13,909	5
Total Gross Patient Revenue	2,821,590 *	100	523.10	2,955,528 *	100	546.31	133,938 *	5
Contractual Adjustments	252,273 –	9–	46.77 –	349,853 –	12–	64.67 –	97,580	39
Other Deductions from Revenue	24,677 –	1–	4.57 –	47,183 –	2–	8.72 –	22,506	91
Provision for Bad Debt	42,561 –	2–	7.89 –	36,413 –	1–	6.73 –	6,148 –	14 –
Other Income	36,815	1	6.83	36,729	1	6.79	86 –	
Net Revenue	2,538,894 **	90	470.69	2,578,807 **	87	472.98	19,913 **	1
Payroll	908,582	32	168.44	901,719	31	166.68	6,863 –	1 –
Employee Benefits	168,494	6	31.24	152,800	5	28.24	15,694 –	9 –
Supplies	388,356	14	72.00	384,301	13	71.04	4,055 –	1 –
Professional Fees	62,712	2	11.63	65,252	2	12.06	2,540	4
Other Operating Expenses	269,981	10	50.05	241,709	8	44.68	28,272 –	10 –
Total Operating Expenses	1,798,125 *	64	333.36	1,745,783 *	59	322.70	52,342 –*	3 –
Management Fees	114,532	4	21.23	114,532	4	21.17	—	
Depreciation & Amortization	166,152	6	30.80	161,151	5	29.79	5,001 –	3 –
Interest	137,085	5	25.41	135,105	5	24.97	1,980 –	1 –
Inter-Company Interest	21,000-	1–	3.89	43,456	1 –	8.03	22,456	107
Other Fixed Expenses	32,347	1	6.00	33,851	1	6.26	1,504	5
Total Fixed Expenses	429,116 *	15	79.55	401,184 *	14	74.16	27,932 *	7 –
Total Expenses	2,227,241 **	79	412.91	2,146,967 **	73	396.85	80,274 –**	4 –
Net Pretax Profit/Loss *CR*	311,653 **	11	57.78	411,840 **	14	76.13	100,187 **	32
Over/Under *CR* Budget				100,187				
Licensed Beds	400 Beds			400 Beds			0 Beds	
Patient Days/Occupancy %	5,394 PD/44%			5,410 PD/44%			16 PD/%	
Total Paid Hours/Inpatient Day	19.61			19.82			.21	

AR Days Outstanding Actual 40

[a] Name has been changed.
[b] P.D. = patient day.
* and ** indicate items of major economic importance.

salaried labor, but not physicians, based on standards for labor hours per unit of activity (e.g., per-calendar day, test, dose, visit, etc.) (see Table 9.2). The standards were determined from time and motion studies and considered "ideals." Because they might not be attainable in the short run, Humana also set budgeted targets for each department. Biweekly comparisons were reported among the actual, budget, and standard hours per unit of activity for each department within a hospital. Specific departments were compared on a regional and company-wide level (see Table 9.3). Performance ratios of actual to standard and actual to budget were used for the comparison (a ratio of greater than 1, or 100%, indicated favorable performance).

- The third performance measurement system, the patient business system, tracked patient origin, charges generated, patient days, admissions, and bad debt by physicians. The information was used to evaluate the revenue-generating and marketing performance of individual physicians and hospitals.

INCENTIVE COMPENSATION SYSTEM

Incentives accounted for a large portion of the total compensation of Humana managers. Each manager was paid a base salary and a bonus based on performance in relation to specified goals. Under this highly leveraged compensation structure, a manager who performed well could earn more at Humana than at the other hospital management companies. The performance measure used and the magnitude of the bonus in relation to base salary varied by level and by type of management (e.g., operations or corporate).

Hospital administrators received a basic bonus of up to 50% of their salary if they met predetermined performance goals for their hospital. The key performance measures were pretax profit, days of accounts receivable outstanding, bad debts, and growth in census. They were then eligible for an additional stock bonus at market value for up to 50% of their salary. Under this system, a six-figure salary was possible for a young Humana hospital administrator. Regional vice presidents received similar incentive compensation, but their performance goals were based on the performance of their region. Corporate managers received bonuses based solely on EPS. Four levels existed in the structure for corporate bonuses, ranging from 25–60% of salary.

RECRUITING, TRAINING, AND PROMOTION

New managers were brought into the company at the entry level. Each year 60 to 70 recent college graduates were recruited to participate in Humana's one-year administrator training program or two-year financial manager training program, which combined formal classroom study with on-the-job training. They then became hospital assistant administrators or assistant financial managers. Approximately half of Humana's operating executives were trained in these programs. Because hospital operations and corporate staff remained relatively separate, some tension existed between the two groups.

Because the size of the hospital determined the salary range and other rewards, the typical advancement pattern was to move from smaller to larger hospitals. No purely lateral or downward moves were permitted. The company's regional vice presidents had moved up through the hospital ranks. Almost every position was posted and filled internally; outsiders were rarely hired, except at entry level.

There was a fairly high turnover in the training program, some turnover at the hospital administrator level; but almost none at the regional vice president or corporate levels.

POINTS TO PONDER

1. Should Humana invest in this hospital? Be prepared to discuss both the financial and managerial implications of your decision.

Table 9.2 The Hospital Replacement Decision: Biweekly Productivity Management Report

Tully Memorial Hospital[a]

IV—Mid-South

Licensed Beds 155 % Occupancy 53

Inpatient Day 1,141; Average Daily Census 1982

Department	Volume	Unit of Measurement	Regular Hours	Overtime Hours	Total Production Hr	Total Paid Hr	Index (Hr./Unit)				Ratio	
							Std.	Budg.	Act.	Y.T.D.	Std.	Budg.
600 NURS AD	14	CAL D[b]	160.0	.0	160.0	160.0	11.43	15.900	11.420	14.080	100%	139%
601 NURS AD	14	CAL D	428.6	.8	429.4	440.4	22.80	21.200	30.670	28.420	74	59
610 MED/SUR	1,098	PAT D	5,086.8	19.9	5,106.7	5,994.1	4.900	4.934	4.561	4.784	105	106
650 I.C.U.	43	PAT D	631.8	7.6	639.4	727.0	15.000	15.710	14.870	16.520	101	106
688 INSU ED	14	CAL D	72.0	.0	72.0	80.0	5.143	5.300	5.143	4.691	100	103
689 PSRO AC	14	CAL D	32.0	.0	32.0	32.0	2.286	8.500	2.286	2.666	100	372
NURSING SVC. SUBTOTAL			6,411.2	28.3	6,439.5	7,433.5						
701 SURGERY	90	VISIT	700.3	24.8	725.1	810.1	9.390	8.514	8.057	9.185	117	106
704 RECY RM	0	VISIT	154.7	1.5	156.2	226.2	.000	1.887	.000	2.427	0	0
712 PHARM	16,981	DOSES	409.8	.0	409.8	451.1	.028	.034	.024	.026	116	141
718 M&S SUP	6,106	LINEI	400.0	.0	400.0	407.5	.069	.089	.066	.064	105	136
722 ANESTHE	14	CAL D	.0	.0	.0	.0	.000	.000	.000	.000	0	0
728 X-RAY	613	PROCS	585.4	52.4	637.8	671.8	1.017	1.017	1.040	1.046	98	98
729 ULTRASO	11	PROCS	80.0	.0	80.0	80.0	3.590	.000	7.273	4.492	49	0
736 LABORAT	33,818	C A P	618.0	3.4	621.4	675.4	.019	.019	.018	.018	103	103
744 E.K.G.	159	TESTS	75.0	.0	75.0	75.0	.500	.500	.472	.455	106	106
748 E.E.G.	9	TESTS	13.5	.0	13.5	13.5	1.500	.000	1.500	1.522	100	0
754 RESP TH	1,365	TREAT	458.5	.0	458.5	474.5	.377	.300	.336	.327	112	89
762 PHYS TH	1,119	MODAL	517.7	.0	517.7	577.7	.353	.438	.463	.364	76	95
763 NUC MED	14	CAL D	80.0	.0	80.0	80.0	5.714	5.300	5.714	5.743	100	93
768 SOC SV	14	CAL D	80.0	.0	80.0	80.0	5.714	5.300	5.714	5.328	100	93
780 EMERGEN	204	VISIT	287.4	.0	287.4	399.9	1.599	1.599	1.409	1.758	113	113
800 DIETARY	5,411	MEALS	1,396.9	.0	1,396.9	1,452.9	.264	.264	.258	.264	102	102
810 HOUSEKP	1,141	T.P.D.	1,107.5	.0	1,107.5	1,130.0	1.204	1.104	.971	1.097	124	114
820 LINEN	14	CAL D	75.0	.0	75.0	7.50	5.357	5.300	5.357	5.221	100	99

830 PLANT	14	CAL D	378.5	.0	378.5	446.5	27.04	26.50	27.03	30.57	100%	98%
832 SYSTEMS	14	CAL D	78.0	.0	78.0	78.0	5.571	5.300	5.571	5.030	100	95
835 SECURITY	14	CAL D	133.0	.0	133.0	140.5	9.500	9.500	9.500	9.551	100	100
840 MED REC	1,141	GTPD	476.3	.0	476.3	529.8	.493	.446	.417	.420	118	107
855 UTIL RE	14	CAL D	48.0	.0	48.0	48.0	3.429	.000	3.429	2.741	100	0
900 ADMIN	14	CAL D	395.0	.0	395.0	395.0	22.20	21.20	28.21	20.31	79	75
902 ACCTG	14	CAL D	308.4	.0	308.4	308.4	22.02	23.30	22.03	20.85	100	106
903 FIN MGT	14	CAL D	160.0	.0	160.0	160.0	11.43	15.90	11.42	10.85	100	139
904 CREDIT	14	CAL D	380.4	.0	380.4	387.9	27.17	31.90	27.17	26.62	100	117
905 PATBILL	14	CAL D	130.4	.0	130.4	167.9	9.31	10.60	9.314	9.691	100	114
906 ADMIT	14	CAL D	187.7	.0	187.7	232.7	13.41	20.20	13.40	16.94	100	151
907 RESERV	14	CAL D	70.0	.0	70.0	70.0	5.000	7.440	5.000	5.242	100	149
908 D.P.	14	CAL D	194.9	.0	194.9	194.9	13.92	15.40	13.92	14.74	100	111
910 P.B.X.	14	CAL D	233.4	.0	233.4	270.9	16.67	22.30	16.67	18.58	100	134
912 MAT MGT	14	CAL D	222.5	.0	222.5	231.1	15.89	15.90	15.89	17.68	100	100
914 SPEE BUS	14	CAL D	197.0	.0	197.0	197.0	14.07	13.30	14.07	13.31	100	95
916 PERS	14	CAL D	232.4	1.5	233.9	233.9	14.30	13.30	16.70	13.98	86	80

[a]Name has been changed.
[b]CAL D = calendar days; PAT D = patient days; PROCS = procedures.

Table 9.3 The Hospital Replacement Decision: Humana, Inc., Gross Revenue and Operating Expense Analysis

Department: Radiology

Period Covered: Fiscal Year

Patient Days	Hospital[a]	Volume	Volume per Pa- tient Day	Rank	Average Rates	Rank	Payroll as a % of Revenue (%)	Rank
23110	1	10273	.44	77	$ 41.09	72	16.59	57
43745	2	33221	.76	31	43.47	68	16.02	50
63959	3	42229	.66	39	52.88	41	13.01	11
17474	4	16760	.96	10	86.54	2	10.00	2
20794	5	18599	.89	16	29.21	84	14.07	23
91121	6	56659	.62	48	64.10	18	13.26	17
37798	7	41229	1.09	2	74.65	7	12.77	9
17264	8	17612	1.02	8	66.25	15	16.01	49
85390	9	51577	.60	54	67.95	12	13.13	13
33652	10	16601	.49	69	67.38	14	14.77	30
24908	11	11368	.46	76	58.14	25	13.32	19
27609	12	9744	.35	84	39.50	77	13.87	22
66304	13	56397	.85	22	47.44	58	14.97	31
97787	14	46017	.47	73	61.52	19	14.99	33
38266	15	35015	.92	15	64.20	17	16.54	55
53568	16	25560	.48	71	74.73	6	13.29	18
21559	17	17161	.80	25	49.44	51	14.70	29
46716	18	40496	.87	20	45.62	64	15.15	37
16848	19	9043	.54	65	39.77	76	16.62	58
42434	20	35286	.83	23	39.86	75	15.28	38
31834	21	17866	.56	61	64.52	16	14.32	25
28360	22	13205	.47	74	51.31	46	14.98	32
163703	23	111970	.68	38	99.48	1	10.36	3
64452	24	37523	.58	58	52.65	42	16.43	53
40971	25	41926	1.02	7	51.13	47	13.11	12
31294	26	32671	1.04	4	40.86	73	17.48	63
40058	27	19084	.48	72	53.96	35	11.21	7
30028	28	19159	.64	44	73.73	8	15.47	42
20429	29	12363	.61	53	47.76	56	14.52	27
27803	30	17193	.62	50	38.00	80	17.17	59
18787	31	19318	1.03	5	79.80	4	10.75	6
63784	32	39607	.62	49	45.22	66	15.86	46
55045	33	32638	.59	55	53.90	36	14.31	24
31887	34	20596	.65	43	37.80	81	19.06	72
59018	35	60457	1.02	6	40.52	74	14.67	28

Percentiles:

High (Outstanding)	111970	10.09		$ 99.48		10.36
90th	51577	.98		70.68		12.77
80th	41229	.88		64.20		13.26
70th	35638	.80		57.71		14.47
60th	32638	.72		54.93		15.05
(Median) 50th	20825	.65		52.01		15.51
Low (Poor)	1450	.32		29.21		19.06

[a]Hospitals' identities are disguised by numbers.

continues

Table 9.3 continued

Department: Radiology

Supplies as a % of Revenue (%)	Rank	Pro. Fee as a % of Revenue	Rank	Other as a % of Revenue (%)	Rank	Profit Margin (%)	Rank	Profit per Patient Day ($)	Rank
11.21	28	.00	0	2.61	1	69.59	1	$ 12.71	7
11.07	27	.00	0	3.71	4	69.20	2	22.84	2
13.29	53	.00	0	4.65	7	69.06	3	24.11	2
7.32	6	.00	0	14.00	60	68.69	4	57.02	
13.79	57	.00	0	3.47	3	68.67	5	17.94	5
12.16	38	.00	0	6.68	12	67.91	6	27.07	1
9.17	13	.55	10	9.64	38	67.87	7	55.26	
5.92	1	.00	0	10.85	45	67.22	8	45.43	
13.15	50	.00	0	6.86	16	66.85	9	27.44	1
12.06	36	.61	11	6.84	15	65.73	10	21.85	3
10.03	18	1.11	14	10.38	42	65.15	11	17.29	5
9.95	17	.00	0	11.04	46	65.14	12	9.08	8
13.77	56	.00	0	6.37	10	64.89	13	26.18	1
12.35	39	.00	0	8.12	27	64.54	14	18.68	4
11.58	31	.00	0	8.92	35	62.97	15	36.99	
12.79	47	.00	0	11.08	47	62.84	16	22.41	2
14.01	60	.00	0	8.44	31	62.84	17	24.73	2
10.32	19	.26	5	11.46	49	62.82	18	24.84	2
16.34	75	.00	0	4.37	6	62.67	19	13.38	7
15.74	71	.00	0	6.76	13	62.22	20	20.62	3
12.03	35	.72	12	10.71	44	62.22	21	22.53	2
12.72	46	.00	0	10.17	40	62.13	22	14.84	6
7.93	9	15.13	21	4.67	8	61.91	23	42.13	
14.75	66	.00	0	7.33	20	61.49	24	18.85	4
13.98	59	.00	0	11.68	51	61.22	25	32.03	
13.50	54	.00	0	8.11	26	60.91	26	25.98	1
9.11	12	3.57	18	15.21	64	60.90	27	15.66	5
10.97	26	.00	0	13.00	57	60.56	28	28.49	1
13.03	49	.03	4	12.06	53	60.36	29	17.45	5
15.81	73	.00	0	7.36	22	59.72	30	14.03	6
13.27	52	.00	0	16.53	71	59.45	31	48.79	
15.77	72	.00	0	9.40	36	58.98	32	16.56	5
14.18	62	.00	0	13.02	58	58.49	33	18.69	4
15.35	69	.00	0	7.34	21	58.25	34	14.22	6
14.81	67	.00	0	12.40	54	58.11	35	24.12	2
5.92		.00		2.61		69.59		57.02	
7.93		.03		5.34		66.85		32.03	
9.95		.32		6.91		62.84		25.98	
10.97		.55		8.11		60.91		23.01	
11.97		1.11		8.88		58.25		21.85	
12.51		2.58		10.60		57.01		18.69	
15.81		15.13		27.32		19.18		4.44	

2. What are the key success factors that will enable Humana to maintain its rapid rate of growth?

3. Outline the control and human resource management systems used by Humana. Do they help or hinder Humana in achieving the key factors you identified in Question 2?

Appendix 9-A

Feasibility Study of Replacement Hospital

Memo To: Kelly Bolton
From: Jane Lloyd, Corporate
Subject: Feasibility Study: Replacement Hospital

Attached is the completed financial feasibility study for a replacement facility. Please review the assumptions closely to be sure they accurately reflect your assessment of the existing market. Based on these assumptions, this project generates the minimum return required for capital projects (15 %).

Pursuant to our telephone conversation, however, listed below are reservations raised about these assumptions:

Marketing Considerations

- The certificate of need application for the new facility indicates that the SMSA has had minimal population growth and a higher than average percentage of the population over age 65.

- Two nearby hospitals have spent considerable capital funds over the years to increase their market share. Both would represent formidable opponents in any market share battles.

- There currently is an out-migration of patients to nearby communities. Though I have not confirmed this, it could be that the patients going to the city require the sophisticated services of the teaching hospitals, and we are capturing some of the remaining patients at our other hospitals in this area. Therefore, the actual significance

of this out-migration may not be what it seems.

- The ability of the new hospital to increase patient days for the current 26,000 annual volume is conditional upon the ability of five recruited physicians to establish successful practices. Again, given the stable nature of this market, this will be difficult.

Patient Days

- The attached *pro-formas* assume patient days in the first year of approximately 32,000 due to impact of recruited physicians and new location of hospital, and assume subsequent years will grow at a compound annual growth rate of 2.4%. This compares to a less than 1% growth rate during the past decade.

- Based upon information presented in the above section and the existing volume of 26,000 patient days, the likelihood of this occurring could be seriously questioned.

Cost-Based Patient Days

- The *pro-forma* assumes that the cost-based patient days will be 57% during the first year of operation versus approximately 63.4% now, because when the hospital last operated at a 32,000 annual patient day volume, 57% of the patient days were cost-based.

- Therefore, the new hospital will not only result in a substantial increase in patient days (32,000 – 26,000 = 6,000), but 70% of the increase in patient days will be charge paying.

- Again, given the market, the likelihood of this occurring could be seriously questioned.

Based on this information, a hypothetical *pro-forma* was developed changing only the following assumptions:

- Patient days
  —First year operation: 26,000 (present number)
  —Subsequent years: Grow by $1/2$% per year (present SMSA GROWTH)

- Cost-based patient days
  —Current actual (63.4%) held constant for subsequent years

The *pro-forma* return for this project is reduced from 15% to 10%, well below the required return. Pre-tax margins are depressed to the extent that the present actual margin (8%) is not obtained until the seventh year of operation.

Prior to submitting the enclosed feasibility for approval, I believe we should take one last look at the assumptions to be sure they are reasonable.

Exhibit 9-A.1 Notes to Projected Income Statement (see Table 9-A.2)

1. Revenue. Total patient days have declined at the present hospital from 38,782 eight years ago. The primary factors contributing to this decline in patient days are:

- deteriorating condition of the existing facility
- existing facility location in downtown
- nearby hospital completing a $20 million renovation and expansion project last year
- another nearby hospital expanding bed capacity three times during the last eight years
- local unemployment rate of 19%
- failure to attract new physicians to the hospital (no physicians have been recruited in six years)

These factors have contributed to the hospital's loss of market share from 19.5% of total SMSA patient days eight years ago to 15.4% now. To resolve this problem, a new 128-bed facility is proposed that will address these problems in the following manner:

- New location to enhance geographic accessibility to the hospital.
- New physical plant to aid in attracting needed physicians to the area (in anticipation of the new hospital, five physicians have been recruited).

Therefore it has been assumed that the new facility will have approximately 5,300 more patient days in the first year of operation than experienced this year. This patient day volume (32,093) is approximately equal to the hospital's patient day volume four years ago. Patient days are projected to grow at a rate that will produce a patient day volume in 1994 that is approximately equal to the actual patient days for this facility eight years ago.

Revenue per patient day, including effects of intensity increases, is projected to grow by 11% per year. No additional rate increases are projected to cover the cost of the new facility.

2. Contractual Allowance. For the past four years, patient days have declined by 5,300 of which 70% (3,700 patient days) were charge-paying patient days. Therefore, it has been assumed that 70% of the increase in patient days will be charge-paying, resulting in total charge-paying patient days being approximately 43% of the total during the first year of operation. Subsequent years are projected assuming 43% of total patient days are charge-based.

3. Other Deductions from Revenue. Estimated to be .7% of revenue, which is consistent with the hospital's current experience.

4. Bad Debt. Estimated to be 3.5% of revenue. This is higher than the current experience (2.1%) because of planned increases in emergency room and outpatient business.

5. Other Revenue. Estimated to be 2.2% of revenue, which is consistent with the hospital's current experience.

6. Payroll and Other Operating Expenses. These are projected using current expense/patient day increased at a 10% annual inflation rate.

7. Management Fees. Management fee is projected at 5% of revenue.

continues

Exhibit 9-A.1 continued

8. Depreciation.

Building	20 Years	$13,999,000
Fixed major and minor moveable equipment	10 Years	3,752,860

Additionally, equipment originally costing $1.5 million (with accumulated depreciation of $600,000) will be transferred from the old facility to the new facility. The net book value ($900,000) was depreciated over 6 years, the average remaining useful life of the transferred equipment.

9. Interest. Fixed major and minor moveable equipment is 70% financed at 15%, payable in 84 equal monthly installments. The building is 70% financed at 15%. Interest payments only are made for the first 5 years, with the principal balance retired in 15 equal annual installments thereafter.

Additionally, the existing facility will have unretired Hospital Revenue Bonds when the new facility opens. It is assumed that the new facility will retire these bonds during the first year of operation. This additional expenditure has been added to the project cost of the new facility for the internal rate of return calculation.

10. Other Fixed Expenses. Estimated to be .8% of revenue, which is consistent with the hospital's current experience.

11. Income Taxes. Income taxes are calculated using an effective annual rate of 48.2%, less the applicable investment tax credit.

12. Return on Equity. Computed at 15% of past year's Stockholders' Equity less Inter-Company Receivables.

Table 9-A.1 Hospital Financial Profile, Fiscal Years 0, 1, and 2

Project: Replacement Facility
Summary Income Statement[a]

(dollars in thousands)

	FY 'X0 Actual	% of Revenue	FY 'X1 Actual	% of Revenue	FY 'X2 Actual	% of Revenue
Inpatient Revenue	$ 8,841	95%	$ 10,307	95%	10,094	95%
Outpatient Revenue	449	5	540	5	530	5
Gross Patient Revenue	9,290	100	10,847	100	10,624	100
Revenue Adjustment[b]	(1,265)	(14)	(1,725)	(16)	(1,810)	(17)
Net Revenue	8,025	86	9,122	84	8,814	83
Operating Expenses	5,853	63	6,659	61	6,549	62
Fixed Expenses	1,102	12	1,159	11	1,274	12
Total Expenses	6,955	75	7,818	72	7,823	74
Pretax Profit	$ 1,070	11%	$ 1,304	12%	991	9%
Financial/Operating Statistics						
Patient Days	32,093		31,834		26,801	
Occupancy	64%		63%		53%	
Beds	138		138		138	
Gross Revenue/P.D.	$ 289.46		$ 340.74		$ 396.42	
Pretax Profit/P.D.	$ 33.35		$ 40.96		$ 36.98	

[a]All financial data include operations of the medical office building.
[b]Includes contractual allowance, other deductions from revenue, bad debts, and other income.

Table 9-A.2 Projected Income Statement—Kelly Bolton's Estimates

(dollars in thousands)

	1	2	3	4	5
Gross Revenue	$ 17,661	$ 20,401	$ 23,549	$ 27,162	$ 31,305
Bad Debts	618	714	824	951	1,096
Contractuals	1,362	1,775	2,599	3,525	4,572
Net Revenue	15,682	17,912	20,126	22,686	25,637
Expenses					
Operating Exp.	10,522	12,047	13,783	15,755	17,997
Management Fee	870	1,005	1,160	1,338	1,542
Depreciation	1,197	1,197	1,197	1,197	1,197
Amortization	0	0	0	0	0
Interest	1,849	1,812	1,769	1,719	1,661
Total Expenses	14,438	16,061	17,909	20,009	22,397
Pretax Income	1,244	1,851	2,217	2,677	3,240
Income Tax	311	892	1,068	1,290	1,561
Net Income	$ 933	$ 959	$ 1,149	$ 1,387	$ 1,679
Operational Stat.					
Revenue/Day	$ 542	$ 602	$ 668	$ 741	$ 823
Oper. Exp./Day	$ 324	$ 356	$ 391	$ 431	$ 474
Mgt. Fee/Day	$ 27	$ 30	$ 33	$ 37	$ 41
Pretax Mgn. (%)	7.0	9.1	9.4	9.9	10.4
Bed Size	128	128	128	128	128
Patient Days	32,093	33,401	34,733	36,090	37,474
Occupancy	68.7	71.5	74.3	77.2	80.2
PROJECTED FUND FLOW					
Net Income	$ 933	$ 959	$ 1,149	$ 1,387	$ 1,679
Depreciation	1,197	1,197	1,197	1,197	1,197
Deferred Taxes	515	584	483	415	354
Amortization	0	0	0	0	0
Tax Effected Int.	958	938	916	891	861
AWC[b]	−1,425	−230	−265	−303	−352
Reinvest Assumpt.	0	0	0	0	0
Net Funds Flow	$ 2,178	$ 3,448	$ 3,480	$ 3,587	$ 3,739

Note: Initial investment = $19,252,000. IRR (including residual value of two times the last year's income) = 15%.

[a]CGR = compounded growth rate.
[b]AWC = average working capital.

continues

Table 9-A.2 continued

(dollars in thousands)

6	7	8	9	10	CGR[a]
$ 35,130	$ 39,425	$ 44,242	$ 49,649	$ 55,716	13.6
1,230	1,380	1,548	1,738	1,950	13.6
5,622	6,780	7,949	9,288	10,797	25.9
28,278	31,265	34,745	38,623	42,969	11.9
20,017	22,264	24,763	27,542	30,633	12.6
1,731	1,942	2,179	2,446	2,745	13.6
1,197	1,047	1,047	1,047	1,047	−1.5
0	0	0	0	0	.0
1,496	1,321	1,176	1,078	980	−6.8
24,441	26,574	29,165	32,113	35,405	10.5
3,838	4,692	5,580	6,510	7,564	22.2
1,850	2,261	2,689	3,138	3,646	31.5
$ 1,988	$ 2,431	$ 2,891	$ 3,372	$ 3,918	17.3
$ 914	$ 1,014	$ 1,126	$ 1,249	$ 1,387	11.0
$ 521	$ 573	$ 630	$ 694	$ 763	10.0
$ 46	$ 51	$ 56	$ 62	$ 69	11.0
10.9	11.9	12.6	13.1	13.6	7.6
128	128	128	128	128	.0
37,886	38,303	38,724	39,150	39,580	2.4
81.1	82.0	82.9	83.8	84.7	2.4

PROJECTED FUND FLOW

$ 1,988	$ 2,431	$ 2,890	$ 3,372	$ 3,918	
1,197	1,047	1,047	1,047	1,047	
−171	−146	−165	−165	−165	
0	0	0	0	0	
775	684	609	558	508	
−333	−376	−429	−480	−541	
0	0	0	0	0	
$ 3,456	$ 3,639	$ 3,952	$ 4,332	$ 4,767	

Table 9-A.3 Replacement (Alternative Case) Income Statement—Jane Lloyd's Corporate Estimates

(dollars in thousands)

	1	2	3	4	5
Gross Revenue	$ 14,578	$ 16,264	$ 18,143	$ 20,239	$ 22,577
Bad Debts	510	569	635	708	790
Contractual Allo.	850	1,090	1,719	2,398	3,137
Net Revenue	$ 13,218	$ 14,605	$ 15,789	$ 17,133	$ 18,650
Expenses					
Operating Exp.	$ 8,686	$ 9,603	$ 10,618	$ 11,740	$ 12,980
Management Fee	718	801	894	997	1,112
Depreciation	1,197	1,197	1,197	1,197	1,197
Amortization	0	0	0	0	0
Interest	1,849	1,812	1,769	1,719	1,661
Total Expenses	$ 12,450	$ 13,413	$ 14,478	$ 15,653	$ 16,950
Pretax Income	$ 769	$ 1,192	$ 1,311	$ 1,480	$ 1,699
Income Tax	$ 82	$ 575	$ 632	$ 713	$ 819
Net Income	$ 687	$ 617	$ 679	$ 767	$ 880
Operational Stat.					
Revenue/Day	$ 542	$ 602	$ 668	$ 741	$ 823
Oper. Exp./Day	$ 324	$ 356	$ 391	$ 431	$ 474
Mgt. Fee/Day	$ 27	$ 30	$ 33	$ 37	$ 41
Pretax Mgn. (%)	5.3	7.3	7.2	7.3	7.5
Bed Size	128	128	128	128	128
Patient Days	26,493	26,626	26,759	26,893	27,027
Occupancy	56.7	57.0	57.3	57.6	57.8

PROJECTED FUND FLOW

	1	2	3	4	5
Net Income	$ 687	$ 617	$ 679	$ 767	$ 880
Depreciation	1,197	1,197	1,197	1,197	1,197
Deferred Taxes	515	584	483	415	354
Amortization	0	0	0	0	0
AWC	−927	−104	−118	−128	−508
Principal Paymts.	−267	−309	−359	−417	−1,137
Reinvest Assumpt.	0	0	0	0	0
Net Cash Flow	$ 1,205	$ 1,985	$ 1,882	$ 1,834	$ 1,802

[a]CGR = compounded growth rate.

continues

Table 9-A.3 continued

(dollars in thousands)

	6	7	8	9	10	CGR[a]
	$ 25,186	$ 28,097	$ 31,344	$ 34,966	$ 39,006	11.6
	882	983	1,097	1,224	1,365	11.6
	4,007	4,948	5,849	6,877	8,028	28.3
	$ 20,297	$ 22,166	$ 24,398	$ 26,865	$ 29,613	9.4
	$ 14,352	$ 15,867	$ 17,543	$ 19,398	$ 21,446	10.6
	1,241	1,384	1,544	1,723	1,922	11.6
	1,197	1,047	1,047	1,047	1,047	−1.5
	0	0	0	0	0	0
	1,496	1,321	1,176	1,078	980	−6.8
	$ 18,286	$ 19,619	$ 21,310	$ 23,246	$ 25,395	8.2
	2,011	2,547	3,088	3,620	4,218	20.8
	$ 969	$ 1,228	$ 1,489	$ 1,745	$ 2,055	42.9
	$ 1,042	$ 1,319	$ 1,599	$ 1,875	$ 2,163	13.7
	$ 914	$ 1,014	$ 1,126	$ 1,249	$ 1,387	11.0
	$ 521	$ 573	$ 630	$ 694	$ 763	10.0
	$ 46	$ 51	$ 56	$ 62	$ 69	11.0
	8.0	9.1	9.9	10.4	10.8	8.3
	128	128	128	128	128	.0
	27,162	27,298	27,435	27,572	27,710	.5
	58.1	58.4	58.7	59.0	59.3	.5

PROJECTED FUND FLOW

	6	7	8	9	10	
	$ 1,042	$ 1,319	$ 1,599	$ 1,875	$ 2,185	
	1,197	1,047	1,047	1,047	1,047	
	−171	−146	−165	−165	−165	
	0	0	0	0	0	
	−157	−826	−301	−333	−375	
	−1,215	−653	−653	−653	−653	
	0	0	0	0	0	
	$ 696	$ 741	$ 1,599	$ 1,771	$ 2,039	

Case Study 10

Humana, Inc.

BACKGROUND

Humana, Inc., headquartered in Louisville, Kentucky, operated acute care hospitals and ambulatory care centers and sold health insurance products.

Historical Growth

David Jones and Wendell Cherry, Louisville law associates, founded Humana in 1961 to build, own, and operate a chain of proprietary nursing homes that became the largest firm in the nursing home industry. In 1969, their focus shifted from nursing homes to a business they perceived to be more profitable—hospitals. For the next three years, the company acquired a hospital a month by swapping stock with the doctors who owned them. In 1972, Humana divested itself of nursing homes and turned from acquisition to construction, building 27 hospitals in three years.

Humana's largest acquisition was the unfriendly 1978 takeover of American Medicorp (AMC), an investor-owned hospital chain roughly equal to it in size, for cash, preferred stock, and 11.7% subordinated debentures. Humana acquired 39 hospitals containing 7,838 beds at a price of approximately $57,000 per bed. The number of Humana hospitals declined from 96 in 1978 to 90 in 1980, and the number

Note: This case was prepared by Professor Regina E. Herzlinger and Richard B. Siegrist, Jr.

of Humana beds rose only slightly from 16,214 to 16,765, primarily by construction. Forty-one of Humana's 87 hospitals were built by the company. During 1981, 1982, and 1983 Humana added 15 hospitals and sold 15 hospitals that did not produce high profit margins or have the potential to be leaders in their markets.

Humana's next major acquisition attempt occurred in 1981 with a bid for Brookwood Health Services common stock of $77 million cash in total ($26.50 per share for stock then selling for $14 per share). It was ultimately defeated by American Medical International (AMI) for a tax-free swap of AMI common stock equivalent to $50 for each Brookwood share. The *New York Times* commented that

> Humana, Inc. has a reputation for dismissing the management of companies it takes over. "Humana takes no prisoners" has become a widespread comment among industry competitors and analysts. It is that reputation that apparently disturbed Brookwood [who] encouraged the entry of a white knight into the fray.

Humana reports that AMI subsequently dismissed Brookwood's management team.

Second Stage

By 1983, Humana viewed itself as an integrated health care delivery company, creating Group Health and Health Services Divisions to explore delivery system changes. One pilot project involved the creation of 68 primary care centers—free-standing facilities for basic community medical needs, excluding surgery, called Humana MedFirst.

They were marketed through soft-sell ads, complemented with discounts. Their primary customer was viewed as a price-sensitive woman aged 25–49, whose membership in a two-career or one-head-of-household family constrained her receipt of health care services to evenings or weekends. They were staffed with four to five doctors and open 12–14 hours per day, seven days a week.

Humana also developed prepaid health plans, administered under its Group Health Division, a separate profit center. Begun in 1984, these programs were sold for two- to five-year terms and charged higher deductibles and/or copayments for health services delivered in non-Humana hospitals or outpatient facilities. Initially their contracts were guaranteed to rise no faster than the Consumer Price Index for up to four years. An extensive utilization review system backed them up. The Group Health Division bought services at a discount from other Humana divisions. (See Tables 10.1 to 10.3 for operating statistics on these new ventures.) Of the 201 hospitals included in the health plans, 86 were Humana's. In Chicago, for example, Humana had only one hospital but signed agreements with 14 others to treat health plan patients. (See Table 10.4 for locations.)

Most of the insurance products were offered to employers through insurance brokers or internal employee benefits personnel. Extensive TV advertising introduced the product to employees. The first wave of ads were of the soft-sell, general image variety. The next wave were humorous; for example, one showed a broker spewing forth an incomprehensible list of initials representing different products, such as a PPO, IPA, HMO, etc., to a dazed prospective corporate buyer. Humana employed 40 sales representatives for this and 50 people in telemarketing for another product, designed to supplement Medicare.

Financial Performance

Humana's high rates of growth were reflected in its stock prices. A share selling for $8 in 1968 was worth $900 after stock splits in 1985. Institutional ownership of Humana stock increased significantly, expanding from 9% in 1976 to over 40% by 1985. Humana's management and directors controlled 14% of the stock at that time.

Humana financed its growth from funds generated from operations, common and preferred stock, bank loans, subordinated debentures, hospital and equipment leases, and traditional mortgage notes.

Sources of Hospital Revenues

Humana derived revenues primarily from patient charges in its hospitals. Humana's patient revenue depended on the occupancy level, payer mix, type of service provided, average length of stay, and the pricing policy of its competitor hospitals (see Tables 10.5 to 10.7). Table 10.8 compares Humana's performance in these areas with its largest competitors.

A new source of hospital revenues was developed in 1984 with Humana's agreement to provide all health care for the indigent residents of Jefferson County in Kentucky for a fixed payment from the government, whose price would rise at either the rate of growth of tax receipts or the Consumer Price Index, whichever was lower.

Location of Hospitals

Seventy-six percent of Humana's domestic hospital beds were concentrated in the South, an area with little state regulation of health care; 18% in the West/Midwest; and none in the Northeast. Florida (22% of Humana's beds), Texas (16%), and Kentucky (11%) were the states with the largest Humana presence. Many hospitals were located in areas in which other hospitals were present. In 1980, 16 of Humana's 90 hospitals monopolized the local market; 2 more were first among competitors. In 1985, Humana signed affiliations for its insurance products with many non-Humana hospitals.

Table 10.1 Humana, Inc.: Profitability of Group Health Division (GHD)

(dollars in thousands, except for per-member and per-day data)

	1984	1985E[a]	1986E[a]
Profits			
If Humana Hospitals are costed at their charges to GHD:			
Revenues	$ 7,833	$ 106,870	$ 362,897
Expenses (–)	–13,204	–120,448	–384,199
Profit (Loss)	$ (5,371)	$ (13,578)	$ (21,302)
Margin (%)	–68.6 %	–12.7 %	–5.9 %
If Humana Hospitals are costed at zero:			
Revenues	$ 7,833	$ 106,870	$ 362,897
Expenses (–)	–9,410	–83,732	–281,962
Profit (Loss)	$ (1,577)	$ 23,138	$ 80,935
Margin (%)	–20.1 %	21.7 %	22.3 %
Assumptions			
Membership (ending)	141,000	300,000	800,000
Membership (average)	13,009	170,050	550,000
Premium/Member	$ 600	$ 624	$ 657
Hospital Days/1,000 Members	600	550	500
% of Hospital Days in Humana Hospitals	90 %	67.5 %	58.8 %
Humana Hospital's Charges to GHD/Day[b]	$ 540	$ 580	$ 632
Humana Hospital's Average Cost/Day	$ 472	$ 544	$ 560
Other Hospitals' Costs	$ 358	$ 15,027	$ 60,890
Hospital Days in Non-Humana Hospitals	780	30,477	113,300
Charge/Day, Non-Humana Hospitals	$ 459	$ 493	$ 537
Total Hospital Costs			
At Charges to GHD	$ 4,152	$ 51,743	$ 163,127
At Hospitals' Costs	$ 3,662	$ 49,469	$ 151,419
Physician Costs/Member	$ 213	$ 217	$ 221
Interest on Income	$ 33	$ 443	$ 1,506
SG & A Variable Costs/Member	$ 231	$ 115	$ 120
SG & A Fixed Costs	$ 2,591	$ 2,850	$ 3,135

[a]E = estimate.
[b]Reflecting a 20% discount.

Sources: Humana, Inc., and Salomon Brothers, Inc., estimates.

Humana's international operations were limited to three hospitals, two in England and one in Switzerland. The 105-bed Wellington Hospital in London, purchased in 1976, was one of England's few private hospitals and attracted an elite patient clientele. The 240-bed Hopital de la Tour in Geneva was purchased in fiscal 1980. During fiscal 1983, Humana sold a Spanish hospital and built the 120-bed Wellington II Hospital in London.

Differentiation

To establish a brand name, "Humana" was used in the name of each hospital. Centers of

Table 10.2 Humana, Inc.: Health Services Division, 1982–86E[a]

(dollars in thousands, except for per-visit and per-day data)

	1982	1983	1984	1985E[a]	1986E
Offices (ending)	45	67	68	180	266
Offices (average)	23	56	68	124	223
Visits per Day	22.6	29.5	36.5	33.8	34.5
Visits, Total	190,000	603,000	900,000	1,531,981	2,810,684
Division Revenues					
Office Revenues	$ 6,650	$ 22,613	$ 36,000	$ 64,343	$123,670
• Total Charges per Visit	35.00	37.50	40.00	42.00	44.00
Physician Payment	3,080	9,043	12,229	25,277	48,414
Gross Division Revenues	3,570	13,570	23,771	39,066	75,256
• Bad Debts	70	270	450	766	1,476
Net Division Revenues	$ 3,500	$ 13,300	$ 23,321	$ 38,300	$ 73,780
Per Visit	$ 18.42	$ 22.39	$ 25.00	$ 25.00	$ 26.25
Expenses					
Depreciation	$ 871	$ 2,112	$ 2,420	$ 4,451	$ 7,996
Total Interest	690	1,680	2,025	3,720	6,690
Total Capital Costs	1,561	3,792	4,445	8,171	14,686
Operating Expenses	9,839	22,309	25,055	41,866	77,325
• Per Office Day	1,172	1,092	1,017	925	950
Total Expenses	$ 11,400	$ 26,101	$ 29,500	$ 50,037	$ 92,012
Total Profits	$ (7,900)	$(12,801)	$ (6,179)	$(11,737)	$(18,232)
Total Cash Flow	$ (7,029)	$(10,688)	$ (3,759)	$ (7,286)	$(10,236)
Office Stage (Number of Offices)					
First Year	45	22	13	100	86
Second Year	0	45	22	13	100
Mature	0	0	45	67	80

[a]E = estimate.

Sources: Humana, Inc., and Salomon Brothers, Inc., estimates.

Excellence were designated in hospitals providing outstanding specialty services. Among these was a burn unit in Humana Hospital–Augusta, which conducted clinical research and provided outstanding care for burn victims. Twenty-two other Centers of Excellence were designated by 1987.

Perhaps the most ambitious differentiation effort was Humana's artificial heart program, which supported research at Humana's Heart Institute International and uninsured hospital costs for up to 100 artificial heart implants. The institute was studying alternatives for heart replacement and developing an international program for treatment of cardiovascular disease. In 1985, it established a relationship with the only surgeon authorized by the government to perform implantation of artificial hearts in humans. By 1985, nine Humana hospitals conducted open-heart surgery programs, including one in England and Switzerland.

Table 10.3 Humana, Inc.: Actual Results, Group Health and Health Services Division, 1985 and 1986

	1986	1985
GROUP HEALTH DIVISION		
Revenues	$ 308.0	$ 89.1
Income	$ (66.8)	$ (9.2)
Number of Markets	51	50
Enrollment, Ending	616,500	194,500
Enrollment, Average	520,000	150,000
Medical Claims/Revenues	94.9%	80.9%
Administration and Marketing/Revenue	22.2%	13.0%
Humana Hospital		
Patient Days	138,700	44,500
Admissions	27,700	9,300
Length of Stay (days)	5.0	4.8
Patient Days/1,000 Enrollees	553	525
Humana Hospital Share of Patient Days	48.3%	56.6%
HEALTH SERVICES DIVISION		
Revenues	$ 64.8	$ 38.0
Income	$ (23.3)	$ (14.7)
Number of Units	153	143
Visits/Center/Day	29	25

MANAGEMENT AND CORPORATE STRATEGY

In 1986, David Jones noted:

It seems logical to predict that the growth of high-quality, integrated systems such as Humana Care Plus will lead to many hospitals joining similar systems, which will compete with each other in improving access, quality, and affordability for value-conscious employers and employees, thus providing "the emerging solution." Within five years it's going to be as easy to get to a doctor as it will be to buy a bag of groceries.

With finite resources being called on to meet myriad, diverse priorities, consumers are telling us very clearly that they will turn to those providers who have developed a high level of quality at affordable prices, no matter how confused the external environment. Our role is to maintain the productivity and profitability that will enable us to offer consumers what they desire and need. In doing so, we must integrate the financial system with the delivery system in a way that is sensitive for the participants. It's not an easy task, but no ground-breaking task is ever easy. And those who do tomorrow what they did yesterday are likely to be caught short.

Management

Humana had the same top management in 1987 as it did in 1961—David Jones, chairman, and Wendell Cherry, president. Both were viewed as aggressive and innovative managers who exerted tight control over Humana's operation. They were credited with turning Humana into a billion-dollar company through such enterprising actions as shifting from nursing homes to hospitals, acquiring and rapidly assimilating American Medicorp, and astute financing.

Operating Strategy

Humana was a tightly managed company characterized by centralized decision making and stringent financial and operating controls. It was functionally organized: The hospital operations function was subdivided into geographic regions headed by vice presidents. The home office in Louisville provided each hospital with a variety of centralized management services, including financing, recruiting, personnel development, accounting, data processing, legal advice, consulting, and purchasing. The latter program alone was estimated to save $15 million annually and to provide consistent quality and delivery. Marketing was done both centrally and in local offices.

Humana considered itself a pioneer in formulating measurable quality goals for patient care. It employed a process management staff to determine what was important in each hospital area and to develop appropriate operating goals against which to measure actual performance. Jones stressed his commitment to this process:

We insist on consistent measurable quality in the things that are critical in serving customers. The most important element…is for each department in every hospital to have an absolutely clear sense of its purpose.

Humana also enhanced the position of its nurses by naming the company's (and the industry's) first vice president for nursing, improving salaries, increasing the responsibility of nurses, and creating managerial career paths for those who chose to follow them.

Pricing and Financial Strategy

Hospital prices were set at headquarters. The company's policy was to price services to cover all "costs" and provide a reasonable return on "equity," with both measured on a replacement cost basis. Jones commented,

A careful adherence to that policy is one reason why we have the highest rate of return in the industry. We think it's ethical, moral, sensible, and effective.

Pricing of the insurance and MedFirst products reflected Humana's belief that the market was very cost sensitive. Humana hospitals were transfer-priced to the insurance division at a discount. Humana intended to have the best profit margin in the industry and accordingly tried to maintain the lowest ratio of operating expense to gross revenue of any hospital company. Other financial goals included minimizing the dilution of its common stock and paying out at least 25% of earnings in dividends.

Marketing Strategy

Humana's marketing focused on attracting physicians to its hospitals, especially those who handled a preponderance of privately insured patients. One method was to offer them space at a large discount in office buildings built by the company next to its hospitals and operated at a loss by Humana. In addition, Humana actively recruited physicians from Canada and

Table 10.4 Humana, Inc.: Geographic Analysis

Market	SMSA	SMSA Data		1983 Regional Hospital Statistics	
		1980 Population (thousands)	Growth 1970–80 (%)	Number of Hospitals	Number of Beds
ALABAMA	Montgomery[a]	273	21	7	1,414
	Florence[a]	135	15	4	1,047
	Huntsville[a]	197	6	3	961
	Misc. Counties[a]	NA	NA	NA	NA
ALASKA	Anchorage	174	38	7	579
ARIZONA	Phoenix[a]	1,509	55	22	5,567
CALIFORNIA	Anaheim[a]	11,498	15	181	36,932
COLORADO	Denver[a]	1,818	31	19	5,989
FLORIDA	Daytona Beach[a]	259	53	7	1,350
	Miami[a]	2,844	40	32	9,400
	Orlando[a]	700	54	11	3,268
	Tampa[a]	1,817	46	35	8,032
	W. Palm Beach[a]	577	85	12	2,617
	Melbourne[a]	273	19	4	960
	Ft. Walton[a]	110	25	NA	NA
	Plantation	NA	NA	NA	NA
GEORGIA	Augusta[a]	346	19	4	1,477
	Atlanta	2,188	27	45	9,690
ILLINOIS	Chicago[a]	7,937	2	89	31,587
	Springfield[a]	188	10	5	1,910
INDIANA	Indianapolis	1,187	5	17	5,655
KANSAS	Kansas City	519	8	10	2,427
	Dodge City	18	NA	NA	NA
KENTUCKY	Louisville[a]	957	6	12	4,199
	Lexington[a]	318	19	9	1,788
	Misc. Counties	NA	NA	NA	NA
LOUISIANA	Shreveport	333	13	9	2,292
	New Orleans	1,256	14	27	6,815
	Lake Charles				
	Misc. Counties	NA	NA	NA	NA

continues

Table 10.4 continued

1983 Regional Hospital Statistics			1984 Humana Data		Humana Hospital % of Region	
Admissions (1,000 pop.)	Inpatient Days (1,000 pop.)	Length of Stay (Days)	Number of Hospitals	Number of Beds	Number of Hospitals (%)	Number of Beds (%)
192	1,302	6.8	1	150	14	11
228	1,376	8.7	1	155	25	15
200	1,371	6.8	1	315	33	33
NA	NA	NA	3	363		
140	871	6.2	1	199	14	34
144	995	6.9	2	434	9	8
114	762	6.4	4	802	2	2
142	966	6.8	2	450	11	8
166	1,311	7.9	1	214	14	18
119	971	8.1	4	1,133	13	12
192	1,279	8.9	3	634	27	19
172	1,380	8.0	5	1,132	14	14
176	1,266	7.2	1	182	8	6
155	1,023	8.6	1	133	25	14
NA	NA	NA	1	238		
NA	NA	NA	1	204		
151	1,212	8.0	1	374	25	25
180	1,147	6.4	3	326	7	3
127	1,083	8.4	1	356	1	1
336	1,690	8.0	1	200	20	11
173	1,435	8.3	1	150	6	3
146	1,125	7.7	1	400	10	18
NA	NA	NA	1	110		
183	1,242	7.6	4	1,418	33	34
226	1,577	7.0	1	170	11	10
NA	NA	NA	2	265		
262	1,659	6.3	2	260	22	11
184	1,396	7.6	1	150	4	2
			1	80		
NA	NA	NA	4	343		

continues

Table 10.4 continued

Market	SMSA	SMSA Data		1983 Regional Hospital Statistics	
		1980 Population (thousands)	Growth 1970–80 (%)	Number of Hospitals	Number of Beds
MISSISSIPPI	Natchez	22	NA	NA	NA
NEVADA	Las Vegas[a]	483	70	8	1,812
NORTH CAROLINA	Charlotte	971	16	12	4,045
	Greensboro	852	15	14	3,613
TENNESSE	Chattanooga[a]	427	15	11	1,990
	Knoxville[a]	566	19	12	3,182
	Nashville[a]	851	22	22	5,649
	Memphis[a]	913	10	15	5,734
TEXAS	San Antonio[a]	1,072	21	17	4,728
	Dallas[a]	2,831	25	52	8,837
	Houston	3,101	43	55	14,344
	Abilene	111	13	2	570
	Corpus Christi[a]	326	15	9	1,717
UTAH	Ogden/Salt Lake City	910	33	13	2,951
VIRGINIA	Richmond[a]	761	13	15	4,401
	Richlands[a]	52	27	NA	NA
	Norfolk[a]	1,160	10	18	4,410
WASHINGTON	Tacoma	486	18	8	1,367
WEST VIRGINIA	Lewisberg	54	17	NA	NA
	Bluefield	18	NA	NA	NA
TOTAL DOMESTIC		54,615	21	884	220,384
TOTAL INTERNATIONAL			NA	NA	NA
TOTAL HUMANA					

continues

Table 10.4 continued

1983 Regional Hospital Statistics			1984 Humana Data		Humana Hospital % of Region	
Admissions (1,000 pop.)	Inpatient Days (1,000 pop.)	Length of Stay (Days)	Number of Hospitals	Number of Beds	Number of Hospitals (%)	Number of Beds (%)
NA	NA	NA	1	101		
150	955	6.4	1	670	13	37
145	1,170	8.1	1	88	8	2
181	1,242	7.7	1	130	7	4
195	1,171	6.0	1	128	9	8
242	1,634	6.8	1	135	8	4
226	1,869	8.3	1	159	5	3
207	1,746	8.4	1	50	7	1
171	1,172	6.9	3	839	18	18
118	796	6.7	1	545	2	6
170	1,228	7.2	5	1,173	9	8
223	1,455	6.5	1	160	50	28
207	1,435	6.9	1	263	11	15
143	821	5.7	1	110	8	4
192	1,613	8.4	1	200	7	5
NA	NA	NA	1	200		
134	1,003	7.5	1	256	6	6
124	708	5.7	1	155	13	11
NA	NA	NA	1	122	NA	NA
NA	NA	NA	1	79	NA	NA
146	1,064	7.2	82	16,999	9	8
NA	NA	NA	4	707		
			87	17,706		

[a]Location of Humana Care Plus participating hospitals as of January 30, 1987.

Source: Dean Witter, *Humana, Inc.*, May 31, 1985, p. 4.

the United States to relocate near its rural hospitals.

Humana's extensive patient marketing efforts included the expressed goal that anyone seeking treatment in a Humana hospital emergency would be seen by a medical professional within 60 seconds. It also created InstaCare cards that enabled a patient to receive immediate emergency care without filling out forms. It also offered programs designed for women. Fifty-three of its hospitals offered a flat-rate for a 24-, 36-, or 48-hour obstetrical visit so that the expectant mother could know the hospital costs in advance of the delivery date. Free prenatal and postnatal educational programs offered seminars, newsletters, and merchant discounts. Seventeen hospitals offered mammogram screening, half for as much as 50% less than the regular market price.

The screening included education in self-examination, with female technicians instructing the patients. Seven hospitals offered osteoporosis screening, four had fertility programs with *in vitro* labs, and two offered eating disorder programs. One hospital offered a day care program for the sick children of working parents.

POINTS TO PONDER

1. What opportunities is the company fulfilling?
2. What skills are necessary for fulfilling these opportunities?
3. How well is Humana implementing these skills?

Table 10.5 Humana, Inc.: Income Statements, 1976–1985, Selected Years

(millions, except per share)

	1985	1984	1983	1982	1981	1980	1976
Gross Revenues	$ 2,875.0	$ 2,606.4	$ 2,298.6	$ 1,923.5	$ 1,703.6	$ 1,392.4	$ 300.3
Contractual Adjustments and Doubtful Accts.	687.0	645.2	533.5	407.2	360.7	275.6	39.7
Net Revenues	$ 2,188.0	$ 1,961.2	$ 1,765.1	$ 1,516.3	$ 1,342.9	$ 1,116.8	$ 260.6
Operating Expenses Including G & A	1,546.0	1,420.4	1,310.4	1,154.4	1,036.9	842.7	212.0
Depreciation and Amortization	147.0	120.6	94.7	78.2	69.2	59.2	17.4
Interest Expense	119.0	87.9	71.2	55.9	59.9	85.4	16.9
Other (Income) Expense						9.6	
	1,812.0	1,628.9	1,476.3	1,288.5	1,166.0	996.9	246.3
Income before Taxes	376.0	332.3	288.8	227.8	176.9	119.9	14.3
Income Taxes	160.04	139.0	128.1	100.7	83.7	55.3	5.5
Minority Interest							
Net Income	$ 216.0	$ 193.3	$ 160.7	$ 127.1	$ 93.2	$ 64.6	$ 8.8
EPS	$ 2.19	$ 1.94	$ 1.64	$ 1.34	$ .97	$ .64	$ .12
Stock Price	$ 31.00	$ 31.13	$ 27.70	$ 19.88	$ 13.75	$ 11.13	$ .91

Table 10.6 Humana, Inc.: Balance Sheets, 1975–1985, Selected Years

(millions)

	1985	1984	1983
Assets			
Cash	$ 82.3	$ 261.0	$ 250.0
Accounts Receivable	365.9	257.7	200.5
Inventories	50.9	45.3	41.5
Other Current Assets	39.5	41.2	29.6
Total Current Assets	538.6	605.4	521.6
Land	181.2	165.4	147.1
Buildings	1,449.6	1,228.7	1,024.1
Equipment	791.7	681.8	540.9
Construction in Progress	91.2	160.1	161.3
	2,513.7	2,236.0	1,873.4
Accumulated Depreciation	562.3	452.6	357.0
	1,951.4	1,783.3	1,516.4
Other Assets	230.0	189.2	179.8
Goodwill	——	——	——
Total Assets	$ 2,720.0	$ 2,577.9	$ 2,217.8
Liabilities and Stockholders' Equity			
Short-Term Debt	$ ——	$ ——	$ ——
Accounts Payable	85.3	140.7	83.4
Accrued Expenses	173.0	97.9	136.5
Income Taxes	49.0	60.0	34.9
LTD—Current	57.8	53.7	50.7
Total Current Liabilities	365.1	352.3	304.5
Long-Term Debt	1,205.6	1,286.5	1,067.7
Deferred Credits and Other Credits	246.5	195.9	176.4
Total Liabilities	1,817.2	1,482.4	1,244.1
Preferred Stock	——	——	60.6
Common Stock	16.2	16.1	13.3
Paid-in Capital	223.4	219.2	212.2
Retained Earnings	679.3	527.2	395.9
Translation Adjustment	(16.1)	(19.3)	(12.8)
Total Stockholders' Equity	902.8	743.2	669.2
Total Liabilities and Stockholders' Equity	$ 2,720.0	$ 2,577.9	$ 2,217.8

continues

Table 10.6 continued

<table>
<thead>
<tr><th colspan="5">(millions)</th></tr>
<tr><th>1982</th><th>1981</th><th>1980</th><th>1976</th><th>1975</th></tr>
</thead>
<tbody>
<tr><td>$ 209.5</td><td>$ 197.4</td><td>$ 116.3</td><td>$ 5.2</td><td>$ 6.1</td></tr>
<tr><td>167.8</td><td>149.7</td><td>128.4</td><td>45.5</td><td>33.1</td></tr>
<tr><td>34.4</td><td>30.0</td><td>28.5</td><td>7.8</td><td>7.8</td></tr>
<tr><td>14.8</td><td>11.4</td><td>9.8</td><td>3.2</td><td>3.5</td></tr>
<tr><td>426.5</td><td>388.5</td><td>283.0</td><td>61.7</td><td>50.5</td></tr>
<tr><td>128.1</td><td>95.9</td><td>82.7</td><td>18.0</td><td>16.8</td></tr>
<tr><td>827.3</td><td>702.4</td><td>675.7</td><td>183.5</td><td>147.3</td></tr>
<tr><td>405.7</td><td>329.1</td><td>296.7</td><td>68.1</td><td>55.8</td></tr>
<tr><td>92.7</td><td>75.2</td><td>37.4</td><td>16.5</td><td>34.6</td></tr>
<tr><td>1,453.8</td><td>1,202.6</td><td>1,092.5</td><td>286.1</td><td>254.5</td></tr>
<tr><td>280.1</td><td>223.8</td><td>173.0</td><td>39.9</td><td>26.7</td></tr>
<tr><td>1,173.7</td><td>978.8</td><td>919.5</td><td>246.2</td><td>227.8</td></tr>
<tr><td>145.0</td><td>134.9</td><td>66.1</td><td>26.3</td><td>26.4</td></tr>
<tr><td>——</td><td>——</td><td>58.0</td><td>6.0</td><td>6.5</td></tr>
<tr><td>$ 1,745.2</td><td>$ 1,502.2</td><td>$ 1,326.6</td><td>$ 340.2</td><td>$ 311.2</td></tr>
<tr><td>$ ——</td><td>$ ——</td><td>$ ——</td><td>$ 9.0</td><td>$ 7.0</td></tr>
<tr><td>67.5</td><td>53.0</td><td>46.1</td><td>12.3</td><td>9.3</td></tr>
<tr><td>105.0</td><td>78.4</td><td>63.0</td><td>11.4</td><td>9.1</td></tr>
<tr><td>61.4</td><td>100.2</td><td>60.3</td><td>3.7</td><td>2.3</td></tr>
<tr><td>39.9</td><td>43.1</td><td>34.8</td><td>7.4</td><td>8.6</td></tr>
<tr><td>273.8</td><td>274.7</td><td>204.2</td><td>43.8</td><td>36.3</td></tr>
<tr><td>864.4</td><td>733.1</td><td>722.4</td><td>205.7</td><td>195.0</td></tr>
<tr><td>161.2</td><td>133.2</td><td>117.8</td><td>17.2</td><td>13.7</td></tr>
<tr><td>1,025.6</td><td>866.3</td><td>840.2</td><td>222.9</td><td>208.7</td></tr>
<tr><td>60.5</td><td>63.9</td><td>65.9</td><td>——</td><td>——</td></tr>
<tr><td>12.6</td><td>9.3</td><td>6.0</td><td>2.5</td><td>2.5</td></tr>
<tr><td>96.0</td><td>91.2</td><td>79.1</td><td>33.7</td><td>33.8</td></tr>
<tr><td>286.1</td><td>196.8</td><td>131.2</td><td>37.3</td><td>29.9</td></tr>
<tr><td>(9.4)</td><td>——</td><td>——</td><td>——</td><td>——</td></tr>
<tr><td>445.8</td><td>361.2</td><td>282.2</td><td>73.5</td><td>66.2</td></tr>
<tr><td>$ 1,745.2</td><td>$ 1,502.2</td><td>$ 1,326.6</td><td>$ 340.2</td><td>$ 311.2</td></tr>
</tbody>
</table>

Table 10.7 Humana, Inc.: Hospital Data, 1976–1985

	1985	1983	1982
Hospitals Operated, U.S.	83	87	86
Beds	16,999	16,783	15,821
Hospitals Operated, International	4	3	3
Beds	854	465	465
Total Hospitals	87	90	89
Total Beds	17,853	17,248	16,286
Admissions	525,400	582,200	578,700
Occupancy	48%	58%	60%
% of Gross Revenue			
Medicare	41%	43%	42%
Medicaid	4	4	3
Other Cost Based	2	2	3
Charge Based	53	51	52
	100%	100%	100%
% of Gross Revenue			
Routine		30	31
Ancillary		70	69
	NA	100%	100%
Patients Days (thousands)	3,069.1	3,579.0	3,549.0

continues

Table 10.8 Performance Comparison of Disguised Hospital Chains and Humana, 1983 and 1985

Hospital Chain	Inpatient Revenue per Patient Day		Patient Days (in thousands)		% Inpatient Revenues	
	1983	1985	1983	1985	1983	1985
1. X	$ 640	$ 837	2,784	2,351	80%	74%
2. Y	514	667	6,205	5,502	81	75
3. HUM	577	779	3,579	3,069	90	85
4. Z	672	831	1,461	1,421	46	40

Table 10.7 continued

1981	1980	1978	1977	1976
87	88	95	59	59
16,086	16,421	16,110	8,403	8,266
2	2	1	1	1
345	344	104	104	104
89	90	96	60	60
16,431	16,765	16,214	8,563	8,370
570,200	NA	NA	NA	NA
61%	59%	57%	54%	55%
40%	39%	38%	34%	32%
5	5	5	5	5
5	5	6	6	6
50	51	51	55	57
100%	100%	100%	100%	100%
33	34	36	38	40%
67	66	64	62	60
100%	100%	100%	100%	100%
3,723.0	3,611.3	2,724.3	1,693.6	1,658.1

Case Study 11

Hyatt Hill Health Center

"These numbers do not mean a thing," said Hank Clemens. "They do not reflect what my department does and needlessly make us look terrible."

Mr. Clemens was talking to Dr. Steven Kyler, the executive director of the Hyatt Hill Health Center (HHHC), at their weekly executive committee meeting. The subject of Hank's ire was the cost-accounting system recently installed in the health center.

BACKGROUND

The Hyatt Hill Health Center was established in Boston. It was sponsored by the Massachusetts General Hospital, widely viewed as among the leading hospitals in the United States for the quality of its medical care, research, and teaching. HHHC was established on an experimental basis to provide community-centered health care to the residents of the community of Bedford, in which it was located. Bedford was a lower-income area with a high incidence of medical, dental, and psychiatric problems; for example, over 40% of Bedford's adults needed dental plates and many were alcoholics and drug abusers.

Because few physicians lived in Bedford, its residents used the emergency room of the Massachusetts General Hospital as a substitute for a

Note: This case was prepared by Professor Regina E. Herzlinger. The organization, location, date, and data of the health center are disguised.

family physician. As a result, they received sporadic therapeutic medical care and little preventive care, such as yearly check-ups.

The purpose of the health center was to provide adequate preventive and therapeutic care and become an accepted force in the Bedford community. This was not an easy mission. Bedford was geographically isolated from the rest of Boston and its residents, largely composed of one closely knit ethnic group, were traditionally suspicious of any "outsiders." Despite a heavy incidence of emotional problems, they were particularly resistant to the services of social workers and psychiatrists. The personnel in these departments spent a great deal of time in the community trying to break down this resistance.

ORGANIZATION AND PERSONNEL

The health center was organized into the following departments: pediatrics, internal medicine, nursing, mental health, social service, nutrition, dental, and specialists. Most of its high professional caliber practitioners held joint appointments at the hospital and incurred substantial opportunity costs by working at HHHC. They were dedicated to demonstrating that a community health center can indeed provide effective therapeutic and preventive medical care and, thus, have a significant impact on its target area.

The HHHC also served as a training ground for members of the hospital or Boston Department of Health staff who were interested in community medicine. Training activities were conducted in all of HHHC's departments but were particularly concentrated in the mental health, social service, and nutrition departments.

FUNDING

The health center's yearly operating budget of nearly $1 million originated from a variety of sources, including the hospital. It was hoped that the HHHC would shortly become financially self-sufficient and not require hospital funds for its operation. At the present time, the federal government accounts for the largest portion of its funds. In return, the health center provides quarterly reports of its patients' characteristics, the kinds of services they receive, and the impact of the center on the community. To gather these data, all practitioners complete the encounter form displayed in Exhibit 11.1 immediately after every patient visit. The encounter form data are then entered into the hospital's system.

THE CONTROL SYSTEM

Background

Late in 1989, a health care cost researcher visited the health center. At the time, Dr. Steven Kyler, the health center's executive director, was increasingly concerned about its achieving financial self-sufficiency. Although the center had a good financial accounting system for billing and external reporting, it lacked managerial accounting data. Because he did not know the total costs of his departments, different kinds of cases, and practitioners, Dr. Kyler could not assess the feasibility of his center's accomplishing its financial self-sufficiency goals. He thus agreed to the installation of a management control system to provide him with the data he wanted.

Mechanics

The management control system was based on the existing data system and provided the following reports for each of the HHHC's departments:

1. Average monthly cost, per encounter and per hour spent in seeing patients, for each practitioner.
2. Average monthly cost of the different kinds of encounters entered on the encounter form.
3. A comparison of actual costs to a standard cost, based on the average costs, in the past, of that department

A sample of the data for the social service department in a typical month is contained in Table 11.1. The formulas used to compute the costs are in Exhibit 11.2 and the total cost data are in Table 11.2.

These data were distributed to Dr. Kyler and his department chiefs about two weeks after the end of each month. They enabled the HHHC's management to compare the efficiency of different practitioners in performing the same kind of work and the relative efficiency and utilization of capacity of different departments.

The key data input for the control system was the time entered by the practitioner on the encounter form for each service performed. To verify the data, a time sheet was completed by all the practitioners, on a daily basis, for a full month, once every three months. For each practitioner, the time entered in the direct patient care category on the time sheet should have equalled the time entered on all the encounter forms. Continual comparisons reconciled the total time derived from the two forms. The time sheet data for the social service department are in Table 11.3.

THE PROBLEM

Although HHHC's practioners performed a number of activities other than providing direct patient care, only the direct patient care activities generated revenue. For HHHC to be self-sufficient, revenues created by the practitioners' medical care activities must absorb the costs of all their other activities. Thus, the financial data produced by the control system included the costs of all the time spent by the

Exhibit 11.1 Hyatt Hill Health Center Mental Health Visit Form

2 ▷	Professional no.:	1 ▷	Date:
	H ☐ ☐		☐☐ ☐☐ ☐☐
			mo. day year

3 ▷ Visit:
- 1 ○ walk-in
- 2 ○ visit kept
- 3 ○ visit broken

Date of Birth
_____

Visit location:
- 1 ○ HHHC
- 2 ○ Home
- 3 ○ School
- 4 ○ Other

➡ Unit No. ☐☐☐ ☐☐ ☐☐

8 ▷ Family no.: A ☐ ☐☐☐☐

Name:

---

10 ▷ Duration of visit:
☐☐ minutes

Modification of charges: ☐ half charge   ☐ no charge

---

12 ▷ Assessment status:
- 1 ○ not started
- 2 ○ in process
- 3 ○ complete this visit
- 4 ○ complete prior visit

Current status of treatment planned at assessment:
- 1 ○ not needed
- 2 ○ short-term, in process
- 3 ○ short-term, completed
- 4 ○ long-term

13 ▷ Activity during this contact consisted of: (check one)

60 ☐ patient-interview	63 ☐ group therapy
61 ☐ others in family-interview	64 ☐ psych. testing
62 ☐ patient and family-interview	65 ☐ other

Additional services:

---

14 ▷ Primary problem: (code primary problem and enter *only* code)

─ mild
─ moderate
─ severe

A. Enter CODE   B. presumptive   confirmed   C.

P ☐☐☐   1 ☐   2 ☐   1 ☐ 2 ☐ 3 ☐

---

15. Referrals:

Made to:	A in HHHC	B Out-side	C Hospital	Received from:	D In HHHC	E Out-side	F Hospital	Check If Current In-volvement
1. nursing				1.				☐
2. dental health				2.				☐
3. nutrition				3.				☐
8. medical and specialties				8.				☐
10. mental health				10.				☐
13. JFK Center				13.				☐
14. schools				14.				☐
15. state hospital				15.				☐
16. police/courts				16.				☐
17. self/friend				17.				☐
18. VNA/LSA				18.				☐
12. other agencies				12.				☐

Exhibit 11.2 Hyatt Hill Health Center: Cost-Accounting Formulas

Symbol	*Meaning*
$X	Fixed cost of the department
$Y	Salary per minute of physician j
Z_j	Time, in minutes, that physician j was available
N_{ij}	Number of encounters of type i by physician j
T_{ij}	Time spent on encounters of type i by physician j

1. The total time spent in patient care by physician j:

$$T_j = \sum_i T_{ij}$$

2. The direct labor cost of physician j:

$$\$DLC_j = (T_j)(\$Y_j)$$

3. The total time spent in nonpatient care activities by physician j:

$$Q_j = Z_j - T_j$$

4. The direct overhead cost of physician j:

$$\$DOH_j = (Q_j)(\$Y_j)$$

5. The total time spent in nonpatient care activities by physicians in the department:

$$Q = \sum_j Q_j$$

6. The fixed overhead cost of physician j:

$$\$FOH_j = \left(\frac{Q_j}{Q}\right)(\$x)$$

7. The total cost of physician j:

$$\$TC_j = \$DLC_j + \$DOH_j + \$FOH_j$$

8. The proportion of the total cost of physician j attributable to encounters of type i:

$$\$TC_{ij} = \left(\frac{T_{ij}}{T_j}\right)(\$TC_j)$$

9. The average cost of encounters of type i for physician j:

$$\$AC_{ij} = \frac{\$TC_{ij}}{N_{ij}}$$

10. The average cost for the department of an encounter:

$$\$AC_w = \frac{\sum_j TC_j}{\sum_{i,j} N_{ij}}$$

continues

Exhibit 11.2 continued

11. The total cost for the department of encounters of type i:

$$\$TC_i = \sum_j TC_{ij}$$

12. The average cost for the department of encounters of type i:

$$\$AC_i = \frac{\$TC_i}{\sum_j N_{ij}}$$

practitioners in HHHC—whether spent in seeing patients or in the other activities listed on the time sheets.

On the basis of these data, the social work department did not appear to be very efficient in the first quarter. Its costs per encounter were higher than those of any other department and its practitioners used less of their time for seeing patients (see Table 11.4).

Dr. Kyler questioned these results at the executive committee meeting. "Why are your costs per encounter so high?" he asked Hank Clemens. "Your department's average costs are twice as high as those of the medical department, and yet the social workers' salaries are half of those of the physicians. You fellows had better shape up. You are costing all of us a lot of money and the Massachusetts General Hospital's Director is very concerned about this. After all, it started the HHHC to lower its costs!"

POINTS TO PONDER

1. What is the purpose of the HHHC?
2. How do you interpret the results shown in Table 11.4?
3. Is the control system consistent with the purposes of the health center? If not, how should it be modified?

Table 11.1 Hyatt Hill Health Center: Cost Data, Social Service Department, Typical Month

	Entire Department	Practitioner: 1	2	3	4
Total Hours Available	400	100	100	100	100
Total Hours Spent in Patient Care	100	20	20	50	10
Hours Spent/Hours Available	25%	20%	20%	50%	10%
Cost per Hour Spent in Patient Care	$100.00	$131.00	$131.00	$ 43.00	$278.00
Cost per Encounter	$100.00	$262.00	$131.00	$ 43.00	$278.00
Initial Interview, Alone		$262.00	$131.00	$ 43.00	$278.00
Initial Interview, Family		$262.00		$ 43.00	$278.00
Additional Interviews, Alone			$131.00	$ 21.50	$278.00
Additional Interviews, Family				$ 64.50	

Table 11.2 Hyatt Hill Health Center: Cost Data, Social Service Department, Typical Month

	Salaries						Departmental Fixed Costs								
	Direct Patient Care	Direct Overhead	Fringe	Furniture and Equipment	Supplies	Rent	Heat and Power	Evaluation	Medical Records and Accounting	Adminis- tration	Service Repre- sentatives	HHHC Outpatient	General	Total	% of Total
Pediatrics	$ 2,400	$ 2,956	$ 610	$ 16	$ 441	$ 162	$ 20	$ 1,117	$ 817	$ 490	$ 220	$ 40	$ 330	$ 8,609	12.9 %
Internal Medicine	3,336	1,331	653	23	467	189	33	894	1,170	533	239	43	359	9,270	12.9
Nutrition	537	260	68	4	—	42	7	381	264	189	81	15	127	1,975	2.7
Nursing	4,148	4,371	657	62	320	398	60	394	455	2,313	931	187	1,557	15,853	22.0
Dental	1,140	2,407	493	84	150	162	20	333	0	877	—	71	590	6,327	8.8
Mental Health	737	4,814	554	41	—	382	47	331	187	1,246	243	101	838	9,278	12.8
Social Services	502	4,906	421	30	—	301	40	458	258	1,720	243	139	1,158	10,176	14.1
Specialists	854	447	—	14	—	—	—	269	413	112	51	9	75	2,244	3.1
Eye Clinic	478	172	29	96	—	126	13	165	253	267	—	22	179	1,800	2.5
Laboratory	1,147	645	143	46	275	41	7	—	666	567	243	46	382	4,208	5.8
Radiology	139	392	49	189	272	68	7	—	387	189	80	15	127	1,914	2.7
Therapists	—	—	—	7	—	47	7	39	25	95	40	8	64	332	.5
Total	$ 15,418	$ 21,701	$ 3,677	$ 612	$ 1,925	$ 1,918	$ 261	$ 4,381	$ 4,895	$ 8,598	$ 2,128	$ 696	$ 5,786	$ 71,986	

Table 11.3 Hyatt Hill Health Center: Social Service Department Time Allocation

	Direct Patient Care	Indirect Patient Care	Community Development	Training	Lunch, Breaks, Administrative Activities
Time Spent (hours)	100	100	80	80	40
Percentage of Total Time Available	25%	25%	20%	20%	10%
Monthly Costs of Activity	$2,500	$2,500	$2,000	$2,000	$1,000

Table 11.4 Hyatt Hill Health Center: Sources of Difference between Standard and Actual Cost per Visit, First Quarter

(in dollars)

Department	Standard Cost per Visit ($)	Actual Cost per Visit ($)	Difference (Variance) between Standard and Actual Cost ($)	Differential Effect of Change in Efficiency[a] ($)	Differential Effect of Change in Utilization of Capacity[b] ($)
Social Service	61.10	54.65	6.45	+1.00	+5.45
Mental Health	53.65	27.77	+ 25.88	+ .23	+ 25.65
Dental Health	42.88	25.72	+ 17.16	+ .41	+ 16.75
Nutrition	34.97	20.45	+ 14.52	+ 6.04	+ 8.48
Pediatrics	25.64	22.16	+ 3.48	− .57	+ 4.05
Internal Medicine	24.72	24.00	+ .72	− .14	+ .86
Nursing	28.34	36.20	− 7.86	−11.15	+ 3.29

[a]Efficiency effects result from changes in the time spent with each patient.

[b]Utilization of capacity effects result from changes in the percentage of their available time that practitioners devote to seeing patients.

Mediplex Group, Inc.

Abe Gosman, president and owner of 60% of Mediplex, a nursing home, substance abuse treatment, and turnkey construction company, stated in his direct, businesslike way:

> I see substantial growth in the "sub-acute" segment of the health care industry: psychiatric care, alcoholism treatment, and nursing facilities. Part of this is a temporary result of the DRG prospective payment system in acute care hospitals, which causes decreases in their length of stay and occupancy rates. Because hospitals are looking for another way to fill up their empty beds, there is an opportunity for companies like ours to set up "managed beds" to provide alcoholism treatment or psychiatric services. After all, we know how to serve this segment efficiently. It wouldn't make sense for hospitals to use their expensive staff to serve the sub-acute patient. They pay RNs $12 per hour; we pay $9 per hour. We are more efficient.
>
> We also see substantial revenues coming from the alcoholism treatment business. The nursing home business is not quite as profitable, but is almost risk-free. There is phenomenal growth in the retirement living business. Our clients are both individuals and church groups. We provide them "one-stop shopping" by offering financing, planning, and designing, with assistance in obtaining the Certificate of Need. Our clients have no cost overruns, because we provide our services for a flat fee.
>
> The size of our inpatient alcoholism treatment facilities makes it feasible for us to offer special services, such as the cocaine program; for example, Spofford Hall has 134 beds, whereas many other inpatient facilities have only 20 or 30 beds. Each special program needs a group of patients large enough to conduct effective group therapy and to justify hiring a specialist. The size of our facilities allows us to reach certain economies of scale and diversify into new services.
>
> But the largest area of growth for us will be in congregate living facilities, in which residents have their own apartments with back-up nursing and medical facilities. That will be a $50 billion industry in the next decade.

INTRODUCTION

Abraham Gosman, Mediplex's founder and driving force, entered the business in 1959 through a college roommate who convinced him to invest $10,000 in a nursing home:

> We got one nursing home partnership and another and gradually started expanding. Nursing homes in the 1950s were mostly converted mansions. They were inexpensive to buy, and I got a lot of experience in rehabilitating them.

Mr. Gosman sold the nursing home company and agreed to stay out of the health care

Note: This case was prepared by Joyce Lallman under the supervision of Professor Regina E. Herzlinger. It is partially based on the prospectus for Mediplex's 1984 equity offering.

business for three years. Using his rehab experience, he went into real estate development. After the three years, he returned to nursing homes, expanding in 1980 to alcohol and substance abuse treatment facilities. Mediplex was incorporated in July 1983 as a consolidation of these activities.

Mediplex was organized into three divisions: (1) *long-term care*, with eight nursing facilities containing 750 skilled and 590 intermediate care beds; (2) *alcohol and substance abuse*, with three inpatient treatment facilities containing 257 licensed beds and five outpatient offices; and (3) *development*, with, in 1984, four turnkey contracts to design, construct, and develop long-term care facilities for third parties (see Table 12.1).

In October 1983, Mediplex had its initial public offering of 700,000 shares of common stock, priced at $15 per share.[1] To improve investor liquidity, Mediplex brought a second public offering of 725,000 shares of common stock to market on October 11, 1984, priced at $20.75 per share.

In October 1984, Mediplex planned to spend $43.7 million on construction of eight nursing facilities containing a total of 1,008 beds and was negotiating the acquisition of a 236-bed nursing facility. It also had purchased $8.1 million of land for the development of life care and retirement centers and had contracts to develop six health care facilities (with a total of 600 beds) for sale or lease to third parties, with a total projected cost of $34.9 million (of which approximately $14.2 million had been expended). Mediplex planned to add a total of 222 beds to its alcohol and substance abuse facilities. In February 1984 it purchased a $2.7 million general acute care hospital in Queens, New York, to be converted to a 100-bed psychiatric hospital at an additional cost of approximately $4.4 million.

EXISTING OPERATIONS

Nursing Facilities

Mediplex's skilled nursing care services required technical or professional personnel,

such as registered or licensed practical nurses, and were provided in an inpatient setting. Its intermediate nursing services were for individuals who did not require hospital or skilled nursing services, but whose mental or physical condition still required inpatient care and service above the level of room and board. Rehabilitative services included therapeutic exercises or activities; gait evaluation and training; maintenance therapy; hydrotherapy; and tests and measurements for functional disabilities, including perceptual, speech, and hearing disorders.

Mediplex provided for both the health care and daily needs of its patients. Health care services were provided by a director of nursing; licensed nurses; physical, occupational, and recreational therapists; social workers; and other personnel. The company also provided food and housekeeping services and scheduled social activities. Each nursing home had a full dining room, a kitchen, a treatment and examining room, hairdressing and barber facilities, and rehabilitative facilities. It was located near at least one hospital and had transfer agreements to accept patients discharged from hospitals. (The average occupancy rate for each facility owned and operated by Mediplex can be found in Table 12.2. The percentage of revenues from private, Medicare, and Medicaid patients and the Mediplex per diem room rates are in Tables 12.3 and 12.4.)

The company's nursing facility patient census averaged a high 40.9 percent private patients—attributed to the quality of its nursing care, its reputation with the local community and hospitals, and the location, appearance, and condition of each of its facilities.

Timothy Coburn, vice president of nursing facilities, described the Mediplex strategy for nursing home operation:

> Our goal is to maximize private pay patients, but if a resident runs out of personal funds, he or she is retained under Medicaid and gets the same (or better) treatment. Medicaid patients are guaranteed physical therapy and other therapies that are figured into the overall Medicaid

Table 12.1 Mediplex Group, Inc.: Revenues and Income of Business Divisions

(dollars in thousands)

| | Twelve Months Ended December 31 | | | | | Six Months Ended June 30 | | | |
| | 1981 | | 1982 | | 1983 | | 1983 | | 1984 | |
	Amount	%	Amount	%	Amount	%	Amount	%	Amount	%
Revenues:										
Alcohol and Substance Abuse	$ 4,409	18.4	$ 6,698	23.6	$ 9,969	25.8	$ 4,719	26.9	$ 6,384	24.7
Nursing	19,496	81.6	21,723	76.4	24,951	64.6	11,482	65.7	14,283	55.4
Development/Construction	—	—	—	—	3,708	9.6	1,288	7.4	5,123	19.9
Total	$ 23,905	100.0	$ 28,421	100.0	$ 38,628	100.0	$ 17,489	100.0	$ 25,790	100.0
Income before Income Taxes:										
Alcohol and Substance Abuse	$ 362	26.3	$ 1,079	29.9	$ 3,181	46.8	$ 1,399	46.6	$ 2,427	46.6
Nursing	1,016	73.7	2,529	70.1	2,743	40.4	1,354	45.1	1,950	37.5
Development/Construction	—	—	—	—	870	12.8	249	8.3	829	15.9
Total	$ 1,378	100.0	$ 3,608	100.0	$ 6,794	100.0	$ 3,002	100.0	$ 5,206	100.0
Average for Industry:										
Revenues	NA		$ 91,400		$107,200					
Profits	NA		4,600		6,800					
1983 Assests ($ in millions):										
Health Care	$ 37.2									
Development	$ 10.4									

Note: NA = not available.

Table 12.2 Mediplex Group, Inc.: Average Occupancy Rate of Nursing Facilities

Facility/Location	Number of Beds[a]	Operated by the Company Since	Average Occupancy Rate, 1983[b]
Connecticut			
Mediplex of Danbury (Danbury)	180	1976	98.0%
Mediplex of Newington (Newington)	180	1978	98.4
Mediplex of Westport (Westport)	120	1977	98.9
Mediplex of Wethersfield (Wethersfield)	240	1976	97.0
Cheshire Convalescent Center (Cheshire)	120	1983	98.1
Massachusetts			
Mediplex of Beverly (Beverly)	190	1980	98.8
Mediplex of Lexington (Lexington)	120	1979	98.1
Mediplex of Newton (Newton)	190	1979	97.8
All Locations	1,340		98.0%

INPATIENT ALCOHOL AND SUBSTANCE ABUSE FACILITIES

Spofford Hall Chesterfield, N.H.	134	August 1980	94.6%
Arms Acres Carmel, N.Y.	65	August 1982	81.7
Conifer Park Scotia, N.Y.	105	November 1983	49.9

[a]The number of beds represents the number of available beds, which in each case represents the maximum number of beds permitted in the facility under its state license.

[b]Average occupancy rates were obtained by dividing the number of patient days in each period by the number of licensed bed days in such period.

Table 12.3 Mediplex Group, Inc.: Sources of Nursing Home Revenues

Revenue Source	Year Ended December 31			Six Months Ended June 30, 1984
	1981	1982	1983	
Private Patients	39.6%	41.0%	45.2%	48.3%
Medicare Patients	0.8	1.1	1.5	1.8
Medicaid Patients	59.6	57.9	53.3	49.9
Total	100.0%	100.0%	100.0%	100.0%

reimbursement rate, while private patients may choose to forgo them.

To attract private pay patients, we stress community involvement, maintaining high staffing ratios and presenting a positive image to local physicians. In Wethersfield, Connecticut, we sponsored a free service for shut-ins in the community. Residents of that nursing home called shut-ins at a certain time every day and if there was no answer alerted local social service people to check on the shut-in. This program was credited with helping a shut-in who had fallen and broken her hip. Another nursing home serves as the location for the senior diners club, to which elderly people are brought for meals and activities.

All of our nursing facilities provide respite care to community residents.

Physicians are impressed by our high staff-to-patient ratios, by our regular medical staff meetings, and by the fact that our patients are well groomed and well cared for. We keep abreast of changes in equipment; for example, our new Century Tubs bathe patients using a whirlpool, thereby offering them an increased measure of privacy and dignity.

I supervise a centralized management team which is responsible for reimburse-ment, physical plant maintenance, purchasing, quality assurance, and operations. Our physical plant engineer sets specification standards for facilities and equipment, making inspection rounds daily. A nurse is in charge of setting policies and procedures and organizing staff training for quality assurance. Our purchasing system is computerized; it can automatically select the vendor who offers the lowest price.

Our nursing home administrators are encouraged to create an individual identity for each home. They meet with the central management team on a monthly basis. Our social workers, food service workers, and other groups meet with their counterparts in other Mediplex nursing facilities on a quarterly basis. We have economies of scale at Mediplex through central purchasing, central billing, and employee benefits.

We are planning a new addition to our nursing home in Lexington, Massachusetts. It will enable us to offer multilevel care in which a patient will be able to move from skilled care to intermediate care and vice versa. Offering a range of services is a good marketing strategy, and there is more profit in a higher level of care.

Table 12.4 Mediplex Group, Inc.: Per Diem Room Rates

	Wethers-field	Danbury	Westport	Newing-ton	Cheshire	Newton	Lexington	Beverly
Billed Rate								
Skilled								
Private	$82.03	$83.80	$92.00	$85.83	$85.30	$115.00		$95.00
Semi-Private	68.37	71.14	76.00	74.50	72.90	92.00		82.00
ICF (Level III) Private Bath	89.13							
Private—Shared Bath	89.13	64.56	75.00	64.40	67.19	105.00	$83.00	90.00
Semi-private	58.04	51.12	53.61	52.50	58.85	87.00	70.00	77.00
Medicaid Rates								
Skilled/Level II	54.71	56.48	61.60	58.51	60.50	55.68		51.38
ICF/Level III	39.70	39.69	44.21	41.63	50.50		42.94	
Medicare/Level I	50.90	65.70	67.20	60.40	51.30	81.00		55.00

Life-Care and Retirement Living Centers

Mediplex viewed the life-care and retirement living field as an extension of its nursing facility business. Retirement living centers offer active elderly residents an opportunity for an independent life-style. Many centers are built with nursing facilities to provide a continuum of care. Charges for center services are paid from private funds with assistance from governmental programs. In certain states, retirement living centers must be licensed and are regulated.

Mediplex expected to derive revenues from providing consulting, marketing, development, construction, and management services to retirement living projects. Because the development phase of these projects was lengthy, Mediplex was prepared to expend substantial funds on feasibility, marketing, and other preliminary studies prior to receiving commitments from prospective project sponsors.

As a part of its expansion into retirement living, in 1984 it purchased 20% of the capital stock of Retirement Centers of America, Inc. (RCAI), with a one-year option to purchase the remaining 80% interest. RCAI provided consulting, marketing, and management services to retirement living projects. In the last five years, it had supervised the development of completed facilities in five states and was supervising the development of retirement living centers in six others.

Alcohol and Substance Abuse Treatment

Mediplex operated or managed an integrated network of alcohol and substance abuse programs in both inpatient and outpatient settings.

The network consisted of three inpatient facilities containing 257 licensed treatment beds, with Certificate of Need applications pending for an additional 189 beds at two of these facilities, and five outpatient offices in Massachusetts.

Inpatient Facilities

Inpatient services were provided at Spofford Hall in New Hampshire, and at Arms Acres and Conifer Park in upstate New York (see Table 12.2). All facilities were accredited by the Joint Commission on Accreditation of Healthcare Organizations. The inpatient setting utilized an interdisciplinary team of professional administrators, psychiatrists, psychologists, alcohol counselors, social workers, licensed nurses, and other professional and paraprofessional personnel. The comprehensive treatment program was built around Alcoholics Anonymous. Inpatient treatment began with primary care, including medical evaluation and detoxification where appropriate, followed by intermediate care, consisting of an individually tailored four- to six-week treatment program. Daily schedules included individual and group therapy, educational meetings, activities therapy, written assignments, and special treatment group meetings. Patients went through a transitional program to help them readjust for their return home. Once there, they were provided with an outpatient program to reinforce the gains made during their inpatient treatment. It included ongoing therapeutic support through the company's inpatient facilities, outpatient offices managed by the company, and offices of other professionals with whom the company had contractual agreements.

Mediplex developed a number of specialized programs. The adolescent program for 13- to 17-year-old patients required parental participation, provided tutorial services to minimize the effects of lost school time, and emphasized the development of individual responsibility. The family program was designed to involve the spouse and children of the patient in the treatment program. The chronic relapse program was a longer and more intense program for individuals who had difficulty maintaining sobriety after treatment. As a result of growing use of cocaine and problems of polyaddiction, the company developed a special cocaine program at its Spofford Hall facility.

Outpatient Facilities

Mediplex managed outpatient alcohol and substance abuse offices for a related party, Bay Colony Health Service, Inc., with five offices in Massachusetts. It provided a full range of alcohol and substance abuse–related outpatient mental health services in addition to its aftercare service. Each of the five offices had a psychologist, social workers, and addiction counselors on its staff who provided group, family, and individual therapy on a fee-for-service basis. Bay Colony had an arrangement with several corporations and the court of Quincy, Massachusetts, to test and interview individuals with alcohol and substance abuse problems and refer them to appropriate treatment settings.

Sources of Revenues

Spofford Hall's revenues were determined by the per diem charges, not subject to state or federal regulations. Approximately 90% of the patients at Spofford Hall were covered by health insurance carriers and the remaining 10% paid for their own care. Income attributable to Spofford Hall constituted a significant portion of the company's total income.

There were several sources of revenues from Arms Acres and Conifer Park. Due to regulatory requirements, the company leased the real property to corporations wholly owned by the company's president and received rent in excess of debt service and depreciation. For its management services, it received management fees based upon a formula related to certain expenses (the fees may be subject to the approval of the New York Division of Alcoholism and Alcohol Abuse). Accordingly, the company's revenues from these facilities were not directly tied to the facilities' revenues or profitability.

Management of Services

Bill Hartegan, vice president of the alcohol and substance abuse division, noted:

The key to profitability in this business is occupancy. The profit is in filling the last 20 to 40 beds in one of our facilities.

We need about 340 referrals per month to keep our 257 inpatient beds full. We get about 80 referrals per month from Bay Colony, our outpatient service network, and other referrals from other affiliated outpatient programs. Outpatient services are not that profitable. Bay Colony was established primarily to serve as a feeder to our inpatient facilities, a provider of aftercare services, and a community base. I have a real public relations problem with our 100% occupancy; it can be difficult to get people admitted. The Bay Colony outpatient services function as a cushion by working with family members and keeping a client "on hold" until a bed opens up.

The large working-class population is our primary target group, because other alcohol and substance abuse programs have already targeted the "carriage class." We are sensitive to the needs of special populations; for example, our census of adult clients in alcoholism treatment usually drops over the Christmas holiday, when they want to be home. Because cocaine abusers and adolescents have increased crises during the holidays, our census for these groups increases and we maintain our high occupancy rates throughout the holiday season.

We use many marketing methods. Community service is a major part of our marketing; for example, I train a group called "Freedom from Chemical Dependency," which works with local prep schools. We sponsor conferences on alcoholism and drug abuse and provide speakers for talk shows. We also develop brochures, TV ads, and radio ads. Our TV ads are often shown in conjunction with special TV programs on alcoholism or drug abuse. We are careful not to appear too commercial, because we are sensitive to what consumers think about for-profit health care. Our ads serve a social purpose by building awareness and educating the public about alcoholism and drug abuse. We are sometimes sought out by the media; for example, *Fortune* magazine will be visiting Spofford Hall soon to research a story on alcoholism treatment for executives. Mediplex employs a physician who is a member of the Harvard Medical School faculty. This enhances our image as a quality service provider.

Our marketing staff consists of five in-house people who specialize in different topic areas (community service, media, etc.) and 20 local representatives who give us broad geographic coverage. They work in our treatment facilities or their homes and are responsible for referral sources such as outpatient counselors, employee assistance program counselors, and mental health professionals. I hire only people with clinical backgrounds to do our marketing. In addition to bringing in clients, they help identify local service needs.

My basic marketing model was developed in Massachusetts and is applied to other communities. My 90-day marketing plan allows me to put the appropriate marketing efforts in place before new facilities open. This can be tricky. I need to have marketing projects in place that will have an effect when the beds open, but not before.

Our alcoholism and substance abuse treatment model is based on large facilities in attractive settings. Our charge for inpatient care, from $200 to $280 per day, is much lower than fees charged by psychiatric or general hospitals. We charge $7,000 for a four-week cocaine program, where a New York hospital would charge $7,000 per week. We get no state or federal reimbursement for our alcoholism and substance abuse treatment program. The insurance industry covers this treatment because it saves insurers money on future health, auto, and life insurance claims.

Mediplex has successfully operated in a regulatory environment, but the regulatory processes of obtaining licensing and Certificates of Need must be viewed as a risk. Other problems are a shortage of qualified professionals to manage our treatment facilities and the growth of health maintenance organizations (HMOs). HMOs are a threat, because they make money by *not* treating people, and we are watching them carefully.

Development and Related Services, Including Construction

Mediplex's management had broad experience in the development of health-related facilities. The company constructed new projects and rehabilitated, converted, and added to existing buildings. Development work included preparing feasibility and marketing studies, furnishing program evaluation and consultation, providing planning and design services, managing construction, and providing or arranging financing. It also assisted in obtaining CONs (a prerequisite for new facilities or services) and zoning and other governmental approvals.

Mediplex's development and construction services were provided on a fee-for-service basis. Its secondary mortgage financing resulted in interest income. Some of the facilities were developed for long-term lease. Fee-for-service revenues were recognized using the percentage-of-completion method.

Planning and Certificates of Need

Steve Garfinkle, vice president of government affairs, described the process of planning and filing Certificates of Need:

Planning at Mediplex is based on bed need. Although some states have already projected bed need, we always do our own demographic analysis. We look at the following factors: (1) economic base, (2) ethnic composition, (3) availability of staff, (4) proximity to a hospital, and (5) accessibility for families. We don't necessarily locate our facilities in high-income areas; we also consider working-class communities where residents have

accumulated savings and pension benefits. Ethnic composition is an issue for
alcoholism services. Availability of staff
can really be a problem. We found it
difficult to get aides for our Beverly,
Massachusetts, nursing home, so we had
to transport them from Salem. In other
geographic locations, we can't get nurses.

Once we identify a community, we
prepare the CON application. Mediplex
has filed 14 CONs in the past $2^{1}/_{2}$ years;
and all of them have been approved,
except in one case where we were denied
12 beds for an alcoholism treatment
facility. We don't file junk applications or
ones we will get in a fight over. We
maintain cooperative relationships with
the state agencies. To me, the CON
process is equivalent to the state's
franchising services.

Recently there has been a big increase
in the number of organizations filing
CONs for nursing home facilities, due
partly to the increased availability of
conventional financing. To us, this
presents an opportunity for more turnkey
business, because many of these
organizations don't have experience in
developing nursing homes. Within one
community there may be competition
among nursing homes for paying patients,
but overall competition in the nursing
home industry is limited.

States vary on whether they will let
nursing homes keep the profits they could
make under the prospective reimbursement schemes they are contemplating. I
believe prospective reimbursement systems are good. There is no danger of
excessive cost-cutting in nursing homes
under these systems, because there are
other ways to guarantee quality. However, I expect that state controls will get
tighter and tighter due to the demographic
situation. The rapid increase in our elderly population will place too many
demands on the system.

The reimbursement situation for
alcoholism treatment is mixed. It will be
increasingly scrutinized by insurance
companies, especially in states that mandate insurance coverage for alcoholism
treatment. In states that have just recently
mandated coverage, there will be growth
in alcoholism reimbursement.

Management and Employees

Mediplex had 13 executive officers and
directors as of October 1984. The company employed approximately 1,270 persons, of whom
1,137 were hourly employees and 133 were salaried. Approximately 78 of the company's
employees were at its headquarters in Newton,
Massachusetts. Its directors included a former
Massachusetts U.S. senator, a former New
York State governor, and a Catholic priest.

Results of Operations

Annual revenues increased in 1983 by 36%
and by 19% in 1982. The revenue increase for
both years resulted from occupancy rates at the
alcohol and substance abuse facilities
increasing by 44% in 1983 and by 15% in
1982; the number of nursing and alcohol and
substance abuse beds operated or managed by
the company increasing by 178 beds (or 12.4%)
in 1983 and 105 beds (or 7.9%) in 1982; the
number of nursing facility private patient days
increasing by 13.9% in 1983 and 6.2% in 1982;
and per diem rate increases for patients at all of
the company's facilities. Additionally, the
company recognized $3,707,890 of revenue
from its new development/construction activities in 1983.

Of the 1982 increase in total revenues, 45%
was attributable to the increased occupancy at
the company's alcohol and substance abuse
facilities, with the balance primarily due to an
increase in per diem rates for patients at the
company's nursing facilities.

Operating expenses, as a percentage of
revenues, excluding interest expense, declined
by 3.2% in 1983 and by 5.6% in 1982, because
of higher utilization. The ratio of revenue to
expense was expected to stabilize as facility
utilization was maximized. Development/con-
struction expenses for 1983 amounted to
$2,957,762.

Government Regulations

Licensing

Mediplex's facilities complied with the licensing requirements of federal, state, and local health agencies and with municipal building codes, health codes, and local fire departments. Under New York regulations, a corporation could not be licensed to operate alcoholism or mental health facilities unless all of its shareholders are individuals. Therefore, Mediplex provided only management services to such facilities.

Government Health Care Reimbursement Programs for Nursing Facilities

In Connecticut and Massachusetts, the nursing facilities' per diem rate for Medicaid patients was based on reasonable costs incurred in providing services plus a return on equity, subject to cost ceilings. There was also a limited incentive allowance for providers whose costs were less than certain ceilings. The provider could not bill the patient for more than the amount of Medicaid's payment. Although the company generally had increased patient per diem rates to reflect inflation, the new Connecticut Medicaid program payments for nursing patients were not expected to reflect inflation fully.

Medicare covered only skilled nursing care services with an amount equal to the direct and indirect cost of the services furnished to Medicare patients and a rate of return on equity capital. It paid for a maximum of 100 days per patient illness spell.

Determination of Charges for Private Patients for Nursing Facilities

In Connecticut, maximum charges paid by private patients were established by the state for each level of care provided by each facility. The maximum private patient rate allowed was the facility's Medicaid rate plus a percentage of the statewide median Medicaid rate. The percentage depends on the number of patients per room. In Massachusetts, charges for private patients were not subject to regulatory control.

Competition

The company had many competitors, some of them solely nursing home companies and some the nursing home operations of more diversified health care or lodging companies. In 1983, the average daily costs of for-profit nursing homes were $64, nonprofits had costs of $82, and the costs of hospital-attached homes were $102.

POINTS TO PONDER

1. What opportunity is Mediplex fulfilling?
2. What are the managerial skills critical to its success? How well have they been implemented to date? If your evaluation is negative, specify the changes needed.
3. How successful has Mediplex been to date? Back up your assessment with a financial analysis (Table 12.5 and Exhibit 12.1 contain additional financial data).

NOTE

1. "The Mediplex Group, Inc. (MPLX-21 BID)," Donaldson, Lufkin, & Jenrette, September 12, 1984.

Table 12.5 Mediplex Group, Inc.: Consolidated Balance Sheets at December 31, 1982, December 31, 1983, and June 30, 1984

| | December 31 | | June 30 |
	1982	1983	1984 (unaudited)
ASSETS			
Current Assets			
Cash and Short-Term Cash Investments	$ 285,165	$ 8,879,942	$ 6,264,663
Accounts Receivable Less Allowance for Doubtful Accounts of			
$350,000 in 1982, $500,000 in 1983, and $241,000 in 1984	2,106,812	3,101,723	3,712,781
Due from Principal Shareholder	4,915,605	—	—
Unbilled Revenues on Uncompleted Construction Contracts	—	3,082,661	4,020,922
Prepaid Expenses and Other Current Assets	459,753	369,766	860,452
Current Portion of Equipment: Lease Receivable from Related Party	100,000	100,000	100,000
Property Held for Sale to Others	—	1,907,334	5,908,409
Total Current Assets	7,867,335	17,441,426	20,867,227
Long-Term Mortgage Receivable, Net of Unearned Interest Income of			
Approximately $617,000	—	—	1,081,743
Unbilled Revenues on Uncompleted Construction Contracts—Long	—	625,229	761,200
Term	750,000	750,000	750,000
Certificate of Deposit Held in Escrow	325,000	225,000	175,000
Equipment Lease Receivable	15,021,400	27,639,003	40,520,097
Property and Equipment, Net	187,259	1,122,033	1,303,496
Other Assets	$ 24,150,994	$ 47,602,691	$ 65,458,763
Total Assets			
LIABILITIES AND SHAREHOLDERS' EQUITY			
Current Liabilities			
Current Portion of Long-Term Debt	$ 1,025,481	$ 1,094,289	$ 1,073,262
Due to Principal Shareholder	—	432,437	—
Accounts Payable	619,452	1,657,629	2,103,660
Accrued Liabilities	873,306	1,645,120	1,592,689
Payable to Third-Party Payers	200,000	735,689	268,380
Construction Borrowings	—	2,009,720	7,327,827
Federal and State Income Taxes Payable	316,980	2,690,034	37,239
Deferred Income Taxes	465,800	552,263	1,151,163
Total Current Liabilities	3,501,019	10,817,181	13,554,220
Long-Term Debt, Less Current Portion	16,463,991	21,912,901	32,438,721
Long-Term Construction Borrowings	—	2,023,370	3,612,020
Deferred Income Taxes	1,008,239	1,555,766	1,925,166
Commitments and Contingencies	—	—	—
Shareholders' Equity:			
Predecessor Entities			
Common Stock	106,000	—	—
Earnings Retained by Combined Entities	3,071,745	—	—
The Mediplex Group, Inc.			
Common Stock, $.10 par Value, Authorized 10,000,000 Shares;			
Issued and Outstanding 3,228,000 Shares	—	322,800	322,800
Paid-in Capital	—	8,107,428	8,107,428
Retained Earnings	—	2,863,245	5,498,408
Total Shareholders' Equity	3,177,745	11,293,473	13,928,636
Total Liabilities and Shareholders Equity	$ 24,150,994	$ 47,602,691	$ 65,458,763

Note: Exhibit 12.1 is an integral part of these financial statements.

Exhibit 12.1 Mediplex Group, Inc.: Edited Notes to the Financial Statements (Tables 12.1 and 12.5)

---

2. Basis of Presentation

The unaudited balance sheet as of June 30, 1984, the unaudited statements of operations (with *pro forma* data for 1983) and changes in financial position for the six months ended June 30, 1983 and 1984, and the unaudited statement of changes in shareholders' equity for the six months ended June 30, 1984 include, in the opinion of management, all adjustments, consisting of only normal recurring adjustments, necessary for a fair presentation of such financial statements. For the six months ended June 30, 1984, such adjustments included a reversal of previously established reserves for doubtful accounts amounting to approximately $260,000 due to favorable collection experience on patient billings.

3. Summary of Significant Accounting Policies
Patient Care Revenues

In addition to health care services paid for by patients, revenues include amounts for services provided that are reimbursable by Medicaid, Blue Cross, Medicare, and other third-party payers under various reimbursement formulas and regulations. Revenues earned for patient services provided at the company's alcohol and substance abuse facilities are on the basis of charges established by the company. Final determination of amounts earned for nursing home patient services is subject to review or audit by the third-party payers. In the opinion of management, adequate provision has been made for any adjustments that may result from these reviews or audits. To the extent that final determination results in amounts that vary from management estimates, future earnings will be charged or credited.

Construction Revenues

Revenues on construction contracts for others are recorded for financial statement purposes using the percentage-of-completion method. Under this method, revenues are recognized according to the ratio of costs incurred to currently estimated total contract costs, which include an allowance for any costs expected to be incurred in excess of the original contract cost estimate. Continual reviews of estimated total contract costs are made during the life of such contracts, based on information then available, and may result in current period adjustments to revenues previously recorded.

Unbilled revenues and costs on uncompleted construction contracts in progress represent costs incurred and revenue recognized on contracts for which billings have not been presented to the customer at the balance sheet date. Generally such revenues are expected to be billed within one year of commencement of construction and be paid through cash, the assumption of the construction borrowings by the customer or the company's receipt of an interest-bearing second mortgage note from the customer or a combination thereof. In cases where a second mortgage note is received, construction revenues are recognized only to the extent of its discounted present value and the related unearned interest income is recognized as earned over the life of the mortgage note.

Property and Equipment

Property and equipment, including significant renewals and betterments, are capitalized at cost. Maintenance and repairs are charged to operations as incurred. Depreciation is provided for on a straight-line basis, over the expected lives of the assets for financial reporting, while accelerated and straight-line methods are used for income tax reporting.

Capitalized Interest

The company follows the practice of capitalizing interest expense related to borrowing incurred with respect to construction activities for third parties as part of construction costs. Interest included in construction costs and expensed during the year ended December 31, 1983, amounted to $94,557. For the six months ended June 30, 1984, interest expense of $236,537 was included in construction costs and $213,548 of interest expense was capitalized to projects intended to be owned, leased, or sold to third parties by the company.

Income tax credits are recognized as a reduction of income tax under the flow-through method of accounting.

Exhibit 12.1 continued

Distribution of Equity

Entities operated as proprietorships distributed a portion of their earnings prior to the combination to the sole proprietor, who is the company's principal shareholder.

15. Related Party Transactions

At December 31, 1983, a noninterest-bearing balance of $432,437 was due to the principal shareholder of the Company. This balance was paid to the company's principal shareholder subsequent to December 31, 1983. At December 31, 1982, the company's principal shareholder had been advanced $4,915,605, which was paid to the company in 1983, principally through the proceeds of the sale of common stock of the company held by the principal shareholder and a contribution to the company of certain real property relating to Arms Acres. Other related party transactions affect Mediplex of New Hampshire, Inc. (Spofford Hall); Bay Colony Health Service, Inc. (Bay Colony); Conifer Park, Inc; and Arms Acres. All involve the company's principal shareholder.

Case Study 13

New England Critical Care, Inc.

Patrick Smith, president of New England Critical Care, Inc. (NECC), said:

> We are known as the company with the most intensive level of clinical support in the home infusion market. Our quality is high, and we present a conservative New England image. We have invested in providing *service* while our competitors primarily sell supplies.

NECC was founded in 1981. The company's primary business consisted of infusing a solution of nutrients, antibiotics, or other substances into the bloodstream of patients with impaired gastrointestinal tracts, infections, or other disorders. Advances in technology and clinical practice made infusion therapy in patients' homes possible, resulting in cost savings and the possibility of improved quality of life.

NECC's services included solution compounding, assistance in obtaining insurance coverage, nursing and delivery services, and communication of patient progress to physicians. By September 1984, it had five branches in major metropolitan areas on both coasts and was pursuing a strategy of rapid growth.

Note: This case was prepared by Joyce Lallman under the supervision of Assistant Professor Nancy M. Kane and subsequently revised by Professor Regina E. Herzlinger.

COMPANY BACKGROUND

The company's 32-year-old founder and president, Patrick Smith, pursued a pre-medical undergraduate degree. He explained, "About one week before I was scheduled to enter medical school, I realized my plans were based on financial motives rather than a true interest in medicine. I decided instead to become a medical products salesman." From 1976 through 1981, he worked for a company specializing in the sales and distribution of intravenous (IV) infusion devices and other medical equipment, reaching the position of director of sales and marketing.

Noted Mr. Smith,

> During the early seventies, I found it most lucrative to sell cardiac monitoring and operating room equipment, because hospitals competed on the basis of having the "latest and best." My best sales pitch was "the hospital down the street has it." This period was really a nightmare in terms of health care costs. Small, rural hospitals were buying four-unit cardiac care units when they didn't even know how to use them. However, they knew they would be reimbursed.
>
> In 1979, I did a study to help my employer determine the future direction of his company. I could see that the hospitals were starting to put the brakes on spending. The market was moving toward the home as technology got better. I ran across a company that provided home health services to patients with digestive problems. I went to visit this company

and asked a lot of questions of it and others in the industry.

After conducting this research, I presented a business plan to my employer for getting into home health care. When he and I failed to agree on whether or how the plan should be implemented, I left to develop this business on my own.

Mr. Smith's selected a location for the business with the criteria of (l) high number of hospital beds, (2) high hospital occupancy rates, (3) large population, (4) geographic concentration of hospitals, and (5) prestigious medical community. They led him to locate in Boston. NECC obtained $1 million of equity in December 1982 from individual investors in the Midwest. This came shortly after Home Health Care went public, a time of considerable excitement about the home infusion industry on Wall Street. The company's first financing was the result of an exhaustive search that took Mr. Smith to both venture capitalists and individual investors. According to Mr. Smith:

The hardest thing an entrepreneur goes through is raising money. People don't believe you, and they don't understand your business. It took from February to December to get a million dollars.

The first patient was accepted in November 1982, and volume in Boston took off. In June 1983, Mr. Smith opened an office in New Jersey with a skeleton operation "to prove to skeptics that we could successfully operate this business in another market." It took until December 1983 to get additional equity financing of $3 million.

By September 1984, the company had a major presence in the Boston, New York, and Baltimore markets and had recently opened offices in San Diego and Buffalo. (See Tables 13.1 and 13.2 for financial results and forecasts.)

OVERVIEW OF HOME INFUSION

Home infusion therapy was a small but rapidly growing segment of the $5.5 billion home health care industry. It consisted of the infusion of a solution of needed substances directly into a blood stream, through IV needles placed in veins. The process was powered by gravity or an infusion pump and took place sometimes overnight or continuously over a period of days. Infusion therapy was administered in hospitals and, increasingly, in patients' homes. Following are descriptions of various infusion therapies.

Total parenteral nutrition (TPN) consists of the intravenous infusion of nutrients (amino acids, glucose, fats, electrolytes, vitamins, and trace materials) to patients who were unable to digest food via their gastrointestinal (GI) tracts because they suffered from GI disorders. The solution flowed from a plastic bag through a pump, which infused it at a steady rate into a catheter in a central vein, generally for periods of about ten hours per day. This treatment required intense initial education of the patient and family. Patients receiving TPN therapy historically needed it for their lifetime, but shorter term applications of several months were becoming more common.

Enternal nutrition (EN) consists of the infusion of a nutritional formula to the functioning portion of a patient's partially compromised GI tract, via a small feeding tube that was often passed through the nose and into the stomach or small intestine. Home EN patients included victims of head, neck, or abdominal cancer, inflammatory bowel disease, obstructions, or neurological disorders such as stroke that could impair swallowing. Patients were usually on service for their lifetime and required limited nursing support.

IV antibiotic therapy treats patients diagnosed with the following: osteomyelitis, endocarditis, pyelonephritis, cellulitis, infections resulting from cystic fibrosis, and many other bone, joint, and soft tissue infections. It was usually the modality of choice for treating infections of the denser tissues, which do not absorb blood quickly. Home treatment lasted anywhere from several days to several weeks. Skilled nursing is a critical element in provision of this service because the IV site must be changed every 2–3 days.

Table 13.1 New England Critical Care, Inc.: Consolidated Forecast of Operations—1984, 1985, Home Infusion Business

	Estimated 1985 ($)	Estimated 1984 ($)
NET REVENUES	29,828,006	9,607,544
COST OF REVENUES		
Materials	7,457,002	2,658,732
Branch Operations	10,285,696	4,009.062
GROSS MARGIN	12,085,308	2,939,750
Percentage of Net Revenues	41%	31%
OPERATING EXPENSES		
Marketing	835,373	495,554
Selling	2,436,824	1,223,000
General & Administrative	7,044,081	4,363,252
Total Operating Expense	10,316,278	6,081,806
OPERATING PROFIT (LOSS)	1,769,030	(3,142,056)
INTEREST EXPENSE, NET	150,071	120,946
PRE-TAX INCOME (LOSS)	1,618,959	(3,263,002)

Source: NECC records.

Continuous IV chemotherapy consists of the continuous infusion of drugs into cancer patients. Its duration depends on the protocols set by the patient's physician, but most patients were terminally ill. Nurses specially trained in oncology were needed to provide this service.

Line maintenance service is for patients whose intravenous lines were used for intermittent drug administration and who needed the integrity of the lines maintained between therapies.

Continuous pain management service is highly effective for controlling pain in terminally ill cancer patients. Depending on the route of access, central or peripheral line, nursing support was more or less intensive.

Hydration therapy is for patients suffering from cancer or gross electrolyte imbalances due to cancer or renal failure or those receiving home pain management or chemotherapy.

Hambrecht & Quist, Incorporated, estimated the 1984 market for TPN, EN, IV antibiotic

therapy, and continuous chemotherapy to be $277 million and projected it to grow at 33% annually to reach roughly $1 billion by 1988.[1] (See Table 13.3 for revenue estimates for these four segments and Tables 13.4 and 13.5 for the distribution of patients by disease.)

Expected Growth Rates

TPN was projected to slow its growth rate from 24% in 1984 to 14% in 1988 as awareness of home TPN was established. Duration of therapy was also expected to decline, decreasing revenue growth.

Depressed growth rates for EN were predicted through the end of 1985, due to Medicare's reluctance to reimburse for home EN. Toward the end of the decade, growth was expected to pick up as EN solutions and techniques became more sophisticated, allowing patients with more complicated disor-

Table 13.2 New England Critical Care, Inc.: Individual Start-Up Branch, Sample Months

	Month 1 ($)	Month 2 ($)	Month 3 ($)	Month 10 ($)	Month 11 ($)	Month 12 ($)	Total Year ($)
REVENUES	0	0	12,000	144,000	164,000	188,000	980,000
Less: Cont. Allow.	0	0	480	5,760	6,560	7,520	39,200
Free Care Allow.	0	0	120	1,440	1,640	1,880	9,800
NET REVENUES	0	0	11,400	136,800	155,800	178,600	931,000
MATERIALS COST	0	0	2,851	34,214	38,966	44,669	232,847
BRANCH OPERATIONS							
Salaries	4,167	6,833	9,500	23,040	26,240	30,080	191,861
Fringe Benefits	583	957	1,330	3,226	3,674	4,211	26,860
Facilities	0	0	6,000	6,000	6,000	6,000	60,000
Travel Expense	625	1,025	1,425	3,456	3,936	4,512	28,779
Leased Equipment	0	0	1,500	1,500	1,500	1,500	15,000
Freight Expense	0	0	60	720	820	940	4,900
Office Expense	2,000	2,000	3,000	5,000	5,000	5,000	52,000
Depreciation	0	0	2,000	2,000	2,000	2,000	20,000
	7,375	10,815	24,815	44,942	49,170	54,243	399,400
GROSS MARGIN	-7,375	-10,815	-16,266	57,644	67,664	79,688	298,753
Percentage of Net Revenues				42.14%	43.43%	44.62%	32.09%
SELLING EXPENSE							
Salaries	3,000	3,000	3,000	9,000	9,000	9,000	69,000
Fringe Benefits	420	420	420	1,260	1,260	1,260	9,660
Travel	750	750	750	2,250	2,250	2,250	17,250
Promotion Expense	0	0	29	346	394	451	2,353
	4,170	4,170	4,199	12,856	12,904	12,961	98,263
BAD DEBT EXPENSE	0	0	912	10,944	12,464	14,288	74,480
TOTAL OPERATING COSTS	4,170	4,170	5,111	23,800	25,368	27,249	172,743
CONTRIBUTION MARGIN	-11,545	-14,985	-21,377	33,844	42,296	52,439	126,010
Percentage of Net Revenues	NA	NA		24.74%	27.15%	29.36%	13.53%

Table 13.3 New England Critical Care, Inc.: Revenue Estimates for the Four Segments of the Home Infusion Therapy Industry

(dollars in millions)

Therapy	1983E	1984E	1985E	1986E	1987E	1988E	Compound Annual Growth Rate
TPN	$ 170	$ 210	$ 250	$ 300	$ 350	$ 400	19%
EN	75	95	115	150	190	250	27
IV Antibiotic Therapy	15	50	125	200	275	350	88
Continuous (or Home IV) Chemotheraphy	5	10	20	40	65	85	76
TOTAL	$ 265	$ 365	$ 510	$ 690	$ 880	$1,085	33%

Source: Hambrecht & Quist, Incorporated. Reprinted with permission.

ders who once would have required TPN to be adequately nourished via EN. Moreover, the more sophisticated EN techniques would command a higher price, enhancing revenue growth. On average, EN was expected to grow 27% annually from 1984 to 1988.

IV antibiotic therapy was projected to contribute the majority of the industry's growth, with an annual growth rate of 80%. However, the increased effectiveness of other drug delivery systems posed risk of substitution. For example, some physicians found that osteomyelitis could be treated effectively with careful oral antibiotic therapy following only three or four days of infusion therapy. In addition, the antibiotic market was more labor intensive than TPN and EN.

The continuous intravenous chemotherapy market, still in its infancy, was thought to have significant growth potential. Penetration was not necessarily expected to escalate dramatically if the government agreed to extend Medicare coverage to home chemotherapy. The growth of this market was directly dependent upon the medical community's acceptance of continuous chemotherapy as an effective means of treatment.

In addition to the presumed improvement in quality of life with at-home treatment, economic incentives fuel the growth of the market. Home TPN costs were $125–$250 per day versus hospital costs of $300–$600. Home EN

costs were $30–$60 per day versus the $150–$300 of hospital costs. The cost of a three- to six-week course of home IV antibiotic therapy was about $4,000 versus an in-hospital cost of about $11,000. The cost differential was attributable to the costs of room, board, and other ancillary services and the higher nursing and laboratory service charges of the hospital.

Initially, infusion therapy was practiced only in large teaching institutions. Through education within the medical community, the therapy slowly migrated to other large urban hospitals, suburban hospitals, and finally to smaller hospitals in rural settings. Hambrecht & Quist research revealed that 36% of home infusion therapy patients were being discharged from hospitals with more than 600 beds, 48% came from hospitals with 301–600 beds, and 16% came from hospitals with 50–299 beds. With the patient base spreading to smaller hospitals, the hospitals operated by large hospital management companies and the smaller independent hospitals became "gatekeepers" to home infusion patients.

Administration of Infusion Therapy

Experts had varied opinions on the proper administration of home infusion therapies. For example, home TPN could involve the use of either premixed or self-mixed solutions. In their article, Blackburn and Baptista explained:

Table 13.4 New England Critical Care, Inc.: Distribution of Patients on Home Infusion Therapy by Disease

Therapy/Disease	Number of Patients Discharged with the Disease	1983 Patient Base Receiving Home Infusion Therapy		1988 Patient Base Receiving Home Infusion Therapy	
		Estimated Number	% of Patients Discharged	Estimated Number	% of Patients Discharged
TPN					
Abdominal Cancer	294,000	1,176	0.4	5,270	1.8
Inflammatory Bowel Disease	44,000	616	1.4	2,760	6.3
Short Bowel and Ischemic Syndromes	37,000	448	1.2	2,000	5.4
Others	35,000	560	1.6	2,500	7.1
Total	410,000	2,800		12,530	
EN					
Head and Neck Cancer	42,000	1,200	2.9	3,750	9.8
Abdominal Cancer, Including Esophageal	314,000	1,800	0.6	5,200	1.7
Esophageal Stricture	41,000	1,200	2.9	3,325	8.1
Central Nervous System Disease	375,000	1,650	0.4	4,575	1.2
Others	84,000	1,650	2.0	3,950	4.7
Total	856,000	7,500		20,800	
IV Antibiotic					
Osteomyelitis	64,000	4,200	6.6	35,200	55
Pyelonephritis	50,000	50	0.1	15,000	30
Cystic Fibrosis	18,000	50	0.3	9,000	50
Septic Arthritis	11,000	—	—	6,000	55
Endocarditis	17,000	500	2.9	6,800	40
All Other Infections	—	200	—	15,000	—
Total	160,000	5,000		87,000	
Continuous Home IV Chemotherapy					
All Cancer	855,000	2,500	0.003	42,750	0.005

Note: The purpose of this exhibit is to depict the uncommon usage of IV therapy in treating some very common diseases. It is not the intent to imply that the home infusion therapy market will approach the size of these patient bases.

Source: Hambrecht & Quist. Reprinted with permission.

Table 13.5 New England Critical Care, Inc.: Service Characteristics

Therapy	Intensity of Nursing Services	Average Duration of NECC Service	Reasons for Discontinuing Therapy
Total Parenteral Nutrition (TPN)	Nurse visits patient every day during the 2- to 4-week training period; then visits taper off so that after 6 months, patient is seen once every 2 weeks	120–150 days; range is from a few weeks to several months	Patient is transferred to EN therapy, is readmitted to the hospital, or dies
Enteral Nutrition (EN)	Nurse visits patient every day for the 2- to 4-week training period; then nurse visits are discontinued. Subsequent problems are handled by phone if possible; nurse will visit patient if necessary	6 months	Therapy is continued throughout the patient's life
Intravenous Antibiotic Therapy	Nurse visits patient every 3 days to change the IV site (very intensive nursing services)	20 days	Patient recovers from disease, except in the case of cystic fibrosis, which is chronic
Chemotherapy	Same as above	No data available; estimate is one year	Patient goes into remission or dies from cancer
Pain Management	Same as above	180 days	Same as above
Hydration Therapy	Same as above. (This therapy is often an adjunct to chemotherapy and pain management.)	180 days	Same as above
Line Maintenance	Nurse visits patient intermittently between therapies (low intensity of nursing service)	No data available	NA

The TPN patient may become a "mixer," where complete solution compounding is required or receive "pre-mixed" solutions, where the TPN solution is compounded by an outside vendor.... We prefer the self-mix approach.... Mixers become more intimately involved in their own care. The cost savings are considerable.[2]

They added, "In the years to come, perhaps small bowel transplantation will render [home TPN] an outdated modality."

According to a recent article:

One relatively new system [to administer medication] is the totally implantable continuous infusion pump, which can deliver a steady flow of drugs directly into the bloodstream of a target organ or part of the body. Many of them are still experimental. The pumps have been applied in a variety of medical contexts.[3]

NEW ENGLAND CRITICAL CARE, INC.

As of September 1984, NECC's clients were receiving IV antibiotic therapy (16%), EN

(40%), TPN (10%), line maintenance (24%), and continuous IV chemotherapy, continuous pain management, and hydration therapy (10%). The company conducted ongoing efforts to identify new home infusion therapies; for example, it was working with Eli Lilly to study the effectiveness of treating congestive heart failure in the home with dobutamine. Other advances in infusion technology that the company followed were treatment of Alzheimer's disease using an implantable pump to deliver medication and treatment of infertility through pulsatile infusions of gonadotropins.

Company Organization

NECC's corporate office, located in Marlborough, Massachusetts, housed operations, finance, sales, marketing, and corporate development functions. Branch offices in Massachusetts, New Jersey, Maryland, New York, and California housed patient service staff and pharmaceutical compounding facilities. As of October 1984, NECC had 28 corporate employees and 75 field employees (including sales staff and branch employees). All employees received equity after 6 months.

Branch managers were responsible for supervising pharmacy, nursing, materials, and patient services; they reported to the vice president of operations in the corporate office. According to Mr. Smith:

> The branch managers will eventually have profit and loss responsibility, and the sales staff will report to them instead of to corporate headquarters. We've had a few problems with the current structure. If the sales people don't meet their quotas, they blame it on their branch. No one has ultimate responsibility; it all comes back up to me.

Sales and Marketing

Keith Trowbridge, vice president of marketing, described his situation as follows:

> Marketing this kind of product is difficult. You can advertise in industry journals, but it is hard to convince someone that your product is better; when what they see is a polyvinyl chloride bag filled with a solution that looks like water. One very important fact about this business is that people are key. The service is intangible, and there can be quick changes, because the service is ongoing.

The company sought people with five to ten years experience in medical sales and offered average cash and equity compensation levels. Rather than using "headhunters," NECC gave the sales force bonuses for recruiting new members. According to Mr. Trowbridge, "We know where the good salespeople are, and sometimes we even choose new sites based on the location of the good salespeople."

NECC's sales force of 11 (as of September 1984) operated out of the company's main offices in Boston, New York, Baltimore, San Diego, and Buffalo, with satellite offices elsewhere partially funded by Eli Lilly, as part of the research project.

Most referrals came from acute care hospitals with over 200 beds and at least an 80% occupancy rate and home health agencies, such as visiting nurse associations. Tertiary teaching hospitals were a major target, since they treated more patients with diagnoses suitable for home care.

Sales calls were directed to clinicians who treated the patients amenable to home therapies, such as surgeons, gastroenterologists, oncologists, infectious disease and pulmonary specialists, internists, nurse specialists in TPN and oncology, continuing care nurses, and pharmacists. The selling process involved much personal communication to educate these decision makers about home health technology and convince them of the quality and reliability of NECC.

The company planned to spend $100,000 over a 15-month period for advertisements in six medical journals, conduct a direct mail campaign, issue press releases about new therapies, and attend trade shows. At the trade shows, the company planned to offer special programs, such as raffles with the theme "New England Getaway." It also planned to produce a $20,000 slide show to be used for sales support. A patient education manual was being developed for $40,000. Long-term plans to enhance the company's image involved the formation of a medical advisory commission and the sponsoring of medical research in home therapies.

According to Mr. Trowbridge:

> Communication will become a problem as we grow. In a way, this company is becoming the kind of structured organization that a lot of our young salespeople and managers were trying to get away from.

Service Process

Referral sources were put in touch with the patient service coordinator, who collected the client's biographical data, insurance coverage, and treatment protocol and transferred the information to the reimbursement and nursing departments. The reimbursement department decided whether to accept the client, based on confirmation of insurance coverage. The nursing department at the branch office determined whether the company provided the type of therapy required. If not, nursing contacted the reimbursement department to halt the time-consuming process of verifying insurance coverage.

Once a client was accepted, the treatment protocol was sent to the pharmacy for planning pharmaceutical purchases. An NECC nurse confirmed protocols with the referring physician and obtained permission to meet with the client in the institution to provide training on use of the home therapy system. The training process, which took from 4 to 40 hours depending on the therapy, enabled the nurse to find out whether the client could handle the responsibility of home therapy. NECC's pharmacy also obtained the client's prescription and discussed the infusion system the patient was using.

At the client's home, the nurse observed how the client managed the home therapy procedures. They then agreed on the nurse's visit schedule; for antibiotic therapy, nurse visits occurred every three days, while the nutrition therapies frequency of visits declined as the client's independence grew. Although the company planned to begin billing according to the number of nursing visits, company policy dictated that nursing personnel were not to be involved in fiscal issues.

Every client visit or significant phone call was documented in weekly progress notes to the client's primary providers. According to Enid Gillman, director of nursing:

> We recognize that our clients bond closely to their primary providers, and we try not to disrupt this relationship. With all of these people involved in the client's care, fragmentation could easily occur. However, we don't see ourselves as competing with these other care givers. We cope with the fragmentation issue by sending out progress notes to everyone. In fact, this policy provides good PR and referrals.

The patient status was also monitored by the delivery representatives, who, by counting the number of bags a client used, could often determine whether the client was complying with the treatment regimen. According to Smith:

> I would like to streamline communications to doctors. In the future, I would like to have a system where physicians could tap into our database to see what is happening with their patients. In fact, real time communication with automatic patient monitors would be ideal.

Reimbursement

The reimbursement department decided whether to accept the patient by contacting the patient's insurance company to find out if home infusion therapy was covered. If the insurance would not provide coverage, the patient was asked if he or she were willing to pay for the service out of pocket. In general, NECC did not accept patients who could not pay. Exceptions were made in certain cases; for example, if a strong referring relationship had been developed with a particular hospital or clinician, the company accepted a patient referred from that source even if he or she could not pay. Rough estimates of the average monthly bill for the company's services were: EN, $1,500/month; IV antibiotic therapy, $4,000/month (depending on the drug); and TPN, $7,000/month.

Due to the "newness" of home infusion therapy, the reimbursement department found it necessary to spend time educating insurance claims agents about the service. According to Karen Tasi, director of reimbursement:

> When I ask insurance companies if they pay for antibiotic therapy, most say no. However, when I break the service into its components—prescriptions, durable medical equipment, and needles and syringes—the insurers do find they reimburse for these items. Nursing coverage is usually reimbursable as well. We break our bills down into components and sometimes highlight them with magic markers to make it easy for insurers.
>
> Because home infusion therapies are new, *all* of our claims go through the insurance companies' medical review. This slows down payment. It takes at least 90 days to receive payment, and from three to six months in some cases. We collect on virtually 100% of our claims because we check with insurance companies for coverage before we accept patients.

The company received reimbursement from Blue Cross, commercial insurers, Medicare, Medicaid, self-paying patients, and other institutions. The coverage of particular patients, however, varied considerably. Prices were set to cover the cost of materials, direct labor, and corporate overhead, with a small allowance for nonpaying patients. Blue Cross and commercial insurers usually paid NECC's charges. Medicare and Medicaid usually paid for only

the cost of the materials, plus a markup of 20–25%. Medicare and Medicaid determined the allowable cost of materials by reviewing published manufacturers' prices and, from these, calculating the average wholesale price. NECC paid slightly less than the average wholesale price for materials it purchased because it obtained bulk discounts. Medicare and Medicaid had the right to audit the company's books to check material costs and client billing.

Federal reimbursement policies had both positive and negative effects on the company's business. The prospective payment system for Medicare patients encouraged hospitals to discharge Medicare patients as quickly as possible. However, there was concern among government officials that the home infusion therapy market would become analogous to the renal dialysis market, where Medicare's cost for dialysis escalated from $229 million to $2 billion in ten years. In response, controls on reimbursement for home nutrition therapy tightened. The changes were not contained in public documents, but in altered instructions given to the insurance companies that review claims for home care patients on behalf of the government (intermediaries). According to Ms. Tasi:

> Much more documentation is required under the new Medicare rules. This is a big issue for us, because we have horrible cooperation from physicians in writing up the necessary reports. It is really the patients' responsibility to see that it's done, but they are too sick. Our nurses and reimbursement staff have taken on the task of filling out the forms, so the doctors only have to sign off on them.

Medicaid policies for covering home infusion therapies vary by state. Management accepted Medicaid patients only from Massachusetts, the only state that reimbursed based on usual, customary, and reasonable charges instead of a mark-up on supply cost. This caused some unhappiness among NECC referral sources. As Ms. Tasi stated:

Physicians require payment up front for their services, but yet they're upset that we reject Medicaid clients. Social workers are the most concerned. They're being squeezed—neither the hospital nor home health wants their patients. We realize that we will have to help physicians serve these people, perhaps by selling them the prescriptions without the service. They then can get their IV changed at a hospital emergency room and purchase supplies from their local pharmacy.

The company's chances of being reimbursed at full charge varied with the type of therapy provided. Cost cutting by Medicare for TPN was unlikely. However, with indications that EN was being used for convenience, particularly in nursing homes in feeding uncooperative or handicapped patients, they expected Medicare to discourage overutilization of that therapy. Ms. Tasi explained that cystic fibrosis patients, who needed antibiotic therapy, were usually well insured; in Massachusetts, Blue Cross offered them 100% coverage. The company also had a good chance of receiving full reimbursement for patients on antibiotic therapy. The company's chances of being fully reimbursed for such services as EN and line maintenance were not as great.

Ms. Tasi supervised four people in the company's reimbursement department. Each was assigned to particular branch offices to become an expert on home infusion reimbursement policies there. The company was considering two options for organization of the reimbursement function: keeping it at corporate headquarters (which was how the competitors were organized) or moving it to the branch level under the branch manager's jurisdiction. Because the reimbursement department was designing a new management information system, it did not expect to become decentralized in the near future.

PHARMACY SERVICES

NECC invested a substantial amount in compounding facilities at each of its branch offices to avoid the risk of product contamination. Whereas hospitals prepared infusion solutions for use within 24 hours, the solutions provided by the company were stored in the home for periods of up to one month. If the solutions for home use were not sterile, the logarithmic growth of bacteria occurring over the storage period could cause the patient to contract a life-threatening infection. NECC's standards for cleanliness exceeded those of the compounding facilities in most hospital pharmacies. Its quality assurance goal was to ensure that the chance of product contamination was less than 0.1%.

An example of staffing requirements and capacity was provided by the Boston compounding facility. This facility was open from 7:00 A.M. to 6:00 P.M. Monday through Friday and from 7:00 A.M. to 3:00 P.M. on Saturday. There were three pharmacists at this facility; together they provided 24-hour/day on-call coverage. The two technicians on staff worked at full capacity (8:00 A.M. to 4:30 P.M. weekdays) to serve the Boston office's 80 to 90 patients. Each clean room was built with space sufficient for eight work stations. The Boston facility was equipped with two. The compounding machines used at that time could compound three liters of solution in 20–25 minutes. However, some inventive workers were developing a new machine that could compound three liters in 10 minutes. At a cost of $8,500, the new machine could be extremely cost-effective, considering that the average technician salary was $15,000/year.

According to Mr. Mitrano, director of pharmacy services:

> Our high standards for quality in the compounding process are actually part of our business strategy. Right now there is no regulation of home infusion therapy. It is very profitable and therefore has a high potential to become regulated. We want to be at the forefront of setting standards and have the competition catch up.
>
> At the present time the only regulations we must meet are state and federal regulations requiring each compounding facility to be licensed as a pharmacy. This

means we have to have registered pharmacists on staff; be open a certain number of hours; have a pH meter (which would never be used in the infusion business); have a light box (which costs $50); and have a facility that is air conditioned (providing positive pressure). Our competition doesn't have to go beyond these licensing requirements. Our typical clean room costs $65,000 to $70,000, and is equipped with $15,000 worth of equipment. Some of our competitors use a room with carpet and four walls that would cost $3,000–$4,000 to construct, equipped with $5,000 to $6,000 worth of equipment.

At this point the state boards of pharmacy do not know what they want to regulate. Many state boards have approached the U.S. Pharmacopoeia about writing standards for home infusion therapy. [It is an independent organization comprising a panel of pharmacists and physicians.] Although it is not a government agency, it works closely with the Food and Drug Administration, and state boards of pharmacy usually mandate the standards it sets. This organization is looking for volunteers to provide assistance in developing standards for home infusion therapy. Our company has a good chance of being very instrumental in this process. I expect it will take about a year or a year and a half for a draft of the proposed standards to appear.

NURSING

Enid Gillman, director of nursing, explained:

Our goal is to deliver high-quality services, and we have individualized, flexible programs. If a hospital uses brand X pump and brand Y dressing technique, we incorporate that system in our therapy and help the clients build on what they've already learned. Other companies have a rigid system, the client has to fit whatever they offer.

One of the biggest differences between us and our competitors is that we have our own nursing staff. This is very important for quality assurance because it gives us control. Our competitors hire nurses on a "per diem" or "case-by-case" basis, or they farm out their clients to visiting nurse associations.

It is surprising how well people do on sophisticated therapies. There are a lot of biases by clinicians that unschooled patients can't do this. They seem to think, "If I went through specialized training to learn these therapies, how can they be learned by someone without a high school education?"

Ms. Gillman stated that most of the company's nurses had 10 to 12 years of experience, with well-developed IV therapy skills in such areas as pediatrics, geriatrics, or chemotherapy. The company provided individualized "hands-on" training based on each nurse's needs. Compensation was competitive with that provided by teaching hospitals, and according to Ms. Gillman:

Our company gives nurses career options within the realm of patient care, rather than the traditional move to administration. Here they can use their specialized clinical skills and get different rewards, such as the autonomy that comes with managing your own client load.

Ms. Gillman also explained:

Staffing ratios are very difficult for us to determine right now. We go with a 1:10 or 1:15 nurse:patient ratio, although we don't really have the facts to justify it. When a new branch office is opened with only one nurse, they have a 24-hour/day commitment. I have to watch for burnout. Recruitment and retention are important to us because we're growing so fast. Because the hiring process takes about two months, we really have to plan ahead.

Ms. Gillman was responsible for development of treatment protocols and quality assurance procedures. Quality assurance audits involved reviewing client records and accompanying nurses on client visits. Plans were to decentralize auditing in the future so nursing managers would audit each other's branches.

MATERIALS MANAGEMENT

The materials management function involved ordering pharmaceutical supplies and infusion equipment from vendors, rotating stock, and checking equipment. According to Mr. Smith, "We're the only company that tests the electronic equipment before it goes out to the patients and brings it back again monthly for testing."

The job performed by the delivery representatives was also part of materials management. They delivered medical supplies to patients' homes and hospitals, took inventory, rotated and stored supplies in patients' homes and hospitals, and represented the company in providing nonclincial information. They were required to be on call, rotating weekends and evenings. Qualifications for this position were a high school diploma and a valid Class D driver's license. The annual salary was $16,000. NECC had designed a career path to enable delivery representatives to move into management positions, first through becoming a supervisor, and then a materials planner. Noted Mr. Smith, "We look for friendly people who smile readily and are outgoing in this job."

COMPETITION

NECC faced an impressive line-up of competitors, attracted by the industry's high growth potential and profit margins. (Materials cost represented only about 18–22% of a home infusion therapy company's revenues.) Table 13.6 briefly describes the major industry participants and their projected revenue and market share.

PLANS FOR THE FUTURE

Mr. Smith's goal was for NECC to become the quality leader in the home health industry. He explained,

> Home health is a $1 billion market now. It will be $5 billion by 1990. I'm not concerned about half a million here or there. Our current losses are caused by going after market share. By December 1985, we plan to have $40 to $50 million in revenue in twelve centers, and we expect to be profitable in the fourth quarter.
>
> Our niche is *quality*. We've invested in experienced IV therapists, quality control in the pharmaceutical compounding process, and experts in reimbursement. The management team I've put together will run a $50–$70 million company. My philosophy is, if you believe in the market and can support a loss for a few years, invest in service, in the very best people.

POINTS TO PONDER

1. What opportunity should NECC be fulfilling?
2. Review its management initiatives. Is it focusing on the appropriate issues? How well is it implementing them?

Table 13.6 New England Critical Care, Inc.: Home Infusion Therapy Market Revenue Estimates

(dollars in millions)

Company	1983E	1984E	1988E	Compound Annual Growth
Baxter Travenol	$ 46	$ 65	$ 195	34%
Home Health Care of America	43	55	160	30
American ContinueCare	11	22	160	71
Abbott Home Care	5	12	90	78
HNS (Healthdyne)	10	20	72	48
Omnicare	5	12	55	62
Investor-owned Hospitals	—	3	80	127
Other Hospitals	50	68	133	22
Other Providers	95	108	140	8
Total	$ 265	$ 365	$1,085	33%

Source: Hambrecht & Quist.

NOTES

1. Bama B. Rucker and Kimberley A. Holmsted, *Home Infusion Therapy Industry* (San Francisco: Hambrecht & Quist Incorporated, March 1984).

2. George L. Blackburn and Richard J. Baptista, "Home TPN: State of the Art," *American Journal of Intravenous Therapy and Clinical Nutrition*, February 1984.

3. Kim Friedman, "Implantable Pump Targets Medication," *Boston Globe*, October 22, 1984.

Case Study 14

North Shore Birth Center

INTRODUCTION

Dorothy Kuell, who prompted Beverly Hospital to set up a birth center, described the vision of the center's founders:

> At a birth center, birth would be a true family experience. There would be no limit on visiting hours or on the number of family and friends attending the birth. A mother would not be confined to one room: She could walk outside, sit in the living room, rest in the bedroom, or take a bath. She could deliver squatting, lying, or sitting. The nurse-midwives would support and assist the mother and her family throughout labor and delivery, unlike the physician, who usually appears only at the delivery, or the labor nurses, who leave when their shifts change.[1]

This vision became reality when the North Shore Birth Center (named for its North Shore of Massachusetts location) opened in November 1980.

INDUSTRY OVERVIEW

History

The North Shore Birth Center was one of a growing number of alternatives to the hospital birth experience. Birth centers were the culmi-

Note: This case was prepared by Professor Regina E. Herzlinger and also by Joyce Lallman under the supervision of Assistant Professor Nancy Kane. It is a companion to Case Study 1, Beverly Hospital.

nation of a long evolution in the preferred birthing location and the professional management of the delivery process.[2]

During the 18th and 19th centuries, childbirth in the United States underwent a gradual shift away from the earlier "social childbirth," in which the woman in labor was surrounded by female friends and relatives and was attended by an experienced (often salaried) midwife. Male physicians gradually became more relied upon, especially in the event of delivery complications. In the 1950s, childbirth became more specialized, with obstetricians replacing general practitioners. The number of lay or "granny" midwives practicing in the United States declined from an estimated 20,700 in 1948 to approximately 1,800 in 1976, and they were located mostly in low-income or remote areas, where no other professional services were available.

As management of the child delivery process became more technical, so did the birth setting. At the beginning of the 20th century over 95% of deliveries in the United States took place at home, but by 1955 almost 95% took place at the hospital. This shift was prompted by advances in medical science, particularly the development of anesthesia and safer surgical intervention techniques for obstetrical emergencies. Hospitals became the only setting with the technical and professional capacity necessary to respond to all medical complications.

During the past decade, the hospital delivery model was challenged. One article cites the following factors:

> The women's movement has affected maternity services, reacting ... against the

perceived male domination of the medical profession.... In addition, there has been growing concern about the rising rates of cesarean deliveries and levels of medication and the psychological consequences of the often impersonalized hospital atmosphere. Nurse-midwives have asserted their competence to perform uncomplicated maternity care.[3]

Nurse-Midwives

A nurse-midwife is a registered nurse with additional training in obstetrics from a school accredited by the American College of Nurse-Midwives. The college certified approximately 250 nurse-midwives each year from 1980 through 1983, and by May 1984 there were 3,018 certified nurse-midwives. In order to practice, certified nurse-midwives must establish an alliance agreement with a physician and health care protocols for consultation and referral when complications arise.

Internationally, nurse-midwives have achieved widespread recognition—for example, they perform many of the deliveries in England and the Netherlands—but a U.S. voluntary hospital did not accept a nurse-midwife on its professional staff until 1964. In 1971 the American College of Obstetricians and Gynecologists recognized that nurse-midwives, as part of a medical team, "may assume responsibility for the complete care and management of uncomplicated maternity patients." By 1984, nurse-midwifery was legal in every state except North Dakota.

The number and proportion of hospital deliveries attended by midwives increased continuously to 63,063 hospital births (1.7% of all births) in 1982.

Cesarean Births

Cesarean births in hospitals, jumped from less than 6% in 1970 to over 18% in 1983 in the United States and to 20% in the Northeast. One study cites these causal factors:

Changing expectations about pregnancy outcomes and an increasing emphasis on delivering the "perfect baby...." Reluctance to accept the risks associated with midforceps deliveries; cesareans, to a large extent, have replaced them. New medical technologies, in particular the fetal heart monitor which electronically measures the fetal heart rate...changes in maternal age.... Fear of malpractice suits is the most frequent reason given by physicians for the increase....Many health insurance plans offer more extensive coverage for cesarean births, [which] may be financially attractive to hospitals.[4]

Birth Centers

Birth centers were designed to offer a more homelike setting than the hospital. Women and their companions often take classes in nutrition, relaxation, and breathing and can spend up to ten times as many hours with nurse-midwives than they would spend with an obstetrician before a typical hospital birth.

Birth centers' costs were one-third the cost of a typical $2,500 to $3,500 hospital birth, including the physician fee. Many insurers included reimbursement of approved birth centers as a regular part of their medical coverage. "We're in favor of anything that saves money without endangering anybody," said a spokesperson for the industry. In 1984, 18 states had regulated birth centers, 20 (including the District of Columbia) were exploring or drafting regulations, and 13 had not started the rule-making process.

The first birthing center demonstration project, the Childbearing Center in New York City, began operation in 1975. Between 1981 and 1984 the number of centers grew to 120 and they were located in many parts of the United States. Births in nonhospital settings and attended by midwives, although a small proportion of total births, increased 12% from 12,754 in 1981 to 14,375 in 1982.

The corporate structure of birth centers reflects their grassroots development. A 1982 survey found 50% organized as nonprofit corporations and only 34% as private professional corporations. Although nurse-midwives provided the impetus for their development, 28% were run by doctors. In 1983, Dr. John S. Short, executive vice president of a multihospital system based in Houston, started a chain of birthing centers to be developed in joint ventures with obstetricians. He predicted that from 30% to 40% of births would be done in one-day stays within five years. Birth centers would compete on the basis of their lower costs. In his experience, a 7,500-square-foot center cost $1.2 million to build, with facilities for elective and emergency surgery. A 5,000- to 6,000-square-foot center without operating rooms would cost $500,000 to build. His first center experienced a 25% drop-out rate in the pre-natal period.[5]

Safety Issues

The American College of Obstetricians and Gynecologists stated that the hospital setting provided the safest environment for mothers and infants during labor, delivery, and the postpartum period. From 10% to 20% of women using birth centers for delivery have to be transferred to hospitals. Dr. Bruce Shepard, author of *The Complete Guide to Women's Health*, expressed reservations about birth centers despite his advocacy of more "humanistic" obstetrics:

> It's difficult to prove with statistics that the birth center is less safe than the hospital, but my strong inclination is that it would be less safe. I would rather see birth-center practices in fully equipped hospitals because when you have an emergency in obstetrics, you have just minutes for intervention. Between 10% and 30% of high-risk situations emanate from low-risk mothers. You can't select those that need to deliver in a hospital in advance.[6]

Other physicians, however, support birth centers. A representative of Dr. Short said, "We are already finding doctors more interested in

the idea, either in joint ventures with entrepreneurs or in establishing their own centers. They want to protect their market, and they are responding to insurers' outcry about rising medical costs."

A matched sample of a large number of women at a birth center comparable to the one at Beverly Hospital and the maternity service at a large teaching hospital revealed more favorable outcomes for the women at the birth center. However, the percentage of babies with unfavorable risk profiles was higher at the birth center.[7]

Consumers

Consumer surveys indicated that despite the increased family involvement in the childbirth process, most consumers preferred hospitals over birth centers; in one, 79% of the female respondents planning to have children preferred hospitalization to a free-standing birthing center. Eighty-five percent preferred a doctor at the childbirth, whether in a hospital or free-standing birthing center, to a nonphysician practitioner or midwife; 4% preferred birth in a hospital assisted by a nonphysician medical practitioner or midwife instead of a doctor; and 11% preferred childbirth in a separate birthing center not attached to a hospital but with a physician present.[8]

The Childbearing Center found that

> the population delivering at [the Childbearing Center] is clearly atypical of the total childbearing population in New York City. The women are likely to be between 25 and 34 years of age, white, and better educated than the general population of women bearing children. Few of them depend on Medicaid. The occupation of almost half of the women is either professional or managerial.[9]

Birth Rates

There were 3,680,537 births in the U.S. in 1982. The last decade has shown a marked shift in childbearing to later ages. For example, while the proportion of all births to teenagers fell from 19 percent in 1975 to 14 percent in 1982, the proportion occurring to mothers aged 30 years and older increased from 17 to 22 percent. Because the incidence of impaired fertility rises sharply with advancing age, continued delay of motherhood by these women may reduce the number of children they ultimately have.

The birth rates per 1,000 population increased by 2 percent or less in four geographic divisions, including New England.[10] Massachusetts resident births continued to increase in 1981 to 73,931, a 1.8% rise over 1980. Of these, 99.2% occurred in hospitals. Fifty-eight hospitals operated maternity units then, with the number of births ranging from a low of 61 at one to 7,099 at Boston's Brigham and Women's Hospital. Almost 26% of births occurred in only four hospitals.[11]

NORTH SHORE BIRTH CENTER

Development

Before the establishment of the birth center, Beverly Hospital's 16-bed maternity unit was running at 50–60% occupancy. Births had dropped from 1,300 in the late 1960s to 518 in 1976, caused by a decline in the overall birth rate and increased competition. The nearby Hunt Hospital in Danvers had grown from 250–300 births per year in the early 1960s to 500 births by 1976 (see Tables 14.1 and 14.2). Home births in the Beverly area were increasing, to an estimated 100—120 per year in the late 1970s. The obstetricians at Beverly Hospital during this period developed innovative practices, such as allowing fathers to attend most deliveries.

When Dorothy Kuell came to Beverly Hospital in 1977 as the new maternity coordinator, she joined local consumers and midwives in the effort to establish a birth center. It opened in November 1980 with two certified nurse-midwives as staff who were already well known by the consumers

supporting natural childbirth and who brought many potential clients with them. Fran Ventre, director of the center, explained her involvement:

> My interest in natural childbirth started with the birth of my own children. I felt ripped off by the natural childbirth classes I attended, because during the birth I wasn't in control. Doctors used the same procedures and rules as for drugged women, including restrictions on nursing or even holding the baby. I joined a well-educated group of women who wanted a healthier, more family-centered approach to childbirth.
>
> I became a childbirth educator and labor coach and went back to school and became a nurse, and then a nurse-midwife. By the time I met Dorothy Kuell, I had been working for over eight years for a doctor who was very supportive of the natural childbirth movement.

Services

A client was first screened to determine risk status. Risky clients (for example, diabetics or women with previous cesarean births), were referred to the maternity services within Beverly Hospital, where they were followed by an obstetrician and, if they chose, a nurse-midwife. "Normal low risks" returned to the birth center for education on such topics as nutrition and exercise. Each client's partner was encouraged to accompany her on these visits so the couple could do their own pre-natal check-ups, urine tests, and recordkeeping. The nurse-midwives met weekly with the medical director to review client care and to refer high-risk clients. A client with no complications could deliver her baby without ever seeing a doctor or stepping into a hospital.

When a client was admitted to the birth center for delivery, the nurse-midwife performed a complete evaluation, including reassignment of risk status, if appropriate. The nurse-midwife stayed with the client during labor to provide physical and emotional support, including breathing and relaxation exer-

Table 14.1 North Shore Birth Center: Births by Hospital of Occurrence, 1970, 1975, 1980, and 1981

Name and Location of Hospital	1970	1975	1980	1981	Percentage Change 1975–80	1981–82
Addison Gilbert, Gloucester	443	342	372	333	8	(10)
Anna Jacques, Newburyport	448	572	771	666	35	(14)
Beverly Hospital, Beverly	951	560	711	852	27	20
Hunt Memorial, Danvers	397	487	480	500	0	4
Lynn Hospital, Lynn	1,400	1,362	1,344	1,289	0	(4)
Salem Hospital, Salem	1,358	962	1,143	1,146	19	0
Union Hospital, Lynn	854	0	0	0	N/A	N/A

Table 14.2 North Shore Birth Center: Distance from Beverly Hospital

	Distance (miles)	Drive Time (minutes)
Hunt Memorial, Danvers	4.2	12
Salem Hospital, Salem	4.5	19
Atlanti-Care Medical Centers		
Union Hospital, Lynn	12.5	19
Lynn Hospital, Lynn	7.9	33
Addison Gilbert Hospital, Gloucester	13.4	18

Source: Beverly Hospital.

cises; to implement client wishes regarding physical position during delivery; and to administer local anesthetics if deemed appropriate.

If any emergencies arose, the mother and/or baby were transferred immediately to the hospital. Those without complications were generally discharged after 4 hours and before 12 hours postpartum; most went home after 5 hours. In about 90% of the cases, clients were visited by their pediatrician before discharge.

Although Beverly Hospital administrators predicted about 75 births for the center's first year, between November 1980 and mid-January 1981, 61 clients were accepted into the program. The total 70 intrapartum transfers and the 774 Birth Center births experienced 23 unexpected complications (Table 14.3). A survey of clients showed that 65% were from Beverly Hospital's normal service area and 35% were from towns as far away as Cambridge. When asked where else they would have delivered, 31% cited Beverly Hospital, 27% cited other hospitals, and 16% claimed they would have delivered at home.

Operations

The center was located 400 feet from the driveway of the hospital's emergency room in a building constructed in 1950 as a residence for the hospital's chief administrative officer. It was equipped for use as a birth center at a cost of approximately $20,000. It could accommodate four women in labor or delivery at one time; there were two beds and two fold-out couches. The atmosphere was homelike and cozy; emergency equipment (such as oxygen) was hidden behind bedroom closet doors.

When the center first opened, it was staffed by two midwives. Because each birth was attended by both, they were on call continuously. They also conducted home visits the day after each baby was born. Their starting salaries were about $18,000 per year.

By 1984, three midwives were employed (including the director). Two were at the center on any one day, except that all three were present on Thursdays for consultation with the medical director. Responsibility for being "in charge" of clinical services and births was rotated among the three midwives.

Administration

For clinical purposes the director of the birth center reported to the chief of obstetrics. During their weekly meetings, they discussed pre-natal patients' risk status. For administrative purposes, the director met weekly with the hospital's executive vice president. The birth center did not have its own business manager, but instead relied on the hospital's business staff.

According to Beverly Hospital's budget director:

> The midwives at first had difficulty accommodating to institutional policies. When they were asked to choose a director, they resisted, saying, "No, we are all equals." They also resisted the idea of merit evaluation. They made statements to the press without consulting the hospital's public relations staff and expenditures without proper budgetary authority. I've spent a lot of time teaching them about administration. When it comes to marketing, though, the midwives themselves are the best marketing tool—their clients respect them so much.

Ms. Ventre explained, "I believe in consensus management and a system of peer review with input from the medical director."

Charge Structure and Financing

In 1984, services cost an all-inclusive $1,045 at the birth center. Beverly Hospital's fees alone were $2,200, exclusive of physician fees (usually around $1,000). In a survey of birth center clients, 32% were covered by Blue Cross, 35% were covered by commercial insurers, 5% were covered by Medicaid, and 27% were self-paying clients.

Insurance coverage was initially in doubt for some patients. According to the budget director:

> Blue Cross and Medicaid recognized reimbursement for birth center services as a pilot. However, some commercial insurers were initially reluctant to recognize payment for midwifery services without a physician or a hospital even though they would save $2,000 per birth.

Beverly Hospital conducted seminars for the commercial insurers and eventually succeeded in getting coverage for birth center services from most commercial insurers as well as two health maintenance organizations.

If a birth center client was transferred to the hospital for the delivery, the client paid the birth center rate for prenatal care, plus the regular hospital charge for the delivery, plus a transfer charge of $165 to cover the midwives'

Table 14.3 North Shore Birth Center: Birth Center Statistics

	1983–84	1982–83	1981–82
Total Births	228	213	225
Transfers	19	16	23
Unexpected Complications	5	9	5
Risked Out	28	24	24
Infant Transfers	2	3	2

time. The bad debt rate at the center was slightly lower than the hospital's overall bad debt rate, because many of the clients felt that they were "part of" the center.

BEVERLY HOSPITAL–BIRTH CENTER RELATIONSHIP

The birth center and Beverly Hospital had some conflicts. Not unexpectedly, there were some initial difficulties in developing the initial medical procedures to be followed at the birth center and over certain issues, such as the point at which a woman experiencing a difficult labor should be transferred to the hospital's delivery room or how the baby should be handled immediately after delivery.

Nevertheless, the positive effects of the birth center on Beverly Hospital may well outweigh the start-up difficulties. Dorothy Kuell explained:

> Many of the midwives' ideas have spread to the hospital. We also have an assertive nursing staff at the hospital. The hospital set up a "women's health service," staffed by a certified nurse-midwife, who runs an in-house pre-natal service and maternity service on similar protocols as the birth center.

According to Robert Fanning, Beverly Hospital's CEO:

> In thinking of the birth center as a business, I believe you have to look at the problems you face getting a counterculture group to integrate. It's essential to have dedicated commitment from the clinical people. The chief of obstetrics can destroy the entire concept.

The birth center fits well with our marketing strategy. This hospital's traditional market is Beverly and areas to the north. We are now targeting our secondary market with a new ad campaign that will focus on maternity care. "Beautiful Beginnings" is the theme. We hope to maintain a relationship with maternity patients that will lead to continued use of Beverly Hospital. We want to present the image: "This is a progressive hospital. We'll provide a birth experience that will meet your expectations."

See Tables 14.4 to 14.10 for financial results.

THE FUTURE

Ms. Ventre expressed the following views on the future:

> I believe it is a good thing that consumers today have more options. I don't tell people that the birth center is the only place to have a child. I think the consumer movement for natural childbirth will continue to thrive. However, consumers can be fooled. Hospitals are building beautiful facilities for childbirth, but it is the medical practice that really makes the difference.

POINTS TO PONDER

1. What opportunity does the North Shore Birth Center represent?
2. Is it a good idea for the Beverly Hospital to sponsor it?
3. What managerial skills are critical to its success? How well are these being implemented?

Table 14.4 North Shore Birth Center: Obstetrics Service, Beverly Hospital Statistics, 1976–1984

	1976	1977	1978	1979	1980	1981	1982	1983	1984
Obstetrics—Unit Deliveries	518	568	639	670	711	744	865	876	913
Alternative Birth Center Deliveries	—	—	—	—	—	108	225	213	228
Total Deliveries	518	568	639	670	711	852	1,090	1,089	1,141
Number of Beds									
In-House	16	16	16	14[a]	14	14	14	14	14
Birth Center						4	4	4	4
Occupancy (%) In-House	40%	43%	48%	52%	58.5%	73.3%	83.0%	79.6%	79.5%
Birth Center Gross Revenue						$ 82,600	$189,800	$210,400	$251,900
Birth Center Direct Expense						$ 71,708	$101,100	$117,800	$135,600
Birth Center Indirect Expense						61,733	75,251	83,241	94,920
Birth Center Total Expense						$133,441	$176,351	$201,041	$230,520

[a]Licensed beds reduced to 14 in February 1979.

Table 14.5 North Shore Birth Center: Direct Expense Breakdown—Obstetrics Service

	Department	
	Obstetrics	Newborn
Salaries and Wages	$ 305,300	$ 213,800
M.D. Compensation	0	0
Supplies and Expenses	$ 20,400	$ 14,100
Expenses for Major Movable Equipment	$ 1,619	$ 4,091
Reclassification	0	0
Recovery	0	0
Total Direct Expense	$ 327,319	$ 231,991

Note: Contractual allowances and bad debts are not available on a department basis.

Table 14.6 North Shore Birth Center: Allocated Expense Breakdown—Obstetrics Service

	Department	
	Obstetrics	Newborn
Interest and Depreciation	$ 53,063	$ 21,593
Fringe Expense	30,635	35,459
Administration	107,539	75,309
Plant	74,712	30,403
Laundry	18,037	21,292
Housekeeping	30,387	12,365
Cafeteria	10,150	7,324
Dietary	74,587	——
Nursing Administration	32,586	23,513
Central Service	3,270	4,067
Pharmacy	105	153
Medical Records	33,947	32,368
Medical Review	24,078	20,647
Social Service	6,205	——
Total Allocated Expense	$ 499,301	$ 284,463

Table 14.7 North Shore Birth Center: Gross Patient Service Revenue, by Service, FY ending September 30, 1984

Service	Routine	Ancillary	Total
Inpatient			
Medical-Surgical	$ 9,304,837	$ 10,616,861	$ 19,921,698
Pediatric	468,892	559,616	1,028,508
Obstetrics	740,807	859,332	1,600,139
Psychiatric	1,194,313	149,504	1,343,817
ICU	1,772,976	3,021,428	4,794,404
Newborn	493,950	65,240	559,190
Subtotal Inpatient	13,975,775	15,271,981	29,247,756
Ambulatory			
Emergency	1,947,755	1,039,674	2,987,429
Clinic	539,742	2,930,415	3,470,157
Satellite Clinic	0	2,786,660	2,786,660
Surgery	219,976	1,148,021	1,367,997
Ambulatory Dialysis	0	1,845,407	1,845,407
Subtotal Ambulatory	2,707,473	9,750,177	12,457,650
Total Patient Care	$ 16,683,248	$ 25,022,158	$ 41,705,406

Table 14.8 North Shore Birth Center: Ancillary Expenses, by Service

(dollars in thousands)

Service	Total Ancillary	Direct	Allocated
Inpatient			
Medical-Surgical	$ 6,593	$ 4,256	$ 2,337
Pediatric	367	239	128
Obstetrics	869	565	304
Psychiatric	90	59	31
ICU	1,740	1,131	609
Newborn	187	122	65
Subtotal Inpatient	$ 9,846	$ 6,372	$ 3,474
Outpatient			
Emergency	$ 874	$ 568	$ 306
Clinic	2,277	1,480	797
Satellite Clinic	2,315	1,505	810
Surgery	658	428	230
Ambulatory Dialysis	1,642	1,067	575
Subtotal Outpatient	$ 7,766	$ 5,048	$ 2,718
Total Expenses	$ 17,612	$ 11,420	$ 6,192

Table 14.9 Accounting for the Costs of Each Beverly Hospital Department—Beverly Hospital Stepdown Expenses (basis of allocation) (in dollars)

| | Direct Expenses | Allocated | Total Expense for Stepdown | (sq. ft.) Interest and Depreciation | (payroll dollars) | | (sq. ft.) Plant | (pounds laundry) Laundry |
					Fringes	Adminis-tration		
Depreciation and Long-Term Interest	2,506,890	0	2,506,890	—	—	—	—	—
Fringe Benefits	2,941,074	15,359	2,956,433	15,359	—	—	—	—
Administration and Short-Term Interest	4,580,160	793,284	5,373,444	366,935	426,349	—	—	—
Plant Operations and Maintenance	2,011,225	669,527	2,680,752	251,542	119,878	254,600	—	—
Laundry and Linen	265,085	227,807	492,892	51,358	33,336	70,801	77,312	—
Housekeeping	655,486	365,578	1,021,064	38,668	87,222	185,244	59,444	0
Cafeteria	303,326	251,937	555,263	35,246	47,019	99,861	49,627	0
Dietary	890,339	448,252	1,338,591	53,783	77,437	164,462	80,726	1,231
Nursing Administration	513,176	517,333	1,030,509	82,496	81,550	173,197	126,153	688
Central Service	122,417	200,982	323,399	50,383	13,285	28,215	75,939	5,321
Pharmacy	356,136	301,368	657,504	38,159	54,400	115,535	56,727	0
Medical Records	422,875	366,601	789,476	51,203	62,759	133,288	77,093	0
Medical Care Review	135,466	59,214	194,680	2,790	15,093	32,054	4,437	0
Social Service	199,979	195,255	395,234	29,067	32,557	69,145	45,926	0
Subtotal Overhead	15,903,634	—	—	1,066,988	1,050,885	1,326,402	653,384	7,240

Table 14.9 continued

(hours service) House-keeping	*(FTE)* Cafeteria	*(# Meals)* Dietary	*(nursing hours)* Nursing Administration	*(costed requisitions)* Central Service	Pharmacy	*(% time)* Medical Records	*(# patients reviewed)* Medical Review	*(# cases)* Social Service	*Total Expense After Stepdown*
—	—	—	—	—	—	—	—	—	—
—	—	—	—	—	—	—	—	—	—
—	—	—	—	—	—	—	—	—	—
—	—	—	—	—	—	—	—	—	—
—	—	—	—	—	—	—	—	—	—
—	—	—	—	—	—	—	—	—	—
20,184	—	—	—	—	—	—	—	—	—
30,799	44,814	—	—	—	—	—	—	—	—
47,242	16,007	0	—	—	—	—	—	—	—
28,852	3,987	0	0	—	—	—	—	—	—
21,852	13,602	0	0	4,093	—	—	—	—	—
29,322	17,932	0	0	4	0	—	—	—	—
1,598	3,750	0	0	0	0	0	—	—	—
16,646	6,912	0	0	2	0	0	0	—	—
196,495	107,004	0	0	4,099	0	0	0	0	—

continues

Table 14.9 continued

	Direct Expenses	Allocated	Total Expense for Stepdown	Allocated Expenses				
				(sq. ft.) Interest and Depreciation	(payroll dollars) Fringes	Adminis- tration	(sq. ft.) Plant	(pounds laundry) Laundry
Surgery, Recovery, Anesthesia	1,136,228	—	—	158,270	114,803	243,822	222,842	67,771
Labor	395,964	—	—	37,339	55,113	117,050	52,573	11,581
Intravenous	572,720	—	—	4,529	31,761	67,454	6,377	0
Medical Supplies	832,000	—	—	0	0	0	0	0
Drugs	969,092	—	—	0	0	0	0	0
Lab	2,839,706	—	—	120,344	213,253	452,912	169,443	2,364
Cardiac Catheter and EKG	400,055	—	—	8,449	12,074	25,643	11,896	1,329
Diagnostic Radiology	1,218,101	—	—	185,477	106,925	227,090	261,150	7,195
CT Scan	92,900	—	—	0	4,594	9,757	0	0
Nuclear Medicine	145,300	—	—	0	8,376	17,788	0	0
Respiratory and Pulmonary Therapy	572,698	—	—	36,830	58,662	124,588	51,857	0
EMG/EEG	146,637	—	—	10,309	6,286	13,350	14,515	1,181
Rehabilitation	527,579	—	—	65,732	80,704	171,401	92,409	3,054
Psychiatric	210,353	—	—	41,824	24,297	51,603	58,887	0
Renal Dialysis	1,138,431	—	—	88,597	92,330	196,093	124,744	16,214
Other	170,588	—	—	4,152	17,779	37,760	5,847	0
Subtotal Ancillary	11,368,352	—	—	761,752	826,957	1,756,311	1,072,541	110,689
Medical-Surgical	3,604,036	—	—	287,883	568,908	1,208,259	405,336	245,105
Pediatric	360,203	—	—	51,048	57,286	121,664	71,875	20,305
Obstetric	327,319	—	—	53,063	50,635	107,539	74,712	18,037
Psychiatric	644,591	—	—	44,470	82,827	175,909	62,613	11,581
Intensive Care	1,004,939	—	—	80,171	152,966	324,872	112,879	23,704
Newborn	231,991	—	—	21,593	35,459	75,309	30,403	21,292
Subtotal Inpatient Routine	6,173,079	—	—	538,228	948,081	2,013,552	757,818	340,024
Emergency	1,327,065	—	—	54,015	87,023	184,821	76,053	28,583
Clinic	241,885	—	—	73,571	34,166	72,562	103,587	6,356
Surgery	58,582	—	—	12,336	9,321	19,796	17,369	0
Subtotal Ambulatory	1,627,532	—	—	139,922	130,510	277,179	197,009	34,939
Total Patient Care	35,072,597	—	—	2,506,890	2,956,433	5,373,444	2,680,752	492,892

Note: See notes to financial statements (Exhibit 1.4).

Table 14.9 continued

Allocated Expenses

(hours service) House-keeping	(FTE) Cafeteria	(# Meals) Dietary	(nursing hours) Nursing Ad-ministration	(costed requisitions) Central Service	Pharmacy	(% time) Medical Records	(# patients reviewed) Medical Review	(# cases) Social Service	Total Expense After Stepdown
90,635	25,447	0	81,697	93,343	7,878	0	0	0	2,242,409
21,382	10,455	0	33,566	9,069	762	0	0	0	744,854
2,594	6,003	0	19,272	2,456	0	0	0	0	713,166
0	0	0	0	69,477	0	0	0	0	901,477
0	0	0	0	0	630,220	0	0	0	1,599,211
68,916	52,268	0	0	18,797	47	0	0	0	3,938,050
4,838	4,108	0	0	615	3	0	0	0	469,010
106,215	28,845	0	0	2,989	348	0	0	0	2,144,335
0	810	0	0	0	0	0	0	0	108,061
0	1,726	0	0	0	0	0	0	0	173,090
21,090	13,747	0	0	18,136	274	0	0	0	897,882
5,904	1,589	0	0	0	0	0	0	0	200,200
37,584	19,803	0	0	2,035	13	0	0	0	1,000,214
23,951	6,614	0	0	7	12	0	0	0	417,548
50,736	20,910	0	67,133	13,844	111	0	0	0	1,809,143
2,378	3,299	0	10,593	603	10	0	0	0	253,009
436,223	195,624	0	212,261	231,371	639,678	0	0	0	17,611,759
164,858	142,554	1,031,750	457,672	50,664	2,027	447,633	109,258	357,903	9,083,846
29,233	12,044	51,346	38,667	3,705	187	23,684	15,529	6,411	863,187
30,387	10,150	74,587	32,568	3,270	105	33,947	24,878	6,205	847,420
25,466	20,712	91,910	66,496	620	103	39,474	5,228	0	1,272,000
45,910	30,335	78,895	97,390	13,962	753	27,632	19,140	14,684	2,028,232
12,365	7,324	0	23,513	4,067	153	32,368	20,647	0	516,484
308,219	223,119	1,328,488	716,324	76,288	3,328	604,738	194,680	385,203	14,611,169
30,932	18,550	0	59,556	6,567	10,385	44,211	0	1,138	1,928,899
42,131	9,103	0	36,386	4,708	4,090	140,527	0	8,893	777,965
7,064	1,863	10,103	5,982	366	23	0	0	0	142,805
80,127	29,516	10,103	101,924	11,641	14,498	184,738	0	10,031	2,849,669
1,021,064	555,263	1,338,591	1,030,509	323,399	657,504	789,476	194,680	395,234	35,072,597

Source: Schedule XV, RSC-403 (12/81)

Table 14.10 North Shore Birth Center: Payer Mix, by Service

Service	Total	Blue Cross	Medicare	Medicaid	Industrial Accident	Commercial Insurance	Self-Pay
			INPATIENT DAYS				
Inpatient							
Medical-Surgical	52,873	4,054	32,315	4,104	356	10,872	1,172
Pediatric	2,758	1,068	102	291	13	1,112	172
Obstetrics	4,074	1,949	5	243	0	1,546	331
Psychiatry	4,659	1,336	538	1,246	0	1,036	503
Intensive Care	4,664	845	2,962	95	1	569	192
Newborn	3,414	1,640	0	214	0	1,283	277
Total Inpatient	72,442	10,892	35,992	6,193	370	16,418	2,647
			VISITS				
Outpatient	48,440	18,534	8,015	2,893	2,224	13,003	3,771
			DOLLARS (thousands)				
Gross Patient Service Revenue	$ 41,705	$ 9,353	$ 19,230	$ 2,494	$ 464	$ 8,205	$ 1,959
Deductions							
Contractual	4,644	941	2,601	1,080	22	0	0
Free Care	584	0	0	0	0	0	584
Bad Debt	1,028	0	0	0	0	514	514
Total Deductions	$ 6,256	$ 941	$ 2,601	$ 1,080	$ 22	$ 514	$ 1,098
Net Revenue	$ 35,449	$ 8,412	$ 16,629	$ 1,414	$ 442	$ 7,691	$ 861
			DAYS				
Average Days Receivable	53	41	37	96	120	64	251

NOTES

1. Deborah Cramer, "Birth without Doctors," *Boston Globe*, April 12, 1981.

2. L. Cannoodt, S. Sieverts, and M. Schachter, "Alternatives to the Conventional In-Hospital Delivery: The Childbearing Center Experience," *Acta Hospitalia* 22, no. 4 (Winter 1982): 324–339.

3. Cannoodt et al.

4. Massachusetts Department of Public Health, *Cesarean Births in Massachusetts*. (Boston, Mass.: Massachusetts Department of Public Health, 1984), pp. 8–9.

5. Donald E.L. Johnson, "40% of Births in Hospitals Could be Borne by Birthing Centers," *Modern Healthcare* 13, no. 12, December 1983: 1240.

6. J.R. Brandstrader, "As More Women Have Babies in Birth Centers, Doctors, Hospitals Rethink Obstetric Procedures," *Wall Street Journal*, November 29, 1983.

7. Gigliola Baruffi, Woodrow S. Dellinger, Jr., Donna M. Stobino, Alice Rudolph, Rebecca Y. Timmons, and Alan Ross, "A Study of Pregnancy Outcomes in a Maternity Center and a Tertiary Care Hospital," *American Journal of Public Health* 74, no. 9 (September 1984): 973–978.

8. Bill Jackson and Joyce Jensen, "Home Care Tops Consumers' List," *Modern Healthcare,* May 1, 1984: 88–90.

9. Canoodt, Sieverts, and Schachter, "Alternatives to the Conventional In-Hospital Delivery: The Childbearing Center Experience."

10. National Center for Health Statistics, *Monthly Vital Statistics Report* 33, no. 6 (1984).

11. Registry of Vital Statistics, *1981 Annual Report of Vital Statistics of Massachusetts,* Massachusetts Department of Public Health, Document No. 1.

Case Study 15

Novel Combination of Two Drugs

While performing a somewhat routine course of investigation in 1986, David O'Leary, M.D., Ph.D., made a startling discovery: Combining two of the most widely used treatments for gastrointestinal (GI) problems created a new drug with considerably improved efficacy.

Tagamet, SmithKline Beecham's "homerun" drug, had revolutionized the market by providing a treatment, not just a palliative, for ulcers. With sales in the billions, Tagamet (cimetidine) spawned a host of competing drugs (Exhibit 15.1 and Table 15.1). All were in pill form; Dr. O'Leary's insight was to create a cimetidine tablet that, when dissolved in water, created an effervescent product akin to Alka-Seltzer.

Drug development was of minor interest to Dr. O'Leary, one of the brightest young (age 34) stars at the Brigham and Women's Hospital (BWH) in Boston. Working in a somewhat stark, industrial-looking laboratory, far removed from the patient wings at BWH, Dr. O'Leary conducted research on the basic structure of human proteins and other areas of biochemistry research. Now that he had made his discovery, however, he wondered how best to develop its commercial potential. He knew

Note: The specific new drug discussed does not exist, to our knowledge. For reasons of confidentiality, the names of the researcher, drugs, and companies involved are disguised. The identities of the Brigham and Women's venture group personnel are not disguised. Case Study 18, Technology Transfer, discusses a related topic.

This case was prepared by Richard Benedict under the supervision of Professor Regina E. Herzlinger.

many people at Cobb and believed them to be likely candidates to develop his discovery. He was also aware that BWH had created a new ventures group to help its researchers transfer technology to the commercial sector. Dr. O'Leary resolved to have discussions with both.

THE PRODUCT

The combination had several distinct advantages, including a longer duration of treatment (1 per day) without the prolonged elevation of serum gastrin levels of other potent agents. Also, where cimetidine was used primarily to treat ulcers, the combination was useful for heartburn, acid indigestion, gas, nausea/upset stomach, and several other minor, but common, GI disorders (Table 15.2).

Because this was a novel combination, it appeared to be patentable. The crucial test was that there be no record of "prior art" or that the combination not represent knowledge or practice so common in the field as to render the invention "anticipated" or "obvious." Although research into new and "me too" GI drugs was one of the hottest areas of drug development in the world, a literature search yielded no previous published material about combining these two products.

FINDING A COMMERCIALIZATION PARTNER

Dr. O'Leary approached the new ventures group at BWH to explore having the discovery commercialized. He had preliminary discus-

Exhibit 15.1 Novel Combination of Two Drugs: H$_2$ Inhibitor Anti-Ulcer Pharmaceuticals

Anti-ulcer products in general, and H$_2$ inhibitors in general, are the fastest growing prescription drug sector. Sales figures for the FDA approved products are noted below. (Searle and Syntex are reported to be developing therapeutically better ulcer remedies than any of the four H$_2$ class brands and are awaiting FDA approval.)

Drug	Company	1987 Market Share (in percent)
Tagamet	SmithKline Beecham	41.6
Zantac	Glaxo	41.2
Pepcid	Merck	5.4
Axid	Lilly	0

Note: Tagamet went off patent in 1992 (U.K.) and will do so in 1994 (U.S.).
Source: Data courtesy of Jerome Brimeyer of Dean Witter, New York.

sions with Cobb, a company that had granted him unrestricted research funds for the past 2 years. Cobb, like most pharmaceuticals, knew that the general expansion of basic scientific knowledge was crucial for its continued success, as was goodwill and personal contacts with scientists likely to make discoveries with important pharmaceutical potential. Dr. O'Leary felt very positive about this relationship.

The new ventures group at BWH included three managers with considerable industry experience whose charter was to enable the scientists and hospital to receive the best return for their discoveries. Aiding them was the hospital's assistant general counsel, outside patent attorneys, and a market-research firm.

Table 15.1 Novel Combination of Two Drugs: Anti-Ulcer/Antacid World Drug Market Shares

Company	November 1984 Percentages
SmithKline Beecham	65
Glaxo	31
All Others	4
Total patients:	1,961,000

Note: No other company had a greater than 4% market share.
Source: SCRIP, March 4, 1985, p. 17.

When Dr. O'Leary and Maria Marmarinos from the new ventures group met with an R & D bench scientist and a business development manager from Cobb to discuss commercialization, they did so under a strict confidentiality agreement. As important, however, was the trust that Dr. O'Leary had in the company. A disreputable firm could later enter a patent fight by claiming that it had unpublished research in the same field or by using the basic discovery to create additional products.

The business development manager proposed that Cobb would conduct all necessary developmental research, pay BWH a 6% royalty on all sales, continue its support of Dr. O'Leary's basic research, and probably increase the grant significantly.

Tagamet sales worldwide of $1.14 billion represented only about a 40% market share. A royalty of 6% on $1 billion in sales would dwarf all sponsored research even at BWH, whose 1987 total of $60 million was one of the largest research budgets of any U.S. hospital.

TAGAMET AND OTHER H$_2$ RECEPTOR ANTAGONISTS

Tagamet represented a new research methodology. Drug discovery usually involves chemists' making serendipitous discoveries (e.g.,

Table 15.2 Novel Combination of Two Drugs: Common Stomach Ailments

Ailment	Cause	Remedy
1. Heartburn	Presence of acid in the lower esophagus	Antacids
2. Acid Indigestion	Excess acid secretion	Antacids
3. Gas	Presence of air in the digestive system	Simethicone
4. Nausea/Upset Stomach	Perception of need to regurgitate	Antacids
5. Chronic Ailments/Ulcer	Excess acid, pepsin	Antacids, H_2 Blockers

Note: All common ailments are caused fundamentally by some form of excess acid.

penicillin) or small rearrangements of existing products. Tagamet's discovery created another approach to drug hunting. Its discoverer, Nobel Prize winner Sir James Black, noted in *The Economist*:

> Instead of looking for compounds and seeing what they do, why not look at what needs to be done, and design a compound that does it?

He did this both for beta-blocker heart drugs and the class of anti-ulcer drugs known as H_2 receptor antagonists. "Knowing that overproduction of gastric acid was a factor in the formation of ulcers and that the action of histamine on the gut wall stimulated its production, he developed a drug to block the interaction of histamine with the stomach wall" (*The Economist*, February 7, 1987, p. 9).

Tagamet was the first H_2 receptor antagonist, but several others soon followed. Glaxo's Zantac became the number one selling H_2 anti-ulcer drug because of its reputation with physicians as being more effective.

THE DECISION

As Maria contemplated the Cobb offer later that afternoon, she was unsure whether to negotiate only with Cobb or to put the new drug out to bid among several companies.

Maria developed the following lists of pros and cons:

Negotiate Only with Cobb: Pros

- Maintains the good relationship among Cobb, Dr. O'Leary, and the hospital.
- Increases revenues with low risk for the hospital (Cobb does all development work).
- Uses Cobb's considerable expertise in patenting drugs.
- Limits the possibility of unauthorized disclosure of the discovery.
- Builds on Cobb's "hunger" to enter this market.

Negotiate Only with Cobb: Cons

- May not get as high a price as would be possible through competitive bidding.
- Cobb has little expertise with GI drugs.
- Since Cobb would do all of the development work, it could also "go beyond" BWH's patent, thus diminishing BWH's royalty income.

Put Product Out to Bid: Pros

- Likely to generate the highest revenue stream for BWH.
- Could require all bidders sign confidentiality agreements, thus limiting risk of disclosure.

- The bidding process itself would increase visibility of the new ventures group within the pharmaceutical community.

Put Product Out to Bid: Cons

- Drawn-out process, difficult logistics, increases the potential of a patent fight.
- Could undermine relationship between scientist and Cobb.
- Would a company already in GI market really be committed to a new product or would it bid a high license fee and then go slow on development?

Maria knew of no easy way to sort out the two options. She examined the financial and market data available on the major players (see Tables 15.3 and 15.4) and made informal calls to colleagues in the industry. She promised Cobb that she would respond within a week, however, and it was time to create a plan of action.

POINTS TO PONDER

1. What option should Maria choose and why?
2. Delineate her plan of action.

Table 15.3 Novel Combination of Two Drugs: Financial Results for Major Pharmaceutical Companies

Company	All Figures for 1987 (dollars in millions)				Research and Development Expenses		
	Net Sales	Net Income	Total Assets	Net Worth	Total	1987/1986	% of Sales
Abbott Laboratories	$4,387.9	$632.6	$4,385.7	$2,093.5	$361.3	26.8%	8.2%
American Home Products	5,028.3	845.1	3,956.9	1,878.2	247.3	8.9	4.9
Bristol-Myers	5,401.2	709.6	4,549.4	3,046.7	341.7	9.8	6.3
Eli Lilly	3,643.8	410.5	4,859.2	2,646.9	466.3	10.9	12.8
Glaxo	2,785.3	774.4	2,357.0	1,737.0	239.9	31.9	8.6
Merck	5,061.3	906.4	5,533.2	1,969.9	565.7	17.9	11.2
Pfizer	4,919.8	690.2	6,684.7	3,644.5	401.0	19.5	8.2
Schering-Plough	2,699.3	320.7	3,053.2	1,317.3	250.7	18.2	9.3
SmithKline Beecham	4,328.8	570.1	4,005.6	1,144.0	423.7	12.4	9.8
Cobb	2,156.5	358.4	2,782.4	1,525.5	221.4	35.8	10.3
Upjohn	2,521.0	305.0	3,043.1	1,673.5	355.5	13.2	14.1
Warner-Lambert	3,484.7	295.8	2,396.5	795.0	231.8	14.6	6.7

Source: Chemical and Engineering News, annual reports.

Table 15.4 Novel Combination of Two Drugs: Selected Sales Information

(dollars in millions)

	1986	1987	1988	1989
Glaxo Worldwide Sales by Line[a]				
Zantac	$ 909.0			$1,837.5
United States	382.5			832.5
Europe	459.0			855.0
Japan	67.5			150.0
Antibiotics	348.0			825.0
Zinacef	115.5			165.0
Ceftazidime	75.0			285.0
Ceporex	97.5			90.0
Ceftin	—			225.0
Other	60.0			60.0
Antiasthma Products	430.5			712.5
Dermatologicals	135.0			150.0
Cardiovasculars	120.0			172.5
All Others	168.0			262.5
Total Revenue	$2,110.5			$3,960.0
Merck U.S. Sales by Sector				
Antihypertensives and Cardiovasculars		$ 1,299		$ 1,947
Antiinflammatories		686		669
Antibiotics		655		730
Others[b]		1,423		1,602
SmithKline Beecham Worldwide Sales by Product Line[c]				
Tagamet	$1,015.0		$1,140.0	
Dyazide	360.0		265.0	
Other Hypertensive/Cardiovascular	30.0		25.0	
Cephalosporin Antibiotics	145.0		175.0	
Ridaura	23.0		60.0	
Calcitonin	38.0		85.0	
Vaccines	30.0		100.0	
Other	254.5		420.0	
Total Ethical	$1,895.5		$2,615.0	
Consumer Health Care	$ 173.7		$ 200.0	
Animal Health Care	250.5		355.0	
Eye and Skin Care	433.0		775.0	
Instruments and Supplies	619.6		795.0	
Clinical Laboratory Supplies	373.1		490.0	
Total Revenue	$3,745.4		$4,870.0	
Cobb U.S. Sales by Sector				
Cardiovasculars	$ 697	$ 941		
Antibiotics	160	180		
Antiinflammatories	123	122		
Antifungals	99	107		
Diagnostics	103	165		
Other	339	328		
Total	$1,521	$1,843		

[a]1989 sales figures for Glaxo are estimated.
[b]Pepcid sales in 1986 were $40 million.
[c]1988 sales figures for SmithKline Beecham are estimated.

Sources: Nomura Securities and SCRIP.

Shouldice Hospital Limited

Two shadowy figures, enrobed in slippers, walked slowly down the semidarkened hall of the Shouldice Hospital. They didn't notice Alan O'Dell, the hospital administrator, and his guest, who had just emerged from the basement boiler room on a tour of the facility. Once they were out of earshot, O'Dell remarked good naturedly, "By the way they act, you'd think our patients own this place. And while they're here, in a way they do."

Following a visit to the five operating rooms, also located on the first of three levels, O'Dell and his visitor once again encountered the same pair of patients still engrossed in discussing their hernia operations, which had been performed the previous morning.

HISTORY

Born on a farm in Bruce County, Ontario, Dr. Earle Shouldice, who was to found the hospital bearing his name, first displayed his interest in medical research at the age of 12. He performed a post-mortem on a calf that, he discovered, had died from an intestinal obstruction. After a year of following the wishes of his parents that he study for the ministry, Shouldice persuaded them to let him enroll in medicine at the University of Toronto.

An attractive brochure that was recently printed, although neither dated nor distributed

---

to prospective patients, described Earle Shouldice as follows:

> While carrying on a private medical and surgical practice in the years between the two World Wars and holding a post as lecturer in anatomy at the University of Toronto, Dr. Shouldice continued to pursue his interest in research. He did pioneer work towards the cure of pernicious anemia, intestinal obstruction, hydrocephalic cases, and other areas of advancing medical knowledge.
>
> His interest in early ambulation stemmed, in part, from an operation he performed in 1932 to remove the appendix from a seven-year-old girl and the girl's subsequent refusal to stay quietly in bed. In spite of her activity, no harm was done, and the experience recalled to the doctor the postoperative actions of animals upon which he had performed surgery. They had all moved about freely with no ill effects. Four years later he was reminded of the child when he allowed washroom privileges immediately following the operations to four men recovering from hernia repair. All had trouble-free recovery.

By the outset of World War II in 1940, Shouldice had given extensive thought to several factors that contributed to early ambulation following surgery. Among them were the use of a local anesthetic, the nature of the surgical procedure itself, the design of a facility to encourage movement without unnecessarily causing discomfort, and the postoperative regimen designed and communicated by the medical team. With all of these things in mind, he had begun to develop a surgical technique for repairing hernias that was superior to others.[1] He offered his services in correcting hernias for army inductees who otherwise would not qualify for service. Because hospital beds often were not available, sometimes the surgery took place in the emergency department of the Toronto General Hospital, and the patients were transported later in the day to a medical fraternity where they were cared for by medical students for two to three days.

By the war's end, word of the Shouldice technique had spread sufficiently that 200 civilians had contacted the doctor and were awaiting surgery upon his discharge from the army. Because of the scarcity of hospital beds, particularly for an operation that was considered elective and of relatively low priority, he started his own hospital. Dr. Shouldice's medical license permitted him to operate anywhere, even on a kitchen table, and consequently he received authorization from the provincial government to open his first hospital in a six-room nursing home in downtown Toronto in July 1945. As more and more patients requested operations, Dr. Shouldice extended his facilities by buying a rambling 130-acre estate with a 17,000-square-foot main house in the suburb of Thornhill, 15 miles north of downtown Toronto. Initially, a 36-bed capacity was created in Thornhill, but after some years of planning, a large wing was added to the house to provide a total capacity of 89 beds.

At the time of his death in 1965, Dr. Shouldice's long-time associate, Dr. Nicholas Obney, was named surgeon-in-chief and chairman of the board of Shouldice Hospital Limited, the corporation formed to operate both the hospital and clinical facilities. Under Dr. Obney's leadership, the volume of activity continued to increase, reaching a total of 6,850 operations in the 1982 calendar year.

THE SHOULDICE METHOD

Only external types of abdominal hernias were repaired at Shouldice Hospital. Internal types, such as hiatus (or diaphragmatic) hernias, were not treated. As a result, most first-time repairs (called primaries) involved straightforward operating procedures that required about 45 minutes. Primaries represented approximately 82% of all operations performed at Shouldice in 1982. The remaining 18% involved patients suffering recurrences of hernias previously repaired elsewhere.[2]

In the Shouldice method, the muscles of the abdominal wall were arranged in three distinct layers, and the opening was repaired—each layer in turn—by overlapping its margins in much the same manner as the edges of a coat might be overlapped when buttoned. The end result was to reinforce the muscular wall of the abdomen with six rows of sutures (stitches) under the skin cover, which was then closed with clamps that were removed within 48 hours after the operation. (Other methods might not separate muscle layers, often involved fewer rows of sutures, and sometimes involved the insertion of screens or meshes under the skin.)

The typical first-time repair could be completed with the use of preoperative sedation (sleeping pill) and analgesic (pain killer) plus a local anesthetic, an injection of Novocain in the region of the incision. This allowed immediate patient ambulation and facilitated rapid recovery. Many of the recurrences and the very difficult hernia repairs, being more complex, could require up to 90 minutes and more. In some circumstances, a general anesthetic was administered.

THE PATIENTS' EXPERIENCE

It was thought that most potential Shouldice patients learned about the hospital and its methods from past patients who had already experienced them. Although over 1,000 doctors had referred patients, doctors were less likely to recommend Shouldice because of the generally regarded simplicity of the surgery, often considered a "bread and butter" operation. Typically, many patients had their problem diagnosed by a personal physician and then took the initiative to contact Shouldice. Many more made this diagnosis themselves and contacted the hospital directly.

The process experienced by Shouldice patients depended on whether or not they lived close enough to the hospital to visit the facility to obtain a diagnosis. Approximately 42% of all Shouldice patients came from the United States. Another 2% originated from provinces other than Ontario and from European countries. These out-of-town patients often were diagnosed by mail, using the Medical Information questionnaire shown in Exhibit 16.1.

Of every eight questionnaires sent, seven were returned to the hospital in completed form. Based on information in the questionnaire, a Shouldice surgeon would determine the type of hernia the respondent had and whether there were signs that some risk might be associated with surgery (for example, an overweight or heart condition, or a patient who had suffered a heart attack or a stroke in the past six months to a year, or whether a general or local anesthetic was required). At this point, a patient was given an operating date, the medical information was logged into a computerized database, and the patient was sent a confirmation card; if necessary, a sheet outlining a weight-loss program prior to surgery and a brochure describing the hospital and the Shouldice method were also sent. A small proportion were refused treatment, either because they were too fat or represented an undue medical risk or because it was determined that they did not have a hernia.

If confirmation cards were not returned by the patient three days or more prior to the scheduled operation, that patient was contacted by phone. Upon confirmation, the patient's folder was sent to the reception desk to await his or her arrival.[3]

Arriving at the clinic between 1:00 P.M. and 3:00 P.M. the day before the operation, a patient might join up with 30 to 34 other patients and their friends and families in the waiting room. After a typical wait of about 20 minutes—depending on the availability of surgeons—a patient was examined in one of six examination rooms staffed by surgeons who had completed their operating schedules for the day. This examination required no more than 15 to 20 minutes, unless the patient needed reassurance. (Patients typically exhibited a moderate level of anxiety until their operation was completed.) At this point it occasionally was discovered that a patient had not corrected his or her weight problem; others might be found not to have a hernia after all. In either case, the patient was sent home.

Following his or her examination, a patient might experience a wait of 5 to 15 minutes to see one of two admitting personnel in the accounting office. Here, health insurance coverage was checked, and various details were discussed in a procedure that usually lasted no more than 10 minutes. Patients sometimes exhibited their nervousness by asking many questions at this point, requiring more time of the receptionist.

Patients next were sent to one of two nurses' stations where, in 5 to 10 minutes and with little wait, their hemoglobin (blood) and urine were checked. At this point, about an hour after arriving at the hospital, a patient was directed to the room number shown on his or her wrist band. Throughout the process, patients were asked to keep their luggage (usually light and containing only a few items suggested by the hospital) with them.

All private rooms at the hospital were semi-private, containing two beds. Patients with similar jobs, backgrounds, or interests were assigned to the same room to the extent possible. Upon reaching their rooms, patients busied themselves unpacking, getting acquainted with roommates, changing into pajamas, "prepping" themselves (shaving themselves in the area of the operation), and providing a urine sample.

At 5:00 P.M. a nurse's orientation provided the group of incoming patients with information about what to expect, the drugs to be administered, the need for exercise after the operation, the facility, and the daily routine. According to Alan O'Dell, "Half are so nervous they don't remember much from the orientation." Dinner was served from 5:30 to 6:00 P.M. in a 100-seat dining room on a first-come, first-served basis. Following further

Exhibit 16.1 Shouldice Hospital Limited: Medical Information Questionnaire

SHOULDICE HOSPITAL

7750 Bayview Avenue
Box 370, Thornhill, Ontario L3T 4A3 Canada
Phone (416) 889-1125

(Thornhill — One Mile North Metro Toronto)

MEDICAL
INFORMATION

Patients who live at a distance often prefer their examination, admission and operation to be arranged all on a single visit—to save making two lengthy journeys. The whole purpose of this questionnaire is to make such arrangements possible, although, of course, it cannot replace the examination in any way. Its completion and return will not put you under any obligation.

Please be sure to fill in both sides.

This information will be treated as confidential.

continues

Exhibit 16.1 continued

FAMILY NAME (Last Name)	FIRST NAME	MIDDLE NAME

STREET & NUMBER (or Rural Route or P.O. Box)   Town/City   Province/State

County	Township	Zip or Postal Code	Birthdate: Month Day Year

Telephone Home _____ If none, give Work _____ neighbor's number _____	Married or Single	Religion

NEXT OF KIN: Name   Address   Telephone #

INSURANCE INFORMATION: Please give name of Insurance Company and Numbers.   Date form completed

HOSPITAL INSURANCE: (Please bring hospital certificates)   OTHER HOSPITAL INSURANCE:
O.H.I.P.   BLUE CROSS   Company Name _____
Number _____   Number _____   Policy Number _____

SURGICAL INSURANCE: (Please bring insurance certificates)   OTHER SURGICAL INSURANCE:
O.H.I.P.   BLUE SHIELD   Company Name _____
Number _____   Number _____   Policy Number _____

WORKMEN'S COMPENSATION BOARD Claim No. _____	Approved Yes No	Social Insurance (Security) Number

Occupation   Name of Business   Are you the Owner?   If Retired — Former Occupation
                                               Yes   No

How did you hear about Shouldice Hospital? (If referred by a doctor, give name & address)

Are you a former patient of Shouldice Hospital?   Yes   No   Do you smoke?   Yes   No

Have you ever written to Shouldice Hospital in the past?   Yes   No

What is your preferred admission date? (Please give as much advance notice as possible)

No admissions Friday, Saturday or Sunday.

FOR OFFICE USE ONLY

Date Received	Type of Hernia	Weight Loss lbs.

Consent to Operate ☐ Heart Report ☐	Special Instructions	Approved

Referring Doctor Notified   Operation Date

continues

Exhibit 16.1 continued

THIS CHART IS FOR EXPLANATION ONLY

Ordinary hernias are mostly either
at the navel ("belly-button") or just above it

or down in the groin area on either side

An "incisional hernia" is one that bulges through the scar of any other
surgical operation that has failed to hold—wherever it may be.

THIS IS YOUR CHART—PLEASE MARK IT!

(MARK WITH AN "X" THE POSITION OF EACH HERNIA YOU WANT REPAIRED)

APPROXIMATE SIZE . . .
Walnut (or less)   ☐   ☐
Hen's Egg or Lemon   ☐   ☐
Grapefruit (or more)   ☐   ☐

ESSENTIAL EXTRA INFORMATION

Use only the sections that apply to your hernias and put a check in each box that seems appropriate.

	Yes	No
NAVEL AREA (AND JUST ABOVE NAVEL) ONLY		
Is this navel (belly-button) hernia your FIRST one?	☐	☐

If it's NOT your first, how many repair attempts so far?   ☐

	RIGHT GROIN		LEFT GROIN	
GROIN HERNIAS ONLY	Yes	No	Yes	No
Is this your FIRST GROIN HERNIA ON THIS SIDE?	☐	☐	☐	☐

How many hernia operations in this groin already?   Right ☐   Left ☐

DATE OF LAST OPERATION ☐

INCISIONAL HERNIAS ONLY (the ones bulging through previous operation scars)
Was the original operation for your Appendix? ☐ , or Gallbladder? ☐ ,
or Stomach? ☐ , or Prostate? ☐ , or Hysterectomy? ☐ , or Other? ☐_____

How many attempts to repair the hernia have been made so far? ☐

continues

Exhibit 16.1 continued

PLEASE BE ACCURATE!: Misleading figures, when checked on an admission day, could mean postponement of your operation until your weight is suitable.

HEIGHT _____ ft. _____ in.   WEIGHT _____ lb.   Recent gain? _____ lb.

Nude or just pajamas   Recent loss? _____ lb.

Waist (muscles relaxed) _____ in.   Chest (not expanded) _____ in.

GENERAL HEALTH

Age _____ years   Is your health now GOOD ☐ , FAIR ☐ , or POOR ☐

Please mention briefly any **severe past illness**—such as a "heart attack" or a "stroke," for example, from which you have just now recovered (and its approximate date)

_____

We need to know about other present conditions, even though your admission is <u>NOT</u> likely to be refused because of them.

Pleast tick ☑ any condition for which you are having regular treatment.		Name any prescribed pills, tablets or capsules you take regularly:
Blood Pressure	☐	
Excess Body Fluids	☐	
Chest Pain ("angina")	☐	
Irregular Heartbeat	☐	
Diabetes	☐	
Asthma & Bronchitis	☐	
Ulcers	☐	
Anticoagulants (to delay blood-clotting or to "thin the blood")	☐	
Other _____		

Did you remember to MARK AN "X" on your body chart to show us where each of your hernias is located?

recreation, tea and cookies were served at 9:00 P.M. in the lounge area. Nurses emphasized the importance of attendance at that time because it provided an opportunity for preoperative patients to talk with those whose operations had been completed earlier that same day. Nearly all new patients were "tucked into bed" between 9:30 and 10:00 P.M. in preparation for an early awakening prior to their operations.

Patients to be operated on early in the day were awakened at 5:30 A.M. to be given preop sedation and to be dressed in an O.R. (operating room) gown. An attempt was made to schedule operations for roommates at approximately the same time. Patients were taken to the preoperating room where the circulating nurse administered Demerol, an analgesic, 45 minutes before surgery. A few minutes prior to the first operation at 7:30 A.M., the surgeon assigned to each patient administered Novocain. During the operation, it was the responsibility of the circulating nurse to monitor the patient's comfort, to note times at which the Novocain was administered and the operation begun, and to arrange for the administration of Demerol to the patient scheduled next on the operating table, depending on the progress of the surgery under way. This was in contrast to the typical hospital procedure in which patients were sedated in their rooms prior to being taken to the operating rooms.

Upon the completion of the operation, during which a few patients were "chatty" and fully aware of what was going on, patients were invited to get off the operating table and walk to the postoperating room with the help of their surgeons. According to Ursula Verstraete, director of nursing,

> Ninety-nine percent accept the surgeon's invitation. While we put them in wheelchairs to return them to their rooms, the walk from the operating table is for psychological as well as physiological [blood pressure, respiratory] reasons. Patients prove to themselves that they can do it, and they start their all-important exercise immediately.

Throughout the day after their operation, patients were encouraged to exercise by nurses and housekeepers alike. By 9:00 P.M. on the day of their operations, all patients were ready and able to walk down to the dining room for tea and cookies, even if it meant climbing stairs, to help indoctrinate the new "class" admitted that day.

Patients in their second or third day of recovery were awakened before 6:00 A.M. so they could loosen up for breakfast, which was served between 7:45 and 8:15 A.M. in the dining room. Good posture and exercise were thought to aid digestion and deter the buildup of gas that could prove painful. After breakfast on the first day after surgery, all of the skin clips (resembling staples) holding the skin together over the incision were loosened and some removed. The remainder were removed the next day. On the fourth morning, patients were ready for discharge.

During their stay, patients were encouraged to take advantage of the opportunity to explore the premises and make new friends. Some members of the staff felt that the patients and their attitudes were the most important element of the Shouldice program. According to Dr. Byrnes Shouldice, the 53-year-old son of the founder, who is vice president of the corporation, a surgeon on the staff, and a 50% owner of the hospital

> Patients sometimes ask to stay an extra day. Why? Well, think about it. They are basically well to begin with. But they arrive with a problem and a certain amount of nervousness, tension, and anxiety about their surgery. Their first morning here they're operated on and experience a sense of relief from something that's been bothering them for a long time. They are immediately able to get around, and they've got a three-day holiday ahead of them with a perfectly good reason to be away from work with no sense of guilt. They share experiences with other patients, make friends easily, and have the run of the hospital. In summer, the most common after-effect from the surgery is sunburn. They kid

with the staff and make this a positive experience for all of us.

The average patient stay for comparable operations at other hospitals was thought to be five to seven or eight days, but it had been declining because of a shortage of beds and the tendency to give elective surgery a low priority for beds. Shouldice patients with jobs involving light exercise could return to work within a week after their operations, but those involved in more strenuous work, whose benefits were insured, received four weeks of benefits and recuperation. All self-employed persons returned to work much earlier. In general, typical times for recuperation from similar operations at other hospitals were two weeks for those in jobs requiring light exercise and eight weeks for those in more strenuous jobs, due largely to long-established treatment regimens.

THE NURSES' EXPERIENCE

The nursing staff comprised 22 full-time and 19 part-time members. They were divided into four groups (as shown in Figure 16.1), with supervisors for the hospital, operating room, laboratory, and central supply reporting to Ursula Verstraete, the director of nursing.

While the operating rooms were fully staffed from about 7 A.M. through the last operation ending in the mid- to late afternoon, the hospital was staffed with three shifts beginning at 7 A.M., 3 P.M., and 11 P.M. Even so, minimal patient needs for physical assistance allowed Shouldice to operate with a much lower nurse-to-patient ratio than the typical hospital. Shouldice nurses spent an unusually large proportion of their time in counseling activities. As one supervisor commented, "We don't use bed-pans." In a typical year, Verstraete estimated that she might experience a turnover of four nurses.

THE DOCTORS' EXPERIENCE

The hospital employed 12 full-time surgeons, 7 part-time assistant surgeons, and 1 anesthe-

tist. Each operating team required a surgeon, an assistant surgeon, a scrub nurse, and a circulating nurse. The operating load varied from 30 to 36 operations per day. As a result, each surgeon typically performed three or four operations each day.

A typical surgeon's day started with a scrubbing shortly before the first scheduled operation at 7:30 A.M. If the first operation was routine, it usually was completed by 8:15 A.M. At its conclusion, the surgical team helped the patient walk from the room and summoned the next patient. While the patient was being prepared and awaiting the full effects of the Demerol to set in, the surgeon completed the previous patient's file by dictating five or so minutes of comments concerning the operation. Postoperative instructions were routine unless specific instructions were issued by the surgeon. After scrubbing, the surgeon could be ready to operate again at 8:30 A.M.

Surgeons were advised to take a coffee break after their second or third operation. Even so, a surgeon could complete three routine operations and a fourth involving a recurrence (a 60- to 90-minute procedure) and still be finished in time for a 12:30 P.M. lunch in the staff dining room.

Upon finishing lunch, as many as six of the surgeons not scheduled to operate in the afternoon moved upstairs to examine incoming patients between 1:00 and 3:00 P.M. A surgeon's day ended by 4:00 P.M. In addition, a surgeon could expect to be on call one weekday night in ten and one weekend in ten. Alan O'Dell commented that the position appealed to doctors who "want to watch their children grow up. A doctor on call is rarely called to the hospital and has regular hours."

According to Dr. Obney, chief surgeon:

> When I interview prospective surgeons, I look for experience and a good education. I try to gain some insight into their domestic situation and personal interests and habits. Naturally, as in any field, we try to avoid anyone with a drinking or drug problem. Oftentimes these people can hide their illness very well and it can

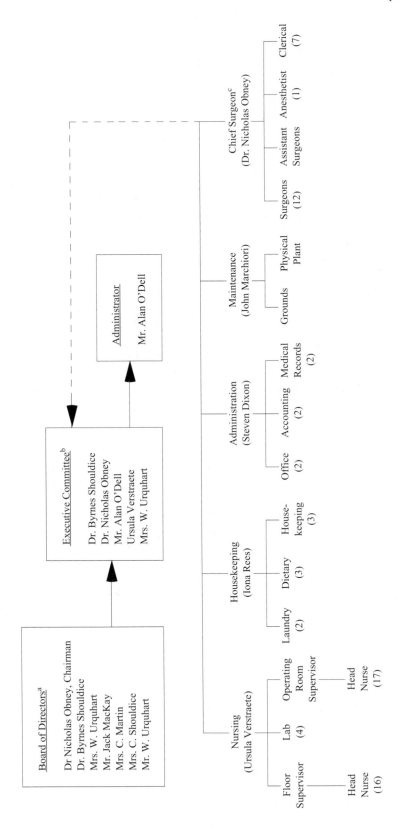

Figure 16.1 Shouldice Hospital Limited: Organization Chart

Board of Directors[a]

Dr Nicholas Obney, Chairman
Dr. Byrnes Shouldice
Mrs. W. Urquhart
Mr. Jack MacKay
Mrs. C. Martin
Mrs. C. Shouldice
Mr. W. Urquhart

Executive Committee[b]

Dr. Byrnes Shouldice
Dr. Nicholas Obney
Mr. Alan O'Dell
Ursula Verstraete
Mrs. W. Urquhart

Administrator

Mr. Alan O'Dell

Nursing
(Ursula Verstraete)

Floor Supervisor — Head Nurse (16)

Lab (4)

Operating Room Supervisor — Head Nurse (17)

Housekeeping
(Iona Rees)

Laundry (2)

Dietary (3)

House-keeping (3)

Administration
(Steven Dixon)

Office (2)

Accounting (2)

Medical Records (2)

Maintenance
(John Marchiori)

Grounds

Physical Plant

Chief Surgeon[c]
(Dr. Nicholas Obney)

Surgeons (12)

Assistant Surgeons

Anesthetist (1)

Clerical (7)

[a]Meets three times a year or as needed.
[b]Meets as needed (usually twice a month).
[c]Informally reports to Executive Committee.

take a while before it is detected. Here, sometimes, recommendations can be of great help. I also try to find out why a surgeon wants to switch positions. And I try to determine if he's willing to perform the repair exactly as he's told. This is no place for prima donnas.

Dr. Shouldice added,

Our surgeons enjoy operating, but sometimes are less interested in the more mundane office routines that all vocations have. Traditionally a hernia is often the first operation that a junior resident in surgery performs. Hernia repair is regarded as a relatively simple operation compared to other major operations. This is quite wrong, as is borne out by the resulting high recurrence rate. It is a tricky anatomical area and occasionally very complicated, especially to the novice or those doing very few hernia repairs each year. But at Shouldice Hospital a surgeon learns the Shouldice technique over a period of several months. He learns when he can go fast and when he must go slow. He develops a pace and a touch. If he encounters something unusual, he is encouraged to consult immediately with other surgeons. We teach each other and try to encourage a group effort. And he learns not to take risks to achieve absolute perfection. Excellence is the enemy of good.

Dr. Obney assigned surgeons to an operating room on a daily basis by noon of the preceding day. This allowed surgeons to examine the specific patients that they were to operate on. Surgeons and assistants were rotated every few days. Scrub nurses and circulating nurses were assigned to a new operating room every two weeks and four weeks, respectively. Unless patients requested specific doctors, cases were assigned to give doctors a nonroutine operation (often involving a recurrence) several times a week. More complex procedures were assigned to more senior and experienced members of the staff, including Dr. Obney himself. Where possible, former Shouldice patients suffering

recurrences were assigned to the doctor who performed the first operation "to allow the doctor to learn from his mistake."

As Dr. Obney commented:

If something goes wrong, we want to make sure that we have an experienced surgeon in charge, and we don't like surgeons who work too fast. Experience is most important. The typical general surgeon may perform 25 to 50 hernia operations per year. Ours perform 600 or more.

The 12 full-time surgeons were paid a straight salary. A typical starting salary at that time for someone with five to ten years of experience was $50,000. In addition, bonuses to doctors were voted by the board of directors twice a year, depending on profit and performance. The total bonus pool paid to the surgeons in a recent year was approximately $500,000. Assisting surgeons were part-time, and they received 51% of the $60 fee that was charged to patients who received their services.

The anesthetist was hired for $300 per day from a nearby partnership. Only one was required to be on duty on any given day and could supervise all five operating rooms in addition to administering an occasional general anesthetic to a patient with a complex case or to a child.

Training in the Shouldice technique was important because the procedure could not be varied. It was accomplished through direct supervision by one or more of the senior surgeons. The rotation of teams and frequent consultations allowed for an ongoing opportunity to appraise performance and take corrective action.

According to Dr. Obney:

We haven't had to let anyone go because they couldn't learn, or continue to adhere to, the method. However, a doctor must decide after several years whether he wants to do this for the rest of his life because, just as in other specialities—for example, radiology—he loses touch with other medical disciplines. If he stays for five years, he doesn't leave. Even among younger doctors, few elect to leave.

THE FACILITY

A tour of the facility with Alan O'Dell yielded some interesting information. The Shouldice Hospital comprised two basis facilities in one building—the hospital and the clinic.

On the first-level opening to grade at the back of the building, the hospital contained the kitchen and dining rooms as well as the office of the supervisor of housekeeping. The second level, also opening to grade but at the front of the building, contained a large, open lounge area, the admissions offices, patient rooms, and a spacious glass-covered Florida room. The third level had additional patient rooms, a large lounge, and a recreational area.

Throughout the tour, patients could be seen visiting in each other's rooms, walking up and down hallways, lounging in the sunroom, and making use of light recreational facilities ranging from a pool table to an exercycle.

Alan O'Dell pointed out some of the features of the hospital:

> The rooms contain no telephones or television sets. If a patient needs to make a call or wants to watch television, he or she has to take a walk. The steps are designed specially with a small rise to allow patients recently operated on to negotiate the stairs without undue discomfort. Every square foot of the hospital is carpeted to reduce the hospital feeling and the possibility of a fall. Carpeting also gives the place a smell other than that of disinfectant.
>
> This facility was designed by Dr. Byrnes Shouldice. He thought about it for years and made many changes in the plan before the first concrete was poured. A number of unique policies were also instituted. Because Dr. Shouldice started out to be a minister, ministers are treated gratis. And you see that mother and child in the next room? Parents accompanying children here for an operation stay free.

You may wonder why we can do it, but we learned that we save more in nursing costs than we spend for the patient's room and board. Children may present difficulties in a hospital environment, but when accompanied by a parent, the parent is happier and so is the child.

While patients and staff were served food prepared in the same kitchen, the staff was required to pick up its food from a cafeteria line placed in the very center of the kitchen. This provided an opportunity for everyone to chat with the kitchen staff several times a day as they picked up a meal or stopped for coffee. Patients were served in the adjoining patient dining room.

According to O'Dell:

> We use all fresh ingredients and prepare the food from scratch in the kitchen. Our kitchen staff of three prepares about 100 breakfasts, 200 lunches, and 100 dinners each day at an average raw food cost of $1.10 per meal.

Iona Rees, director of housekeeping, pointed out:

> We do all of our own laundry in the building with two full-time employees. And I have only three on my housekeeping staff for the entire facility. One of the reasons for so few housekeepers is that we don't need to change linens during a patient's four-day stay. They are basically well, so there is no soiling of bed linens. Also, the medical staff doesn't want the patients in bed all day. They want the nurses to encourage the patients to be up socializing, comparing notes [for confidence], encouraging each other, and walking around, getting exercise.
>
> Of course, we're in the rooms straightening up throughout the day. This gives the housekeepers a chance to josh with the patients and to encourage them to exercise.

The bottom level of the clinic housed five operating rooms, a laboratory, the patient-recovery room, and a central supply area where surgical instruments were cleaned and sterilized. This was the only area of the entire facility that was not carpeted, to prevent static electricity from forming in areas where potentially explosive anesthetics might be used. In total, the estimated cost to furnish an operating room was no more than $30,000. This was considerably less than for other hospitals requiring a bank of equipment with which to administer anesthetics for each room. At Shouldice, two mobile units were used by the anesthetist when needed. In addition, the complex had one "crash cart" per floor for use if a patient should suffer a heart attack or stroke during his or her hospital stay.

The first floor of the clinic contained admissions and accounting offices, a large waiting room with a capacity for as many as 50 people, and 6 examination rooms. On the second floor of the clinic, situated in much of what was the original house, was found the administrative offices. A third floor contained 14 additional hostel rooms where patients could be held overnight awaiting the assignment of a room and their operations. At such times when the hospital was particularly crowded, doctors were asked to identify those postoperative patients who could be released a day early. Often these were local residents or children.

ADMINISTRATION

Alan O'Dell, while he walked, described his job:

> I'm responsible for a little of everything around here. We try to meet people's needs and make this as good a place to work as possible. My door is always open. And members of our staff will come in to seek advice about everything from medical to marital problems. There is a strong concern for employees here. Nobody is fired. [This was later reinforced by Dr. Shouldice, who described a situation involving two employees who confessed to theft in the hospital. They agreed to seek psychiatric

help and were allowed to remain on the job.] As a result, turnover is low.

> We don't have a union, but we try to maintain a pay scale higher than the union scale for comparable jobs in the area. For example, our nurses receive from $15,000 to $25,000 per year, depending on the number of years' experience. We have a profit-sharing plan that is separate from the doctors'. Last year the employees divided up $65,000.

> If work needs to be done, people pitch in to help each other. A unique aspect of our administration is that I insist that each secretary is trained to do another's work and in an emergency is able to switch to another function immediately and enable the more vital workload to proceed uninterrupted. With the exception of the accounting staff, every secretary, regardless of her or his position in the hospital, is trained to handle the hospital switchboard and work at the reception desk. If necessary, I'll go downstairs and type billings if they're behind. We don't have an organization chart. A chart tends to make people think they're boxed into jobs.[4]

> In addition to other activities, I try to stay here one night a week having dinner and listening to the patients to find out how things are really going around here.

ADMINISTRATIVE STRUCTURE

The hospital was operated on a nonprofit basis and the clinic on a for-profit basis. Dr. Shouldice and Mrs. W. Urquhart, his sister, each owned 50% of each.

O'Dell, as administrator of the hospital, was responsible for all of its five departments: surgery, nursing, administration, maintenance, and housekeeping. Medical matters were the domain of Dr. Obney, the chief surgeon. Both Alan O'Dell and Dr. Obney reported directly to an executive committee comprising Dr. Shouldice and Dr. Obney, Alan O'Dell, Ursula Verstraete (director of nursing), and Mrs. Urquhart. The executive committee met as needed, usually twice a month, and in turn reported to an inside board (as shown in Figure

16.1). In addition to executive committee members (except Ursula Verstraete), the board included the spouses of Dr. Shouldice and Mrs. Urquhart, two former long-time employees, and Jack MacKay. The board met three times per year, or when necessary.

OPERATING COSTS

It was estimated by the casewriter that the 1983 budgets for the hospital and clinic were close to $2.8 million and $2 million, respectively.[5]

THE MARKET

Hernia operations were among the most common performed on males. In 1979, for example, it was estimated that 600,000 such operations were performed in the United States alone. Only in the early 1980s had the hospital begun to organize information about either its client base of 140,000 "alumni" or the market in general.

According to Dr. Shouldice:

> When our backlog of scheduled operations gets too large, we begin to wonder how many people decide instead to have their local doctor perform the operation. Every time we have expanded our capacity, the backlog has declined briefly, only to climb once again. Right now, at 1,200 it is larger than it has ever been at this time of year [January].

The hospital relied entirely on word-of-mouth advertising, the importance of which was suggested by the results of a poll carried out by students of DePaul University as part of a project (Exhibit 16.2 shows a portion of these results). Although little systematic data about patients had been collected, Alan O'Dell remarked that "if we had to rely on wealthy patients only, our practice would be much smaller."

Patients were attracted to the hospital, in part, by its reasonable rates. For example, charges for a typical operation were four days of hospital stay at $111 per day, a $450 surgical fee for a primary inguinal (the most common hernia) operation, and a $60 fee for the assistant surgeon.[6] If a general anesthetic was required, an additional fee of $75 was assessed. These were the charges that compared with total costs of $2,000 to $4,000 for operations performed elsewhere.

Round-trip fares for travel to Toronto from various major cities on the North American continent ranged from roughly $200 to $600.

In addition to providing free services to the clergy and to parents of hospitalized children, the hospital also provided annual checkups to its alumni, free of charge. Many of them occurred at the time of the annual reunion. The most recent reunion, featuring dinner and a floor show, was held at a first-class hotel in downtown Toronto and was attended by 1,400 former patients, many of them from outside Canada.

The reunion was scheduled to coincide with the mid-January decline in activity at the hospital, when an average of only 145 operations per week were performed. This was comparable to a similar lull in late summer and contrasted with the peak of activity in September, when as many as 165 operations per week might be performed.

It was thought that patients from outside Canada were discouraged from coming to Toronto in midwinter by often misleading weather reports. Vacations interfered with plans in late summer. For many of the same reasons, the hospital closed for two weeks late in December each year. This allowed time for major maintenance work to be performed. Throughout the year, no operations were scheduled for Saturdays or Sundays, although patients whose operations were scheduled late in the week remained in the hospital over the weekend.

PROBLEMS AND PLANS

When asked about major questions confronting the management of the hospital, Dr. Shouldice cited a desire to seek ways of in-

Exhibit 16.2 Shouldice Hospital Limited: Shouldice Hospital Annual Patient Reunion, January 15, 1983

Direction: For each question, please place a check mark as it applies to you.

1. *Sex*
   - Male   95.35%
   - Female   4.65%

2. *Age*
   - 20 or less   —
   - 21–40   9.30%
   - 41–60   39.54%
   - 61 or more   51.16%

3. *Nationality*
   Directions: Please place a check mark in the nation you represent and please write in your province, state or country where it applies.

   - Canada 88.37%   Province _____
   - America 11.63%   State _____
   - Europe _____   Country _____
   - Other _____

4. *Education level*
   - Elementary   11.63%
   - High School   41.86%
   - College   30.23%
   - Graduate Work   16.28%

5. *Occupation*   _____

6. Have you been overnight in a hospital other than Shouldice before your operation?
   - Yes 74.1%
   - No 25.9%

7. What brought Shouldice Hospital to your attention?

   Friend 53.49%   Doctor 20.93%   Relative 16.28%   Article _____   Other 9.30%
   (Please explain)

8. Did you have a single 58.14% or double 41.86% hernia operation?

9. Is this your first Annual Reunion? Yes 46.51% No 53.49%

   If no, how many reunions have you attended? _____

   - 2–5 reunions 47.83%
   - 6–10 reunions 21.73%
   - 11–20 reunions 17.39%
   - 21–36 reunions 13.05%

10. Do you feel that Shouldice Hospital cared for you as a person?

    Most definitely 86.05%   Definitely 13.95%   Very little _____   Not at all _____

11. What impressed you the most about your stay at Shouldice? Please check one answer for each of the following.

    A. *Fees charged for operation and hospital stay*
       Very Important 23.00%   Important 6.90%   Somewhat Important 13.80%   Not Important 55.20%

    B. *Operation procedure*
       Very Important 76.74%   Important 20.93%   Somewhat Important 2.33%   Not Important _____

    C. *Physician's Care*
       Very Important 72.10%   Important 27.90%   Somewhat Important _____   Not Important _____

    D. *Nursing Care*
       Very Important 65.12%   Important 32.56%   Somewhat Important _____   Not Important _____

continues

Exhibit 16.2 continued

E. *Food Service*

Very		Somewhat	Not
Important 53.48%	Important 25.59%	Important 16.28%	Important 4.65%

F. *Shortness of Hospital Stay*

Very		Somewhat	Not
Important 39.53%	Important 34.88%	Important 18.60%	Important 6.98%

G. *Exercise; Recreational Activities*

Very		Somewhat	Not
Important 39.53%	Important 32.56%	Important 27.91%	Important ⎯

H. *Friendships with Patients*

Very		Somewhat	Not
Important 58.15%	Important 23.25%	Important 11.63%	Important 6.98%

I. *"Shouldice Hospital hardly seemed like a hospital at all."*

Very		Somewhat	Not
Important 58.15%	Important 30.23%	Important 11.63%	Important ⎯

12. In a few words, give the MAIN REASON why you returned for this annual reunion.

_____

_____

_____

creasing the hospital's capacity while at the same time maintaining control over the quality of the service delivered, the future role of government in the operations of the hospital, the use of the Shouldice name by potential competitors, and the selection of the next chief surgeon.

As Dr. Shouldice put it:

I'm a doctor first and an entrepreneur second. For example, we could refuse permission to other doctors who want to visit the hospital. They may copy our technique and misapply it or misinform their patients about the use of it. This results in failure, and we are concerned that the technique will be blamed for the recurrences. But we're doctors, and it is our obligation to help other surgeons learn. On the other hand, it's quite clear that others are trying to emulate us. Look at this ad. [The advertisement is shown in Figure 16.2.]

This makes me believe that we should add to our capacity, either here or elsewhere. Here, for example, we could go to Saturday operations and increase our capacity by 20% or, with an investment of perhaps $2 million and permission from the provincial government, we could add another floor of rooms to the hospital, expand our number of beds by 50%, and schedule the operating rooms more heavily.

On the other hand, with government regulation being what it is, do we want to invest more money in Toronto? Or should we establish another hospital with similar design outside Canada? I have under consideration a couple of sites in the United States where private hospital operations are more common. Then, too, there is the possibility that we could diversify at other locations into other specialties offering similar opportunities such as eye surgery, varicose veins, or hemorrhoids.

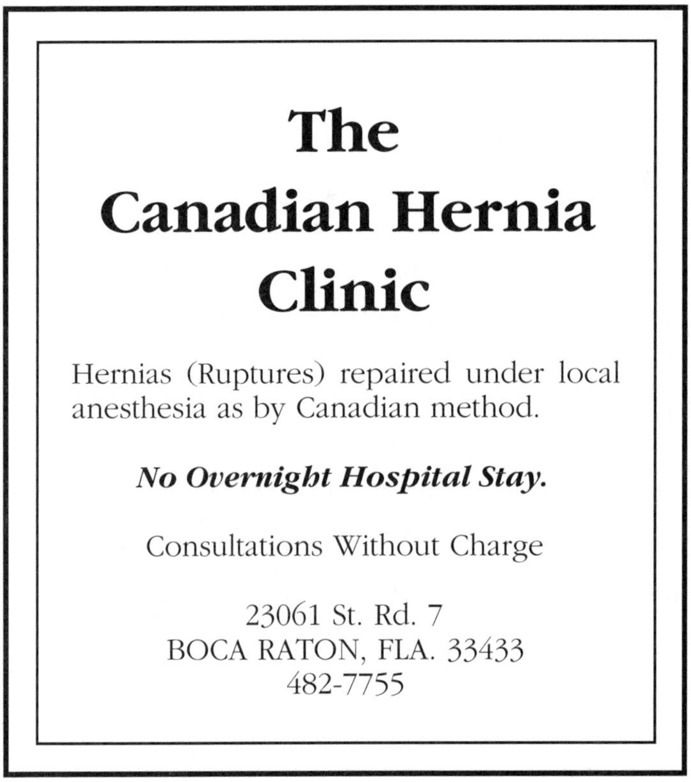

Figure 16.2 Shouldice Hospital Limited: Advertisement by a Shouldice Competitor

For now, I have my hands full thinking about the selection of someone to succeed Dr. Obney when he retires. He's 65, you know. And for good reason, he's resisted changing certain successful procedures that I think we could improve on. We had quite a time changing the schedule for the administration of Demerol to patients to increase their comfort level during the operation. Dr. Obney has opposed a Saturday operating program on the premise that he won't be here and won't be able to maintain proper control.

Alan O'Dell added his own concerns:

How should we be marketing our services? Right now, we don't. We're even afraid to send out this new brochure we've put together for fear it will generate too much demand. We know that both patients and doctors believe in what we do. Our records show that just under 1% of our patients are medical doctors, a significantly high percentage. How should we capitalize on that? And should we try to control the misuse of the hospital's name by physicians who say they use our techniques but don't achieve good results? We know it's going on, because we get letters from patients of other doctors claiming that our method didn't work.

On the other hand, I'm concerned about this talk of Saturday operations. We are already getting good utilization of this facility. And if we expand further, it will be very difficult to maintain the same kind of working relationships and attitudes. Already there are rumors floating around among the staff about it. And the staff is not pleased.

We still have some improvements to make in our systems. With more extensive computerization, for example, we could improve our admitting procedures.

The matter of Saturday operations had been a topic of conversation among the doctors as well. Four of the older doctors were opposed to it. While most of the younger doctors were indifferent or supportive, at least two who had been at the hospital for some time were particularly concerned about the possibility that the issue would drive a wedge between the two groups. As one put it, "I'd hate to see the practice split over the issue."

POINTS TO PONDER*

1. What opportunity is the Shouldice Hospital fulfilling?
2. What are the managerial skills critical to its success?
3. Should the hospital expand? If yes, which of the ways discussed in the case should it choose for expansion? If not, why not?

NOTES

1. Most hernias, known as external abdominal hernias, were protrusions of some part of the abdominal contents through a hole or slit in the muscular layers of the abdominal wall that was supposed to contain them. Well over 90% of these hernias occurred in the groin area. Of these, by far the most common were inguinal hernias, many of which were caused by a slight weakness in the muscle layers brought about by the passage of the testicle in male babies through the groin area shortly before birth. Aging also caused inguinal hernias to develop. The other, much less common, external hernias were called "femoral," in which a protrusion appeared in the top inch or so of the thigh. Because of the cause of the affliction, 85% of all hernias occurred in males.

2. Based on a careful tracking of its patients over more than 30 years, it was estimated that the gross recurrence rate for all operations performed at Shouldice was 0.8%. Recurrence rates reported in the literature for these types of hernia varied greatly. However, one text published around that time stated, "In the United States the gross rate of recurrence for groin hernias approaches 10%."

3. Patients living within 50 miles from the hospital (about 40% of all patients) were encouraged to come to the clinic on a walk-in basis for an examination, usually requiring no more than 15 or 20 minutes for the physical and completion of an information questionnaire. If the doctor performing the examination diagnosed the problem as an external hernia, the individual could obtain immediately a future booking for the operation. On occasion, when a previously booked patient canceled at the last minute, a walk-in patient, or one selected from a special waiting list, could be scheduled for the next day. At the time of booking, the potential patient was given a specific date for the operation, a letter estimating the total cost of the operation (as required by the Ontario provincial government for all Ontario residents), and information supplied to out-of-province patients.

4. The chart in Figure 16.1 was prepared by the casewriter, based on conversations with hospital personnel.

5. The latter figure included the bonus pool for doctors.

6. At the time this case was written, a Canadian dollar was worth about 80% of an American dollar.

---

*These were added by Professor Herzlinger and are not part of Professor Heskett's case study.

Case Study 17

Spacelabs

Spacelabs, one of Squibb's medical product companies, manufactured an ambulatory blood pressure (ABP) monitor that recorded blood pressure and heart rate readings over a 24-hour time period (see Table 17.1 and Exhibit 17.1). One January day at Spacelabs' headquarters in Bellevue, Washington, Brad Harlow, the energetic 27-year-old manager for ABP products, contemplated his upcoming presentation to Spacelabs' engineers, marketing staff, and managers:

> We have not had much competition in the past, but I expect competitors to enter the market soon. We must make some improvements in our ABP monitor if we are going to fend off this competition. I have identified some changes that would improve our product [see Tables 17.2 and 17.3], but have I set the correct priorities?

AMBULATORY BLOOD PRESSURE MONITORING

Purpose

Between 28 and 60 million Americans suffer from hypertension, or high blood pressure. For 90% to 95% of hypertensives, no specific cause can be determined, although this problem is occasionally a response to kidney disease, a heart defect, or other medical problem. Those

with normal blood pressure have elastic artery walls that stretch and contract in response to the variation in the force of blood flow as the heart constricts and relaxes. Hypertensives have a faulty arterial pressure control mechanism and their small arteries stay constricted, making it more difficult for blood to pass. Untreated, hypertension contributes to heart disease, stroke, and several other illnesses. Treatment is effective in reducing the complications of hypertension, although patients do not always adhere to the physician's regimen because hypertension has no visible symptoms.

Blood pressure is easily measured using a sphygmomanometer, a blood pressure cuff attached to a gauge, and a stethoscope. The cuff is placed above a person's elbow and inflated briefly to stop the circulation. The stethoscope is placed over the artery just beneath the cuff. As air is released from the cuff, a pulsing sound can be heard when blood begins to flow. The reading on the gauge at that moment is the systolic pressure, or the maximal blood pressure during the heart beat. With continued air release, the sound disappears and the gauge indicates diastolic pressure, the pressure while the heart is resting.

Hypertension is diagnosed with three separate readings taken at different time periods. Several years ago, blood pressure recordings taken at home by patients became an additional tool in the evaluation of hypertension. Because home readings were often lower than those taken at the office, it was unclear whether the lower home readings were a result of untrained personnel taking the blood pressure or of the patient being hypertensive only in the office. The appropriate management of "labile hyper-

Table 17.1 Spacelabs: Price List

Model	Item	Price*	Description/Configuration
5200	Ambulatory Monitor	$3,450	Micro-processor–based unit (non-invasive ausculatory and oscillometric), includes RAM PACK, adult cuff, and carry case
5300	Portable Operating Station (POS)	$8,300	Mini-computer, telephone modem, POS software, one (1) Ambulatory Monitor and one case (20 count) of Procedure Kits
5600	RAM PACK PC Interface	$7,900	Includes RAM PACK interface box and cable, board for IBM PC or PCXT, Report Generator software, Operators Manual, one (1) Ambulatory Monitor, and one case (20 count) of Procedure Kits
5250	RAM PACK	$500	One (1) additional RAM PACK for use with any Ambulatory Monitor
015-0010-00D	Large Adult Cuff	$180	33–47 cm Arm Circumference
015-0008-00D	Small Adult Cuff	$180	18–26 cm Arm Circumference
015-0009-00D	Adult Cuff	$180	25–35 cm Arm Circumference
—	Carrying Case	$35	Carrying case for Ambulatory Monitor (includes case, belt, and shoulder strap)
016-0028-00	Report Generator Software	$1,995	Includes POS to PC/PXT cable, Report Generator software (Lotus 1-2-3 and ABP Operating Diskette), and Operators Manual

*Prices are effective November 1984 and are subject to change without notice.

Note: All products are covered by a 90-day warranty. Approximate gross margins are 5200 = 74%; 5300 = 72%; 5600 = 78%; 5250 = 82%.

tensives," whose blood pressures fluctuate above and below the level separating them from normotensive persons, was also unclear.

Twenty-four–hour blood pressure monitoring was a method of answering these questions. It gave more physiological data throughout a life cycle and was not dependent upon the patient's reliability or involvement. It could associate changes in blood pressure with the patient's environment or behavior and establish the degree of "lability" by measuring the total range of systolic and diastolic pressure in 24 hours. Automatic, indirect ambulatory blood pressure monitoring could also be used to establish the optimum drug dosage time and period and to evaluate the effectiveness of the medication over an entire 24-hour period.

Blood Pressure Monitoring Technologies

Both invasive (intra-arterial) and noninvasive technologies have been developed for ambulatory monitoring of blood pressure. The

Exhibit 17.1 Spacelabs: Ambulatory BP Report

Patient Name: John Doe   Medication: None
Sex: M   Height: 5'11"   Weight: 200   Reason for Test: Hypertension

SUMMARY TABLE

	24 HR			NIGHTTIME			DAYTIME		
	MIN	MAX	MEAN	MIN	MAX	MEAN	MIN	MAX	MEAN
SYSTOLIC[a]	83	191	120	83	191	127	87	142	119
DIASTOLIC[a]	36	102	80	36	91	82	56	102	93
MEAN[a]	61	116	93	77	116	97	68	107	95
HEART RATE[b]	50	144	78	58	144	85	54	103	78

NUMBER OF SYSTOLICS > 140 (mm Hg): 8%
NUMBER OF DIASTOLICS > 90 (mm Hg): 23%

[a]Systolic, diastolic, and mean blood pressures reported in mm Hg.
[b]Heart rate reported in beats per minute.

HOURLY AVERAGED READINGS

HOUR	# of READINGS	SYSTOLIC	DIASTOLIC	MEAN	PP	HEART RATE
8	3	124	81	96	28	90
9	4	127	92	101	26	92
10	3	114	87	96	18	71
11	3	124	91	101	23	75
12	3	128	83	97	31	73
13	2	121	85	97	25	88
14	3	120	83	95	25	84
15	3	125	88	100	25	85
16	3	130	91	105	25	93
17	2	120	85	98	23	86
18	3	126	83	103	22	80
19	5	145	73	97	48	101
20	1	142	86	90	52	108
21	3	117	90	99	18	79
22	3	122	91	101	21	81
23	3	111	76	87	24	64
0	2	113	72	85	28	68
1	1	116	68	83	80	80
2	1	95	57	72	23	73
3	2	109	63	78	32	62
4	1	83	50	61	22	50
5	1	93	52	66	27	59
6	3	92	58	69	22	56
7	3	102	75	83	19	57

Table 17.2 Spacelabs: ABP Product/Market Requirements

Item	Comments
New Monitor	Smaller, lighter with new BP algorithm; will position us against any new market entrance
Tie-in to Current Products	"Package sale to ambulatory customer—can upgrade Holter to ABP—lock out ABP competitors
Algorithm Improvement	Less motion and noise sensitivity; potential use with stress testing and corporate fitness; large new market potential
Cost	Lower standard costs for improving margins and insurance against low-cost competitive entry
Data Analysis	Long-term BP diagnostic/predictive software. This would impact favorably on reimbursement and widen applications screening population
ABP Networking	Integrate BP monitor over network for both research (multisite) and Scanning Service use

Note: BP = blood pressure.

Table 17.3 Spacelabs: R & D Priorities

Priority	Project	Marketing Requirement?	Engineering Commitment?*
1	New Monitor	Yes	No
2	Finish 5600	Yes	Yes
3	New BP Algorithm	No	?
4	New Report Format	No	No

*Commitment defined as an engineering/R & D project that is on the 1985 schedule and being tracked.

risks and costs associated with the invasive direct arterial measurement led to a search for noninvasive procedures. By 1982, the most widely used ambulatory blood pressure recording system was manufactured by Del Mar Avionics. It contained a solid state memory, a miniature pump powered by a rechargeable battery, and a cuff-imbedded microphone and could be programmed to yield between 125 and 200 blood pressure readings over a 24-hour period. The 4.5-pound device was worn on the patient's side and supported by a belt and shoulder strap. The correlations between the Avionics device and conventional methods of blood pressure recording approximated .90 for both systolic and diastolic pressure. Generally, about 15–30% of the readings obtained with the Avionics device were unusable or suspect.

The market for ambulatory blood pressure monitoring equipment was expected to develop much as the market for ambulatory electrocardiography (ECG) monitoring equipment (Holter monitors) had. The first ambulatory ECG monitoring units, named after their designer, Norman Holter, Ph.D., became commercially available in 1963 from the Del Mar Avionics Company. Holter recorders were sold to hospitals and physicians, as well as to the commercial scanning services that sprang up to interpret the data provided by the Holter recorders. The data were read either manually and/or with the use of a computer program that isolated deviant ECG characteristics. The commercial services were small for-profit firms (150 in 1982). Scanning services were also offered by hospitals and by cardiologists who incorporated themselves, bought scanning equipment, and provided these services. (See Tables 17.4 and 17.5 for market data on ambulatory ECG monitoring equipment.)

SPACELABS

From 1980 to 1982, Squibb, a major pharmaceutical company, acquired six companies that manufactured the following medical electronic monitoring equipment: ultrasound, Holter cardiac and stress monitors, public blood pressure screening and testing, portable patient monitoring systems and defibrillators. These companies became part of the Squibb Medical Products Group, which by 1984 had sales of $396 million. In 1983, the four companies with cardiology-related products were integrated under the Spacelabs name, primarily to enhance brand awareness. They projected revenues of over $100 million in 1985.

The four companies that composed Spacelabs became functional organizations, with product managers for each product group and centralized administration and engineering. Spacelabs employed one sales force to sell its ambulatory monitors and another to sell its hospital monitoring systems. The product managers at Spacelabs were responsible for both marketing and product development. They served as advocates for their particular product lines, competing for engineers and other resources. According to Mr. Harlow:

> For projects under a certain dollar amount, you sometimes go outside the normal channels, not using Spacelabs' engineers, and not telling everyone what you're doing. For example, when I needed some new software for my product, I went outside and got Lotus 1-2-3.

Table 17.4 Spacelabs: Ambulatory ECG Monitoring Procedures Growth

(numbers in thousands)

		1978	1979	1980	1981	1982E	1983E	1984E	1985E	1986E
Commercial Services	#	435	525	775	975	1,225	1,500	1,800	2,100	2,400
	%	62	61	60	56	51	43	40	39	39
Growth	%	—	20.7	47.6	25.8	25.6	22.4	20	16.7	14.3
Patient Care Facilities	#	250	350	500	750	1,200	1,950	2,700	3,300	3,750
	%	38	39	40	44	49	57	60	61	61
Growth	%	—	40	42.8	50	60	62.5	38.5	22.6	13.6
TOTAL		685	875	1,275	1,725	2,425	3,450	4,500	5,400	6,150
% Growth of Total over Previous Year		—	28	46	35	41	42	30	20	14
Sales of Ambulatory Cardiac Monitoring Systems		6,565	6,960	6,431	7,049	8,260	11,275	11,725	11,350	11,675

Source: "The Ambulatory Cardiac Monitoring Market," Frost & Sullivan, Inc., March 1982. Reprinted with permission.

Table 17.5 Spacelabs: Unit Shipments of Ambulatory Cardiac Monitoring Systems

	1978	1979	1980	1981	1982	1983	1984	1985	1986
Holter Recorders	5,275	5,450	4,860	4,400	4,325	4,100	3,625	2,725	2,275
Growth (%)	—	3.3	(14.0)	(9.5)	(1.7)	(5.2)	(11.6)	(24.8)	(16.5)
Holter Scanners	550	650	611	699	810	725	700	625	550
Growth (%)	—	18.5	(6.0)	14.4	15.9	(10.5)	(3.4)	(10.7)	(12.0)
Intermittent Recording Systems	540	600	700	1,400	2,800	4,200	4,200	4,200	4,200
Growth (%)	—	11.1	16.7	100.0	100.0	50.0	—	—	—
Real-time Recording Systems	200	260	260	550	1,125	2,250	3,200	4,000	4,650
Growth (%)	—	30.0	—	111.5	104.5	100.0	42.2	25.0	16.3

Source: "The Ambulatory Cardiac Monitoring Market," Frost & Sullivan, Inc., March 1982. Reprinted with permission.

When I needed new parts for my product, I went to a production line where they were making plastic boxes for another product and said, "Hey, could you make an extra ten of those for me?"

In addition to lobbying for their own product line, product managers conducted market research, telemarketing, and sales force training. The salary range for product managers was $30,000 to $60,000, and some were on a bonus system.

The Spacelabs sales network consisted of 3 regional managers, 16 salespeople, and 5 distributors. Three compensation plans were used: (1) base salary and expenses plus commission (for salespeople in dense, urban areas); (2) straight commission; or (3) a dealership arrangement, with commission (for independent dealers who covered large geographic areas and handled many product lines). Under the first plan, the average salesperson earned $50,000–$60,000, with top salespeople earning $80,000–$90,000. The average salesperson under the second plan earned $75,000–$85,000, with top salespeople earning up to $150,000. Randy Miskimon, sales director, explained:

Recruiting good salespeople is our most difficult problem. They have only one to two sales calls per physician customer to bring the message across, and they spend only 10 to 15 minutes in front of the customer during a sales call. This requires a great deal of product knowledge, as well as knowledge about our competitors. We look for people who can sell in a rapid turn situation, such as people experienced in selling copiers or pharmaceuticals. What we offer is a company with a good image; one that can give them a secure future.

Our ambulatory sales force took a chance in picking up the ABP monitor. I believe they are to be commended for doing this. Instead of a technical sell, this product really involves an educational sell, similar to that of the Holter monitor 20 years ago.

DEVELOPMENT OF THE ABP MONITOR

Jim Taylor, vice president of marketing and business development for Spacelabs, explained how the ABP monitor came into existence:

In 1982, I was responsible for a small company in the blood pressure monitoring business, which was acquired by Spacelabs. We had seven engineers and one product manager. By 1982, there was a great deal of competition in the blood pressure monitor market, especially in terms of pricing, and we didn't have much to offer. Our survival depended upon the evolution of the ABP monitor. We had no charter to make this product, but the guys did their best to hammer it out in the back room.

The technology involved in this product was not awe-inspiring, the reimbursement wasn't there, and there were clinical questions. It is hard to do market projections on a product that people aren't using and don't know they need and that may or may not be reimbursed. If we had another profitable line, we probably wouldn't have pursued this business.

However, there was an American College of Cardiology trade show coming up, so we took all the existing technology we could get together. We programmed the Epson Computer, which had been out for about three months, to do what we needed. We used a computer case design from a sister company to avoid tooling charges. We put the basic system in a suitcase so it looked portable and "packaged." At the show we took a couple of units and put them on good-looking fashion models, who paraded up and down the aisles. We thought if the product didn't attract any interest, at least we didn't have that much invested.

We got about 100 leads at that show, a large number for this type of product. It helped that our competitor's equipment was priced at $22,000 for a total system. We priced our system at $6,500 to break the price resistance barrier and said that because the cost of our equipment was low, reimbursement wasn't that important.

Our belief at the time was that monitoring blood pressure over an extended period of time would eventually become a standard practice, that reimbursement wouldn't come until people started to use long-term blood pressure monitors, and that there was money to be made early. We reallocated about $25,000 from various projects to finish the ABP monitor after the show.

THE SPACELABS PRODUCT DEVELOPMENT PROCESS

Mr. Taylor went on to explain how new products were managed at Spacelabs in 1985:

> Two major channels are used for new product development. The first is traditional strategic planning, which assigns engineering time and other resources to a particular product related to our current businesses. For products outside the realm of Spacelabs' current products, our people sometimes go around the normal channels and become pirates, engaging in what we call "back room operations." Some companies have tried to formalize this process, but I would guess this will slow things down. In this field changes take place fast, and big companies often don't do well on the cutting edge of technology. Because there is good communication, trust, and a willingness to take risks in small companies, they can frequently come up with technologically superior ideas. But for a small company within a large corporation, it is hard to get visibility. A small company can easily lose its competitive advantage in technology.
>
> Many companies combine marketing with strategic planning. They're hard to do together, and they're different. Marketing of today will generally drive out the planning for tomorrow.
>
> We don't always use formal financial criteria to guide our decisions on new products. This is difficult to calculate when one product is a by-product of other products or where markets are not yet well defined. I will say that the ambulatory blood pressure monitoring business is more profitable than most of our businesses.

Marketing the ABP Monitor

In 1984, revenues for Spacelabs' ambulatory products were approximately $13 million, with $11 million coming from the Holter and stress monitoring products and almost $2 million coming from the ambulatory blood pressure monitor. Mr. Harlow explained:

> The end users [patients] for whom we are marketing this product are 25- to 55-year-old people in the work place. From their perspective the advantage of the ambulatory blood pressure monitor is that it will limit the drug regimens prescribed as a result of misdiagnosis of high blood pressure. Not only can there be adverse health consequences to the drugs, but these prescriptions can cost $60 per month.

Mr. Taylor added:

> Physician decisions on hypertension aren't based on 24-hour blood pressure monitoring. Even if most doctors got the 24-hour data they would not know what to do with it, because their prescribing patterns are based on getting only a few blood pressure measurements. For this reason we marketed the ambulatory blood pressure monitor first to clinical researchers and pharmaceutical researchers. We hoped to get the applications for our product written up in clinical journals and thereby educate the rest of the medical community. General public relations and mass media activities were also pursued.

Mr. Harlow described the rationale behind his 1985 marketing plan for ambulatory blood pressure products (see Tables 17.6 to 17.9):

> We perceive the market to consist of the following segments: researchers; cardiologists; general practitioners, family practitioners, and internal medicine specialists; scanning services and hospitals; other; and international. The research segment consists primarily of government researchers with many uses for our product, such as monitoring the blood pressure of military personnel. We supply their monitors at a reduced cost or on a loan basis. Cardiologists are the first doctors to purchase products such as ours. General practitioners, family practition-

ers, and specialists in internal medicine are the last to come to market, but together they constitute the largest group. Scanning services represent a good vehicle for marketing our product, but they can reduce the cost of ambulatory blood pressure monitoring and compete with our physician customers in pricing. Currently Blue Shield and some private insurance carriers reimburse physicians for monitoring at the full price (charge) of $130–$200; they reimburse scanning services at the price of $80.

The "other" segment consists of nonmedical users, such as psychologists (to determine what situations affect clients' blood pressure) police (to monitor the pressure reaction of recruits) and even corporations (to check the health profile of top executives). We never anticipated this market. These groups call us even though we don't do any active marketing to reach them.

In the international segment, we are targeting England, Germany, France, and Italy. In these countries physicians formerly used the "Oxford" blood pressure monitoring devices, which were based on invasive technology. We feel our product represents a significant improvement over that technology. Our international customers are "easier sells," because the health care system in these countries is more organized. When one government subdivision decides to reimburse for our product, it opens up many potential new sales. There are some barriers in this market, however. Our computer poses a problem in some countries, due to technology export restrictions. The Politburo leaders in the Eastern Bloc countries want our product because they are so far behind in medical technology, but we can't sell to all of this market due to U.S. trade restrictions. Our international sales are handled through the Squibb Medical Systems international sales force.

Our projections of market size are based on the existence of 19 salespeople in the United States (16 at Spacelabs and 3 at Del Mar), and 10 to 15 in the foreign markets. I've got to admit that the market

Table 17.6 Spacelabs: ABP Market Size by Segment

(dollars in millions)

	1983	1984	1985	1986
Domestic				
Research	$ 0.3	$ 0.5	$ 0.6	$ 0.6
Cardiology	0.6	0.5	0.6	0.9
GP/FP/IM[a]	0	0.4	0.8	1.4
Scanning Service/Hospital	0	0.2	0.6	0.8
Other	0	0.3	0.3	0.8
Subtotal	$ 0.9	$ 1.9	$ 2.9	$ 4.5
International	0.5	1.0	2.9	4.5
Total	$ 1.4	$ 2.9	$ 5.8	$ 9.0

[a]GP = general practice; FP = family practice; IM = internal medicine.

Table 17.7 Spacelabs: ABP Monitor Sales History

Year	Domestic	International[a]	Total
1983	$ 630,000	$ 30,000	$ 660,000
1984	1,350,000[b]	300,000	1,650,000
1985 (est.)	2,100,000	1,850,000	3,950,000

[a]Billings to customers (not transfer prices).
[b]Preliminary data.

Table 17.8 Spacelabs: Total Market Potential (5 to 10 Years)

Market	Number	X	Market Acceptance	X	Average Sale	X	Market (millions)
Cardiologists	12,000	X	50%	X	$ 10K	=	$ 60.0
GPs and FPs	63,000		25%		6K		94.5
IMs	65,000		30%		6K		117.0
Scanning Service	200		90%		20K		3.6
Research	200		30%		50K		3.0
International	—		—		—		100.0
	140,400						$ 378.1

Note: At 5 years = $75 million annually; at 10 years = $38 million annually. Gross margin between 72% and 82%.

Table 17.9 Spacelabs: Customer Profile

	1984 *Average $/Sale*	Projected 1985 *Average $/Sale*
	(dollars in thousands)	
Cardiologists	$11K	$11K
Primary Uses: Hypertension Management Drug Efficacy and Titration[a]		
GP/IM/FP	8K	10K
Primary Uses: Hypertension Diagnosis Diabetic Management Chronobiology[b]		
Scanning Service/Hospital	17K	20K
Primary Uses: Nephrology[c] Evaluations Hypertension Management Holter Screening		
Research	65K	20K
Primary Uses: New Drug Studies (Phase I and II) Circadian Variations[d] Psychology Evaluations Biofeedback OB Studies		

[a]Adjusting the drug dosage according to the patient's response.
[b]The study of body functions that vary over time periods longer than one day.
[c]The study of kidney function.
[d]The study of body functions that vary with a cycle of one day.

acceptance figures in my marketing plan are optimistic.

Our sales of ambulatory blood pressure monitors in 1984 equaled $1.65 million (see Table 17.7). Until mid-1984, all domestic sales were made by three people, including me. From mid-1984 to now, sales have been made by 7 out of the 16 people in Spacelabs' ambulatory sales force. With a larger domestic sales force behind this product, plus our international sales force, I expect 1985 sales to come close to $4 million.

Our only domestic competitor up to this point has been Del Mar Avionics (see Exhibit 17.2). They haven't made any significant product changes in four years.

We feel that their main focus is the Holter monitor and that they are milking their blood pressure product. I've never lost a head-to-head sale with Del Mar. One of our competitors in England is Remlar, but again, they haven't been strong. We expect a number of competitors to enter this market, however, especially the pacemaker companies.

He explained his positioning strategy for the ABP monitor:

Our goal is to become the market leader in quality, price, and service. Our pricing allows us good gross margins. In terms of accuracy, our readings are within plus or

Exhibit 17.2 Spacelabs: Competition

Existing

Del Mar Avionics
    1984 Sales: $150K   # of Systems: 8

    1985 Sales: $100K   # of Systems: 5

    Product: P-II/III—A system with 2 Monitors, $17–25K

    Features: 5.0 lb., ECG leads, slow pump, report can be tied to an Apple II

    Strategies: Will try to recoup investment without spending additional dollars. Sold as an add-on to present Holter base. No new products, little sales attention.

Projected

Del Mar: No new products expected.

Medtronic: Prototype being evaluated at Cornell Medical Group, NYC.

Hewlett-Packard: Actively recruiting for product manager in BP. Could be an easy technical extension for them.

Remlar: Does not appear to be entering fully automatic ABP market. Competes as semi-automatic device in Europe.

Others: DMI, General Electric Medical, and Paramed have all expressed interest in the ABP market.

---

minus 5 millimeters of mercury, while doctor's office readings are within plus or minus 8 millimeters of mercury (due to variations in hearing acuity).

We had early problems with service. Because some of our RAM PACKs (data storage units) failed, I asked all our users to send back their entire systems. We cleaned all the equipment, replaced the RAM PACKs, and returned them to our customers, all at no charge. We felt it was important to handle this situation quickly to maintain our product's reputation. We provide service on a mail order basis. Currently, 3 of the 120 Spacelabs' service people work on the ambulatory blood pressure monitor. If on-site service becomes a competitive issue, we could provide service through Spacelabs' ten regional service centers.

Commenting on the future, Harlow noted,

The ABP monitor hasn't reached the limit of technology. We are vulnerable to competition. The cuff on our product is new (the competitors' monitors needed ECG leads), but the blood pressure detection methods could be improved. The amount of engineering time charged to the ABP monitor now is about 1 FTE [full-time equivalent] software engineer and 0.3 FTE hardware engineer. There are also about six or seven engineers who help out on this product, although their time is not charged to the product. I have given engineering my projections for the number of product enhancements we'll need in 1985.

In addition to evaluating our product design and operational status, I've developed a promotion budget for the coming year (see Table 17.10). We promote the ambulatory blood pressure monitor through seminars, telemarketing, medical shows, and direct mail. We try to get on medical talk shows and in journals. This product has great market pull; once the end users see it, they want it. To assist our salespeople, we've developed a revenue analysis that presents the economics of our product from the physician's perspective (see Exhibit 17.3).

I've got to convince our engineers, marketing people, and managers to invest enough resources in my product to ensure that it remains competitive. I know that Squibb wants to invest a higher than average amount of funds into research and development at Spacelabs, but priorities change. For example, next year could be an engineering year or it could be a marketing year. Overall, Spacelabs spends about 3% of sales for marketing. My marketing budget for the ambulatory blood pressure monitor equals roughly 7% of its projected sales. I wonder if they'll buy my plan and its priorities.

Table 17.10 Spacelabs: ABP Promotion Expenses

(dollars in thousands)

Seminars/Symposia	*Budget*
Seven Seminars co-sponsored with local hospital or Scanning Service. A noted researcher presents a paper on the clinical value of ABP. The local representative and sponsor provide demonstrations of the equipment and answer queries at a reception following.	$ 10K
Three (3) Symposia sponsored by E. R. Squibb. Spacelabs can exhibit equipment at drug conferences.	2K
Research grants, white papers, and luminary support. Includes one (I) demo system continually being used in 2–3 month studies.	10K
Miscellaneous	3K
Direct Mail	
Two mailings to Scanning Services (n = 200), two mailings to cardiologists (with Holter), one mailing to nephrologists, and two mailings to high prescription writers (Squibb list). Cost includes letter and brochure for each physician.	40K
Two mailings to local physicians to promote ABP Scanning Service (includes mailing and cover letter development).	10K
Telemarketing	
Lead generation and data samples from Scanning Services and Research groups. Telelecture ("800" lecture on the benefits of ABP) set-up and running.	10K
Marketing Materials	
New brochure—development and printing	35K
Data sheet—Model 5600 RAM PACK^{TM} PC Interface	15K
Patient booklet—description of ABP procedure	5K
Total	$ 140K

Exhibit 17.3 Spacelabs: Marketing Letter

Dear Doctor:

You have probably been reading about the growing use of ambulatory blood pressure monitoring. Researchers have found it extremely helpful in conducting drug efficacy studies. And more and more office-based physicians such as yourself are discovering its benefits in diagnosing hypertension—particularly the mild hypertensive, a common and sometimes elusive patient.

Whether you're interested in diagnosis or in monitoring the effects of the medication you have prescribed, ambulatory blood pressure monitoring allows you to easily correlate periodic monitoring of blood pressure over a 24-hour period with events in that patient's life at that moment…to determine whether readings of 150/95 are frequent or rare…to observe what percentage of blood pressures exceed a given level…to verify that medication once or twice a day maintains pressures all day.

If you agree that this capability could benefit you and your patients, then you should consider ICR's Ambulatory Blood Pressure system, for these reasons:

It's easy for the patient—it uses no electrodes, provides multiple cycle times, and is the lightest weight system of its kind available.

It's easy for you— accurate, reliable data are easily retrieved or transmitted to a variety of locations via its telephone modem and computer link—and 24-hour blood pressure monitoring is reimbursable in many states by Blue Cross and other private carriers.

It's an ICR product—we have more than 20 years' experience in ambulatory Holter monitoring.

It's accompanied by outstanding service provided by Spacelabs' expanded national network of dedicated, expert service representatives—and a special 800 "hot line" for your questions.

It's backed by Spacelabs, a Squibb company—trusted names in cardiovascular medicine.

Please read the enclosed brochure for a more detailed description of this system, and its benefits to you. Then return the enclosed postage-paid reply card to request additional information or a call from our representative in your area, or call me toll-free at 800-xxx-xxxx. We'll be happy to show you how little it costs to add this exciting new capability to your practice.

Sincerely,

Brad R. Harlow
Manager, Ambulatory BP Products

continues

Exhibit 17.3 continued

Ambulatory Blood Pressure Revenue Analysis

System Price	$:	9,000	Depreciation (Months)	:	60
Monthly Payment	$:	228.54	Depreciation Method	:	SL
Sales Tax Rate	%:	6.0	Revenue per Test	$:	150.00
Financing Rate (APR)	%:	18.0	Supply Cost per Test	$:	5.00
Customer Tax Bracket	%:	35.0	Residual Value	$:	900.00

			Year		
	1985	1986	1987	1988	1989
Depreciation	$ 1,620	$ 1,620	$ 1,620	$ 1,620	$ 1,620
Interest	1,523	1,284	999	658	250
Sales Tax Deduction	540	—	—	—	—
TOTAL EXPENSES	3,685	2,904	2,619	2,278	1,870
Tax Deduction	1,289	1,016	917	797	655
Investment Tax Credit	900	—	—	—	—
TOTAL TAX SAVINGS	2,189	1,016	917	797	655
Sum of Monthly Payments	2,742	2,742	2,742	2,742	2,742
After-Tax Expenses[a]	553	1,726	1,825	1,945	2,087
Net Monthly Cost[b]	$ 46	$ 144	$ 152	$ 162	$ 174

Note: Your average monthly cost is only $136 per month.
[a]Depreciation is not an out-of-pocket expense, but is a tax credit.
[b]System includes 1-POS, 1-RAM PACK, and 1 Large Adult Cuff.

POINTS TO PONDER

1. What kind of opportunity does the ABP represent?

2. Is it a good idea for Spacelabs? For Squibb?

3. What are the managerial skills critical to its success?

Technology Transfer: Anti-Inflammatory Discovery

Susan Dubé, vice president of new ventures at Brigham and Women's Hospital, mulled over how best to commercialize a basic scientific discovery recently made at the hospital. The issue was familiar. While drugs, procedures, or services were fairly easy to commercialize through licensing, joint ventures, or establishing new companies, basic scientific discoveries were more difficult to commercialize because they provided no immediate, tangible product or because they represented so many potentials that no one commercial venture could realize all of them.

The discovery in the paper before Susan was the latter case, what she described as an "enabling base technology." The invention disclosure by Bernie Mitchell, M.D., concerned endothelial cells and blood cell surfaces. The technology could be used for leukocyte adhesion inhibition (LAI),[*] an anti-inflammatory treatment for several important areas (see Table 18.1), including:

- Therapy for leukocyte-mediated vascular injury such as reperfusion damage and adult respiratory distress syndrome.
- Treatment for acute inflammation of joint and capsules (e.g., tendonitis, bursitis, rheumatoid and juvenile arthritis).
- Dermatological applications, including the replacement of topical steroid creams.
- Therapy for inflammation secondary to viral, bacterial, and parasitic infection.
- Diagnostic tests for better and earlier identification of cardiac and other inflammatory disorders.

The issue with this exciting technology was if any one firm would be willing or able to utilize all of its potential. Cellex had been suggested by Dr. Mitchell, but Susan wondered if this was the right choice. Dr. Mitchell was impressed with its development facilities and was eager to begin work with the company. Susan wanted to prepare her recommendations concerning Cellex's suitability as a business partner. (See Table 18.2 for Cellex financials and Table 18.3 for information on other biotechnology firms.)

TECHNOLOGY TRANSFER AT BRIGHAM AND WOMEN'S

Scientific discovery in the United States came from the government and private research institutions involved in basic research and the commercial firms that had long dominated the development stage.

Pressure had mounted in recent years to increase the speed with which basic discoveries became commercial products. The pressure

---

[*]*Epithelial*: The layer of cells forming the epidermis of the skin and the surface layer of mucous and serum membranes. Epithelium serves the purposes of protection, absorption, secretion, movement of substances through ducts, production of germ cells, and reception of stimuli. *Endothelium*: A form of squamous (flat, scaly) epithelium cells that line the blood and lymphatic vessels, the heart, and various other body cavities. *Leukocyte*: White blood corpuscles.

Note: This case was prepared by Richard Benedict under the supervision of Professor Regina E. Herzlinger. The identity of the product, physician, and biotechnology company involved has been disguised. Case Study 15, Novel Combination of Two Drugs, discusses a related topic.

Table 18.1 Technology Transfer: Anti-Inflammatory Discovery: Persons with Selected Chronic Conditions, by Age and Sex, 1983

Chronic Condition	Persons with Condition (thousands)	Incidence per 1,000						
		Total	Under 18 Years	18–44 Years	45–64 Years	65 Years and Over	Male	Female
Heart Conditions	18,978	82.8	19.4	37.1	143.3	303.0	79.3	86.0
High Blood Pressure (Hypertension)	27,813	121.3	1.9[a]	62.1	263.6	387.9	104.1	137.4
Varicose Veins of Lower Extremities	6,838	29.8	.2[a]	22.1	55.1	87.1	11.6	46.8
Hemorrhoids	10,924	47.6	1.0[a]	57.5	76.5	74.2	46.1	49.1
Chronic Bronchitis	10,864	47.4	59.3	37.9	44.7	58.3	42.0	52.4
Asthma	8,787	38.3	45.2	36.1	34.6	36.4	34.5	41.9
Chronic Sinusitis	30,767	134.2	49.5	162.8	182.4	149.6	119.0	148.4
Hay Fever, Allergic Rhinitis without Asthma	19,771	86.2	55.4	109.7	91.9	63.1	83.7	88.6
Dermatitis, including Eczema	9,108	39.7	37.4	40.8	43.9	34.0	29.6	49.2
Diseases of Sebaceous Glands[b]	6,192	27.0	28.5	38.2	12.9	5.8	25.9	28.1
Arthritis	30,115	131.3	2.2[a]	53.6	284.8	471.6	94.9	165.3
Diabetes	5,613	24.5	1.8[a]	9.0	58.2	79.5	21.3	27.5
Migraine	7,258	31.6	6.4	47.0	42.5	16.9	15.8	46.5
Diseases of Urinary System	7,061	30.8	9.4	29.8	43.1	65.3	14.4	46.1
Visual Impairments	8,081	35.2	10.3	29.5	49.7	92.1	42.7	28.2
Hearing Impairments	20,698	90.3	18.8	49.8	148.4	314.8	107.1	74.5
Deformities or Orthopedic Impairments	22,152	96.0	27.0	105.9	136.8	161.6	93.8	99.2

[a]Figures do not meet standards of reliability or precision.
[b]Acne and sebaceous skin cyst.

Table 18.2 Technology Transfer: Anti-Inflammatory Discovery: Cellex Financial Data

(dollars in millions)

	1986	1987	1988	1989	1990	1991
Revenues						
Product Revenues						
Alpha-Interferon		$ 1.8	$ 3.0	$ 6.0	$ 11.0	$ 14.0
Gamma-IF, R. Arthritis		—	1.2	2.1	3.6	4.0
Gamma-IF, Cancer		—	—	1.0	2.0	2.0
IL-2		—	—	—	—	1.0
TPA		—	—	—	1.0	3.0
TNF		—	—	—	—	—
Factor VIII		—	—	—	—	—
GM-CSF		—	—	—	—	1.0
MIS		—	—	—	—	—
Malaria Vaccine		—	—	—	—	—
Hepatitis B Vaccine		—	—	1.0	2.0	3.0
Royalties from Hepatitis B Patent		—	2.0	4.0	6.0	6.0
Porcine Growth Hormone		—	—	2.0	5.0	7.0
Anti-Inflammatories		—	—	—	—	—
Total Product Revenues		$ 1.8	$ 6.2	$ 16.1	$ 30.6	$ 41.0
Contract Revenues		6.8	10.6	11.2	10.5	11.0
Interest Income		3.9	3.5	3.2	3.0	3.0
Total Revenues		$ 12.5	$ 20.3	$ 30.5	$ 44.1	$ 55.0
Other Financial Ratios						
Current Assets	$ 73.6	$ 57.8				
Total Assets	$ 100.9	$ 80.7				
Current Liabilities	$ 7.2	$ 7.6				
Stockholders' Equity	$ 89.2	$ 67.9				
Retained Earnings	$ (82.0)	$(104.6)				
Cash	$ 29.7	$ 27.0				

Sources: Biotechnology Stocks—Industry Report, Cable Howse & Ragen. Cellex annual report.

came from an increasingly competitive marketplace and from research institutions whose research was increasingly expensive. Most observers agreed that basic scientific research would continue to originate from independent research institutions. Thus a major concern was to aid the transfer of technology from research to commercial entities.

In 1985, Brigham and Women's Hospital created a corporate ventures office to provide managerial advice to its scientists in the commercialization of their products. Other major institutions, such as Stanford and MIT, had created similar offices, and many other institutions would follow suit in the years to follow. The office was headed by Susan Dubé, and

Table 18.3 Technology Transfer: Anti-Inflammatory Discovery: Biotechnology Firms Sales, Profits, and Assets, 1986

(dollars in millions)

Firm	Sales ($)	1986/1985 (%)	Profits ($)	1986/1985 (%)	Assets ($)
Applitex	127.3	56	−352.20	NA	376
Electro-Nucleonics	63.0	11	1.53	−6	50
Applied Biosystems	54.9	4	10.37	50	91
Alza	51.6	20	9.01	78	137
Cetus	39.6	−13	1.10	−10	204
Centocor	27.1	36	−39.02	NA	121
Amgen	21.1	198	0.55	NA	94
Immunogenetics	18.4	3	0.61	NA	18
Genzyme	12.1	26	0.04	NA	33
California Biotechnology	10.8	43	−18.97	NA	97
Collaborative Research	10.4	36	−2.35	NA	22
Monoclonal Antibodies	9.5	87	−0.07	NA	18
Calgene	7.4	424	−0.91	NA	41
Cellex	6.4	−57	−28.15	NA	101
Genex	3.3	−80	−12.08	NA	15

Sources: *Chemical Week* and *Standard & Poor's*.

included Maria Marmarinos, who focused on new technologies, and another person, who was responsible for new service ventures. Working closely with them was a lawyer, who assisted in contract negotiation and patent applications.

In their experience, although a few products had been developed by establishing separate companies and some service opportunities were developed through joint ventures, most opportunities were commercialized through license agreements. For ceding the rights to the new science, the institution received a steady stream of income from the sale of the commercialized product. But the institution received nothing if the technology proved difficult to commercialize or if the licensing party proved indifferent to its potential.

If a new technology were successfully commercialized, the licensing agreement could produce a significant stream of income (the University of Wisconsin continues to receive royalties from its patent of Vitamin D in milk from the 1920s). Most of the "upside potential" for successful products accrued to the commercial partner, however. Once development costs were amortized and learning curve

economies realized, the commercial partner gained increasing rewards, while the research institution continued to receive a flat fee.

DEVELOPING AND LICENSING THE LAI DISCOVERY

A development partner for the LAI discovery was needed not only for financial reasons but also to aid in refining, synthesizing, and cloning the protein used in research. No organization could provide these services on a contract basis. Large pharmaceutical companies often did not have the expertise, and smaller biotechnology firms usually were fully utilizing their facilities for protein production.

Dr. Mitchell knew that Cellex had a specific application for the anti-inflammatory technology and could produce LAI in large, purified quantities. Dr. Mitchell's research up until this point had used the naturally occurring form of LAI, which was found in human umbilical cords. Such a natural source could not produce either enough LAI or sufficiently pure LAI for advanced research and commercial development.

The issue of purity was especially important. Dr. Mitchell's test equipment would demonstrate activity, but could not identify other contributing substances. Isolating a pure form of the protein required human expertise and extremely sensitive and expensive equipment. Once it was identified, it could be cloned and reproduced (it would be recorded as a particular sequence of DNA). Cloning and growing additional copies of the protein also required specialized expertise in fermentation and other techniques.

OPENING NEGOTIATIONS

Susan and Maria Marmarinos approached Cellex. The negotiation involved considerable exploratory work. In the early stages, Cellex discussed only very general concepts and no specific applications of the therapy. Cellex also insisted on exclusive rights to all uses. Cellex realized that if it were to become commercially viable, it needed basic laboratory skills from Dr. Mitchell.

Susan and Maria believed that if Cellex were to develop all LAI applications, then Brigham and Women's should have an equity stake in the project. Maria made this proposal to Cellex at the first meeting and later received its response (Exhibit 18.1).

Dr. Mitchell was eager to begin working with a development partner. He wanted to publish his findings, and it was difficult to disclose too much until a commercial contract was signed. He was also increasingly in need of the purified protein to continue his research. Susan knew that the ethos at Brigham and Women's was that scientific discovery must always take precedence over business concerns. She also knew, however, that her job was to recommend the best possible deal for the institution. She thought some more about the proposal and began to formulate specific negotiation results and tactics.

POINTS TO PONDER

Recommend a strategy for Susan's negotiation.

Exhibit 18.1 Technology Transfer: Anti-Inflammatory Discovery: License Agreement and Research Collaboration between Cellex and Brigham and Women's Hospital (Draft Proposal for Discussion Only)

February 17, 1988

Purpose: To establish a research collaboration in the field of endothelial cell–leukocyte interactions, with the goal of developing commercial products based on licensed patents and technology. The products shall include LAI and ELAM-l, and may also include new discoveries emerging from the research collaboration.

1. *Subject:* LAI, ELAM-l, and Monoclonal Antibodies H4/18 and H18/7.

2. *Licensed Patents and Technology*: Patents, including those in preparation, related to the purification of the subject proteins; patents on recombinant forms of the subject proteins; patents on inventions developed by Brigham and Women's or jointly by Cellex and Brigham and Women's as part of the research collaboration; any other patents or technology owned by Brigham and Women's that are necessary to commercialize the subject proteins.

3. *Field of Use*: Exclusive right to test, develop, manufacture, sell, and sublicense products covered by licensed patents and technology, for all uses. Brigham and Women's retains nonexclusive rights to licensed patents and technology for use by Dr. Mitchell and his academic collaborators for noncommercial research purposes only.

4. *Territory*: Worldwide.

5. *Research Gift*: Cellex will pay Dr. Mitchell's laboratory a gift of $120,000 per year for three years, in $30,000 quarterly payments, to be used on research projects chosen solely by Dr. Mitchell. This gift is contingent upon Brigham and Women's filing for U.S., European, and Japanese patent protection (with the assistance of Cellex) on LAI and ELAM-l before the first public, enabling disclosure of each of these technologies.

6. *Additional Payments*:

   a. $120,000 if within three years LAI is demonstrated by Dr. Mitchell's lab to have a therapeutically relevant effect in a mutually agreeable, pre-clinical model of an important human disease or condition.

   b. $120,000 if within three years ELAM-l, a fragment of ELAM-l, or antibodies to ELAM-l are demonstrated by Dr. Mitchell's lab to have a therapeutically relevant effect, as in paragraph 6(a).

7. *Publication*: Cellex will not publish research results related to licensed technology without the prior review of Dr. Mitchell. Dr. Mitchell will allow Cellex to review research manuscripts related to the licensed technology at least 30 days prior to submission for publication, for the purpose of evaluating patent potential.

8. *Royalties*:

   • 2% of Cellex's net sales of products covered by licensed patents; *or*
   • 7% of net revenue earned by Cellex from sublicensing of products covered by licensed patents.

9. *Terms of Royalties*: Life of the patents, on the country-by-country basis, or 10 years from the first sale, whichever is less.

10. *Patent Prosecution and Enforcement:* Cellex will be responsible and will assume the cost of patent prosecution and enforcement. Dr. Mitchell and Brigham and Women's will cooperate fully in the enforcement of licensed patents and provide free access to laboratory records essential to their defense. Patents on joint inventions that are the result of collaborative research will be jointly owned.

Case Study 19

Trinity University

Trinity University, a well-regarded Texan private liberal arts institution, was contemplating two changes in the health care benefits of its employees. One possible change reduced the four categories and two plans presently used for Aetna policies to a smaller number, and the second implemented a flexible benefits plan. Each change is discussed in greater detail in Exhibits 19.1 and 19.2, respectively. In considering the changes, the administration placed its highest priority on the concept of budgetable costs: It wanted to budget costs accurately for each program for a period of at least five years. Its other priority was to position Trinity as a progressive, academically superior institution whose environment and benefits would attract faculty and professional staff from around the world.

Trinity spent $17 million on salaries and another $3.4 million on employee benefits in the fiscal year 1987. These sums had increased an average of 19% annually throughout the decade, a rate substantially higher than the rate of endowment or tuition increases and one that had not been predicted. The administration did not want to increase funding of current operating expenses through the endowment. The university's endowment, comprising primarily equities and oil-related investments such as mineral and royalty interests, was valued at approximately $240 million. While the endowment was considered large for a university with an enrollment of 2,500 students, the variability of its investment value caused concern. The administration felt that future benefit increases would reduce funds available for salaries.

Table 19.1 shows the distribution of benefit costs by employee groups and benefit categories. The three employee groups composed three different constituencies: (1) faculty and professional staff; (2) contract employees (all on salary); and (3) classified employees (all paid hourly). Because of the depressed South Texas economy, the salaries for classified employees averaged only $14,000. Contract employees' salaries averaged in the $25,000 range. Faculty and professional staff salaries were competitive with those in other universities across the country.

Many faculty and staff were vocal and proactive and wished to be full participants in the decision-making process regarding conditions of employment. The University Fringe Benefits Committee reviewed all employee benefit programs. It was chaired by a professor of mathematics and included both faculty and staff as members. The committee was viewed differently by different constituencies. Faculty and staff members viewed it as their voice with the administration, while hourly employees saw the committee and the administration as one and the same. The Faculty Senate was a vocal critic of the existing benefit structure. Its president was a single parent.

Note: This case was prepared by Donna Gardner under the supervision of Professor Regina E. Herzlinger.

POINTS TO PONDER

1. Should the number of Aetna premium categories be reduced from four to two and why?

420

Exhibit 19.1 Trinity University: Reducing Aetna Categories from Four to Two and Aetna Plans A and B from Two to One

Deductible—the amount the insured must pay before health insurance payments begin. Out-of-pocket maximum—after the insured has paid this amount, health insurance pays all remaining expenses.

Presently, Aetna offers two plans: A, with $100 per person deductible and $500 annual out-of-pocket maximum payments, and B, with a $500 deductible an a $2,500 out-of-pocket maximum. Their costs and enrollments are shown below. Alternatively, we can offer one Aetna plan with a $200 per person deductible and a $1,000 out-of-pocket limit and limit it to a single employee or employees with dependents category. The alternative plan would bring Aetna's policies at or below the cost of staff and IPA HMOs we offer. The alternative Aetna policy would cost $78.00 for a single employee and $199.00 for employees with dependents per month. Trinity may cancel its Aetna contract on 30 days notice.

Trinity will pay 60% of the costs of any of these plans. It will maintain the staff HMO and IPA plans that presently exist, regardless of the decision about the Aetna plans.

Present Health Insurance Premium Rates

Enrollees, Total Number	Type of Health Insurance	Number of Employees by Type of Employee Group[*]			Total Monthly Premium
		cl	ct	fa	
	Aetna-Option A				
58	Employee only	20	12	26	$ 93.07
13	Employee/child	6	1	6	200.48
25	Employee/spouse	7	4	14	234.12
63	Employee/family	6	9	48	275.13
159		39	26	94	
	Aetna-Option B				
17	Employee only	8	5	4	$ 72.93
8	Employee/child	4	2	2	137.10
9	Employee/spouse	2	1	6	157.31
9	Employee/family	3	1	5	221.48
43		17	9	17	
	Staff HMO				
49	Employee	21	10	18	$ 78.94
10	Employee/child	9	1	0	161.83
14	Employee/spouse	4	2	8	190.25
41	Employee/family	13	3	25	222.61
114		47	16	51	
	PruCare (IPA)				
104	Employee	46	22	36	$ 69.04
30	Employee/child	23	1	6	133.72
29	Employee/spouse	14	6	9	146.68
56	Employee/family	22	5	29	229.98
219		105	34	80	
535	Total with Trinity coverage	208	85	242	
140	Total without Trinity coverage	80	29	31	

[*]cl = classified employees; ct = contract employees; fa = faculty/administrative employees.

Exhibit 19.2 Trinity University: Flexible Benefits Plan

Section 125 of the Internal Revenue Code allows employees to participate in employee benefits plans on a "tax-free" basis. It provides that any expenses paid on behalf of an employee and paid by an employee for participation in a "covered plan" will not be subject to federal, state (in most cases), Social Security, and FUTA taxes. Other advantages include:

- The perception that this form of plan design is progressive and could serve as a model for other academic institutions.

- The plan can be structured to include benefits that cannot be included in the traditional health care program such as dependent care assistance and medical expenses not reimbursed under the current health care program.

- The plan can be structured to provide benefits for all employees regardless of their ability to pay.

- The plan can be structured so as to ensure that the university's contribution to the health care program could be determined on an annual basis, thus making this contribution capped.

The most significant disadvantage of this program is that if employees fail to utilize their contributions to the benefit plan, they will lose the unused amount of contribution. This rule, referred to as the use-it-or-lose-it rule, is strictly enforced by the IRS.

If Trinity adapted a flexible benefit plan, it might contribute a fixed amount of money for the benefits of each employee. The employees could then allocate this money as they desired among medical and other benefits. The medical benefits would include the Aetna plan(s) and the two HMOs.

2. Should the number of Aetna plans be changed from two to one and why?

3. Estimate the cost of a flexible benefit plan to Trinity. Should it be adopted and why?

4. What new venture opportunities do the circumstances of this case bring to your mind? Be specific in your answer, listing the exact products or services these new ventures will provide.

Table 19.1 Trinity University: Salary and Benefits

Item	FAC/ADM		Contract		Classified		Total	
	Amount	% of Salary	Amount	% of Salary	Amount	% of Salary	Amount	% of Salary
Salaries	$ 8,727	NA	$ 3,726	NA	$ 4,066	NA	$ 16,519	NA
Pension	873	10.00%	373	10.00%	213	5.24%	1,459	8.83%
Medical	307	3.52	80	2.20	206	5.07	595	3.60
AETNA B	19	0.22	6	0.16	15	0.37	40	0.24
AETNA A	146	1.67	34	0.91	46	1.13	226	1.37
IPA HMO	81	0.93	26	0.70	96	2.36	203	1.23
Staff HMO	61	0.70	14	0.38	49	1.21	124	0.75
Benefits, Other	638	7.31	277	7.44	313	7.70	1,228	7.44
Total Pension, Medical, and Other Benefits	$ 1,818	20.83%	$ 730	19.64%	$ 732	18.01%	$ 3,282	19.87%

United States Health Care Systems, Inc.

Below are excerpts from a prospectus issued November 20, 1985.

THE COMPANY

United States Health Care Systems owns four federally qualified health maintenance organizations (HMOs). They serve the market areas of southeastern Pennsylvania; New Jersey; Florida, to serve the three market areas of Jacksonville, Orlando, and Tampa; and the greater Chicago marketplace, which includes parts of Illinois and Indiana. Additionally, the Company expects to begin operations in the metropolitan area of New York City and Connecticut during 1986. The Company's primary care physicians use its proprietary system to influence the economics of medical delivery, substantially reducing medical costs without sacrificing the quality of medical care. Its services, marketed to employer groups, are provided through a network of selected, independent primary care physicians who coordinate each member's individual medical program. In addition to providing primary physician care, specialist care, and hospital services, the Company offers home health care and other outpatient services as well as optional prescription drug and vision care plans. The Company owns four primary care offices that it leases to primary care physicians and also offers financial and management services to its private participating physicians.

The Company has developed prospective compensation arrangements and incentives with its independent primary care physicians, specialist physicians, hospitals, and other health care providers in order to improve the efficiency and effectiveness of health care delivery.

The Company believes its system offers the following important advantages:

- To the member—a coordinated, more comprehensive health and preventive care program than is normally available from traditional health plans, and without substantial copayments or deductible features.

- To the physician—an opportunity to participate in a system that has attracted an increasing number of people interested in cost-effective, quality medical care; more effectively influence health care planning; enjoy stable and timely remuneration; reduce bad debt experience and billing and other paperwork.

- To the employer—an improvement in the breadth and quality of benefit programs available to employees and their families without increase in cost or administrative burdens.

On September 30, 1985, the Company's HMOs had contractual relationships with

Note: The physician compensation system described in this case study has been superseded by a system that utilizes both quality and efficiency measures in determining the amount and frequency of payments to primary care physicians.

This case was prepared by Professor Regina E. Herzlinger.

approximately 1,680 primary care physicians in 1,100 physicians' offices, 8,570 specialty physicians, 170 hospitals, and 1,370 pharmacies. The Company markets directly to employers and prospective members through its direct sales force of 86 sales representatives and 17 marketing managers.

The common stock was traded at the prices shown below:

	High	*Low*
1983	$ 5	$2 $^1/_2$
1984	10 $^1/_2$	3 $^1/_4$
1985	22 $^1/_8$	8 $^3/_4$

OPERATIONS

Nine Months Ended September 30, 1985, Compared to Nine Months Ended September 30, 1984

The Company's HMOs grew by 167,000 members during the first nine months of 1985, representing a 29% increase over the 129,000 members added during the same period of 1984 (Table 20.1). The growth was primarily due to continued penetration of the Company's existing marketplaces.

Premium revenues increased $113,657,000 or 82%. The average consolidated premium on a per member basis increased 10%.

1984 Compared to 1983

Premium revenue increases resulted primarily from a 79% rise in average membership. Increases in membership for Pennsylvania, New Jersey, and Florida (which commenced operation in March 1984) were 93,000, 53,000, and 30,000 members respectively. The average premium on a per member basis increased 12%. It represents a higher rate of increase in Pennsylvania, partially offset by lower premium rates in the other HMOs.

Premium revenue increases for each of the Company's HMOs are shown in Table 20.2.

1983 Compared to 1982

Premium revenue increases resulted primarily from new members enrolling in HMO of Pennsylvania and HMO of New Jersey. The average premium on a per member basis increased 14%.

Premium revenue increases for each of the Company's HMOs are shown in Table 20.3.

Table 20.1 United States Health Care Systems, Inc.: Membership Data and Operating Statistics

	December 31,					*September*
	1980	*1981*	*1982*	*1983*	*1984*	*30, 1985*
Number of Members (rounded)	59,000	87,000	126,000	222,000	398,000	565,000
Number of Employer Groups (rounded)	1,100	1,500	1,700	2,900	5,000	6,800
Medical Expenses as a Percentage of Premium Revenue	86.3%	89.9%	87.2%	85.8%	82.2%	78.8%
Annualized Hospital Days per One Thousand Members	526	496	456	425	369	364

Table 20.2 United States Health Care Systems, Inc.: Premium Revenue Increases, 1983 to 1984

(dollars in thousands)

	1984 Premiums	Total Increase	Increases Due to:	
			Additions to Membership	Rate Change
HMO of Pennsylvania	$157,451	$ 68,848	$ 58,507	$ 10,341
HMO of New Jersey	35,800	31,869	31,360	509
HMO of Florida	6,006	6,006	6,006	—
	$199,257	$106,723	$95,873	$ 10,850

Table 20.3 United States Health Care Systems, Inc.: Premium Revenue Increases, 1982 to 1983

(dollars in thousands)

	1983 Premiums	Total Increase	Increases Due to:	
			Additions to Membership	Rate Change
HMO of Pennsylvania	$ 88,603	$ 38,175	$ 31,071	$ 7,104
HMO of New Jersey	3,931	3,931	3,931	—
	$ 92,534	$ 42,106	$ 35,002	$ 7,104

LIQUIDITY AND CAPITAL RESOURCES

For the period ended September 30, 1985, funds provided from operations decreased by 70% from the same period in 1984. The funds provided by increasing profitability were partially offset by an acceleration of payment of medical claims. Net income as a percentage of revenues was 6.5% for the nine-month period ended September 30, 1985, compared to 4.8% for the comparable period in 1984, and the Company's current ratio declined to 1.0:1 from 1.6:1. The decrease was primarily due to the purchase of long-term securities, including $12,670,000 of restricted reserves that are held in trust to meet certain state and federal regulatory agencies' requirements for HMOs. In 1982, 1983, and 1984 the current ratio was 1.3:1, 3.4:1, and 1.3:1, respectively.

The Company's current expansion into new service areas and growth in existing service areas will be financed by funds provided from operations. The Company believes that its cash and capital resources are sufficient to fund current and forecasted operations.

THE COMPANY'S HMO

In exchange for a fixed monthly payment, members receive virtually complete health care coverage with minimal out-of-pocket expenditures, unlike many conventionally designed health plans that contain substantial copayment and deductible features. When an individual enrolls, he or she selects a primary care physician from among the physicians associated with that HMO. The primary care physicians are family practitioners, general practitioners, internists, or pediatricians who provide all necessary preventive and routine medical care and are responsible for making referrals to specialists. Except in emergency situations, Company-insured hospital care requires the prior approval of the member's primary care physician and takes place in hospitals affiliated with the Company. When emergency circumstances arise that require medical care by physicians or hospitals unaffiliated with the Company, however, the cost of such medical care is paid by the Company.

The Company's HMOs also market to members, for additional premiums, the Company's own optional supplemental prescription drug and vision care plans that provide, respectively, all prescription drugs and medications at a member cost per prescription of $2.50, and eye examinations with the Company paying $35 or $70 (depending upon the coverage elected) every 24 months toward the cost of corrective lenses (including contact lenses). At September 30, 1985, of the approximately 565,000 HMO members, approximately 56% were enrolled in the prescription drug plan and nearly 100% were enrolled in the vision care plan.

In 1985 the Company entered into annual contracts with the federal government to provide health care services to Medicare. The federal government will pay the Company at a rate equal to 95% of the estimated average cost for services per Medicare beneficiary that would have been incurred for treatment of such beneficiaries by other providers located in similar geographic areas. Terms of these contracts, including amounts payable to the Company under them, are subject to periodic unilateral revision by the federal government.

Other members join the Company's program through employer groups. In most instances, employers offer employees a choice of traditional health insurance or membership in an HMO. During a designated period (usually 1 month annually), employees may select their desired health coverage. New employees make their choices at the time of employment. Employers may pay all or part of the monthly charges and agree to make payroll deductions for any portion not provided as a benefit. Management believes that among the most significant factors motivating its members to select its HMOs are the comprehensive benefits

and savings of out-of-pocket expenses they provide.

Appendix 20.A sets forth financial information concerning the Company's four HMOs.

RELATIONSHIP WITH PRIMARY CARE PHYSICIANS

In the Company's system, the primary care physician plays the key role in practicing preventive medicine and also acts as a "gatekeeper" and medical ombudsman to regulate the use of specialist physicians, hospitals, and other alternative forms of health care. Company-affiliated physicians have non-HMO patients in addition to members of the Company's program.

Ann MacDowell, who worked at United States Health Care Systems from 1979 to 1984, most recently as a Director of Provider Relations, explained the system as of 1984:

> At United States Health Care Systems, each premium dollar is divided 19% for primary care, 21% for specialty care, 42% for hospital care, and 18% for administrative expenses and profit. These allocations are distributed to provide incentives for primary care physicians to utilize resources effectively. A capitation amount is calculated for each primary care physician based on the ages of patients who have chosen to be served by him or her. Eighty percent of the annual capitation amount is paid to the physician in equal monthly installments. Twenty percent is placed into a pooled fund and held in reserve until the end of the year. Separate allocations are also made to cover specialty care and hospital care.
>
> Except in an emergency, patients are first seen by the primary care physician, who refers them to specialist care if needed. Specialists are paid on a fee-for-service basis. Each payment to a specialist is debited to the primary care physician's specialty fund. If money remains in this fund at year-end, one-half of it is paid to the physician. If the physician's specialty fund is depleted

before year-end, funds from the 20% reserve pool are used to cover the cost of specialty care. Funds remaining in the 20% pooled reserve at the end of the year are paid to the primary care physicians based on their original contribution. Because spending from the 20% pooled reserve reduces every primary care physician's share, there is an incentive for peer review; physicians will question a colleague's practice patterns if he/she utilizes specialists to excess.

The hospital care fund is managed much like the specialty care fund. Actuarial research is used to predict the hospital admissions expected from a primary care physician's United States Health Care Systems member base. If the number of hospitalizations is less than the number predicted, the physician gets a payment, after reduction to pay for specialist charges in excess of actuarially estimated specialist charges. The distribution is pro rated to each primary care physician based inversely on the use of hospital services by his or her patients. The average payment received by a primary care physician from all funds equals 10% to 30% of the primary care capitation.

The primary care physicians receive monthly reports on patient utilization of services and the status of all funds. Physician coordinators visit the physicians regularly to assist them in interpreting the reports and to raise awareness of the incentive program.

To support earlier discharge of patients from the hospital, United States Health Care Systems pays for and coordinates home health care. When a member is admitted to a hospital, a nurse employed by United States Health Care Systems receives information such as the patient's diagnosis and physician. If the diagnosis is appropriate for home care, the nurse contacts the physician and tracks the status of patients in the hospital and acts as a go-between with home health care agencies.

At United States Health Care Systems, control systems and incentives are continually

refined and improved. As stated by Ann Mac-Dowell,

> It is a big change for primary care physicians to pay attention to financial data and take responsibility for the cost of specialist and hospital care. Most physicians compare what they would have made in private practice with what they make under the United States Health Care Systems capitation, and they are amazed that the capitation system works. The capitation system is really the big selling point for physicians, with the additional payments being just "gravy."

Cost Control

The Company has capitated arrangements for maternity care, mental health care, diagnostic laboratory services, radiology and diagnostic imaging services, podiatric treatment, and prescription drugs. It also has contracts for all inclusive per diem hospitalization rates and specific rates for emergency room services. Unnecessary hospital days are reduced through a requirement that elective admissions generally occur only Sunday through Thursday thus avoiding charges for less productive weekend hospitalization. In addition, the Company carefully monitors the expected and actual length of all hospital admissions.

All hospital admissions are reviewed by at least one of the Company's 10 full-time medical directors or 12 primary care physicians who serve on a part-time basis as medical directors. When a primary care physician admits a patient to the hospital, he or she must send a written referral form to the hospital. The Company's utilization review department obtains all pertinent data regarding the patient and admitting physician, verifies coverage, estimates the expected length of stay, and records the member's status and projected utilization into its computer system according to the hospital and type of care. The medical directors and their staff monitor the care of hospitalized members on a daily basis. The utilization review department coordinates the activities of the primary care physician and the specialist in planning the member's care in the hospital, discharge, and subsequent transition to the home environment, including provision for home health care if necessary.

Any services to be performed by a physician who is not associated with the Company, other than emergency care, must be approved by one of the Company's medical directors. The primary care physician must complete an out-of-plan service form to justify the need for service.

The Company's computer-based medical information data base provides the primary care physicians with a monthly printout of services and costs in their practice. This report contains the budgeted and actual monthly cost and utilization statistics relating to primary care services, specialist expenses, and hospitalization. Hospital data are further analyzed by the type of medical service, days paid, and actual and average length of stay by type of admission. The information for each practice is then related to the median performance of the entire Company, and practices that deviate significantly from the norm are reviewed by a medical director.

The data base also enables the Company to continually monitor its membership enrollment eligibility and histories of the use and cost of various services. Twice weekly, the Company performs a comprehensive claims verification process to eliminate duplicate claims and identify situations requiring a medical review.

These procedures and controls are augmented by additional financial safeguards designed to preserve the Company from the cost of hospital utilization in excess of that estimated. The Company has established reserves for unreported specialist and hospital costs for services that have been performed and has a reinsurance contract as protection against major individual claims. At September 30, 1985, each of the Company's HMOs has a reinsurance contract with Employers Reinsurance Corporation. HMO of Pennsylvania's and HMO of New Jersey's reinsurance contracts limit their annual exposure per claim to $100,000 plus 10% of the next $900,000 and 100% of any

excess over $1,000,000; HMO of Florida's and HMO Great Lakes' reinsurance contracts limit their annual exposure per claim to $50,000 plus 10% of the next $950,000 and 100% of any excess over $1,000,000. The Company currently incurs a reinsurance premium cost of approximately $.31 per member per month, which aggregated to approximately $1,428,000 in the first nine months of 1985.

QUALITY ASSURANCE

The Company compiles various statistical information concerning the utilization of services including x-ray, pediatric referrals, emergency room care, outpatient care, short procedure unit care, and psychiatric hospitalization. Underutilization as well as overutilization of care is closely evaluated in an effort to provide a high quality of care to the plans' members.

The Company has peer review procedures whereby physicians on the Company's staff periodically review and evaluate the quality of health care delivered by individual primary care physicians and specialist physicians. In addition to the medical directors, approximately 13 primary care physicians in Pennsylvania, 14 in New Jersey, 8 in Florida, and 6 in Illinois participate in quality assurance and peer review committees. The medical directors of the Company and quality assurance committees perform various medical care evaluation studies that entail a detailed review of the tests and procedures performed by physicians for specific diagnoses. On a periodic basis, the five most frequent diagnoses are determined and medical care evaluation studies are performed on those diagnoses. In the event a standard test or procedure was not performed, the medical directors investigate the case to determine whether the treatment pattern was appropriate.

The Company's member relations department deals directly with members concerning their health care and grievances. On a routine basis, surveys are sent to members questioning them about the quality of care that they receive.

The quality assurance committees review problems presented by the member relations department.

Each primary care physician is obligated to carry professional liability insurance no less than the greater of the minimum amount required in the state in which the physician is licensed or the Company's requirements. The Company also carries professional liability insurance and general umbrella liability insurance.

MARKETING

At September 30, 1985, the Company provided its health care programs and services to approximately 6,800 employer groups that represent approximately 5,100 employers. The distribution of those groups among the Company's HMOs is shown in Table 20.4.

For certain employers, the Company develops individual marketing and benefit groups for separate divisions, locations, or benefit classes within the same employer. Accordingly, an individual corporation or government agency can include more than one employer group. The Company is attempting to increase its market share by enrolling new members from new and existing employer groups.

A direct sales force of 86 sales representatives and 17 marketing managers are supported by extensive market research and a computerized data base that identifies prospects, grades them, and establishes specific enrollment goals by territory, old and new employer groups, and sales representative. The marketing efforts are also supported by an advertising program that includes television, radio, billboards, and print media. Medicare marketing is done through direct mail and media advertising directed at individuals rather than groups.

The Company's 25 largest customers account for 578 employer groups that in the aggregate composed 34% of its members at September 30, 1985.

For the 9 months ended September 30, 1985, premiums billed to the federal government, for the Federal Employees Health Benefits Plan, which represented approximately 270 employer groups, were approximately 14% of total premium revenues.

The Company's agreements with employer groups are for a term of 12 months and subject to renewal annually.

OTHER SERVICES

The Company has designed home health programs to reduce the incidence of hospitalization and the length of stay in hospitals. Among the services available are x-ray examinations, diagnostic tests and electrocardiograms, homemakers and home health aides, and mental health services. In addition, the Company has established the "L'il Appleseed" program, which consists of a home visit by a specially trained pediatric nurse to assist mothers and newborn children on the day following their early discharge from the hospital.

In order to place physicians' offices in desired geographical areas, the Company will assist primary care physicians associated with its HMOs in either opening new offices or expanding and improving current physicians' offices. The assistance rendered to physicians may include one or more of the following services: loans for the establishment, renovation, or operation of medical offices; consultative services on the establishment and operation of medical offices; and administration and management of the medical office for the physician on a contract basis. In addition, the Company currently owns four buildings and leases a fifth that are, in turn, leased to primary care physicians for medical offices; the Company intends to acquire additional facilities for the purpose of assisting physicians in establishing offices in desired geographical areas.

COMPETITION

The Company has a number of competitors, including substantially larger commercial insurance carriers. The most significant com-

Table 20.4 United States Health Care Systems, Inc.: HMO Data

	HMO of Pennsylvania		HMO of New Jersey		HMO of Florida		HMO Great Lakes	
	December 31, 1984	*September 30, 1985*	*December 31, 1984*	*September 30, 1985*	*December 31, 1984*	*September 30, 1985*	*December 31, 1984[a]*	*September 30, 1985*
Number of Members	288,000	354,000	80,000	142,000	30,000	59,000	—	10,000
Number of Primary Care Physicians	560	760	26	400	120	220	—	300
Number of Primary Care Physician Offices	360	480	170	250	110	160	—	210
Number of Specialist Physicians	3,530	4,830	1,630	2,000	390	880	—	860
Number of Hospitals	62	74	25	58	9	14	—	24
Number of Pharmacies	450	510	220	440	110	260	—	160

[a] HMO Great Lakes commenced operations in June 1985.

petitors in Pennsylvania are the Blue Cross and Blue Shield plans serving the greater Philadelphia and Lehigh Valley areas that insured approximately 2.2 million and 420,000 people, respectively, at December 31, 1984. In addition, four other HMOs operate in the Philadelphia area and had a combined membership of approximately 97,000 people at December 31, 1984.

HMO of New Jersey competes primarily with Blue Cross and Blue Shield of New Jersey. The nine HMOs in the Company's New Jersey service area served approximately 253,000 people at December 31, 1984.

HMO of Florida competes with Blue Cross and Blue Shield of Florida, Inc., and several commercial insurance carriers. Prudential Insurance Company and CIGNA each have HMOs in Florida.

HMO Great Lakes competes primarily with Blue Cross and Blue Shield in the greater Chicago area of Illinois, Indiana, and Wisconsin. There are approximately 22 other HMOs in the area being served by HMO Great Lakes, with a combined membership in excess of 780,000 at December 31, 1984.

STOCK OPTION PLANS

The Company has an incentive stock option plan for its employees (the "Employee Option Plan") that provides for the grant of options to purchase an aggregate of approximately 854,295 shares of the Company's common stock. At September 30, 1985, options for 702,319 shares had been granted to employees of the Company, of which options for 136,323 were granted during the last fiscal year; an additional 38,328 were granted during the current fiscal year. Options for 127,590 shares were exercised in the last fiscal year. During the first nine months of 1985, an additional 114,811 options were exercised. The weighted average per share exercise price of the options in 1985 was $1.81. The exercise price per share was the fair market value on the date of grant.

The Company has a stock option plan for its primary care physicians (the "Physicians Option Plan") that provides for the grant of options to purchase an aggregate of approximately 854,295 shares of common stock. Options for 854,295 shares have been granted to approximately 163 primary care physicians' offices, of which options for 176,953 shares were granted during the first nine months of 1985. Options for 51,732 shares were exercised in the last fiscal year. During the first nine months of 1985 an additional 121,138 options were exercised. The options granted are exercisable in five equal annual installments. The exercise price per share of the options granted in 1985 is $13.11.

POINTS TO PONDER

1. What opportunity is the company fulfilling?
2. Describe United States Health Care's managerial control and human resource management systems. Are they consistent with the goals of the company?
3. Evaluate the company's financial success and the reasons for its growth. How much of the growth in profits is attributable to changes in volume, price, and ability to control its costs?

United States Health Care Systems, Inc., Financial Data

Table 20.A.1 United States Health Care Systems, Inc.: Consolidated Balance Sheets

(dollars in thousands)

	December 31, 1983	December 31, 1984	September 30, 1985 (unaudited)
ASSETS			
Total Current Assets	$ 56,234	$ 59,807	$ 46,825
Property, Plant, and Equipment, at Cost, Less Accumulated Depreciation	2,133	9,186	14,068
Intangible Assets, at Cost, Less Accumulated Amortization	1,235	2,556	5,617
Long-Term Marketable Securities	—	30,118	49,219
Long-Term Notes Receivable, Less Current Portion	148	331	1,019
Deferred Expenses	—	818	4,011
	$ 59,750	$102,916	$120,759
LIABILITIES AND SHAREHOLDERS' EQUITY			
Current Liabilities			
Medical Claims and Capitation Costs Payable	$ 10,579	$ 40,444	$ 37,581
Unearned Premiums	1,091	1,938	4,761
Accounts Payable and Accrued Liabilities	2,532	1,251	989
Income Taxes Payable	1,583	1,624	3,262
Accrued Employee Compensation and Benefits	692	2,437	2,251
Liability to Department of Health and Human Services	226	226	226
Current Portion of Long-Term Debt	7	7	6
Total Current Liabilities	16,710	47,927	49,076
Long-Term Debt, Net of Current Portion	200	192	187
Deferred Income Taxes	213	707	659
Commitments	—	—	—
Shareholders' Equity			
Par Value	46	105	237
Capital in Excess of Par Value	38,401	39,797	41,619
Retained Earnings	4,180	15,008	30,918
Common Stock in Treasury, at Cost 101,000 and 138,000 Shares in 1984 and 1985		(820)	(1,937)
Total Shareholders' Equity	42,627	54,090	70,837
	$ 59,750	$102,916	$120,759

Note: See accompanying notes in Exhibit 20.A.1.

Table 20-A.2 United States Health Care Systems, Inc.: Consolidated Statement of Income

(dollars in thousands except per share data)

| | Year Ended December 31, | | | Nine Months Ended September 30, | |
	1982	1983	1984	1984 (unaudited)	1985 (unaudited)
Revenues					
Premiums	$ 50,428	$ 92,534	$ 199,257	$ 138,101	$ 251,758
Other, Primarily Interest	796	3,144	6,398	4,314	7,201
	51,224	95,678	205,655	142,415	258,959
Expenses					
Medical Claims and Capitation					
Costs Net of Reinsurance Recoveries	43,979	79,360	163,854	115,651	198,391
Salaries and Related Costs	2,816	5,135	10,781	6,949	13,206
Other Administrative and					
Marketing Costs	2,323	4,868	9,670	6,401	13,748
	49,118	89,363	184,305	129,001	225,345
Income before Income Taxes	2,106	6,315	21,350	13,414	33,614
Provision for (Benefit from) Income Taxes					
Current	1,040	2,940	10,847	6,971	16,315
Deferred	15	169	(325)	(430)	363
	1,055	3,109	10,522	6,541	16,678
Net Income	$ 1,051	$ 3,206	$ 10,828	$ 6,873	$ 16,936
Net Income per Common Share and Common Share Equivalent	$ .03	$ .07	$ .23	$ .15	$ .35
Weighted Average Number of Common and Common Equivalent Shares	31,489	43,982	47,520	47,369	48,233

Note: See accompanying notes in Exhibit 20.A.1.

Exhibit 20-A.1 United States Health Care Systems, Inc.: Edited Notes to Consolidated Financial Statements

December 31, 1982, 1983, and 1984, and September 30, 1985
(all references to September 30, 1984, and 1985 are unaudited)

1. Organization and Significant Accounting Policies

* * * *

Reinsurance
Reinsurance premiums incurred net of related reinsurance recoveries are classified as medical expense in the financial statements. Reinsurance recoveries on paid claims are classified as current receivables at the balance sheet date.

Capitation Costs
Capitation costs represent monthly charges paid to participating physicians as retainers for providing continuing medical care.

* * * *

2. Receivables and Reinsurance Agreements
Receivables comprise the following:

(dollars in thousands)

| | December 31, | | September 30, |
	1983	1984	1985
Premiums (net of allowance for uncollectible accounts of $88,000, $537,000, and $1,150,000 in 1983, 1984, and 1985, respectively)	$ 4,202	$ 11,798	$ 23,871
Reinsurance	685	849	930
Interest Receivable	899	2,069	1,853
Other	129	128	443
Accounts Receivable	$ 5,915	$ 14,844	$ 27,097

For the years ended December 31, 1983, and 1984 and the 9 months ended September 30, 1985, premiums billed to the Federal government represented 11%, 14%, and 14%, respectively, of total premium revenues.

The Company and its subsidiaries have various reinsurance agreements to limit their losses on individual claims.

Intangible assets comprise the following:

(dollars in thousands)

| | December 31, | | September 30, |
	1983	1984	1985
Computer Software	$ 364	$ 772	$ 1,179
Subscriber Lists and Contracts	425	425	425
Organization Costs (primarily start-up costs)	380	1,739	5,002
Cost in Excess of Net Assets of Business Purchased	558	558	558
Other	11	11	11
	1,738	3,505	7,175
Less Accumulated Amortization	503	949	1,558
Net Intangible Assets	$ 1,235	$ 2,556	$ 5,617

Deferred expenses comprise the costs of developing HMOs where operations have not yet commenced. At commencement of operations, such costs are reclassified as intangible assets.

Appendix A

The Structure of the Health Care Industry

This note provides background material to aid in understanding the health care industry.

Because the largest segment of expenses were for hospital care, 38%, we will discuss first the nature and extent of this system, touching briefly on its short history, and outlining the types of institutions, their characteristics of size, ownership, patient mix, and other relevant information.

Physicians' services accounted for the next largest segment of the health dollar outlay, 20%. Physicians' behavior is held to influence costs throughout the system to a much greater extent than their share of health expense indicates because their decisions affect the nature and extent of services received by the public. We will describe the changes in physicians' methods of practice and their availability, geographical distribution, specialty choices, and incomes. We will outline governmental attempts to influence them.

Although other segments of health care impact less on the health dollar, their cost is still substantial and will be discussed briefly: Nursing home expense accounted for 8%, drugs for about 7% of health expenditures, dentistry about 6%, eyeglasses 1%, and research about 1%. Some 5% of health expense went for administration of health programs. (See Table A-1 for health expenditure data.)

Affecting the way in which money is spent on health care are the sociodemographics of the population. A disproportionate amount was spent on the elderly and on those whose behavior adversely affects their health (e.g.,

those who smoke, drink alcohol, or take drugs in excessive amounts). The age, sex, residence, wealth, and health insurance coverage of the population all play a role in their use of health services and are taken into account in describing the industry.

BACKGROUND: THE HOSPITAL SYSTEM

The acute care general hospital has existed in this country for only a century, coming with urbanization, industrialization, and greater mobility of the population after the Civil War. People left home and families to move to jobs in the cities and to settle the West. Associated with the industrialization of the country was a decline in the number of domestic servants available to help care for the sick. Hospitals became acceptable to the general population with the advent of antiseptics. Better hygiene and less infection in hospitals made them something more than they had been: places where the poor and homeless went to die. The invention of anesthesia played an important role in vastly increasing the number of operations that surgeons could carry out. The automobile made it possible for both doctors and patients to reach a convenient central place.

The number of hospitals grew rapidly from fewer than 200 in 1873 to some 4,000 in 1910 and to 6,000 in 1946. The average number of beds was small, since each community and group of doctors wanted its own institution, both for emergencies and for prestige. Some excess in capacity was expected, since infectious diseases in a preantibiotics era made

Note: Appendix A is adapted from the "Note on the Health Care Industry," 9-186-169, last revised in 1988.

437

Table A-1 National Health Expenditures, by Source of Funds and Type of Expenditure, 1988 and 1989

(dollars in billions)

Year and Type of Expenditure	All Sources	All Private	Private				Government		
			Private Total	Consumer		Other	Total	Federal	State and Local
				Consumer Direct	Private Insurance				
1988 National Health Expenditures	$ 544.0	$ 315.8	$ 291.5	$ 115.5	$ 176.0	$ 24.3	$ 228.2	$ 156.7	$ 71.5
Health Service and Supplies	524.1	307.9	291.5	115.5	176.0	16.5	216.2	147.5	68.7
Personal Health Care	480.0	287.4	271.4	115.5	155.9	16.0	192.7	141.7	51.0
Hospital Care	211.7	97.8	87.5	11.3	76.2	10.3	113.9	85.7	28.2
Physician Services	105.1	70.2	70.2	20.1	50.1	0.0	34.9	28.1	6.8
Dentist Services	29.4	28.7	28.7	16.3	12.4	—	0.7	0.4	0.3
Other Professional Services	23.8	19.2	16.6	7.6	8.9	2.6	4.6	3.5	1.1
Home Health Care	4.5	1.2	0.8	0.5	0.3	0.3	3.4	2.6	0.7
Drugs and Medical Sundries	41.5	36.8	36.8	30.4	6.5	—	4.7	2.2	2.5
Eyeglasses and Appliances	12.0	9.7	9.7	8.7	1.0	—	2.2	2.0	0.3
Nursing Home Care	42.8	21.8	21.0	20.6	0.5	0.8	20.9	12.6	8.3
Other Personal Health Care	9.3	1.9	—	—	—	1.9	7.4	4.7	2.7
Program Administration and Net Cost of Private Health Insurance	27.9	20.6	20.1	—	20.1	0.5	7.3	3.9	3.4
Government and Public Health Activities	16.2	—	—	—	—	—	16.2	1.9	14.3
Research and Construction of Medical Facilities	19.8	7.8	—	—	—	7.8	12.0	9.2	2.8
Noncommercial Research	10.3	0.7	—	—	—	0.7	9.6	8.3	1.3
Construction	9.5	7.1	—	—	—	7.1	2.4	0.9	1.5
1989 National Health Expenditures	604.1	350.9	324.5	124.8	199.7	26.3	253.3	174.4	78.8
Health Service and Supplies	583.5	342.7	324.5	124.8	199.7	18.2	240.8	164.8	76.1
Personal Health Care	530.7	315.3	297.7	124.8	172.9	17.6	215.4	158.4	57.0
Hospital Care	232.8	108.3	96.9	12.7	84.2	11.4	124.5	92.9	31.6
Physician Services	117.6	78.5	78.4	22.4	56.1	0.0	39.2	31.8	7.4
Dentist Services	31.4	30.7	30.7	17.2	13.4	—	0.7	0.4	0.3
Other Professional Services	27.0	21.6	18.7	8.5	10.2	2.9	5.4	4.1	1.4
Home Health Care	5.4	1.3	1.0	0.6	0.4	0.3	4.1	3.1	0.9
Drugs and Medical Sundries	44.6	39.3	39.3	32.3	7.0	—	5.3	2.5	2.8
Eyeglasses and Appliances	13.5	11.0	11.0	9.8	1.2	—	2.5	2.2	0.3
Nursing Home Care	47.9	22.7	21.8	21.3	0.5	0.9	25.2	16.2	9.0
Other Personal Health Care	10.5	2.1	—	—	—	2.1	8.4	5.2	3.3
Program Administration and Net Cost of Private Health Insurance	35.3	27.4	26.8	—	26.8	0.5	8.0	4.3	3.6
Government and Public Health Activities	17.5	—	—	—	—	—	17.5	2.1	15.4
Research and Construction of Medical Facilities	20.6	8.2	—	—	—	8.2	12.4	9.7	2.8
Noncommercial Research	11.0	0.8	—	—	—	0.8	10.2	8.8	1.4
Construction	9.6	7.4	—	—	—	7.4	2.2	0.8	1.4

Notes: 0.0 denotes less than $50 million. Research and development expenditures of drug companies and other manufacturers and providers of medical equipment and supplies are excluded from "research expenditures," but are included in the expenditure class in which the product falls. Numbers may not add to totals because of rounding.
Source: Helen C. Lazenby and Suzanne W. Letsch, "National Health Expenditures, 1989," *Health Care Financing Review,* Winter 1990, page 17.

hospitals crowded at some periods and relatively empty at others. The early community hospitals were started by white Protestant groups, financed by philanthropy, and staffed by a largely closed panel of physicians. The number of hospitals increased as each wave of immigrants came to the United States. Roman Catholics and Jews developed their own hospitals, both to satisfy the religious needs of the patients and to furnish a workplace for their doctors. Public hospitals in metropolitan areas that cared for the poor had somewhat more open staffing policies in response to political pressures from new residents.

Hospitals were labor intensive, using low-paid workers. Nurses performed maintenance and cleaning functions as part of their training, during which time they received little more than board and room. Physicians in training worked in the hospitals in similar fashion, with no salary. (Few, if any, full-time doctors or nurses were employed by the hospitals.) In a nontechnical era when few tests and procedures were carried out on patients, the cost of care was relatively low by today's standards. Despite this, the cost was a burden to many, and individual hospitals offered prepaid plans to cover possible hospital care as early as the 1920s. These led eventually to the formation in 1937 of the nonprofit Blue Cross hospital insurance plans and 10 years later to Blue Shield plans covering doctors' fees. Both plans were sponsored by the providers for whose services they paid.

In 1940 the number of hospital beds averaged 3.2 for every 1,000 people in the country. The health of the population had been adversely affected by a decade of depression, evidenced by the medical examinations of draftees during World War II. A national health insurance plan that would cover all medical care was widely discussed and seemed near at hand in the United States when it was adopted in Great Britain after the war. This didn't happen, but to answer perceived health needs, and with the help of lobbying by the American Hospital Association, Congress passed the Hospital Construction Act, known as Hill-Burton, in 1946. Its aim was to increase the number of hospital beds to a maximum of 4.5 per 1,000 population and to even the distribution of hospitals by raising the number in poor states. This guideline for a maximum number of beds soon became a minimum standard; guidelines that had been arrived at fairly arbitrarily and that should have been interpreted according to local circumstances became national standards (Cowen, 1981; Institute of Medicine, 1980). Hill-Burton required, as well, that a "reasonable amount" of free hospital services be given to the poor—a provision never defined or enforced. Hill-Burton is credited for raising the number of hospitals in poor states, but help went largely to middle-class communities (Clark et al., 1980).

Postwar Changes

World War II can be seen as a watershed in the history of medical treatment and hospital care. The discovery of penicillin and other antibiotics greatly reduced the number of deaths from infection, presaging the increase in the length of life of the population. This discovery, along with the cure for polio in the 1950s, began popular support for research and for the federally supported National Institutes of Health. Subsequent technological advances demanded better skills from hospital personnel and the demand for women industrial workers during the war gave women ambitions beyond low-paid nursing jobs. The cost of hospital care rose as more employees per patient were required and as those employees demanded better pay than in the past. Unions, restricted by wage controls during the war years, had pressed for health insurance as a nontaxed benefit. Medical insurance as an employee benefit soon became widespread in most industries. Insurance companies reimbursed hospitals for whatever prices they charged, encouraging increases in hospital expenditures. Because more people were living longer—an event brought about by postwar prosperity (better hygiene, working conditions, diet) as well as by advances in medicine—they required far greater amounts of hospital care.

1965: Medicare and Medicaid

During the period when other Western countries adopted universal health insurance, the United States rejected the idea; but a major concession to those most vulnerable to illness and least able to pay for it was made by the Johnson administration in its aim to achieve a "Great Society." In 1965, Congress added provisions to the Social Security Act that paid a large part of hospital and other health expenses for those over 65 (Medicare) and financed grants to the states for medical assistance for the poor (Medicaid). Payments to hospitals followed the pattern set by private insurance by reimbursing costs. The social aim was to change the kind of health care available to the poor from charity in public hospitals to treatment equal to that received by the rest of the population. It was achieved to such an extent that beds in public hospitals were closed as the poor purchased care elsewhere. Giving greater access to care to those who need it most without restrictions on cost had a predictable (in retrospect) result. Government financing in 1972 under Medicare of kidney dialysis, a recent innovation at the time in treating kidney disease patients who would otherwise have died, was to prove much more expensive than anticipated. Even before this impact, by 1972 the Medicare budget had risen to a point where public concern forced Congress to enact some price controls and to introduce a program aimed at reducing the quantity of services provided Medicare recipients without, hopefully, reducing the quality. Physicians were required to review each other's medical practices in hospitals to discourage unnecessary procedures. These Professional Standards Review Organizations, or PSROs, had only slight effect on costs, and the search for effective cost containment continued.

1980s: Too Much Health Care?

By 1980 the number of hospital beds had reached the maximum proposed by the hospitals in 1946 (4.5 per 1,000 population),

but the cost of hospital care had risen from about $12 per day in the 1940s to over $284 per day in 1981. Even allowing for inflation and more complex medical care, many saw this as excessive. They began to question the 4.5 figure and thought the country needed fewer hospital beds. The bed-occupancy rate of the hospitals had changed little over the years. In 1940, it averaged 69.9%, and in 1982, 75.3%, and by 1984, it was estimated at 67%. An occupancy rate of 80% was thought to minimize costs (Anderson, 1985). Such "over-bedding"—once acceptable—now was seen as contributing to high costs. The incentive for hospitals now was to keep their beds occupied.

In the 1970s a variety of measures to contain hospital costs were introduced, and by the end of the decade almost every state had a program designed to limit hospital construction by requiring Certificates of Need from a governmental body before construction could begin. The process was judged largely ineffectual, primarily causing delays in expansion rather than abandonment of plans. In 1983 the government introduced prospective budgeting to limit Medicare expenditures for the 30 million people who receive benefits from the program. By 1986 only one state (New Jersey) retained a waiver; all others had to adopt the method proposed by Medicare that set a price (taking into account regional variations) for each case of illness regardless of how long the person was in the hospital. In addition, corporations altered their health insurance policies to provide incentives for employees to economize with health care costs. Among the changes were programs reviewing the utilization patterns of providers and cost-sharing policies to reduce consumption of health care, particularly expensive hospital care.

Possibly as a result, hospital inpatient admissions declined from 9.4 million in the first quarter of 1982 to 8.6 million in the same period in 1986, and outpatient visits increased from 54.4 million in 1982 to over 63 million in 1986. Admissions for those under 65 fell at a sharper rate than for the over-65 group. Lengths of stay also fell. Cost per admission rose, as did the cost per case—from an average of \$2,400 in 1982 to \$3,400 in 1986. The number of hospital full-time employees fell from 2.65 million in 1982 to 2.55 million in 1986, while part-time employees increased from 950,000 to 978,000 and beds declined by 20,000.

The overall effect was to raise hospital profitability to record levels in 1985. Nevertheless, between 1980 and 1985, 109 rural hospitals and 190 urban hospitals with fewer than 300 beds were closed, and an increasing number affiliated with others to form chains. Lastly, many formed holding companies with for-profit subsidiaries to aid the financing of the nonprofit hospital. The integration of hospitals took place both horizontally and vertically. Horizontal integration was exemplified by the formation of new nonprofit chains such as the VHA (Voluntary Hospital Association); chains accounted for 38% of the beds in 1985. Of the 692 million nonprofit beds in 1985, 207 million were in chains; 100 million of the 119 million for-profit beds also belonged to a chain. Vertical integration could involve hospitals in joint ventures with insurance companies, free-standing ambulatory care and surgery ventures, consolidated diagnostic and laboratory facilities, nursing homes, hospices, and birthing centers.

THE PRESENT HOSPITAL SYSTEM

Type of Hospital

The hospital system can be characterized by:

- type of ownership (government and nongovernment; within the latter category, nonprofit and proprietary)
- length of patient stay (short-term—under 30 days—acute care or long-term chronic disease care)
- size of hospital (full-service or tertiary care is usually found in hospitals with 250 beds and over)

Some essential parameters of the hospital system are shown in Table A-2.

Government-Owned Hospitals

The federal government owns and operates 8% of the country's hospital beds, in armed services and Veterans Administration hospitals and public health service and prison hospitals. States administer and fund long-term psychiatric and chronic disease hospitals and those attached to state university medical schools. Cities and counties operate hospitals, which were in the past primarily for the indigent. Government programs that pay health benefits (Medicare and Medicaid) introduced in 1965 have widened the hospital choices for many of the country's poor and reduced the census in public hospitals.

Government hospitals are staffed by salaried physicians. Private physicians who collect fees for service admit their patients to private community hospitals.

Nongovernment-Owned Hospitals

The 3,300 nonprofit community hospitals in 1986 treated patients with acute health problems requiring short-term stays averaging 7.2 days. These hospitals required an average of four employees to serve each patient in the country as a whole, with the highest number employed in the Pacific states and the lowest in the Southeast. They are often known as "voluntary" hospitals, a name stemming from the time when they were supported entirely by charity and fees from patients. By the 1980s, philanthropy had become insignificant as hospitals relied largely on government payments for the poor and the elderly and private insurance reimbursement. The number of hospital beds averaged 4.2 per 1,000 population, up from 3.2 in 1940 and down slightly from a high of 4.6 in 1975. The occupancy rate in these hospitals averaged 66.8% in 1986, continuing a steady decline from the 1970 post–World War II high of 80%. The smaller the hospital, the lower the occupancy rate, in general.

These hospitals may be run by a board of trustees drawn from the community at large, a religious group, or an organization with a specific purpose (e.g., the Shriners hospital for

Table A-2 The Hospital System by Size and Ownership in the United States, 1986

	5,800 Hospitals Percentage by Size	1 Million Beds, Percentage by Size of Hospitals	Percentage of Beds
Size			
Under 100 Beds	45%	14%	
100–299 Beds	36	37	
Over 300 Beds	18	49	
Ownership			
Government			
Federal			7%
State and Local			17
Proprietary			10
Nonprofit			65

Note: These statistics are for general short-stay hospitals.
Source: Compiled with permission from *AHA Hospital Statistics*, copyright © 1987 by The American Hospital Association.

burn injuries). Religious or ethnic discrimination against physicians admitted to hospital staffs began to disappear after World War II and is no longer common, but the religious identities of the hospitals persist.

Proprietary Hospitals

Small hospitals owned for profit and run privately by doctors co-existed before 1900 with the nonprofits. Their number remained small partly because the advent of more complex and effective medical technology than had existed earlier required substantial support not easily provided by individual investors. Also, the reputation of for-profits had been tarnished by the Carnegie Foundation's renowned Flexner Report that criticized existing medical standards in 1910, especially those in the many for-profit medical schools and hospitals.

Proprietary hospitals accounted for 36% (2,400) of all hospitals in the United States in 1928, but made up only 11% (770) by 1968 (Steinwald and Neuhauser, 1970). They existed most commonly in the West and Southwest, where philanthropy played less of a role than in the East and profits were necessary. They were largely surgical centers. The successful nonprofit health insurance plans started by hospitals in the 1930s did not encourage for-profits; the plans paid lower rates to for-profit chains than to nonprofits (Schlesinger, 1985).

The 1970s saw the advent of chains of hospitals owned by corporations such as Humana and Hospital Corporation of America (HCA) and an upturn in the proprietary ownership of hospitals. American Hospital Association (AHA) statistics show 834 proprietary hospitals in 1986; the number of beds in for-profits had almost doubled since 1970, to some 107,000 short-term beds and about 8,000 long-term, including psychiatric. Their distribution varied: For-profits accounted for 11% of the general short-term beds, but 52% of the short-term psychiatric beds and only 6% of the long-term psychiatric beds. Short-term admissions were largely covered by health insurance, while prolonged stays were not: Most of the long-term patients were in public institutions. Occupancy rates in for-profits averaged 57% in 1984, having fallen steadily from a 1970 high of 72%.

Large corporations owned the majority of all these proprietaries in 1985. They also contracted to manage some 300 voluntary nonprofits. The regional distribution of proprietaries continued to be largely western and southern. In an effort to combat prejudice against the quality of care offered by for-profits, chains in the late 1970s were seeking alliances with academic medical centers (Schlesinger, 1985).

Proprietary short-term hospitals in 1982 employed fewer people per 100 patients than did nonprofits and paid them slightly less. Their payroll as a proportion of all expenses declined over the ten years from 1971, as did that of the nonprofits.

Characteristics of the General Hospital

Type of Accommodation

Hospitals in the United States imitated the still-current European model of open wards of 20 or more beds when they originated as charity hospitals; as befits "rich America," wards gradually gave way to a preponderance of semi-private (2 to 4 beds to a room) or private accommodations. Government funding of hospitals after World War II modernized and built many hospitals in the latter mode. The hotel function of the hospital varies according to the wealth of the user, with the public hospital often deficient in amenities.

Type of Care

The hospital treatment (or "service") is divided into two major categories of medical and surgical (operating) services and further categorized by some 35 specialties such as mental health or psychiatry, respiratory or lung therapy, rehabilitation for stroke or accident injury, obstetrics and gynecology, and pediatrics.

In a community with many hospitals, not every specialty will be found in every hospital. Some Boston hospitals, for example, have closed their services for children (pediatrics) because Children's Hospital can serve the population adequately. Competition often blocks such cooperation, however, with every institution eager to perform the latest technology such

as heart transplants. A danger in this is that a number of studies have indicated that a certain volume of practice is necessary to maintain the skills of those operating.

The range of services available in the community hospital varies widely, affected both by the community's needs and the expense. Almost all community hospitals had emergency rooms in the 1980s (94%), post-operation recovery rooms (93%), and physical therapy (88%), but only 10% had facilities for open heart surgery and 20% had capacity for x-ray therapy. Many had blood banks (76.5%), but very few had organ banks for transplants (3.5%). Psychiatric services could be found in only about 10% of the hospitals and kidney dialysis facilities were not readily available (24% inpatient and 13% outpatient). Genetic counseling and family planning were rare (7–8%).

Outpatient or ambulatory care for patients not sick enough to need admission to the hospital was offered in about 40% of the hospitals, more frequently in the East Coast states than in the South. Typically patients visit clinics by appointment; in some arrangements, patients may see the same doctor at each visit.

Emergency rooms (ERs) are designed to treat victims of sudden illness or accident, but in many hospitals—especially in large cities—they serve people without a private doctor who are not always acutely ill. Such use of the ER is an expensive alternative and a less satisfactory one to seeing a doctor regularly in an out-of-the-hospital setting. ERs are frequently staffed by doctors employed elsewhere who "moonlight" for extra payment.

As medical technology has increased, ancillary services—those outside the hotel and nursing functions—have become important revenue producers in the hospital. Laboratories, radiology (x-ray and other imaging devices) departments, and pharmacies are typical ancillary services for which patients are charged on a use-of-service basis. Costs of these services have accounted for a large part of the increase in hospital expenses in the past decade and have also been responsible for much of the hospital income.

Utilization Patterns

Use of the hospital is reflected in the number of patients admitted, the length of time they remain in the hospital, the number of outpatient visits they make, the occupancy rate of the hospital beds, and the number of staffed beds maintained.

The number of days of care per 1,000 population declined 18% between 1983 and 1985; the decline was reflected in those over 65 as well as in younger people, with days of care for the older group down 20%. The hospital occupancy, which had risen slightly during the 1970s, declined by 1989 to 65% from nearly 74% in 1983. Outpatient visits increased in response to cost pressures as well as technological changes that made more outpatient diagnosis and therapy possible.

Nature of the Organization

"Throw-away" supplies from the kitchen to the bedside have replaced some of the need for routine maintenance of equipment by employees, but patient care is still labor intensive, with salaries and benefits accounting for about half of the hospital's short-term expense. The professional staff of doctors and nurses—and, of course, the patients—are supported by the services of employees in administration, maintenance, admissions, medical records, housekeeping, transportation, and pharmacy, as well as by dietitians, clerks, and laboratory technicians.

Special training for hospital administrators is given in graduate programs largely set up since the 1960s and greatly expanded in the 1970s. Administration of a hospital has been influenced in the past by the physicians on the staff, but as management responsibilities and financial complexities have increased, the administrators have risen in status. The chief administrator, once known as the director, is now frequently called the president of the hospital.

The past administrator concentrated on budgeting and managing the nonmedical or support areas of the hospital. Today, administrators are not only concerned with reducing costs, but must consider ways to increase revenues. Hospital administrators discuss marketing strategies to encourage patients to use hospital services.

Physicians in private practice who use the hospital remain somewhat outside the authority of the administration. Administrators depend on the physicians' practices to bring patients into the hospital. Physicians who are not employed by the institution may admit patients to more than one hospital, are legally responsible for their own actions, and in theory at least are free to react independently to administrative rulings. Physicians employed by the hospital also command authority and can act with discretion in carrying out their duties. Permission to admit patients to a hospital is frequently controlled by the established medical staff. Physicians are key to a hospital's utilization. Their major concerns in affiliating with a hospital are with the hospital's quality of care, its ability to deal with alternative care delivery systems, the availability of a new technology, and the decision-making process.

Nursing was a low-prestige occupation well into the 1930s in the United States, consisting of hard work at low wages for lower-middle-class women. The war in the 1940s, prosperity, and the women's movement played their roles in raising wages. The increasing complexity of medicine raised the educational standards of nursing, and many of the tasks formerly performed by nurses were turned over to less skilled personnel. Hospitals that relied before 1940 on student nurses and employed very few graduate nurses typically began employing graduates who managed less skilled and lower paid licensed practical nurses and nurse's aides. Nursing used half the hospital payroll in the 1980s.

Nursing as a profession remains limited, however, with few opportunities for advancement. Seniority and experience are generally not rewarded, and there have been few inducements to prevent nurses moving from one hospital to another. Turnover has been reported at 50% in recent years and has predictably been more of a problem in acute care city hospitals, where patients were less likely to be middle class and more likely to have complicated illnesses than in suburban or private specialty hospitals. Proprietary hospitals have made better use of part-time employees than have the nonprofits, and proprietary chains like Humana stressed the good working conditions they provided as an inducement to nurses to stay with them.

A systemwide "nursing shortage" in the 1980s has been attributed to cost cutting (*Economist*, 1988b). Hospitals claim they are unable to pay U.S. nurses enough to keep them working, although 14% more qualified nurses existed in 1988 (1.9 million registered nurses; 1.5 million working) than in 1980, and had resorted to importing foreign nurses under five-year visas. Beginning with Medicare prospective payment in 1983, hospitals cut back on nursing help as fewer hospital beds were needed. Hospitals then decided that it was more cost effective to employ fully trained nurses than medical technicians and aides; they had cut back on practical nurses (33,000 fewer in 1986 than 1984) but were employing more (38,000 more in 1986 than 1984) registered nurses, a practice that will be limited by the falling off in nursing school enrollments. A 40% decrease in nursing school enrollments in Massachusetts occurred between 1983 and 1988. High school students interviewed claimed that nursing offered insufficient status, challenge, or salary. Hospitals have not only had to raise salaries, but those that accorded nurses professional status and authority in managing patients appeared to have the best chance of retaining them (Freudenheim, 1988c).

The Teaching Hospital

Only 12% of the 7,000 government and nongovernment hospitals in the 1980s were affiliated with medical schools, but they accounted for 27% of the beds: One-third of the affiliated hospitals have more than 500 beds. Two-fifths of the affiliated hospitals were owned by state and local governments. Almost all Veterans Administration hospitals serve as a teaching resource, as do many municipal public hospitals and state mental hospitals.

Both graduate medical education and post-graduate training of physicians and surgeons demand practical, supervised teaching of "clinical" skills (a term derived from treatment of patients in clinics) by experienced doctors in a hospital setting. Only the first two years in most medical schools are devoted solely to basic science courses in a classroom and laboratory.

The next two years are spent in rotations among the basic medical and surgical services and the many specialty services. Supervising the medical students in their care of patients is a hierarchy of physicians further along in their training, who are in turn overseen by professors in the medical school and/or by private-practice physicians. The first postgraduate year is spent as an intern, or first-year resident, during which the physicians in training take turns sleeping at the hospital in order to maintain 24-hour patient care. Several more years will be spent in residency, the amount of time depending on the nature of the specialized training. Interns and residents are known as "house staff" and are paid low salaries by the hospitals (during the 1980s, in the range of $18,000 to $35,000 per year).

The teaching hospital is generally staffed by a group of doctors who are specialists in their fields, have appointments at an associated medical school, conduct research studies, and are in most cases on salary, and employed full time by the hospital and the university, although they often can see private patients at the hospital in faculty group practices. Doctors in private practice may also contribute several hours per week without pay to student supervision. The privilege of being able to admit one's patients to a teaching hospital is generally coveted by private physicians, not the least because doctors in training, who take turns being "on call" at the hospital, provide a useful back-up function for the practitioner.

Covering the relatively high costs of patient care in teaching hospitals has increasingly become an issue, with insurers objecting to paying for research and teaching. Hospitals argue that high costs are an inevitable result of their complicated cases, skilled staff, up-to-date equipment, and need to provide comprehensive training and patient care.

In 1983, the government initiated a cost containment system under which hospitals would be paid for treatment of Medicare patients based on a predetermined price rather than the traditional payment of whatever the cost of treatment had been (retrospective reimbursement) used by other insurers. That prospective price was to be based on a designated amount arrived at in advance to pay for each of 467 different disease entities, known as diagnosis-related groups or DRGs. Teaching hospitals succeeded in getting an additional payment to cover their special needs because DRGs did not allow for the severity of illness within the same disease condition.

Rural Hospitals

Some 1,500 hospitals or 36% of general short-stay hospitals in 1986 had fewer than 100 beds and were classified as rural hospitals (some exceptions exist within cities but no data are collected to show geographical differences). About half the rural hospitals are owned by their communities and subsidized by taxes, compared with about 28% of all community hospitals. Some 35% of the elderly in the United States live in rural areas compared with 25% of the population in general. Rural hospitals are thus more vulnerable to Medicare's prospective payment restrictions than are urban hospitals. Occupancy rates in small nonprofit hospitals were significantly lower than those in large ones; very small institutions (6 to 24 beds) had occupancy rates of 30% in 1986, those with 25 to 49 beds had a rate of 40%, and those with 50 to 99 beds were 53% occupied. In contrast, the largest hospitals (500 beds or more) had an occupancy rate of 74%.

People in rural areas are slightly less likely to have health insurance than is the nonfarm population (86% compared with 90%), and

they are much more likely to rely on individual policies because farmers are self-employed (26% of farmers compared with 7.5% of the total population had individual policies) (Trippler, 1986). Farmers have a higher accident rate, but are generally healthier than the rest of the population.

Small hospitals may be more expensive to run than large ones, and their dependence on the local economy (declining in the rural heartland in the 1980s) adds to their difficulties. Staffing at rural hospitals declined nearly 8% from 1983 to 1985, and there were 3.2% fewer acute care beds. In 1986 the reductions slowed somewhat to a cut of 2% in staffed beds. Rural hospitals have increased their affiliations with multihospital chains; in 1982 one-fourth of the rural hospitals were owned or managed by chains, but in 1987 one-third had such ties. Systems control even more (40%) in the South Atlantic, Mountain, and Pacific states. Operating margins of rural hospitals are said to be "so thin that one expensive patient can push the hospital in the red" (Robinson, 1987). For-profit entrepreneurs entered the market for rural health care in areas where, because of tourism or some light manufacturing, people were expected to be able to pay for care (Fasse, 1986).

Turning excess beds in rural hospitals to nursing home use was effective in meeting long-term care needs; it provided care near patients' homes and avoided building of expensive nursing homes (Richardson and Kovner, 1986). Since 1980 such "swing beds" have been permitted to serve Medicare (skilled nursing) and Medicaid (intermediate care) patients in small hospitals—first those with fewer than 50 beds, then in 1988 those with under 100 beds. Swing-bed days, largely for Medicare patients, made up nearly one-fourth of the patient days in a sample of 26 hospitals between 1982 and 1985. With prospective budgeting by Medicare limiting the acute care days permitted, easy transfer of patients from acute care to nursing home care (a transfer on paper) is an advantage to small hospitals that would otherwise have trouble finding long-term care beds for their patients.

OTHER HEALTH CARE FACILITIES

Psychiatric Hospitals

The trend since World War II has been to "mainstream" patients with mental illness through general hospitals for evaluation and short-term treatment rather than to isolate them in separate hospitals. As state hospitals reduced their census, federally funded community mental health centers (CMHCs) and general hospitals increased their care of patients with mental problems. The 717 CMHCs accounted for 38% of all admissions to mental health facilities and more than half the outpatient visits in 1980 (see Table A-3). These reforms coincided with the introduction in the 1950s of psychoactive drugs that control symptoms of mental disturbance and made out-of-hospital care feasible for many patients. The adequacy of such deinstitutionalization has been questioned; in many cities, the "homeless" population is believed to be made up of many of these "deinstitutionalized" patients.

State, municipal, and county hospitals serve those unable to pay for care. The average daily census in state hospitals fell from 560,000 in 1955 to 216,000 in 1974; by 1984, it had fallen to 122,000 (AHA, 1987). Private hospitals serve short-term patients who pay for the cost of treatment through health insurance or private funds. Private insurance did not cover mental illness for many years, but provider lobbying resulted in legislation that required such coverage in health insurance policies. By 1984 Blue Cross and commercial insurers covered 99% of full-time employees in medium and large firms, according to the Bureau of Labor Statistics, but coverage was subject to many

Table A-3 Mental Health Facilities: 1983 Admissions, Inpatient Cases, and 1988 Expenditures, by Type of Facility

Psychiatric Facility	Number	Admissions (thousands)	Inpatients[a] (thousands)	1988 Expenditures (millions)
State and County Hospitals	280	350	150	$ 6,990
Private Hospitals	185	110	13	4,604
Veterans Administration Neuropsychological Hospitals	22			1,290
General Hospitals with Psychiatric Unit	1,347	1,300	18	3,617
Outpatient Clinics, Free-standing	1,054	820		668
CMHCs[b]	717	1,160		NA
Inpatient		280	10	
Outpatient		880	NA	NA
Total		2,990	191	23,071

Note: Numbers are approximate. Not included are services provided by office-based practice or on general wards of private general hospitals, where many psychiatric patients are served. Nursing homes also have psychiatric patients, not shown here.

[a]Average daily census.

[b]Only data for CMHCs that received federal funds are shown here.

Source: 1983 data compiled from data issued by the Division of Biometry, National Institute of Mental Health, 1987, Statistical Notes 182, 185; 1988 data compiled from *Health United States*, 1990, p. 218.

more restrictions and copayments than was coverage for other illness.

In 1984, the 216 short-term psychiatric hospitals had an average daily census of 15,000. Three-fifths of these hospitals were for-profit, most of them owned by corporations. For-profit management of psychiatric hospitals was led by HCA, which entered the psychiatric field as recently as 1981, but had 40 hospitals in 1984, with some 3,600 beds and plans for 700 more.

Although psychoactive drugs have reduced the length of hospitalization, hospitalization is still frequently lengthy and expensive. Public hospitals generally have treated more of those with chronic conditions such as schizophrenia and severe alcohol abuse problems than have private hospitals, while the latter tended to treat affective disorders such as depression and neuroses. The AHA reports that average length of stay in public hospitals was 155 days in 1982; in private hospitals it was 33 days. Private psychiatric hospitals in the 1980s were increasingly offering specialized treatment for identifiable disorders such as eating problems among adolescents and drug and alcohol dependency.

Long-Term Care Facilities

In addition to psychiatric care, long-term care is given in nursing homes, "old age" homes, and rehabilitation centers that serve patients with illnesses that do not require the acute care technology and the number and kind of personnel of the general hospitals. With rising concern about cost of care in the general hospital, the demand for these forms of institutional care has increased. Nursing homes accounted for 8.5% of all health expenditures in 1987, or about $42 billion.

The nursing home segment of the health care industry expanded rapidly in the decade after Medicaid liberalized payments for such care for the poor in 1965. Government aid was accompanied by an increase in the population who were living past 85 years of age and had the greatest need for nursing home care.

Medicaid provided a major source of payment for both proprietary and nonprofit homes— 50% in the former and 44% in the latter in 1985. Some 76% of an estimated 26,000 nursing homes and 70% of the 1.8 million beds were owned by private investors in 1986 (National Center for Health Statistics data). The proportion in proprietary homes has been rising from 60% in 1964. Proprietaries charged about 30% more in 1964 than did nonprofits, but by 1977 the proprietaries were about 9% cheaper than the others. Some of this adjustment in charges may be due to limits on Medicaid payments. Variations existed by state in the number of beds available; for example, fewer beds per elderly population were available in Florida, with its high proportion of elderly residents, than in Wisconsin (22 compared with 94).

Although only 43% of the over 65 population in 1990 were expected to spend any time in a nursing home, the number who need such care varies by age group. Fifty-one percent of those admitted to nursing homes stay less than three months, but six percent stay more than five years. The greatest use of nursing homes comes, as might be expected, from those in the oldest age groups. Less than 5% of those under 45 years of age who died in 1986 used a nursing home, in contrast to 71% of those over 95. Women used nursing homes much more than men (Kemper and Murtaugh, 1991). Family members provide most of the help to the elderly with limitations who continue to live in the community, and the absence of sustaining helpers is the most critical factor in nursing home entry. Perceived poor health, incontinence, and mental confusion are other important reasons for admission to a nursing home.

About half of nursing home care was paid for by Medicaid, less than 3% by Medicare, and the rest was paid for privately. Medicaid pays nursing home fees only for those with almost no income. With custodial-care nursing homes costing from $1,000 to $2,500 per month and skilled nursing facilities costing up to $3,000, patients commonly "spend down" whatever funds they have after six months in a nursing home, after which they qualify for public aid

(Scanlon and Feder, 1984). Contrary to public expectations, Medicare covers very little nursing home care, since coverage is largely restricted to skilled nursing for a short time and does not pay for custodial care. The Catastrophic Care Act, passed in 1988, amended Medicare to protect a small number, statistically, against unusual expense, but does not cover custodial nursing care. The burden of private payment to care for the aging population has stimulated bills in Congress to protect the income of spouses remaining at home and has spurred an increase in the marketing of private long-term care insurance, which in 1987 accounted for only 1% of nursing home expenditures and had interested only 2% of those over 65.

Estimates varied as to how much insurance the affected population would be able or willing to pay for. Data estimating the assets as well as the income of the elderly show that only one-fourth had a net worth of more than $100,000 in 1986. The median net worth of householders over 65 was about $60,000, and with the value of their homes excluded, it was $18,000. Both income and net worth were lower for the single survivors, most vulnerable to nursing home need. Although there has been much discussion of converting home equity into funding for care, little conversion has occurred, and it is unlikely that such home conversion could pay for a significant amount of long-term care.

Economists calculate that half the elderly could afford premiums of up to $49 per month for long-term care insurance if they were willing to spend 10% of their discretionary resources (Cohen, et al., 1987). Other researchers claim that 25% to 40% of the high income elderly would buy some insurance over the next 30 years, but that the effect on Medicaid would be minor; Medicaid spending for nursing home care is expected to triple by 2020 (Wiener and Rivlin, 1988). Demand for insurance products may be stimulated by offerings that meet the varied needs of different groups among elderly consumers.

A major problem for nursing homes is the nationwide shortage of nurses in the late 1980s. Nursing homes were typically less desirable places to work and paid lower salaries than acute care hospitals. Unskilled long-term care staff were difficult to find and keep; yearly turnover was estimated at 100% in 1987 (Kenkel, 1987).

Proprietary nursing homes have gone out of business at a high rate. One study showed that 68% of them had failed in New York between 1967 and 1974 (Smith, 1981). Nursing homes have been subject to "scandals" about the kind of care given since the 1930s. A Texas corporation (Autumn Hills Convalescent Centers of Houston) was indicted in 1985 for the murder of one of its residents who was alleged to have received inferior, negligent care (Reinhold, 1985). The vulnerability of aged residents is heightened by the loss of family presence for a variety of social and economic reasons.

Nursing home chains grew in the last decade. They owned about 15% of nursing home beds in 1985 (Punch, 1985). Most grew by acquisition rather than construction, largely because state government restrictions hampered building—the theory of health planners had been that the more beds, the more demand and the higher the costs. Beverly was the largest of the investor-owned chains, with 127,000 beds in 1986, up from 90,000 in 1983. Its rapid acquisition of beds was expected to fall off; it had operating losses of $60 million in 1987. The poor financial condition of these and other for-profit homes was blamed by the industry on low Medicaid payments, especially in southern states. The 30 largest nonprofit nursing homes together had 39,000 beds in 1984. Nursing home care as a percentage of national health expenditures has increased from 5% in 1965 to 8.4% in 1987.

Life-care centers are a fairly new concept; many are owned or operated by nursing home chains. They typically consist of apartment complexes built near an associated nursing home. Residents pay entrance fees of $25,000 and up, sometimes partly refundable if the resident dies or moves out, and monthly maintenance fees of $450 to $1,500 and up. Dining facilities and an activity center are typical, and nursing home care, for which they pay additional fees, is available when residents cannot manage on their own. There were about 600 life-care communities in 1988. Many have had financial problems, causing residents to lose their investment and their placement since they do not own the housing. Centers usually restrict entry by age and health status.

Rehabilitation, Hospice, and Dialysis Facilities

In 1985, *short-term rehabilitation centers* were developing in answer to patients' needs. *Hospices* designed for patients who are terminally ill offer pain relief and supportive psychological help for family and patients rather than conventional medical treatment. Hospices are not equipped to handle every terminal illness, however, and there are indications that they serve an additional purpose rather than act as a substitute for hospital care (*Economic Report of the President*, 1985). *Dialysis centers* were established as an answer to the development in the 1960s of the mechanical technique known as hemodialysis that cleanses impurities from the blood in imitation of the kidney. It enabled many patients who would otherwise have died of kidney disease to be given years of useful life as long as they continued to be dialyzed regularly.

There have been accusations that the profits to be made from dialysis centers have resulted in substantially fewer kidney transplants (which eliminate the need for dialysis) and less home dialysis (cheaper in the past than at a center) than would otherwise have occurred. Medicare recently began to offer reimbursement for home care at the same rate as in a center. Centers were soon offering home care. Reimbursement per average treatment was $131 in a hospital-based center and $127 in a free-standing (for-profit) one in 1985. Typically a patient receives three treatments per week. Kidney dialysis cost $2.5 billion in 1986 for treatment of 100,000 patients.

In 1984 there were 1,330 dialysis facilities, 9% more than in 1983. In 1974, only 10% of the centers were out of hospital while in 1984 their number had grown to 50%. Hospitals are unlikely to relinquish dialysis entirely because it is often needed only temporarily for acutely ill patients with a variety of disease complications.

HOME HEALTH CARE

The aging of the population in the United States and concern about hospital costs have sparked interest in the home health care market. Elderly people are most in need of support systems; if they can be maintained in their own homes, the societal cost can be less than if they must be institutionalized. At present, informal care by family (typically by daughters, many of whom are elderly themselves) makes up most of the help given to disabled elderly people needing assistance. Formal sources of care accounted for less than 15% of all "helper days" measured by the Department of Health and Human Services in a 1982 survey (Doty, Liu, and Wiener, 1985). More formal sources of help will be needed, it is anticipated, as the number of those over 75—most at risk of chronic disease and disability—becomes a significant percentage of the population.

Prospective payment mechanisms instituted by Medicare in 1983 to reduce the number of days patients spend in hospitals increase the need for out-of-hospital help for recovering patients. Anticipating this, Medicare expanded its minimal home health coverage in 1981, encouraging and sometimes confusing the home health care market (Edmondson, 1985). Some providers expected that certain services would be covered, only to find that they had been mistaken. Medicare expenditures for home health increased from $119 million in 1974 to $770 million in 1980 and to $1.5 billion in 1983. This rapid increase is said to have alarmed government officials even though home health represents only 3% of Medicare costs. Responding to the public's preference for home care over institutions, however, Medicare was expected to pay $2.8 billion for short-term home care in 1988.

Estimates of current annual revenues for home health care technology and services range from $3.9 billion to $6 billion; they may reach $13 billion to $24 billion by the 1990s. Technology can be employed in providing intravenous infusions of nutrients, antibiotics, and chemicals (cancer therapy), in peritoneal dialysis that can be done at home, and in respiratory and physical therapy. Other home care involves the employment of skilled nurses, speech therapists, homemakers and aides, and medical social workers.

Several large firms have taken a leading role in expanding home health care. Baxter-Travenol's method of dialysis allows more mobility and easier home dialysis than was possible in the past; the market for this so-called "continuous ambulatory peritoneal dialysis" (the abdominal cavity is washed out rather than the blood stream) has reached $100 million per year. Several other companies have entered the field (see Table A-4) and it is expected that hospitals will contract with companies to supply home services if these still new techniques prove feasible (see Table A-5). Marketing is directed at providers of health care at present rather than to patients. The companies expect to supply the necessary products and train the professionals in their use. Providers will, in turn, train the patients. Presumably this will mitigate the risk to the company of errors by patients and will lessen resentment of doctors who fear loss of income because of fewer visits to doctors' offices and hospitals.

Direct marketing to the consumer is being pursued by a number of companies that sell specialized products for incontinence. Procter & Gamble sold $150 million of such disposable products, and Kimberly-Clark and Johnson & Johnson are also in the market.

Home health care providers of service include private firms and the nonprofit Visiting Nurses Association. Not all of the 4,000 home health agencies qualified for the Medicare certification, which increases greatly their viability.

THE ROLE OF THE PHYSICIAN IN THE HEALTH CARE SYSTEM

Number and Distribution

In 1987 there were some 550,000 physicians in the United States, 430,000 in patient care. Their number varied widely by state; overall, there were 180 physicians in patient care in 1985 per 100,000 population (up from 135 in 1975), but New York had 252 and Massachusetts had 254, while South Dakota had only 123. The South Central states generally had low numbers of physicians, and the Northeast high proportions relative to the population. The availability of primary care physicians has been a continued problem in rural areas. A goal of one primary care physician to a population of 3,500 was proposed by federal health planners in the 1970s, indicating that this minimum standard had not been met in many areas. Some 60% of the population in Mississippi and 40% in Alabama, for example, lived in such health manpower shortage areas, compared with 14% in California and 9% in New Jersey (Lefkowitz, 1983).

Maldistribution occurs because physicians gravitate to areas where earnings will be adequate, hospital facilities are available, and they can interact with their peers and find good schools and job opportunities for their spouses. Physicians also tend to stay in or near the city in which they complete their training.

It was thought in the 1960s that if more physicians were graduated, they would "trickle out" to the less desirable underserved areas of the country—rural areas and inner cities, especially—as competition forced them out of more affluent areas. To this end, more medical schools were organized from the 1960s on—rising from 79 schools in 1950 to 126 in 1980—and the federal government aided by giving capitation grants to medical schools and loans to medical students from 1963 on through the 1970s to encourage enlarged classes. The number of students graduated each year rose from 7,000 in 1960 to 16,800 in 1985. Some

Table A-4 Home Infusion Providers

(dollars in millions)

Companies	1987	1988	1989	1990E	1991E
Caremark (Baxter Inc.)					
% of Market Share	41.5%	37.3%	33.0%	30.5%	29.3%
Total Revenues	$ 355	$ 440	$ 542	$ 680	$ 850
Company Growth Rate		23.9%	23.2%	25.5%	25.0%
New England Critical Care					
% of Market Share	3.6%	4.1%	5.1%	6.1%	7.1%
Total Revenues	$ 31	$ 48	$ 84	$ 137	$ 205
Company Growth Rate		34.6%	75%	63.1%	49.7%
Home Nutritional Services					
% of Market Share	4.1%	4.0%	4.0%	4.1%	4.2%
Total Revenues	$ 35	$ 47	$ 66	$ 91	$ 122
Company Growth Rate		34.6%	40.1%	37.9%	34.1%
HMSS					
% of Market Share	2.5%	3.0%	3.5%	4.0%	4.7%
Total Revenues	$ 21	$ 35	$ 57	$ 90	$ 135
Company Growth Rate		66.7%	62.9%	57.9%	50.0%
National Medical Care (W.R. Grace)[a]					
% of Market Share	2.3%	2.5%	4.0%	4.0%	4.2%
Total Revenues	$ 20	$ 29	$ 66	$ 90	$ 121
Company Growth Rate		45.0%	127.6%	36.4%	34.9%
Care Plus					
% of Market Share	2.3%	1.9%	2.1%	2.2%	2.4%
Total Revenues	$ 20	$ 22	$ 34	$ 49	$ 69
Company Growth Rate		10.0%	54.5%	44.1%	40.8%
Continental Affiliates					
% of Market Share	2.3%	2.8%	2.4%	2.3%	2.2%
Total Revenues	$ 20	$ 31	$ 40	$ 51	$ 64
Company Growth Rate		55.0%	29.0%	28.7%	24.3%
T^2					
% of Market Share	2.3%	2.8%	2.8%	2.8%	2.7%
Total Revenues	$ 20	$ 33	$ 46	$ 62	$ 79
Company Growth Rate		65.0%	39.4%	34.8%	28.0%
Other					
% of Market Share	38.9%	41.9%	43.1%	43.9%	43.3%
Total Revenues	$ 333	$ 494	$ 707	$ 978	$1,255
Company Growth Rate		48.3%	43.1%	38.3%	28.3%
Total Market Size	$ 855	$1,179	$1,642	$2,228	$2,901
Industry Growth Rate		37.9%	39.3%	35.7%	30.2%
3-Year Compound Moving Growth Rate		41.0%	40.4%	37.6%	35.0%

[a]W.R. Grace completed its acquisition of Infusion Care from Avon on 1/24/89; Infusion Care is now part of National Medical Care. Our revenue projections for National Medical Care incorporate both companies.

Source: Company reports and Prudential-Bache estimates, March 1990.

Table A-5 Total Home Infusion Market Size and Growth

(dollars in millions)

Therapy	1986	1987	% Change	1988	% Change	1989	% Change	1990E	% Change	1991E	% Change
Total Parenteral Nutrition	$ 270	$ 338	25.2%	$ 405	19.8%	$ 475	17.3%	$ 546	14.9%	$ 622	13.9%
% of Market	46%	40%		34%		29%		25%		21%	
Enteral Nutrition (Home Only)	$ 123	$ 167	35.8%	$ 200	19.8%	$ 231	15.5%	$ 255	10.4%	$ 280	9.8%
% of Market	21%	20%		17%		14%		11%		10%	
Total Home Antibiotics (A/B)	$ 130	$ 210	61.5%	$ 355	69.0%	$ 580	63.4%	$ 910	56.9%	$1,275	40.1%
% of Market	22%	25%		30%		35%		41%		44%	
A/B without AIDS	$ 115	$ 183	59.1%	$ 275	50.3%	$ 385	40.0%	$ 530	37.7%	$ 700	32.1%
% of Market	19%	21%		23%		23%		24%		24%	
Chemotherapy	$ 30	$ 48	60.0%	$ 72	50.0%	$ 105	45.8%	$ 150	42.9%	$ 205	36.7%
% of Market	5%	6%		6%		6%		7%		7%	
Pain Therapy	$ 10	$ 27	170.0%	$ 46	70.4%	$ 70	52.2%	$ 92	31.4%	$ 115	25.0%
% of Market	2%	3%		4%		4%		4%		4%	
Other	$ 30	$ 65	116.7%	$ 101	55.4%	$ 181	79.2%	$ 275	51.9%	$ 404	46.9%
% of Market	5%	8%		9%		11%		12%		14%	
Total Market	$ 593	$ 855	44.2%	$1,179	37.9%	$1,642	39.3%	$2,228	35.7%	$2,901	30.2%
Compound Growth (3-Year Moving Average)			41.0%		40.4%		37.6%		35.1%		

Source: Company Reports and Prudential-Bache estimates, March 1990.

3,000 foreign-educated physicians augmented the supply each year. By the 1980s the consensus was that there were too many physicians rather than too few. The number of active physicians per 100,000 population has grown 51% since 1965, although the number per capita in general practice is down 25% (American Medical Association [AMA], data). Medical school applications fell from 42,000 in 1976 to 31,000 in 1986. By 1988 researchers were again predicting that a shortage of doctors would be evident by the year 2000 as shrinking enrollments, the aging population, new techniques, and the AIDS epidemic brought a need for more physicians.

The idea that if more physicians were trained they would serve the 40 million people living in areas needing them had proved true to some degree by the 1980s, with suburbs of large metropolitan areas and small towns better supplied with board-certified specialists than they were before 1960 (McConnel and Tobias, 1986). It has been questioned whether this represents a real gain, however, since specialists often replaced general practice physicians (Sidel and Sidel, 1984). Sparsely settled areas and inner cities were still underserved in the 1980s. In the northern Great Plains some 10% of the people live more than 20 miles from a physician while in the Northeast only .2% and in the Great Lakes area only 1% must travel that distance for medical care.

Medical Education

Graduate physicians compete each year for the most desirable training positions in the United States, leaving less popular positions to be filled by foreign medical graduates (FMGs) (many of whom are U.S. citizens studying abroad), who made up 16% of the residents in training in 1986–1987 (AMA statistics), down from a peak of 45% in 1973. The increase in domestically trained physicians in recent years and the poor reputation of some of the foreign schools combined to influence public policy toward reducing the number of FMGs allowed to practice in the United States. Amendments to

the Immigration and Naturalization Act in 1976, 1977, and 1981 made it more difficult for FMGs to practice, and in 1984 the test to admit FMGs to residency training was made more difficult. The limitations were a problem for large municipal hospitals and mental health institutions that have depended heavily on such graduates. By 1988, qualifications were once again being eased.

Another approach to solving the maldistribution problem was the 1976 legislation to require medical schools to increase the number of primary care residencies—designed to encourage physicians to train in "primary care" or general practice rather than to specialize. (Actually, general practice is now a "specialty," but the training period is shorter than that for many other specialities.)

Over the last ten years there has been a steady decline in the number applying to medical schools. Lower prestige, less freedom to practice as they wish (as third-party payers influence behavior), static incomes, high education costs, and long years of training have all been blamed as discouraging factors (Easterbrook, 1987). The number in the student age group as a proportion of the population declined slightly (1%) since 1980 and is expected to fall further in the next decade.

More than half the 31,000 applicants to medical school were accepted for enrollment in 1986, a higher proportion than in the past—1.7 applicants per accepted student compared with a peak of 2.8 in 1975. More than 60% of the 1986 class had earned at least a 3.5 grade point average in college, however, indicating little decline so far in grade point averages; grades on the entry examination fell slightly. Continued decline in applications is expected to bring less qualified applicants or reduced class size, as has occurred in dental schools (O'Neil, 1988). Women made up 36% of those accepted and their increased interest and acceptance in medical schools kept the decline in applicants from being as steep as it would otherwise have been (Jolly, 1988). Women made up less than 10% of the applicants until the 1970s, when women's organizations sued the medical schools, charging discrimination.

Researchers have found that certain characteristics, such as being raised in a small town, being among the younger siblings in a family, and exhibiting strong socialization patterns in school, correlate with the choice of primary care as a specialty, and they have urged medical schools to consider these characteristics in evaluating applicants (Stefanu et al., 1980). The recommendation is unlikely to be adopted as long as medical school entry remains competitive and strongly influenced by grades on entrance examinations.

Median tuition in 1987 averaged $15,000 at private medical schools and $4,600 at public schools. As debt to pay for medical training rose to an average of $33,000 or more in 1987, depending on the study, its effect on specialty training has been appraised (Bazzoli, 1985). Although factors other than debt are thought by some to have a greater influence on specialty choice (e.g., marital status, spouse's earnings, educational level of parents), most commentators agreed that with 82% of medical school graduates in 1986 in debt at more than twice the 1980 level, it significantly affected practice decisions. For minorities, the average debt was $40,000, and nearly a third had borrowed more than $50,000.

Armed forces scholarship loans with a payback in service accounted for 10% of the $473 million in aid to students in 1985–1986. The National Health Service Corps, with a payback requiring work in underserved areas, accounted for a negligible amount ($1.9 million to 113 students). Loans were the main source of funds (76%). Scholarships were minor, averaging less than $2,000 per student, including service-related ones. The low-interest guaranteed student loan (GSL) was the most popular, with 60% of medical students receiving some money from it, the average being $4,700 (the maximum is $5,000, soon to rise to $7,500). Those who needed more than this resorted to market rate loans that accrued interest throughout school and residency.

Full-time faculty increased more than five times between 1960 and 1986. Expansion of biomedical science research and patient care activity mostly accounted for this, although the number of schools increased as well under government urging and help to expand the number of doctors. This faculty taught 66,000 medical students, 54,000 residents, 20,000 graduate students in science, and 7,500 clinical fellows *(Journal of the American Medical Association*, 1987).

Less than half of today's students enter primary care areas of medicine. The number of graduates surveyed who planned a general internal medicine residency fell off from 13.5% of all graduates in 1981 to 8.5% in 1987.

The number of hours residents worked rose 3% between 1983 and 1987 despite much publicity about the danger of overworked, sleep-deprived doctors making sometimes fatal errors. The assumption is that some hospitals are taking advantage of residents at their relatively low salaries during the training period when they must remain at one hospital. Salaries did not increase while indebtedness rose. All residents worked long hours. The median ranged from 50 hours per week in pathology and psychiatry to 89 in OB/GYN and 87 in surgery. Ten percent of surgeons worked more than 122 hours per week. The median for internal medicine was 73 hours and for pediatrics, 80. The average resident spent eight nights per month on call at the hospital.

Women make up about 30% of physicians in training. More of them are specializing in psychology (11%), pediatrics (19%), and OB/GYN (9%) than are found in the totals for men and women together; fewer women than men are becoming surgeons.

Physicians' Incomes

Specialists earn what is thought by many to be a disproportionate amount. Their hourly reimbursement is about four times that of primary care physicians. Surgeons are paid largely for specific procedures once something has gone wrong, while general practitioners can charge only so much for an office visit that might maintain health (see Table A-6). A government-sponsored study by Harvard Public Health School researchers aimed at finding

Table A-6 Average Net Income from Medical Practice by Specialty

Specialty	Number of Non-federal Physicians in Patient Care 1985	Average Net Yearly Income					
		1970	1976[a]	1978	1981	1984	1986
Total for All Patient Care[b]	427,000	$41,800	$59,500	$65,500	$ 93,000	$ 108,400	$ 119,500[c]
General Family Practice	53,000	33,900	47,400	54,600	72,200	71,100	80,300
Internal Medicine	52,000	40,300	60,500	63,800	85,100	103,200	—
Surgery	25,000	50,700	73,200	82,600	118,600	151,800	162,400
Pediatrics	22,000	34,800	47,000	51,200	65,100	74,500	81,800
Obstetrics and Gynecology	23,000	47,100	65,800	70,300	110,800	116,200	—
Psychiatry	32,500	39,900	47,600	50,200	70,600	85,500	—
Anesthesiology	19,500	39,400	60,100	74,200	118,600	145,400	—
Radiology	—						168,000

[a]Projected by respondents at time of survey.
[b]Physicians whose specialties are classified as Radiology and "Other" are included in this total.

From 1970 to 1981, net income from medical practice increased 122 percent for all specialties. Net income for surgeons increased 134 percent in the same period. However, when physicians' incomes for all specialties are adjusted for inflation, real income decreased by 5 percent from 1970 to 1981. Surgeons' income decreased by .13 percent in the same period. Of the specialties listed above, psychiatrists lost the most buying power, 24.5 percent, while anesthesiologists increased their buying power by 28.5 percent.

[c]*Medical Economics*, May 16, 1988, states $112,790 as the average net income for all specialties in 1986 and $146,430 as the average for surgeons.

Source: American College of Surgeons: *Socio-Economic Factbook*, 1982, *Profile of Medical Practice*, 1981, and *SMS Report*, June 1982. American Medical Association: *Socioeconomic Characteristics of Medical Practice*, 1985, 1987.

ways to even out physicians' fees has been published recently (Hsaio et al., 1988).

In the United States, a physician's average income is 5.5 times that of an average worker's wage; in France, it is 7 times a worker's wage; in West Germany, under a cost-control law, it is 6 times a worker's; while in Britain, under the National Health Service it is 2.5 times that of a worker. Canadian doctors earn about 5 times the average industrial wage. About 21% of income is derived directly from patients' fees, 20% from commercial insurers, 18% each from Blue Shield and Medicare, and the rest from prepaid practices.

Physicians' incomes have not kept pace with the cost of living, especially among general practitioners. In the past, doctors were often able to raise their fees to compensate for reduced income, but cost saving pressure from government and corporate insurers discourages such practices as large purchasers shop for competitive prices (Easterbrook, 1987).

The fees charged for office visits, especially for established patients, did not vary appreciably by physician specialty, although general practice and pediatrics fees were lower (see Table A-7). Fees for office visits do not reflect charges for procedures. Fees for established patients increased 5.5% in 1984, but only 3% for new patients, perhaps reflecting competition from health maintenance organizations (HMOs) in attracting patients. The amount charged by physicians in nonmetropolitan areas was about 30% less than

in large metropolitan areas. The difference was less pronounced among family practitioners and pediatricians than for the other specialties.

The money spent by physicians on training should be considered in evaluating earnings. Private medical schools were charging about $15,000 per year for tuition alone for four years in the late 1980s; state schools charged less ($2,000 to $5,000), but were not free. Training continues for another four years, at minimum, during which young physicians earned $25,000 or less per year—well below a beginning lawyer's or MBA's income. Surgical training takes several more years past the minimum internship and residency. The average debt of a graduating physician was $33,000 in 1987, according to one source (Easterbrook, 1987), while others cite a median of $79,000 for men and $56,000 for women (Farber, 1986).

Physician Utilization

The mean number of patient visits per week was higher for patients who used physicians in group practice than for those who visited solo practitioners in 1984, although the margin was not wide. Doctors in large metropolitan areas saw considerably fewer patients per week (106) than those in nonmetropolitan areas (144), where the number of physicians in proportion to the population was much lower. Self-employed physicians had 125 visits a week, versus 100 for physicians employed in

---

Table A-7 Physicians' Mean Fee for Office Visits, by Specialty, 1983 and 1984

	New Patient		Established Patient	
	1983	*1984*	*1983*	*1984*
All Physicians	$45.83	$47.21	$24.74	$26.09
General Practice	29.72	30.37	19.95	20.71
Internal Medicine	68.51	71.00	27.82	29.89
Surgery	42.95	43.92	24.80	25.65
Pediatrics	33.54	34.46	22.89	24.11
OB/GYN	46.11	47.32	28.79	31.16

Source: AMA Data, *Socioeconomic Survey*, 1985.

hospitals or by health plans. Patients of self-employed physicians had shorter hospital stays (5.8 days) than did patients of employed physicians (8.8). It is possible that employed physicians are influenced to keep the hospital full, but part of the explanation may also lie in the tertiary (more complicated) care given by many employed physicians. The average number of visits is highest in the regions (North and South Central) where the supply of physicians is lowest. Over a ten-year period the average number of patient visits has declined in all regions and for all practice modes.

The Medicaid population used physicians in 1980 significantly more than the rest (5,605 visits per 1,000 person-years versus 3,960), reflecting the large proportion of Medicaid that goes toward long-term care of disabled people (Health Care Financing Administration [HCFA], 1984). For office visits to physicians, women saw physicians 3 times a year, on average, while men saw them 2 times in 1981. White people visited physicians 2.7 times a year while other races saw them 2.1 times. Predictably, the visit rate rose with the age of the patient, with each patient over 65 seeing physicians an average of 4 times a year and those aged 15 to 44 seeing them only twice (National Center for Health Statistics, *Health United States, 1989*).

A large number (83%) of consumers of health care report that they have a regular physician who provides routine medical care, (Jensen and Miklovic, 1986). About 10% switched physicians in 1985. Predictably, age, sex, and residence influenced the number who had a regular physician; the proportion was higher for women (83%) than for men (72%); higher for those over 65 (85%) than for younger people (75% of those 24–34); higher among those who have lived in one place for five years (80%) than for newcomers (50% for two-year residents); higher in the North and Central states than in the West, where HMOs are available and where many residents are recent migrants. A regular relationship with the same physician that has lasted at least five years was reported by 66% of those surveyed. Physicians were selected 53% of the time by

the female head of the household. Long-term loyalty was most pronounced in areas with few physicians relative to the population. Women were more likely than men to use specialists as regular physicians (25% versus 16%). The more education consumers had, the more likely they were to use specialists (37% of postgraduates versus 17% with a high school education). Use of specialists also correlated with their availability, with higher availability than usual in metropolitan areas.

The poor, probably as a result of Medicaid, now have better access to physicians. In 1964, those with a minimum family income had the fewest visits, but by 1981 poor people had the highest rate of physician visits. Blacks averaged fewer visits per year than whites in 1988—4.8 visits per year for blacks and 5.5 for whites; however, approximately the same percentage of both races had seen a doctor within the past year (National Center for Health Statistics, *Health United States*, 1989).

Malpractice Issues

The average annual number of malpractice claims nearly tripled in the years from 1980 to 1985, rising from 3 per 100 physicians to 8.6 (AMA data). Nationally, the average was 5%. Surgeons were at greatest risk; they averaged 14 claims per 100 physicians from 1980 to 1985. Their malpractice premiums were 4 times those of non-surgical physicians (*Medical Economics*, 1989). The average liability premium increased from $4,170 in 1983 to $10,950 in 1988.

The malpractice insurance system reached a crisis in 1975 when many insurance carriers refused to write policies and others drastically increased premiums; tort reforms instituted since then by the states have not solved the problem.

A number of explanations have been advanced for the increase in malpractice suits and the associated rise in insurance cost: Too little policing is done by the medical establishment to discipline the relatively few physicians who are guilty of bad practices;

competition among an increasing number of lawyers has led some to be willing to advertise for malpractice cases and to press marginal cases, hoping for settlements; insurance companies raised premiums in the mid-1980s to recoup losses from past sales to poor risks when interest rates were high; higher insurance rates are justified because the law now allows claims to be made long after an injury is reputed to have occurred; physicians and hospitals practice poor "risk management" by not emphasizing preventive measures that would avoid suits; juries award occasional large amounts, against which insurers must protect themselves, that are based on compassion rather than cause.

Fear of malpractice suits brings associated costs. Doctors practice "defensive" medicine, ordering tests and procedures to protect themselves from possible negligence claims; the AMA estimates that 20% of all procedures may be defensive. The St. Paul Insurance Companies reported that "bad results" of treatment was the leading cause of liability claims, reflecting the public's often too-optimistic expectations from modern medicine; "delay or omission of treatment" and "wrong diagnosis" were also significant causes for suit. Other associated costs result from payment for defense of suits that are dropped or found without merit and time lost in court appearances and preparation.

Physicians have lodged protests and "job actions" over the burden of paying malpractice insurance. Early in 1985, doctors in Albany, Syracuse, and Buffalo refused new patients to force legislation to reduce insurance rates. Rate increases of 50% had resulted in physicians in high-risk specialities such as obstetrics paying more than $100,000 a year for insurance. Most states have passed some sort of tort reform since 1975. They have included pretrial screening to eliminate frivolous claims, caps on the amount of damages that can be awarded, and reductions in the amount of the award that the plaintiff's attorney is allowed—for example, a sliding scale allowing the attorney as much as 40% of the first $150,000 but only 25% of anything over $500,000. (It is common for plaintiffs' attorneys to charge from 33% to 40% of awards since they accept cases judged to have merit without advance payment.) Such sliding scales seem to have reduced malpractice premiums in California, but have not done so in Indiana. A Rand Corporation study that assessed the effect of reforms over a limited period found that pretrial screening panels have not reduced the total number of claims and that limitations on contingency fees had not affected the frequency or the severity (measured by the amount of settlement) of claims. Caps on awards did reduce the severity of claims, but not the frequency (Curran, 1983). It is also unproven that better regulation of physicians would lower premiums, although no one argues that better performance review should not be carried out.

Mode of Practice

The great majority of American physicians have practiced independently, charging a fee for each service to a patient (the "fee-for-service" mode). Some came together to practice as a group, augmenting each other's expertise. A few group practices became very well known: the Mayo Clinic in Rochester, Minnesota, which had started in the 1890s, the Crile Clinic in Cleveland, the Lahey Clinic in Boston, and Ochsner Clinic in New Orleans. These group practices charged patients a fee for service, but the senior founding physicians usually retained ownership of the group and paid salaries to younger doctors invited to join the practice, who might later be offered shares in it. Benefits for the group lay in sharing expenses, in rotating duty for patient responsibility on weekends and evenings, and in allowing vacations for one another. Groups that developed a reputation for quality medicine because of "stars" like the Mayo brothers, who were skilled surgeons, enjoyed a marketing advantage and were often opposed by independent physicians in their communities. Proprietary clinics were more common in the West than in the East, because there were fewer major hospitals there offering centers for specialists.

In 1984 some 139,000 or 28% practiced in groups (AMA, 1984). Two-thirds were in small groups of three to four physicians rather than in large group clinics. Three types of practice prevailed: general, single specialty, (70%), and multiple specialty (18%). By 1984, in addition to the usual economies of joint practice, groups benefited from earnings from ancillary charges for x-rays and laboratory tests. Physicians' groups could buy an expensive CAT scanner, for example, that might be denied to a hospital by state Certificate of Need programs.

The groups' relationships with hospitals were varied. Over 30% of the groups had a hospital as a landlord, but only 2% were hospital operated. Over 47% had no hospital relationship, with a higher percentage of the three- and four-person groups having no relationship. The percentage of specialists in groups ranged from over 90% of radiologists to 39% of anesthesiologists and 12% of psychiatrists.

In 1986, about 25% of all physicians worked as employees of hospitals or health plans rather than as independent practitioners. The proportion was higher among young doctors (39%) under age 36, some of whom may later become independent. The high costs of medical education and of malpractice insurance made private practice less attractive; more predictable hours and help with administration and billing were also advantages of employment, despite somewhat lower earnings than for independent practice. Another advantage of employment was that the employer either provided no free care or absorbed the cost, while private practitioners were unable to avoid giving substantial amounts of free care (Oshfeldt, 1985). But employment required some sacrifices of physicians' autonomy and freedom to practice their own brand of medicine.

HMO

A variation on group practice, with an important difference, is the prepaid group health arrangement, popularly known today as an HMO. The idea may have originated with the ancient Chinese: The obligation of the phy-

sician to keep patients well rather than to treat them only when they were sick. To this end, the HMO requires a fixed payment for the year in advance from the patient or customer, and the physician receives a salary. There is thus no incentive for physicians to institute extra procedures to augment their fees. If the customer is healthy, the HMO operates at an advantage. Many studies have shown that hospitalization rates are lower for enrollees of HMOs than for those of private physicians in traditional practice; why this is true is the subject of considerable debate. (See the section on "Effectiveness of HMOs," below.)

The largest HMO, Kaiser-Permanente in California, is the only one to have grown without opposition, perhaps because it was started during World War II for shipyard workers who had been displaced from their home physicians and because Kaiser built its own hospitals (Anderson, 1985). In 1984, the Kaiser plan had an enrollment of 4.7 million people, and the Health Insurance Plan of New York City, 900,000. Throughout the country there were some 660 plans with a total enrollment of some 30 million people by 1987. Plans with more than 100,000 members dominated—28 plans accounted for 58% of the enrollment. HMOs originated under a mission of improving the quality of patient care by providing prepaid preventive care. The apparent "cost containment" ability of HMOs is a more recent aspect.

As cost consciousness has increased, health planners and government payers have endorsed HMOs. Encouragement for expansion of such plans was given by Congress in the Health Maintenance Organization Act of 1973 and in extensions of the act in 1976 and 1978. Government-funded HMOs were to serve especially in rural and inner city areas. Despite endorsement by planners and government, however, enrollment in HMOs still accounted for only 7% of the population by 1984. Social security Amendments in 1984 allowed Medicare to contract on a prospective capitation basis with HMOs and comprehensive medical providers, but by 1988 only a few demonstration projects were in effect. In the 1980s, for-profit hospital chains had begun to form their own HMOs. Large urban hospitals increasingly accepted affiliation with an HMO (*Hospitals*, 1985). The HMO concept has been better received in urban areas than elsewhere.

The traditional HMO is a "staff" model with salaried physicians who see only the HMO enrollees. An IPA type of HMO is "open"; it consists of physicians who may see all patients whether HMO enrollees or not. Some HMOs are "group" because they enlist a medical group to provide their services. It is much less costly to start an IPA type of HMO, and this model is the most attractive to consumers because it gives them the widest variety of choice.

The preferred provider organization (PPO) is another practice concept that has evolved recently under which a group of physicians and/or hospitals offer their services at reduced rates to a third party who can guarantee a sufficient volume of patients and prompt payment of fees, such as a large employer. Enrollees generally pay little or nothing for use of the preferred provider services, but 20% or more of the cost of seeing other providers.

Effectiveness of HMOs

It is not clear what role self-selection plays in the lower costs of caring for people in HMOs. It is possible that healthier people, oriented toward prevention of illness, are more likely to enroll in one and that physicians who elect to join an HMO are satisfied with a practice style that emphasizes low usage of resources (Luft, 1981). It is not clear to what degree the lower hospitalization rate for HMOs can be attributed to the style of practice, since Blue Cross has shown a downward trend in hospitalization, and there are significant variations geographically in hospital usage attributed to varying styles of medical practice (Wennberg and Gittelsohn, 1973). HMO hospital days per 1,000 enrollees range from 350–500, while traditional insurance policy days are from 600–800 per thousand.

Some contend that HMOs skim the healthy, employed customers from the rest of the health system. Although HMO enrollment is open to anyone, their services are generally located in areas where they are likely to attract middle-class patients. The Harvard Health Plan, with offices in Boston suburbs, for example, has fewer than 1% Medicaid enrollees and a low percentage of Medicare payers. (Medicaid patients have had no financial incentive to restrain their access to care, and until 1984 Medicare patients could not join an HMO on a risk contract basis.) Another objection to HMOs is that it is difficult to establish whether patients suffer from too little attention. Most HMOs operate with a primary care physician as gatekeeper to specialists, a system that in some cases may affect the quality of care received and result in low patient satisfaction. It is probable that HMOs will remain one mode of practice in a multiple system.

DENTISTRY

The number of dentists in the country increased during the 1970s in response to a perceived need for them and in conjunction with rising incomes. The number of applicants to dental schools began to fall off in the late 1970s, however, and the decline continued—down to 4,370 in 1987 from 6,000 in 1980—as it became apparent that dental caries were declining appreciably at the same time that the population of children and young adults was falling off. This meant that the "bread and butter" of dentistry, filling cavities afflicting young people, would decline. Public health experts do not expect that dentistry will die out, however (Exter, 1985). They expect that changes in dental practices that have tended to preserve teeth rather than extract them in the years since 1950 will shift attention from cavities to periodontal and other problems of older people—attention previously unneeded because the elderly had lost their teeth.

The decline in dental caries has been attributed largely to fluoridation, but some experts caution that it is too soon to be sure of the cause of the decline or to predict that it will continue. The decline has apparently occurred in areas without fluoride in the water supply, indicating that socioeconomic factors and better dental care may also be causes.

The number of dentists in the country in 1984 (132,750) represented only 56 per 100,000 population, many fewer than the ratio for physicians. A 1976 study by the Carnegie Council on Policy Studies in Higher Education showed that one-fourth of the population had not seen a dentist in the last five years. In contrast to 4.9 visits per year to a physician, the average for dental visits was 1.7 per person each year. The number of visits depended on the ability to pay. These visit rates may improve if dental insurance coverage increases. In 1981 only half as many people had access to such insurance as had medical insurance, and few elderly people carried it; 40% of those under 65 had dental insurance, but only 6% of those over 65 did.

Dentists have responded to the need to increase their business by organizing corporate facilities, opening street-front offices, participating in HMOs, and working in nursing homes and hospitals in addition to operating independently in their traditional solo practices. They employ dental assistants, hygienists, and laboratory technologists to expand productivity. Other marketing ideas common now range from movies and music in the office to advertisements for painless, cosmetic enhancement of teeth (Lefferts, 1985) and tooth implants.

In 1986, nearly $30 billion was spent on dental services. Medicaid paid for $600 million, and private insurance accounted for about a third of the amount spent on dentistry. Such insurance had covered only 1% of dental services in 1965.

DRUGS

Prescription drugs, over-the-counter drugs, and other medical products sold through retail stores rather than dispensed by doctors or hospitals accounted for some 6% of personal health care expenditures in 1986, or $30 billion. Consumers paid for three-fourths of these drugs directly and for another 15% through private health insurance. Government programs paid for about 10%. Prescriptions accounted for about 57% of the money spent on drugs.

Although spending for drugs has increased over the last ten years, it has grown at a slower rate than expenses for health care overall. Part of this is attributed to a relatively low inflation rate in the cost of drugs, but the government also attributes it to the low level of coverage by third parties (HCFA, 1984). Price consciousness by the consumer may have held spending down (Gibson et al., 1984). Third parties paid for about one-fourth of drug costs, but this was far below the nearly four-fifths of total health care spending financed by government and other insurance. The increase in spending for drugs was 9% per year from 1973 to 1983, while the overall increase in health spending was 13.4% per year.

Since 1906 the drug industry has been regulated by the Pure Food and Drug Act, culminating in a campaign at the turn of the century by the AMA and by journalists to end then-prevalent deceptive advertising to the general public of often dangerous and addictive drugs. The AMA set up an independent Council on Drugs that joined with the government in testing medical products. It refused to advertise patent medicines in its journal. Newspapers agreed to block advertisements that the AMA claimed were dishonest. Over the years, the bulk of drug purchasing has been channeled through the physician, enhancing the status of the profession, but leaving doctors vulnerable to charges that they are often co-opted by the pharmaceutical companies (Klaw, 1975). Prescription drugs are marketed today through the physician whose awareness of them is aroused by drug advertising that is accepted in medical journals. "Detail men" from pharmaceutical companies regularly visit doctors' offices to explain their products, leave samples, and urge their use. So many new compounds are marketed each year that most doctors welcome the companies' information. Too few, say critics, are likely to read evaluations of comparable drugs or keep up adequately with medical literature. Evidence that questionable products had again become a problem prompted amendments to the Food and Drug Act in recent years, which forced manufacturers to show that products were not only safe, but effective. In line with the new directives, the FDA investigated approved drugs as well and found many to be expensive but worthless.

Pharmaceutical companies in the United States are required to perform more rigorous testing of each new product than in most foreign countries (except Sweden and Canada) before government approval is given. Companies complain that the testing time and the subsequent typically lengthy review by the FDA eats into their patent protection time. They argued for some years that Congress should allow them longer than the usual 17 years of monopoly on patented compounds so that the expense of testing could be offset, and Congress recently agreed. Companies have also sought to build their trademark images so that doctors will continue to prescribe a patented drug even when a generic one has become available.

In 1985, pharmaceutical and biotechnology companies urged Congress to allow them to sell drugs not approved for use in the United States to countries overseas (Sun, 1985). Such sales have been prohibited for the past 40 years. Companies claim they lose sales to foreign firms at present and that sufficient safeguards would be in place to prevent abuse. Critics think proper monitoring by the FDA would be impossible, but Congress, interested in protecting American industry, passed legislation allowing foreign sales in 1986.

Despite FDA controls, marketing of drugs carries risks. Complications may not show up for many years, as in the case of DES (diethylstilbestrol), which caused cancer 20 years or more later in the female offspring of women who took it when pregnant. Lingering problems ensued with Chloromycetin, an antibiotic marketed by Parke Davis. Since it is useful in specific cases, it was kept on the market after the discovery in the 1950s that it could cause fetal aplastic anemia. In 1967, a Senate subcommittee faulted the company for continuing to urge its use for minor ailments that should have been treated with a safer drug.

Pharmaceutical companies and chemical companies that also sell drugs are among the *Fortune 500* companies with sales in billions of dollars yearly. Many of them sponsor research in universities as well as internally. They pay physicians outside the company for clinical tests of their products.

HEALTH STATUS OF THE POPULATION

The amount and kind of health care needed by the population can be shown to some extent by the mortality or death rates for major diseases—a statistic easy to gather (see Table A-8). Less straightforward are morbidity (illness) data, which are gathered from a number of sources. Estimating the cost of various types of disease calls for tabulating the direct costs of treatment and adding to that the indirect cost of earnings foregone through sickness and death. Costs of diseases where the mortality is high and death often occurs at a relatively young age (e.g., cardiovascular diseases, injuries) will be appreciably different from those that are chronic and debilitating but do not result in early death (e.g., diseases of the digestive system). See Table A-9 for estimates of both direct and indirect costs for the major disease categories.

Mortality

Probably the most popular measure of improved health status is an increase in length of life. Over the last 25 years, life expectancy at birth has lengthened, although again blacks overall do not live as long as whites (Table A-10).

Heart disease was the leading killer of all Americans in 1984, with cancer next, followed by accidents and stroke (see Table A-8). The death rate for heart disease (184/100,000) and cancer (133/100,000) dominated, with stroke (33/100,000) and accidents (35/100,000) less

Table A-8 Death Rates per 100,000 Population, by Disease, for Blacks and Whites, Both Sexes, 1950–1984

| | 1950 | | | | 1970 | | | | 1984 | | | | |
| | Men | | Women | | Men | | Women | | Men | | Women | | |
	White	Black	White	Black	White	Black	White	Black	White	Black	White	Black	Total
Heart Disease	380	415	224	350	350	380	170	250	250	300	124	187	184
Stroke	87	122	103	128	70	125	56	108	34	63	29	52	33
Cancer	130	126	120	132	154	198	110	124	159	235	109	131	133
Lung	20	17	5	4	50	60	10	10	60	80	19	20	38
Breast	—	—	23	19	—	—	23	22	—	—	23	26	23
Pneumonia and Influenza	27	64	19	50	26	54	15	29	16	25	9	11	12
Liver Disease	12	9	6	6	19	33	9	18	13	23	7	10	10
Diabetes	11	10	16	23	13	20	13	31	9	17	8	21	10
Accidents	81	106	30	40	76	120	27	35	51	65	19	20	35
Motor	36	40	10	10	40	50	14	14	28	27	11	8	19
Suicide	18	7	5	2	18	10	7	3	20	11	6	2	12
Homicide	4	50	1	10	7	80	2	15	8	51	3	11	8

Note: Death rates are age adjusted. Also, numbers are rounded.

Source: Compiled from *Health United States, 1986,* DHHS No. 87-1232, 1987.

Table A-9 Estimated Amounts and Percentage of Distribution of Total Economic Costs of Major Disease Categories, by Diagnosis and Type of Cost, 1980

(dollars in millions)

Diagnosis	Total	Direct Cost	Indirect Costs		Total	Direct Cost	Indirect Costs	
			Morbidity	*Mortality*[a]			*Morbidity*	*Mortality*
Total	$415,918	$211,143	$67,827	$136,948	100.0%	100.0%	100.0%	100.0%
Infectious and Parasitic Diseases	9,793	4,300	4,107	1,386	2.4	2.0	6.1	1.0
Neoplasms	45,821	13,049	5,778	26,994	11.0	6.2	8.5	19.7
Endocrine, Nutritional, and Metabolic Diseases and Immunity Disorders	12,211	7,329	2,237	2,645	2.9	3.5	3.3	1.9
Diseases of Blood and Blood-forming Organs	1,900	1,155	281	464	0.5	0.5	0.4	0.3
Mental Disorders	30,312	19,824	8,917	1,571	7.3	9.4	1.3	1.1
Diseases of the Nervous System and Sense Organs	22,087	17,123	2,616	2,339	5.3	8.1	3.9	1.7
Diseases of the Circulatory and Cardiovascular System	79,658	32,488	11,448	35,722	19.2	15.4	16.9	26.1
Diseases of the Respiratory System	31,872	16,661	10,146	5,065	7.7	7.9	15.0	3.7
Diseases of the Digestive System (includes dentistry)	41,109	30,974	3,441	6,694	9.9	14.7	5.1	4.9
Diseases of the Genitourinary System	15,171	12,313	1,762	1,096	3.6	5.8	2.6	0.8
Diseases of the Skin and Subcutaneous Tissue	6,578	5,940	539	99	1.6	2.8	0.8	0.0
Diseases of the Musculoskeletal System and Connective Tissue	20,489	13,124	6,938	427	4.9	6.2	10.2	0.3
Congenital Anomalies	4,057	1,345	—	2,712	1.0	0.6	—	2.0
Symptoms, Signs, and Ill-defined Conditions	8,959	3,815	1,847	3,297	2.2	1.8	2.7	2.4
Injury and Poisoning	67,995	18,684	7,234	42,077	16.3	8.8	10.7	30.7
Other Conditions[b]	13,642	8,746	536	4,360	3.3	4.1	0.8	3.2
Unallocated Expenditures	4,265	4,265	—	—	1.0	2.0	—	—

Note: Numbers and percentages may not add up due to rounding.

[a] Present value of lifetime earnings discounted at 6%.

[b] Includes complications of pregnancy, childbirth, and puerperium and certain conditions originating during the prenatal period.

Source: Rice, D.P., Hodgson, T.A., and Kopstein, A.N., "The Economic Cost of Illness: Update," *Health Care Financing Review* (Fall 1985): 61–80.

Table A-10 Life Expectancy at Birth for Blacks and Whites

	1960	1982	1985
Black Women	65.9	72.8	73.5
White Women	74.1	78.7	78.7
Black Men	61.8	64.8	65.3
White Men	68.4	71.4	71.9

Note: Life expectancy is about the same in Britain but is longer in Sweden and Japan.

significant; the four causes accounted for three out of four deaths. Men are twice as likely as women to die of heart disease. Blacks are more vulnerable to high blood pressure and resulting heart diseases than are whites. The difference in the rate of death due to heart disease between black and white women was more pronounced than that between black and white men, but has been narrowing over the years. Since heart disease mainly affects people over 65 and that segment of the population is rising, we might expect the death rates to have gone up since 1950, but in fact this has not happened. An overall decline in heart disease mortality has been attributed to better diet, more exercise, and better health care, but no reliable proof of cause has been given.

Although the death rate for *stroke* has been declining in the 30-year period, the difference between blacks and whites remains startling, with blacks almost twice as vulnerable as whites. High blood pressure is an important risk factor in stroke, as it is in heart disease.

Overall, *cancer* mortality rates have changed little since 1950. Although therapies against cancers have been successful in children and young adults, advances have been offset by cancer deaths in the aging population, especially by a rise in incidence of deaths from lung cancer among both sexes. Cancer is an important cause of death for black women, especially those from age 25 to 44, and for white women from age 25 to 64. Lung cancer is taking its toll of women, with the mortality rate four times that of women in 1950. Black men, who had a slightly lower rate of death from lung cancer than white men in 1950, had exceeded them by a wide margin by 1984.

Some 40,000 women died of breast cancer in 1985, 60,000 were estimated to have the first stage of the disease in 1987.

Accidents of all kinds remain an important cause of death for all young people—a leading cause below age 45. Black men are more likely to die of accidents than are white men, but their mortality rate has declined since 1970, probably attributable to the aging of the postwar "baby boom." Homicide is a significantly more important cause of death among black men than among white men and this is especially true for young black men (15 to 24).

Infant mortality. The death rate for black infants has more than halved since 1960, down from 42 per 1,000 births to 18 in 1984, but this is still twice as high as that for white infants. The rate for the United States overall (11.2) is double that for the countries with the best rate (6.5 in Finland and Japan) and higher than the infant mortality rate in most of the Western countries.

Morbidity

National health surveys report the number of days in which people had to restrict activity because of illness or accident, counting both days spent at home and in the hospital. The poorer and the less educated the person surveyed, the more days were spent in restricted activity and in days in bed. Those with family income under $10,000 had about a month per year of low activity, while those with an income of $25,000 or more reported 13 days lost in the early 1980s. Blue collar workers were ill more than white collar workers, but the differences were small. Farming, by this measure, is a healthy occupation, with 8 days of limitations, and only two in bed. Women were ill slightly more often than men.

A more specific measure of the incidence of disease can be seen from the diagnoses of the patients discharged from short-stay hospitals each year (National Center for Health Statistics, 1987). The 34 million hospital discharges in 1986 included those on whom operations or other procedures had been performed as well as many who had been admitted because of medical problems for which no distinct procedure may have been carried out. Throughout this discussion it should be kept in mind that many patients will have more then one condition affecting them.

Heart disease is the most important reason for hospitalization, with 5.6 million discharges affected, fairly evenly divided between men and women, the majority (3.3 million) over 65 years old. Some 300,000 heart attack victims were treated under Medicare in 1986. Cancer and respiratory disease also affect older people disproportionately. Among younger people (aged 15–44), mental disorders, injuries and poisoning, and diseases of the digestive system and the genitourinary system were most significant, accounting for some 1 million victims in each category.

Procedures

Some 38 million procedures were carried out in hospitals in 1986 on the 34 million discharges (NCHS, 1987). Diagnostic and therapeutic procedures using radiology and computer technology (CAT scans, ultrasounds, radioisotopes, etc.) to discover and define as well as treat disease accounted for the largest number (9.8 million). Problems with the digestive system called for some 5.7 million hospital procedures. Births were next in number, with 3.6 million babies born, 720,000 of them delivered by cesarean section. There were 3.5 million operations on the musculoskeletal system (repairing fractures, replacing

knee and hip joints, etc). Nearly as many operations were performed on women's genital organs (3.0 million) and on the cardiovascular system (2.7 million). Procedures on the urinary system (1.9 million), on the nose, mouth, and pharynx (1.0 million), and on the respiratory system (1.0 million) were next in frequency. The many other procedures carried out included mastectomy, other cancer operations, replacement of the lens in the eye, etc.

Morbidity Cost Estimates

A more complete estimate of morbidity includes those who are affected by being hospitalized. Estimates of the economic costs of a disease vary, depending on whether indirect losses in earning power are considered. Although treatments such as dialysis and transplants alter the rule, generally incidence of disease governs the amount spent to cure or mitigate the effects of it (see Table A-9).

Cardiovascular disease manifests itself in the population outside the hospital in large numbers. Overall, some 59 million people were estimated by the American Heart Association to suffer from high blood pressure in the mid-1980s; although some 15 million of those affected had only mild hypertension without further complication, others had a more serious form of the disease that can bring on heart failure, kidney failure, and/or strokes. More than 4.5 million people had serious coronary artery disease and 2 million have had a stroke. An estimated 90 million people had higher than normal cholesterol levels, sometimes leading to coronary artery disease.

Treatment of this large population accounted for direct costs of some $32.5 billion in 1980, including all circulatory diseases such as stroke, and for the sales of more than $3.6 billion in cardiovascular products. Drugs are especially important in treating high blood pressure, accounting for about one-fourth of the expenditures for that condition.

Beta blockers, drugs that lower blood pressure, sold some $800 million alone in 1987. A new genetically engineered drug, TPA, was approved in 1988; it is a highly effective anticlotting drug for heart attack survivors, but at more than $2,000 per dose has elicited protests from hospitals that are constrained by Medicare's limit of $6,500 per heart attack patient but worried about malpractice if they refuse the drug (Freudenheim, 1988a). An estimated 120,000 Medicare patients might benefit from TPA, but Medicare has resisted extra payment for it.

Aspirin and other drugs to reduce pain and swelling helped the 37 million patients with arthritis, lupus, and other rheumatic diseases in 1987. Steroids may also be added in the most serious cases. Osteoporosis, a thinning of the bones, especially in the spine, afflicted 24 million women. Ninety percent of women over 75, especially thin, white women, have some degree of disability from this disease. Hormones and calcium supplements provide some improvement in the condition. Direct costs of musculoskeletal diseases were estimated at $13 billion in 1980.

Gastrointestinal problems, often leading to ulcers, affect millions of people; treatment begins with antacids and may include antimuscarines, such as bismuth, and histamine receptors, such as Tagamet, the world's largest selling drug in 1984. Diseases of the digestive system were estimated to cost some $31 billion in 1980, but about half of this was spent on dentistry, included in this category.

Kidney diseases affect about 13 million. Kidney dialysis for end-stage renal disease has been covered under Medicare since 1972; some 100,000 patients of all ages were served largely by for-profit centers in 1987, the largest being National Medical Care, which treated about one-fifth of those needing dialysis. Government financing encouraged treatment in centers; the centers provided consistent, convenient care at a price the government accepted. They may have resulted in the decrease. The cost of the end-stage kidney disease program was about $2.5 billion in 1986 (Benjamin, 1988). Diseases of the genitourinary system cost some $12 billion in 1980.

Anxiety causes distress to millions; estimates are that some 15% of the adult population use anti-anxiety drugs such as Valium or its generic equivalent. For those suffering from more serious psychiatric difficulties, psychotropic drugs have made patients more manageable and able to function outside institutions. Many experts feel that a large fraction of the U.S. population that needs mental health services are untreated. Direct costs of mental disorders were estimated at $20 billion in 1980. Some 1.8 million inpatient care episodes and 2.8 million outpatient treatments occurred at mental health organizations in 1986 (National Center for Health Statistics, *Health United States*, 1987).

The most common psychiatric condition is depression, affecting some 10 million each year. The cause is unknown but drugs are effective in 70% of those treated. About 5 million people have moderate dementia and 1.5 million have severe dementia (Alzheimer's disease); this figure is likely to increase to 7.4 million by 2040 as the number of aged in the population rises (Office of Technology Assessment, 1987). No useful treatment is yet known and nursing home care is usually needed as patients deteriorate.

Approximately 10 million people were estimated to have cancer; about 1 million new cases occurred in 1986—predictions are that only 50% will be alive in five years. The highest incidence rates occurred in cancer of the lung, the large bowel, the prostate, and the breast.

Some 8 million people (2 to 3 million children) are estimated to be affected by asthma. The death rate is small (1.8 deaths per 100,000 population, compared with 180 deaths per 100,000 for cardiovascular diseases), but the disability can be serious. Drugs such as cromolyn and steroids used in inhalers bring relief, as does preventive treatment to diagnose allergies that bring on attacks.

Some 10 million injuries occur in the workplace each year, 4,000 of them fatal in 1984 (U.S. Public Health Service, 1986). About 400,000 workers become ill after exposure to hazardous substances and 100,000 are thought to die prematurely from the effects of such pollutants. An equal number of workers lose some degree of hearing as a result of noise in the workplace. Others suffer from lung and other cancer, musculoskeletal injuries, cardiovascular problems, and reproductive disorders that are work related. Traffic accidents injure 1.5 million automobile occupants each year and kill about 22,000.

Infectious diseases among children still exist despite vaccination because vaccines are not reaching all children. About 86% receive DPT vaccination (for diphtheria, pertussis, and tetanus), and 82% were immunized against measles; 77% received mumps and rubella vaccine, and 74% were given polio vaccine.

Glaucoma, damage to the optic nerve, affects the eyes of some 2 million people.

Because drinking alcohol and smoking tobacco have been shown to be significant causes of serious diseases, the numbers of people using these substances affect morbidity. About 43 million people were smokers in 1987, increasing their chances of developing heart disease and lung cancer. About 33% of men and 28% of women were smoking in 1985, but these proportions represented a decline from 1980 levels (38% and 30% respectively). The surgeon general blamed 320,000 deaths annually on tobacco smoking in 1988.

Alcoholism affects some 13 million people, among them 3 million teenagers. Studies have shown alcoholism a factor in some 30% to 50% of hospital admissions. Excessive drinking leads to liver disease and contributes to other physical disabilities as well as to vehicular accidents and abusive behavior. From 100,000 to 200,000 deaths each year are attributed to alcoholism.

Abuse of other substances affects fewer people but has destructive results both personally for the user and for society in drug-related crime. Drugs misused most frequently are opioids (heroin, codeine); stimulants (amphetamines and cocaine), and hallucinogenics (marijuana, PCP, and LSD). Half a million people were estimated to be addicted to heroin, and estimates were that 2.5 million had serious drug problems. Some 8,000 deaths per year and 300,000 medical emergencies were attributed to drug abuse. About 4,000 deaths occurred in 1987 because of heroin overuse and about 2,000 from cocaine, up from 615 deaths from abuse of cocaine in the United States in 1985 (*Economist*, 1988a).

There are more than 10 million cases of sexually transmitted diseases in the United States each year. Gonorrhea and Chlamydia infect three million people each annually, causing 75,000 ectopic pregnancies that kill the fetus and endanger the life of the mother. Some 2.5 million teenagers contract a sexually transmitted disease each year (*New York Times*, 1986). Genital herpes infects over 500,000.

Intravenous drug use and sexual activity have been implicated in spreading the deadly AIDS virus. Since 1981 when the virus became apparent in the United States, some 56,000 people have died, equaling the number killed in the Vietnam War. Another 54,000 were active cases in 1988 in the United States, most of them living in the large cities. Many more (estimates vary from 1.5 to 3 million) are infected with the HIV virus that in about half the cases will develop into AIDS. Although victims of AIDS live a variable period after diagnosis, treatment is not yet effective and an early death is usual. The increasing caseload was expected to cost hospitals in New York City alone $2 billion by 1991 (Marriott, 1988).

Obesity, a condition that contributes to heart disease, diabetes, and other problems, exists in nearly a third of the adults aged 35 to 74. Overweight affects fewer men than women and does not increase appreciably by age group in men, remaining at about 30% from age 35 to 64 and falling off to 26% after that; among women, the proportion who are overweight increases from 25% at age 35–44 to 37% at 65–74.

REFERENCES

American College of Surgeons. 1982. *Socio-Economic Factbook for Surgery*. Chicago: American College of Surgeons.

American Hospital Association. 1983, 1987. *Hospital Statistics*. Chicago: American Hospital Association.

American Medical Association. 1981. *Profile in Medical Practice*.

——— 1984. *Medical Groups in the United States*.

——— 1985, 1987. *Socioeconomic Characteristics of Medical Practice*.

Anderson, O.W. 1985. *Health Services in the United States.* Ann Arbor, Mich.: Health Administration Press.

Bazzoli, G. 1985. "Medical School Indebtedness," *Health Affairs* 4(2): 98–104.

Benjamin, M. 1988. "Medical Ethics and Economics of Organ Transplantation." *Health Progress* (March): 47–52.

Carper, W., and Lischert, R. 1983. "Strategic Power Relationships in Contemporary Profit and Nonprofit Hospitals." *Academy Management Journal* 26: 311–20.

Clark, L.J., et al. 1980. "Impact of Hill-Burton." *Medical Care* 18: 532–50.

Cohen, M.A., et al. 1987. "The Financial Capacity of the Elderly to Insure for Long-Term Care." *The Gerontologist* 27(4): 494–502.

Cowen, J.B. 1981. "The National Guidelines." *Hospitals* (April 16): 7–80.

Curran, W.J. 1983. "Medical Malpractice Claims Since the Crisis of 1975." *New England Journal of Medicine* 309: 1107–8.

Doty, P., Liu, K., and Wiener, J. 1985. "An Overview of Long-Term Care." *Health Care Financing Review* (Spring): 69–78.

Easterbrook, G. 1987. "The Revolution in Modern Medicine." *Newsweek*, January 26, pp. 407–74.

Economic Report of the President. 1985. Washington, D.C., February.

Economist. 1988a. March 5, p. 23.

Economist. 1988b. "Where Have All the Nurses Gone?" May 14, p. 30.

Edmondson, D. 1985. "The Home Health Care Market." *American Demographics* (April): 29–51.

Exter, T.G. 1985. "Dental Demographics." *American Demographics* (February): 31.

Farber, L.. 1986. "Why Women Doctors Don't Have a Lot of Money." *Medical Economics* (November 23): 62.

Fasse, J. 1986. "Rx for Rural Hospitals." *Venture*, March.

Freudenheim, M. 1988a. "Cost Cutting Gain in TPA Debate." *New York Times*, April 5, D2.

———. 1988b. "Nursing Homes Face Pressures." *New York Times*, May 28, Al.

———. 1988c. "Nursing Shortage Is Costing Billions." *New York Times*, May 31, D2.

Gibson, R.M., et al. 1984. "National Health Expenditures, 1983." *Health Care Financing Review*, Winter.

Hadley, J., and Feder, J. 1984. "Troubled Hospitals: Poor Patients or Management?" *Business & Health* (September): 15–19.

Health Care Financing Administration. 1984. *Medicare and Medicaid Data Book.*

Health Insurance Association of America. 1982–83, 1987–88. *Source Book of Health Insurance Data.* Washington, D.C.

Hospitals. 1985. "Most Metro Hospitals Will Link with HMOs." September 1.

Hsiao, W., Braun, P., Yntema, D.B., and Becker E.R. 1988. "Estimating Physicians' Work for a Resource-based Relative Value Scale." *New England Journal of Medicine* 319: 836–841.

Institute of Medicine. 1980. *Health Planning in the United States.* Washington, D.C.: National Academy of Sciences, March.

Jensen, J., and Miklovic, N. 1986. "Fewer Consumers Report They Have Physicians Who Provide Routine Care." *Modern Healthcare* (January 3): 90.

Jolly, P. 1988. "Medical Education in the United States." *Health Affairs* (Suppl.): 144–57.

Journal of the American Medical Association. 1987. Medical Education Issue, August 28.

Kemper, P., and Murtaugh, C.M. 1991. "Lifetime Use of Nursing Home Care." *New England Journal of Medicine* 324: 595–600.

Kenkel, P.J. 1987. "More Hospitals Enter Long-Term Care Business." *Modern Healthcare* (November 20): 30.

Klaw, S. 1975. *The Great American Medicine Show.* New York: Viking Press.

Knowles, J.H. 1977. "The Responsibility of the Individual." *Daedalus* (Winter): 57–80.

Lefferts, N.E. 1985. "What's New in Dentistry." *New York Times*, September 8, F15.

Lefkowitz, B. 1983. *Health Planning: Lessons for the Future.* Gaithersburg, Md.: Aspen Publishers.

Luft, H.S. 1981. *Health Maintenance Organizations: Dimensions of Performance.* New York: Wiley-Interscience.

Marriott, M. 1988. "New York City Asks State and United States for AIDS Help." *New York Times*, May 17, B1.

McConnel, C.E., and Tobias, L.A. 1986. "Distributional Change in Physician Manpower." *American Journal of Public Health Association* 76: 638–42.

Medical Economics. 1989. "Just How Heavy Is the Burden of Malpractice Insurance?" January 16, p. 168.

Modern Healthcare. 1985. "HMOs." May 24.

———. 1986. "Hospital Selection Factors." August 15, p. 49.

National Center for Health Statistics. 1982, 1985, 1988. *Health United States, 1981* (DHHS Pub. No. 82-1232). *Health United States, 1984* (DHHS Pub. No. 85-1232). *Health United States, 1987* (DHHS Pub. No. 88-1232). *Health United States, 1989* (DHHS Pub. No. 90-1232).

———. 1987. "National Hospital Discharge Survey, 1986 Summary." Advance data from Vital and Health Statistics. No. 145. DHHS Pub. No. PHS 87-1250. Hyattsville, Md.: Public Health Service.

New York Times. 1985. "Medical Insurance: High Costs in New York." October 13.

Office of Technology Assessment. 1987. "Losing a Million Minds." April 7.

O'Neil, E.H. 1988. "The Changing Profile of Education in Health Professions." *Health Affairs* (Suppl.): 136–43.

Oshfeldt, R. 1985. "Uncompensated Medical Services Provided by Physicians and Hospitals." *Medical Care*: 1338–44.

Punch, L. 1985. "Investor-owned Chains of Nursing Homes." *Modern Healthcare*, June 7.

Reinhold, R. 1985. "Trial Opens in Death at Texas Nursing Home." *New York Times*, October 1, A17.

Richardson, H., and Kovner, A.R. 1986. "Implementing Swing-Bed Services in Small Rural Hospitals." *Journal of Rural Health* 2(1): 46–60.

Robinson, M. 1987. "Rural Providers Ask: 'What's a Hospital?'" *Hospitals (*December 5): 48.

Scanlon, W.J., and Feder, J. 1984. "Long-Term Care Marketplace." *Healthcare Financial Management* (January): 18.

Schlesinger, M. 1985. "The Rise of Proprietary Health Care." *Business & Health* (January-February): 7–12.

Sidel, V.W., and Sidel, R. 1984. *Reforming Medicine.* New York: Pantheon. See Chapter 11 on holism and self-care.

Smith, D. 1981. *Long-term Care in Transition: Regulation of Nursing Homes.* Washington, D.C.: AUPHA Press.

Stefanu, C., Korman, M., Pate, M.L., and Chapman, J.S. 1980. "Selection of Primary Care as a Medical Career." *Southern Medical Journal* 73:924–27.

Steinwald, B., and Neuhauser, D. 1970. "Role of Proprietary Hospital." *Journal of Law and Contemporary Problems* 35:817–38.

Sun, M. 1985. "New Momentum for Drug Export Bill." *Science* (November 22): 926.

Trippler, A.K. 1986. "Health Care Coverage in America's Heartland." *Business and Health* (May): 32–34.

U.S. Public Health Service, Office of Disease Prevention and Health Promotion. 1986. *1990 Health Objectives.* Washington, D.C.: Government Printing Office.

Wennberg, J.E., and Gittelsohn, A. 1973. "Small Area Variations in Health Care Delivery." *Science* 182: 1102.

Wiener, J., and Rivlin, A. 1988. *Caring for the Disabled Elderly: Who Will Pay?* Washington, D.C.: Brookings.

Appendix B

The Financing of the Health Care Industry

Health insurance, private and governmental, paid about 75% of personal health care expenses and some 94% of hospital costs in 1989. Reimbursement of health care costs by insurance has resulted in increased demands for health services and their liberal provision by doctors and hospitals, according to many commentators on the health scene. When someone other than patients or their doctors paid for services offered, the result was an inflationary effect on the amount and cost of health services provided (See Table B-1). Regulatory efforts by the government to control the expansion of the industry have been made in a political context that attempted to satisfy many interest groups. Until recently, the states have taken the lead in attempting to reduce health costs. In 1983, the Medicare program brought the federal government into the hospital rate-setting picture by introducing a fixed payment for each type of illness.

Although government interest in the health care industry has most recently centered on containment of costs, regulation has a long history in this country, beginning with protection of the public against infectious disease and unlicensed practitioners. Next came laws designed to increase access to health care as medical practice became more sophisticated and effective than it had been in earlier years. Once access had been expanded, the emphasis turned to planning to distribute health services more equitably and to promote efficiency by reducing duplication of services. Planning also involved limiting the increases in health costs as these occurred in the 1970s. Maintaining the quality of the care given became the next objective when cost containment measures were instituted, since it was feared that price restraints might adversely affect the kind of medical care the public had come to expect.

Recognizing that capital investment in improvements brings interest, depreciation, and operating costs that then influence the costs of hospital care, state governments as early as the 1960s, and the federal government later through the Health Planning Law of 1974, attempted to restrict capital expenditures of hospitals by requiring that they satisfy government agencies that there was a need for rebuilding, addition of beds, or purchase of expensive equipment. The effect of these "Certificate of Need" laws will be discussed.'

A small but important sector of the health care industry is the research establishment, half funded by the federal government. The growth of academic medicine and of the National Institutes of Health will be sketched. The results of research play a role in preventing disease and in enhancing the quality of life for those who are ill. At the same time, technology developed through research is blamed for increasing the cost of health care, especially in the last years of people's lives. Payment of the research training costs in teaching hospitals is in flux, with third-party payers reluctant to absorb them.

Table A-1 (p. 440) shows the payment sources for the major health sectors and the amount spent on each sector; it provides a base for the ensuing discussion of finances. The sources of

Appendix B is adapted from the "Note on Financing of the Health Care Industry," 9-186-170, last revised in 1989. Both were written by Sherrie Epstein under the supervision of Professor Regina E. Herzlinger.

Table B-1 Rise in Health Care Costs

Item	Fourth Quarter[a]	Past 12 Months[b]
All Items	5.5	4.6
All Services	6.5	5.1
Medical Care	8.1	8.5
Medical Care Commodities	6.9	8.2
Prescription Drugs	9.1	9.5
Non-Prescription Drugs and Medical Supplies	3.8	5.8
Medical Care Services	8.4	8.6
Professional Medical Services[c]	7.2	6.5
Physicians' Services[c]	6.7	7.2
Dental Services	6.1	6.4
Eye Care	3.2	3.4
Services by Other Medical Professionals[d]	3.9	5.7
Hospital and Related Services	9.0	11.3
Hospital Rooms	10.8	11.0
Other Inpatient Hospital Services[e]	7.8	11.5
Outpatient Services	9.7	11.7

[a]Seasonally adjusted annual rate (percent change) for 3 months ending December 31, 1989, consumer price index for all urban consumers.
[b]Unadjusted percent change from December 31, 1988, to December 31, 1989, consumer price index for all urban consumers.
[c]Includes general practitioners, specialists, and surgeons.
[d]Includes chiropractors, optometrists, psychologists, and independent medical laboratories.
[e]Includes nursing and convalescent care.

Source: Compiled from the Bureau of Labor Statistics by *Medical Benefits,* February 1989, p .8.

financing are distributed in different ways. The single largest source, private insurance, pays primarily for hospital and physician services. Patients' out-of-pocket payments are used little for hospitals and primarily for nursing homes and dental services. Medicare and Medicaid expenditures differ from each other and from the patterns of usage of other sources.

Discussion of the financing and regulating programs in the 1980s follows, beginning with private health insurance, continuing with public health insurance (Medicare and Medicaid), and ending with a discussion of regulatory and quality control programs.

HEALTH INSURANCE

History

Health insurance evolved in Europe as "sick benefits" to replace wages lost when a worker was ill. As early as the 1880s in Germany and Austria wage earners in some industries received such benefits and by the turn of the century in Sweden, Denmark, and Switzerland the state provided incentives for workers to participate in voluntary funds. Social unrest in European countries contributed to the growth of such "sick" plans to placate workers. In the United States only a few voluntary sick funds existed; there were few unions and little socialist activity compared to the European countries of the period. A few sickness and accident policies were sold by commercial insurance companies but they were expensive to administer and appealed only to the middle class. Theodore Roosevelt campaigned in 1912 to sponsor some form of health insurance but his defeat by Wilson ended such political advocacy for many years.

The insurance companies were opposed to state-sponsored health insurance early in the century, thinking it might erode the market for their profitable death-benefit insurance. Employers, through the National Association of Manufacturers, opposed it, and physicians who initially liked the idea soon became fearful that if capitation payments (fees paid them for the number of patients cared for rather than by services given) were instituted, their incomes would be reduced. The First World War interrupted discussion of insuring against illness and after the war the concept became associated with "Bolshevism."

The first prepayment plan, presaging Blue Cross, began in 1920 with the Baylor Hospital's enrollment of school teachers in Dallas, Texas, a large number of whom had been delinquent in payment of their hospital bills. The plan guaranteed 21 days of hospital care at Baylor for $6 a year. The Depression in the 1930s pressured doctors and hospitals to look for a reliable source of income and for the public to look for a way to avoid debt if they became ill. People were paying medical bills last, if ever, and funds from those who could pay no longer subsidized the care of the poor.

The Blue Cross plans were underwritten by the hospitals in the localities in which they were started. Instead of providing conventional capital reserves, required by state insurance departments for commercial carriers, the Blues were able to substitute the hospitals' guarantee of benefits (hospitals were paid for services provided rather than paying the subscriber an indemnity for a claim). Hospital trustees and administrators were required to sit on the boards of the new plans. Single hospital plans gave way to areawide ones and were soon supported by the American Hospital Association (AHA), which urged service benefits. By 1939, 25 states had allowed these hospital service plans. Insurance commissioners were empowered to review rates and supervise the finances of the plans. The Blues had the advantage of being declared nonprofit and exempt from taxes.

Attention shifted during the Depression to unemployment insurance rather than national health insurance, and by the time the post-World War II recovery was underway, private health insurance had made great strides. Once the elderly and disabled and poor were covered by government programs in 1965, the debate for a national health plan seemed ended.

By 1982, about 82% of the population had private insurance for health expenses, but it was no longer only Blue Cross or even predominantly Blue Cross. Commercial insurance companies began to sell health policies in substantial numbers during World War II, and by 1960 the number enrolled in commercial plans exceeded those in Blue Cross. Commercial carriers were able to offer employers good rates during the war when health benefits (nontaxed) replaced wage increases denied workers during wartime wage freezes. The Blues were many different plans organized on a regional basis, while commercial companies were nationwide.

In 1986 the number of persons with some kind of hospital insurance coverage reached 180 million. Benefits paid by commercial insurers were consistently lower than the amount paid by Blue Cross in the 1980s despite their higher enrollment (see Table B-2). Employers spent $158 billion annually by 1987 on health insurance: 37% of expenditures for insurance companies, 32% for Blue Cross/Blue Shield, and 31% for independent and related plans. The benefits were a business expense and employees were not taxed for them. Estimates were that $25 billion in federal tax revenues were forgone (Regula, 1987). Federal and state governments were beginning to question the tax exemptions of hospitals and of Blue Cross in the late 1980s. In 1986 Blue Cross was required by the IRS to pay a 20% minimum tax—lower than the corporate rate paid by commercial insurers, but a new and unwelcome obligation. The same ruling may affect some tax-exempt HMOs, usually long-established network-model plans. Some states were questioning their hospitals' tax exemptions as they sought ways to cover the health care of the uninsured (see discussion under "Uninsured and Underinsured" below.)

Insurance Modes

In the early days, Blue Cross, as a nonprofit plan, insured its subscribers without deductibles—paying the so-called "first dollar." The Blues also insured for whatever services would

Table B-2 Persons Covered and Benefit Payments of Private Health Insurance, 1980 and 1988

	Number of Persons (millions)		Claims Requests (billions)	
	1980	1988	1980	1988
Commercial Insurance Companies*	105.5	93.3	$37.0	$83.0
Group	97.4	105.1	33.0	76.4
Individual/Family	33.8	17.2	4.0	6.6
Blue Cross/Blue Shield	86.1	74.0	25.5	48.2
Other Plans**	25.5	71.3	16.2	62.8
Totals All Insurers*	187.4	182.3	$76.3	$171.7

* Totals eliminate duplication of people who have coverage from more than one source and duplicate administrative expenses.
**Other Plans = self-insured and self-administered plans; plans with third-party administrators; and HMOs.
  Source: *Source Book of Health Insurance Data*, 1990 (Washington, D.C.: Health Insurance Association of America, 1991).

be needed, going against the theory of insurance that dictated covering only a known and defined risk. Commercial insurers—with few exceptions—adhered to insurance against particular risks; the benefits in these "indemnity" policies varied with the plan chosen and the amount paid in insurance.

Indemnity benefits were paid to the policyholder, not to the medical care provider. At times the indemnity was kept by the insured, who did not pay the medical bill. As a result, such policies now often require the insured to "assign" the benefit to the hospital or physician, who collects it from the insurer. Indemnity policies may prevent people from choosing expensive providers or treatments since the excess over the indemnity is paid by the insured. Similarly, deductibles (patient out-of-pocket payments before insurance coverage begins) and requirements to pay part of the charges (coinsurance) have been shown to hold down use and expense. Preferred practitioner organizations (PPO) sometimes agree to accept the indemnity in full, and insured people are encouraged or required to go to those PPOs. The indemnity is pegged at the charge of a low-priced provider. Usually the PPO must be guaranteed a certain volume of patients before agreeing to the arrangement.

An ambitious and expensive study has attempted to answer the effect of cost sharing on health status. The Rand Corporation carried out three- to five-year studies of healthy adults under 65 over a seven-year period to determine whether coinsurance discouraged use (they

thought it did) and whether cost sharing endangered health (they thought it didn't).

Unlike the traditional commercial carriers, the Blues at first offered community enrollment, allowing everyone to join and to pay the same rate. Commercial insurers charged rates to groups based on their own health experience (a practice known as experience rating). Over the years, the two approaches have converged. Blue Cross could not compete with the commercial carriers, who rapidly overtook them, without giving up its community rating. Low-risk groups otherwise would buy commercial insurance and eventually Blue Cross would be left with the highest risk groups. Blue Cross eventually gave up most of its first-dollar coverage, too.

Most of the commercial and Blue Cross enrollees are group members who pay lower rates than those who subscribe individually. Groups are drawn from the working population where health "experience" is likely to be good. Group enrollment also helps to avoid the high costs of collecting premiums on insurance sold by individual agents. Usually an employer takes care of the accounting and sometimes pays the claims, leaving the insurance carrier only the medical review of claims.

Recent Trends in Private Health Insurance

An increasing number of firms were not offering health insurance in the 1980s. The number of people insured for hospital expense with private insurance dropped from a 1982 high of 188 million. Some 56% of the uninsured were employed year round in 1980, up about 7% from 1977. Employers who did offer insurance increasingly asked their workers to contribute to the premiums: 53% of employers paid the full cost in 1980 but by 1984 only 38% did. Many more group plans were asking for deductibles of $100 or more in 1984 than had done so four years earlier. Over the past decade there has been a significant increase in the number of employers who have opted to self-insure their work force, especially when it was a relatively young one. Only 5% of those insured in 1965 were in self-insured groups and the proportion had reached only 8% by 1976, but by 1985 those covered by self-insured or health maintenance plans accounted for 30% of the total insured (Health Insurance Association of America, 1986-1987). In 1985 some 40% of employers with 100 or more employees were self-insured (Employee Benefit Research Institute, 1986); in 1986 three-fourths of employers with 1,000 or more employees were self-insuring (McDonnell, 1986). By doing so employers saved premium taxes and could potentially avoid supplying state mandated benefits, although most had followed practices required by state insurance commissions. (The Employee Retirement and Income Security Act had prohibited states from requiring employers to provide employee benefits.) The larger the company, the more likely it was to self-insure; four out of five companies with more than 5,000 employees were doing so, while fewer than one in ten of those with 100 or fewer employees self-insured. Some large companies administered their own plans, but most used outside administrators, usually commercial insurers.

Health maintenance plans in which medical care is offered enrollees at a set yearly rate paid in advance have increased greatly since the 1970s. Seen as a way to contain costs, private insurance companies and Blue Cross had started their own HMOs or preferred provider organizations. Although indemnity or service-benefit plans still accounted for most of the health insurance coverage in the United States,

an estimated $26 billion of the $158 billion being spent on privately financed health insurance went to HMOs enrolling some 30 million people in 1987. Commercial insurers began to enter the HMO market in the 1980s. Enthusiasm for these plans seemed to have ebbed by 1988 as enrollment slowed; many plans lost money and were forced to raise their premiums and to cut back on the amount paid their doctors.

Nevertheless, these developments were indicative of changes in health care financing methods. Private fee-for-service physicians, individual nonprofit hospitals, and traditional insurance still dominated, but not to the same extent as in the past. Physicians practiced in groups and increasingly had some involvement with HMOs or PPOs (preferred providers who offered discounts for groups of clients). Hospitals had joined multi-hospital systems, marketed their services to consumers, and sometimes eliminated services on which they lost money. Departing from their former role of selling insurance only, private insurers administered health plans for self-insured employers, and offered them stop-loss protection from unusual claims; such protection sometimes hinged on purchase of other more profitable insurance such as life insurance. By 1988 insurance companies were often returning to their role as insurer rather than administrator by operating HMOs for companies and guaranteeing that the company subscribers' costs would not exceed a certain amount (Kramon, 1988). Blue Cross largely administered Medicare (although private companies serviced Medicare in many states); Blue Cross also sponsored HMOs.

Uncompensated Care

Uncompensated care is a term used to lump together the charity and bad debt that is increasingly a problem in the health care industry as the various payers object to shouldering the burden. Estimates vary because the term is defined differently by various providers, the definition often depending on which category was reimbursed. Medicare and

Medicaid pay a share of charity care but not of bad debt. The AHA, the trade association for nonprofits, in 1986 said that bad debt and charity cost hospitals $7.9 billion and that three-fourths of this was bad debt.

The term is not precise because much of this shortfall has been compensated by someone: by philanthropy, by public funds, by cost shifting from those who pay their medical charges, and by discretionary funds of hospitals (Mulstein, 1984). Public hospitals provide the majority of the uncompensated care. From 10% to 15% of hospitals service the neediest populations and give the most free care. The AHA data showed, too, that hospitals with a high number of obstetrical beds and neonatal care and hospitals that received a high proportion of funds from outpatient care, were also likely to have high proportions of uncompensated care.

Uninsured and Underinsured

Interest has focused on determining how many people have no health insurance or have inadequate amounts to insure against what to them would be catastrophic costs, as hospitals find it increasingly difficult to cope with patients who cannot pay. Estimates of this population vary because of differences in survey methods. The Current Population Survey conducted by the Census Bureau estimated that from 32 million to 37 million were uninsured in 1986. From one-half to nearly two-thirds of them were employed adults and their dependents. Three-fourths of the uninsured were classified as poor (family income below 100% of poverty). In addition to the uninsured, most health insurance offered no protection against the catastrophic costs of nursing home care (see Table B-3).

Governmental Attempts To Cover the Uninsured

Legislation

Because so many of the uninsured were employed, expanding employer-based insurance was seen as one way to improve access to medical care. In 1985 the Consolidated Omnibus Budget Reconciliation Act (COBRA) required employers with 20 or more employees to provide interim coverage for employees who were laid off or whose hours of employment were reduced below the level for benefit coverage. Coverage also was mandated for survivors (including dependents) of employees who died and for spouses who were divorced. Employers were not required to continue their contributions and could charge employees 102% of the cost of the premium for the insurance, although administration of the insurance was expected to cost more than the 2% allowed. Terminated employees had coverage for 18 months and others for 36 months, presumably allowing enough time for them to secure other health insurance. In 1986 COBRA was amended so that retirees of a company that declared bankruptcy could purchase their prior health benefits rather than having them cut off or reduced because of the company's difficulties.

The states have tried in a number of ways to arrange for health insurance for those who would not otherwise qualify for it in order to avoid paying for charity care if they become ill. Pregnant women made up a large number of the uninsured needing hospital services, and 24 states responded quickly to a law allowing pregnant women and children above the poverty level to participate in Medicaid, thus procuring preventive services (with federal sharing) that were likely to save trouble and expense later. Health insurance pools for those at high risk of illness who could not buy private insurance have been created in 15 states.

Many states (e.g., Maine, Michigan) have provided incentives to small employers to encourage them to furnish health insurance. Others have set up trust funds from contributions from all hospitals and insurers; the funds are then distributed according to need to those hospitals that give charity care.

Massachusetts, following Hawaii, has made the most ambitious effort to provide health insurance. It passed a law in April 1988 requiring employers of 6 or more people to offer health benefits; the remaining uninsured would be

Table B-3 Health Care Coverage by Type of Coverage, Percent of Population, Persons under 65 Years of Age, 1980 and 1989

	Private Insurance		Medicaid		Not Covered	
	1980	1989	1980	1989	1980	1989
Total	78.8%	76.6%	5.9%	6.4%	12.5%	15.7%
Age						
Under 15 Years	74.7	71.7	10.2	11.4	12.8	15.9
15–44 Years	79.3	76.6	4.2	4.3	14.2	18.1
45–64 Years	83.6	83.3	3.1	3.4	8.6	10.6
Sex						
Male	79.5	76.9	4.7	5.2	12.7	16.4
Female	78.2	76.2	7.1	7.6	12.2	14.9
Race						
White	81.9	79.7	3.9	4.5	11.4	14.5
Black	60.1	59.2	17.9	17.1	19.0	22.0
Family Income						
Less than $14,000	38.6	34.6	27.6	26.6	31.0	37.3
$14,000–24,999	61.1	71.4	9.2	4.8	25.9	21.4
$25,000–34,999	79.0	87.9	3.0	1.2	15.0	9.3
$35,000–49,999	90.2	92.4	1.1	0.8	6.2	5.6
$50,000 or more	93.7	95.7	0.6	0.4	3.9	3.2

Source: Health United States, 1990.

covered through a group plan sponsored by the state at premiums adjusted for those who cannot pay the full price. There is national congressional support for this bill as well; but in 1991 a newly elected governor urged that it be repealed in Massachusetts.

Taxing Nonprofit Hospitals

In another approach to finding funds to cover the cost of care for those who cannot pay, some states have attempted to tax nonprofit hospitals. As voluntary hospitals began opening profit making subsidiaries, signing research agreements with pharmaceutical companies, and eliminating services on which they lost money, they became vulnerable to altering the public's view of their service mission, thus putting their tax-free status at risk. They were presumably providing care to indigents in exchange for exemption from property and income taxes. In

1985 the Supreme Court ruled that hospitals were no longer automatically excused from paying property taxes. In order to retain their exemption they would have to prove they did not operate commercial ventures and that they provided a sufficient amount of services to the poor without expectation of payment. In a 1990 report, the General Accounting Office demonstrated that for-profit hospitals frequently provided as much charity care as nonprofits and that the value of their charity care did not equal the value of the nonprofit hospitals' tax-exemptions. (See also R.E. Herzlinger and W.S. Krasker, "Who Profits from Nonprofits?", *Harvard Business Review*, January/February 1987.)

A few states taxed nonprofit hospitals; for example, Utah had been successful by 1987 in imposing property taxes on four nonprofits and six ambulatory care centers (a ruling that was being appealed), and the hospital associations were worried about future actions (Greene, 1987). In a related move, the U.S. Supreme Court decided that it was unconstitutional to exempt interest on municipal bonds. Outstanding bonds were not affected, but it opened the way for Congress to tax such bonds, useful in raising money to fund hospitals.

MEDICARE AND MEDICAID

Background

By the 1950s, voluntary health insurance was well established in covering risks for the employed segment of the population. Attention shifted to the needs of the elderly. Senate hearings and opinion polls pressured the government for help and resulted in a congressional proposal by Republicans for medical benefits for the elderly poor. Liberals were able to pass a law that guaranteed medical care to all those over 65 regardless of income when the 1964 election brought a Democratic majority to Congress.

The plan, known as Medicare, enacted in Title XVIII of the Social Security Amendments in 1965, combined hospital insurance under Social Security (known as Part A) with voluntary insurance to cover doctors' bills, paid partly by the government and partly by the recipient (known as Part B) (see Exhibit B-1). The government financed the hospital insurance by putting a portion of the public's Social Security contributions into a trust fund. Medicare benefits were subject to copayments and deductibles. Copayments have increased over the years and in the 1980s Medicare paid about half the medical expenses of the elderly.

An additional part of the plan (Title XIX) became Medicaid. General tax revenues were used to help the states pay for medical care of poor families with dependent children and of the poor elderly and disabled. (Medicaid pays Medicare charges for those who are below poverty levels.) Federal contributions ranged from a base in the 13 wealthier states of 50% up to 77% in Mississippi in the 1980s. Eligibility and benefits varied widely according to the politics and as the wealth of the states fluctuated with fiscal crises. (A number of those below the poverty line did not qualify for Medicaid help in the 1980s; nearly 38% of those earning less than $14,000 a year in 1989 were uninsured.)

The medical establishment had successfully fought off earlier attempts at anything resembling national health insurance and it was not enthusiastic about this proposal. The government agreed to pay "reasonable costs" of hospitals and "reasonable charges" of physicians to secure the cooperation of physicians and hospitals. The hospital costs included, at the urging of the hospital industry, accelerated depreciation. "Fiscal intermediaries" were appointed to reimburse and to audit the accounts of the hospitals (to distance government from the job). In most cases Blue Cross and Blue Shield became the intermediaries and were paid a fee for the work entailed. (In the 1980s, Blue Cross and Blue Shield still were predominantly acting as intermediaries.)

By 1972, it was apparent that Medicare costs were higher than had been expected. The rate of increase per year had gone up faster than the rate for health care expenditures overall. In addition, the proportion of elderly in the population was increasing. Also, those affected by end-stage renal disease were added to the Medicare rolls in 1972. Dialysis treatments for this population were to prove much more expensive than anticipated. Congress amended the law, promising funding for demonstration projects to test whether a prospective payment system would lower costs without seriously affecting the kind of care given. The law also authorized limits on hospitals' per diem "reasonable costs." Experiments in prospective payment were carried out in a number of states for the next decade. (See section on "Rate Setting.")

Medicare and Medicaid Financing

Medicare in the 1980s was financed largely by a payroll tax on employers and employees of 1.3% on the first $45,000 of wages.

Exhibit B-1 Medicare Coverage, 1985

Part A—Hospital

Government pays for

90 days/spell of illness
+60 reserve days

100 days SNF*/spell of illness

Home health visits

Beneficiary pays

$400 deductible for 1st hospital day
$100 coinsurance for hospital days 61–90
$200 coinsurance for each reserve hospital day
$40 coinsurance for days 21 to 100 of SNF

Part B—Physician (voluntary)

Government pays for

80% of reasonable charges

Beneficiary pays

$75 deductible, annually
20% (cost sharing) of charges
$15.50/month insurance premium

Medicare hospital reimbursement

- Pays prospective rate per DRG at discharge
- Pays retroactive cost of capital and medical education
- Pays only bad debt attributable to Medicare patients

Creates incentives for hospital to

- Unbundle services[†]
- Increase admissions
- Reclassify to high-cost DRGs
- Increase capital and medical education expenses

*Skilled nursing facility.
[†]Shifting costs to reimbursable areas.

Medicare enrollees also paid in some $4 billion in premiums toward their voluntary (supplementary) insurance to pay physicians. General revenues paid 30% of the Medicare financing. Some 70% of Medicare benefits go to hospitals since beneficiaries are responsible themselves for a large proportion of physicians' charges and the costs of nursing homes, dentistry, and drugs (see Table B-4). Capital expenditures account for about 7% of the amount spent on hospitals; depreciation and interest make up most of the expense, with a small percentage (7%) charged to return on equity to proprietary

hospitals. Capital costs are less than 10% of operating costs for most of the hospitals (80%); only a few (5%) show costs of capital from 15% to 20%. (Further details of the Medicare payment system and the reforms begun in 1983 follow under the heading of "Medicare Reform and DRGs.")

The federal share of payment for Medicaid varies with the income level in the state, and eligibility varies with state rules. Usually it hinges on being eligible for federally assisted cash welfare payments, but some people below the poverty line do not receive benefits and

Table B-4 Medicare and Medicaid Benefits, 1980–1989

	1980	1985	1987	1989
Medicare Benefits[a]				
Enrollees (millions)	28.5	31.1	32.4	33.6
Amount (billions), Total Insurance	$ 36.8	$ 72.3	$ 82.0	$100.6
Hospital Insurance	25.6	48.4	50.3	60.8
Hospitals	65%	62%	57%	54%
Physicians	22%	24%	28%	27%
Home Health	2%	1%	3%	3%
Nursing Homes	2%	1%	1%	3%
Outpatient Hospital	5%	6%	7%	8%
Other	4%	6%	4%	5%
Medicaid Benefits[b]				
Recipients (millions)	21.6	21.8	23.1	23.5
Vendor Payments (billions)	$ 23.3	$ 37.5	$ 45.0	$ 54.5
Hospitals	31%	28%	28%	28%
Physicians	8%	6%	6%	6%
Nursing Homes[c]	34%	32%	30%	29%
Drugs, Prescribed	6%	6%	7%	7%

[a]13% went to disabled (especially dialysis for end-stage renal disease) under age 65; the rest to those over 65.

[b]One-fourth of the benefits in 1986 went to families with dependent children (AFDC), who made up 70% of recipients; three-fourths went to the elderly (Medicaid pays Medicare enrollment and other charges for the poor) and the blind or disabled, who accounted for 30% of recipients.

[c]Excluding the intermediate care facilities for the mentally retarded.

Source: National Center for Health Statistics, *Health United States 1990*.

some who are above the line receive them. Three-fourths of Medicaid benefits were spent for the elderly, blind, or disabled, who made up less than one-third of the recipients, while the smaller percentage of benefits went to aid the much larger number of families with dependent children (AFDC). Medicaid pays for nursing home and other institutional care for the impoverished. The number of Medicaid recipients grew between 1972 and 1977 (from 18 million to nearly 23 million), but had declined slightly by 1982 as the Reagan administration revised eligibility rules to disqualify many.

Other proposals for keeping "the lid" on costs have included a cap on federal contributions: Federal payments to each state were reduced a little more each year, reductions going from 3% in 1981 up to 4.5% in 1984.

Some $41 billion was spent on Medicaid in 1986, roughly 50 percent of that spent on Medicare. Despite efforts to reduce the rolls of recipients, less attention seems to have been paid to Medicaid reform than to Medicare, perhaps because the federal role is less and also because the recipients are unfortunates for whom there is little other recourse.

In paying physicians, Medicaid specified that they must accept the designated amount. As a result, participation by community physicians often has been low and patients have been seen by older physicians or foreign medical graduates, usually not board-certified specialists.

Table B-4 compares the Medicare program with Medicaid. One significant difference is in the payment of physicians. Until 1985 Medicare continued its original method of paying "reasonable charges" judged by what was "customary and prevailing" in the area. Participation by physicians was much better for Medicare than for Medicaid. In addition, the Medicare rules allowed physicians to collect more than the "reasonable charge" if they thought a case warranted it. They were able to refuse "assignment" wherein they were guaranteed payment directly from Medicare. (Many doctors had liked the idea of assignment since it reduced the risk that the patient would collect from Medicare and not pay the physician.) Physicians could instead collect from the patient and charge more than the Medicare fee. Known as "balance billing," this practice has come under fire from those who claim it is regressive for poor Medicare participants who are already paying the same coinsurance as their wealthier peers. Massachusetts passed a law in November 1985 barring physicians from licensure if they participate in Medicare and refuse to accept Medicare's payment in full.

Medicare Reform and DRGs

In 1982 Congress sought to extend limits on "reasonable costs" paid to hospitals in a new law known as TEFRA (Tax Equity and Fiscal Responsibility Act); this time all the costs of hospital services, not just the daily charge, were to be limited. This and other changes in hospital reimbursements that put control in the hands of the government were never fully implemented, however. The law was superseded by the Social Security Amendments of 1983, which introduced the concept of payment of a fixed-in-advance sum for each type of illness. Loosely termed "prospective payment," it was more accurately prospective rate setting.

Hospitals (especially the smaller ones) accepted this DRG rate setting as preferable to the global budgeting threatened by TEFRA. Payment fixed by the type of illness had been proposed as a cost containment measure for some time. Hospitals had pointed out that differences in case mix (the degree of illness of the patients treated) had to be considered in comparing hospital costs. Defining each kind of illness had been a problem—classifications numbered in the thousands and were too unwieldy for practical use. The DRG system proposed by researchers at Yale condensed these into 467 groups—presumed few enough for computer assimilation.

The logic behind the DRG was that variations in medical practice and in the costs of performing medical services had been noted by researchers for some time and by reviewers in the professional standards review organization (PSRO) program. As a "prudent buyer" of medical services, Medicare was obligated, the government said, to look for a way to pay the same price for comparable services.

Since regulators had been unable to find a consistent correlation between quality and price, there seemed to be justification for trying to set a rate for payment that would not depend solely on a given hospital's own costs. It had been difficult to classify and compare the units being measured among hospitals. There seemed to be no common denominator in making comparisons (Kalison and Averill, 1984). Regulators had tried looking at the number of beds, the length of a patient's stay, and the number of admissions in trying to find desirable norms. Now they would try to eliminate differences in case mix in comparing costs among hospitals. DRGs was the method adopted.

A uniform national classification of an individual patient's illness was not easy to reach, and critics of the system claimed it had not yet been done. Some fault DRGs because they do not explain a large proportion of the variance in costs or consider sufficiently the "severity of illness," and they propose more elaborate classification (Horn, 1985). Others thought that without a control over volume of admissions, DRGs could only have a limited success in containing costs (Wennberg, McPherson, and Caper, 1984). The need to discourage excess treatment or indeed to decide what was excessive was not addressed or controlled by DRGs (Moore, 1985). There have been numerous accusations that hospitals can classify a given illness in several ways and still fall within the DRG guidelines—one classification may be rewarded by a low payment, however, and another equally valid one may be paid at a much higher rate. When DRGs were instituted in 1983, it was feared that the Hospital Trust Fund would run out of money by 1991 and that Medicare beneficiaries would not collect what had been promised to them. By 1988 the fund looked secure at least until 2005. Admissions to hospitals declined between 1983 and 1987, as contrasted with the increase that occurred between 1972 and 1982. Length of stay also fell.

Credit for these successes cannot be attributed to DRGs as such. Other contributing factors were that contributions to the trust fund remained high because employment was high, more people over 65 were staying in the work force, the hospitals cut back on employment for the first time since World War II, and the number of hospital closings doubled to 244 during the five-year period, compared with 1980–83. Rural hospitals were especially vulnerable, threatening access to care for rural residents. Hospitals claimed that one-third of them had negative Medicare operating margins. Hospitals complained that DRGs did not allow for increases in labor costs (thereby exacerbating the nursing shortage) or for advances in technology.

DRG Payment Method

The appropriate DRG is determined by first classifying it into one of 23 diagnostic categories based on the body systems or organs; for example, diagnostic category 16 covers diseases and disorders of the blood and blood-forming organs and immunological dis-

orders (see Exhibit B-2). The specific DRG within this category is selected on the basis of the patient's age, sex, or complicating factor. These DRGs are assigned weights that are applied to the cost of the DRG, as determined by the daily costs in the traditional Medicare cost reports. Thus, 397 has a weight of .9863; 398 a weight of .8500; and 399 a weight of .8459. Each is also assigned a mean length of stay, such as 6.7 days for DRG 397.

DRG payments have been modified in several ways. A "day outlier" was a patient whose length of stay was greater than the mean by the lesser of 20 days or 1.94 standard deviations from the mean. This patient was reimbursed at 60% of the per diem for days that lie beyond the length of stay and 1.94 standard deviations or 20 days. A "cost outlier" incurs costs 1.5 times greater than the DRG. It was also reimbursed at 60% of costs beyond the threshold.

Special facilities were also adjusted in the DRG scheme. Sole community hospitals, cancer hospitals, referral centers, and teaching institutions can qualify for higher DRG reimbursement. Indirect medical education reimbursement is based on the ratio of interns and residents to beds; it was 8.1% per discharge as a base for 1986. Also, hospitals in states that had experimental statewide reimbursement systems received DRG waivers because these systems were seen as fairer mechanisms. Small and large urban and rural hospitals were guaranteed an area total outlier payment. Capital costs, subject to planning restraints (CON), were "passed through" (paid retroactively); by fiscal year 1987, they were paid for at actual cost less 3.5%.

The only payment for bad debt under DRGs is the amount attributable to unpaid deductibles and coinsurance related to the services given the insured Medicare patients. Similarly, Medicare pays only the proportion of malpractice premium expense related to malpractice losses attributable to its beneficiaries. Routine costs and costs of ancillary services are screened for "reasonableness."

The government view in setting out DRG payment methods was that as an insurance

Exhibit B-2 DRG Classification Method and Discharge Procedure

Classification Method:

1. From the International Classification of Diseases (12,000 diagnoses);

2.. Twenty-three categories of major diagnoses are made, according to organ systems (kidney, heart, etc.);

3. From these are drawn 467 distinct groups of "medically meaningful" diagnoses, defined as those in which all patients in a given grouping will be treated in a way that will, on average, result in equal use of hospital resources.

Discharge Procedure:

A. In assigning a case to a DRG, the hospital admitting physician completes step 1, below and the attending physician completes steps 2 through 5, entering information on a discharge "face sheet."

    1. Principal diagnosis and up to four complications
    2. Treatments performed
    3. Age of patient
    4. Sex of patient
    5. Discharge status

B. Hospital medical records department reviews and codes the diagnoses.

C. Information is sent to a Medicare fiscal intermediary who determines the DRG and calculates payment based on

DRG Weight	*Dollar Weight*
An index number representing hospital resources used in treatment	A federally established dollar rate combined with a hospital-specific rate based on the hospital's cost experience during a three-year transition period; afterward, 100% federal rate.

Source: "DRGs and the Prospective Payment System," *AMA Guide for Physicians*, Chicago, 1984.

company it was free to act in its own economic interest (Kalison and Averill, 1984). Experimental or undesirable procedures are not given a weight and thus no price (Smits and Watson, 1984). The government could thus veto procedures it did not approve. Bills are coded according to the International Classifications, which are revised only periodically. Coding of new procedures has led to problems and to a high rate of coding error. The DRG system encourages innovation in high-priced surgical specialties like vascular surgery as opposed to low-priced procedures like those in urology. Its application to free-standing ambulatory surgery

centers was mandated as of October 1987, as was its application to independent laboratories. The applicability of the methodology to physicians and prepaid health plans is currently being studied.

RBRVS

Resource-based relative value scales (RBRVS) will be used to compensate physicians for care to Medicare patients. They are estimated to increase the payments for non-specialists—internal medicine up to 16% and family practice by 37%—and reduce those for specialists, like radiologists, whose payments will decrease by 21%, and thoracic surgeons, whose payments will be reduced by 20%.

RATE SETTING

"Costs" and "Charges" Explained

The cost of health care and the charges made for it are often confused and spoken of interchangeably. Charges are usually considerably higher than the actual per patient cost of care because hospitals seek to make up in the charge to those who can afford to pay what they lose in bad debt, charity cases, and restrictions on reimbursements by some of the third-party payers.

Traditionally, hospitals have been reimbursed for "reasonable costs" by Medicare, Medicaid, and Blue Cross, and physicians have been reimbursed for "reasonable charges." Defining "reasonable" was left to the insurers, who arrive at their decision by reviewing what was "customary and usual" in physician charges and the norms of hospital costs for similar-sized institutions in comparable geographic areas. They considered, too, the "case mix" of the hospital—community hospitals usually have less severely ill, less complicated patients than does a university teaching hospital. These reimbursement methods gave way to prospective rate setting in the 1980s.

Commonly referred to as "rate setting," the term encompasses various attempts to set reimbursement rates for health care in hospitals prospectively rather than retroactively. Its purpose is to restrict the ability of hospitals to charge whatever they determined to have been the costs of care. There have been some voluntary efforts at setting such rates—notably, the hospital industry's voluntary effort between 1977 and 1980—but rate setting generally is held to mean a mandated regulation by an authority outside the hospital that encompasses prospective payment to at least some payers.

Without prospective rate setting, hospitals have had no incentive to limit services. Presumably if a hospital knew in advance that it would receive only so much payment, it would try to increase its efficiency in the hope of keeping the difference or at least avoiding losses. As hospital costs rose, particularly after the enactment of Medicare and Medicaid in 1965, the constituency for rate setting also increased, especially in those states that were generous in paying the health costs of the poor. State officials worried about the increasing costs of paying their share of Medicaid bills. Blue Cross officials and subscribers also were concerned about rising insurance rates, and private payers were complaining to their legislators about medical bills.

In the early 1970s, rate-setting programs that affected one or more payers grew from 2 to 27, most administered by Blue Cross for hospitals in each Blue Cross plan's region. In 1985, only ten states had rate-setting systems in effect (Eby and Cohodes, 1985) and most were being dropped. The reception by hospitals of Medicare's 1983 cost-saving mechanism of setting rates by fixing the amount paid for each hospitalization according to its "disease-related group" has been good, attributed by health commentators to the desire of hospitals to be in control of such mechanisms rather than having control vested in a government body.

The federal government lent support to rate-setting regulation by the states but did not embrace it itself until 1983. The 1972 amendments to the Social Security Act and the 1974 Health Planning Act both gave federal aid to state experiments. These experiments evolved from then-current practice and essentially tried to hold this year's rates down to last year's. They all tried to regulate the hospital charges to one or more of the major payers: Blue Cross, Medicaid, self-pay patients, and, less frequently, Medicare. The rates were set sometimes by voluntary agreements with Blue Cross and at other times mandated by an agency of the state or by an independent commission appointed by the governor. The effectiveness of these programs seems to have been limited but is difficult to evaluate because they usually did not regulate all the payers and because enforcement often was weak or was resisted strongly.

Most of the programs limited per diem or per admission costs and none addressed per capita population costs. Setting rates was done by a review of the budget of each hospital being regulated, by comparing institutions, and by taking into consideration changes in the cost of living and recommendations of health planning agencies.

Global Budgeting

In Massachusetts, a total hospital budget was set in 1983, weighted by the volume of business, inflation, and costs beyond the control of the hospital, under Chapter 372 of the Commonwealth laws. Total or "global" budgeting like this was an unpopular concept for the hospital industry, which saw such budgeting as loss of control of its business to government regulators. Health planners countered by maintaining that piecemeal setting of rates had little chance of success in controlling costs. Also global budgeting, which used the prior year's costs as a base for determining the budget, rewarded inefficient hospitals with many slack resources and penalized efficient ones whose costs were already lean.

The Rate Setting Commission in Massachusetts issued a review of the first two years under Chapter 372 at the end of 1985. It showed increases in patient care costs continuing but at a lower rate: The increase had been 6.7% in 1982–1983, but was 6.2% in 1983–1984. Despite this, the profitability of the hospitals had not been harmed—it had, in fact, also increased. Nevertheless, the system had proved unpopular with the hospitals, which had earlier supported it. In the spring of 1985 the Massachusetts Hospital Association voted to drop its support for extending the all-payer system under a Medicare waiver. Commented James Stowe of the Health Data Institute, "Hospitals appear to be rethinking support for the all-payer approach because many have concluded that the constraints of that regulatory model outweigh the value of its protection" (Stowe, 1985).

CERTIFICATE OF NEED

History

The first CON law was enacted by New York in 1964 and 26 other states followed its lead in the next decade. The law was designed to limit capital expansion (and its resulting influence on medical costs) by requiring a review and approval by a state agency of any expenditure exceeding (usually) $100,000–$150,000 or the addition of beds or services by hospitals and nursing homes. State regulators, it was assumed, would consider the overall needs of the community, not the demands of each institution.

In 1972, the federal government encouraged CON by writing into the Social Security Amendments a "Section 1122" that denied Medicare and Medicaid payment for capital costs if they had not been approved by a state government agency. In 1974, the National Health Planning Law added additional sanctions, withholding other federal health funds if states did not have a CON program. The law provided funds for health planning that helped pay for state CON programs.

By 1982, every state except Louisiana had a CON program. By then most programs covered hospitals, nursing homes, kidney dialysis, and ambulatory surgical centers. The capital limit before review was necessary had risen to $600,000. Medical equipment for patient use costing more than $400,000 was usually under review, and so were new services with operating costs above a certain limit (usually $200,000). Some states have put ceilings or "caps" on the total capital value of projects approved in one year so that agencies will be forced to evaluate the relative merits of differing projects rather than only comparable ones. Others have included out-of-hospital settings like doctors' offices to prevent attempts to get around acquisition of expensive equipment, such as imaging devices like computer-assisted tomography (CAT) scanners and magnetic resonance imaging (MRI) machines.

In 1980, the Reagan administration came in with an antiregulatory, procompetitive ideology and cut back on health planning funds. Although seven states dropped their programs after 1982, they have retained some sort of moratorium on capital expansion, usually at fairly high thresholds. Predictions are that states will retain some kind of CON but that they will reduce the number of projects reviewed by raising the capital threshold and dropping review of expenditures that supposedly will not affect patient charges appreciably, such as mechanical repair, replacement of plant, or elimination of safety hazards (Simpson, 1985).

Congress opted in 1983 to reimburse for capital under the DRG system instituted for Medicare on an incurred-cost basis. Until this is changed, Medicare will not pay capital costs unless they have been approved by a CON program under Section 1122.

Effectiveness

How effective have CON programs been? Studies conducted indicate that CON does not limit capital expansion or control cost increases as well as had been hoped. The best results have been in holding down the number of acute care beds. Approval rates of proposals for expansion were very high (93%) when they were being studied under the National Health Planning Law in 1979. A high approval rate did not always indicate cursory review. In many areas, health planners were able to discourage applications unlikely to be approved before they were sent through the review process. Proponents of the CON idea argue that hospital expansion would have been greater than it has been without the review mechanism. CON's greatest effect may have been in delaying construction, not in avoiding it.

Experience has shown a need for better standards. Even where standards for determination of need are relatively clear cut, such as in the number of beds needed in an area, there have been appeals from providers for changes. As a result, standards have been adjusted to allow more beds per population in rural areas, where accessibility to a hospital is important,

for example, and adjustments have been made in standards of occupancy for hospitals that have a larger than usual proportion of elderly patients.

Many CON determinations have been stricter in judging new facilities than old ones, serving to discourage competition. A CON license is a distinct competitive advantage, significantly increasing the value of the organization holding it. CON has resulted in a great deal of costly litigation. Most of the suits challenging CON determinations have been unsuccessful.

PROFESSIONAL REVIEW ORGANIZATIONS

Professional Review Organizations (PROs) were mandated under the Social Security Amendments of 1983 that provided for prospective payment via DRGs for all participating hospitals.

These organizations are an outgrowth of the Professional Standards Review Organizations (PSROs) set up by the 1972 amendments to the Social Security law and designed to monitor quantity and quality of medical care under Medicare and Medicaid. The new PROs differ somewhat from the old, especially in modifying the nonprofit status of the old by allowing for-profit organizations to qualify for the HCFA contract, introducing the possibility of competition among the organizations. The PROs are funded under the Medicare trust fund—from 1977 on the PSROs received funds for hospital review through unpredictable congressional appropriations—thus returning funding to the original method set out in 1972.

Historically, the success of the PSRO program has been much debated. A number of congressional reviews concluded that the cost of the program exceeded the savings brought about by it. Supporters criticized the limited scope of the reviews and also claimed that the effect of the program was subtle and not easily measured by such studies. They said that physicians who were aware that their practices were being reviewed by an organization of their peers would be more careful to see that their practices conformed to desirable norms than they would have been without review. In the past, the emphasis of the PSROs has been on holding down the quantity of procedures given Medicare and Medicaid patients and on restricting the length of stay in the hospital, although some attention was paid to the need for admission. Review was not easy to accomplish and effectiveness was not easy to measure. Physicians, who largely constituted the peer review organizations, gave them lukewarm support, viewing government requests for accountability as insulting and interfering. In addition, it was genuinely difficult to define "medical necessity and appropriateness" since the mode of practice for a given condition could vary within acceptable norms and could be complicated by individual circumstances.

The Bureau of Health Standards and Quality, which had administered the PSRO program, had complained of high unit costs of review and had tried in 1980 to substitute "focused" review on problem areas to reduce those costs. The bureau claimed that a third of acute care hospitals were not covered by review mechanisms because the bureau could not afford coverage. Total program appropriation was $144 million in 1980, with $85 million going for hospital review and the rest for program administration.

RESEARCH

The Second World War was not only a watershed in the history of medical progress, it marked the start of a great expansion in federal investment in medical research.

From 1900 until the war, private funds in universities largely supported research. The American Medical Association and a few independent centers like the Rockefeller Institute in New York and the Mayo Clinic in Minnesota also sponsored medical research. Most of this was basic research that looked for fundamental scientific understanding. Applied research in medicine was carried out in pharmaceutical houses. In 1945 more than twice as much ($40

million) was being spent on applied as on basic research.

Until the 1930s the Department of Agriculture housed the major federally sponsored health research. It enforced the Food and Drug Act and did work on pesticides, veterinary medicine, and soil chemistry. Some of this aided later researchers in their work on antibiotics.

The Public Health Service (PHS) was organized in 1912 and grew out of a laboratory formed in Washington, D.C., to regulate vaccines. It soon was authorized to study infectious disease as well. The laboratory was named the National Institutes of Health (NIH) in 1930 and given a large private tract of land in 1938 in Bethesda, a suburb of Washington, D.C. In 1937, Congress granted the PHS the right to award grants to researchers outside its government laboratories. Funding for the PHS was small in 1938 ($2.8 million) compared to funding for the Department of Agriculture ($26 million). The war spurred medical research funding in nongovernment laboratories. Decisions about how these grants were to be awarded were made by groups of university scientists, and this became the precedent for later government granting through the NIH.

Although the PHS carried out other medical duties (e.g., medical service for seamen, prisoners, and migrants, and control of venereal disease and tuberculosis), research was soon centered in the NIH. The direction of research followed a formula of calling attention to one disease at a time, as poliomyelitis researchers had done with the very successful March of Dimes. This focused appeal had brought in a disproportionate amount of money in relation to the threat of polio to the public in the 1930s and 1940s.

This categorical approach, as it came to be known, was aided by Mary Lasker, the wife of a wealthy advertising man, who was extremely successful from the 1960s on in lobbying Congress and presidents for more money for health research in the areas that interested her: cancer, heart disease, and stroke. The NIH soon comprised several institutes—eleven in 1987, each with its own budget and constituency.

Today, the director of NIH has almost no legislated capability to allocate resources among the institutes. Thus he cannot decide which disease entity deserves how much of a share of the research budget. The level of funding for each institute does not correspond with the level of morbidity or mortality of the disease entities.

While some research is done in the NIH laboratories and in its Clinical Center (its hospital), the bulk (80%) of the research funded by the NIH is conducted extramurally, largely in universities and medical schools. The recipients of grants and contracts for research are chosen by review committees made up of the researchers' scientific peers, not by the government.

The growth of the research establishment after the war greatly altered and strengthened academic medicine. The average medical school income rose from $500,000 per year before the war to $4 million by 1958 and $15 million by 1968. Full-time faculty, which had been sparse, increased greatly. An average department of internal medicine in a medical school might have had 15 members before the war but by 1970 might number 150. Physicians employed by the government and by institutions accounted for 12.8% of the total number of physicians in 1940, but 26.5% by 1957. The growth in full-time faculty meant that there was much less need for physicians in private practice to function as part-time teachers in the medical schools. There has been an increasing tension between the academic and practicing medical communities as they competed for patients and for the use of hospital resources.

The research establishment has shared somewhat in the 1970s' public disillusionment with medicine, or, more accurately, with the cost of it. Funding has just about kept up with inflation in biomedical research and development expenses since 1975. Grants have become more competitive as the pool of researchers has continued to expand. Although all researchers have been affected, this has been especially discouraging to younger investigators who have no track record with which to influence peer recognition.

NIH grants are applied for by researchers who direct their applications describing the project they hope to carry out to the Division of Research Grants. The division oversees the 64 Study Sections, made up of scientific experts in their disciplines, drawn from universities and medical schools, who usually serve on the Study Sections for several years (paid only nominal amounts for meeting days) and meet periodically to grade the applications, giving each a priority score. Disciplines cut across institute lines and Study Sections typically review grant applications for several institutes. The institutes then must approve applications before they can be funded, usually selecting them on the basis of the priority score within the constraints of their budgets. About 19% of the applications are sent to two institutes, but funding is shared in only a few cases (Institute of Medicine, 1984).

Some research-related programs have been cut from the federal budget. The government has cut out programs that selected schools through a peer review system to receive funds for building research facilities. In recent years individual schools have been appealing successfully to their congressmen to appropriate money for these facilities. Boston University in November 1985 received $19 million for a science and engineering center, joining others like Northwestern, which received $20 million for a research park in 1984, and Columbia University, which received $20 million for an organic chemistry center. These independent "pork-barrel" awards have been criticized because they represent a lack of planning in allocating government money for the overall needs of the research community (Maeroff, 1985).

Some $7 billion was spent on health research and development in 1986 by the federal government, of which $5 billion went to NIH. The rest of the federal outlay went to other agencies, especially the Defense Department. State and local government spent about $1 billion and private nonprofit foundations and health agencies provided another $700 million. Industry spent an estimated $6 billion on research and development in 1986, most of it in its own laboratories and the bulk of it on development; drug companies' research is included here. Industry funding is growing at much faster rates than governmental capital. It was estimated to have surpassed government spending in magnitude in 1990.

REFERENCES

American Hospital Association. 1982. *Survey of Medical Care for the Poor.*

Darling, H. 1985. "Cost Management Update." *Business & Health* (December): 38.

Eby, C.E., and Cohodes, D.R. 1985. "What Do We Know about Rate Setting?" *Journal of Health Politics* (Summer): 299.

Economic Report of the President. 1985. Washington, D.C., February.

Employee Benefit Research Institute. 1986. *Features of Employer Health Plans.* Washington, D.C.: Employee Benefit Research Institute.

Greene, J. 1987. "Ten Not-for-Profit Providers Denied Tax Exemptions." *Modern Healthcare* (November 20).

Health Insurance Association of America. 1982–83, 1984–85, 1986–87. *Source Book.*

Herzlinger, R.E., and Krasker, W. 1987. "Who Profits from Nonprofits?" *Harvard Business Review* (January-February).

Horn, S.D. 1985. "A Plan to Modify DRGs." *Business & Health* (September): 32.

Institute of Medicine. 1984. *The Organizational Structure of the NIH.* Washington, D.C.: National Academy of Sciences Press, October.

Kalison, M.J., and Averill, R.F. 1984. "Responding over Time: Regulation vs. Contract." *Health Care Financial Management* (May): 104.

Kramon, G. 1988. "Employers Test New Ways to Shift Risk on Health Costs." *New York Times*, June 27, Al.

Maeroff, G.I. 1985. "Universities Lobby in Washington for Research Funds." *New York Times*, November 19, Cl.

McDonnell, P., et al. 1986. "Self-Insured Health Plans." *Health Care Financing Review* (Winter).

Moore, F.D. 1985. "Who Should Profit from the Care of Your Illness?" *Harvard Magazine* (November-December): 45.

Mulstein, S. 1984. "The Uninsured and the Financing of Uncompensated Care." *Inquiry* (Fall): 214.

NIH Data Book. 1985. Washington, D.C.: National Institutes of Health.

Pear, R. 1985. "Changes Sought in Doctors' Pay under Medicare." *New York Times*, December 7, 8.

Regula, R. 1987. "National Policy and the Medically Uninsured." *Inquiry* (Spring): 48.

Simpson, J.B. 1985. "State CON Programs." *American Journal of Public Health* 75: 1225.

Smits, H.L., and Watson, R.E. 1984. "DRGs and Surgical Practice." *New England Journal of Medicine* 311: 1612.

Stowe, J. B. 1985. "All Payer Savings." *Business & Health* (December): 38.

U.S. General Accounting Office. 1990. *Nonprofit Hospitals—Better Standards Needed for Tax Exemption.* Gaithersburg, Md.: U.S. General Accounting Office.

Wennberg, J.E., McPherson, K., and Caper, P. 1984. "Will Payment Based on DRGs Control Hospital Costs?" *New England Journal of Medicine* 311:295–300.

Appendix C

Pharmaceuticals

This appendix describes the categories and major types of drugs.

DRUG PRODUCTS

The three types of pharmaceutical products are proprietary drugs (over-the-counter, or OTC), generic ethical drugs, and patented ethical drugs.

Proprietary drugs are defined by the FDA as those safe for use without supervision by the professional. They are sold directly to consumers without prescription and include aspirin (Bufferin, Anacin), acetaminophen (Tylenol), and many steroid creams. They make up 12% of the worldwide market for all medicines. New proprietary drugs tend to be reformulations of existing products or drugs that the FDA's OTC drug review has approved as being safe to use without supervision (almost any drug is unsafe if taken in the wrong dosage or taken the wrong way). Competition in this market emphasizes brand names, advertising, and low-cost production. Companies with significant OTC market share include Johnson & Johnson, American Home Products, Warner-Lambert, Schering-Plough, and Bristol-Myers Squibb.

Patented ethical drugs are those whose developers were given exclusive but temporary

Appendix C is adapted from the "Note on the Pharmaceutical Industry," 9-189-076, written by Brandon Fradd, and the "Note on Medical Technology," 9-187-110, written by Sherrie Epstein, both last revised in 1988 and written under the supervision of Professor Regina E. Herzlinger. The full versions of the notes are published by the Harvard Business School, Boston, Massachusetts.

rights by the government. The 17-year patent allows its owner to charge a price premium, promising high returns to the developer.

Generic ethical drugs are off-patent, well-established ethical drugs (sold only by prescription). Made by more than 600 generic drug companies or by divisions of large research-based companies, they account for about 23% of the ethical drug market and are a growing segment because of efforts to contain costs. Although the branded segment is the largest, the unbranded segment is faster growing.

DRUG CATEGORIES

Drugs can be categorized by therapeutic benefit or disease being treated. The categorizations are not precise, because there are many ways to group diseases and one drug may be used for many different diseases. There is also no precise correlation between drugs and diseases. For example, the group of calcium antigens originally prescribed for angina (heart pain) were later found to be effective for hypertension and possibly for arrhythmias and arterial constriction. The antibiotics are probably the most diverse category; while most are strongly effective against certain infectious organisms, they may also be useful in a wide variety of infections.

Drugs can also be categorized by whether their use is occasional or chronic. Gastrointestinal agents for ulcers are usually taken regularly for years, but drugs for indigestion are taken only occasionally. The best-selling drugs are taken chronically, with the exception of antibiotics, because their market is determined by the large number of possible infections and because many diseases lead as a secondary consequence to infection, particularly in the hospital, where the incidence of infection is much higher than in the general community.

Major Drug Categories

Discussion of the major categories of drugs produced by the pharmaceutical industry follows.

Antibacterials

Antibacterials or "antibiotics," a term coined in the 1940s by microbiologist Selman Waksman, who won a Nobel Prize for the discovery of streptomycin, introduced the modern era in medical care. They played a crucial role in quelling infections from diseases that had previously been scourges, such as tuberculosis, septicemias (blood poisoning), meningitis, typhoid, scarlet fever, pneumonias, venereal diseases, rheumatic fever, etc. Antibacterials evolved from the path-finding discoveries of bacterial forms of Lister, Koch, and Pasteur in the late 19th century and continued with Ehrlich and his "magic bullet," which found its target, the syphilis spirochete early in the 20th century. Modern antimicrobials began with the discovery of penicillin by Alexander Fleming in London in 1928, although development and production problems were not solved until the 1940s. The first sulfa drugs came from Gerhard Domegk's Bayer laboratory in Germany in 1932.

Antimicrobials have altered the kinds of diseases that cripple or kill Americans. Medical concerns shifted to chronic long-term illnesses as more of the population survived to old age. Not only did the new drugs make recovery much more certain than in the past, they reduced the pain, damage to the patient, and length of hospitalization. Despite the expense of the antibiotics, their existence has reduced overall costs of health care. In the 1930s a streptococcal infection might have entailed a $500 outlay (an estimate that includes not infrequent funeral charges), weeks in the hospital, and discomfort and debilitation. By 1989, the cost might be as little as $10 and the period of illness at home might be only a few days. In addition, the use of antibiotics has made many formerly common and often dangerous operations unnecessary, such as those for mastoid infections and for lung abscesses.

Perhaps the greatest effect of antibacterial treatment has been in expanding surgical possibilities. Major surgery of the heart and lung and many orthopedic procedures, for example, have become possible because surgeons have learned to prevent or cure infection by using antibiotics before, during, and after the wounds have been made. The most recent successes of antibacterials have been in making transplant surgery safer. Many problems remain, however. Infection is still a major cause of difficulty in perfecting the use of artificial hearts. Micro-organisms gain a foothold in the prosthetic materials and devices and are very hard to eradicate. A *caveat* to all this is that the rate of illness from many infectious diseases had begun to decline even before the antibiotics came on the scene and that some of the spectacular results may be attributed to public health measures such as better hygiene, less crowding, better diet, etc.[1]

New antibiotic agents have been developed continuously over the past 40 years to act specifically against infections that may have become resistant to an earlier agent or because it is desirable to have a drug that has fewer side effects, has a wider spectrum of applicability, lasts longer, or costs less than earlier versions. The chemical structure of an antibiotic may be modified to achieve desired characteristics. The earliest antibacterial compounds came from natural sources such as soil molds, and the synthetics developed later have similar molecular structures to the natural forms.

Semisynthetic penicillins such as oxacillin, nafcillin, and methicillin have been used preventively and successfully in surgery, but a significant number of people are allergic to penicillin (5% to 10% of adults). Cephalosporins have supplanted penicillins in surgery in the mid-1980s because the most recent formulations of them are useful against a wider spectrum of bacteria and against those that were resistant to the penicillins. Also, fewer allergic reactions to them have occurred. The new cephalosporins are twice as expensive as penicillins, but they have been marketed with the claim that since fewer doses of the drug will be necessary, their higher cost will be offset by savings in the time of hospital personnel. In 1986 more than 50% of all hospital antibiotics sales were cephalosporins. The market for hospital-based antibiotics is 1.5 times that of office-based antibiotics.[2]

Antihypertensives and Other Cardiovascular Drugs

Deaths from hypertensive heart disease fell precipitously after the discovery of drugs to combat the disease. Deaths per 100,000 population were about 550 in 1950 but had fallen to about 55/100,000 by the 1970s. Hexamethonium and hydralazine (vasodilators) came into use in the 1950s. Coumadin and heparin (anticoagulants) were introduced at the end of the 1940s to keep blood from clotting and diuretics (in the 1950s) to help patients lose unneeded fluid have added to the effectiveness of treatment for hypertension.

With some 40 million people currently affected by heart disease (some estimates are higher if people with mild hypertension are included), the market for cardiovascular products is large. Common practice in treating hypertensives had been to begin with a diuretic and to add other agents as needed over a typically long period of treatment; but as of 1988 a more individualized approach was recommended. Beta blockers made up the second largest segment of the industry, accounting for some $900 million; calcium antagonists, 27%; and ACE inhibitors 21%.[*]

---

*With thanks to Dr. Roy Drucker of Upjohn Pharmaceuticals for his comments on this section.

Antiarthritics

The discovery of the hormone cortisone was an outgrowth of Claude Bernard's work on glands in the 19th century. Discovered at the Mayo Clinic in the 1930s, cortisone was thought at first to be a miracle drug against rheumatoid arthritis. Side effects, however, were severe, with swelling, heart disease, stomach ulcers, and occasional mental disturbances occurring after continued use. Later, it would be shown that in the early years of the disease, treatment with aspirin was just as effective and much less risky. Cortisone's early promise may have been partly due to its placebo effect. (A Latin word for "I will please," a placebo or ineffective drug given by a doctor has often been shown to benefit the patient through the power of suggestion.) Although cortisone derivatives such as prednisone are still being employed in the treatment of arthritis, doctors are aware of the serious complications of steroid therapy. The drugs are deemed worthwhile in life-threatening situations in patients with lupus and other serious rheumatic disorders.

For those with milder forms of arthritis, nonsteroidal anti-inflammatory drugs are useful. Aspirin and other salicylates and such drugs as phenylbutazone, indomethacin, and ibuprofen reduce the signs and symptoms of rheumatoid disease, although they have no effect on the underlying causes and do not reduce damage to joints and tissues.

Antiulcer Drugs

Peptic ulcers occur in the areas of the gastrointestinal tract exposed to acid and pepsin. Various conditions cause secretion of excess acid or poor defense against it. The incidence of the disease is estimated at 18 new cases each year per 10,000 adults. Peptic ulcers are classified as gastric and duodenal ulcers, with the latter more common. Twice as many men as women are victims of duodenal ulcers, while gastric ulcers occur in equal numbers between the sexes. Duodenal ulcers occur in younger people, with the peak occurring at age 40, while the occurrence of gastric ulcer peaks at age 50. Peptic ulcers hospitalized 620,000 people in 1976; one-fourth of them required surgery, according to the Pharmaceutical Manufacturer's Association. They estimated the cost of the disease at $2 billion.

Pharmaceuticals prescribed for the condition are antacids such as Maalox and Mylanta, antimuscarinic drugs that coat the ulcer craters such as Pro-Banthine and Robinul and bismuth compounds, and those that act on a histamine receptor such as cimetidine (Tagamet) and ranitidine (Zantac). In 1977, cimetidine (Tagamet) was introduced in the United States and surgery rates declined. The drug has been most effective against duodenal ulcers. Although it does not cure the disease or prevent recurrence, it heals the ulcer while it is being taken. Typical dosage is from 4 to 7 times daily for a month, followed by lower dosage for six months to a year. Zantac, introduced in the United States more recently, lasts longer and has fewer side effects, although those from cimetidine have not been serious. Treatment for ulcers typically involves a combination of the different kinds of drugs. Antacids and antimuscarinics may be given in conjunction with the histamine blockers. The many side effects from antimuscarinics make them undesirable as a first-line treatment, however.

Psychotropic Drugs

About 70% of the psychotropic drugs used in the United States are hypnotics or anxiolytics. The rest are antidepressants (18%) and antipsychotic substances (10%). The hypnotics (barbiturates) can act as sleeping pills and the anxiolytics (tranquilizers, especially the benzodiazepines) relieve anxiety without causing sleepiness. The effect depends largely on the dosage, because higher dosages of tranquilizers will produce the hypnotic effect and low dosages of hypnotics can act as sedatives and because their chemical structure is similar.

Questionnaires of users and surveys of the drugs sold estimate that 3% to 4% of adults use prescription hypnotics and 15% of adults take tranquilizers. It is more difficult to estimate how often the drugs are used, but surveys indicate that anti-anxiety and hypnotic drugs are among the most frequently prescribed in the United States—especially the benzodiazepines such as Valium and Librium.

A government survey showed some 85 million psychotropic drugs obtained in 1977, accounting for 9% of all medicines prescribed that year.[3] About 9% of the population paid for psychotropic medicines, spending about $513 million for them. Most of this was paid out of pocket, with private insurance and government sources accounting for 15% and 16% respectively.

NOTES

1. Brian Inglis, *The History of Medicine* (Cleveland: World Publishing, 1965).

2. A. Sundel, "Parenteral Antibiotics," *Medical Marketing and Media*, November, 1986.

3. National Center for Health Services Research and Development, *Psychotropic Drugs* (Washington D.C.: U.S. Government Printing Office, 1983).

Index